MW00861790

Joseph Cardinal Ratzinger at the celebration of his seventy-fifth birthday in 2002 in Rome with his brother, Georg Ratzinger, choirmaster emeritus of the cathedral in Regensburg (Photo KNA).

First page of the draft of the lecture "In the Presence of the Angels" (see below, JRCW-11:461–79), which was presented in honor of his brother on the occasion of his retirement from the position of choirmaster at the cathedral in Regensburg.

JOSEPH RATZINGER
COLLECTED WORKS
Volume 11

JOSEPH RATZINGER
COLLECTED WORKS

Edited by Gerhard Ludwig Müller
in conjunction with the
Institut Papst Benedikt XVI. in Regensburg:
Rudolf Voderholzer, Christian Schaller, Gabriel Weiten

Volume 11
Theology of the Liturgy

JOSEPH RATZINGER

Theology of the Liturgy

The Sacramental Foundation
of Christian Existence

Edited by Michael J. Miller

Translated by John Saward,
Kenneth Baker, S.J., Henry Taylor, et al.

IGNATIUS PRESS   SAN FRANCISCO

In collaboration with
LIBRERIA EDITRICE VATICANA
Original German edition:
Theologie der Liturgie: Die sakramentale Begründung christlicher Existenz
(Gesammelte Schriften 11)
© 2008 by Verlag Herder GmbH, Freiburg im Breisgau

Cover design by Roxanne Mei Lum

© 2014 by Ignatius Press, San Francisco
All rights reserved
ISBN 978-1-58617-595-5
Library of Congress Control Number 2011930605
Printed in the United States of America ∞

Contents

PART B
Typos—Mysterium—Sacramentum

PART C
The Celebration of the Eucharist—
Source and Summit of Christian Life

APPENDICES

Pope Benedict XVI

On the Inaugural Volume
of My Collected Works

The Second Vatican Council began its work with deliberation on the
"Schema on the Sacred Liturgy"; then on December 4, 1963, the document was solemnly promulgated with the rank of a constitution as
the first fruit of that great ecclesial gathering. Considered superficially,
the fact that the theme of liturgy was taken up at the start of the
Council's work and that the constitution on that subject turned out to
be its first result was an accident. Pope John had convoked the assembly of bishops out of a desire, which was joyfully shared by all, for a
new updating of Christianity in times that had changed but had set no
definite program for it. A long series of schemas had been composed
by the preparatory commissions. But there was no compass with which
to find the way through this abundance of suggestions. Of all the
projects, the document about the sacred liturgy seemed to be the least
controversial. So it most likely appeared to be a kind of exercise, as it
were, by which the Fathers could learn the method of conciliar work.
What may superficially appear to be an accident proved, in view of
the hierarchy of the themes and duties of the Church, to be intrinsically the right thing also. By starting with the theme of liturgy, God's
primacy, the absolute precedence of the theme of God, was unmistakably highlighted. Beginning with the liturgy tells us: "God first".
When the focus on God is not decisive, everything else loses its orientation. The saying from the Rule of St. Benedict "Nothing is to be
preferred to the liturgy" (43, 3) applies specifically to monasticism,
but as a way of ordering priorities it is true also for the life of the
Church and of every individual, for each in his own way. It may be
useful here to recall that in the word "orthodoxy", the second half,
"-doxa", does not mean "idea" but, rather, "glory": it is not a matter
of the right "idea" about God; rather, it is a matter of the right way
of glorifying him, of responding to him. For that is the fundamental
question of the man who begins to understand himself correctly: How

must I encounter God? Thus learning the right way of worshipping—orthodoxy—is the gift par excellence that is given to us by the faith.

Once I had decided, after some hesitation, to take up the project of an edition of my collected works, it was clear to me that the Council's priorities apply and that, hence, the volume with my writings on the liturgy had to stand at the beginning. The liturgy of the Church has been for me since my childhood the central reality of my life, and in the theological school of teachers like Schmaus, Söhngen, Pascher, and Guardini it became the center of my theological efforts, also. I chose fundamental theology as my field because I wanted first and foremost to examine thoroughly the question: Why do we believe? But also included from the beginning in this question was the other question of the right response to God and, thus, the question of the liturgy. My studies on the liturgy are to be understood from this perspective. I was concerned, not about the specific problems of liturgical studies, but always about anchoring the liturgy in the foundational act of our faith and, thus, also about its place in the whole of our human existence.

This volume now brings together all the short and medium-sized studies with which I have given my views on liturgical questions on various occasions over the years and from various perspectives. After all the essays that had resulted in that way, I was finally compelled to present an overview, which was published in the Jubilee Year 2000 under the title *The Spirit of the Liturgy* and constitutes the central text of this book. Unfortunately almost all the reviews jumped on a single chapter: "The Altar and the Direction of Liturgical Prayer". Readers of these reviews must have concluded that the whole work dealt only with the direction in which Mass is celebrated; that it was all about trying to reintroduce Mass celebrated by the priest "with his back to the people". Given this distortion, I thought for a while about omitting this chapter—nine pages out of a total of two hundred—so that finally a discussion could begin about the essential things in the book about which I had been and am concerned. This would have been possible and that much easier, since in the meantime two excellent studies have been published in which the question about the orientation of prayer in the Church of the first millennium is explained convincingly. I am thinking first of the important little book by U. M. Lang *Turning towards the Lord: Orientation in Liturgical Prayer* (San Francisco: Ignatius Press, 2004), and especially about the major essay by

Stefan Heid "Gebetshaltung und Ostung in der frühchristlichen Zeit" (*RAC* 72 [2006]: 347–404), in which the sources and secondary literature on this question are treated comprehensively. The result is quite clear: The notion that priest and people should look at each other while praying appeared only in the modern era and was completely foreign to ancient Christendom. After all, priest and people pray, not to each other, but to the one Lord. That is why they look in the same direction while praying: either toward the East, as a cosmic symbol for the Lord who is coming, or, when this is not possible, to an image of Christ in the apse, to a cross, or else they simply look up together, as our Lord did during his high-priestly prayer on the evening before his Passion (Jn 17:1). Meanwhile the recommendation that I made at the end of the pertinent chapter in my book has fortunately been adopted more and more widely: not to make structural alterations, but simply to put a cross in the middle of the altar for the priest and the faithful to look at together, so as to allow themselves in this way to be led to the Lord to whom we all pray together.

But with that I may once again have said too much on this point, which is actually only a detail in my book that I could also leave out. The essential purpose of the work was to go beyond the often petty questions about one form or another and to place the liturgy in its larger context, which I tried to present in three concentric circles that are present in all the particular topics. First, there is the intrinsic interrelationship of Old and New Testament; without the connection to the Old Testament heritage, the Christian liturgy is utterly incomprehensible. The second circle is the relationship to the religions of the world. And finally there is also the third circle: the cosmic character of the liturgy, which represents more than the coming together of a more or less large circle of people: the liturgy is celebrated in the expanse of the cosmos, encompassing creation and history at the same time. This was what the orientation of prayer meant: that the Redeemer to whom we pray is also the Creator and, thus, that the liturgy also always contains a love for creation and the responsibility for it. I would be happy if the new edition of my liturgical writings could help others see the greater perspectives of our liturgy and put petty quarrels about external forms in their proper place.

Finally and most importantly I have to express my thanks. I thank first of all the Bishop of Regensburg, Gerhard Ludwig Müller, who took on this project of publishing the collected works and managed the personnel and institutional requirements for carrying it out. Then I would like to thank in a very special way Prof. Dr. Rudolf Voderholzer, who invested an unusual amount of time and energy in collecting and reviewing my writings. I likewise thank Dr. Christian Schaller, who capably assisted him in this work. Finally, my sincere thanks to Herder Publishing Company, which has taken on this difficult and laborious work with great love and care. May the whole effort help the liturgy to be understood more and more profoundly and celebrated worthily. "The joy of the LORD is our strength" (cf. Neh 8:10).

Rome, on the Solemnity of Saints Peter and Paul 2008

Benedict XVI

Editor's Foreword

Pope Benedict XVI is one of the great theologians on the Chair of Peter. In surveying the long series of his predecessors, a comparison with the outstanding scholarly figure of the eighteenth century, Pope Benedict XIV (1740–1758), comes to mind. Likewise one might think of Pope Leo the Great (440–461), who formulated the decisive insight for the christological profession of the Council of Chalcedon (451).

In the long years of his academic career as a professor of fundamental and dogmatic theology, Pope Benedict XVI published an independent corpus of theological work that puts him in the ranks of the important theologians of the twentieth and twenty-first centuries. For more than fifty years, the name Joseph Ratzinger has stood for an original overall concept of systematic theology.

His writings combine the scholarly findings of theology with the living form of the faith. As a science that has its genuine place within the Church, theology can show us the special destiny of man as a creature and image of God.

In his scholarly works, Benedict XVI was always able to refer back to an amazing knowledge of the history of theology and dogma, which he conveyed in such a way that God's vision of man, from which everything is born, comes to light. This becomes accessible for many readers through Joseph Ratzinger's facility with words and language. Complex subjects are not deprived of general comprehensibility by complicated reflections but rather are made transparent, so that their inner simplicity becomes visible. It is always about the fact that God wants to speak to every person and that his word becomes a light that enlightens every man (Jn 1:9).

His academic career led the theology professor Joseph Ratzinger to the colleges and universities of Freising, Bonn, Münster (in Westphalia), Tübingen, and finally to Regensburg, where he worked from 1969 until his appointment as Archbishop of Munich and Freising in 1977.

Joseph Cardinal Ratzinger also felt connected with the city and diocese of Regensburg during his long period of time as Prefect of the Congregation for the Doctrine of the Faith (1982–2005). He regularly visited his brother, Georg Ratzinger, who for many years served as the choirmaster at the cathedral in Regensburg and director of its boys' choir, the Domspatzen (1964–1994). Nor has anyone forgotten the sermons he gave in the Regensburg Cathedral on a wide variety of feast days. The grave of his parents, Josef and Maria Ratzinger, and of his sister, Maria, is located in the cemetery in Regensburg-Ziegetsdorf. About his residence in Pentling outside the gates of the cathedral town of Regensburg he once said: After all the agitated years in different places of employment, "we were again at home."

During his pastoral visit to his Bavarian homeland in 2006, he once again emphasized the intrinsic connection between faith and reason in his Regensburg lecture, which was a stellar moment not only in the history of German universities. Neither reason nor faith can operate independently of the other and still arrive at its proper destination. Reason and faith are preserved from dangerous pathologies by reciprocal correction and purification. Pope Benedict XVI thereby aligns himself with the great tradition of theological sciences, which can prove to be the unifying element in the overall framework of the university.

Thus Regensburg became, so to speak, the *genius loci* [guardian spirit of a place] that intends to collect and safeguard the complete theological works of Joseph Ratzinger. The episcopal See of Regensburg, with its great erudite bishops, St. Albertus Magnus (1260–1262) and Johann Michael Sailer (1821–1832), stands for the unity of the episcopal and the academic magisterium, which confirms the rationality of the faith and the pastoral fruitfulness of scholarship. This tradition was continued by Archbishop Michael Buchberger (1927–1961), under whose direction the *Lexikon für Theologie und Kirche* came into being, which is now an international standard work available in its third edition.

So this cathedral town finally offered itself also as the site of a center for research into the work of Joseph Ratzinger/Benedict XVI. After the Holy Father commissioned me, as the Bishop of Regensburg, to publish his *Collected Works* in sixteen volumes, I founded the *Institut Papst-Benedikt XVI.* [Pope Benedict XVI Institute] in Regensburg to carry out this project. It is meant to become a place in which the life, thought, and work of the theologian, bishop, and pope Joseph Ratzinger/Benedict XVI are comprehensively documented. The compilation and editing of his entire published and unpublished work, the inquiry into the biographical and theological context, and the construction of a special library provide the ideal conditions for a comprehensive examination of his complete theological works.

The overall plan was devised in close consultation with Pope Benedict XVI. Each individual volume has been authorized by the Holy Father himself, not only in its thematic design but also in the selection of the texts. This project strives for completeness. For individual shorter texts, only the place where they were found is noted. So it is fair to speak of a living witness to the theology of Joseph Ratzinger/Benedict XVI, because the central thing is not the mere collection and archiving of texts, but rather the systematic development of a subject area in theology by means of a newly designed arrangement that uncovers connections and makes an overview possible.

At the personal request of Benedict XVI, the *Collected Works* are being published under the name of the author, Joseph Ratzinger.

To the director-in-chief, Prof. Dr. Rudolf Voderholzer of Trier, and his deputy, Dr. Christian Schaller, I must express here my special thanks. They support the publication of the *Collected Works* knowledgeably, circumspectly, and with great theological competence.

I would like to thank sincerely the Holy Father Pope Benedict XVI. The great vote of confidence in me that he expresses by commissioning me to publish his works is simultaneously a joy and a responsibility for me.

Regensburg, the Solemnity of Saints Peter and Paul, 2008

+ Gerhard Ludwig

Bishop of Regensburg

Abbreviations

In Scripture references, books from the Bible are abbreviated as they are in the *Revised Standard Version—Second Catholic Edition* (RSV-2CE).

a	article (in the *Summa theologiae* by Thomas Aquinas)
Adv. Haer.	*Adversus haereses*
AHAW.PH	*Abhandlungen der Heidelberger Akademie der Wissenschaften. Philosophisch-historische Klasse*
Apol.	Apologia
art.	article (in an encyclopedia)
BAC	Biblioteca de Autores Cristianos
BEvTh	*Beiträge zur Evangelischen Theologie*
BR	Bayerischer Rundfunk = Bavarian Radio
BZ	*Biblische Zeitschrift*
CChr	Corpus Christianorum
cf.	compare
CMe	Christliche Meister
Comm. in	Commentary on
Conc (D)	*Concilium* (German edition)
CSEL	Corpus scriptorum ecclesiasticorum latinorum
DH	Denzinger/Hünermann, *Kompendium der Glaubensbekenntnisse und kirchlichen Lehrentscheidungen*, expanded and translated into German by Peter Hünermann, in collaboration with Helmut Hoping (Freiburg, 1991; reprintings)

DS	Denzinger/Schönmetzer, *Enchiridion symbolorum, definitionum et declarationum de rebus fidei et morum*
ed.	editor, edited by
EKD	Evangelische Kirche in Deutschland (Lutheran-Evangelical Church in Germany)
En. in Ps.	*Enarrationes in Psalmos* (Augustine)
FC	Fontes Christiani
FoKTh	*Forum Katholische Theologie*
FS	Festschrift
GCS	Die griechischen christlichen Schriftsteller der ersten drei Jahrhunderte
GdK	*Gottesdienst der Kirche: Handbuch der Liturgiewissenschaft*
HDG	*Handbuch der Dogmengeschichte*
Hom.	Homily
Ibid./ibid.	In the same place
IgnEph.	Ignatius of Antioch, *Letter to the Ephesians*
IgnMagn.	Ignatius of Antioch, *Letter to the Magnesians*
IgnRom.	Ignatius of Antioch, *Letter to the Romans*
IKaZ	*Internationale Katholische Zeitschrift "Communio"* [German edition]
IThS	*Innsbrucker Theologische Studien*
JLW	*Jahrbuch für Liturgiewissenschaft* (from 1950 on, ALW = *Archiv ...*)
JRCW	*Collected Works of Joseph Ratzinger*
JRGS	*Joseph Ratzinger: Gesammelte Schriften* (original German edition)
KKD	*Kleine Katholische Dogmatik*
KKTS	*Konfessionskundliche und kontroverstheologische Studien* (Paderborn, 1959–)

Abbreviations

KlBl	*Klerusblatt*
KLK	*Katholisches Leben und Kirchenreform* (until 1966: *Kämpfen*) *im Zeitalter der Glaubensspaltung*
LThK²	*Lexikon für Theologie und Kirche*, 2nd ed., edited by Josef Höfer and Karl Rahner
LThK³	*Lexikon für Theologie und Kirche*, 3rd ed., edited by Walter Kasper
LWQF	*Liturgiewissenschaftliche Quellen und Forschungen*
LXX	Septuagint (Greek translation of the Hebrew Bible)
MBTh	*Münsterische Beiträge zur Theologie*
MS(D)	*Musica sacra* (German ed.)
MThS.S	*Münchener Theologische Studien, Systematische Abteilung*
n.	note
n.s.	new series
OR	*L'Osservatore Romano*
P.	*Pater* (German title for priest)
PL	Migne, Patrologia Latina
q	question (in the *Summa theologiae* by Thomas Aquinas)
RAC	*Reallexikon für Antike und Christentum*
RB	*Revue biblique*
resp.	*respondeo* [response (in the *Summa theologiae* by Thomas Aquinas)]
RGST	*Reformationsgeschichtliche Studien und Texte*
RHPhR	*Revue d'histoire et de philosophie religieuses*
S.Th.	*Summa theologiae*
SC	Second Vatican Council, Constitution on the Sacred Liturgy *Sacrosanctum concilium*, December 4, 1963
SChr	Sources chrétiennes

StANT	*Studium zum Alten und Neuen Testament*
StdZ	*Stimmen der Zeit*
ThGl	*Theologie und Glaube*
ThJb (L)	*Theologisches Jahrbuch* (Leipzig)
ThLZ	*Theologische Literaturzeitung*
ThQ	*Theologische Quartalschrift* (Tübingen)
ThRv	*Theologische Revue*
ThWAT	*Theologisches Wörterbuch zum Alten Testament*, edited by Gerhard Johannes Botterweck, Helmer Ringgren, and Heinz-Josef Fabry
ThWNT	*Theologisches Wörterbuch zum Neuen Testament*, founded by Gerhard Kittel
TRE	*Theologische Realenzyklopädie*
TThS	*Trierer Theologische Studien*
TThZ	*Trierer Theologische Zeitschrift*
US	*Una Sancta: Rundbriefe für interkonfessionelle Begegnung*
VApS	*Verlautbarungen des Apostolischen Stuhls* [a German periodical similar to *The Pope Speaks*]
VELKD	Vereinigte Evangelisch-Lutherische Kirche Deutschlands (United Evangelical-Lutheran Church of Germany)
VIEG	*Veröffentlichungen des Instituts für Europäische Geschichte Mainz*
vol./vols.	volume/volumes
WA	*Weimarer Ausgabe*, Weimar Edition of the works of Martin Luther
WdF	*Wege der Forschung*
WUNT	*Wissenschaftliche Untersuchungen zum Neuen Testament*
ZKTh	*Zeitschrift für Katholische Theologie*
ZThK	*Zeitschrift für Theologie und Kirche*

PART A

THE SPIRIT OF THE LITURGY

Preface

One of the first books I read after starting my theological studies at the beginning of 1946 was Romano Guardini's first little book, *The Spirit of the Liturgy*. It was published at Easter 1918 as the opening volume in the Ecclesia Orans series edited by Abbot Herwegen, and from then until 1957 it was constantly reprinted. This slim volume may rightly be said to have inaugurated the Liturgical Movement in Germany. Its contribution was decisive. It helped us to rediscover the liturgy in all its beauty, hidden wealth, and time-transcending grandeur, to see it as the animating center of the Church, the very center of Christian life. It led to a striving for a celebration of the liturgy that would be "more substantial" (*wesentlicher*, one of Guardini's favorite words). We were now willing to see the liturgy—in its inner demands and form—as the prayer of the Church, a prayer moved and guided by the Holy Spirit himself, a prayer in which Christ unceasingly becomes contemporary with us, enters into our lives.

I should like to suggest a comparison. Like all comparisons, it is in many ways inadequate, and yet it may aid understanding. We might say that in 1918, the year that Guardini published his book, the liturgy was rather like a fresco. It had been preserved from damage, but it had been almost completely overlaid with whitewash by later generations. In the Missal from which the priest celebrated, the form of the liturgy that had grown from its earliest beginnings was still present, but, as far as the faithful were concerned, it was largely concealed beneath instructions for and forms of private prayer. The fresco was laid bare by the Liturgical Movement and, in a definitive way, by the Second Vatican Council. For a moment its colors and figures fascinated us. But since then the fresco has been endangered by climatic conditions as well as by various restorations and reconstructions. In fact, it is threatened

From *The Spirit of the Liturgy*, trans. John Saward (San Francisco: Ignatius Press, 2000).

with destruction, if the necessary steps are not taken to stop these damaging influences. Of course, there must be no question of its being covered with whitewash again, but what is imperative is a new reverence in the way we treat it, a new understanding of its message and its reality, so that rediscovery does not become the first stage of irreparable loss.

My purpose in writing this little book, which I now lay before the public, is to assist this renewal of understanding. Its basic intentions coincide with what Guardini wanted to achieve in his own time with *The Spirit of the Liturgy*. That is why I deliberately chose a title that would be immediately reminiscent of that classic of liturgical theology. The only difference is that I have had to translate what Guardini did at the end of the First World War, in a totally different historical situation, into the context of our present-day questions, hopes, and dangers. I am not attempting, any more than Guardini was, to involve myself with scholarly discussion and research. I am simply offering an aid to the understanding of the faith and to the right way to give the faith its central form of expression in the liturgy. If this book were to encourage, in a new way, something like a "liturgical movement", a movement toward the liturgy and toward the right way of celebrating the liturgy, inwardly and outwardly, then the intention that inspired its writing would be richly fulfilled.

Joseph Cardinal Ratzinger
The Feast of St. Augustine of Hippo
August 28, 1999
Rome

I. The Essence of the Liturgy

1. Liturgy and Life: The Place of the Liturgy in Reality

What *is* the liturgy? What happens during the liturgy? What kind of reality do we encounter here? In the 1920s the suggestion was made that we should understand the liturgy in terms of "play". The point of the analogy was that a game has its own rules, sets up its own world, which is in force from the start of play but then, of course, is suspended at the close of play. A further point of similarity was that play, though it has a meaning, does not have a purpose and that for this very reason there is something healing, even liberating, about it. Play takes us out of the world of daily goals and their pressures and into a sphere free of purpose and achievement, releasing us for a time from all the burdens of our daily world of work. Play is a kind of other world, an oasis of freedom, where for a moment we can let life flow freely. We need such moments of retreat from the pressure of daily life if its burden is to be bearable. Now there is some truth in this way of thinking, but it is insufficient. It all depends on what we are playing. Everything we have said can be applied to any game, and the trouble is that serious commitment to the rules needed for playing the game soon develops its own burdens and leads to new kinds of purposefulness. Whether we look at modern sport or at chess championships or, indeed, at any game, we find that play, when it does not degenerate into mere fooling about, quickly turns from being another world, a counter-world or non-world, to being a bit of the normal world with its own laws.

We should mention another aspect of this theory of play, something that brings us closer to the essence of the liturgy. Children's play seems in many ways a kind of anticipation of life, a rehearsal for later life, without its burdens and gravity. On this analogy, the liturgy would be a reminder that we are all children, or should be children, in relation to that true life toward which we yearn to go. Liturgy would be a kind of anticipation, a rehearsal, a prelude for the life to come, for eternal life, which St. Augustine describes, by contrast with life in this world, as a fabric woven, no longer of exigency and need, but of the freedom of generosity and gift. Seen thus, liturgy would be the redis-covery within us of true childhood, of openness to a greatness still to come, which is still unfulfilled in adult life. Here, then, would be the concrete form of hope, which lives in advance the life to come, the only true life, which initiates us into authentic life—the life of free-dom, of intimate union with God, of pure openness to our fellow-man. Thus it would imprint on the seemingly real life of daily existence the mark of future freedom, break open the walls that confine us, and let the light of heaven shine down upon earth.

This application of play-theory distinguishes the liturgy by its essence from the ordinary kinds of play, which doubtless always contain a long-ing for the real "game", for a wholly different world in which order and freedom are at one. By contrast with the superficial, utilitarian, or humanly vacuous aspects of ordinary play, the play-theory of liturgy brings out what is special and different about that "play" of Wisdom of which the Bible speaks, the play that can be compared to the lit-urgy. But this analogy still lacks something, something essential. The idea of a life to come appears only as a vague postulate. The reference to God, without whom the "life to come" would only be a waste-land, remains quite indeterminate. I should like to suggest, therefore, a new approach, this time starting from specific biblical texts.

In the accounts of the events leading up to Israel's flight from Egypt, as well as in those that describe the flight itself, the Exodus appears to have two distinct goals. The first, which is familiar to us all, is the reaching of the Promised Land, in which Israel will at last live on its own soil and territory, with secure borders, as a people with the free-dom and independence proper to it. But we also hear repeatedly of another goal. God's original command to Pharaoh runs as follows: "Let my people go, that they may serve me in the wilderness" (Ex 7:16). These words—"Let my people go, that they may serve me"—are repeated four times, with slight variations, in all the meetings of Pha-raoh with Moses and Aaron (cf. Ex 8:1; 9:1; 9:13; 10:3). In the course of the negotiations with Pharaoh, the goal becomes more concrete. Pharaoh shows he is willing to compromise. For him the issue is the Israelites' freedom of worship, which he first of all concedes in the following form: "Go, sacrifice to your God within the land" (Ex 8:25). But Moses insists—in obedience to God's command—that they must go out in order to worship. The proper place of worship is the wilderness: "We must go three days' journey into the wilderness and sacrifice to the LORD our God as he will command us" (Ex 8:27). After the plagues that follow, Pharaoh extends his compromise. He now concedes that worship according to the will of the Deity should take place in the wilderness, but he wants only the men to leave: the women and children, together with the cattle, must stay in Egypt. He is assuming the current religious practice, according to which only men are active participants in worship. But Moses cannot negotiate about the liturgy with a foreign potentate, nor can he subject worship to any form of political compromise. The manner in which God is to be worshipped is not a question of political feasibility. It contains its measure within itself, that is, it can only be ordered by the measure of revelation, in dependency upon God. That is why the third and most far-reaching compromise suggested by the earthly ruler is also rejected. Pharaoh now offers women and children the permission to leave with the men: "Only let your flocks and your herds remain" (Ex 10:24). Moses objects: All the livestock must go too, for "we do not know with what we must serve the LORD until we arrive there" (10:26). In all this, the issue is not the Promised Land: the only goal of the Exodus is shown to be worship, which can only take place according to God's measure and therefore eludes the rules of the game of political compromise.

Israel departs, not in order to be a people like all the others; it departs in order to serve God. The goal of the departure is the still unknown mountain of God, the service of God. Now the objection could be made that focusing on worship in the negotiations with Pharaoh was purely tactical. The real goal of the Exodus, ultimately its only goal, was not worship but land—this, after all, was the real content of the promise to Abraham. I do not think that this does justice to the seriousness that pervades the texts. To oppose land and worship makes no sense. The land is given to the people to be a place for the worship of the true God. Mere possession of the land, mere national autonomy, would reduce Israel to the level of all the other nations. The pursuit of such a goal would be a misunderstanding of what is distinctive about Israel's election. The whole history recounted in the books of the Judges and Kings, which is taken up afresh and given a new interpretation in the Chronicles, is intended to show precisely this, that the land, considered just in itself, is an indeterminate good. It becomes a true good, a real gift, a promise fulfilled, only when it is the place where God reigns. Then it will be, not just some independent state or other, but the realm of obedience, where God's will is done and the right kind of human existence developed. Looking at the biblical texts enables us to define more exactly the relationship of the two goals of the Exodus. In its wanderings, Israel discovers the kind of sacrifice God wants, not after three days (as suggested in the conversation with Pharaoh), but after three months, on the day they come "into the wilderness of Sinai" (Ex 19:1). On the third day God comes down onto the top of the mountain (cf. 19:16, 20). Now he speaks to the people. He makes known his will to them in the Ten Commandments (cf. 20:1–17) and, through the mediation of Moses, makes a covenant with them (cf. Ex 24), a covenant concretized in a minutely regulated form of worship. In this way, the purpose of the wandering in the wilderness, as explained to Pharaoh, is fulfilled. Israel learns how to worship God in the way he himself desires. Cult, liturgy in the proper sense, is part of this worship, but so too is life according to the will of God; such a life is an indispensable part of true worship. "The glory of God is the living man, but the life of man is the vision of God", says St. Irenaeus (cf. *Adv. Haer.* 4, 20, 7), getting to the heart of what happens when man meets God on the mountain in the wilderness. Ultimately, it is the very life of man, man himself as living righteously, that is the true worship of God, but life becomes real life only when it receives its form from looking toward God. Cult exists in order to communicate this vision and to give life in such a way that glory is given to God.

Three things are important for the question we are considering. First of all, on Sinai the people receive not only instructions about worship, but also an all-embracing rule of law and life. Only thus can it become a people. A people without a common rule of law cannot live. It destroys itself in anarchy, which is a parody of freedom, its exaltation to the point of abolition. When every man lives without law, every man lives without freedom. This brings me to my second point. In the ordering of the covenant on Sinai, the three aspects of worship, law, and ethics are inseparably interwoven. This is the greatness of the Sinai covenant but also its limitation, as is shown in the transition from Israel to the Church of the Gentiles, where the interweaving was to unravel, to make room for a diversity of legal forms and political structures. In the modern age this necessary unravelling has led finally to the total secularization of the law and the exclusion of any God-ward perspective from the fashioning of the law. But we must not forget that there is an essential connection between the three orders of worship, law, and ethics. Law without a foundation in morality becomes injustice. When morality and law do not originate in a God-ward perspective, they degrade man, because they rob him of his highest measure and his highest capacity, deprive him of any vision of the infinite and eternal. This seeming liberation subjects him to the dictatorship of the ruling majority, to shifting human standards, which inevitably end up doing him violence. Thus we come to a third point, which takes us back to where we started, to the question of the nature of worship and liturgy. When human affairs are so ordered that there is no recognition of God, there is a belittling of man. That is why, in the final analysis, worship and law cannot be completely separated from each other. God has a right to a response from man, to man himself, and where that right of God totally disappears, the order of law among men is dissolved, because there is no cornerstone to keep the whole structure together.

What does this mean for the question we have been considering? We were looking at the two goals of the Exodus, and we saw that the issue was ultimately about the nature of the liturgy. Now it becomes clear that what took place on Sinai, in the period of rest after the wandering through the wilderness, is what gives meaning to the taking of the land. Sinai is not a halfway house, a kind of stop for refreshment on the road to what really matters. No, Sinai gives Israel, so to speak, its interior land without which the exterior one would be a cheerless prospect. Israel is constituted as a people through the covenant and the divine law it contains. It has received a common rule for righteous living. This and this alone is what makes the land a real gift. Sinai remains present in the Promised Land. When the reality of Sinai is lost, the Land, too, is inwardly lost, until finally the people are thrust into exile. Whenever Israel falls away from the right worship of God, when she turns away from God to the false gods (the powers and values of this world), her freedom, too, collapses. It is possible for her to live in her own land and yet still be as she was in Egypt. Mere possession of your own land and state does not give you freedom; in fact, it can be the grossest kind of slavery. And when the loss of law becomes total, it ends in the loss even of the land. The "service of God", the freedom to give right worship to God, appears, in the encounter with Pharaoh, to be the sole purpose of the Exodus, indeed, its very essence. This fact is evident throughout the Pentateuch. This real "canon in the canon", the very heart of Israel's Bible, is set entirely outside of the Holy Land. It ends on the edge of the wilderness, "beyond the Jordan", where Moses once more sums up and repeats the message of Sinai. Thus we can see what the foundation of existence in the Promised Land must be, the necessary condition for life in community and freedom. It is this: steadfast adherence to the law of God, which orders human affairs rightly, that is, by organizing them as realities that come from God and are meant to return to God.

But, once again, what does all this mean for our problem? First, it becomes clear that "cult", seen in its true breadth and depth, goes beyond the action of the liturgy. Ultimately, it embraces the ordering of the whole of human life in Irenaeus' sense. Man becomes glory for God, puts God, so to speak, into the light (and that is what worship is), when he lives by looking toward God. On the other hand, it is also true that law and ethics do not hold together when they are not anchored in the liturgical center and inspired by it. What kind of reality, then, do we find in the liturgy? As a first answer we can now say this: The man who puts to one side any consideration of the reality of God is a realist only in appearance. He is abstracting himself from the One in whom we "live and move and have our being" (Acts 17:28). It is only, therefore, when man's relationship with God is right that all of his other relationships—his relationships with his fellowmen, his dealings with the rest of creation—can be in good order. As we have seen, law is essential for freedom and community; worship—that is, the right way to relate to God—is, for its part, essential for law. We can now broaden the insight by taking a further step. Worship, that is, the right kind of cult, of relationship with God, is essential for the right kind of human existence in the world. It is so precisely because it reaches beyond everyday life. Worship gives us a share in heaven's mode of existence, in the world of God, and allows light to fall from that divine world into ours. In this sense, worship—as we said when we were discussing play—has the character of anticipation. It lays hold in advance of a more perfect life and, in so doing, gives our present life its proper measure. A life without such anticipation, a life no longer opened up to heaven, would be empty, a leaden life.

That is why there are in reality no societies altogether lacking in cult. Even the decidedly atheistic, materialistic systems create their own forms of cult, though, of course, they can only be an illusion and strive in vain, by bombastic trumpeting, to conceal their nothingness.

And so we come to a final reflection. Man himself cannot simply "make" worship. If God does not reveal himself, man is clutching empty space. Moses says to Pharaoh: "[W]e do not know with what we must serve the LORD" (Ex 10:26). These words display a fundamental law of all liturgy. When God does not reveal himself, man can, of course, from the sense of God within him, build altars "to the unknown god" (cf. Acts 17:23). He can reach out toward God in his thinking and try to feel his way toward him. But real liturgy implies that God responds and reveals how we can worship him. In any form, liturgy includes some kind of "institution". It cannot spring from imagination, our own creativity—then it would remain just a cry in the dark or mere self-affirmation. Liturgy implies a real relationship with Another, who reveals himself to us and gives our existence a new direction.

In the Old Testament there is a series of very impressive testimonies to the truth that the liturgy is not a matter of "what you please". Nowhere is this more dramatically evident than in the narrative of the golden calf (strictly speaking, "bull calf"). The cult conducted by the high priest Aaron is not meant to serve any of the false gods of the heathen. The apostasy is more subtle. There is no obvious turning away from God to the false gods. Outwardly, the people remain completely attached to the same God. They want to glorify the God who led Israel out of Egypt and believe that they may very properly represent his mysterious power in the image of a bull calf. Everything seems to be in order. Presumably even the ritual is in complete conformity to the rubrics. And yet it is a falling away from the worship of God to idolatry. This apostasy, which outwardly is scarcely perceptible, has two causes. First, there is a violation of the prohibition of images. The people cannot cope with the invisible, remote, and mysterious God. They want to bring him down into their own world, into what they can see and understand. Worship is no longer going up to God, but drawing God down into one's own world. He must be there when he is needed, and he must be the kind of God that is needed. Man is using God, and in reality, even if it is not outwardly discernible, he is placing himself above God. This gives us a clue to the second point. The worship of the golden calf is a self-generated cult. When Moses stays away for too long, and God himself becomes inaccessible, the people just fetch him back. Worship becomes a feast that the community gives itself, a festival of self-affirmation. Instead of being worship of God, it becomes a circle closed in on itself: eating, drinking, and making merry. The dance around the golden calf is an image of this self-seeking worship. It is a kind of banal self-gratification. The narrative of the golden calf is a warning about any kind of self-initiated and self-seeking worship. Ultimately, it is concerned, no longer with God, but with giving oneself a nice little alternative world, manufactured from one's own resources. Then liturgy really does become pointless, just fooling around. Or still worse it becomes an apostasy from the living God, an apostasy in sacral disguise. All that is left in the end is frustration, a feeling of emptiness. There is no experience of that liberation which always takes place when man encounters the living God.

2. Liturgy—Cosmos—History

It is a widely accepted opinion in modern theology that in the so-called nature religions, as well as in the non-theistic higher religions, cult is focused on the cosmos, while in the Old Testament and Christianity the orientation is toward history. Islam—like post-biblical Judaism—is familiar only with a liturgy of the Word, which is shaped and ordered by the revelation that took place in history, though, in line with the universal tendency of that revelation, it is definitely meant to have a significance for the world as a whole. The idea of worship being either cosmic or historical is not entirely unfounded, but it is false when it leads to an exclusive opposition. It underestimates the sense of history to be found even in the nature religions, and it narrows the meaning of Christian worship of God, forgetting that faith in redemption cannot be separated from faith in the Creator. In this book we shall discover just how important this question is, even for the apparent externals of liturgical celebration.

I shall try to explain what I am saying in several stages. In the religions of the world, cult and cosmos are always closely bound up with one another. The worship of the gods is never just a kind of act of socialization on the part of the community, the affirmation, through symbols, of its social cohesion. The commonly held idea is that worship involves a circular movement of giving and receiving. The gods sustain the world, while men, by their cultic gifts, feed and sustain the gods. The circle of being has two parts: the power of the gods supporting the world, but also the gift of men, which provides for the gods out of the world's resources. This leads to the idea that man was in fact created in order to sustain the gods and to be an essential link in the circular chain of the universe. However naïve this may seem, it reveals a profound intuition into the meaning of human existence. Man exists for God, and thus he serves the whole. Of course, distortion and abuse also lurk behind the door: man somehow has power over the gods; in some small way, in his relationship to them, he has the key to reality in his hand. The gods need him, but, of course, he also needs them. Should he abuse his power, he would do harm to the gods, but he would also destroy himself.

In the Old Testament's account of creation (Gen 1:1—2:4) these views are certainly discernible but at the same time transformed. Creation moves toward the Sabbath, to the day on which man and the whole created order participates in God's rest, in his freedom. Nothing is said directly about worship, still less about the Creator needing the gifts of men. The Sabbath is a vision of freedom. On this day slave and master are equals. The "hallowing" of the Sabbath means precisely this: a rest from all relationships of subordination and a temporary relief from all burden of work. Now some people conclude from this that the Old Testament makes no connection between creation and worship, that it leads to a pure vision of a liberated society as the goal of human history, that from the very beginning its orientation is anthropological and social, indeed revolutionary. But this is a complete misunderstanding of the Sabbath. The account of creation and the Sinai regulations about the Sabbath come from the same source. To understand the account of creation properly, one has to read the Sabbath ordinances of the Torah. Then everything becomes clear. The Sabbath is the sign of the covenant between God and man; it sums up the inward essence of the covenant. If this is so, then we can now define the intention of the account of creation as follows: creation exists to be a place for the covenant that God wants to make with man. The goal of creation is the covenant, the love story of God and man. The freedom and equality of men, which the Sabbath is meant to bring about, is not a merely anthropological or sociological vision;

it can only be understood *theo*-logically. Only when man is in covenant with God does he become free. Only then are the equality and dignity of all men made manifest. If, then, everything is directed to the covenant, it is important to see that the covenant is a relationship: God's gift of himself to man, but also man's response to God. Man's response to the God who is good to him is love, and loving God means worshipping him. If creation is meant to be a space for the covenant, the place where God and man meet one another, then it must be thought of as a space for worship. But what does worship really mean? How is it different from the circle of giving and receiving that characterized the pre-Christian world of worship?

Before turning to this vital question, I should like to refer to the text that concludes the giving of the ceremonial law in the book of Exodus. It is constructed in close parallel to the account of creation. Seven times it says, "Moses did as the Lord had commanded him", words that suggest that the seven-day work on the tabernacle replicates the seven-day work on creation. The account of the construction of the tabernacle ends with a kind of vision of the Sabbath. "So Moses finished the work. Then the cloud covered the tent of meeting, and the glory of the LORD filled the tabernacle" (Ex 40:33f.). The completion of the tent anticipates the completion of creation. God makes his dwelling in the world. Heaven and earth are united. In this connection we should add that, in the Old Testament, the verb *bara* has two, and only two, meanings. First, it denotes the process of the world's creation, the separation of the elements, through which the cosmos emerges out of chaos. Secondly, it denotes the fundamental process of salvation history, that is, the election and separation of pure from impure, and therefore the inauguration of the history of God's dealings with men. Thus begins the spiritual creation, the creation of the covenant, without which the created cosmos would be an empty shell. Creation and history, creation, history, and worship are in a relationship of reciprocity. Creation looks toward the covenant, but the covenant completes creation and does not simply exist along with it. Now if worship, rightly understood, is the soul of the covenant, then it not only saves mankind but is also meant to draw the whole of reality into communion with God.

Once again we face the question: What *is* worship? What happens when we worship? In all religions sacrifice is at the heart of worship. But this is a concept that has been buried under the debris of endless misunderstandings. The common view is that sacrifice has something to do with destruction. It means handing over to God a reality that is in some way precious to man. Now this handing over presupposes that it is withdrawn from use by man, and that can only happen through its destruction, its definitive removal from the hands of man. But this immediately raises the question: What pleasure is God supposed to take in destruction? Is anything really surrendered to God through destruction? One answer is that the destruction always conceals within itself the act of acknowledging God's sovereignty over all things. But can such a mechanical act really serve God's glory? Obviously not. True surrender to God looks very different. It consists—according to the Fathers, in fidelity to biblical thought—in the union of man and creation with God. Belonging to God has nothing to do with destruction or non-being: it is rather a way of being. It means emerging from the state of separation, of apparent autonomy, of existing only for oneself and in oneself. It means losing oneself as the only possible way of finding oneself (cf. Mk 8:35; Mt 10:39). That is why St. Augustine could say that the true "sacrifice" is the *civitas Dei*, that is, love-transformed mankind, the divinization of creation and the surrender of all things to God: God all in all (cf. 1 Cor 15:28). That is the purpose of the world. That is the essence of sacrifice and worship.

And so we can now say that the goal of worship and the goal of creation as a whole are one and the same—divinization, a world of freedom and love. But this means that the historical makes its appearance in the cosmic. The cosmos is not a kind of closed building, a stationary container in which history may by chance take place. It is itself movement, from its one beginning to its one end. In a sense, creation *is* history.

This can be understood in several ways. For example, against the background of the modern evolutionary world view, Teilhard de Chardin depicted the cosmos as a process of ascent, a series of unions. From very simple beginnings the path leads to ever greater and more complex unities, in which multiplicity is not abolished but merged into a growing synthesis, leading to the "Noosphere", in which spirit and its understanding embrace the whole and are blended into a kind of living organism. Invoking the epistles to the Ephesians and Colossians, Teilhard looks on Christ as the energy that strives toward the Noosphere and finally incorporates everything in its "fullness". From here Teilhard went on to give a new meaning to Christian worship:

the transubstantiated Host is the anticipation of the transformation and divinization of matter in the christological "fullness". In his view, the Eucharist provides the movement of the cosmos with its direction; it anticipates its goal and at the same time urges it on.

The older tradition starts from a different conceptual model. Its image is not of an upward flying arrow but of a kind of cross-shaped movement, the two essential directions of which can be called *exitus* and *reditus*, departure and return. This "paradigm" is common in the general history of religions as well as in Christian antiquity and the Middle Ages. For Christian thinkers, the circle is seen as the great movement of the cosmos. The nature religions and many non-Christian philosophies think of it as a movement of unceasing repetition. On closer inspection, these two points of view are not as mutually exclusive as at first sight they seem. For in the Christian view of the world, the many small circles of the lives of individuals are inscribed within the one great circle of history as it moves from *exitus* to *reditus*. The small circles carry within themselves the great rhythm of the whole, give it concrete forms that are ever new, and so provide it with the force of its movement. And in the one great circle there are also the many circles of the lives of the different cultures and communities of human history, in which the drama of beginning, development, and end is played out. In these circles, the mystery of beginning is repeated again and again, but they are also the scene of the end of time, of a final collapse, which may in its own way prepare the ground for a new beginning. The totality of the small circles reflects the great circle. The two—the great circle and the small circles—are interconnected and interdependent. And so worship is bound up with all three dimensions of the cross-shaped movement: the personal, the social, and the universal.

Before attempting to explain this in more detail, we must take note of the second, and in many respects more important, possibility lying hidden in the pattern of *exitus* and *reditus*. First there is an idea that received perhaps its most impressive formulation in the work of the great philosopher of late antiquity Plotinus, though, in different forms, it is found in large parts of the non-Christian cults and religions. The exodus by which non-divine being makes its appearance is seen, not as a going out, but as a falling down, a precipitation from the heights of the divine, and by the laws of falling it hurtles into ever greater depths, farther and farther into remoteness from

God. This means that non-divine being is itself, as such, fallen being. Finitude is already a kind of sin, something negative, which has to be saved by being brought back into the infinite. And so the journey back—the *reditus*—begins when the fall is arrested in the outer depths, so that now the arrow points upward. In the end the "sin" of the finite, of not-being-God, disappears, and in that sense God becomes "all in all". The way of *reditus* means redemption, and redemption means liberation from finitude, which is the real burden of our existence. Cult, then, has to do with the movement turning around. It is the sudden awareness that one has fallen, like the prodigal son's moment of remorse, when he looks back to where he has come from. According to many of these philosophies, knowledge and being coincide, and so this new view of the beginning is already an ascent back toward it. Cult in the sense of the looking up to what is before and above all being is, of its very nature, knowledge, and as knowledge it is movement, return, redemption.

The philosophies of cult go off in different directions. One theory is that only philosophers, only minds qualified for higher thought, are capable of the knowledge that constitutes the "way". Only they are capable of the ascent, of the full divinization that is redemption and liberation from finitude. For the others, for the simpler souls not yet capable of the full upward vision, there are the different liturgies that offer them a certain redemption without being able to take them to the height of the Godhead. The doctrine of the transmigration of souls often compensates for these inequalities. It offers the hope that at some time in the wanderings of existence the point will be reached when at last we can find an escape from finitude and its torments. *Knowledge* (*gnosis*) is the real power of redemption here and therefore the highest form of our elevation—union with God. That is why conceptual and religious systems of this kind—individually, they are all very different—are called "Gnosticism". In early Christianity the clash with Gnosticism was the decisive struggle for its own identity. The fascination of such views is very great; they seem so easily identifiable with the Christian message. For example, original sin, so hard otherwise to understand, is identified with the fall into finitude, which explains why it clings to everything stuck in the vortex of finitude. Again, the idea of redemption as deliverance from the burden of finitude is readily comprehensible, and so on. In our own times, too, in a variety of forms, the fascination of Gnosticism is at work. The religions of the Far East have the same basic pattern. That is why the various kinds of teaching on redemption that they offer seem highly plausible. Exercises for relaxing the body and emptying the mind are seen as the path to redemption. They aim at liberation from finitude, indeed, they momentarily anticipate that liberation and so have salvific power.

As we have said, Christian thought has taken up the schema of *exitus* and *reditus*, but, in so doing, it distinguishes the two movements from one another. *Exitus* is not a fall from the infinite, the rupture of being and thus the cause of all the sorrow in the world. No, *exitus* is first and foremost something thoroughly positive. It is the Creator's free act of creation. It is his positive will that the created order should exist as something good in relation to himself, from which a response of freedom and love can be given back to him. Non-divine being is, therefore, not something negative in itself, but, on the contrary, the wholly positive fruit of the divine will. It depends, not on a disaster, but on a divine decree that is good and does good. The act of God's being, which causes created being, is an act of freedom. In this respect, the principle of freedom is present in being itself, from its ground upward. The *exitus*, or rather God's free act of creation, is indeed ordered toward the *reditus*, but that does not now mean the rescinding of created being; rather, it means what we have described above. The creature, existing in its own right, comes home to itself, and this act is an answer in freedom to God's love. It accepts creation from God as his offer of love, and thus ensues a dialogue of love, that wholly new kind of unity that love alone can create. The being of the other is not absorbed or abolished, but rather, in giving itself, it becomes fully itself. Here is a unity that is higher than the unity of indivisible elementary particles. This *reditus* is a "return", but it does not abolish creation; rather, it bestows its full and final perfection. This is how Christians understand God being "all in all". But everything is bound up with freedom, and the creature has the freedom to turn the positive *exitus* of its creation around, as it were, to rupture it in the Fall: this is the refusal to be dependent, saying No to the *reditus*. Love is seen as dependence and is rejected. In its place come autonomy and autarchy: existing from oneself and in oneself, being a god of one's own making. The arch from *exitus* to *reditus* is broken. The return is no longer desired, and ascent by one's powers proves to be impossible.

If "sacrifice" in its essence is simply returning to love and therefore divinization, worship now has a new aspect: the healing of wounded freedom, atonement, purification, deliverance from estrangement. The essence of worship, of sacrifice—the process of assimilation, of growth in love, and thus the way into freedom—remains unchanged. But now it assumes the aspect of healing, the loving transformation of broken freedom, of painful expiation. Worship is directed to the Other in himself, to his all-sufficiency, but now it refers itself to the Other who alone can extricate me from the knot that I myself cannot untie. Redemption now needs the Redeemer. The Fathers saw this expressed in the parable of the Lost Sheep. For them, the sheep caught in the thorn bush and unable to find its way home is a metaphor for man in general. He cannot get out of the thicket and find his way back to God. The shepherd who rescues him and takes him home is the Logos himself, the eternal Word, the eternal Meaning of the universe dwelling in the Son. He it is who makes his way to us and takes the sheep onto his shoulders, that is, he assumes human nature, and as the God-Man he carries man the creature home to God. And so the *reditus* becomes possible. Man is given a homecoming. But now sacrifice takes the form of the Cross of Christ, of the love that in dying makes a gift of itself. Such sacrifice has nothing to do with destruction. It is an act of new creation, the restoration of creation to its true identity. All worship is now a participation in this "Pasch" of Christ, in his "passing over" from divine to human, from death to life, to the unity of God and man. Thus Christian worship is the practical application and fulfillment of the words that Jesus proclaimed on the first day of Holy Week, Palm Sunday, in the Temple in Jerusalem: "I, when I am lifted up from the earth, will draw all men to myself" (Jn 12:32).

The circles of the cosmos and of history are now distinguished. The gift of freedom is the center of created as well as of divine being, and so the historical element has its own irrevocable meaning, but it is not for that reason separated from the cosmic element. Ultimately, despite their differences, the two circles continue to be the one circle of being. The historical liturgy of Christendom is and always will be cosmic, without separation and without confusion, and only as such does it stand erect in its full grandeur. Christianity is uniquely new, but it does not spurn the religious quest of human history. It takes up in itself all the prevailing preoccupations of the world's religions, and in that way it maintains a connection with them.

3. From Old Testament to New: The Fundamental Form of the Christian Liturgy—Its Determination by Biblical Faith

Peace in the universe through peace with God, the union of above and below—that, according to the argument we have presented so far, is how we can describe the essential intention of worship in all the world's religions. But this basic definition of the attributes of worship is marked concretely by an awareness of man's fall and estrangement. Of necessity it takes place as a struggle for atonement, forgiveness, reconciliation. The awareness of guilt weighs down on mankind. Worship is the attempt, to be found at every stage of history, to overcome guilt and bring back the world and one's own life into right order. And yet an immense feeling of futility pervades everything. This is the tragic face of human history. How can man again connect the world with God? How is he supposed to make valid atonement? The only real gift man should give to God is himself. As his religious awareness becomes more highly developed, so his awareness that any gift but himself is too little, in fact absurd, becomes more intense. Historically, this sense of inadequacy has been the source of grotesque and horrific forms of cult. The most extreme example is human sacrifice. Superficially, it seems to give the deity what is best, and yet more deeply it has to be seen as the most horrific evasion of the gift of self, the most horrific and therefore the most to be rejected. Thus, as religion becomes more highly developed, this terrible attempt at atonement is more and more discarded, but it also becomes clearer that in all worship it is not the real gift but a mere replacement that is given.* The sacrificial system of all the world's religions, including Israel's, rests on the idea of representation—but how can sacrificial animals or the fruits of harvest represent man, make expiation for him? This is not representation but replacement, and worship with replacements turns out to be a replacement for worship. Somehow the real thing is missing.

---

*Cardinal Ratzinger here uses the German word *Ersatz*, which is generally translated as "substitute" (as in *Ersatzkaffee*, coffee made out of a substitute for coffee beans such as acorns). I have not used "substitute" because of the more positive theological connotations of that English word when used as a translation of *Stellvertreter*. The Cardinal is contrasting the two ways in which one thing can take the place of another. In the first case, there is mere absence: something that should be there is missing (cf. "a poor substitute for real coffee"). In the second case, there is mysterious presence: somehow one thing is present in the other. This explains the contrast I have put into the English between "replacement" (*Ersatz*) sacrifices and "representation" (*Vertretung*) sacrifices.—Trans.

What, then, is special about the liturgy of Israel? First of all, without doubt, the One to whom it is directed. Other religions frequently direct their worship to subordinate powers. Precisely because they know that the only true God cannot be served by the sacrifice of animals, they leave him without worship. Sacrifices are aimed at the "principalities and powers" with which man has to deal on a daily basis. These are what he has to fear, to propitiate, to placate. Israel did not merely deny the existence of these "gods" but saw them more and more as demons, which increasingly alienate man from himself and from God. Adoration is due to God alone: that is the First Commandment. Now this one God is worshipped through an extensive sacrificial system, the meticulous regulations for which are set out in the Torah. However, when we look at the cultic history of Israel more closely, we run up against a second characteristic, which leads finally, by its inner logic, to Jesus Christ, to the New Testament. It is precisely when we read the New Testament in terms of cultic theology that we see how much it is bound up, in its deepest implications, with the Old. The New Testament corresponds to the inner drama of the Old. It is the inner mediation of two elements that at first are in conflict with one another and find their unity in the form of Jesus Christ, in his Cross and Resurrection. What at first seems to be a break turns out, on closer inspection, to be a real fulfillment, in which all the paths formerly followed converge.

Anyone who reads the book of Leviticus by itself—apart from chapter 26, with its threat of exile and its promise of new blessings—could come to the conclusion that it sets up an eternally valid form of worship. Here is an apparently everlasting world order, with no further history to come, because in the course of the year it constantly brings about new expiation, purification, restoration. It seems to be a static or, if you like, cyclical world order. It always remains the same, because it contains weights and counterweights in perfect balance. But chapter 26, to a certain extent, shatters this appearance. More importantly, Leviticus has to be read in the context of the whole Torah and the whole Bible. It seems to me to be of some importance that, at the beginning of cultic history, Genesis and Exodus place two events in which the problem of representation is quite clearly addressed. First of all, there is Abraham's sacrifice. Out of obedience, Abraham is willing to do something that goes against the mission given by God: to sacrifice his only son, Isaac, the bearer of the promise. In so doing, he would be giving up everything, for, without descendants, the land promised to his descendants has no meaning. At the very last moment God himself stops Abraham from offering this kind of sacrifice. He is given something else to offer instead of the son of God—a male lamb. And so representative sacrifice is established by divine command. God gives the lamb, which Abraham then offers back to him. Accordingly, we offer sacrifice, as the Roman Canon says, "*de tuis donis ac datis*" (from your own gracious gifts). Somehow there always has to be a stinging reminder of this story, an expectation of the true Lamb, who comes from God and is for that very reason not a replacement but a true representative, in whom we ourselves are taken to God. The Christian theology of worship—beginning with St. John the Baptist—sees in Christ the Lamb given by God. The Apocalypse presents this sacrificed Lamb, who lives as sacrificed, as the center of the heavenly liturgy, a liturgy that, through Christ's Sacrifice, is now present in the midst of the world and makes replacement liturgies superfluous (see Rev 5).

My second point concerns the institution of the Passover liturgy in Exodus 12. Here the rules are laid down for the sacrifice of the Passover lamb as the center of the liturgical year and of Israel's memorial of faith, which is at the same time an everlasting foundation of faith. The lamb appears clearly as the ransom through which Israel is delivered from the death of the firstborn. Now this ransom serves also as a reminder. It is ultimately the firstborn itself to which God lays claim: "Consecrate to me all the first-born; whatever is the first to open the womb among the people of Israel, both of man and of beast, is mine" (Ex 13:2). The sacrificed lamb speaks of the necessary holiness of man and of creation as a whole. It points beyond itself. The Passover sacrifice does not, as it were, stop with itself; rather, it places an obligation on the firstborn and, in them, on the people as a whole, on creation as a whole. This fact should help us appreciate the emphatic way in which St. Luke in his infancy narratives describes Jesus as the "first-born" (cf. Lk 2:7). It also helps us understand why the Captivity Epistles present Christ as the "first-born of creation", in whom takes place a sanctification of the firstborn that embraces us all.

But we are still in the Old Testament. Its sacrificial system is constantly accompanied by prophetic disquiet and questioning. Already in 1 Samuel 15:22 [RSV adapted] we meet a primordial word of prophecy that, with some variations, runs through the Old Testament before

being taken up anew by Christ: "More precious than sacrifice is obedience, submission better than the fat of rams!" In Hosea the prophecy appears in this form: "For I desire steadfast love and not sacrifice,
the knowledge of God, rather than burnt offerings" (6:6). In the mouth
of Jesus it assumes a very simple and elementary form: "I desire mercy,
and not sacrifice" (Mt 9:13; 12:7). Thus Temple worship was always
accompanied by a vivid sense of its insufficiency. "If I were hungry, I
would not tell you; for the world and all that is in it is mine. Do I eat
the flesh of bulls, or drink the blood of goats? Offer to God a sacrifice
of thanksgiving, and pay your vows to the Most High" (Ps 50[49]:12–
14). The radical critique of the Temple, which, according to the account
in Acts chapter 7, Stephen delivered in a fiery speech, is certainly
unusual in its form, marked as it is with the new passion of Christian
faith, but it is not without precedent in the history of Israel. At the
end Stephen takes the key sentence of his critique from the prophet
Amos: "I hate, I despise your feasts, and I take no delight in your
solemn assemblies. Even though you offer me your burnt offerings
and cereal offerings, I will not accept them, and the peace offerings of
your fatted beasts I will not look upon. Take away from me the noise
of your songs; to the melody of your harps I will not listen" (Amos 5:21–
23; cf. Acts 7:42f., citing Amos 5:25–27).

The whole of St. Stephen's speech is triggered by the accusation that
he had said "Jesus of Nazareth will destroy this place [that is, the Tem-
ple], and will change the customs which Moses delivered to us"
(Acts 6:14). Stephen responds to this allegation only indirectly, by invoking the line of criticism of Temple and sacrifice that runs through the
Old Testament. He quotes the controversial criticism of cult to be found
in Amos 5:25–27, the original meaning of which is very hard to deci-
pher. He uses the version in the Greek Bible, in which all the worship
of the forty years in the wilderness is aligned with the worship of the
golden calf. This makes Israel's liturgy during the whole of this foundational period seem like a continuation of the first apostasy. "Did you
offer to me slain beasts and sacrifices, forty years in the wilderness,
O house of Israel? And you took up the tent of Moloch, and the star of
the god Rephan, the figures which you made to worship; and I will
remove you beyond Babylon" (Acts 7:42f.; cf. Amos 5:25–27). The
very beasts of sacrifice seem here to be a perversion of worship of the
one God. The words of the prophet, used by Stephen in the version of
the Alexandrian translators, must have come as a violent shock to his

hearers. In fact, he could have added to them the dramatic words of the prophet Jeremiah: "[I]n the day that I brought them out of the land of Egypt, I did not speak to your fathers or command them concerning burnt offerings and sacrifices" (Jer 7:22). Stephen refrains from exploiting such texts, which give us a sense of the difficult internal debates in Israel before the Exile. Instead, he adds three other trains of thought to get across his exposition of the message of Christ.

Moses, he says, made the tent of meeting, in obedience to God's command, according to the pattern he had seen on the mountain (cf. Acts 7:44; Ex 25:40). This means that the earthly Temple is only a replica, not the true Temple. It is an image and likeness, which points beyond itself. David, who found favor with God, prayed God to let him build a tabernacle. "But it was Solomon who built a house for him" (Acts 7:47). The transition from the tent with all its impermanence to the house intended to lodge God in an edifice of stone is seen as a deviance, for "the Most High does not dwell in houses made with hands" (7:48). Finally, Stephen adds something to the idea of impermanence, which was conspicuous in the tent but obscured in the house. He brings out the inner dynamism of the Old Testament, which inevitably strove to get beyond the impermanence. He quotes the Messianic prophecy that in a certain sense forms the climax of Deuteronomy (cf. 18:15) and, for Stephen, provides the key for the interpretation of the whole Pentateuch: "God will raise up for you a prophet from your brethren as he raised me up" (7:37). The essential work of Moses was the construction of the tabernacle and the ordering of worship, which was also the very heart of the order of law and moral instruction. If this is so, then it is clear that the new Prophet, the definitive Prophet, will lead the people out of the age of the tabernacle and its impermanence, out of all the inadequacy of sacrificial animals. He will "destroy" the Temple and indeed "change the customs" that Moses had delivered. The prophets who followed Moses were the great witnesses to the impermanence of all these customs. Raising their voices, they pushed history forward toward the New Moses. This is the prophetic line that reached its destination in the Righteous One on the Cross (cf. Acts 7:51f.).

Stephen does not contest the words he is accused of having spoken. Instead, he tries to prove that they contain a deeper fidelity to the message of the Old Testament and, indeed, to the message of Moses. It is important also to note that the charge brought against the first martyrs of the Church is identical, almost to the letter, with the accusation that plays such a central role in the trial of Jesus. For Jesus was accused of having said: "I will destroy this temple that is made with hands, and in three days I will build another, not made with hands" (Mk 14:58). Of course, the witnesses could not agree about the exact meaning of Jesus' prophecy (cf. 14:59), but it is clear that such words played a central role in the dispute about Jesus. Here we reach the heart of the christological question, the question of who Jesus is, and at the same time we reach the heart of the question of what the true worship of God is. The prophecy of the Temple's destruction, which Jesus is accused of having made, points beyond itself to the incident recorded by all four Evangelists: the cleansing of the Temple. This could not be regarded as just an angry outburst against the abuses that happen in all holy places. No, in the final analysis, this had to be seen as an attack on the Temple cult, of which the sacrificial animals and the special Temple moneys collected there were a part. True, none of the Synoptic Gospels reports any such words of Jesus in this context, but St. John presents them as a prophetic utterance that Jesus makes in explanation of his action: "Destroy this temple, and in three days I will raise it up" (Jn 2:19). Jesus does not say that *he* will demolish the Temple—that version was the false witness borne against him. But he does prophesy that his accusers will do exactly that. This is a prophecy of the Cross: he shows that the destruction of his earthly body will be at the same time the end of the Temple. With his Resurrection the new Temple will begin: the living body of Jesus Christ, which will now stand in the sight of God and be the place of all worship. Into this body he incorporates men. It is the tabernacle that no human hands have made, the place of true worship of God, which casts out the shadow and replaces it with reality. Interpreted at its deepest level, the prophecy of the Resurrection is also a prophecy of the Eucharist. The body of Christ is sacrificed and precisely as sacrificed is living. This is the mystery made known in the Mass. Christ communicates himself to us and thus brings us into a real bond with the living God. We should mention in this connection another detail, which is found in all three of the Synoptic Gospels. They all report that, at the moment of Jesus' death, the veil of the Temple was torn in two, from top to bottom (cf. Mk 15:38; Mt 27:51; Lk 23:45). What they mean to say is this: at the moment of Jesus' death, the function of the old Temple comes to an end. It is dissolved. It is no longer the place of God's presence, his "footstool", into which he has caused his glory to descend. Theologically, the visible destruction of the Temple, which will follow in a few decades, has already been anticipated. Worship through types and shadows, worship with replacements, ends at the very moment when the real worship takes place: the self-offering of the Son, who has become man and "Lamb", the "Firstborn", who gathers up and into himself all worship of God, takes it from the types and shadows into the reality of man's union with the living God. The prophetic gesture of cleansing the Temple, of renewing divine worship and preparing it for its new form, has reached its goal. The prophecy connected with it is fulfilled: "[Z]eal for your house has consumed me" (Ps 69[68]:9; Jn 2:17). At the end it was Jesus' "zeal" for right worship that took him to the Cross. This is precisely what opened the way for the true house of God, the "one not made with human hands"—the risen body of Christ. And the interpretation that the Synoptic Gospels give to Jesus' symbolic act of prophecy is also fulfilled: "My house shall be called a house of prayer for all the nations" (Mk 11:17). The abolition of the Temple inaugurates a new universality of worship, "in spirit and truth" (cf. Jn 4:23), which Jesus foretold in his conversation with the Samaritan woman. Needless to say, the words "spirit and truth" must not be taken in a subjectivist sense, as they were in the Enlightenment. No, they must be seen in the light of him who could say of himself: "I am the truth" (Jn 14:6).

We have so far presented a sketch of the inner dynamism of the idea of worship in the Old Testament and have shown that there was an intense awareness of the impermanence of the Temple sacrifices together with a desire for something greater, something indescribably new. Before trying to pull everything together and draw some conclusions, we must try to hear the voices in which there is already a presentiment of this new thing that is to come. I am thinking of the tendency, which had already become apparent, of taking up an essentially critical attitude toward the previous forms of worship. In pre-exilic Israel one constantly hears voices warning about the rigidifying of the sacrificial system and its degeneration into externalism and syncretism. The Exile came as a challenging opportunity to formulate clearly a positive doctrine about worship and the new thing that was to come. There was no Temple any more, no public and communal form of divine worship as decreed in the law. Deprived as she was of worship, Israel was bound to feel immeasurably poor and pathetic. She stood before God with empty hands. There was no expiation any more, no "holocausts" ascending to God. In this crisis the conviction became ever clearer that Israel's sufferings, through God and for God, the cry of her broken heart, her persistent pleading before the silent God, had to count in his sight as "fatted sacrifices" and whole burnt offerings. It was the very emptiness of Israel's hands, the heaviness of her heart, that was now to be worship, to serve as a spiritual equivalent of the missing Temple oblations. During the new oppression of Jewish worship under Antiochus IV Epiphanes (175–163 B.C.), these ideas, as set forth in the book of Daniel, acquired a new power and profundity. They remained alive even after the restoration of the Temple by the Maccabees. The Qumran community formed an opposition to the priestly monarchy of the Maccabees: it did not recognize the new Temple and saw itself instead as dedicated to "spiritual worship". In Alexandria, the Jews eventually made contact with the Greek critique of cult, and from then on the concept of *logikē latreia* (*thusia*) [worship and sacrifice with spirit and mind], which we encounter in the epistle to the Romans (cf. Rom 12:1), grew increasingly important. This was the Christian response to the cultic crisis of the whole ancient world. The sacrifice is the "word", the word of prayer, which goes up from man to God, embodying the whole of man's existence and enabling him to become "word" (*logos*) in himself. It is man, conforming himself to *logos* and becoming *logos* through faith, who is the true sacrifice, the true glory of God in the world. Israel's experience of suffering during the Exile and the Hellenistic period first brought the word of prayer into prominence as the equivalent of exterior sacrifice. Now, through the word *logos*, the whole philosophy of *logos* in the Greek world is incorporated into the concept. The Greek mind elevates it eventually to the idea of a mystical union with the Logos, the very meaning of all things.

The Fathers of the Church took up this spiritual development. They saw the Eucharist as essentially *oratio*, sacrifice in the Word, and in this way they also showed how Christian worship stood in relation to the spiritual struggle of antiquity, to its quest for man's true path and for his encounter with God. The Fathers call the Eucharist simply "prayer", that is, the sacrifice of the Word, but in so doing, they go beyond the Greek idea of the sacrifice of the *logos* and provide an answer to the question left open by Old Testament theology, which made prayer the equivalent of sacrifice. A striking conflict is evident in the great Old Testament movement toward worship in the "Word". On the one hand, the way is open to a new, positive form of divine worship. On the other hand, there is still an insufficiency. The Word alone is not enough. There is an expectation of a restoration of the Temple in purified form. This explains the apparent contradictions that we find in Psalm 51(50). On the one hand, there is a magnificent unfolding of the new idea of worship: "For you take no delight in sacrifice. . . . The sacrifice acceptable to God is a broken spirit" (vv. 16–17). On the other hand, the whole psalm ends with a stirring vision of a fulfillment to come: "[T]hen will you delight in right sacrifices, in burnt offerings and whole burnt offerings; then bulls will be offered on your altar" (vv. 18–19). For its part, the Hellenistic Logos-mysticism, however grand and beautiful, allows the body to fall into insubstantiality. The hope for spiritual ascent and universal reunion conforms to the Gnostic pattern of which we spoke earlier. Something is missing.

The idea of the sacrifice of the Logos becomes a full reality only in the *Logos incarnatus*, the Word who is made flesh and draws "all flesh" into the glorification of God. When that happens, the Logos is more than just the "Meaning" behind and above things. Now he himself has entered into flesh, has become bodily. He takes up into himself our sufferings and hopes, all the yearning of creation, and bears it to God. The two themes that Psalm 51 (50) could not reconcile, the two themes that throughout the Old Testament keep running toward one another, now really converge. The Word is no longer just the representation of something else, of what is bodily. In Jesus' self-surrender on the Cross, the Word is united with the entire reality of human life and suffering. There is no longer a replacement cult. Now the vicarious sacrifice of Jesus takes us up and leads us into that likeness with God, that transformation into love, which is the only true adoration. In virtue of Jesus' Cross and Resurrection, the Eucharist is the meeting point of all the lines that lead from the Old Covenant, indeed, from the whole of man's religious history. Here at last is right worship, ever longed for and yet surpassing our powers: adoration "in spirit and truth". The torn curtain of the Temple is the curtain torn between the world and the countenance of God. In the pierced heart of the Crucified, God's own heart is opened up—here we see who God is and what he is like. Heaven is no longer locked up. God has stepped out of his hiddenness. That is why St. John sums up both the meaning of the Cross and the nature of the new worship of God in the mysterious promise made through the prophet Zechariah (cf. 12:10). "They shall look on him whom they have pierced" (Jn 19:37). We shall meet this text again, with a new significance, in Revelation 1:7. For the moment we must try to sum up some of the conclusions that emerge from what we have said so far.

1. Christian worship, or rather the liturgy of the Christian faith, cannot be viewed simply as a Christianized form of the synagogue service, however much its actual development owes to the synagogue service. The synagogue was always ordered toward the Temple and remained so, even after the Temple's destruction. The synagogue's liturgy of the Word, which is celebrated with magnificent profundity, regards itself as incomplete, and for that reason it is very different from the liturgy of the Word in Islam, which, together with pilgrimage and fasting, constitutes the whole of divine worship as decreed by the Koran. By contrast, the synagogue service is the divine worship that takes place in the absence of the Temple and in expectation of its restoration. Christian worship, for its part, regards the destruction of the Temple in Jerusalem as final and as theologically necessary. Its place has been taken by the universal Temple of the risen Christ, whose outstretched arms on the Cross span the world, in order to draw all men into the embrace of eternal love. The new Temple already exists, and so too does the new, the definitive sacrifice: the humanity of Christ opened up in his Cross and Resurrection. The prayer of the man Jesus is now united with the dialogue of eternal love within the Trinity. Jesus draws men into this prayer through the Eucharist, which is thus the ever-open door of adoration and the true Sacrifice, the Sacrifice of the New Covenant, the "reasonable service of God". In modern theological discussion, the exclusive model for the liturgy of the New Covenant has been thought to be the synagogue—in strict opposition to the Temple, which is regarded as an expression of the law and therefore as an utterly obsolete "stage" in religion. The effects of this theory have been disastrous. Priesthood and sacrifice are no longer intelligible. The comprehensive "fulfillment" of pre-Christian salvation history and the inner unity of the two Testaments disappear from view. Deeper understanding of the matter is bound to recognize that the Temple, as well as the synagogue, entered into Christian liturgy.

2. This means that universality is an essential feature of Christian worship. It is the worship of an open heaven. It is never just an event in the life of a community that finds itself in a particular place. No, to celebrate the Eucharist means to enter into the openness of a glorification of God that embraces both heaven and earth, an openness effected by the Cross and Resurrection. Christian liturgy is never just an event organized by a particular group or set of people or even by a particular local Church. Mankind's movement toward Christ meets Christ's movement toward men. He wants to unite mankind and bring about the one Church, the one divine assembly, of all men. Everything, then, comes together: the horizontal and the vertical, the uniqueness of God and the unity of mankind, the communion of all who worship in spirit and in truth.

3. Accordingly, we must regard St. Paul's concept of *logikē atreia*, of divine worship in accordance with *logos*, as the most appropriate way of expressing the essential form of Christian liturgy. This concept is the confluence of several different streams: the spiritual movement of the Old Testament, the process of inner purification within the history of religion, human quest, and divine response. The *logos* of creation, the *logos* in man, and the true and eternal Logos made flesh, the Son, come together. All other definitions fall short. For example, one could describe the Eucharist, in terms of the liturgical phenomenon, as an "assembly", or, in terms of Jesus' act of institution at the Last Supper, as a "meal". But this seizes on individual elements while failing to grasp the great historical and theological connections. By contrast, the word "Eucharist" points to the universal form of worship that took place in the Incarnation, Cross, and Resurrection of Christ, and so it can happily serve as a summary of the idea of *logikē latreia* and may legitimately serve as an appropriate designation for Christian worship.

4. Finally, all these insights open up an essential dimension of Christian liturgy, which we must consider more concretely in the next chapter. As we have seen, Christian liturgy is a liturgy of promise fulfilled, of a quest, the religious quest of human history, reaching its goal. But it remains a liturgy of hope. It, too, bears within it the mark of impermanence. The new Temple, not made by human hands, does exist, but it is also still under construction. The great gesture of embrace emanating from the Crucified has not yet reached its goal; it has only just begun. Christian liturgy is liturgy on the way, a liturgy of pilgrimage toward the transfiguration of the world, which will only take place when God is "all in all".

II. Time and Space in the Liturgy

1. The Relationship of the Liturgy to Time and Space: Some Preliminary Questions

Can there really be special holy places and holy times in the world of Christian faith? Christian worship is surely a cosmic liturgy, which embraces both heaven and earth. The epistle to the Hebrews stresses that Christ suffered "outside the gate" and adds this exhortation: "Therefore let us go forth to him outside the camp, bearing abuse for him" (13:12). Is the whole world not now his sanctuary? Is sanctity not to be practiced by living one's daily life in the right way? Is our divine worship not a matter of being loving people in our daily life? Is *that* not how we become like God and so draw near to the true sacrifice? Can the sacral be anything other than imitating Christ in the simple patience of daily life? Can there be any other holy time than the time for practicing love of neighbor, whenever and wherever the circumstances of our life demand it?

Whoever asks questions like these touches on a crucial dimension of the Christian understanding of worship, but overlooks something essential about the permanent limits of human existence in this world, overlooks the "not yet" that is part of Christian existence and talks as if the New Heaven and New Earth had already come. The Christ-event and the growth of the Church out of all the nations, the transition from Temple sacrifice to universal worship "in spirit and truth", is the first important step across the frontier, a step toward the fulfillment of the promises of the Old Testament. But it is obvious that hope has not yet fully attained its goal. The New Jerusalem needs no Temple because Almighty God and the Lamb are themselves its Temple. In this City, instead of sun and moon, it is the glory of God and its lamp, the Lamb, that shed their brilliance (cf. Rev 21:22f.). But this City is not yet here. That is why the Church Fathers described the various stages of fulfillment, not just as a contrast between Old and New Testaments, but as the three steps of shadow, image, and reality. In the Church of the New Testament the shadow has been scattered by the image: "[T]he night is far gone, the day is at hand" (Rom 13:12). But, as St. Gregory the Great puts it, it is still only the time of dawn, when darkness and light are intermingled. The sun is rising, but it has still not reached its zenith. Thus the time of the New Testament is a peculiar kind of "in-between", a mixture of "already and not yet". The empirical conditions of life in this world are still in force, but they have been burst open, and must be more and more burst open, in preparation for the final fulfillment already inaugurated in Christ.

This idea of the New Testament as the between-time, as image between shadow and reality, gives liturgical theology its specific form. It becomes even clearer when we bear in mind the three levels on which Christian worship operates, the three levels that make it what it is. There is the middle level, the strictly liturgical level, which is familiar to us all and is revealed in the words and actions of Jesus at the Last Supper. These words and actions form the core of Christian liturgical celebration, which was further constructed out of the synthesis of the synagogue and Temple liturgies. The sacrificial actions of the Temple have been replaced by the Eucharistic Prayer, which enters into what Jesus did at the Last Supper, and by the distribution of the consecrated gifts. But this properly liturgical level does not stand on its own. It has meaning only in relation to something that really happens, to a reality that is substantially present. Otherwise it would lack real content, like bank notes without funds to cover them. The Lord could say that his Body was "given" only because he *had* in fact given it; he could present his Blood in the new chalice as shed for many only because he really *had* shed it. This Body is not the ever-dead corpse of a dead man, nor is the Blood the life-element rendered lifeless. No, sacrifice has become gift, for the Body given in love and the Blood given in love have entered, through the Resurrection, into the eternity of love, which is stronger than death. Without the Cross and Resurrection, Christian worship is null and void, and a theology of liturgy that omitted any reference to them would really just be talking about an empty game.

In considering this foundation of reality that undergirds Christian liturgy, we need to take account of another important matter. The crucifixion of Christ, his death on the Cross, and, in another way, the act of his Resurrection from the grave, which bestows incorruptibility on the corruptible, are historical events that happen just once and as such belong to the past. The word *semel* (*ephapax*), "once for all", which the epistle to the Hebrews emphasizes so vigorously in contrast to the multitude of repeated sacrifices in the Old Covenant, is strictly applicable to them. But if they were no more than facts in the past, like all the dates we learn in history books, then there could be nothing contemporary about them. In the end they would remain beyond our reach. However, the exterior act of being crucified is accompanied by an interior act of self-giving (the Body is "given for you"). "No one takes [my life] from me," says the Lord in St. John's Gospel, "but I lay it down of my own accord" (10:18). This act of giving is in no way just a spiritual occurrence. It is a spiritual act that takes up the bodily into itself, that embraces the whole man; indeed, it is at the same time an act of the Son. As St. Maximus the Confessor showed so splendidly, the obedience of Jesus' human will is inserted into the everlasting Yes of the Son to the Father. This "giving" on the part of the Lord, in the passivity of his being crucified, draws the passion of human existence into the action of love, and so it embraces all the dimensions of reality—Body, Soul, Spirit, Logos. Just as the pain of the body is drawn into the pathos of the mind and becomes the Yes of obedience, so time is drawn into what reaches beyond time. The real interior act, though it does not exist without the exterior, transcends time, but since it comes from time, time can again and again be brought into it. That is how we can become contemporary with the past events of salvation. St. Bernard of Clairvaux has this in mind when he says that the true *semel* ("once") bears within itself the *semper* ("always"). What is perpetual takes place in what happens only once. In the Bible the Once for All is emphasized most vigorously in the epistle to the Hebrews, but the careful reader will discover that the point made by St. Bernard expresses its true meaning. The *ephapax* ("once for all") is bound up with the *aiōnios* ("everlasting"). "Today" embraces the whole time of the Church. And so in the Christian liturgy we not only receive something from the past but become contemporaries with what lies at the foundation of that liturgy. Here is the real heart and true grandeur of the celebration of the Eucharist, which is more, much more than a meal. In the Eucharist we are caught up and made contemporary with the Paschal Mystery of Christ, in his passing from the tabernacle of the transitory to the presence and sight of God.

Let us go back to where we started. We said that there is, first, the level of the event of institution and, secondly, the liturgical making present, the real liturgical level. I have tried to show how the two levels are interconnected. Now if past and present penetrate one another in this way, if the essence of the past is not simply a thing of the past but the far-reaching power of what follows in the present, then the future, too, is present in what happens in the liturgy: it ought to be called, in its essence, an anticipation of what is to come. But we must not be overhasty. The idea of the *eschaton*, of the Second Coming of Christ, immediately comes to mind, and rightly so. But there is yet another dimension to be considered. This liturgy is, as we have seen, not about replacement, but about representation, vicarious sacrifice [*Stellvertretung*]. Now we can see what this distinction means. The liturgy is not about the sacrificing of animals, of a "something" that is ultimately alien to me. This liturgy is founded on the Passion endured by a man who with his "I" reaches into the mystery of the living God himself, by the man who is the Son. So it can never be a mere *actio liturgica*. Its origin also bears within it its future in the sense that representation, vicarious sacrifice, takes up into itself those whom it represents; it is not external to them, but a shaping influence on them. Becoming contemporary with the Pasch of Christ in the liturgy of the Church is also, in fact, an anthropological reality. The celebration is not just a rite, not just a liturgical "game". It is meant to be indeed a *logikē latreia*, the "logicizing" of my existence, my interior contemporaneity with the self-giving of Christ. His self-giving is meant to become mine, so that I become contemporary with the Pasch of Christ and assimilated unto God. That is why in the early Church martyrdom was regarded as a real eucharistic celebration, the most extreme actualization of the Christian's being a contemporary with Christ, of being united with him. The liturgy does indeed have a bearing on everyday life, on me in my personal existence. Its aim, as St. Paul says in the text already referred to, is that "our bodies" (that is, our bodily existence on earth) become "a living sacrifice", united to the Sacrifice of Christ (cf. Rom 12:1). That is the only explanation of the urgency of the petitions for acceptance that characterize every Christian liturgy. A theology that is blind to the connections we have been considering can only regard this as a contradiction or a lapse into pre-Christian ways, for, so it will be said, Christ's Sacrifice was accepted long ago.

True, but in the form of representation it has not come to an end. The *semel* ("once for all") wants to attain its *semper* ("always"). This Sacrifice is complete only when the world has become the place of love, as St. Augustine saw in his *City of God*. Only then, as we said at the beginning, is worship perfected and what happened on Golgotha completed. That is why, in the petitions for acceptance, we pray that representation become a reality and take hold of us. That is why, in the prayers of the Roman Canon, we unite ourselves with the great men who offered sacrifice at the dawn of history: Abel, Melchizedek, and Abraham. They set out toward the Christ who was to come. They were anticipations of Christ, or, as the Fathers say, "types" of Christ. Even his predecessors were able to enter into the contemporaneousness with him that we beg for ourselves.

It is tempting to say that this third dimension of liturgy, its suspension between the Cross of Christ and our living entry into him who suffered vicariously for us and wants to become "one" with us (cf. Gal 3:28), expresses its moral demands. And without doubt Christian worship does contain a moral demand, but it goes much farther than mere moralism. The Lord has gone before us. He has already done what we have to do. He has opened a way that we ourselves could not have pioneered, because our powers do not extend to building a bridge to God. He himself became that bridge. And now the challenge is to allow ourselves to be taken up into his being "for" mankind, to let ourselves be embraced by his opened arms, which draw us to himself. He, the Holy One, hallows us with the holiness that none of us could ever give ourselves. We are incorporated into the great historical process by which the world moves toward the fulfillment of God being "all in all". In this sense, what at first seems like the moral dimension is at the same time the eschatological dynamism of the liturgy. The fullness of Christ, of which the Captivity Epistles of St. Paul speak, becomes a reality, and only thus is the Paschal event completed throughout history. The "today" of Christ lasts right to the end (cf. Heb 4:7ff.).

When we look back on our reflections hitherto in this chapter, we see that we have twice encountered—in different contexts—a three-step process. The liturgy, as we saw, is characterized by tension that is inherent in the historical Pasch of Jesus (his Cross and Resurrection) as the foundation of its reality. The ever-abiding form of the liturgy has been shaped in what is once and for all; and what is everlasting—the second step enters into our present moment in the liturgical action and—the third step—wants to take hold of the worshipper's life and ultimately of all historical reality. The immediate event—the liturgy—makes sense and has a meaning for our lives only because it contains the other two dimensions. Past, present, and future interpenetrate and touch upon eternity. Earlier we became acquainted with the three stages of salvation history, which progresses, as the Church Fathers say, from shadow to image to reality. We saw that in our own time, the time of the Church, we were in the middle stage of the movement of history. The curtain of the Temple has been torn. Heaven has been opened up by the union of the man Jesus, and thus of all human existence, with the living God. But this new openness is only mediated by the signs of salvation. We need mediation. As yet we do not see the Lord "as he is". Now if we put the two three-part processes together—the historical and the liturgical—it becomes clear that the liturgy gives precise expression to this historical situation. It expresses the "between-ness" of the time of images, in which we now find ourselves. The theology of the liturgy is in a special way "symbolic theology", a theology of symbols, which connects us to what is present but hidden.

In so saying, we finally discover the answer to the question with which we started. After the tearing of the Temple curtain and the opening up of the heart of God in the pierced heart of the Crucified, do we still need sacred space, sacred time, mediating symbols? Yes, we do need them, precisely so that, through the "image", through the sign, we learn to see the openness of heaven. We need them to give us the capacity to know the mystery of God in the pierced heart of the Crucified. Christian liturgy is no longer replacement worship but the coming of the representative Redeemer to us, an entry into his representation that is an entry into reality itself. We do indeed participate in the heavenly liturgy, but this participation is mediated to us through earthly signs, which the Redeemer has shown to us as the place where his reality is to be found. In liturgical celebration there is a kind of turning around of *exitus* to *reditus*, of departure to return, of God's descent to our ascent. The liturgy is the means by which earthly time is inserted into the time of Jesus Christ and into its present. It is the turning point in the process of redemption. The Shepherd takes the lost sheep onto his shoulders and carries it home.

2. Sacred Places—The Significance of the Church Building

Even the staunchest opponents of sacred things, of sacred space in this case, accept that the Christian community needs a place to meet, and on that basis they define the purpose of church buildings in a non-sacral, strictly functional sense. Church buildings, they say, make it possible for people to get together for the liturgy. This is without question an essential function of church buildings and distinguishes them from the classical form of the temple in most religions. In the Old Covenant, the high priest performed the rite of atonement in the Holy of Holies. None but he was allowed to enter, and even he could do so only once a year. Similarly, the temples of all the other religions are usually, not meeting places for worshippers, but cultic spaces reserved to the deity. The Christian church building soon acquired the name *domus ecclesiae* (the house of the Church, the assembly of the People of God), and then, as an abbreviation, the word *ecclesia* ("assembly", "church") came to be used, not just of the living community, but also of the building that housed it. This development is accompanied by another idea: Christ himself offers worship as he stands before the Father. He becomes his members' worship as they come together with him and around him. This essential difference between the Christian place of worship and the temples of the other religions must not, of course, be exaggerated into a false opposition. We must not suggest a break in the inner continuity of mankind's religious history, a continuity that, for all the differences, the Old and New Testaments never abolish. In his eighteenth catechesis (23–25), St. Cyril of Jerusalem makes an interesting point about the word *convocatio* (*synagogē-ekklēsia*, the assembly of the people called together and made his own by God). He rightly points out that in the Pentateuch, when the word first makes its appearance with the appointment of Aaron, it is ordered toward worship. Cyril shows that this applies to all the later passages in the Torah, and, even in the transition to the New Testament, this ordering is not forgotten. The calling together, the assembly, has a purpose, and that purpose is worship. The call comes from worship and leads back to worship. It is worship that unites the people called together and gives their being together its meaning and worth: they are united in that "peace" which the world cannot give. This also becomes clear in relation to that great Old and New Testament archetype of the *ekklēsia*, the community on Sinai. They come together to hear God's Word and to seal everything with sacrifice. That is how a "covenant" is established between God and man.

But instead of continuing with these theoretical considerations, let us look more closely at the process by which church buildings took concrete form. Using the research of E. L. Sukenik, Louis Bouyer has shown how the Christian house of God comes into being in complete continuity with the synagogue and thus acquires a specifically Christian newness, without any dramatic break, through communion with Jesus Christ, the crucified and risen Lord. This close connection with the synagogue, with its architectural structure and liturgical form, does not in any way contradict what we said above about the Christian liturgy not just continuing the synagogue but also incorporating the Temple. For the Jews saw the synagogue in relation to the Temple. The synagogue was never just a place for instruction, a kind of religious classroom, as Bouyer puts it. No, its orientation was always toward the presence of God. Now, for the Jews, this presence of God was (and is) indissolubly connected with the Temple. Consequently, the synagogue was characterized by two focal points. The first is the "seat of Moses", of which the Lord speaks in the Gospel (cf. Mt 23:2). The rabbi does not speak from his own resources. He is not a professor, analyzing and reflecting on the Word of God in an intellectual way. No, he makes present the Word that God addressed and addresses to Israel. God speaks through Moses today. What the seat of Moses stands for is this: Sinai is not just a thing of the past. It is not mere human speech that is happening here. God is speaking.

The seat of Moses, then, does not stand for itself and by itself, nor is it simply turned toward the people. No, the rabbi looks—as does everyone else in the synagogue—toward the Ark of the Covenant, or rather the shrine of the Torah, which represents the lost Ark. Up to the Exile, the Ark of the Covenant was the only "object" allowed inside the Holy of Holies. That is what gave the Holy of Holies its special dignity. The Ark was seen as an empty throne, upon which the Shekinah—the cloud of God's presence—came down. The cherubim—representing, as it were, the elements of the world—served as "assistants at the throne". They were not self-subsistent deities, but an expression of the created powers that worship the only God. God is addressed as "thou who art enthroned between the cherubim". The heavens cannot contain him, but he has chosen the Ark as the "footstool" of his presence. In this sense, the Ark embodies something like the real presence of God among his own. At the same time it is an impressive sign of the absence of images from the liturgy of the Old Testament, which maintains God in his sovereignty and holds out to him, so to speak, only the footstool of his throne. During the Exile, the Ark of the Covenant was lost, and from then on the Holy of Holies was empty. That is what Pompeius found when he strode through the Temple and pulled back the curtain. He entered the Holy of Holies full of curiosity and there, in the very emptiness of the place, discovered what is special about biblical religion. The empty Holy of Holies had now become an act of expectation, of hope, that God himself would one day restore his throne.

The synagogue, in its shrine of the Torah, contains a kind of Ark of the Covenant, which means it is the place of a kind of "real presence". Here are kept the scrolls of the Torah, the living Word of God, through which he sits on his throne in Israel among his own people. The shrine is surrounded, therefore, with signs of reverence befitting the mysterious presence of God. It is protected by a curtain, before which burn the seven lights of the menorah, the seven-branch candlestick. Now the furnishing of the synagogue with an "Ark of the Covenant" does not in any way signify that the local community has become, so to speak, independent, self-sufficient. No, it is the place where the local community reaches out beyond itself to the Temple, to the commonality of the one People of God as defined by the one God. The Torah is in all places one and the same. And so the Ark points beyond itself to the one place of its presence that God chose for himself—the Holy of Holies in the Temple in Jerusalem. This Holy of Holies, as Bouyer puts it, remained "the ultimate focus of the synagogal worship" (p. 15). "Thus have all the synagogues, at the time of Our Lord and since that time, been oriented" (p. 15). The rabbi and the people gaze at the "Ark of the Covenant", and in so doing, they orient themselves toward Jerusalem, turn themselves toward the Holy of Holies in the Temple as the place of God's presence for his people. This remained the case even after the destruction of the Temple. The empty Holy of Holies had already been an expression of hope, and so, too, now is the destroyed Temple, which waits for the return of the Shekinah, for its restoration by the Messiah when he comes.

This orientation toward the Temple, and thus the connection of the synagogue's liturgy of the Word with the sacrificial liturgy of the Temple, can be seen in its form of prayer. The prayers said at the unrolling and reading of the scrolls of Scripture developed out of the ritual prayers originally linked to the sacrificial actions in the Temple and now regarded, in accord with the tradition of the time without the Temple, as an equivalent of sacrifice. The first of the two great prayers of the synagogue rite comes to a climax in the common recitation of the *Kiddush*, of which the hymn of the seraphim in Isaiah chapter 6 and the hymn of the cherubim in Ezekiel chapter 3 are a part. Bouyer makes this comment: "But the truth must be that the association of men with these heavenly canticles, in the worship of the Temple, had probably been a central feature of the offering of the sacrifice of incense morning and evening of every day" (p. 22). Who would not be reminded of the Trisagion of the Christian liturgy, the "thrice holy" hymn at the beginning of the Canon? Here the congregation does not offer its own thoughts or poetry but is taken out of itself and given the privilege of sharing in the cosmic song of praise of the cherubim and seraphim. The other great prayer of the synagogue culminates in "the recitation of the *Abodah* which, according to the rabbis, was formerly the consecration prayer of the daily burnt offering in the Temple" (p. 22). The petition added to it about the coming of the Messiah and the final restoration of Israel may be seen, according to Bouyer, "as the expression of the essence of the sacrificial worship" (p. 22). Let us remind ourselves here of that transition from animal sacrifices to "worship in harmony with *logos*" which characterizes the path from the Old Testament into the New. Finally, we must mention the fact that no special architectural form was created for the synagogue. The "typical Greek building for public meetings: the basilica", was used (p. 17). Its aisles, divided off by rows of columns, enabled people entering the building to circulate around it.

I have lingered over this description of the synagogue because it exhibits already the essential and constant features of Christian places of worship. Once again we see clearly the essential unity of the two Testaments. Not surprisingly, in Semitic, non-Greek Christianity, the original form of church buildings generally retains the close connection of church with synagogue, a pattern of religious continuity and innovation. (I am thinking here of the Monophysite and Nestorian Churches of the Near East, which broke away from the Church of the Byzantine Empire during the christological debates of the fifth century.) Christian faith produced three innovations in the form of the synagogue as we have just sketched it. These give Christian liturgy its new and proper profile. First of all, the worshipper no longer looks toward Jerusalem. The destroyed Temple is no longer regarded as the place of God's earthly presence. The Temple built of stone has ceased to express the hope of Christians; its curtain is torn forever. Christians look toward the east, the rising sun. This is not a case of Christians worshipping the sun but of the cosmos speaking of Christ. The song of the sun in Psalm 19(18) is interpreted as a song about Christ when it says: "[The sun] comes forth like a bridegroom leaving his chamber.... Its rising is from the end of the heavens, and its circuit to the end of them" (vv. 5f.). This psalm proceeds directly from applauding creation to praising the law. Christians interpret it in terms of Christ, who is the living Word, the eternal Logos, and thus the true light of history, who came forth in Bethlehem from the bridal chamber of the Virgin Mother and now pours out his light on all the world. The east supersedes the Jerusalem Temple as a symbol. Christ, represented by the sun, is the place of the Shekinah, the true throne of the living God. In the Incarnation, human nature truly becomes the throne and seat of God, who is thus forever bound to the earth and accessible to our prayers. In the early Church, prayer toward the east was regarded as an apostolic tradition. We cannot date exactly when this turn to the east, the diverting of the gaze from the Temple, took place, but it is certain that it goes back to the earliest times and was always regarded as an essential characteristic of Christian liturgy (and indeed of private prayer). This "orientation"* of Christian prayer has several different meanings. Orientation is, first and foremost, a simple expression of looking to Christ as the meeting place between God and man. It expresses the basic christological form of our prayer.

The fact that we find Christ in the symbol of the rising sun is the indication of a Christology defined eschatologically. Praying toward the east means going to meet the coming Christ. The liturgy, turned toward the east, effects entry, so to speak, into the procession of history toward the future, the New Heaven and the New Earth, which we encounter in Christ. It is a prayer of hope, the prayer of the pilgrim as he walks in the direction shown us by the life, Passion, and Resurrection of Christ. Thus very early on, in parts of Christendom, the eastward direction for prayer was given added emphasis by a reference to the Cross. This may

---

*The word "orientation" comes from *oriens*, "the East". "Orientation" means "easting", turning toward the east.

have come from linking Revelation 1:7 with Matthew 24:30. In the first of these, the Revelation of St. John, it says: "Behold, he is coming with the clouds, and every eye will see him, every one who pierced him; and all tribes of the earth will wail on account of him. Even so. Amen." Here the seer of the Apocalypse depends on John 19:37, where, at the end of the account of the crucifixion, the mysterious text of the prophet Zechariah (12:10) is quoted, a text that suddenly acquires a wholly new meaning: "They shall look on him whom they have pierced." Finally, in Matthew 24:30 we are given these words of the Lord: "[T]hen [on the Last Day] will appear the sign of the Son of man in heaven, and then all the tribes of the earth will mourn [cf. Zech 12:10], and they will see the Son of man coming on the clouds of heaven [cf. Dan 7:13] with power and great glory." The sign of the Son of Man, of the Pierced One, is the Cross, which has now become the sign of victory of the Risen One. Thus the symbolism of the Cross merges with that of the east. Both are an expression of one and the same faith, in which the remembrance of the Pasch of Jesus makes it present and gives dynamism to the hope that goes out to meet the One who is to come. But, finally, this turning toward the east also signifies that cosmos and saving history belong together. The cosmos is praying with us. It, too, is waiting for redemption. It is precisely this cosmic dimension that is essential to Christian liturgy. It is never performed solely in the self-made world of man. It is always a cosmic liturgy. The theme of creation is embedded in Christian prayer. It loses its grandeur when it forgets this connection. That is why, wherever possible, we should definitely take up again the apostolic tradition of facing the east, both in the building of churches and in the celebration of the liturgy. We shall come back to this later, when we say something about the ordering of liturgical prayer.

The second innovation in regard to the synagogue is as follows. A new element has appeared that could not exist in the synagogue. At the east wall, or in the apse, there now stands an altar on which the Eucharistic Sacrifice is celebrated. As we saw, the Eucharist is an entry into the liturgy of heaven; by it we become contemporaries with Jesus Christ's own act of worship, into which, through his Body, he takes up worldly time and straightway leads it beyond itself, snatching it out of its own sphere and enfolding it into the communion of eternal love. Thus the altar signifies the entry of him who is the Orient into the assembled community and the going out of the community from the prison of this world through the curtain now torn open, a participation in the Pasch, the "passing over" from the world to God, that Christ has opened up. It is clear that the altar in the apse both looks toward the *Oriens* and forms part of it. In the synagogue the worshippers looked beyond the "Ark of the Covenant", the shrine of the Word, toward Jerusalem. Now, with the Christian altar, comes a new focal point. Let us say it again: on the altar, what the Temple in the past foreshadowed is now present in a new way. Yes, it enables us to become the contemporaries of the Sacrifice of the Logos. Thus it brings heaven into the community assembled on earth, or, rather, it takes that community beyond itself into the communion of saints of all times and places. We might put it this way: the altar is the place where heaven is opened up. It does not close off the church, but opens it up—and leads it into the eternal liturgy. We shall have more to say about the practical consequences of the significance of the Christian altar, because the question of the correct position for the altar is at the center of the postconciliar debate.

But first we must finish what we were saying about the different ways in which Christian faith transformed the synagogue. The third point to be noted is that the shrine of the Word remained, even with regard to its position in the church building. However, of necessity, there is a fundamental innovation here. The Torah is replaced by the Gospels, which alone can open up the meaning of the Torah. "Moses", says Christ, "wrote of me" (Jn 5:46). The shrine of the Word, the "Ark of the Covenant", now becomes the throne of the Gospel. The Gospel does not, of course, abolish the "Scriptures" or push them to one side; rather, it interprets them, so that henceforth and forever they form the Scriptures of Christians, without which the Gospel would have no foundation. The practice in the synagogue of covering the shrine with a curtain, in order to express the sacredness of the Word, is retained. Quite spontaneously, the new, second holy place, the altar, is surrounded by a curtain, from which, in the Eastern Church, the Iconostasis develops. The fact that there are two holy places had significance for the celebration of the liturgy. During the Liturgy of the Word, the congregation gathered around the shrine of the Sacred Books, or around the seat associated with it, which evolved quite spontaneously from the seat of Moses to the bishop's throne. Just as the rabbi did not speak by his own authority, so the bishop expounds the Bible in the name, and by the mandate, of Christ. Thus, from being a written word from the past, it again becomes what it is: God's addressing us here and now. At the end of the Liturgy of the Word, during which the faithful stand around the bishop's seat, everyone walks together with the bishop to the altar, and now the cry resounds: "*Conversi ad Dominum*", Turn toward the Lord! In other words, look toward the east with the bishop, in the sense of the words from the epistle to the Hebrews: "[Look] ... to Jesus the pioneer and perfecter of our faith" (12:2). The Liturgy of the Eucharist is celebrated as we look up to Jesus. It *is* our looking up to Jesus. Thus, in early church buildings, the liturgy has two places. First, the Liturgy of the Word takes place at the center of the building. The faithful are grouped around the *bema*, the elevated area where the throne of the Gospel, the seat of the bishop, and the lectern are located. The Eucharistic celebration proper takes place in the apse, at the altar, which the faithful "stand around". Everyone joins with the celebrant in facing east, toward the Lord who is to come.

Finally, we must mention one last difference between the synagogue and the earliest church buildings. In Israel only the presence of men was deemed to be necessary for divine worship. The common priesthood described in Exodus chapter 19 was ascribed to them alone. Consequently, in the synagogue, women were only allowed into the tribunes or galleries. As far as the apostles were concerned, as far as Jesus himself is concerned, there was no such discrimination in the Church of Christ. Even though the public Liturgy of the Word was not entrusted to women, they were included in the liturgy as a whole in exactly the same way as men. And so now they had a place—albeit in separation from men—in the sacred space itself, around both the *bema* and the altar.

3. The Altar and the Direction of Liturgical Prayer

The reshaping so far described, of the Jewish synagogue for the purpose of Christian worship, clearly shows—as we have already said—how, even in architecture, there is both continuity and newness in the relationship of the Old Testament to the New. As a consequence, expression in space had to be given to the properly Christian act of worship, the celebration of the Eucharist, together with the ministry of the Word, which is ordered toward that celebration. Plainly, further developments became not only possible but necessary. A place set aside for

Baptism had to be found. The Sacrament of Penance went through a long process of development, which resulted in changes to the form of the church building. Popular piety in its many different forms inevitably found expression in the place dedicated to divine worship. The question of sacred images had to be resolved. Church music had to be fitted into the spatial structure. We saw that the architectural canon for the liturgy of Word and sacrament is not a rigid one, though with every new development and reordering the question has to be posed: What is in harmony with the essence of the liturgy, and what detracts from it? In the very form of its places of divine worship, which we have just been considering, Christianity, speaking and thinking in a Semitic way, has laid down principles by which this question can be answered. Despite all the variations in practice that have taken place far into the second millennium, one thing has remained clear for the whole of Christendom: praying toward the east is a tradition that goes back to the beginning. Moreover, it is a fundamental expression of the Christian synthesis of cosmos and history, of being rooted in the once-for-all events of salvation history while going out to meet the Lord who is to come again. Here both the fidelity to the gift already bestowed and the dynamism of going forward are given equal expression.

Modern man has little understanding of this "orientation". Judaism and Islam, now as in the past, take it for granted that we should pray toward the central place of revelation, to the God who has revealed himself to us, in the manner and in the place in which he revealed himself. By contrast, in the Western world, an abstract way of thinking, which in a certain way is the fruit of Christian influence, has become dominant. God is spiritual, and God is everywhere: Does that not mean that prayer is not tied to a particular place or direction? Now, we can indeed pray everywhere, and God is accessible to us everywhere. This idea of the universality of God is a consequence of Christian universality, of the Christian's looking up to God above all gods, the God who embraces the cosmos and is more intimate to us than we are to ourselves. But our knowledge of this universality is the fruit of revelation: God has shown himself to us. Only for this reason do we know him; only for this reason can we confidently pray to him everywhere. And precisely for this reason is it appropriate, now as in the past, that we should express in Christian prayer our turning to the God who has revealed himself to us. Just as God assumed a body and entered the time and space of this world, so it is appropriate to prayer—at least to communal liturgical prayer—that our speaking to God should be "incarnational", that it should be christological, turned through the incarnate Word to the triune God. The cosmic symbol of the rising sun expresses the universality of God above all particular places and yet maintains the concreteness of divine revelation. Our praying is thus inserted into the procession of the nations to God.

But what about the altar? In what direction should we pray during the eucharistic liturgy? In Byzantine church buildings the structure just described was by and large retained, but in Rome a somewhat different arrangement developed. The bishop's chair was shifted to the center of the apse, and so the altar was moved into the nave. This seems to have been the case in the Lateran basilica and in St. Mary Major well into the ninth century. However, in St. Peter's, during the pontificate of St. Gregory the Great (590–604), the altar was moved nearer to the bishop's chair, probably for the simple reason that he was supposed to stand as much as possible above the tomb of St. Peter. This was an outward and visible expression of the truth that we celebrate the Sacrifice of the Lord in the communion of saints, a communion spanning all times and ages. The custom of erecting an altar above the tombs of the martyrs probably goes back a long way and is an outcome of the same motivation. Throughout history the martyrs continue Christ's self-oblation; they are like the Church's living altar, made not of stones but of men, who have become members of the Body of Christ and thus express a new kind of cultus: sacrifice is mankind becoming love with Christ.

The ordering of St. Peter's was then copied, so it would seem, in many other stational churches in Rome. For the purposes of this discussion, we do not need to go into the disputed details of this process. The controversy in our own century was triggered by another innovation. Because of topographical circumstances, it turned out that St. Peter's faced west. Thus, if the celebrating priest wanted—as the Christian tradition of prayer demands—to face east, he had to stand behind the people and look—this is the logical conclusion—toward the people. For whatever reason it was done, one can also see this arrangement in a whole series of church buildings within St. Peter's direct sphere of influence. The liturgical renewal in our own century took up this alleged model and developed from it a new idea for the form of the liturgy. The Eucharist—so it was said—had to be celebrated *versus populum* (toward the people). The altar—as can be seen in the normative model of St. Peter's—had to be positioned in such a way that priest and people looked at each other and formed together the circle of the celebrating community. This alone—so it was said—was compatible with the meaning of the Christian liturgy, with the requirement of active participation. This alone conformed to the primordial model of the Last Supper. These arguments seemed in the end so persuasive that after the Council (which says nothing about "turning toward the people") new altars were set up everywhere, and today celebration *versus populum* really does look like the characteristic fruit of Vatican II's liturgical renewal. In fact it is the most conspicuous consequence of a reordering that not only signifies a new external arrangement of the places dedicated to the liturgy, but also brings with it a new idea of the essence of the liturgy—the liturgy as a communal meal.

This is, of course, a misunderstanding of the significance of the Roman basilica and of the positioning of its altar, and the representation of the Last Supper is also, to say the least, inaccurate. Consider, for example, what Louis Bouyer has to say on the subject:

> The idea that a celebration facing the people must have been the primitive one, and that especially of the last supper, has no other foundation than a mistaken view of what a meal could be in antiquity, Christian or not. In no meal of the early Christian era, did the president of the banqueting assembly ever face the other participants. They were all sitting, or reclining, on the convex side of a sigma table, or of a table having approximately the shape of a horse shoe. The other side was always left empty for the service. Nowhere in Christian antiquity, could have arisen the idea of having to 'face the people' to preside at a meal. The communal character of a meal was emphasized just by the opposite disposition: the fact that all the participants were on the same side of the table. (pp. 53–54)

In any case, there is a further point that we must add to this discussion of the "shape" of meals: the Eucharist that Christians celebrate really cannot adequately be described by the term "meal". True, the Lord established the new reality of Christian worship within the framework of a Jewish (Passover) meal, but it was precisely this new reality, not the meal as such, that he commanded us to repeat. Very soon the new reality was separated from its ancient context and found its proper and suitable form, a form already predetermined by the fact that the Eucharist refers back to the Cross and thus to the transformation of Temple sacrifice into worship of God that is in harmony with *logos*. Thus it came to pass that the synagogue liturgy of the Word, renewed and deepened in a Christian way, merged with the remembrance of Christ's death and Resurrection to become the "Eucharist", and precisely thus was fidelity to the command "Do this" fulfilled. This new and all-encompassing form of worship could not be derived simply from the meal but had to be defined through the interconnection of Temple and synagogue, Word and sacrament, cosmos and history. It expresses itself in the very form that we discovered in the liturgical structure of the early Churches in the world of Semitic Christianity. It also, of course, remained fundamental for Rome. Once again let me quote Bouyer:

> Never, and nowhere, before that [that is, before the sixteenth century], have we any indication that any importance, or even attention, was given to whether the priest celebrated with the people before him or behind him. As Professor Cyrille Vogel has recently demonstrated it, the only thing ever insisted upon, or even mentioned, was that he should say the eucharistic prayer, as all the other prayers, facing East.... Even when the orientation of the church enabled the celebrant to pray turned toward the people, when at the altar, we must not forget that it was not the priest alone who, then, turned East: it was the whole congregation, together with him. (pp. 55–56)

Admittedly, these connections were obscured or fell into total oblivion in the church buildings and liturgical practice of the modern age. This is the only explanation for the fact that the common direction of prayer of priest and people were labelled as "celebrating toward the wall" or "turning your back on the people" and came to seem absurd and totally unacceptable. And this alone explains why the meal—even in modern pictures—became the normative idea of liturgical celebration for Christians. In reality what happened was that an unprecedented clericalization came on the scene. Now the priest—the "presider", as they now prefer to call him—becomes the real point of reference for the whole liturgy. Everything depends on him. We have to see him, to respond to him, to be involved in what he is doing. His creativity sustains the whole thing. Not surprisingly, people try to reduce this newly created role by assigning all kinds of liturgical functions to different individuals and entrusting the "creative" planning of the liturgy to groups of people who like to, and are supposed to, "make their own contribution". Less and less is God in the picture. More and more important is what is done by the human beings who meet here and do not like to subject themselves to a "pre-determined pattern". The turning of the priest toward the people has turned the community into a self-enclosed circle. In its outward form, it no longer opens out on what lies ahead and above, but is closed in on itself. The common turning toward the east was not a "celebration toward the wall"; it did not mean that the priest "had his back to the people": the priest himself was not regarded as so important. For just as the congregation in the synagogue looked together toward Jerusalem, so in the Christian liturgy the congregation looked together "toward the Lord". As one of the fathers of Vatican II's Constitution on the Liturgy, J. A. Jungmann, put it, it was much more a question of priest and people facing in the same direction, knowing that together they were in a procession toward the Lord. They did not close themselves into a circle; they did not gaze at one another; but as the pilgrim People of God they set off for the *Oriens*, for the Christ who comes to meet us.

But is this not all romanticism and nostalgia for the past? Can the original form of Christian prayer still say something to us today, or should we try to find our own form, a form for our own times? Of course, we cannot simply replicate the past. Every age must discover and express the essence of the liturgy anew. The point is to discover this essence amid all the changing appearances. It would surely be a mistake to reject all the reforms of our century wholesale. When the altar was very remote from the faithful, it was right to move it back to the people. In cathedrals this made it possible to recover the tradition of having the altar at the crossing, the meeting point of the nave and the presbyterium. It was also important clearly to distinguish the place for the Liturgy of the Word from the place for the properly eucharistic liturgy. For the Liturgy of the Word is about speaking and responding, and so a face-to-face exchange between proclaimer and hearer does make sense. In the psalm the hearer internalizes what he has heard, takes it into himself, and transforms it into prayer, so that it becomes a response. On the other hand, a common turning to the east during the Eucharistic Prayer remains essential. This is not a case of something accidental; rather, it is a

49

matter of what is essential. Looking at the priest has no importance. What matters is looking together at the Lord. It is now a question, not of dialogue, but of common worship, of setting off toward the One who is to come. What corresponds with the reality of what is happening is not the closed circle but the common movement forward, expressed in a common direction for prayer.

Häussling has levelled several objections at these ideas of mine, which I have presented before. The first I have just touched on. These ideas are alleged to be a romanticism for the old ways, a misguided longing for the past. It is said to be odd that I should speak only of Christian antiquity and pass over the succeeding centuries. Coming as it does from a liturgical scholar, this objection is quite remarkable. As I see it, the problem with a large part of modern liturgiology is that it tends to recognize only antiquity as a source, and therefore normative, and to regard everything developed later, in the Middle Ages and through the Council of Trent, as decadent. And so one ends up with dubious reconstructions of the most ancient practice, fluctuating criteria, and never-ending suggestions for reform, which lead ultimately to the disintegration of the liturgy that has evolved in a living way. On the other hand, it is important and necessary to see that we cannot take as our norm the ancient in itself and as such, nor must we automatically write off later developments as alien to the original form of the liturgy. There can be a thoroughly living kind of development in which a seed at the origin of something ripens and bears fruit. We shall have to come back to this idea in a moment. But in our case, as we have said, what is at issue is not a romantic escape into antiquity, but a rediscovery of something essential, in which Christian liturgy expresses its permanent orientation. Of course, Häussling thinks that turning to the east, toward the rising sun, is something that nowadays we just cannot bring into the liturgy. Is that really the case? Are we not interested in the cosmos any more? Are we today really hopelessly huddled in our own little circle? Is it not important, precisely today, to pray with the whole of creation? Is it not important, precisely today, to find room for the dimension of the future, for hope in the Lord who is to come again, to recognize again, indeed to live, the dynamism of the new creation as an essential form of the liturgy?

Another objection is that we do not need to look toward the east, toward the crucifix—that, when priest and faithful look at one another, they are looking at the image of God in man, and so facing one another is the right direction for prayer. I find it hard to believe that the famous critic thought this was a serious argument. For we do not see the image of God in man in such a simplistic way. The "image of God" in man is not, of course, something that we can photograph or see with a merely photographic kind of perception. We can indeed see it, but only with the new seeing of faith. We can see it, just as we can see the goodness in a man, his honesty, interior truth, humility, love—everything, in fact, that gives him a certain likeness to God. But if we are to do this, we must learn a new kind of seeing, and that is what the Eucharist is for.

A more important objection is of the practical order. Ought we really to be rearranging everything all over again? Nothing is more harmful to the liturgy than a constant activism, even if it seems to be for the sake of genuine renewal. I see a solution in a suggestion that comes from the insights of Erik Peterson. Facing east, as we heard, was linked with the "sign of the Son of Man", with the Cross, which announces the Lord's Second Coming. That is why very early on the east was linked with the sign of the Cross. Where a direct common turning toward the east is not possible, the cross can serve as the interior "east" of faith. It should stand in the middle of the altar and be the common point of focus for both priest and praying community. In this way we obey the ancient call to prayer: "*Conversi ad Dominum*", Turn toward the Lord! In this way we look together at the One whose death tore the veil of the Temple—the One who stands before the Father for us and encloses us in his arms in order to make us the new and living Temple. Moving the altar cross to the side to give an uninterrupted view of the priest is something I regard as one of the truly absurd phenomena of recent decades. Is the cross disruptive during Mass? Is the priest more important than the Lord? This mistake should be corrected as quickly as possible; it can be done without further rebuilding. The Lord is the point of reference. He is the rising sun of history. That is why there could be a cross of the Passion, which represents the suffering Lord who for us let his side be pierced, from which flowed blood and water (Eucharist and Baptism), as well as a cross of triumph, which expresses the idea of the Second Coming and guides our eyes toward it. For it is always the one Lord: Christ yesterday, today, and forever (Heb 13:8).

4. The Reservation of the Blessed Sacrament

The Church of the first millennium knew nothing of tabernacles. Instead, first the shrine of the Word, and then even more so the altar, served as sacred "tent". Approached by steps, it was sheltered, and its sacredness underscored, by a "ciborium", or marble baldacchino, with burning lamps hanging from it. A curtain was hung between the columns of the ciborium (Bouyer, pp. 46–48). The tabernacle as sacred tent, as place of the Shekinah, the presence of the living Lord, developed only in the second millennium. It was the fruit of passionate theological struggles and their resulting clarifications, in which the permanent presence of Christ in the consecrated Host emerged with greater clarity. Now here we run up against the decadence theory, the canonization of the early days and romanticism about the first century. Transubstantiation (the substantial change of the bread and wine), the adoration of the Lord in the Blessed Sacrament, eucharistic devotions with monstrance and processions—all these things, it is alleged, are medieval errors, errors from which we must once and for all take our leave. "The Eucharistic Gifts are for eating, not for looking at"— these and similar slogans are all too familiar. The glib way such statements are made is quite astonishing when we consider the intense debates in the history of dogma, theology, and ecumenism undertaken by the great theologians in the nineteenth century and the first half of the twentieth. All that seems now to be forgotten.

It is not the intention of this little book to enter into these theological discussions in detail. It is plain for all to see that already for St. Paul bread and wine become the Body and Blood of Christ, that it is the risen Lord himself who is present and gives himself to us to eat. The vigor with which the Real Presence is emphasized in John chapter 6 could hardly be surpassed. For the Church Fathers, too, from the earliest witnesses onward—just think of St. Justin Martyr or St. Ignatius of Antioch—there is no doubt about the great mystery of the Presence bestowed upon us, about the change of the gifts during the Eucharistic Prayer. Even a theologian of such a spiritualizing tendency as St. Augustine never had a doubt about it. Indeed, he shows just how far confession of faith in the Incarnation and Resurrection, which is so closely bound up with eucharistic faith in the bodily presence of the risen Lord, has transformed Platonism. "Flesh and blood" have received a new dignity and entered into the Christian's hope for eternal life. An important finding of Henri de Lubac has often been misunderstood. It has always been clear that the goal of the Eucharist is our own transformation, so that we become "one body and spirit" with Christ (cf. 1 Cor 6:17). This correlation of ideas—the insight that the Eucharist is meant to transform *us*, to change mankind itself into the living temple of God, into the Body of Christ—was expressed, up to the early Middle Ages, by the twin concepts of *corpus mysticum* and *corpus verum*. In the vocabulary of the Fathers, *mysticum* meant, not "mystical" in the modern sense, but, rather, "pertaining to the mystery, the sphere of the sacrament". Thus the phrase *corpus mysticum* was used to express the sacramental Body, the corporeal presence of Christ in the Sacrament. According to the Fathers, that Body is given to us, so that we may become the *corpus verum*, the real Body of Christ. Changes in the use of language and the forms of thought resulted in the reversal of these meanings. The Sacrament was now addressed as the *corpus verum*, the "true Body", while the Church was called the *corpus mysticum*, the "Mystical Body", "mystical" here meaning no longer "sacramental" but "mysterious". Many people have drawn the conclusion from de Lubac's careful description of the linguistic change that a hitherto unknown realism, indeed naturalism, was now forcing its way into eucharistic doctrine, and the large views of the Fathers were giving way to a static and one-sided idea of the Real Presence.

It is true that this linguistic change also represented a spiritual development, but we should not describe it in the slanted way just mentioned. We can agree that something of the eschatological dynamism and corporate character (the sense of "we") of eucharistic faith was lost or at least diminished. As we saw above, the Blessed Sacrament contains a dynamism, which has the goal of transforming mankind and the world into the New Heaven and New Earth, into the unity of the risen Body. This truth was not seen so vividly as before. Again, the Eucharist is not aimed primarily at the individual. Eucharistic personalism is a drive toward union, the overcoming of the barriers between God and man, between "I" and "thou" in the new "we" of the communion of saints. People did not exactly forget this truth, but they were not so clearly aware of it as before. There were, therefore, losses in Christian awareness, and in our time we must try to make up for them, but still there were gains overall. True, the Eucharistic Body of the Lord is meant to bring us together, so that we become his "true Body". But the gift of the Eucharist can do this only because in it the

Lord gives us *his true Body*. Only the true Body in the Sacrament can build up the true Body of the new City of God. This insight connects the two periods and provides our starting point.

The early Church was already well aware that the bread once changed remains changed. That is why they reserved it for the sick, and that is why they showed it such reverence, as is still the case today in the Eastern Church. But now, in the Middle Ages, this awareness is deepened: the gift *is* changed. The Lord has definitively drawn this piece of matter to himself. It does not contain just a matter-of-fact kind of gift. No, the Lord himself is present, the Indivisible One, the risen Lord, with Flesh and Blood, with Body and Soul, with Divinity and Humanity. The whole Christ is there. In the early days of the Liturgical Movement, people sometimes argued for a distinction between the "thing-centered" view of the Eucharist in the patristic age and the personalistic view of the post-medieval period. The Eucharistic Presence, they said, was understood, not as the presence of a Person, but as the presence of a gift distinct from the Person. This is nonsense. Anyone reading the texts will find that there is no support anywhere for these ideas. How is the Body of Christ supposed to become a "thing"? The only presence is the presence of the whole Christ. Receiving the Eucharist does not mean eating a "thing-like" gift (Body and Blood?). No, there is a person-to-person exchange, a coming of the one into the other. The living Lord gives himself to me, enters into me, and invites me to surrender myself to him, so that the Apostle's words come true: "[I]t is no longer I who live, but Christ who lives in me" (Gal 2:20). Only thus is the reception of Holy Communion an act that elevates and transforms a man.

"He is here, he himself, the whole of himself, and he remains here." This realization came upon the Middle Ages with a wholly new intensity. It was caused in part by the deepening of theological reflection, but still more important was the new experience of the saints, especially in the Franciscan movement and in the new evangelization undertaken by the Order of Preachers. What happens in the Middle Ages is not a misunderstanding due to losing sight of what is central, but a new dimension of the reality of Christianity opening up through the experience of the saints, supported and illuminated by the reflection of the theologians. At the same time, this new development is in complete continuity with what was always believed hitherto. Let me say it again: This deepened awareness of faith is impelled by the knowledge that in the consecrated species *he* is there and remains there. When a man experiences this with every fiber of his heart and mind and senses, the consequence is inescapable: "We must make a proper place for this Presence." And so little by little the tabernacle takes shape, and more and more, always in a spontaneous way, it takes the place previously occupied by the now disappeared "Ark of the Covenant". In fact, the tabernacle is the complete fulfillment of what the Ark of the Covenant represented. It is the place of the "Holy of Holies". It is the tent of God, his throne. Here he is among us. His presence (Shekinah) really does now dwell among us—in the humblest parish church no less than in the grandest cathedral. Even though the definitive Temple will only come to be when the world has become the New Jerusalem, still what the Temple in Jerusalem pointed to is here present in a supreme way. The New Jerusalem is anticipated in the humble species of bread.

So let no one say, "The Eucharist is for eating, not looking at." It is not "ordinary bread", as the most ancient traditions constantly emphasize. Eating it—as we have just said—is a spiritual process, involving the whole man. "Eating" it means worshipping it. Eating it means letting it come into me, so that my "I" is transformed and opens up into the great "we", so that we become "one" in him (cf. Gal 3:16). Thus adoration is not opposed to Communion, nor is it merely added to it. No, Communion reaches its true depths only when it is supported and surrounded by adoration. The Eucharistic Presence in the tabernacle does not set another view of the Eucharist alongside or against the Eucharistic celebration; it simply signifies its complete fulfillment. For this Presence has the effect, of course, of keeping the Eucharist forever in church. The church never becomes a lifeless space but is always filled with the presence of the Lord, which comes out of the celebration, leads us into it, and always makes us participants in the cosmic Eucharist. What man of faith has not experienced this? A church without the Eucharistic Presence is somehow dead, even when it invites people to pray. But a church in which the eternal light is burning before the tabernacle is always alive, is always something more than a building made of stones. In this place the Lord is always waiting for me, calling me, wanting to make me "eucharistic". In this way, he prepares me for the Eucharist, sets me in motion toward his return.

The changes in the Middle Ages brought losses, but they also provided a wonderful spiritual deepening. They unfolded the magnitude of the mystery instituted at the Last Supper and enabled it to be experienced with a new fullness. How many saints—yes, including saints of the love of neighbor—were nourished and led to the Lord by this experience! We must not lose this richness. If the presence of the Lord is to touch us in a concrete way, the tabernacle must also find its proper place in the architecture of our church buildings.

5. Sacred Time

As we begin to consider the significance of sacred time in the structure of Christian liturgy, we must remember all that we said in the first chapter of this second part about the significance of time and space in Christian worship. All time is God's time. When the eternal Word assumed human existence at his Incarnation, he also assumed temporality. He drew time into the sphere of eternity. Christ is himself the bridge between time and eternity. At first it seems as if there can be no connection between the "always" of eternity and the "flowing away" of time. But now the Eternal One himself has taken time to himself. In the Son, time co-exists with eternity. God's eternity is not mere time-lessness, the negation of time, but a power over time that is really present with time and in time. In the Word incarnate, who remains man forever, the presence of eternity with time becomes bodily and concrete.

All time is God's time. On the other hand, as we saw above, the time of the Church is a "between" time, between the shadow and the reality, and so its special structure demands a sign, a time specially chosen and designated to draw time as a whole into the hands of God. This, of course, is one of the marks of the Bible's universalism: it is not based on some general, transcendental character of mankind; rather, it strives to attain the whole through an election. But now there can be no escaping the question: What *is* time? Needless to say, this is not the place to plumb the depths of this question, which has exercised the minds of all the great thinkers of history. However, a few hints at an answer are imperative if the contact of the liturgy with time is to be properly understood. The first thing to say is that time is a cosmic reality. The orbiting of the sun by the earth (or, as the ancients thought, of the earth by the sun) gives existence the rhythm that we call time—from hour to hour, from morning to evening and evening to morning, from spring through summer and autumn to winter. In addition to this rhythm of the sun there is the shorter rhythm of the moon—from its slow growth to its disappearance with the new moon and the new beginning. The two rhythms have created two measures, which appear in the history of culture in various combinations. Both show how much man is woven into the fabric of the universe. Time is first of all a cosmic phenomenon. Man lives with the stars. The course of the sun and the moon leaves its mark on his life.

But beside and beneath this there are other rhythms, each with its own measure, at the various levels of being. Plants have their time. For example, the rings in the trunk of a tree display the tree's own internal time, which is, of course, inseparably intertwined with cosmic time. Again, man, as he matures and declines, has his own time. We could say that his heartbeat is like the internal rhythm of his own time. In the time of man the different levels of life, the organic and the spiritual-intellectual, enter into a mysterious synthesis, which is inserted into the immensity of the universe but also into a common history. The path of man that we call history is a specific form of time.

All of this is present in the liturgy and in the liturgy's own particular way of relating to time. The sacred space of the Christian worship of God is itself already opened toward time. Facing east means that when one prays, one is turned toward the rising sun, which has now become a subject of historical significance. It points to the Paschal Mystery of Jesus Christ, to his death and new rising. It points to the future of the world and the consummation of all history in the final coming of the Redeemer. Thus time and space are interconnected in Christian prayer. Space itself has become time, and time has, so to speak, become spatial, has entered into space. And just as time and space intertwine, so, too, do history and cosmos. Cosmic time, which is determined by the sun, becomes a representation of human time and of historical time, which moves toward the union of God and world, of history and the universe, of matter and spirit—in a word, toward the New City whose light is God himself. Thus time becomes eternity, and eternity is imparted to time.

In the piety of the Old Testament we find a double division of time: one determined by the weekly rhythm, which moves toward the Sabbath, and the other by the feast days, which are determined partly by the theme of creation (seed-time and harvest, in addition to feasts of the nomadic tradition) and partly by the remembrance of God's actions in history. These two sources are frequently interconnected. This basic arrangement still applies in Christianity. Even in its ordering of time, Christianity retains a profound, interior continuity with its Jewish heritage, in which, in turn, the heritage of the world's religions is taken up and dedicated to the one God, albeit purified and illuminated by him.

Let us begin with the weekly rhythm. We have already seen that the Sabbath brought the sign of the covenant into time, tied creation and covenant together. This fundamental ordering of things, which was also incorporated into the Decalogue, was still taken for granted in Christianity. But now the covenant was raised up to a new level through the Incarnation, Cross, and Resurrection, so that henceforth we must speak of a "New Covenant". God has acted once more in a new way, in order to give the covenant its universal breadth and definitive form. But this divine action had something to do with the rhythm of the week. Its climax, toward which everything else was ordered, was the Resurrection of Jesus "on the third day". In our reflections on the Last Supper we saw that Supper, Cross, and Resurrection belong together. Jesus' giving of himself unto death gives the words he speaks at the Supper their realism. On the other hand, his self-giving would be meaningless were death to have the last word. Thus only through the Resurrection does the covenant come fully into being. Now man is forever united with God. Now the two are really bound together indissolubly. Thus the Day of Resurrection is the new Sabbath. It is the day on which the Lord comes among his own and invites them into his "liturgy", into his glorification of God, and communicates himself to them. The morning of the "third day" becomes the hour of Christian worship of God. St. Augustine showed—in regard to the connection of Supper, Cross, and Resurrection—how through their inner unity the Supper has become quite spontaneously the morning sacrifice, and precisely thus is the task entrusted to the apostles at the time of the Last Supper fulfilled. The transition from Old to New Testament is plainly revealed in the transition from Sabbath to Day of Resurrection as the new sign of the covenant, and in the process Sunday takes over the significance of the Sabbath. There are three different names for this day. Seen from the Cross, it is the third day—in the Old Testament the third day was regarded as the day of theophany, the day when God entered into the world after the time of expectation.

In terms of the weekly schedule, it is the first day of the week. Finally, the Fathers added another consideration: seen in relation to the whole preceding week, Sunday is the eighth day.

Thus the three symbolisms are interlocked. Of the three the most important is that of its being the first day of the week. In the Mediterranean world in which Christianity came into being, the first day of the week was regarded as the day of the sun, while the other days were allotted to the various planets then known. The Christians' day of worship was determined by the remembrance of God's action, the date of the Resurrection of Jesus. But now this date came to carry the same cosmic symbolism that also determined the Christian direction of prayer. The sun proclaims Christ. Cosmos and history together speak of him. And to this a third factor was added: the first day is the beginning of creation. The new creation takes up the old creation. The Christian Sunday is also a festival of creation: thanksgiving for the gift of creation, for the "Let there be . . ." with which God established the being of the world. It is thanksgiving for the fact that God does not let creation be destroyed but restores it after all of man's attempts to destroy it. The "first day" contains St. Paul's idea of the whole creation waiting for the revelation of the sons of God (cf. Rom 8:19). Just as sin wrecks creation (as we can see!), so it is restored when the "sons of God" make their appearance. Sunday thus explains the commission given to man in the account of creation: "Subdue [the earth]!" (Gen 1:28). This does not mean: Enslave it! Exploit it! Do with it what you will! No, what it does mean is: Recognize it as God's gift! Guard it and look after it, as sons look after what they have inherited from their father. Look after it, so that it becomes a true garden for God and its meaning is fulfilled, so that for it, too, God is "all in all". This is the orientation that the Fathers wanted to express by calling the Day of the Resurrection the "eighth day". Sunday looks not only backward but forward. Looking toward the Resurrection means looking toward the final consummation. With the Day of the Resurrection coming after the Sabbath, Christ, as it were, strode across time and lifted it up above itself. The Fathers connected with this the idea that the history of the world as a whole can be seen as one great week of seven days corresponding to the ages of a man's life. The eighth day, therefore, signifies the new time that has dawned with the Resurrection. It is now, so to speak, concurrent with history. In the liturgy we already reach out to lay hold of it. But at the same time it is ahead of us. It is the sign of God's definitive world, in which shadow and image are superseded in the final mutual indwelling of God and his creatures. It was to reflect this symbolism of the eighth day that people liked to build baptisteries, baptismal churches, with eight sides. This was meant to show that Baptism is birth into the eighth day, into the Resurrection of Christ and into the new time that opened up with the Resurrection.

Sunday is thus, for the Christian, time's proper measure, the temporal measure of his life. It is not based on an arbitrary convention that could be exchanged for another; rather, it contains a unique synthesis of the remembrance of history, the recalling of creation, and the theology of hope. For Christians, it is the weekly returning feast of the Resurrection, though it is one that does not render a specific remembrance of Christ's Passover superfluous. It is quite clear from reading the New Testament that Jesus approached his "hour" with full awareness. The phrase emphasized in St. John's Gospel, the "hour of Jesus", certainly has many layers of meaning. But first and foremost it refers to a date: Jesus did not want to die on just any date. His death had a significance for history, for mankind, for the world. That is why it had to be woven into a very particular cosmic and historical hour. It coincides with the Passover of the Jews as set out and regulated in Exodus chapter 12. St. John and the epistle to the Hebrews show in a special way how it incorporates the content of other feasts, especially the Day of Atonement, but its proper date is Passover. The Lord's death is not any kind of accident. It is a "feast". It brings to an end what is symbolically opened up in the Passover. He takes it—as we have seen—from replacement to reality, to the vicarious ministry of his self-oblation.

The Passover is the "hour" of Jesus. It is precisely in connection with this date that we see the universal significance of Jesus' death for human history. At first Passover was the feast of nomads. From Abel to the Apocalypse the sacrificed lamb is a type of the Redeemer, of his pure self-giving. We do not need to go farther into the importance of nomadic culture in the origins of biblical religion. What is significant is this, that monotheism was not able to develop in the great cities and fertile countryside of Mesopotamia. No, it was in the wilderness, where heaven and earth face each other in stark solitude, that monotheism was able to grow—in the homelessness of the wanderer, who does not deify places but has constantly to put his trust in the God who wanders with him. It has recently been pointed out that the date of Passover coincides with the constellation of Aries the Ram—the Lamb. This was of no more than marginal importance for the fixing of the date of Easter. What was essential was the connection with the date of the death and Resurrection of Jesus, which was of its very nature linked with the Jewish liturgical calendar. Now this link, raising as it does the question of the relation of New Testament to Old and of the newness of Christianity, was to have explosive potential. In the second century A.D. it led to the Easter controversy, which was not to be settled, at least for the Great Church, until the Council of Nicaea (325). On the one hand, there was the custom in Asia Minor of conforming to the Jewish calendar and always celebrating the Christian Easter on 14 Nisan, the date of the Jewish Passover. On the other hand, there was the custom, especially in Rome, of regarding Sunday, the day of the Resurrection, as the determining factor: the Christian Easter should, therefore, be celebrated on the Sunday after the first full moon of spring. The Council of Nicaea promulgated this decision. Through its ruling, the solar and lunar calendars were interconnected, and the two great cosmic forms of ordering time were linked to each other in association with the history of Israel and the life of Jesus. But let us return to the image of the lamb (or ram). In the fifth century there was a controversy between Rome and Alexandria about what the latest possible date for Easter could be. According to Alexandrian tradition, it was April 25. Pope St. Leo the Great (440–461) criticized this very late date by pointing out that, according to the Bible, Easter should fall in the first month, and the first month did not mean April but the time when the sun is passing through the first part of the Zodiac—the sign of Aries. The constellation in the heavens seemed to speak, in advance and for all time, of the Lamb of God, who takes away the sins of the world (Jn 1:29), the one who sums up in himself all the sacrifices of the innocent and gives them their meaning. The mysterious story of the ram, caught in the thicket and taking the place of Isaac as the sacrifice decreed by God himself, was now seen as the pre-history of Christ. The fork of the tree in which the ram was hanging was seen as a replica of the sign of Aries, which in turn was the celestial foreshadowing of the crucified Christ. We should also say that Jewish tradition gave the date of March 25 to Abraham's sacrifice. Now, as we shall see presently, this day was also regarded as the day of creation, the day when God's Word decreed: "Let there be light." It was also considered, very early on, as the day of Christ's death and eventually as the day of his conception. We may see a reflection of these connections in the first epistle of St. Peter, which describes Christ as the lamb "without blemish" demanded by Exodus 12:5 and "destined before the foundation of the world" (1 Pet 1:20). The mysterious words in Revelation 13:8 about the "Lamb slain from the beginning of the world" [translated from the German] could also perhaps be interpreted in the same way—though other translations are possible that tone down the paradox. These cosmic images enabled Christians to see, in an unprecedented way, the world-embracing meaning of Christ and so to understand the grandeur of the hope inscribed in Christian faith. This is most illuminating. It seems clear to me that we have to recapture this cosmic vision if we want once again to understand and live Christianity in its full breadth.

I should like to make two further remarks about the celebration of Easter. In our reflections so far, we have seen how deeply Christianity is marked by the symbolism of the sun. The dating of Easter, finally fixed at Nicaea, incorporated the feast into the solar calendar, but it did not break its link with the lunar calendar. In the world of religion, the moon, with its alternating phases, is frequently seen as the symbol of the feminine, but especially as a symbol of transitoriness. Thus the cosmic symbolism of the moon corresponds to the mystery of death and resurrection, which is celebrated in the Christian Passover. When the Sunday after the first full moon of spring comes to be the date of Easter, the symbolism of sun and moon are linked together. Transitoriness is taken up into what never passes away. Death becomes resurrection and passes into eternal life.

Finally, we should add that, for Israel, Passover was not simply a cosmic festival but was essentially aimed at historical remembrance. It is the feast of the Exodus out of Egypt, the feast of Israel's liberation, with which it begins its own journey in history as the People of God. Israel's Passover is the recalling of an act of God that was liberation and thus the foundation of the community. This content of the feast also entered into Christianity and helped it understand the depth of meaning in the Resurrection of Christ. Jesus had consciously connected his final journey with Israel's Passover. He defined it as his "hour". There must, therefore, be an inner connection between Israel's remembrance and the new event of Christendom's sacred triduum. Man's last enemy is death. Man is fully set free only when he is set free from death. The oppression of Israel in Egypt was indeed a kind of death, which threatened to, and was intended to, destroy the people as such. Death was imposed on all male progeny. But on the night of Passover the angel of death now passes over Egypt and strikes down its firstborn. Liberation is liberation for life. Christ, the Firstborn from the dead, takes death upon himself and, by his Resurrection, shatters death's power. Death no longer has the last word. The love of the Son proves to be stronger than death because it unites man with God's love, which is God's very being. Thus, in the Resurrection of Christ, it is not just the destiny of an individual that is called to mind. He is now perpetually present, because he lives, and he gathers us up, so that we may live: "[B]ecause I live, you will live also" (Jn 14:19). In the light of Easter, Christians see themselves as people who truly *live*. They have found their way out of an existence that is more death than life. They have discovered real life: "And this is eternal life, that they know you the only true God, and Jesus Christ whom you have sent" (Jn 17:3). Deliverance from death is at the same time deliverance from the captivity of individualism, from the prison of self, from the incapacity to love and make a gift of oneself. Thus Easter becomes the great feast of Baptism, in which man, as it were, enacts the passage through the Red Sea, emerges from his own existence into communion with Christ and so into communion with all who belong to Christ. Resurrection builds communion. It creates the new People of God. The grain of wheat that dies all alone does not remain alone but brings much fruit with it. The risen Lord does not remain alone. He draws all mankind to himself and so creates a new universal communion of men. The whole meaning of the Jewish Passover is made present in the Christian Easter. At the same time, it is not about remembering a past and unrepeatable event, but, as we have seen, "once for all" here becomes "forever". The Risen Lord lives and gives life. He lives and brings about communion. He lives and opens up the future. He lives and shows the way. But we must also not forget that this feast of salvation history, open as it is to the future, to what lies ahead, has its roots in a cosmic celebration, roots that it does not relinquish. The dying and rising moon becomes the sign in the cosmos for death and resurrection. The sun of the first day becomes the messenger of Christ, who "comes forth like a bridegroom leaving his chamber, and like a strong man runs its course with joy" (Ps 19[18]:5f.).

That is why the calendar of the Christian feasts is not to be manipulated at will. The "hour" of Jesus makes its appearance, again and again, within the unity of cosmic and historical time. Through the feast we enter into the rhythm of creation and into God's plan for human history.

A question comes up at this point that I should like to discuss briefly before moving to the Christmas season. The cosmic symbolism that I have been describing has its precise setting in the area of the Mediterranean and the Near East in which the Jewish and Christian religions came into being. By and large it applies to the Northern Hemisphere of the globe. Now in the Southern Hemisphere everything is reversed. The Christian Easter falls, not in the spring, but in the autumn. Christmas coincides, not with the winter solstice, but with high summer. This raises the question of "inculturation" with great urgency. If the cosmic symbolism is so important, ought we not to adjust the liturgical calendar for the Southern Hemisphere? G. Voss has rightly responded by pointing out that, if we did this, we would reduce the mystery of Christ to the level of a merely cosmic religion; we would be subordinating history to the cosmos. But the historical does not serve the cosmic; no, the cosmic serves the historical. Only in history is the cosmos given its center and goal. To believe in the Incarnation means to be bound to Christianity's origins, their particularity, and, in human terms, their contingency. Here is the guarantee that we are not chasing myths; that God really has acted in our history and taken our time into his hands. Only over the bridge of this "once for all" can we come into the "forever" of God's mercy. At the same time, we must take account of the full breadth of the symbol and of God's action in history. Voss has very beautifully pointed to the "autumnal" aspects of the Easter mystery, which deepen and broaden our understanding of the feast and give it a special profile appropriate to the Southern Hemisphere. Incidentally, the Scriptures and the liturgy offer their own suggestions for a transferral of the symbols. I have already pointed out that, in interpreting the Passion of Jesus, St. John's Gospel and the epistle to the Hebrews do not just refer to the feast of Passover, which is the Lord's "hour", in terms of date. No, they also interpret it in light of the ritual of the Day of Atonement celebrated on the tenth day of the seventh month (September–October). In the Passover of Jesus there is, so to speak, a coincidence of Easter (spring) and the Day of Atonement (autumn). Christ connects the world's spring

and autumn. The autumn of declining time becomes a new beginning, while the spring, as the time of the Lord's death, now points to
the end of time, to the autumn of the world, in which, according to
the Fathers, Christ came among us.

The liturgical calendar used before the postconciliar reforms contained a strange transferral of the seasons, a use that, of course, had
long eluded people's understanding and was interpreted in a much too
superficial way. Depending on how late or early Easter fell, the time
after Epiphany had to be shortened or lengthened. The Sundays left
out after Epiphany had to be moved to the end of the Church's year.
If one looks carefully at the readings then in use, one finds that the
texts are largely taken up with the theme of sowing the seed, which is
a metaphor for the seed of the Gospel to be scattered throughout the
world. Now these texts and their respective Sundays can be accommodated just as well in the spring as in the autumn. Both seasons are
seed-time. In the spring the farmer sows seed for autumn, in autumn
for the coming year. Sowing seed always points to the future. It belongs
to the waxing year but also to the waning year, for the waning year
also points to a new future. In both seasons the mystery of hope is at
work and reaches its proper depth in the waning year, which leads
beyond decline to a new beginning. It would be a great work of inculturation to develop this approach and to bring it into the common
consciousness of Christians in the two hemispheres, southern and northern. The South could help the North to discover a new breadth and
depth in the mystery, thus enabling us all to draw afresh on its richness.

Let us turn—albeit very briefly—to the second focal point of the
Church's year, the Christmas season, which developed somewhat later
than the cycle that leads to and comes from Easter. Sunday, like the
eastward stance for Christian prayer, is a primordial *datum* of Christianity. It had a fixed place from the beginning and shaped Christian
existence so profoundly that St. Ignatius of Antioch said that we "no
longer observe the Sabbath, but live in the observance of the Lord's
Day" (*Mag.* 9, 1). But already in the New Testament Christians look
back from the Easter mystery to the Incarnation of Christ from the
Virgin Mary. In the Gospel of St. John, which is the concluding
synthesis of New Testament faith, the theology of the Incarnation
stands on equal footing alongside the theology of Easter. Or rather
the theology of the Incarnation and the theology of Easter do not
simply stand alongside each other. No, these are the two inseparable

focal points of the one faith in Jesus Christ, the incarnate Son of God and Redeemer. The Cross and Resurrection presuppose the Incarnation. It is only because the Son, and in him God himself, "came down from heaven" and "became incarnate from the Virgin Mary" that Jesus' death and Resurrection are events that are contemporary with us all and touch us all, delivering us from a past marked by death and opening up the present and future. On the other hand, the Incarnation has as its goal the attainment by the "flesh", by corruptible earthly existence, of an incorruptible form, in other words, an entry into Paschal transformation. Having been recognized as a focal point of faith in Christ, the Incarnation had to be given some expression in liturgical celebration, some place in the rhythm of sacred time. It is hard to say how far back the beginnings of the Christmas feast go. It assumed its definitive form in the third century. At about the same time the feast of the Epiphany emerged in the East on January 6 and the feast of Christmas in the West on December 25. The two feasts had different emphases because of the different religious and cultural contexts in which they arose, but essentially their meaning was the same: the celebration of the birth of Christ as the dawning of the new light, the true sun, of history. The complicated and somewhat disputed details of the development of the two feasts need not detain us in this little book. Here I should simply like to indicate what seems to me to be helpful to understanding the two days. Astonishingly, the starting point for dating the birth of Christ was March 25. As far as I know, the most ancient reference to it is in the writings of the African ecclesiastical author Tertullian (ca. 150–ca. 207), who evidently assumes as a well-known tradition that Christ suffered death on March 25. In Gaul, right up to the sixth century, this was kept as the immovable date of Easter. In a work on the calculation of the date of Easter, written in A.D. 243, and also emanating from Africa, we find March 25 interpreted as the day of the world's creation, and, in connection with that, we find a very peculiar dating for the birth of Christ. According to the account of creation in Genesis 1, the sun was created on the fourth day, that is, on March 28. This day should, therefore, be regarded as the day of Christ's birth, as the rising of the true sun of history. This idea was altered during the third century, so that the day of Christ's Passion and the day of his conception were regarded as identical. On March 25 the Church honored both the Annunciation by the angel and the

Lord's conception by the Holy Spirit in the womb of the Virgin. The feast of Christ's birth on December 25—nine months after March 25—developed in the West in the course of the third century, while the East—probably because of a difference of calendar—at first celebrated January 6 as the birthday of Christ. It may also have been the response to a feast of the birth of the mythical gods observed on this day in Alexandria. The claim used to be made that December 25 developed in opposition to the Mithras myth or as a Christian response to the cult of the unconquered sun promoted by Roman emperors in the third century in their efforts to establish a new imperial religion. However, these old theories can no longer be sustained. The decisive factor was the connection of creation and Cross, of creation and Christ's conception. In the light of the "hour of Jesus", these dates brought the cosmos into the picture. The cosmos was now thought of as the pre-annunciation of Christ, the Firstborn of creation (cf. Col 1:15). It is he of whom creation speaks, and it is by him that its mute message is deciphered. The cosmos finds its true meaning in the Firstborn of creation, who has now entered history. From him comes the assurance that the adventure of creation, of a world with its own free existence distinct from God, does not end up in absurdity and tragedy but, throughout all its calamities and upheavals, remains something positive. God's blessing of the seventh day is truly and definitively confirmed. The fact that the dates of the Lord's conception and birth originally had a cosmic significance means that Christians can take on the challenge of the sun cult and incorporate it positively into the theology of the Christmas feast. There are magnificent texts in the writings of the Fathers that express this synthesis. For example, St. Jerome in a Christmas sermon says this: "Even creation approves our preaching. The universe itself bears witness to the truth of our words. Up to this day the dark days increase, but from this day the darkness decreases.... The light advances, while the night retreats." Likewise, St. Augustine, preaching at Christmas to his flock in Hippo: "Brethren, let us rejoice. The heathen, too, may still make merry, for this day consecrates for us, not the visible sun, but the sun's invisible Creator." Again and again, the Fathers take up the verse about the sun that we have already quoted from Psalm 19(18). For the early Church, this became the real Christmas psalm: the sun, that is, Christ, is like a bridegroom coming forth from his chamber. An echo of the Marian mystery was also heard in this psalm, which was interpreted as a prophecy of Christ. Between the two dates of

March 25 and December 25 comes the feast of the Forerunner, St. John the Baptist, on June 24, at the time of the summer solstice. The link between the dates can now be seen as a liturgical and cosmic expression of the Baptist's words: "He [Christ] must increase, but I must decrease" (Jn 3:30). The birthday of St. John the Baptist takes place on the date when the days begin to shorten, just as the birthday of Christ takes place when they begin again to lengthen. The fabric of this feast is of an entirely Christian weave, without direct precedent in the Old Testament. However, it stands in continuity with the synthesis of cosmos and history, of remembrance and hope, that was already characteristic of the Old Testament feasts and took on a new form in the Christian calendar. The close interweaving of incarnation and resurrection can be seen precisely in the relation, both proper and common, that each has to the rhythm of the sun and its symbolism.

I should like briefly to mention the feast of the Epiphany, celebrated on January 6, which is closely connected with Christmas. Let us leave on one side all the historical details and the many glorious patristic texts on the subject. Let us try to understand it very simply in the form that we have here in the West. It interprets the Incarnation of the Logos in terms of the ancient category of "epiphany", that is, of the self-revelation of God, the God who manifests himself to his creatures. In this perspective the feast links together several different epiphanies: the adoration of the Magi as the beginning of the Church of the Gentiles, the procession of the nations to the God of Israel (cf. Is 60); the Baptism of Jesus in the Jordan, in which the voice from above publicly proclaims Jesus as the Son of God; and the wedding at Cana, where he reveals his glory. The narrative of the adoration of the Magi became important for Christian thought, because it shows the inner connection between the wisdom of the nations and the Word of promise in Scripture; because it shows how the language of the cosmos and the truth-seeking thought of man lead to Christ. The mysterious star could become the symbol for these connections and once again emphasize that the language of the cosmos and the language of the human heart trace their descent from the Word of the Father, who in Bethlehem came forth from the silence of God and assembled the fragments of our human knowledge into a complete whole.

The great feasts that structure the year of faith are feasts of Christ and precisely as such are ordered toward the one God who revealed himself to Moses in the burning bush and chose Israel as the confessor of faith in his uniqueness. In addition to the sun, which is the image of Christ, there is the moon, which has no light of its own but shines with a brightness that comes from the sun. This is a sign to us that we men are in constant need of a "little" light, whose hidden light helps us to know and love the light of the Creator, God one and triune. That is why the feasts of the saints from earliest times have formed part of the Christian year. We have already encountered Mary, whose person is so closely interwoven with the mystery of Christ that the development of the Christmas cycle inevitably introduced a Marian note into the Church's year. The Marian dimension of the christological feasts was made visible. Then, in addition, come the commemorations of the apostles and martyrs and, finally, the memorials of the saints of every century. One might say that the saints are, so to speak, new Christian constellations, in which the richness of God's goodness is reflected. Their light, coming from God, enables us to know better the interior richness of God's great light, which we cannot comprehend in the refulgence of its glory.

III. Art and Liturgy

1. The Question of Images

In the First Commandment of the Decalogue, which underscores the uniqueness of the God to whom alone adoration is due, we read this admonition: "You shall not make for yourself a graven image, or any likeness of anything that is in heaven above, or that is in the earth beneath, or that is in the water under the earth" (Ex 20:4; cf. Deut 5:8). There is a notable exception to this prohibition of images at the very center of the Old Testament, one that concerns the most sacred of places, the gold covering of the Ark of the Covenant, which was regarded as the place of expiation. "There I will meet with you", says God to Moses, "I will speak with you of all that I will give you in commandment for the people of Israel" (Ex 25:22). With regard to the fashioning of the covering, Moses receives the following instructions: "And you shall make two cherubim of gold; of hammered work shall you make them, on the two ends of the mercy seat.... The cherubim shall spread out their wings above.... [T]heir faces [shall be turned] one to another; toward the mercy seat shall the faces of the cherubim be" (Ex 25:18–20). The mysterious beings that cover and protect the place of divine revelation can be represented, precisely to conceal the mystery of the presence of God himself. As we have already seen, St. Paul saw the crucified Christ as the true and living "place of expiation", of whom the "mercy seat", the *kapporeth* lost during the Exile, was but a foreshadowing. In him God has now, so to speak, lifted the veil from his face. The Eastern Church's icon of the Resurrection of Christ takes up this link between the Ark of the Covenant and the Paschal Mystery of Christ when it shows Christ standing on cross-shaped slabs, which symbolize the grave but also suggest a reference to the *kapporeth* of the Old Covenant. Christ is flanked by the cherubim and approached by the women who came to the tomb

70

to anoint him. The fundamental image of the Old Testament is retained, but it is reshaped in the light of the Resurrection and given a new center: the God who no longer completely conceals himself but now shows himself in the form of the Son. This transformation of the narrative of the Ark of the Covenant into an image of the Resurrection reveals the very heart of the development from Old Testament to New. However, if we are to understand it correctly in its totality, we must follow the main lines of the development a little more closely.

The prohibition of images in Islam and in Judaism since about the third or fourth century A.D. has been interpreted in a radical way, so that only non-figurative, geometrical designs are permitted in the ornamentation of the sanctuary. However, in the Judaism at the time of Jesus and well into the third century, a much more generous interpretation of the image-question developed. Paradoxically, in the images of salvation we see exactly the same continuity between synagogue and church that we have already noticed in our discussion of liturgical space. As a result of archaeological discoveries, we now know that the ancient synagogues were richly decorated with representations of scenes from the Bible. They were by no means regarded as mere images of past events, as a kind of pictorial history lesson; rather, they were seen as a narrative (*haggadah*), which, while calling something to mind, makes it present. On liturgical feasts the deeds of God in the past are made present. The feasts are a participation in God's action in time, and the images themselves, as remembrance in visible form, are involved in the liturgical re-presentation. The Christian images, as we find them in the catacombs, simply take up and develop the canon of images already established by the synagogue, while giving it a new modality of presence. The individual events are now ordered toward the Christian sacraments and to Christ himself. Noah's ark and the crossing of the Red Sea now point to Baptism. The sacrifice of Isaac and the meal of the three angels with Abraham speak of Christ's Sacrifice and the Eucharist. Shining through the rescue of the three young men from the fiery furnace and of Daniel from the lions' den we see Christ's Resurrection and our own. Still more than in the synagogue, the point of the images is not to tell a story about something in the past but to incorporate the events of history into the sacrament. In past history Christ with his sacraments is on his way through the ages. We are taken into the events. The events themselves transcend the passing of time and become present in our midst through the sacramental action of the Church.

The centering of all history in Christ is both the liturgical transmission of that history and the expression of a new experience of time, in which past, present, and future make contact, because they have been inserted into the presence of the risen Lord. As we have seen already and now find confirmed anew, liturgical presence contains eschatological hope within it. All sacred images are, without exception, in a certain sense images of the Resurrection, history read in the light of the Resurrection, and for that very reason they are images of hope, giving us the assurance of the world to come, of the final coming of Christ. However inferior the first images of the Christian tradition may often be in their artistic qualities, an extraordinary spiritual process has taken place in them, though one that is in close and deep unity with the iconography of the synagogue. The Resurrection sheds a new light on history. It is seen as a path of hope, into which the images draw us. Thus the images of the early Church have a thoroughly sacramental significance. They have the character of mysteries, going far beyond the didactic function of telling the stories of the Bible.

None of the early images attempts to give us anything like a portrait of Christ. Instead, Christ is shown in his significance, in "allegorical" images—for example, as the true philosopher instructing us in the art of living and dying. He appears as the great teacher, but above all in the form of the shepherd. The reason why this image, which is derived from Sacred Scripture, became so precious to early Christianity is that the shepherd was regarded as an allegory of the Logos. The Logos, through whom all things were made, who bears within himself, so to speak, the archetypes of all existing things, is the guardian of creation. In the Incarnation he takes the lost sheep, human nature, mankind as a whole, onto his shoulders and carries it home. The image of the shepherd thus sums up the whole of salvation history: God's entry into history, the Incarnation, the pursuit of the lost sheep, and the homeward path into the Church of the Jews and Gentiles.

One development of far-reaching importance in the history of the images of faith was the emergence for the first time of a so-called *acheiropoietos*, an image that has not been made by human hands and portrays the very face of Christ. Two of these images appeared in the East at about the same time in the middle of the sixth century. The first of these was the so-called *camulianium*, the imprint of the image of Christ on a woman's gown. The second was the *mandylion*, as it was called later, which was brought from Edessa in Syria to Constantinople and is thought by many scholars today to be identical with the Shroud of Turin. In each case, as with the Turin Shroud, it must have been a question of a truly mysterious image, which no human artistry was capable of producing. In some inexplicable way, it appeared imprinted upon cloth and claimed to show the true face of Christ, the crucified and risen Lord. The first appearance of this image must have provoked immense fascination. Now at last could the true face of the Lord, hitherto hidden, be seen and thus the promise be fulfilled: "He who has seen me has seen the Father" (Jn 14:9). The sight of the God-Man and, through him, of God himself seemed to have been opened up; the Greek longing for the vision of the Eternal seemed to be fulfilled. Thus the icon inevitably assumed in its form the status of a sacrament. It was regarded as bestowing a communion no less than that of the Eucharist. People began to think that there was virtually a kind of real presence of the Person imaged in the image. The image in this case, the image not made by human hands, was an image in the full sense, a participation in the reality concerned, the refulgence and thus the presence of the One who gives himself in the image. It is not hard to see why the images modelled on the *acheiropoietos* became the center of the whole canon of iconography, which meanwhile had made progress and was understood better in its wider implications.

Clearly, though, there was a danger lurking here: a false sacramentalizing of the image, which seemed to lead beyond the sacraments and their hiddenness into a direct vision of the divine presence. And so it is also clear that this new development was bound to lead to violent counter-movements, to that radical rejection of the image that we call "iconoclasm", the destruction of images. Iconoclasm derived its passion in part from truly religious motives, from the undeniable dangers of a kind of adoration of the image, but also from a cluster of political factors. It was important for the Byzantine emperors not to give any unnecessary provocation to Moslems and Jews. The suppression of images could be beneficial to the unity of the Empire and to relations with the Empire's Moslem neighbors. And so the thesis was proposed that Christ must not be represented in an image. Only the sign of the Cross (without a *corpus*) could be, as it were, his seal. Cross or image—that was the choice. In the course of this struggle the true theology of icons matured and bequeathed us a message that has a profound relevance to us today in the iconographic crisis of the West.

The icon of Christ is the icon of the risen Lord. That truth, with all its implications, now dawned on the Christian mind. There is no *portrait* of the risen Lord. At first the disciples do not recognize him. They have to be led toward a new kind of seeing, in which their eyes are gradually opened from within to the point where they recognize him afresh and cry out: "It is the Lord!" Perhaps the most telling episode of all is that of the disciples on the road to Emmaus. Their hearts are transformed, so that, through the outward events of Scripture, they can discern its inward center, from which everything comes and to which everything tends: the Cross and Resurrection of Jesus Christ. They then detain their mysterious companion and give him their hospitality, and at the breaking of bread they experience in reverse fashion what happened to Adam and Eve when they ate the fruit of the tree of the knowledge of good and evil: their eyes are opened. Now they no longer see just the externals but the reality that is not apparent to their senses yet shines through their senses: it is the Lord, now alive in a new way. In the icon it is not the facial features that count (though icons essentially adhere to the appearance of the *acheiropoietos*). No, what matters is the new kind of seeing. The icon is supposed to originate from an opening up of the inner senses, from a facilitation of sight that gets beyond the surface of the empirical and perceives Christ, as the later theology of icons puts it, in the light of Tabor. It thus leads the man who contemplates it to the point where, through the interior vision that the icon embodies, he beholds in the sensible that which, though above the sensible, has entered into the sphere of the senses. As Evdokimov says so beautifully, the icon requires a "fast from the eyes". Icon painters, he says, must learn how to fast with their eyes and prepare themselves by a long path of prayerful asceticism. This is what marks the transition from art to sacred art (p. 188). The icon comes from prayer and leads to prayer. It delivers a man from that closure of the senses which perceives only the externals, the material surface of things, and is blind to the transparency of the spirit, the transparency of the Logos. At the most fundamental level, what we are dealing with here is nothing other than the transcendence of faith. The whole problem of knowledge in the modern world is present. If an interior opening-up does not occur in man that enables him to see more than what can be measured and weighed, to perceive the reflection of divine glory in creation, then God remains excluded from our field of vision. The icon, rightly understood, leads us away from false questions about portraits, portraits comprehensible at the level of the senses, and thus enables us to discern the face of Christ and, in him, of the Father. Thus in the icon we find the same spiritual orientations that we discovered previously when emphasizing the eastward direction of the liturgy. The icon is intended to draw us onto an inner path, the eastward path, toward the Christ who is to return. Its dynamism is identical with the dynamism of the liturgy as a whole. Its Christology is trinitarian. It is the Holy Spirit who makes us capable of seeing, he whose work is always to move us toward Christ. "We have drunk deeply of the Spirit," says St. Athanasius, "and we drink Christ" (Evdokimov, p. 204). This seeing, which teaches us to see Christ, not "according to the flesh", but according to the Spirit (cf. 2 Cor 5:16), grants us also a glimpse of the Father himself.

Only when we have understood this interior orientation of the icon can we rightly understand why the Second Council of Nicaea and all the following councils concerned with icons regard it as a confession of faith in the Incarnation and iconoclasm as a denial of the Incarnation, as the summation of all heresies. The Incarnation means, in the first place, that the invisible God enters into the visible world, so that we, who are bound to matter, can know him. In this sense, the way to the Incarnation was already being prepared in all that God said and did in history for man's salvation. But this descent of God is intended to draw us into a movement of ascent. The Incarnation is aimed at man's transformation through the Cross and to the new corporeality of the Resurrection. God seeks us where we are, not so that we stay there, but so that we may come to be where he is, so that we may get beyond ourselves. That is why to reduce the visible appearance of Christ to a "historical Jesus" belonging to the past misses the point of his visible appearance, misses the point of the Incarnation.

The senses are not to be discarded, but they should be expanded to their widest capacity. We see Christ rightly only when we say with Thomas: "My Lord and my God!" We have just established that the icon has a trinitarian scope, and now we must come to terms with its ontological proportions. The Son could become incarnate as man only because man was already planned in advance in relation to him, as the image of him who is in himself the image of God. As Evdokimov again says so strikingly, the light of the first day and the light of the eighth day meet in the icon. Present already in creation is the light that will shine with its full brightness on the eighth day in the Resurrection of the Lord and in the new world, the light that enables us to see the splendor of God. The Incarnation is rightly understood only when it is seen within the broad context of creation, history, and the new world. Only then does it become clear that the senses belong to faith, that the new seeing does not abolish them, but leads them to their original purpose. Iconoclasm rests ultimately on a one-sided apophatic theology, which recognizes only the Wholly Other-ness of the God beyond all images and words, a theology that in the final analysis regards revelation as the inadequate human reflection of what is eternally imperceptible. But if this is the case, faith collapses. Our current form of sensibility, which can no longer apprehend the transparency of the spirit in the senses, almost inevitably brings with it a flight into a purely "negative" (apophatic) theology. God is beyond all thought, and therefore all propositions about him and every kind of image of God are in equal proportions valid and invalid. What seems like the highest humility toward God turns into pride, allowing God no word and permitting him no real entry into history. On the one hand, matter is absolutized and thought of as completely impervious to God, as mere matter, and thus deprived of its dignity. But, as Evdokimov says, there is also an apophatic Yes, not just an apophatic No, the denial of all likeness. Following Gregory Palamas, he emphasizes that in his essence God is radically transcendent, but in his existence he can be, and wants to be, represented as the Living One. God is the Wholly Other, but he is powerful enough to be able to show himself. And he has so fashioned his creature that it is capable of "seeing" him and loving him.

With these reflections we once again make contact with our own times and therefore also with the development of liturgy, art, and faith in the Western world. Is this theology of the icon, as developed in the East, true? Is it valid for us? Or is it just a peculiarity of the Christian East? Let us start with the historical facts. In early Christian art, right up to the end of the Romanesque period, in other words up to the threshold of the thirteenth century, there is no *essential* difference between East and West with regard to the question of images. True, if we think of St. Augustine or St. Gregory the Great, the West emphasized, almost exclusively, the pedagogical function of the image. The so-called *Libri Carolini*, as well as the synods of Frankfurt (794) and Paris (824), came out against the poorly understood

Seventh Ecumenical Council, Nicaea II, which canonized the defeat of iconoclasm and the rooting of the icon in the Incarnation. By contrast, the Western synods insist on the purely educative role of the images: "Christ", they said, "did not save us by paintings" (cf. Evdokimov, p. 167).

But the themes and fundamental orientation of iconography remained the same, even though now, in the Romanesque style, plastic art emerges, something that never had a foothold in the East. It is always the risen Christ, even on the Cross, to whom the community looks as the true *Oriens*. And art is always characterized by the unity of creation, Christology, and eschatology: the first day is on its way toward the eighth, which in turn takes up the first. Art is still ordered to the mystery that becomes present in the liturgy. It is still oriented to the heavenly liturgy. The figures of the angels in Romanesque art are essentially no different from those in Byzantine painting. They show that we are joining with the cherubim and seraphim, with all the heavenly powers, in praise of the Lamb. In the liturgy the curtain between heaven and earth is torn open, and we are taken up into a liturgy that spans the whole cosmos.

With the emergence of Gothic, a change slowly takes place. Much remains the same, especially the fundamental inner correspondence between the Old Testament and the New, which for its part always has a reference to what is still to come. But the central image becomes different. The depiction is no longer of the *Pantocrator*, the Lord of all, leading us into the eighth day. It has been superseded by the image of the crucified Lord in the agony of his Passion and death. The story is told of the historical events of the Passion, but the Resurrection is not made visible. The historical and narrative aspect of art comes to the fore. It has been said that the mysterial image has been replaced by the devotional image. Many factors may have been involved in this change of perspective. Evdokimov thinks that the turn from Platonism to Aristotelianism during the thirteenth century played a part. Platonism sees sensible things as shadows of the eternal archetypes. In the sensible we can and should know the archetypes and rise up through the former to the latter. Aristotelianism rejects the doctrine of Ideas. The thing, composed of matter and form, exists in its own right. Through abstraction I discern the species to which it belongs. In place of seeing, by which the super-sensible becomes visible in the sensible, comes abstraction. The relationship of the spiritual and the material has changed and with it man's attitude to reality as it appears to him. For Plato, the category of the beautiful had been definitive. The beautiful and the good, ultimately the beautiful and God, coincide. Through the appearance of the beautiful we are wounded in our innermost being, and that wound grips us and takes us beyond ourselves; it stirs longing into flight and moves us toward the truly Beautiful, to the Good in itself. Something of this Platonic foundation lives on in the theology of icons, even though the Platonic ideas of the beautiful and of vision have been transformed by the light of Tabor. Moreover, Plato's conception has been profoundly reshaped by the interconnection of creation, Christology, and eschatology, and the material order as such has been given a new dignity and a new value. This kind of Platonism, transformed as it is by the Incarnation, largely disappears from the West after the thirteenth century, so that now the art of painting strives first and foremost to depict events that have taken place. Salvation history is seen less as a sacrament than as a narrative unfolded in time. Thus the relationship to the liturgy also changes. It is seen as a kind of symbolic reproduction of the event of the Cross. Piety responds by turning chiefly to meditation on the mysteries of the life of Jesus. Art finds its inspiration less in the liturgy than in popular piety, and popular piety is in turn nourished by the historical images in which it can contemplate the way to Christ, the way of Jesus himself, and its continuation in the saints. The separation in iconography between East and West, which took place at the latest by the thirteenth century, doubtless goes very deep: very different themes, different spiritual paths, open up. A devotion to the Cross of a more historicizing kind replaces orientation to the *Oriens*, to the risen Lord who has gone ahead of us.

Nevertheless, we should not exaggerate the differences that developed. True, the depiction of Christ dying in pain on the Cross is something new, but it still depicts him who bore *our* pains, by whose stripes we are healed. In the extremes of pain it represents the redemptive love of God. Though Grünewald's altarpiece takes the realism of the Passion to a radical extreme, the fact remains that it was an image of consolation. It enabled the plague victims cared for by the Antonians to recognize that God identified with them in their fate, to see that he had descended into their suffering and that their suffering lay hidden in his. There is a decisive turn to what is human, historical, in Christ, but it is animated by a sense that these human afflictions of his belong to the mystery. The images are consoling, because they make visible the overcoming of our anguish in the incarnate God's sharing of our suffering, and so they bear within them the message of the Resurrection. These images, too, come from prayer, from interior meditation on the way of Christ. They are identifications with Christ, which are based in turn on God's identification with us in Christ. They open up the realism of the mystery without diverging from it. As for the Mass, as the making present of the Cross, do these images not enable us to understand that mystery with a new vividness? The mystery is unfolded in an extremity of concreteness, and popular piety is enabled thereby to reach the heart of the liturgy in a new way. These images, too, do not show just the "surface of the skin", the external sensible world; they, too, are intended to lead us through mere outward appearance and open our eyes to the heart of God. What we are suggesting here about the images of the Cross applies also to all the rest of the "narrative" art of the Gothic style. What power of inward devotion lies in the images of the Mother of God! They manifest the new humanity of the faith. Such images are an invitation to prayer, because they are permeated with prayer from within. They show us the true image of man as planned by the Creator and renewed by Christ. They guide us into man's authentic being. And finally, let us not forget the glorious art of Gothic stained glass! The windows of the Gothic cathedrals keep out the garishness of the light outside, while concentrating that light and using it so that the whole history of God in relation to man, from creation to the Second Coming, shines through. The walls of the church, in interplay with the sun, become an image in their own right, the iconostasis of the West, lending the place a sense of the sacred that can touch the hearts even of agnostics.

The Renaissance did something quite new. It "emancipated" man. Now we see the development of the "aesthetic" in the modern sense, the vision of a beauty that no longer points beyond itself but is content in the end with itself, the beauty of the appearing thing. Man experiences himself in his autonomy, in all his grandeur. Art speaks of this grandeur of man almost as if it were surprised by it; it needs no other beauty to seek. There is often scarcely a difference between the depictions of pagan myths and those of Christian history. The tragic burden of antiquity has been forgotten; only its divine beauty is seen. A nostalgia for the gods emerges, for myth, for a world without fear of sin and without the pain of the Cross, which had perhaps been too overpowering in the images of the late Middle Ages. True, Christian subjects are still being depicted, but such "religious art" is no longer sacred art in the proper sense. It does not enter into the humility of the sacraments and their time-transcending dynamism. It wants to enjoy today and to bring redemption through beauty itself. Perhaps the iconoclasm of the Reformation should be understood against this background, though doubtless its roots were extensive.

Baroque art, which follows the Renaissance, has many different aspects and modes of expression. In its best form it is based on the reform of the Church set in motion by the Council of Trent. In line with the tradition of the West, the Council again emphasized the didactic and pedagogical character of art, but, as a fresh start toward interior renewal, it led once more to a new kind of seeing that comes from and returns within. The altarpiece is like a window through which the world of God comes out to us. The curtain of temporality is raised, and we are allowed a glimpse into the inner life of the world of God. This art is intended to insert us into the liturgy of heaven. Again and again, we experience a Baroque church as a unique kind of *fortissimo* of joy, an Alleluia in visual form. "The joy of the LORD is your strength" (Neh 8:10). These words from the Old Testament express the basic emotion that animates this iconography. The Enlightenment pushed faith into a kind of intellectual and even social ghetto. Contemporary culture turned away from the faith and trod another path, so that faith took flight in historicism, the copying of the past, or else attempted compromise or lost itself in resignation and cultural abstinence. The last of these led to a new iconoclasm, which has frequently been regarded as virtually mandated by the Second Vatican Council. The destruction of images, the first signs of which reach back to the 1920s, eliminated a lot of *kitsch* and unworthy art, but ultimately it left behind a void, the wretchedness of which we are now experiencing in a truly acute way.

Where do we go from here? Today we are experiencing, not just a crisis of sacred art, but a crisis of art in general of unprecedented proportions. The crisis of art for its part is a symptom of the crisis of man's very existence. The immense growth in man's mastery of the material world has left him blind to the questions of life's meaning that transcend the material world. We might almost call it a blindness of the spirit. The questions of how we ought to live, how we can overcome death, whether existence has a purpose and what it is—to all these questions there is no longer a common answer.

Positivism, formulated in the name of scientific seriousness, narrows the horizon to what is verifiable, to what can be proved by experiment; it renders the world opaque. True, it still contains mathematics, but the *logos* that is the presupposition of this mathematics and its applicability is no longer evident. Thus our world of images no longer surpasses the bounds of sense and appearance, and the flood of images that surrounds us really means the end of the image. If something cannot be photographed, it cannot be seen. In this situation, the art of the icon, sacred art, depending as it does on a wider kind of seeing, becomes impossible. What is more, art itself, which in impressionism and expressionism explored the extreme possibilities of the sense of sight, becomes literally object-less. Art turns into experimenting with self-created worlds, empty "creativity", which no longer perceives the *Creator Spiritus*, the Creator Spirit. It attempts to take his place, and yet, in so doing, it manages to produce only what is arbitrary and vacuous, bringing home to man the absurdity of his role as creator.

Again we must ask: Where do we go from here? Let us try to sum up what we have said so far and to identify the fundamental principles of an art ordered to divine worship.

1. The complete absence of images is incompatible with faith in the Incarnation of God. God has acted in history and entered into our sensible world, so that it may become transparent to him. Images of beauty, in which the mystery of the invisible God becomes visible, are an essential part of Christian worship. There will always be ups and downs in the history of iconography, upsurge and decline, and therefore periods when images are somewhat sparse. But they can never be totally lacking. Iconoclasm is not a Christian option.

2. Sacred art finds its subjects in the images of salvation history, beginning with creation and continuing all the way from the first day to the eighth day, the day of the resurrection and Second Coming, in which the line of human history will come full circle. The images of biblical history have pride of place in sacred art, but the latter also includes the history of the saints, which is an unfolding of the history of Jesus Christ, the fruit borne throughout history by the dead grain of wheat. "You are not struggling against icons", said St. John Damascene to the iconoclastic emperor Leo III, "but against the saints." In the same period, and with the same view in mind, Pope St. Gregory III instituted in Rome the feast of All Saints (cf. Evdokimov, p. 164).

3. The images of the history of God in relation to man do not merely illustrate the succession of past events; they display the inner unity of God's action. In this way they have a reference to the sacraments, above all, to Baptism and the Eucharist, and, in pointing to the sacraments, they are contained within them. Images thus point to a presence; they are essentially connected with what happens in the liturgy. Now history becomes sacrament in Christ, who is the source of the sacraments. Therefore, the icon of Christ is the center of sacred iconography. The center of the icon of Christ is the Paschal Mystery: Christ is presented as the Crucified, the risen Lord, the One who will come again and who here and now hiddenly reigns over all. Every image of Christ must contain these three essential aspects of the mystery of Christ and, in this sense, must be an image of Easter. At the same time, it goes without saying that different emphases are possible. The image may give more prominence to the Cross, the Passion, and in the Passion to the anguish of our own life today, or again it may bring the Resurrection or the Second Coming to the fore. But whatever happens, one aspect can never be completely isolated from another, and in the different emphases the Paschal Mystery as a whole must be plainly evident. An image of the crucifixion no longer transparent to Easter would be just as deficient as an Easter image forgetful of the wounds and the suffering of the present moment. And, centered as it is on the Paschal Mystery, the image of Christ is always an icon of the Eucharist, that is, it points to the sacramental presence of the Easter mystery.

4. The image of Christ and the images of the saints are not photographs. Their whole point is to lead us beyond what can be apprehended at the merely material level, to awaken new senses in us, and to teach us a new kind of seeing, which perceives the Invisible in the visible. The sacredness of the image consists precisely in the fact that it comes from an interior vision and thus leads us to such an interior vision. It must be a fruit of contemplation, of an encounter in faith with the new reality of the risen Christ, and so it leads us in turn into an interior gazing, an encounter in prayer with the Lord. The image is at the service of the liturgy. The prayer and contemplation in which the images are formed must, therefore, be a praying and seeing undertaken in communion with the seeing faith of the Church. The ecclesial dimension is essential to sacred art and thus has an essential connection with the history of the faith, with Scripture and tradition.

5. The Church in the West does not need to disown the specific path she has followed since about the thirteenth century. But she must achieve a real reception of the Seventh Ecumenical Council, Nicaea II, which affirmed the fundamental importance and theological status of the image in the Church. The Western Church does not need to subject herself to all the individual norms concerning images that were developed at the councils and synods of the East, coming to some kind of conclusion in 1551 at the Council of Moscow, the Council of the Hundred Canons. Nevertheless, she should regard the fundamental lines of this theology of the image in the Church as normative for her. There must, of course, be no rigid norms. Freshly received intuitions and the ever-new experiences of piety must find a place in the Church. But still there is a difference between sacred art (which is related to the liturgy and belongs to the ecclesial sphere) and religious art in general. There cannot be completely free expression in sacred art. Forms of art that deny the *logos* of things and imprison man within what appears to the senses are incompatible with the Church's understanding of the image. No sacred art can come from an isolated subjectivity. No, it presupposes that there is a subject who has been inwardly formed by the Church and opened up to the "we". Only thus does art make the Church's common faith visible and speak again to the believing heart. The freedom of art, which is also necessary in the more narrowly circumscribed realm of sacred art, is not a matter of do-as-you-please. It unfolds according to the measure indicated by the first four points in these concluding reflections, which are an attempt to sum up what is constant in the iconographic tradition of faith. Without faith there is no art commensurate with the liturgy. Sacred art stands beneath the imperative stated in the second epistle to the Corinthians. Gazing at the Lord, we are "changed into his likeness from one degree of glory to another; for this comes from the Lord who is the Spirit" (3:18).

But what does all this mean practically? Art cannot be "produced", as one contracts out and produces technical equipment. It is always a gift. Inspiration is not something one can choose for oneself. It has to be received, otherwise it is not there. One cannot bring about a renewal of art in faith by money or through commissions. Before all things it requires the gift of a new kind of seeing. And so it would be worth our while to regain a faith that sees. Wherever that exists, art finds its proper expression.

2. Music and Liturgy

The importance of music in biblical religion is shown very simply by the fact that the verb "to sing" (with related words such as "song", and so forth) is one of the most commonly used words in the Bible. It occurs 309 times in the Old Testament and thirty-six in the New. When man comes into contact with God, mere speech is not enough. Areas of his existence are awakened that spontaneously turn into song. Indeed, man's own being is insufficient for what he has to express, and so he invites the whole of creation to become a song with him: "Awake, my soul! Awake, O harp and lyre! I will awake the dawn! I will give thanks to you, O Lord, among the peoples; I will sing praises to you among the nations. For your steadfast love is great to the heavens, your faithfulness to the clouds" (Ps 57[56]:8f.). We find the first mention of singing in the Bible after the crossing of the Red Sea. Israel has now been definitively delivered from slavery. In a desperate situation, it has had an overwhelming experience of God's saving power. Just as Moses as a baby was taken from the Nile and only then really received the gift of life, so Israel now feels as if it has been, so to speak, taken out of the water: it is free, newly endowed with the gift of itself from God's own hands. In the biblical account, the people's reaction to the foundational event of salvation is described in this sentence: "[T]hey believed in the LORD and in his servant Moses" (Ex 14:31). But then follows a second reaction, which soars up from the first with elemental force: "Then Moses and the people of Israel sang this song to the LORD" (15:1). Year by year, at the Easter Vigil, Christians join in the singing of this song. They sing it in a new way as their song, because they know that they have been "taken out of the water" by God's power, set free by God for authentic life. The Apocalypse of St. John draws the bow back even farther. The final enemies of the People of God have stepped onto the stage of history: the satanic trinity, consisting of the beast, its image, and the number of its name. Everything seems lost for the holy Israel of God in the face of such overwhelming odds. But then the Seer is given the vision of the conquerors, "standing beside the sea of glass with harps of God in their hands. And they sing the song of Moses, the servant of God, and the song of the Lamb" (Rev 15:3). The paradox now becomes even more powerful. It is not the gigantic beasts of prey, with their power over the media and their technical strength, who win the victory. No, it is the sacrificed Lamb that conquers. And so once again, definitively, there resounds the song of God's servant Moses, which has now become the song of the Lamb.

Liturgical singing is established in the midst of this great historical tension. For Israel, the event of salvation in the Red Sea will always be the main reason for praising God, the basic theme of the songs it sings before God. For Christians, the Resurrection of Christ is the true Exodus. He has stridden through the Red Sea of death itself, descended into the world of shadows, and smashed open the prison door. In Baptism this Exodus is made ever present. To be baptized is to be made a partaker, a contemporary, of Christ's descent into hell and of his rising up therefrom, in which he takes us up into the fellowship of new life. On the very next day after the joy of the Exodus, the Israelites had to accept that they were now exposed to the wilderness and its terrors, and even entry into the Promised Land did not put a stop to the threats to their life. But there were also the mighty deeds of God, which were new every day. These were cause for singing Moses' song anew and proved that God is a God, not of the past, but of the present and future. Of course, while singing the song, they realized it was only provisional, and so they longed for the definitive new song, for the salvation that would no longer be followed by a moment of anguish but would be a song only of praise. The man who believes in the Resurrection of Christ really does know what definitive salvation is. He realizes that Christians, who find themselves in the "New Covenant", now sing an altogether new song, which is truly and definitively new in view of the wholly new thing that has taken place in the Resurrection of Christ. What we discovered in the first part about the "in-between" state of Christian reality (no longer a shadow, but still not full reality, only an "image") applies again here. The definitively new song has been intoned, but still all the sufferings of history must be endured, all pain gathered in and brought into the sacrifice of praise, in order to be transformed there into a song of praise.

Here, then, is the theological basis for liturgical singing. We need now to look more closely at its practical reality. In addition to the various witnesses that are found throughout Scripture to the singing of the individual and of the community, as well as to the music of the Temple, the book of Psalms is the proper source for us to rely on here. Because it lacks musical notation, we are unable to reconstruct the "sacred music" of Israel, but it does give us an idea of the richness of both the instruments and the different kinds of singing used in Israel. In their prayed poetry, the Psalms display the whole range of human experiences, which become prayer and song in the presence of God. Lamentation, complaint, indeed accusation, fear, hope, trust, gratitude, joy—the whole of human life is reflected here, as it is unfolded in dialogue with God. It is striking that even complaints made in desperate affliction almost always end with words of trust, with an anticipation, as it were, of God's saving act. In a certain sense, one might describe all these "new songs" as variations on the song of Moses. Singing before God rises up, on the one hand, out of an affliction from which no earthly power can save man—his only refuge is God. But at the same time it emerges out of a trust that, even in utter darkness, knows that the crossing of the Red Sea is a promise that will have the last word in life and in history. Finally, it is important to say that the Psalms frequently come from very personal experiences of suffering and answered prayer, and yet they always flow into the common prayer of Israel. They are nourished out of the common store of God's saving deeds in the past.

With regard to the singing of the Church, we notice the same pattern of continuity and renewal that we have seen in the nature of the liturgy in general, in church architecture, and in sacred images. Quite spontaneously, the Psalter becomes the prayer book of the infant Church, which, with equal spontaneity, has become a Church that sings her prayers. That applies first of all to the Psalter, which Christians, of course, now pray together with Christ. In its canon of Scripture, Israel had ascribed most of the Psalms to King David and had given them a definite interpretation in terms of theology and the history of salvation. For Christians, it is clear that Christ is the true David, that David in the Holy Spirit prays through and with the One who is to be his Son and who is the only begotten Son of God. With this new key, Christians entered into the prayer of Israel and came to realize that, precisely through them, that prayer was to become the new song. The Holy Spirit, who had inspired David to sing and to pray, moved him to speak of Christ, indeed caused him to become the very mouth of Christ, thus enabling us in the Psalms to speak through Christ, in the Holy Spirit, to the Father. Now this exegesis of the Psalms, at once christological and pneumatological, not only concerns the text but also includes the element of music. It is the Holy Spirit who teaches us to sing—first David and then, through him, Israel and the Church. Yes, singing, the surpassing of ordinary speech, is a "pneumatic" event. Church music comes into being as a "charism", a gift of the Spirit. It is the true *glossolalia*, the new tongue that comes from the Holy Spirit. It is above all in Church music that the "sober inebriation" of faith takes place—an inebriation surpassing all the possibilities of mere rationality. But this intoxication remains sober, because Christ and the Holy Spirit belong together, because this drunken speech stays totally within the discipline of the Logos, in a new rationality that, beyond all words, serves the primordial Word, the ground of all reason. This is a matter to which we must return.

We have already seen how in the Apocalypse the horizon is widened by the confession of faith in Christ: the song of the conquerors is described as the song of God's servant Moses and of the Lamb. Now this opens up a further dimension of singing before God. In Israel's Bible we have so far discovered two principal motivations of this singing before God: affliction and joy, distress and deliverance. Man's relationship with God was doubtless too strongly marked by reverential fear of the Creator's eternal might for anyone to dare to see these songs to God as love songs. Ultimately, love lies hidden in the trust that deeply marks all these texts, but the love remains diffident, precisely hidden. The alliance of love and song came into the Old Testament in a rather curious way, namely, through the acceptance of the Song of Songs. This was a collection of thoroughly human love songs, but almost certainly its acceptance involved a far deeper interpretation. These very beautiful love poems of Israel could be seen as the inspired words of Sacred Scripture because of the conviction that, in this serenading of human love, the mystery of the love of God and Israel shines through. The prophets described the worship of foreign gods as harlotry, a term that in this case has an exact meaning, because fertility rites and temple prostitution were part of the fertility cults. Conversely, the election of Israel now appears as the love story of God and his people. The covenant is expounded through the analogy of betrothal and marriage, as the binding of God's love to man and of man to God. Thus human love was able to serve as a profoundly real analogy for God's action in Israel. Jesus took up this line in Israel's tradition and presented himself, in an early parable, as the Bridegroom. When asked why his disciples, unlike John's and the Pharisees, did not fast, he replied: "Can the wedding guests fast while the bridegroom is with them? As long as they have the bridegroom with them, they cannot fast. The days will come, when the bridegroom is taken away from them, and then they will fast in that day" (Mk 2:19f.). This is a prophecy of the Passion but also an announcement of the marriage that constantly appears in Jesus' parables of the wedding banquet and that, in the Apocalypse, the last book of the New Testament, becomes the central theme. Everything moves through the Passion toward the wedding of the Lamb. Since, in the visions of the heavenly liturgy, that wedding seems always to be already anticipated, Christians came to see the Eucharist as the presence of the Bridegroom and thus as a foretaste of the wedding feast of God. In the Eucharist a communion takes place that corresponds to the union of man and woman in marriage. Just as they become "one flesh", so in Communion we all become "one spirit", one person, with Christ. The spousal mystery, announced in the Old Testament, of the intimate union of God and man takes place in the Sacrament of the Body and Blood of Christ, precisely through his Passion and in a very real way (cf. Eph 5:29–32; 1 Cor 6:17; Gal 3:28). The singing of the Church comes ultimately out of love. It is the utter depth of love that produces the singing. "*Cantare amantis est*", says St. Augustine, singing is a lover's thing. In so saying, we come again to the trinitarian interpretation of Church music. The Holy Spirit is love, and it is he who produces the singing. He is the Spirit of Christ, the Spirit who draws us into love for Christ and so leads to the Father.

We must turn once more from these inner driving forces of liturgical music to more practical questions. The expression used in the Psalms for "singing" has its etymological roots in the common stock of ancient oriental languages and denotes an instrumentally supported singing, the instruments probably being stringed. The singing was clearly related to a text and always, with regard to content, directed to a particular statement. It presumably involved a kind of speech-song that allowed changes of note in the melody only at the beginning and end. The Greek Bible translated the Hebrew *zamir* by the word *psallein*, which in Greek meant "to pluck" (especially in the sense of a stringed instrument) but now became the word for the special kind of instrumental playing used in Jewish worship and later described the singing of Christians. Several times there is an additional expression, the meaning of which is obscure, but in any case it refers in some way to ordered artistic singing. Thus, in the musical sphere, biblical faith created its own form of culture, an expression appropriate to its inward essence, one that provides a standard for all later forms of inculturation.

The question of how far inculturation can go soon became a very practical one for early Christianity, especially in the area of music. The Christian communities had grown out of the synagogue and, along with the christologically interpreted Psalter, had also taken over the synagogue's way of singing. Very soon new Christian hymns and canticles came into being: first, with a wholly Old Testament foundation, the Benedictus and Magnificat, but then christologically focused texts, preeminently the prologue of St. John's Gospel (1:1–18), the hymn of Christ in the epistle to the Philippians (2:6–11), and the song of Christ in the first epistle to Timothy (3:16). In his first epistle to the Corinthians, St. Paul provides us with some very interesting information about the order of service in early Christian liturgy: "When you come together, each one has a hymn, a lesson, a revelation, a tongue, or an interpretation. Let all things be done for edification" (14:26). Through the Roman author Pliny, who informed the emperor about the religious services of the Christians, we know that, at the beginning of the second century A.D., singing to the glory of Christ in his divinity was at the very heart of Christian liturgy. One can well imagine that with these new Christian texts came a more varied use of the singing than hitherto and the composition of new melodies. It would seem that one of the ways in which Christian faith was developed was precisely in the writing of canticles, which arose at this time in the Church as "gifts of the Spirit". Herein lay hope but also danger. As the Church was uprooted from her Semitic soil and moved into the Greek world, a spontaneous and far-reaching fusion took place with Greek *logos* mysticism, with its poetry and music, that eventually threatened to dissolve Christianity into a generalized mysticism. It was precisely hymns and their music that provided the point of entry for Gnosticism, that deadly temptation which began to subvert Christianity from within. And so it is understandable that, in their struggle for the identity of the faith and its rooting in the historical figure of Jesus Christ, the Church authorities resorted to a radical decision. The fifty-ninth canon of the Council of Laodicea forbids the use of privately composed psalms and non-canonical writings in divine worship. The fifteenth canon restricts the singing of psalms to the choir of psalm-singers, while "other people in church should not sing." That is how post-biblical hymns were almost entirely lost. There was a rigorous return to the restrained, purely vocal style of singing taken over from the synagogue. We may regret the cultural impoverishment this entailed, but it was necessary for the sake of a greater good. A return to apparent cultural poverty saved the identity of biblical faith, and the very rejection of false inculturation opened up the cultural breadth of Christianity for the future.

When we look at the history of liturgical music, we can see extensive parallels with the evolution of the image question. The East, at least in the Byzantine world, kept to purely vocal music. True, among the Slavs, probably under Western influence, it has been extended into polyphony. The male-voice choirs of this tradition, through their sacral dignity and restrained power, touch the heart and make the Eucharist a true feast of faith. In the West, in the form of Gregorian chant, the inherited tradition of psalm-singing was developed to a new sublimity and purity, which set a permanent standard for sacred music, music for the liturgy of the Church. Polyphony developed in the late Middle Ages, and then instruments came back into divine worship—quite rightly, too, because, as we have seen, the Church not only continues the synagogue, but also takes up, in the light of Christ's Pasch, the reality represented by the Temple. Two new factors are thus at work in Church music. Artistic freedom increasingly asserts its rights, even in the liturgy. Church music and secular music are now each influenced by the other. This is particularly clear in the case of the so-called "parody Masses", in which the text of the Mass was set to a theme or melody that came from secular music, with the result that anyone hearing it might think he was listening to the latest "hit". It is clear that these opportunities for artistic creativity and the adoption of secular tunes brought danger with them. Music was no longer developing out of prayer but, with the new demand for artistic autonomy, was now heading away from the liturgy; it was becoming an end in itself, opening the door to new, very different ways of feeling and of experiencing the world. Music was alienating the liturgy from its true nature.

At this point the Council of Trent intervened in the culture war that had broken out. It was made a norm that liturgical music should be at the service of the Word; the use of instruments was substantially reduced; and the difference between secular and sacred music was clearly affirmed. At the beginning of the last century, Pope St. Pius X made a similar intervention. The age of the Baroque, albeit in different forms in the Catholic and Protestant worlds, achieved an astounding unity of secular music-making with the music of the liturgy. It succeeded in dedicating the whole luminous power of music, which reached such a high point in this period of cultural history, to the glorifying of God. Whether it is Bach or Mozart that we hear in church, we have a sense in either case of what *gloria Dei*, the glory of God, means. The mystery of infinite beauty is there and enables us to experience the presence of God more truly and vividly than in many sermons. But there are already signs of danger to come. Subjective experience and passion are still held in check by the order of the musical universe, reflecting as it does the order of the divine creation itself. But there is already the threat of invasion by the virtuoso mentality, the vanity of technique, which is no longer the servant of the whole but wants to push itself to the fore. During the nineteenth century, the century of self-emancipating subjectivity, this led in many places to the obscuring of the sacred by the operatic. The dangers that had forced the Council of Trent to intervene were back again. In similar fashion, Pope Pius X tried to remove the operatic element from the liturgy and declared Gregorian chant and the great polyphony of the age of the Catholic Reformation (of which Palestrina was the outstanding representative) to be the standard for liturgical music. A clear distinction was made between liturgical music and religious music in general, just as visual art in the liturgy has to conform to different standards from those employed in religious art in general. Art in the liturgy has a very specific responsibility, and precisely as such does it serve as a well-spring of culture, which in the final analysis owes its existence to cult.

After the cultural revolution of recent decades, we are faced with a challenge no less great than that of the three moments of crisis that we have encountered in our historical sketch: the Gnostic temptation, the crisis at the end of the Middle Ages and the beginning of modernity, and the crisis at the beginning of the twentieth century, which formed the prelude to the still more radical questions of the present day. Three developments in recent music epitomize the problems that the Church has to face when she is considering liturgical music. First of all, there is the cultural universalization that the Church has to undertake if she wants to get beyond the boundaries of the European mind. This is the question of what inculturation should look like in the realm of sacred music if, on the one hand, the identity of Christianity is to be preserved and, on the other, its universality is to be expressed in local forms. Then there are two developments in music itself that have their origins primarily in the West but that for a long time have affected the whole of mankind in the world culture that is being formed. Modern so-called "classical" music has maneuvered itself, with some exceptions, into an elitist ghetto, which only specialists may enter—and even they do so with what may sometimes be mixed feelings. The music of the masses has broken loose from this and treads a very different path. On the one hand, there is pop music, which is certainly no longer supported by the people in the ancient sense (pop*ulus*). It is aimed at the phenomenon of the masses, is industrially produced, and ultimately has to be described as a cult of the banal. "Rock", on the other hand, is the expression of elemental passions, and at rock festivals it assumes a cultic character, a form of worship, in fact, in opposition to Christian worship. People are, so to speak, released from themselves by the experience of being part of a crowd and by the emotional shock of rhythm, noise, and special lighting effects. However, in the ecstasy of having all their defenses torn down, the participants sink, as it were, beneath the elemental force of the universe. The music of the Holy Spirit's sober inebriation seems to have little chance when self has become a prison, the mind is a shackle, and breaking out from both appears as a true promise of redemption that can be tasted at least for a few moments.

What is to be done? Theoretical solutions are perhaps even less helpful here. There has to be renewal from within. Nevertheless, by way of conclusion, I am going to try to sum up the principles that have emerged from our look at the inner foundations of Christian sacred music.

The music of Christian worship is related to *logos* in three senses:

1. It is related to the events of God's saving action to which the Bible bears witness and which the liturgy makes present. God's action continues in the history of the Church, but it has its unshakeable center in the Paschal Mystery of Jesus Christ, his Cross, Resurrection, and Ascension. This takes up, interprets, and brings to fulfillment the history of salvation in the Old Testament as well as the hopes and experiences of deliverance in the religious history of mankind. In liturgical music, based as it is on biblical faith, there is, therefore, a clear dominance of the Word; this music is a higher form of proclamation.

Ultimately, it rises up out of the love that responds to God's love made flesh in Christ, the love that for us went unto death. After the Resurrection, the Cross is by no means a thing of the past, and so this love is always marked by pain at the hiddenness of God, by the cry that rises up from the depths of anguish, *Kyrie eleison*, by hope and by supplication. But it also has the privilege, by anticipation, of experiencing the reality of the Resurrection, and so it brings with it the joy of being loved, that gladness of heart that Haydn said came upon him when he set liturgical texts to music. Thus the relation of liturgical music to *logos* means, first of all, simply its relation to words. That is why singing in the liturgy has priority over instrumental music, though it does not in any way exclude it. It goes without saying that the biblical and liturgical texts are the normative words from which liturgical music has to take its bearings. This does not rule out the continuing creation of "new songs", but instead inspires them and assures them of a firm grounding in God's love for mankind and his work of redemption.

2. St. Paul tells us that of ourselves we do not know how to pray as we ought but that the Spirit himself intercedes for us "with sighs too deep for words" (Rom 8:26). Prayer is a gift of the Holy Spirit, both prayer in general and that particular kind of prayer which is the gift of singing and playing before God. The Holy Spirit is love. He enkindles love in us and thus moves us to sing. Now the Spirit of Christ "takes what is [Christ's]" (cf. Jn 16:14), and so the gift that comes from him, the gift that surpasses all words, is always related to Christ, *the* Word, the great Meaning that creates and sustains all life. Words are superseded, but not the Word, the Logos. This is the second, deeper sense in which liturgical music is related to *logos*. The Church's tradition has this in mind when it talks about the sober inebriation caused in us by the Holy Spirit. There is always an ultimate sobriety, a deeper rationality, resisting any decline into irrationality and immoderation. We can see what this means in practice if we look at the history of music. The writings of Plato and Aristotle on music show that the Greek world in their time was faced with a choice between two kinds of worship, two different images of God and man. Now what this choice came down to concretely was a choice between two fundamental types of music. On the one hand, there is the music that Plato ascribes, in line with mythology, to Apollo, the god of light and reason. This is the music that draws

senses into spirit and so brings man to wholeness. It does not abolish the senses but, rather, inserts them into the unity of this creature that is man. It elevates the spirit precisely by wedding it to the senses, and it elevates the senses by uniting them with the spirit. Thus this kind of music is an expression of man's special place in the general structure of being. But then there is the music that Plato ascribes to Marsyas, which we might describe, in terms of cultic history, as "Dionysian". It drags man into the intoxication of the senses, crushes rationality, and subjects the spirit to the senses. The way Plato (and, more moderately, Aristotle) allots instruments and keys to one or other of these two kinds of music is now obsolete and may in many respects surprise us. But the Apollonian/Dionysian alternative runs through the whole history of religion and confronts us again today. Not every kind of music can have a place in Christian worship. It has its standards, and that standard is the Logos. If we want to know with whom we are dealing, the Holy Spirit or the unholy spirit, we have to remember that it is the Holy Spirit who moves us to say, "Jesus is Lord" (1 Cor 12:3). The Holy Spirit leads us to the Logos, and he leads us to a music that serves the Logos as a sign of the *sursum corda*, the lifting up of the human heart. Does it integrate man by drawing him to what is above, or does it cause his disintegration into formless intoxication or mere sensuality? That is the criterion for a music in harmony with *logos*, a form of that *logikē latreia* (reason-able, *logos*-worthy worship) of which we spoke in the first part of this book.

3. The Word incarnate in Christ, the Logos, is not just the power that gives meaning to the individual, not even just the power that gives meaning to history. No, he is the creative Meaning from which the universe comes and that the universe, the cosmos, reflects. That is why this Word leads us out of individualism into the communion of saints spanning all times and places. This is the "broad place" (Ps 31[30]:8), the redemptive breadth into which the Lord places us. But its span stretches still farther. As we have seen, Christian liturgy is always a cosmic liturgy. What does this mean for our question? The Preface, the first part of the Eucharistic Prayer, always ends with the affirmation that we are singing "Holy, Holy, Holy" together with the cherubim and seraphim and with all the choirs of heaven. The liturgy is echoing here the vision of God in Isaiah chapter 6. In the Holy of Holies in the Temple, the prophet sees the throne of God, protected by the sera-

phim, who call to one another: "Holy, holy, holy is the LORD of hosts; the whole earth is full of his glory" (Is 6:1–3). In the celebration of Holy Mass, we insert ourselves into this liturgy that always goes before us. All our singing is a singing and praying with the great liturgy that spans the whole of creation.

Among the Fathers, it was especially St. Augustine who tried to connect this characteristic view of the Christian liturgy with the world view of Greco-Roman antiquity. In his early work "On Music" he is still completely dependent on the Pythagorean theory of music. According to Pythagoras, the cosmos was constructed mathematically, a great edifice of numbers. Modern physics, beginning with Kepler, Galileo, and Newton, has gone back to this vision and, through the mathematical interpretation of the universe, has made possible the technological use of its powers. For the Pythagoreans, this mathematical order of the universe ("cosmos" means "order"!) was identical with the essence of beauty itself. Beauty comes from meaningful inner order. And for them this beauty was not only optical but also musical. Goethe alludes to this idea when he speaks of the singing contest of the fraternity of the spheres: the mathematical order of the planets and their revolutions contains a secret timbre, which is the primal form of music. The courses of the revolving planets are like melodies, the numerical order is the rhythm, and the concurrence of the individual courses is the harmony. The music made by man must, according to this view, be taken from the inner music and order of the universe, be inserted into the "fraternal song" of the "fraternity of the spheres". The beauty of music depends on its conformity to the rhythmic and harmonic laws of the universe. The more that human music adapts itself to the musical laws of the universe, the more beautiful will it be.

St. Augustine first took up this theory and then deepened it. In the course of history, transplanting it into the world view of faith was bound to bring with it a twofold personalization. Even the Pythagoreans did not interpret the mathematics of the universe in an entirely abstract way. In the view of the ancients, intelligent actions presupposed an intelligence that caused them. The intelligent, mathematical movements of the heavenly bodies was not explained, therefore, in a purely mechanical way; they could be understood only on the assumption that the heavenly bodies were animated, were themselves "intelligent". For Christians, there was a spontaneous turn at this point from stellar deities to the choirs of angels that surround God and illuminate the universe. Perceiving the "music of the cosmos" thus becomes listening to the song of the angels, and the reference to Isaiah chapter 6 naturally suggests itself. But a further step was taken with the help of trinitarian faith, faith in the Father, the Logos, and the Pneuma. The mathematics of the universe does not exist by itself, nor, as people now came to see, can it be explained by stellar deities. It has a deeper foundation: the mind of the Creator. It comes from the Logos, in whom, so to speak, the archetypes of the world's order are contained. The Logos, through the Spirit, fashions the material world according to these archetypes. In virtue of his work in creation, the Logos is, therefore, called the "art of God" (*ars* = *technē*!). The Logos himself is the great artist, in whom all works of art—the beauty of the universe—have their origin. To sing with the universe means, then, to follow the track of the Logos and to come close to him. All true human art is an assimilation to *the* artist, to Christ, to the mind of the Creator. The idea of the music of the cosmos, of singing with the angels, leads back again to the relation of art to *logos*, but now it is broadened and deepened in the context of the cosmos. Yes, it is the cosmic context that gives art in the liturgy both its measure and its scope. A merely subjective "creativity" is no match for the vast compass of the cosmos and for the message of its beauty. When a man conforms to the measure of the universe, his freedom is not diminished but expanded to a new horizon.

One final point follows from this. The cosmic interpretation remained alive, with some variations, well into the early modern age. Only in the nineteenth century was there a move away from it, because "metaphysics" seemed so outdated. Hegel now tried to interpret music as just an expression of the subject and of subjectivity. But whereas Hegel still adhered to the fundamental idea of reason as the starting point and destination of the whole enterprise, a change of direction took place with Schopenhauer that was to have momentous consequences. For him, the world is no longer grounded in reason but in "will and idea" (*Wille und Vorstellung*). The will precedes reason. And music is the primordial expression of being human as such, the pure expression of the will—anterior to reason—that creates the world. Music should not, therefore, be subjected to the word, and only in exceptional cases should it have any connection with the word. Since music is pure will, its origin precedes that of reason. It takes us back behind reason to the actual foundation of reality. It is reminiscent of Goethe's recasting of the prologue of St. John: no longer "In the beginning was the Word", but now "In the beginning was the Deed." In our own times this continues in the attempt to replace "orthodoxy" by "orthopraxy"—there is no common faith any more (because truth is unattainable), only common praxis. By contrast, for Christian faith, as Guardini shows so penetratingly in his masterly early work *The Spirit of the Liturgy*, *logos* has precedence over *ethos*. When this is reversed, Christianity is turned upside down. The cosmic character of liturgical music stands in opposition to the two tendencies of the modern age that we have described: music as pure subjectivity, music as the expression of mere will. We sing with the angels. But this cosmic character is grounded ultimately in the ordering of all Christian worship to *logos*.

Let us have one last brief look at our own times. The dissolution of the subject, which coincides for us today with radical forms of subjectivism, has led to "deconstructionism"—the anarchistic theory of art. Perhaps this will help us to overcome the unbounded inflation of subjectivity and to recognize once more that a relationship with the Logos, who was at the beginning, brings salvation to the subject, that is, to the person. At the same time it puts us into a true relationship of communion that is ultimately grounded in trinitarian love.

As we have seen in both chapters of this part of the book, the problems of the present day pose without doubt a grave challenge to the Church and the culture of the liturgy. Nevertheless, there is no reason at all to be discouraged. The great cultural tradition of the faith is home to a presence of immense power. What in museums is only a monument from the past, an occasion for mere nostalgic admiration, is constantly made present in the liturgy in all its freshness. But the present day, too, is not condemned to silence where the faith is concerned. Anyone who looks carefully will see that, even in our own time, important works of art, inspired by faith, have been produced and are being produced—in visual art as well as in music (and indeed literature). Today, too, joy in the Lord and contact with his presence in the liturgy has an inexhaustible power of inspiration. The artists who take this task upon themselves need not regard themselves as the rearguard of culture. They are weary of the empty freedom from which they have emerged. Humble submission to what goes before us releases authentic freedom and leads us to the true summit of our vocation as human beings.

IV. Liturgical Form

1. Rite

For many people today, the word "rite" does not have a very good ring to it. "Rite" suggests rigidity, a restriction to prescribed forms. It is set in opposition to that creativity and dynamism of inculturation by which, so people say, we get a really living liturgy, in which each community can express itself. Before going into the questions raised here, we must first of all see what rite in the Church really means, what rites there are, and how they relate to one another. In the second century, the Roman jurist Pomponius Festus, who was not a Christian, defined *ritus* as an "approved practice in the administration of sacrifice" (*mos comprobatus in administrandis sacrificiis*). He thereby summed up in a precise formula one of the great realities in the history of religion. Man is always looking for the right way of honoring God, for a form of prayer and common worship that pleases God and is appropriate to his nature. In this connection, we must remember that originally the word "orthodoxy" did not mean, as we generally think today, right doctrine. In Greek, the word *doxa* means, on the one hand, opinion or splendor. But then in Christian usage it means something on the order of "true splendor", that is, the glory of God. Orthodoxy means, therefore, the right way to glorify God, the right form of adoration. In this sense, orthodoxy is inward "orthopraxy". If we go back to the word's origins, the modern opposition disappears. It is not a question of theories about God but of the right way to encounter him. This, then, was seen as Christian faith's great gift: we know what right worship is. We know how we should truly glorify God—by praying and living in communion with the Paschal journey of Jesus Christ, by accomplishing with him his *Eucharistia*, in which Incarnation leads to Resurrection—along the way of the Cross. To adapt a saying of Kant, liturgy "covers everything" from the Incarnation to the Resurrection, but only on the way of the Cross. For Christians, then, "rite" means the practical arrangements made by the community, in time and space, for the basic type of worship received from God in faith. And, of course, as we saw in the first part, worship always includes the whole conduct of one's life. Thus rite has its primary place in the liturgy, but not only in the liturgy. It is also expressed in a particular way of doing theology, in the form of spiritual life, and in the juridical ordering of ecclesiastical life.

At this point we must try, as we have just indicated, to get at least a brief overview of the major rites that have left their stamp on the Church. What rites are there? Where do they come from? These are questions that in their details present a multitude of problems, which we cannot discuss here. If we want to get an overview of the whole, then the sixth canon of the First Council of Nicaea may be a helpful starting point. It speaks of three primatial sees: Rome, Alexandria, and Antioch. The fact that all three sees are connected with Petrine traditions need not concern us here. At any rate, all three are points of crystallization in the liturgical tradition. We should also realize that since the fourth century (soon after Nicaea) Byzantium emerged as an additional regulatory center of ecclesiastical, and thus also of liturgical, life. After the transfer of imperial rule to the Bosphorus, Byzantium regarded itself as the "New Rome" and assumed the prerogatives of Rome. But it also increased its influence through the waning importance of Antioch, and indeed the functions of Antioch to a large extent passed over to Byzantium. Thus we may speak of four great circles of liturgical tradition. At the beginning, the relations of Rome and Alexandria were comparatively close, while Byzantium and Antioch were nearer to each other.

Without going into details outside the scope of this book, we must become a little more specific. Antioch was bound to be a center of liturgical tradition. It was here that Gentile Christianity came into being and the name "Christian" was first used (cf. Acts 11:26). It was the capital of Syria and therefore of the cultural and linguistic world in which divine revelation took place. Syria was also the setting for the great theological debates about how rightly to confess faith in Christ, and so it is not surprising that such a culturally dynamic area should become the birthplace of distinctive traditions in the liturgy. On the one hand, there are the West Syrian rites, prominent among which is the Syro-Malankar rite, which still flourishes in India and goes back to the Apostle James. The Maronite rite should also be assigned to the West Syrian family. On the other hand, there are the so-called Chaldean rites (also called East Syrian or "Assyrian"). Their starting point is to be found in the great theological schools of Nisibis and Edessa. These rites were characterized by an extraordinary missionary zeal and spread as far as India, Central Asia, and China. In the early Middle Ages there were about seventy million of the faithful in this ritual family, which suffered irretrievable losses through Islam and the Mongol invasions. At any rate, the Syro-Malabar Church still continues to exist in India. The Chaldean liturgical family goes back to the Apostle Thomas and to Addai and Mari, disciples of the apostles. There is no doubt that it has preserved very ancient traditions, and the tradition that the Apostle Thomas was a missionary in India definitely has to be taken seriously at the historical level.

The great ecclesiastical sphere of Alexandria includes above all the Coptic and Ethiopian rites. The Liturgy of St. Mark, which developed in Alexandria, bears the marks of strong Byzantine influence, to which we shall return. In a category and with a significance all its own is the Armenian rite, which tradition traces back to the Apostles Bartholomew and Thaddeus. St. Gregory the Illuminator (260–323) is to be regarded as its special Father. In its form it largely follows the Byzantine liturgy.

And so we come finally to the two greatest families of rites: the Byzantine and the Roman. As we saw, Byzantium takes up, first and foremost, the tradition of Antioch. The Liturgy of St. John Chrysostom carries the Antiochene heritage to Byzantium, but the influences of Asia Minor and Jerusalem are also taken up, so that there is a confluence here of the rich inheritance of the lands evangelized by the apostles. A large part of the Slavic world adopted the Byzantine liturgy and, by this means, entered into communion of prayer with the Fathers and the apostles. In the West three great ritual groups can at first be discerned. Alongside the Roman liturgy, which was very similar to the Latin liturgy of Africa, stood the old Gaulish or "Gallican" liturgy, to which in turn the Celtic was closely related, as was the old Spanish or "Mozarabic" liturgy. All three ritual domains were at first very similar to one another, but, in contrast to the conservatism of Rome, which in liturgical matters was rather archaic and sober, Spain and Gaul opened themselves to Eastern influences and assimilated them in their own distinctive way. By comparison with the strict brevity of Rome, the Gallican liturgy is characterized by poetic exuberance. From about the end of the first millennium, Rome began to appropriate the Gallican heritage, and the Gallican rite, in its proper grandeur, disappeared, though precious elements of it lived on in the Roman rite. Only with the liturgical reform after the Second Vatican Council, with its concern to restore the Roman tradition in its purity, did the Gallican inheritance more or less completely disappear. For the first time a radical standardization of the liturgy had been carried out, though in the previous century the surviving rites proper to particular places and religious orders had increasingly been disappearing. Since then, of course, what began as a process of making everything uniform has swung to the opposite extreme: a widespread dissolution of the rite, which must now be replaced by the "creativity" of the community.

Before exploring the fundamental question that this once more raises, the question of the meaning and validity of rite, we must draw some conclusions from our perhaps rather tedious sketch of the existing ritual landscape. First, it is important that the individual rites have a relation to the places where Christianity originated and the apostles preached: they are anchored in the time and place of the event of divine revelation. Here again "once for all" and "always" belong together. The Christian faith can never be separated from the soil of sacred events, from the choice made by God, who wanted to speak to us, to become man, to die and rise again, in a particular place and at a particular time. "Always" can only come from "once for all". The Church does not pray in some kind of mythical omnitemporality. She cannot forsake her roots. She recognizes the true utterance of God precisely in the concreteness of its history, in time and place: to these God ties us, and by these we are all tied together. The diachronic aspect, praying with the Fathers and the apostles, is part of what we mean by rite, but it also includes a local aspect, extending from Jerusalem to Antioch, Rome, Alexandria, and Constantinople. Rites are not, therefore, just the products of inculturation, however much they may have incorporated elements from different cultures. They are forms of the apostolic tradition and of its unfolding in the great places of the tradition.

We must add a second point. Rites are not rigidly fenced off from each other. There is exchange and cross-fertilization between them.

The clearest example is in the case of the two great focal points of ritual development: Byzantium and Rome. In their present form, most of the Eastern rites are very strongly marked by Byzantine influences. For its part, Rome has increasingly united the different rites of the West in the universal Roman rite. While Byzantium gave a large part of the Slavic world its special form of divine worship, Rome left its liturgical imprint on the Germanic and Latin peoples and on a part of the Slavs. In the first millennium there was still liturgical exchange between East and West. Then, of course, the rites hardened into their definitive forms, which allowed hardly any cross-fertilization. What is important is that the great forms of rite embrace many cultures. They not only incorporate the diachronic aspect, but also create communion among different cultures and languages. They elude control by any individual, local community or regional Church. Unspontaneity is of their essence. In these rites I discover that something is approaching me here that I did not produce myself, that I am entering into something greater than myself, which ultimately derives from divine revelation. That is why the Christian East calls the liturgy the "Divine Liturgy", expressing thereby the liturgy's independence from human control. The West, by contrast, has felt ever more strongly the historical element, which is why Jungmann tried to sum up the Western view in the phrase "the liturgy that has come to be". He wanted to show that this coming-to-be still goes on—as an organic growth, not as a specially contrived production. The liturgy can be compared, therefore, not to a piece of technical equipment, something manufactured, but to a plant, something organic that grows and whose laws of growth determine the possibilities of further development. In the West there was, of course, another factor. With his Petrine authority, the pope more and more clearly took over responsibility for liturgical legislation, thus providing a juridical authority for the continuing formation of the liturgy. The more vigorously the primacy was displayed, the more the question came up about the extent and limits of this authority, which, of course, as such had never been considered. After the Second Vatican Council, the impression arose that the pope really could do anything in liturgical matters, especially if he were acting on the mandate of an ecumenical council. Eventually, the idea of the givenness of the liturgy, the fact that one cannot do with it what one will, faded from the public consciousness of the West. In fact, the First Vatican Council had in no way defined the pope as an absolute monarch. On the contrary, it presented him as the guarantor of obedience to the revealed Word. The pope's authority is bound to the tradition of faith, and that also applies to the liturgy. It is not "manufactured" by the authorities. Even the pope can only be a humble servant of its lawful development and abiding integrity and identity. Here again, as with the questions of icons and sacred music, we come up against the special path trod by the West as opposed to the East. And here again is it true that this special path, which finds space for freedom and historical development, must not be condemned wholesale. However, it would lead to the breaking up of the foundations of Christian identity if the fundamental intuitions of the East, which are the fundamental intuitions of the early Church, were abandoned. The authority of the pope is not unlimited; it is at the service of sacred tradition. Still less is any kind of general "freedom" of manufacture, degenerating into spontaneous improvisation, compatible with the essence of faith and liturgy. The greatness of the liturgy depends—we shall have to repeat this frequently—on its unspontaneity (*Unbeliebigkeit*).

Let us ask the question again: "What does 'rite' mean in the context of Christian liturgy?" The answer is: "It is the expression, that has become form, of ecclesiality and of the Church's identity as a historically transcendent communion of liturgical prayer and action." Rite makes concrete the liturgy's bond with that living subject which is the Church, who for her part is characterized by adherence to the form of faith that has developed in the apostolic tradition. This bond with the subject that is the Church allows for different patterns of liturgy and includes living development, but it equally excludes spontaneous improvisation. This applies to the individual and the community, to the hierarchy and the laity. Because of the historical character of God's action, the "Divine Liturgy" (as they call it in the East) has been fashioned, in a way similar to Scripture, by human beings and their capacities. But it contains an essential exposition of the biblical legacy that goes beyond the limits of the individual rites, and thus it shares in the authority of the Church's faith in its fundamental form. The authority of the liturgy can certainly be compared to that of the great confessions of faith of the early Church. Like these, it developed under the guidance of the Holy Spirit (cf. Jn 16:13). It was the tragedy of Luther's efforts at reform that they occurred at a time when the essential form of the liturgy was not understood and had to a large extent been obscured. Despite the radicalism of his reversion to the principle of "Scripture alone", Luther did not contest the validity of the ancient Christian creeds and thereby left behind an inner tension that became the fundamental problem in the history of the Reformation. The Reformation would surely have run a different course if Luther had been able to see the analogous binding force of the great liturgical tradition and its understanding of sacrificial presence and of man's participation in the vicarious action of the Logos. With the radicalization of the historical-critical method, it has become very clear today that the *sola scriptura* principle cannot provide a foundation for the Church and the commonality of her faith. Scripture is Scripture only when it lives within the living subject that is the Church. This makes it all the more absurd that a not insignificant number of people today are trying to construct the liturgy afresh on the basis of *sola scriptura*. In these reconstructions they identify Scripture with the prevailing exegetical opinions, thus confusing faith with opinion. Liturgy "manufactured" in this way is based on human words and opinions. It is a house built on sand and remains totally empty, however much human artistry may adorn it. Only respect for the liturgy's fundamental unspontaneity and pre-existing identity can give us what we hope for: the feast in which the great reality comes to us that we ourselves do not manufacture but receive as a gift.

This means that "creativity" cannot be an authentic category for matters liturgical. In any case, this is a word that developed within the Marxist world view. Creativity means that in a universe that in itself is meaningless and came into existence through blind evolution, man can creatively fashion a new and better world. Modern theories of art think in terms of a nihilistic kind of creativity. Art is not meant to copy anything. Artistic creativity is under the free mastery of man, without being bound by norms or goals and subject to no questions of meaning. It may be that in such visions a cry for freedom is to be heard, a cry that in a world totally in the control of technology becomes a cry for help. Seen in this way, art appears as the final refuge of freedom. True, art has something to do with freedom, but freedom understood in the way we have been describing is empty. It is not redemptive; rather, it makes despair sound like the last word of human existence. This kind of creativity has no place within the liturgy. The life of the liturgy does not come from what dawns upon the minds of individuals and planning groups. On the contrary, it is God's descent upon our world, the source of real liberation. He alone can open the door to freedom. The more priests and faithful humbly surrender themselves to this descent of God, the more "new" the liturgy will constantly be, and the more true and personal it becomes. Yes, the liturgy becomes personal, true, and new, not through tomfoolery and banal experiments with the words, but through a courageous entry into the great reality that through the rite is always ahead of us and can never quite be overtaken.

Does it still need to be explicitly stated that all this has nothing to do with rigidity? Whereas, for Moslems, the Koran is God's speech, pure and simple, without any human mediation, Christians know that God has spoken through man and that the human and historical factor is, therefore, part of the way God acts. That, too, is why the Word of the Bible becomes complete only in that responsive word of the Church which we call tradition. That is why the accounts of the Last Supper in the Bible become a concrete reality only when they are appropriated by the Church in her celebration. That is why there can be development in the "Divine Liturgy", a development, though, that takes place without haste or aggressive intervention, like the grain that grows "of itself" in the earth (cf. Mk 4:28). We saw above that each of the various ritual families grew out of the "apostolic sees", the central places of the apostolic tradition, and that this connection with apostolic origins is essential to what defines them. From this it follows that there can be no question of creating totally new rites. However, there can be variations within the ritual families. The Christian West, in particular, well into modern times, saw such variations taking place within the general framework of a fundamental ritual form. An example of this kind of development seems to me to be the Missal that may be used in Zaire (the Congo). It is the Roman rite "in the Zairean mode". It still belongs within the great fellowship of the apostolically rooted Roman rite, but that rite is now, so to speak, clad in Congolese garments, with the addition— this seems to me to make perfect sense—of certain elements from the Christian East. For example, in line with what is said in Matthew 5:23–25, the sign of peace is exchanged, not before Communion, but before the Presentation of the Gifts, which would be desirable for the whole of the Roman rite, insofar as the sign of peace is something we want to retain.

2. The Body and the Liturgy

a. "Active Participation"

To express one of its main ideas for the shaping of the liturgy, the Second Vatican Council gave us the phrase *participatio actuosa*, the "active participation" of everyone in the *opus Dei*, in what happens in the worship of God. It was quite right to do so. The *Catechism of the Catholic Church* points out that the word "liturgy" speaks to us of a common service and thus has a reference to the whole holy People of God (cf. CCC 1069). But what does this active participation come down to? What does it mean that we have to do? Unfortunately, the word was very quickly misunderstood to mean something external, entailing a need for general activity, as if as many people as possible, as often as possible, should be visibly engaged in action. However, the word "part-icipation" refers to a principal action in which everyone has a "part". And so if we want to discover the kind of doing that active participation involves, we need, first of all, to determine what this central *actio* is in which all the members of the community are supposed to participate. The study of the liturgical sources provides an answer that at first may surprise us, though, in the light of the biblical foundations considered in the first part, it is quite self-evident. By the *actio* of the liturgy the sources mean the Eucharistic Prayer. The real liturgical action, the true liturgical act, is the *oratio*, the great prayer that forms the core of the Eucharistic celebration, the whole of which was, therefore, called *oratio* by the Fathers. At first, simply in terms of the form of the liturgy, this was quite correct, because the essence of the Christian liturgy is to be found in the *oratio*; this is its center and fundamental form. Calling the Eucharist *oratio* was, then, a quite standard response to the pagans and to questioning intellectuals in general. What the Fathers were saying was this: The sacrificial animals and all those things that you had and have, and which ultimately satisfy no one, are now abolished. In their place has come the Sacrifice of the Word. We are the spiritual religion, in which in truth a Word-based worship takes place. Goats and cattle are no longer slaughtered. Instead, the Word, summing up our existence, is addressed to God and identified with *the* Word, the Word of God, who draws us into true worship. Perhaps it would be useful to note here that the word *oratio* originally means, not "prayer" (for which the word is *prex*), but solemn public speech. Such speech now attains its supreme dignity through its being addressed to God in full awareness that it comes from him and is made possible by him.

But this is only just a hint of the central issue. This *oratio*—the Eucharistic Prayer, the "Canon"—is really more than speech; it is *actio* in the highest sense of the word. For what happens in it is that the human *actio* (as performed hitherto by the priests in the various religions of the world) steps back and makes way for the *actio divina*, the action of God. In this *oratio* the priest speaks with the I of the Lord— "This is my Body", "This is my Blood." He knows that he is now speaking, not from his own resources, but in virtue of the sacrament that he has received, he has become the voice of Someone Else, who is now speaking and acting. This action of God, which takes place through human speech, is the real "action" for which all of creation is in expectation. The elements of the earth are transubstantiated, pulled, so to speak, from their creaturely anchorage, grasped at the deepest ground of their being, and changed into the Body and Blood of the Lord. The New Heaven and the New Earth are anticipated. The real "action" in the liturgy in which we are all supposed to participate is the action of God himself. This is what is new and distinctive about the Christian liturgy: God himself acts and does what is essential. He inaugurates the new creation, makes himself accessible to us, so that, through the things of the earth, through our gifts, we can communicate with him in a personal way. But how can we participate, have a part, in this action? Are not God and man completely incommensurable? Can man, the finite and sinful one, cooperate with God, the Infinite and Holy One? Yes, he can, precisely because God himself has become man, become body, and here, again and again, he comes through his body to us who live in the body. The whole event of the Incarnation, Cross, Resurrection, and Second Coming is present as the way by which God draws man into cooperation with himself. As we have seen, this is expressed in the liturgy in the fact that the petition for acceptance is part of the *oratio*. True, the Sacrifice of the Logos is accepted already and forever. But we must still pray for it to become *our* sacrifice, that we ourselves, as we said, may be transformed into the Logos (*logisiert*), conformed to the Logos, and so be made the true Body of Christ. That is the issue, and that is what we have to pray for. This petition itself is a way into the Incarnation and the Resurrection, the path that we take in the wayfaring state of our existence. In this real "action", in this prayerful approach to participation, there is no difference between priests and laity. True, addressing the *oratio* to the Lord in the name of the Church and, at its core, speaking with the very "I" of Jesus Christ—that is something that can be done only through sacramental empowerment. But participation in that which no man does, that which the Lord himself and only he can do—that is equally for everyone. In the words of St. Paul, it is a question of being "united to the Lord" and thus becoming "one spirit with him" (1 Cor 6:17). The point is that, ultimately, the difference between the *actio Christi* and our own action is done away with. There is only *one* action, which is at the same time his and ours—ours because we have become "one body and one spirit" with him. The uniqueness of the eucharistic liturgy lies precisely in the fact that God himself is acting and that we are drawn into that action of God. Everything else is, therefore, secondary.

Of course, external actions—reading, singing, the bringing up of the gifts—can be distributed in a sensible way. By the same token, participation in the Liturgy of the Word (reading, singing) is to be distinguished from the sacramental celebration proper. We should be clearly aware that external actions are quite secondary here. *Doing* really must stop when we come to the heart of the matter: the *oratio*. It must be plainly evident that the *oratio* is the heart of the matter, but that it is important precisely because it provides a space for the *actio* of God. Anyone who grasps this will easily see that it is now a matter, not of looking at or toward the priest, but of looking together toward the Lord and going out to meet him. The almost theatrical entrance of different players into the liturgy, which is so common today, especially during the Preparation of the Gifts, quite simply misses the point. If the various external actions (as a matter of fact, there are not very many of them, though they are being artificially multiplied) become the essential in the liturgy, if the liturgy degenerates into general activity, then we have radically misunderstood the "theo-drama" of the liturgy and lapsed almost into parody. True liturgical education cannot consist in learning and experimenting with external activities. Instead one must be led toward the essential *actio* that makes the liturgy what it is, toward the transforming power of God, who wants, through what happens in the liturgy, to transform us and the world. In this respect, liturgical education today, of both priests and laity, is deficient to a deplorable extent. Much remains to be done here.

At this point the reader will perhaps ask: "What about the body? With this idea of a word-based sacrifice (*oratio*), have you not shifted everything over to the spiritual side?" That charge might have applied to the pre-Christian idea of a logos-liturgy, but it cannot be true of the liturgy of the Word incarnate, who offers himself to us in his Body and Blood and, thus, in a corporeal way. It is, of course, the new corporeality of the risen Lord, but it remains true corporeality, and it is this that we are given in the material signs of bread and wine. This means that we are laid hold of by the Logos and for the Logos in our very bodies, in the bodily existence of our everyday life. The true liturgical action is the deed of God, and for that very reason the liturgy of faith always reaches beyond the cultic act into everyday life, which must itself become "liturgical", a service for the transformation of the world. Much more is required of the body than carrying objects around and other such activities. A demand is made on the body in all its involvement in the circumstances of everyday life. The body is required to become "capable of resurrection", to orient itself toward the resurrection, toward the Kingdom of God, in a word: "Thy will be done on earth as it is in Heaven." Where God's will is done, there is heaven, there earth becomes heaven. Surrendering ourselves to the action of God, so that we in our turn may cooperate with him—that is what begins in the liturgy and is meant to unfold further beyond it. Incarnation must always lead through Cross (the transforming of our wills in a communion of will with God) to Resurrection—to that rule of love which is the Kingdom of God. The body must be trained, so to speak, for the resurrection. Let us remember incidentally that the unfashionable word *askēsis* can be simply translated into English as "training". Nowadays we train with enthusiasm, perseverance, and great renunciation for many different purposes—why do we not train ourselves for God and his Kingdom? "I train my body", says St. Paul, "and subdue it" (1 Cor 9:27, RSV adapted). He also uses the discipline of athletes as an image for training in one's own life. This training is an essential part of everyday life, but it has to find its inner support in the liturgy, in the liturgy's "orientation" toward the risen Christ. Let me say once again: it is a way of learning to accept the other in his otherness, a training for love, a training to help us accept the Wholly Other, God, to be shaped and used by him. The body has a place within the divine worship of the Word made flesh, and it is expressed liturgically in a certain discipline of the body, in gestures that have developed out of the liturgy's inner demands and that make the essence of the liturgy, as it were, bodily visible. These gestures may vary in their details from culture to culture, but in their essential forms they are part of that culture of faith which has grown out of Christian cult. They form, therefore, a common language that crosses the borders of the different cultures. Let us have a closer look at them.

b. The Sign of the Cross

The most basic Christian gesture in prayer is and always will be the sign of the Cross. It is a way of confessing Christ crucified with one's very body, in accordance with the programmatic words of St. Paul: "[W]e preach Christ crucified, a stumbling block to Jews and folly to Gentiles, but to those who are called, both Jews and Greeks, Christ the power of God and the wisdom of God" (1 Cor 1:23f.). Again he says: "I decided to know nothing among you except Jesus Christ and him crucified" (2:2). To seal oneself with the sign of the Cross is a visible and public Yes to him who suffered for us; to him who in the body has made God's love visible, even to the utmost; to the God who reigns not by destruction but by the humility of suffering and love, which is stronger than all the power of the world and wiser than all the calculating intelligence of men. The sign of the Cross is a confession of faith: I believe in him who suffered for me and rose again; in him who has transformed the sign of shame into a sign of hope and of the love of God that is present with us. The confession of faith is a confession of hope: I believe in him who in his weakness is the Almighty; in him who can and will save me even in apparent absence and impotence. By signing ourselves with the Cross, we place ourselves under the protection of the Cross, hold it in front of us like a shield that will guard us in all the distress of daily life and give us the courage to go on. We accept it as a signpost that we follow: "If any man would come after me, let him deny himself and take up his cross and follow me" (Mk 8:34). The Cross shows us the road of life—the imitation of Christ.

We connect the sign of the Cross with confession of faith in the triune God—the Father, the Son, and the Holy Spirit. In this way it becomes a remembrance of Baptism, which is particularly clear when we use holy water with it. The Cross is a sign of the Passion, but at the same time it is a sign of the Resurrection. It is, so to speak, the saving staff that God holds out to us, the bridge by which we can pass over the abyss of death, and all the threats of the Evil One, and reach God. It is made present in Baptism, in which we become contemporary with Christ's Cross and Resurrection (cf. Rom 6:1–14). Whenever we make the sign of the Cross, we accept our Baptism anew; Christ from the Cross draws us, so to speak, to himself (cf. Jn 12:32) and thus into communion with the living God. For Baptism and the sign of the Cross, which is a kind of summing up and re-acceptance of Baptism, are above all a divine event: the Holy Spirit leads us to Christ, and Christ opens the door to the Father. God is no longer the "unknown god"; he has a name. We are allowed to call upon him, and he calls us.

Thus we can say that in the sign of the Cross, together with the invocation of the Trinity, the whole essence of Christianity is summed up; it displays what is distinctively Christian. Nevertheless, or rather for this very reason, it also opens the way into the wider history of religion and the divine message of creation. In 1873, on the Mount of Olives, Greek and Hebrew grave inscriptions bearing the sign of a cross were discovered from the time of Jesus. The excavators inevitably assumed that they were dealing with Christians of the earliest times. In about 1945 increasing numbers of Jewish graves with the sign of the cross were being discovered and assigned to more or less the first century after Christ. The discoveries no longer left room for the view that these were first-generation Christians. On the contrary, it had to be recognized that signs of the cross were established in the Jewish *milieu*. How are we to make sense of this? The key is to be found in Ezekiel 9:4f. In the vision described there, God says to his linen-clad messenger, who carries the writing case at his side: "Go through the city, through Jerusalem, and put a mark [*Tav*] upon the foreheads of the men who sigh and groan over all the abominations that are committed in it." In the terrible catastrophe now imminent, those who do not connive in the sin of the world yet suffer from it for the sake of God, suffering impotently yet at a distance from sin, are sealed with the last letter of the Hebrew alphabet, the *Tav*, which was written in the form of a cross (T or + or X). The *Tav*, which as a matter of fact had the form of a cross, becomes the seal of God's ownership. It corresponds to man's longing for God, his suffering for the sake of God, and so places him under God's special protection. E. Dinkler was able to show that cultic stigmatization—on the hands or forehead—was occasionally practiced in the Old Testament and that this custom was also well known in New Testament times. In the New Testament, Revelation 7:1–8 takes up the basic idea in Ezekiel's vision. The discoveries of the graves, in conjunction with the texts of the time, prove that in certain circles within Judaism the *Tav* was a widespread sacred sign—a sign of confession of faith in the God of Israel and at the same time a sign of hope in his protection. Dinkler summarizes his findings by saying that, in the cross-shaped *Tav*, "a whole confession of faith is summed up in *one* sign." "The realities believed in and hoped for", he says, "are read into a visible image, but the image is more than a mere reflection; it is in fact an image in whose saving power one places one's hopes" (p. 24). As far as we know, Christians did not at first take up this Jewish symbol of the cross, but they found the sign of the Cross from within their faith and were able to see in it the summing up of their whole faith. But was Ezekiel's vision of the salvific *Tav*, with the whole tradition built upon it, not bound to appear to Christians later as a glimpse of the One who was to come? Was the meaning of this mysterious sign not now "unveiled" (cf. 2 Cor 3:18)? Did it not now become clear to whom this sign belonged, from whom it derived its power? Could they fail to see in all this a prophecy of the Cross of Jesus Christ, who has transformed the *Tav* into the power of salvation?

The Fathers belonging to the Greek cultural world were more directly affected by another discovery. In the writings of Plato, they found the remarkable idea of a cross inscribed upon the cosmos (cf. *Timaeus* 34ab and 36bc). Plato took this from the Pythagorean tradition, which in its turn had a connection with the traditions of the ancient East. First, there is an astronomical statement about the two great movements of the stars with which ancient astronomy was familiar: the ecliptic (the great circle in the heavens along which the sun appears to run its course) and the orbit of the earth. These two intersect and form together the Greek letter *Chi*, which is written in the form of a cross (like an X). The sign of the cross is inscribed upon the whole cosmos. Plato, again following more ancient traditions, connected this with the image of the deity: the Demiurge (the fashioner of the world) "stretched out" the world soul "throughout the whole universe". St. Justin Martyr (d. ca. 165), the Palestinian-born first philosopher among the Fathers, came across this Platonic text and did not hesitate to link it with the doctrine of the triune God and his action in salvation history in the person of Jesus Christ. He sees the idea of the Demiurge and the world soul as premonitions of the mystery of the Father and the Son—premonitions that are in need of correction and yet also capable of correction. What Plato says about the world soul seems to him to refer to the coming of the Logos, the Son of God. And so he can now say that the shape of the cross is the greatest symbol of the lordship of the Logos, without which nothing in creation holds together (cf. *I Apol.* 55). The Cross of Golgotha is foreshadowed in the structure of the universe itself. The instrument of torment on which the Lord died is written into the structure of the universe. The cosmos speaks to us of the Cross, and the Cross solves for us the enigma of the cosmos. It is the real key to all reality. History and cosmos belong together. When we open our eyes, we can read the message of Christ in the language of the universe, and conversely, Christ grants us understanding of the message of creation.

From Justin onward, this "prophecy of the Cross" in Plato, together with the connection of cosmos and history that it reveals, was one of the fundamental ideas in patristic theology. It must have been an overwhelming discovery for the Fathers to find that the philosopher who summed up and interpreted the most ancient traditions had spoken of the cross as a seal imprinted on the universe. St. Irenaeus of Lyons (d. ca. 200), the real founder of systematic theology in its Catholic form, says in his work of apologetics, the *Demonstration of the Apostolic Preaching*, that the Crucified One is "the very Word of Almighty God, who penetrates our universe by an invisible presence. And for this reason he embraces the whole world, its breadth and length, its height and depth, for through the Word of God all things are guided into order. And the Son of God is crucified in them, since, in the form of the Cross, he is imprinted upon all things" (1, 3). This text of the great Father of the Church conceals a biblical quotation that is of great importance for the biblical theology of the Cross. The epistle to the Ephesians exhorts us to be rooted and grounded in love, so that, together with all the saints, we "may have power to comprehend with all the saints what is the breadth and length and height and depth, and to know the love of Christ which surpasses knowledge" (3:18f.). There can be little doubt that this epistle emanating from the school of St. Paul is referring to the cosmic Cross and thereby taking up traditions about the cross-shaped tree of the world that holds everything together—a religious idea that was also well known in India. St. Augustine has a wonderful interpretation of this important passage from St. Paul. He sees it as representing the dimensions of human life and as referring to the form of the crucified Christ, whose arms embrace the world and whose path reaches down into the abyss of the underworld and up to the very height of God himself (cf. *De doctrina christiana* 2, 41, 62; *Corpus Christianorum* 32, 75f.). Hugo Rahner has assembled the most beautiful patristic texts relevant to the cosmic mystery of the Cross. I should like to add only two more. In Lactantius (d. ca. 325) we read: "In his Passion God spread out his arms and thus embraced the globe as a sign that a future people, from the rising of the sun to its setting, would gather under his wings" (81). An unknown Greek author of the fourth century, contrasting the Cross with the cult of the sun, says that *Helios* (the sun) has now been conquered by the Cross. "Behold, man, whom the created sun in the heavens could not instruct, is now irradiated by the sunlight of the Cross and (in Baptism) enlightened." Then the anonymous author takes up some words of St. Ignatius of Antioch (d. ca. 110), who described the Cross as the cosmic hoist (*mēchanē*) for going up to heaven, and says: "O what truly divine wisdom is this! O Cross, thou hoist to heaven! The Cross was driven into the ground—and behold, idol worship was destroyed. No ordinary wood is this, but the wood that God used for victory" (87f.).

In his eschatological discourse, Jesus had announced that at the end of time "the sign of the Son of man" would appear in heaven (Mt 24:30). The eye of faith was now able to recognize that this sign had been inscribed into the cosmos from the beginning and thus see faith in the crucified Redeemer confirmed by the cosmos. At the same time, Christians thus realized that the paths of religious history converged on Christ, that their expectations, expressed in many different images, led to him. Conversely, this meant that philosophy and religion gave faith the images and concepts in which alone it could fully understand itself.

"[Y]ou will be a blessing", God had said to Abraham at the beginning of salvation history (Gen 12:2). In Christ, the Son of Abraham, these words are completely fulfilled. He is a blessing, and he is a blessing for the whole of creation as well as for all men. Thus the Cross, which is his sign in heaven and on earth, was destined to become the characteristic gesture of blessing for Christians. We make the sign of the Cross on ourselves and thus enter the power of the blessing of

Jesus Christ. We make the sign over people to whom we wish a blessing; and we also make it over things that are part of our life and that
we want, as it were, to receive anew from the hand of Jesus Christ.
Through the Cross, we can become sources of blessing for one another.
I shall never forget the devotion and heartfelt care with which my
father and mother made the sign of the Cross on the forehead, mouth,
and breast of us children when we went away from home, especially
when the parting was a long one. This blessing was like an escort that
we knew would guide us on our way. It made visible the prayer of our
parents, which went with us, and it gave us the assurance that this
prayer was supported by the blessing of the Savior. The blessing was
also a challenge to us not to go outside the sphere of this blessing.
Blessing is a priestly gesture, and so in this sign of the Cross we felt
the priesthood of parents, its special dignity and power. I believe that
this blessing, which is a perfect expression of the common priesthood
of the baptized, should come back in a much stronger way into our
daily life and permeate it with the power of the love that comes from
the Lord.

3. Posture

a. Kneeling/*Prostratio*

There are groups, of no small influence, who are trying to talk us out
of kneeling. "It doesn't suit our culture", they say (which culture?).
"It's not right for a grown man to do this—he should face God on his
feet." Or again: "It's not appropriate for redeemed man—he has been
set free by Christ and doesn't need to kneel any more." If we look at
history, we can see that the Greeks and Romans rejected kneeling. In
view of the squabbling, partisan deities described in mythology, this
attitude was thoroughly justified. It was only too obvious that these
gods were not God, even if you were dependent on their capricious
power and had to make sure that, whenever possible, you enjoyed
their favor. And so they said that kneeling was unworthy of a free
man, unsuitable for the culture of Greece, something the barbarians
went in for. Plutarch and Theophrastus regarded kneeling as an expression of superstition. Aristotle called it a barbaric form of behavior
(cf. *Rhetoric* 1361 a 36). St. Augustine agreed with him in a certain

respect: the false gods were only the masks of demons, who subjected men to the worship of money and to self-seeking, thus making them "servile" and superstitious. He said that the humility of Christ and his love, which went as far as the Cross, have freed us from these powers. We now kneel before that humility. The kneeling of Christians is not a form of inculturation into existing customs. It is quite the opposite, an expression of Christian culture, which transforms the existing culture through a new and deeper knowledge and experience of God.

Kneeling does not come from any culture—it comes from the Bible and its knowledge of God. The central importance of kneeling in the Bible can be seen in a very concrete way. The word *proskynein* alone occurs fifty-nine times in the New Testament, twenty-four of which are in the Apocalypse, the book of the heavenly liturgy, which is presented to the Church as the standard for her own liturgy. On closer inspection, we can discern three closely related forms of posture. First, there is *prostratio*—lying with one's face to the ground before the overwhelming power of God; secondly, especially in the New Testament, there is falling to one's knees before another; and thirdly, there is kneeling. Linguistically, the three forms of posture are not always clearly distinguished. They can be combined or merged with one another.

For the sake of brevity, I should like to mention, in the case of *prostratio*, just one text from the Old Testament and another from the New. In the Old Testament, there is an appearance of God to Joshua before the taking of Jericho, an appearance that the sacred author quite deliberately presents as a parallel to God's revelation of himself to Moses in the burning bush. Joshua sees "the commander of the army of the Lord" and, having recognized who he is, throws himself to the ground. At that moment he hears the words once spoken to Moses: "Put off your shoes from your feet; for the place where you stand is holy" (Josh 5:15). In the mysterious form of the "commander of the army of the Lord", the hidden God himself speaks to Joshua, and Joshua throws himself down before him. Origen gives a beautiful interpretation of this text: "Is there any other commander of the powers of the Lord than our Lord Jesus Christ?" According to this view, Joshua is worshipping the One who is to come—the coming Christ. In the case of the New Testament, from the Fathers onward, Jesus' prayer on the Mount of Olives was especially important. According to St. Matthew (26:39) and St. Mark (14:35), Jesus throws himself to the ground; indeed, he falls to the earth (according to Matthew). However, St. Luke, who in his whole work (both the Gospel and the Acts of the Apostles) is in a special way the theologian of kneeling prayer, tells us that Jesus prayed on his knees. This prayer, the prayer by which Jesus enters into his Passion, is an example for us, both as a gesture and in its content. The gesture: Jesus assumes, as it were, the fall of man, lets himself fall into man's fallenness, prays to the Father out of the lowest depths of human dereliction and anguish. He lays his will in the will of the Father's: "Not my will but yours be done." He lays the human will in the divine. He takes up all the hesitation of the human will and endures it. It is this very conforming of the human will to the divine that is the heart of redemption. For the fall of man depends on the contradiction of wills, on the opposition of the human will to the divine, which the tempter leads man to think is the condition of his freedom. Only one's own autonomous will, subject to no other will, is freedom. "Not my will, but yours . . ."—those are the words of truth, for God's will is not in opposition to our own; rather, it is the ground and condition of its possibility. Only when our will rests in the will of God does it become truly will and truly free. The suffering and struggle of Gethsemane is the struggle for this redemptive truth, for this uniting of what is divided, for the uniting that is communion with God. Now we understand why the Son's loving way of addressing the Father, "Abba", is found in this place (cf. Mk 14:36). St. Paul sees in this cry the prayer that the Holy Spirit places on our lips (cf. Rom 8:15; Gal 4:6) and thus anchors our Spirit-filled prayer in the Lord's prayer in Gethsemane.

In the Church's liturgy today, prostration appears on two occasions: on Good Friday and at ordinations. On Good Friday, the day of the Lord's crucifixion, it is the fitting expression of our sense of shock at the fact that we by our sins share in the responsibility for the death of Christ. We throw ourselves down and participate in his shock, in his descent into the depths of anguish. We throw ourselves down and so acknowledge where we are and who we are: fallen creatures whom only he can set on their feet. We throw ourselves down, as Jesus did, before the mystery of God's power present to us, knowing that the Cross is the true burning bush, the place of the flame of God's love, which burns but does not destroy. At ordinations prostration comes from the awareness of our absolute incapacity, by our own powers, to take on the priestly mission of Jesus Christ, to speak with his "I". While the ordinands are lying on the ground, the whole congregation sings the Litany of the Saints. I shall never forget lying on the ground at the time of my own priestly and episcopal ordination. When I was ordained bishop, my intense feeling of inadequacy, incapacity, in the face of the greatness of the task was even stronger than at my priestly ordination. The fact that the praying Church was calling upon all the saints, that the prayer of the Church really was enveloping and embracing me, was a wonderful consolation. In my incapacity, which had to be expressed in the bodily posture of prostration, this prayer, this presence of all the saints, of the living and the dead, was a wonderful strength—it was the only thing that could, as it were, lift me up. Only the presence of the saints with me made possible the path that lay before me.

Secondly, we must mention the gesture of falling to one's knees before another, which is described four times in the Gospels (cf. Mk 1:40; 10:17; Mt 17:14; 27:29) by means of the word *gonypetein*. Let us single out Mark 1:40. A leper comes to Jesus and begs him for help. He falls to his knees before him and says: "If you will, you can make me clean." It is hard to assess the significance of the gesture. What we have here is surely, not a proper act of adoration, but, rather, a supplication expressed fervently in bodily form, while showing a trust in a power beyond the merely human. The situation is different, though, with the classical word for adoration on one's knees—*proskynein*. I shall give two examples in order to clarify the question that faces the translator. First there is the account of how, after the multiplication of the loaves, Jesus stays with the Father on the mountain, while the disciples struggle in vain on the lake with the wind and the waves. Jesus comes to them across the water. Peter hurries toward him and is saved from sinking by the Lord. Then Jesus climbs into the boat, and the wind lets up. The text continues: "And the ship's crew came and said, falling at his feet, 'Thou art indeed the Son of God'" (Mt 14:33, Knox version). Other translations say: "[The disciples] in the boat worshipped [Jesus], saying . . ." (RSV). Both translations are correct. Each emphasizes one aspect of what is going on. The Knox version brings out the bodily expression, while the RSV shows what is happening interiorly. It is perfectly clear from the structure of the narrative that the gesture of acknowledging Jesus as the Son of God is an act of worship. We encounter a similar set of problems in St. John's Gospel when we read the account of the healing of the man born blind. This narrative, which is structured in a truly "theo-dramatic" way, ends with a dialogue between Jesus and the man he has healed. It serves as a model for the dialogue of conversion, for the whole narrative must also be seen as a profound exposition of the existential and theological significance of Baptism. In the dialogue, Jesus asks the man whether he believes in the Son of Man. The man born blind replies: "Tell me who he is, Lord." When Jesus says, "It is he who is speaking to you", the man makes the confession of faith: "I do believe, Lord", and then he "[falls] down to worship him" (Jn 9:35–38, Knox version adapted). Earlier translations said: "He worshipped him." In fact, the whole scene is directed toward the act of faith and the worship of Jesus, which follows from it. Now the eyes of the heart, as well as of the body, are opened. The man has in truth begun to see. For the exegesis of the text it is important to note that the word *proskynein* occurs eleven times in St. John's Gospel, of which nine occurrences are found in Jesus' conversation with the Samaritan woman by Jacob's well (Jn 4:19–24). This conversation is entirely devoted to the theme of worship, and it is indisputable that here, as elsewhere in St. John's Gospel, the word always has the meaning of "worship". Incidentally, this conversation, too, ends—like that of the healing of the man born blind—with Jesus' revealing himself: "I who speak to you am he" (Jn 4:26).

I have lingered over these texts because they bring to light something important. In the two passages that we looked at most closely, the spiritual and bodily meanings of *proskynein* are really inseparable. The bodily gesture itself is the bearer of the spiritual meaning, which is precisely that of worship. Without the worship, the bodily gesture would be meaningless, while the spiritual act must of its very nature, because of the psychosomatic unity of man, express itself in the bodily gesture. The two aspects are united in the one word, because in a very profound way they belong together. When kneeling becomes merely external, a merely physical act, it becomes meaningless. On the other hand, when someone tries to take worship back into the purely spiritual realm and refuses to give it embodied form, the act of worship evaporates, for what is purely spiritual is inappropriate to the nature of man. Worship is one of those fundamental acts that affect the whole man. That is why bending the knee before the presence of the living God is something we cannot abandon.

In saying this, we come to the typical gesture of kneeling on one or both knees. In the Hebrew of the Old Testament, the verb *barak*, "to kneel", is cognate with the word *berek*, "knee". The Hebrews regarded the knees as a symbol of strength; to bend the knee is, therefore, to bend our strength before the living God, an acknowledgment of the fact that all that we are we receive from him. In important passages of the Old Testament, this gesture appears as an expression of worship. At the dedication of the Temple, Solomon kneels "in the presence of all the assembly of Israel" (2 Chron 6:13). After the Exile, in the afflictions of the returned Israel, which is still without a Temple, Ezra repeats this gesture at the time of the evening sacrifice: "I ... fell upon my knees and spread out my hands to the LORD my God" (Ezra 9:5). The great psalm of the Passion, Psalm 22(21) ("My God, my God, why have you forsaken me?"), ends with the promise: "Yes, to him shall all the proud of the earth fall down; before him all who go down to the dust shall throw themselves down" (v. 29, RSV adapted). The related passage Isaiah 45:23 we shall have to consider in the context of the New Testament. The Acts of the Apostles tells us how St. Peter (9:40), St. Paul (20:36), and the whole Christian community (21:5) pray on their knees. Particularly important for our question is the account of the martyrdom of St. Stephen. The first man to witness to Christ with his blood is described in his suffering as a perfect image of Christ, whose Passion is repeated in the martyrdom of the witness, even in small details. One of these is that Stephen, on his knees takes up the petition of the crucified Christ: "Lord, do not hold this sin against them" (7:60). We should remember that Luke, unlike Matthew and Mark, speaks of the Lord kneeling in Gethsemane, which shows that Luke wants the kneeling of the first martyr to be seen as his entry into the prayer of Jesus. Kneeling is not only a Christian gesture, but a christological one.

For me, the most important passage for the theology of kneeling will always be the great hymn of Christ in Philippians 2:6–11. In this pre-Pauline hymn, we hear and see the prayer of the apostolic Church and can discern within it her confession of faith in Christ. However, we also hear the voice of the Apostle, who enters into this prayer and hands it on to us, and, ultimately, we perceive here both the profound inner unity of the Old and New Testaments and the cosmic breadth of Christian faith. The hymn presents Christ as the antitype of the First Adam. While the latter high-handedly grasped at likeness to God, Christ does not count equality with God, which is his by nature, "a thing to be grasped", but humbles himself unto death, even death on the Cross. It is precisely this humility, which comes from love, that is the truly divine reality and procures for him the "name which is above every name, that at the name of Jesus every knee should bow, in heaven and on earth and under the earth" (Phil 2:5–10). Here the hymn of the apostolic Church takes up the words of promise in Isaiah 45:23: "By myself I have sworn, from my mouth has gone forth in righteousness a word that shall not return: 'To me every knee shall bow, every tongue shall swear.' " In the interweaving of Old and New Testaments, it becomes clear that, even as crucified, Jesus bears the "name above every name"—the name of the Most High—and is himself God by nature. Through him, through the Crucified, the bold promise of the Old Testament is now fulfilled: all bend the knee before Jesus, the One who descended, and bow to him precisely as the one true God above all gods. The Cross has become the world-embracing sign of God's presence, and all that we have previously heard about the historical and cosmic Christ should now, in this passage, come back into our minds. The Christian liturgy is a cosmic liturgy precisely because it bends the knee before the crucified and exalted Lord. Here is the center of authentic culture—the culture of truth. The humble gesture by which we fall at the feet of the Lord inserts us into the true path of life of the cosmos.

There is much more that we might add. For example, there is the touching story told by Eusebius in his history of the Church as a tradition going back to Hegesippus in the second century. Apparently, St. James, the "brother of the Lord", the first bishop of Jerusalem and "head" of the Jewish Christian Church, had a kind of callous on his knees because he was always on his knees worshipping God and begging for forgiveness for his people (2, 23, 6). Again, there is a story that comes from the sayings of the Desert Fathers, according to which the devil was compelled by God to show himself to a certain Abba Apollo. He looked black and ugly, with frighteningly thin limbs, but, most strikingly, *he had no knees*. The inability to kneel is seen as the very essence of the diabolical.

But I do not want to go into more detail. I should like to make just one more remark. The expression used by St. Luke to describe the kneeling of Christians (*theis ta gonata*) is unknown in classical Greek. We are dealing here with a specifically Christian word. With that remark, our reflections return full circle to where they began. It may well be that kneeling is alien to modern culture—insofar as it is a culture, for this culture has turned away from the faith and no longer knows the One before whom kneeling is the right, indeed, the intrinsically necessary gesture. The man who learns to believe learns also to kneel, and a faith or a liturgy no longer familiar with kneeling would be sick at the core. Where it has been lost, kneeling must be rediscovered, so that, in our prayer, we remain in fellowship with the apostles and martyrs, in fellowship with the whole cosmos, indeed, in union with Jesus Christ himself.

b. Standing and Sitting—Liturgy and Culture

We can be considerably more brief in what we say about these two postures, because they are not very controversial these days, and the importance that each has is not hard to see. In the Old Testament, standing is a classic posture for prayer. Let us content ourselves with just one example—the prayer of the childless Hannah, who becomes, in answer to her prayers, the mother of Samuel. In the New Testament, St. Luke paints a portrait of Elizabeth, the mother of John the Baptist, with colors reminiscent of Hannah. After she has weaned the child Samuel, the happy mother comes to the Temple in order to hand over the child of promise to the Lord: "I am the woman", she says, "who was standing here in your presence, praying to the LORD" (1 Sam 1:26). A whole series of New Testament texts show us that in Jesus' time standing was the ordinary posture for prayer among the Jews (cf. Mt 6:5; Mk 11:25; Lk 18:11ff.). Among Christians, standing was primarily the Easter form of prayer. The twentieth canon of Nicaea decrees that Christians should stand, not kneel, during Eastertide. It is the time of the victory of Jesus Christ, the time of joy, in which we show forth the Paschal victory of the Lord, even in the posture of our prayer. This may remind us once again of the passion of St. Stephen. Faced with the fury of his persecutors, he looks up to heaven, where he sees Jesus standing at the right hand of the Father [cf. Acts 7:55]. Standing is the posture of the victor. Jesus stands in God's presence—he stands, because he has trodden death and the power of the Evil One underfoot. At the end of this struggle, he is the one who stands upright, the one who remains standing. This standing is also an expression of readiness: Christ is standing up at the right hand of God in order to meet us. He has not withdrawn. It is for us that he stands, and in the very hour of anguish we can be sure that he will set off and come to us, just as once he set off from the Father and came to his own across the water, when wind and waves were overpowering their boat. When we stand, we know that we are united to the victory of Christ, and when we stand to listen to the Gospel, it is an expression of reverence. When this Word is heard, we cannot remain sitting; it pulls us up. It demands both reverence and courage, when he calls us to set off in some new direction, to do his will and to carry it into our lives and into the world.

Just one further reminder may help us here. We are familiar, from the painting in the catacombs, with the figure of the *orans*, the female figure standing and praying with outstretched hands. According to recent research, the *orans* normally represents, not the praying Church, but the soul that has entered into heavenly glory and stands in adoration before the face of God. This has two important aspects. First, the soul is almost always represented as a woman, because what is specific to human existence in relation to God is expressed in the form of a woman: the bridal element, in regard to the eternal nuptials, and also the ready acceptance of the grace bestowed upon us. The second point is this: it is not the earthly liturgy, the liturgy of pilgrimage, that is represented here but prayer in the state of glory. Thus, once again, this time in light of the *orans*, it becomes clear that standing prayer is an anticipation of the future, of the glory that is to come; it is meant to orient us toward it. Insofar as liturgical prayer is an anticipation of what has been promised, standing is its proper posture. However, insofar as liturgical prayer belongs to that "between" time in which we live, then kneeling remains indispensable to it as an expression of the "now" of our life.

Finally, the liturgy permits sitting during the readings, the homily, and the meditative assimilation of the Word (the responsorial psalm, and so on). Whether it is also appropriate during the Preparation of the Gifts may be regarded as an open question. In recent times, sitting has been introduced here because of a particular understanding of this part of the sacred liturgy. Certain people deny it has a sacred character and regard it as something purely practical. I shall not debate the issue here. New research—including the theological comparison of the different rites—is necessary. Sitting should be at the service of recollection. Our bodies should be relaxed, so that our hearing and understanding are unimpeded.

Today (as, doubtless, in different ways, also in the past) it is noticeable that there is some curious mixing and matching going on with the different postures. Here and there, sitting has become very like the lotus position of Indian religiosity, which is regarded as the proper posture for meditation. Now I do not want absolutely to rule out the Christian use of the lotus position, which is again being practiced, in different ways, by some Christians. However, I do not believe it has any place in the liturgy. If we try to understand the inner language of bodily gestures, then we can begin to understand their origin and spiritual purpose. When a man kneels, he lowers himself, but his eyes still look forward and upward, as when he stands, toward the One who faces him. To kneel is to be oriented toward the One who looks upon us and toward whom we try to look, as the epistle to the Hebrews says, "looking to Jesus, the pioneer and perfecter of our faith" (Heb 12:2; cf. 3:1). Keep your eyes fixed on Jesus—that is a maxim of the Fathers' doctrine of prayer, which takes up again the Old Testament motif of "seeking [God's] face". The man who prays looks beyond himself to the One who is above him and approaches him. He in turn, by his gazing and praying, tries to approach the Lord and thus seeks to enter into nuptial union with him. In the sitting position of oriental meditation, it is all quite different. Man looks into himself. He does not go away from himself to the Other but tends to sink inward, into the nothing that is at the same time everything. True, the Christian tradition is also familiar with the God who is more interior to us than we are to ourselves—the God whom we seek precisely by breaking away from aimless wandering in the external world and going inward. It is there, inside ourselves, that we find ourselves and the deepest ground of our being. In this sense, there are real bridges from the one attitude to the other. With all of today's empiricism and pragmatism, with its loss of soul, we have good reason to learn again from Asia. But however open Christian faith may be, must be, to the wisdom of Asia, the difference between the personal and the a-personal understandings of God remains. We must, therefore, conclude that kneeling and standing are, in a unique and irreplaceable way, the Christian posture of prayer—the Christian's orientation of himself toward the face of God, toward the face of Jesus Christ, in seeing whom we are able to see the Father (Jn 14:9).

Dancing is not a form of expression for the Christian liturgy. In about the third century, there was an attempt in certain Gnostic-Docetic circles to introduce it into the liturgy. For these people, the crucifixion was only an appearance. Before the Passion, Christ had abandoned the body that in any case he had never really assumed. Dancing could take the place of the liturgy of the Cross, because, after all, the Cross was only an appearance. The cultic dances of the different religions have different purposes—incantation, imitative magic, mystical ecstasy—none of which is compatible with the essential purpose of the liturgy of the "reasonable sacrifice". It is totally absurd to try to make the liturgy "attractive" by introducing dancing pantomimes (wherever possible performed by professional dance troupes), which frequently (and rightly, from the professionals' point of view) end with applause. Wherever applause breaks out in the liturgy because of some human achievement, it is a sure sign that the essence of liturgy has totally disappeared and been replaced by a kind of religious entertainment. Such attractiveness fades quickly—it cannot compete in the market of leisure pursuits, incorporating as it increasingly does various forms of religious titillation. I myself have experienced the replacing of the penitential rite by a dance performance, which, needless to say, received a round of applause. Could there be anything farther removed from true penitence? Liturgy can only attract people when it looks, not at itself, but at God, when it allows him to enter and act. Then something truly unique happens, beyond competition, and people have a sense that more has taken place than a recreational activity. None of the Christian rites includes dancing. What people call dancing in the Ethiopian rite or the Zairean form of the Roman liturgy is in fact a rhythmically ordered procession, very much in keeping with the dignity of the occasion. It provides an inner discipline and order for the various stages of the liturgy, bestowing on them beauty and, above all, making them worthy of God. Once again we face the question: What do we have here, liturgy or popular piety? Very often these old forms of religious expression, which could not be inserted as such into the liturgy, have been integrated into the world of faith. Popular piety has a special importance as a bridge between the faith and each culture. Of its very nature, it is directly indebted to its culture. It enlarges the world of faith and gives it its vitality in the various circumstances of life. It is less universal than the liturgy, which connects vast regions with each other and embraces different cultures. Consequently, the various forms of popular piety are farther removed from each other than the liturgies are, and yet they embody the humanity of man, which, for all the differences of culture, remains similar in so many ways. The best-known example in Europe is the spring procession in Echternach.* In a little sanctuary in the middle of the desert of northern Chile, I was once able to attend some Marian devotions that were followed in the open air by a dance, in honor of the Madonna, employing masks that looked rather frightening to me. Doubtless behind this lay very ancient, pre-Columbian traditions. What once might have been marked by a terrifying seriousness, in view of the power of the gods, had now been set free, transformed into an act of homage to the humble woman who can be called the Mother of God and the ground of our trust. Once again it is something different if, after the liturgy, the joy that it contains turns into a "secular" feast, which is expressed in a common meal and dancing but does not lose sight of the reason for the joy, of what gives it its purpose and measure. This connection between the liturgy and cheerful earthiness ("Church and inn") has always been regarded as typically Catholic, and so it is still.

At this point a brief remark about the theme of liturgy and inculturation suggests itself. Needless to say, we cannot go into it too widely and deeply, but by the same token it should not be overlooked. Everywhere these days the liturgy seems to be the proving ground for experiments in inculturation. Whenever people talk about inculturation, they almost always think only of the liturgy, which then has to undergo often quite dismal distortions. The worshippers usually groan at this, though it is happening for their sake. An inculturation that is more or less just an alteration of outward forms is not inculturation at all but a misunderstanding of inculturation. Moreover, it frequently insults cultural and religious communities, from whom liturgical forms are borrowed in an all too superficial and external way. The first and most fundamental way in which inculturation takes place is the unfolding of a Christian culture in all its different dimensions: a culture of cooperation, of social concern, of respect for the poor, of the overcoming of class differences, of care for the suffering and dying; a culture that educates mind and heart in proper cooperation; a political culture and

---

*Echternach, in the Grand Duchy of Luxembourg, holds an annual "Dancing Procession" (*Springprozession, procession dansante*) in honor of St. Willibrord, the Apostle of the Netherlands, who died in 739 in the Abbey of Echternach, which he founded. It is a tradition that goes back to the Middle Ages and takes place on the Tuesday after Pentecost. As the thousands of pilgrims pass around the tomb of the saint and through the streets of the little town, they dance to an ancient melody, hopping twice on the right foot and twice on the left. At the same time they call upon the saint for his protection against epilepsy and St. Vitus' Dance.

a culture of law; a culture of dialogue, of reverence for life, and so on. This kind of authentic inculturation of Christianity then creates culture in the stricter sense of the word, that is, it leads to artistic work that interprets the world anew in the light of God. As the Greeks so rightly saw, culture is, before all else, education, taking that word in its deepest sense as the inner opening up of a man to his possibilities, in which his external abilities are developed in harmony with his gifts. In the religious sphere, culture manifests itself above all in the growth of authentic popular piety. Despite all the inadequacies of the Christian mission in Latin America, and despite the fact that so much still needs to be done, Christian faith has put down deep roots in souls. This can be seen in the popular piety in which the mystery of Christ has come very close to people, in which Christ has become truly their own. Think, for example, of devotion to the Passion, in which these suffering peoples, after the cruelty of the gods of the past, gratefully look upon the God who suffers with them as the answer to their deepest longings. Think, too, of Marian devotion, in which the whole mystery of the Incarnation, the tenderness of God, the participation of man in God's own nature, and the nature of God's saving action are experienced at a profound level. Popular piety is the soil without which the liturgy cannot thrive. Unfortunately, in parts of the Liturgical Movement and on the occasion of the postconciliar reform, it has frequently been held in contempt or even abused. Instead, one must love it, purifying and guiding it where necessary, but always accepting it with great reverence, even when it seems alien or alienating, as the dedicated sanctuary of faith in the hearts of the people. It is faith's secure inner rooting; when it dries up, rationalism and sectarianism have an easy job. Tried and tested elements of popular piety may pass over, then, into liturgical celebration, without officious and hasty fabrication, by a patient process of lengthy growth. Incidentally, the liturgy, without any manipulation of the rite, has always quite spontaneously, through the way it is celebrated, borne the imprint of each culture in which it is celebrated. A liturgy in an Upper Bavarian village looks very different from High Mass in a French cathedral, which in turn seems quite unlike Mass in a southern Italian parish, and again that looks different from what you would find in a mountain village in the Andes, and so on. The decoration and arrangement of the altar and the interior of the church, the style of singing and praying—all of these give the liturgy its own special character, enabling people to feel completely at home. And yet in every place we can experience it as one and the same liturgy, and in this way we experience, too, the great communion of faith. The unity of the rite gives us a real experience of *communio*. When the rite is respected and animated from within, unity and diversity are not in opposition.

4. Gestures

The oldest gesture of prayer in Christendom is prayer with arms extended, the *orans* posture, which we have already briefly mentioned. This is one of the primal gestures of man in calling upon God and is found in virtually every part of the religious world. It is first of all an expression of nonviolence, a gesture of peace. A man opens his arms and thus opens himself to another person. It is also a gesture of seeking and hoping. Man reaches out to the hidden God, stretches out toward him. Arms extended have been compared to wings: man seeks the heights, he wants to be, as it were, carried upward by God on the wings of prayer. But for Christians, arms extended also have a christological meaning. They remind us of the extended arms of Christ on the Cross. The crucified Lord has given this primal human gesture of prayer a new depth. By extending our arms, we resolve to pray with the Crucified, to unite ourselves to his "mind" (Phil 2:5). In the arms of Christ, stretched on the Cross, Christians see a twofold meaning. In his case too, in his case above all, this gesture is the radical form of worship, the unity of his human will with the will of the Father, but at the same time these arms are opened toward us—they are the wide embrace by which Christ wants to draw us to himself (Jn 12:32). Worship of God and love of neighbor—the content of the chief commandment, which sums up the law and the prophets—coincide in this gesture. To open oneself to God, to surrender oneself completely to him, is at the same time—the two things cannot be separated—to devote oneself to one's neighbor. This combining of the two directions of love in the gesture of Christ on the Cross reveals, in a bodily and visible way, the new depth of Christian prayer and thus expresses the inner law of our own prayer.

A later development was the gesture of praying with hands joined. This comes from the world of feudalism. The recipient of a feudal estate, on taking tenure, placed his joined hands in those of his lord—a wonderful symbolic act. I lay my hands in yours, allow yours to enclose mine. This is an expression of trust as well as of fidelity. The gesture has been retained in priestly ordination. The newly ordained man receives his priestly task as a kind of feudal estate held on tenure. He is not the source of his priesthood. He is a priest, not through his own skills and abilities, but by the gift of the Lord, a gift that always remains a gift and never becomes simply his possession, a power of his own. The new priest receives the gift and task of priesthood as a gift from another, from Christ, and recognizes that all he is ever able and allowed to be is a "steward of the mysteries of God" (cf. 1 Cor 4:1), "a good steward of God's varied grace" (cf. 1 Pet 4:10). If this is what he is to become, he must commit his whole existence to the task. And that can only take place in the "house of God" (Heb 3:2–6), the Church, in which the bishop, in the place of Christ, accepts the individual into the priesthood, into a relationship of fidelity to Christ. When the ordinand lays his joined hands in the hands of the bishop and promises him reverence and obedience, he is dedicating his service to the Church as the living Body of Christ, laying his hands in the hands of Christ, entrusting himself to him and giving him his hands, so that they may be his. What within feudalism may be questionable—for all human lordship is questionable and can only be justified if it represents and is faithful to the real Lord—finds its true meaning in the relationship of the believer to Christ the Lord. This, then, is what is meant when we join our hands to pray: we are placing our hands in his, and with our hands we place in his hands our personal destiny. Trusting in his fidelity, we pledge our fidelity to him.

We have already said something about kneeling as a gesture of prayer. I should like at this point to mention bowing. One of the petitions for acceptance in the Roman Canon (Eucharistic Prayer I) begins with the word *supplices*: Bowing low, we implore thee. Here again the bodily gesture and the spiritual process are inseparable and flow into one another. This is the gesture of the tax collector, who knows that he cannot endure the gaze of God and so bows low before it. And yet this prayer asks that our sacrifice may come before the face of God, into his sight, and be for us a blessing. Out of the depths of our insufficiency we call upon God, that he may set us upright, enable us to gaze upon him, and make us such that he may gaze upon us. The *supplices*—our being "bowed low"—is the bodily expression, so to speak, of what the Bible calls humility (cf. "he humbled himself", Phil 2:8).

For the Greeks, humility was the attitude of a slave, and so they rejected it. The transformation of values brought about by Christianity sees in it something different. Humility is the ontologically appropriate attitude, the state that corresponds to the truth about man, and as such it becomes a fundamental attitude of Christian existence. St. Augustine constructed his whole Christology, indeed, I would say his entire apologetics for Christianity, upon the concept of *humilitas*. He took up the teaching of the ancients, of the Greek and Roman world, that *hybris*—self-glorifying pride—is the real sin of all sins, as we see in exemplary form in the fall of Adam. Arrogance, the ontological lie by which man makes himself God, is overcome by the humility of God, who makes himself the slave, who bows down before us. The man who wants to come close to God must be able to look upon him—that is essential. But he must likewise learn to bend, for God has bent himself down. In the gesture of humble love, in the washing of feet, in which he kneels at our feet—that is where we find him. Thus the *supplices* is a gesture of great profundity. It is a physical reminder of the spiritual attitude essential to faith. Astonishingly, several modern translations of the Roman Canon have simply omitted the *supplices*. Perhaps they regarded the physical expression, which as a matter of fact has disappeared, as unimportant. Perhaps, too, they thought it was an unsuitable thing for a modern man to do. To bow low before a human being, to win his favor, is indeed unfitting. But to bow low before God can never be unmodern, because it corresponds to the truth of our being. And if modern man has forgotten this truth, then it is all the more incumbent on Christians in the modern world to rediscover it and teach it to our fellowmen.

Another gesture came into Christianity from the narrative already mentioned of the Pharisee and the Tax Collector (cf. Lk 18:9–14): striking the breast. Apparently, in the North Africa of St. Augustine, it was very popular and practiced in a somewhat exaggerated and superficial manner, so much so, in fact, that the Bishop of Hippo had to remind his flock, with gentle irony, to moderate their "sin-bashing". However, this gesture, by which we point not at someone else but at ourselves as the guilty party, remains a meaningful gesture of prayer. This is exactly what we need, time and again, to do: to see and acknowledge our guilt and so also to beg for forgiveness. When we say *mea culpa* (through my fault), we turn, so to speak, to ourselves, to our own front door, and thus we are able rightly to ask forgiveness of

God, the saints, and the people gathered around us, whom we have wronged. During the *Agnus Dei* (Lamb of God), we look upon him who is the Shepherd and for us became Lamb and, as Lamb, bore our iniquities. At this moment it is only right and proper that we should strike our breasts and remind ourselves, even physically, that our iniquities lay on his shoulders, that "with his stripes we are healed" (Is 53:5).

5. The Human Voice

It is clear that in the liturgy of the Logos, of the Eternal Word, the word and thus the human voice have an essential role to play. In this little book, which is not intended to give instructions for liturgical practice but only insights into the spirit of the liturgy, we do not need to discuss the detailed forms in which the human voice is deployed in the liturgy. We have seen much of this already in early chapters, especially in connection with sacred music. First there is the *oratio*, the priestly mode of prayer, in which the priest, in the name of the whole community, speaks through Christ, in the Holy Spirit, to the Father. Then there are the various forms of proclamation: the readings ("Prophet and Apostle", as they used to say in the early Church, meaning by "prophecy" the whole of the Old Testament), the Gospel (solemnly sung at High Mass), and the homily, which in the strict sense is reserved to the bishop and then to the priest and deacon as well. Then there is the response to the Word [*Ant-Wort*], by which the assembled congregation takes up and accepts the Word. This structure of Word and response, which is essential to the liturgy, is modelled on the basic structure of the process of divine revelation, in which Word and response, the speech of God and the receptive hearing of the Bride, the Church, go together. In the liturgy, the response has different forms. For example, there is the acclamation ("shout"), which is of great importance in the world of ancient law. The responsive acclamation confirms the arrival of the Word and makes the process of revelation, of God's giving of himself in the Word, at last complete. The Amen, the Alleluia, and the *Et cum spiritu tuo*, and so on, are all part of this. One of the important results of the liturgical renewal is the fact that the people really do again respond in the acclamation and do not have to leave it to a representative, the altar server. This is the only way the true structure of the liturgy can be restored, a structure that, as we have just seen, makes concrete in divine worship the fundamental structure of divine action. God, the Revealer, did not want to stay as *solus Deus, solus Christus* (God alone, Christ alone). No, he wanted to create a Body for himself, to find a Bride—he sought a response. It was really for her that the Word went forth. Alongside the acclamation are the various forms of meditative appropriation of the Word, especially in the singing of psalms (but also in hymns), the different forms of which (responsorial and antiphonal) do not need to be discussed in detail here. Then there is the "new song", the great song the Church sings as she goes off toward the music of the New Heaven and New Earth. This explains why, in addition to congregational singing, Christian liturgy of its very nature finds a suitable place for the choir, and for musical instruments, too, which no purism about collective singing should be allowed to contest. The possibilities will, of course, always differ from place to place, but the Church as a whole must, for the sake of God, strive for the best, for from the very nature of the liturgy, by an inner necessity, comes a culture that becomes a standard for all secular culture.

We are realizing more and more clearly that silence is part of the liturgy. We respond, by singing and praying, to the God who addresses us, but the greater mystery, surpassing all words, summons us to silence. It must, of course, be a silence with content, not just the absence of speech and action. We should expect the liturgy to give us a positive stillness that will restore us. Such stillness will not be just a pause, in which a thousand thoughts and desires assault us, but a time of recollection, giving us an inward peace, allowing us to draw breath and rediscover the one thing necessary, which we have forgotten. That is why silence cannot be simply "made", organized as if it were one activity among many. It is no accident that on all sides people are seeking techniques of meditation, a spirituality for emptying the mind. One of man's deepest needs is making its presence felt, a need that is manifestly not being met in our present form of the liturgy.

For silence to be fruitful, as we have already said, it must not be just a pause in the action of the liturgy. No, it must be an integral part of the liturgical event. How is that to be done? In recent times, the attempt has been made to insert two short periods of silence into the liturgy as a way of addressing the problem: a pause for reflection after the homily and a period of silent prayer after the reception of Holy Communion. The pause for silence after the homily has not proved to be very satisfactory: it seems artificial, with the congregation just waiting for as long as the celebrant feels inclined to let it go on. What is more, the homily often leaves questions and contradictions in people's minds rather than an invitation to meet the Lord. As a general rule, the homily should conclude with an encouragement to prayer, which would give some content to the brief pause. But even then it remains just a pause in the liturgy, not something from which a liturgy of silence can develop. More helpful and spiritually appropriate is the silence after Communion. This, in all truth, is the moment for an interior conversation with the Lord who has given himself to us, for that essential "communicating", that entry into the process of communication, without which the external reception of the Sacrament becomes mere ritual and therefore unfruitful. Unfortunately, there are often hindrances that spoil this precious moment. The distribution of Communion continues with the noise of people going back and forth. In relation to the rest of the liturgical action, the distribution often lasts too long, which means that the priest feels the need to move the liturgy on quickly so that there is no empty period of waiting and restlessness, with people already getting ready to leave. Nevertheless, whenever possible, this silence after Communion should be used, and the faithful should be given some guidance for interior prayer.

In some places, the Preparation of the Gifts is intended as a time for silence. This makes good sense and is fruitful, if we see the Preparation, not as just a pragmatic external action, but as an essentially interior process. We need to see that we ourselves are, or should be, the real gift in the "Word-centered sacrifice" through our sharing in Jesus Christ's act of self-offering to the Father (of which we spoke in the first part). Then this silence is not just a period of waiting, something external. Then something happens inwardly that corresponds to what is going on outwardly—we are disposing ourselves, preparing the way, placing ourselves before the Lord, asking him to make us ready for transformation. Shared silence becomes shared prayer, indeed, shared action, a journey out of our everyday life toward the Lord, toward merging our time with his own. Liturgical education ought to regard it as its duty to facilitate this inner process, so that in the common experience of silence the inner process becomes a truly liturgical event and the silence is filled with content.

The structure of the liturgy itself provides for other moments of silence. First there is the silence of the Consecration at the elevation of the consecrated species. It is an invitation to direct our eyes toward Christ, to look at him from within, in a gaze that is at once gratitude, adoration, and petition for our own transformation. There are fashionable objections that would try to talk us out of this silence at the Consecration. The showing of the Gifts, it is said, is a medieval error, which disturbs the structure of the Eucharistic Prayer, the expression of a false and too grossly materialistic piety. The argument is that the elevation is out of keeping with the essential direction of the Eucharist. At this moment, so it is claimed, we should not be worshipping Christ—the whole Canon addresses the Father, to whom we pray through Christ. We do not need to go into these criticisms in detail. The essential answer to them is provided by what was said in chapter 2 about reverence for the Blessed Sacrament and the rightfulness of the medieval developments, which unfolded what had been there from the beginning in the faith of the Church. It is correct to say that the Canon has a trinitarian structure and consequently as a totality moves "through Christ, in the Holy Spirit, to the Father". But the liturgy in this respect knows nothing of rigidity and fixation. The reformed Missal of 1970 itself places on our lips a greeting directed toward the Lord: "We proclaim your death, O Lord, and we confess your Resurrection, until you come [in glory]!" The moment when the Lord comes down and transforms bread and wine to become his Body and Blood cannot fail to stun, to the very core of their being, those who participate in the Eucharist by faith and prayer. When this happens, we cannot do other than fall to our knees and greet him. The Consecration is the moment of God's great *actio* in the world for us. It draws our eyes and hearts on high. For a moment the world is silent, everything is silent, and in that silence we touch the eternal—for one beat of the heart we step out of time into God's being-with-us.

Another approach to the question of content-filled silence is provided by the liturgy itself. There is a silence that is part of the liturgical action, not an interruption. I am thinking of the silent prayers of the priest. Those who hold a sociological or activistic view of the priest's duties in the Mass frown upon these prayers, and, whenever possible, they leave them out. The priest is defined in a narrowly sociological and functionalistic way as the "presider" at the liturgical celebration, which is thought of as a kind of meeting. If that is what he is, then, of course, for the sake of the meeting, he has to be in action all the time. But the priest's duties in the Mass are much more than a matter of chairing a meeting. The priest presides over an encounter with the living God and as a person who is on his way to God. The silent prayers of the priest invite him to make his task truly personal, so that he may give his whole self to the Lord. They highlight the way in which all of us, each one personally yet together with everyone else, have to approach the Lord. The number of these priestly prayers has been greatly reduced in the liturgical reform, but, thank God, they do exist—they have to exist, now as before. First there is the short prayer of preparation before the proclamation of the Gospel. The priest should pray it with real recollection and devotion, conscious of his responsibility to proclaim the Gospel aright, conscious, too, of the need that that entails for a purification of lips and heart. When the priest does this, he shows the congregation the dignity and grandeur of the Gospel and helps them understand how tremendous it is that God's Word should come into our midst. The priest's prayer creates reverence and a space for hearing the Word. Again, liturgical education is necessary if the priest's prayer is to be understood and the people are not only to stand up physically but also to rise up spiritually and open the ears of their hearts to the Gospel. We have already spoken of the Preparation of the Gifts, the significance of which in the new rite is not entirely clear. The priest's reception of Holy Communion is preceded by two very beautiful and profound prayers, from which, to avoid the silence being too long, he is to choose one. Perhaps we shall again one day take the time to use both. But even if only one of them is prayed, the priest should with all the more reason really pray it in recollected silence as a personal preparation for receiving the Lord. This will help to bring everyone else into silence before the Sacred Presence, and then going to Communion will not degenerate into something merely external. This is particularly necessary, because in the present order of the Mass the sign of peace frequently causes a lot of hustle and bustle in the congregation, into which the invitation to "Behold the Lamb of God" then comes as a rather abrupt intervention. If in a moment of quiet the eyes of the hearts of all are directed toward the Lamb, this can become a time of blessed silence. After the priest's reception of Communion another (formerly, there were two) silent prayer of thanksgiving is provided for him, which again can and should be made their own by the faithful.

I should like to mention at this point that old prayer books contain, alongside a lot of kitsch, much that is a valuable resource for prayer, much that has grown out of deep interior experience and can again become today a school for prayer. What St. Paul says in the epistle to the Romans—that we do not know how to pray as we ought (Rom 8:26)—applies even more to us today. So often we are without words in our encounter with God. The Holy Spirit does indeed teach us to pray; he does indeed give us the words, as St. Paul says; but he also uses human mediation. The prayers that have risen up from the hearts of believers under the guidance of the Holy Spirit are a school, provided us by the Holy Spirit, that will slowly open our mute mouths and help us to learn how to pray and to fill the silence.

In 1978, to the annoyance of many liturgists, I said that in no sense does the whole Canon always *have* to be said out loud. After much consideration, I should like to repeat and underline the point here in the hope that, twenty years later, this thesis will be better understood. Meanwhile, in their efforts to reform the Missal, the German liturgists have explicitly stated that, of all things, the Eucharistic Prayer, the high point of the Mass, is in crisis. Since the reform of the liturgy, an attempt has been made to meet the crisis by incessantly inventing new Eucharistic Prayers, and in the process we have sunk farther and farther into banality. Multiplying words is no help—that is all too evident. The liturgists have suggested all kinds of remedies, which certainly contain elements that are worthy of consideration. However, as far as I can see, they balk, now as in the past, at the possibility that silence, too, silence especially, might constitute communion before God. It is no accident that in Jerusalem, from a very early time, parts of the Canon were prayed in silence and that in the West the silent Canon— overlaid in part with meditative singing—became the norm. To dismiss all this as the result of misunderstandings is just too easy. It really is not true that reciting the whole Eucharistic Prayer out loud and without interruptions is a prerequisite for the participation of everyone in this central act of the Mass. My suggestion in 1978 was as follows. First, liturgical education ought to aim at making the faithful familiar with the essential meaning and fundamental orientation of the Canon. Secondly, the first words of the various prayers should be said out loud as a kind of cue for the congregation, so that each individual in his silent prayer can take up the intonation and bring the personal into the communal and the communal into the personal. Anyone who has experienced a church united in the silent praying of the Canon will know what a really *filled* silence is. It is at once a loud and penetrating cry to God and a Spirit-filled act of prayer. Here everyone does pray the Canon together, albeit in a bond with the special task of the priestly ministry. Here everyone is united, laid hold of by Christ, and led by the Holy Spirit into that common prayer to the Father which is the true sacrifice—the love that reconciles and unites God and the world.

6. Vestments

The liturgical attire worn by the priest during the celebration of Holy Mass should, first and foremost, make clear that he is not there as a private person, as this or that man, but stands in place of Another—Christ. What is merely private, merely individual, about him should disappear and make way for Christ. "[I]t is no longer I who live, but Christ who lives in me" (Gal 2:20). These words of St. Paul, in which, from his own, very personal experience of Christ, he describes the newness of the baptized person, apply in a special way to the priest in celebrating Mass. It is not he himself who is important, but Christ. It is not he himself whom he is communicating to men, but Christ. He makes himself the instrument of Christ, acting, not from his own resources, but as the messenger, indeed as the presence, of Another—*in persona Christi*, as the liturgical tradition says. Liturgical vestments are a direct reminder of those texts in which St. Paul speaks of being clothed with Christ: "For as many of you as were baptized into Christ have put on Christ" (Gal 3:27). In the epistle to the Romans, the image is connected with the opposition between two ways of living. To those who waste their lives in immoderate eating and drinking, in debauchery and licentiousness, St. Paul shows the Christian way: "But put on the Lord Jesus Christ, and make no provision for the flesh, to gratify its desires" (Rom 13:14). In the epistles to the Ephesians and Colossians, the same idea is interpreted in an even more fundamental way in relation to the anthropology of the new man: "[P]ut on the new nature, created after the likeness of God in true righteousness and holiness" (Eph 4:24). "[You] have put on the new nature, which is being renewed in knowledge after the image of its creator. Here there cannot be Greek and Jew, circumcised and uncircumcised, barbarian, Scythian, slave, free man, but Christ is all, and in all" (Col 3:10f.). The assumption is that the image of putting on Christ was developed by analogy with a man's putting on of the cultic mask of the deity when he was initiated into mystery cults. For St. Paul, there is no question any more of masks and rituals; rather, it is a matter of a process of spiritual transformation. The goal is the inward renewal of man, his real assimilation to God, and thus his unity, the overcoming of all the barriers that have been, and continue to be, erected in the history of human sinfulness. The image of putting on Christ is, therefore, a dynamic image, bearing on the transformation of man and the world, the new humanity. Vestments are a reminder of all this, of this transformation in Christ, and of the new community that is supposed to arise from it. Vestments are a challenge to the priest to surrender himself to the dynamism of breaking out of the capsule of self and being fashioned anew by Christ and for Christ. They remind those who participate in the Mass of the new way that began with Baptism and continues with the Eucharist, the way that leads to the future world already delineated in our daily lives by the sacraments.

In his two epistles to the Corinthians, St. Paul gives further elaboration to the eschatological orientation of the image of clothing. In the first epistle he says: "[T]his perishable nature must put on the imperishable, and this mortal nature must put on immortality" (15:53). The Apostle gives us an even deeper insight into his own hopes and struggles in the fifth chapter of the second epistle. Paul describes the body of this earthly time as an "earthly tent", which will be taken down, and looks ahead to the house not made with human hands, "eternal in the heavens". He is anxious about the taking down of the tent, anxious about the "nakedness" in which he will then find himself. His hope is to be, not "unclothed", but "further clothed", to receive the "heavenly house"—the definitive body—as a new garment. The Apostle does not want to discard his body, he does not want to be bodiless. He is not interested in any flight of the soul from the "prison of the body", as envisaged by the Pythagorean tradition taken up by Plato. He wants not flight but transformation. He hopes for resurrection. Thus the theology of clothing becomes a theology of the body. The body is more than an external dressing up of man—it is part of his very being, of his essential constitution. And yet this body is subject to decay. It is only a tent. It is provisional. But at the same time it is an anticipation of the definitive body, the definitive and complete form of human existence. The liturgical vestment carries this message in itself. It is a "further clothing", not an "unclothing", and the liturgy guides us on the way to this "further clothing", on the way to the body's salvation in the risen body of Jesus Christ, which is the new "house not made with hands, eternal in the heavens" (2 Cor 5:1). The Body of Christ, which we receive in the Eucharist, to which we are united in the Eucharist ("one Body with him", cf. 1 Cor 6:12–20), saves us from "nakedness", from the bareness in which we cannot stand before God. In the context of this teaching of St. Paul, I am very fond of the old formula for the distribution of Holy Communion: "The Body of our Lord Jesus Christ preserve thy soul unto everlasting life." These words turn the teaching of 2 Corinthians 5:1–10 into prayer. The soul on its own would be a sad fragment. But even before the general resurrection, it enters into the Body of Christ, which in a sense becomes our body, just as we are supposed to become his Body. The Body (of Christ) saves our soul for eternal life—for Greek thought a nonsensical paradox, but because of the risen Christ, living hope. The liturgical vestment has a meaning that goes beyond that of external garments. It is an anticipation of the new clothing, the risen Body of Jesus Christ, that new reality which awaits us when the earthly "tent" is taken down and which gives us a "place to stay" (cf. Jn 14:2: "In my Father's house are many rooms": the word translated "room" here really means "place to stay", highlighting the definitiveness, the privilege of having somewhere we can remain).

When the Fathers were thinking about the theology of clothing, two other biblical texts came to their minds, which I should like to include in my reflections here to give us a better understanding of liturgical vestments. First there is the story of the Prodigal Son, in which the father, having embraced his son on his return, gives this instruction: "Bring quickly the best robe . . ." (Lk 15:22). In the Greek text, it says "the *first* robe", and that is how the Fathers read and understood it. For them, the first robe is the robe in which Adam was created and which he lost after he had grasped at likeness to God. All the clothes subsequently worn by man are only a poor substitute for the light of God coming from within, which was Adam's true "robe". Thus, in reading the account of the Prodigal Son and his return, the Fathers heard the account of Adam's fall, the fall of man (cf. Gen 2:7), and interpreted Jesus' parable as a message about the return home and reconciliation of mankind as a whole. The man who in faith returns home receives back the first "robe", is clothed again in the mercy and love of God, which are his true beauty. The white garment presented at Baptism is meant to suggest these great connections in salvation history, and at the same time it points toward the white garment of eternity, of which the Apocalypse speaks (cf. 19:8)—an expression of the purity and beauty of the risen body. The great arch that connects Adam's creation and fall with the white garment of eternity is contained in the symbolism of liturgical vestments, and the cornerstone supporting the whole arch is Christ: "Put on Christ"—even now be one with him, even now be members of his Body.

7. Matter

The Catholic liturgy is the liturgy of the Word made flesh—made flesh for the sake of the resurrection. And, as we have seen, it is a cosmic liturgy. Thus it is clear that not only do the human body and signs from the cosmos play an essential role in the liturgy but that the matter of this world is part of the liturgy. Matter comes into the liturgy in two ways: first, in the form of many kinds of symbols—the holy fire of Easter night, the candle and the flame that burns on it, the various kinds of liturgical objects such as the bell, the altar cloth, and so on. In the last century, Romano Guardini opened up our understanding of this symbolic world in a new way by his little book *Sacred Signs*. Recently, Bishop Kapellari of Klagenfurt gave us a new book, with many pictures, in which Guardini's insights are developed, deepened, and applied to our present situation. There is no need, therefore, to discuss the matter here.

The second, even more important way in which matter comes into the liturgy is in the sacraments, the sacred actions that go back to Christ himself, which in the strict sense constitute the liturgy—precisely because they were not invented by men but were given to us in their substance by the Lord himself. Three of the seven sacraments relate directly to man as a person at very particular points in his life and consequently do not need any other "matter" than man himself in the situation to which the sacrament is ordered. First there is Penance, in which as sinners we beg for the word of forgiveness and renewal. Then there is Holy Orders, in which the Lord, by the bishop's laying on of hands, gives a man mission and authority in succession to the ministry of the apostles. Finally, there is Matrimony, in which two human beings give themselves to each other for a lifelong union and thereby become a real, living, and tangible image of the covenant between Christ and his Church (cf. Eph 5:27–32).

But then there are four sacraments—Baptism, Confirmation, the Eucharist, and the Anointing of the Sick—in which material things become the vessels of God's action upon us. It is not for this little book to develop a theology of the sacraments. I should just like to highlight the elements that come into the liturgy here as a mediation of the divine action. For these elements, which the Lord himself chose, are full of meaning. We need to meditate on them as such if we are to understand the spirit of the liturgy better. They are: water, (olive) oil, (wheaten) bread, and wine. Let us remember in parenthesis here that of the four elements in antiquity—water, air, fire, earth—the first three are all symbols of the Holy Spirit, while the earth represents man, who comes from the earth and to the earth returns. Fire and air in the form of breath are present in many ways in the symbolism of the liturgy, but only water, which comes from above and yet belongs to the earth, has become, as the primordial element of life, sacramental matter in the strict sense. The Church's tradition discerns a twofold symbolism in water. The salt water of the sea is a symbol of death, a threat and a danger; it reminds us of the Red Sea, which was deadly to the Egyptians, though the Israelites were rescued from it. Baptism is a kind of passing through the Red Sea. A death occurs within it. It is more than a bath or washing—it touches the very depths of existence, as far as death itself. It is a crucifying communion with Christ. This is precisely what is signified by the Red Sea, which is an image of death and resurrection (cf. Rom 6:1–11). On the other hand, water flowing from a spring is a symbol of the source of all life, *the* symbol of life. That is why the early Church laid down that Baptism had to be administered by means of "living water", spring water, so that Baptism could be experienced as the beginning of new life. In this connection, the Fathers always had at the back of their minds the conclusion of the Passion narrative according to St. John: blood and water flow from the opened side of Jesus; Baptism and Eucharist spring from the pierced heart of Jesus. He has become the living spring that makes us alive (cf. Jn 19:34f.; 1 Jn 5:6). At the Feast of Tabernacles Jesus had prophesied that streams of living water would flow from the man who came to him and drank: "Now this he said about the Spirit, which those who believed in him were to receive" (Jn 7:38). The baptized man himself becomes a spring. When we think of the great saints of history, from whom streams of faith, hope, and love really came forth, we can understand these words and thus understand something of the dynamism of Baptism, of the promise and vocation it contains.

When we look at the three other elements in the sacraments of the Church—olive oil, wheaten bread, and wine, we are struck by the characteristic that distinguishes them from the gift of water. Whereas water is the common element of life for the whole earth and is therefore suitable in all places as a door of entry to communion with Christ, in the case of the other three elements we are dealing with the typical gifts of Mediterranean culture. We encounter this triad in explicit association in the glorious psalm of creation, Psalm 104(103), where the Psalmist thanks God for giving man the food of the earth and "wine to gladden the heart of man, oil to make his face shine, and bread to strengthen man's heart" (v. 15). These three elements of Mediterranean life express the goodness of creation, in which we receive the goodness of the Creator himself. And now they become the gift of an even higher goodness, a goodness that makes our face shine anew in likeness to the "Anointed" God, to his beloved Son, Jesus Christ, a goodness that changes the bread and wine of the earth into the Body and Blood of the Redeemer, so that, through the Son made man, we may have communion with the triune God himself.

At this point comes the objection that these gifts have a symbolic force only in the Mediterranean area and that in other growing regions they ought to be replaced by elements appropriate to those regions. This is the same issue that we encountered when we were discussing the inversion of the cosmic symbolism of the seasons in the Southern Hemisphere. The answer we gave there applies again here: in the interplay of culture and history, history has priority. God has acted in history and, through history, given the gifts of the earth their significance. The elements become sacraments through connection with the unique history of God in relation to man in Jesus Christ. As we have said before, Incarnation does not mean doing as we please. On the contrary, it binds us to the history of a particular time. Outwardly, that history may seem fortuitous, but it is the form of history willed by God, and for us it is the trustworthy trace he has imprinted on the earth, the guarantee that we are not thinking up things for ourselves but are truly touched by God and come into touch with him. Precisely through what is particular and once-for-all, the here and now, we emerge from the "ever and never" vagueness of mythology. It is with this particular face, with this particular human form, that Christ comes to us, and precisely thus does he make us brethren beyond all boundaries. Precisely thus do we recognize him: "It is the Lord" (Jn 21:7).

V. Bibliography

General Works on the Liturgy

The presentation of the theology of the liturgy in the *Catechism of the Catholic Church* (CCC) is fundamental (cf. 1077–1112) [see editorial notes on parts C and D in the appendices of JRCW11].

Adam, Adolf, and Rupert Berger. *Pastoralliturgisches Handlexikon.* Freiburg, Basel, and Vienna: Herder, 1980 (new ed., 1999).

Corbon, Jean. *Liturgie de source.* Paris: Cerf, 1980. Translated by Matthew J. O'Connell as *The Wellspring of Worship* (New York: Paulist Press, 1988).

Kunzler, Michael. *Die Liturgie der Kirche.* AMATECA: Lehrbücher zur katholischen Theologie, vol. 10. Paderborn: Bonifatius, 1995.

———. *Porta orientalis: Fünf Ost-West-Versuche über Theologie und Ästhetik der Liturgie.* Paderborn: Bonifatius, 1993.

Lang, Bernhard. *Heiliges Spiel: Eine Geschichte des christlichen Gottesdienstes.* Munich: Beck, 1998.

Martimort, Aimé Georges, ed. *L'Église en prière: Introduction à la liturgie.* New ed. 4 vols. Paris: Desclée, 1983–1984. Translated by Matthew O'Connell as *The Church at Prayer: An Introduction to the Liturgy.* New ed. 4 vols. (Collegeville, Minn.: Liturgical Press, 1986–1988).

Meyer, Hans Bernhard, Hansjörg Auf der Maur, Balthasar Fischer, Angelus Albert Häussling, and Bruno Kleinheyer, eds. *Gottesdienst der Kirche: Handbuch der Liturgiewissenschaft.* Regensburg: Pustet, 1984–.

Nichols, Aidan, O.P. *Looking at the Liturgy: A Critical View of Its Contemporary Form.* San Francisco: Ignatius Press, 1996.

Ratzinger, Joseph. *Das Fest des Glaubens.* Einsiedeln: Johannes Verlag, 1981. Translated by Graham Harrison as *The Feast of Faith: Approaches to a Theology of the Liturgy* (San Francisco: Ignatius Press, 1986) [see editorial notes on parts C and D in the appendices of JRCW11].

————. *Ein neues Lied für den Herrn: Christusglaube und Liturgie in der Gegenwart.* Freiburg, Basel, and Vienna: Herder, 1995. Translated by Martha M. Matesich as *A New Song for the Lord: Faith in Christ and Liturgy Today* (New York: Crossroad, 1996).

Sartore, Domenico, and Achille Maria Triacca, eds. *Nuovo dizionario di liturgia.* Rome: Edizioni Paoline, 1983.

Chapter I.1

Particularly important for the theme of play is Johan Huizinga, *Homo ludens: Proeve eener bealing van het spel-element der cultuur* (Haarlem: Tjeenk Willink, 1938) (translated as: *Homo ludens: A Study of the Play-Element in Culture* [1950; Boston: Beacon Press, 1955]) as well as the precious little book of Hugo Rahner's, drawn entirely from the Fathers: *Der spielende Mensch* (Einsiedeln: Johannes Verlag, 1952), translated by Brian Battershaw and Edward Quinn as *Man at Play* (New York: Herder and Herder, 1967).

In *The Spirit of the Liturgy*, Romano Guardini to a large extent unfolded the special nature of the liturgy with the help of the concept of play. However, in the fourth and fifth printing (1920), he inserted a chapter on "The Seriousness of the Liturgy", which clearly limits the concept of play.

Chapter I.2

On the *exitus-reditus* theme:

Ratzinger, Joseph. *Die Geschichtstheologie des heiligen Bonaventura.* Munich and Zurich, 1959. 2nd ed., St. Ottilien: EOS, 1992. Translated by Zachary Hayes as *The Theology of History in St. Bonaventure.* Chicago, Ill.: Franciscan Herald Press, 1971.

Seckler, Max. *Das Heil in der Geschichte: Geschichtstheologisches Denken bei Thomas von Aquin.* Munich: Kösel, 1954.

Torrell, Jean-Pierre. *Initiation à St. Thomas d'Aquin.* Fribourg: Éditions universitaires, 1993. Translated by Robert Royal as *Saint Thomas Aquinas*, vol. 1 (Washington, D.C.: Catholic Univ. of America Press, 1996).

Chapter I.3

The view set out here, of the path from the Old Testament to the New and of the nature of the liturgy in general, is one I have developed over the course of many years through my acquaintance with the Scriptures and the liturgy. Preliminary sketches for it, together with references to the literature, can be found in the two works of mine mentioned above, *The Feast of Faith* and *A New Song for the Lord*, as well as in the article "Eucharistie und Mission" (*Forum katholische Theologie* 14 [1998]: 81–98), which has been published in several different languages.

Chapter II.1

On the "Church between the Testaments", see:

Ratzinger, Joseph. *Volk und Haus Gottes in Augustins Lehre von der Kirche,* 304–8. 2nd ed. St. Ottilien: EOS, 1992.

On *semel quia semper,* see:

St. Bernard of Clairvaux. *Sermo 5 de diversis* 1. In Bernhard von Clairvaux. *Sämtliche Werke, lateinisch/deutsch,* edited by Gerhard B. Winkler, 9:218. Innsbruck: Tyrolia, 1998.

Chapter II.2

My presentation here takes its bearings from Louis Bouyer. *Architecture et liturgie.* Paris: Cerf, 1991. The page numbers given refer to the English edition: *Liturgy and Architecture* (Notre Dame, Ind.: Univ. of Notre Dame Press, 1967).

From the abundant literature on this matter, I should like to mention only the following:

Norman, Edward Robert. *The House of God: Church Architecture, Style, and History.* New York: Thames and Hudson, 1990.
White, Lloyd Michael. *Building God's House in the Roman World.* Baltimore and London: Johns Hopkins Univ. Press, 1990.

Bibliography

Chapter II.3

Here once again I refer to Bouyer and my own *Feast of Faith*. More of the literature can be found in the latter [see editorial notes on parts C and D in the appendices of JRCW11].

Chapter II.4

On faith in the Real Presence and its unfolding in theology, see:

Betz, Johannes. *Eucharistie in der Schrift und Patristik*, HDG, ed. Schmaus, Grillmeier, Scheffczyk, and Seybold. Vol. 4, pt. 4a. Freiburg, Basel, and Vienna: Herder, 1979.
————. *Die Eucharistie in der Zeit der griechischen Väter*. Vol. 2, pt. 1. Freiburg: Herder, 1961.
Gerken, Alexander. *Theologie der Eucharistie*. Munich: Kösel, 1973.
Lubac, Henri de. *Corpus mysticum: L'Eucharistie et l'Église au moyen âge*. 2nd ed. Paris: Aubier, 1949. Translated by Gemma Simmonds, with Richard Price and Christopher Stephens, as *Corpus Mysticum: The Eucharist and the Church in the Middle Ages: Historical Survey* (Notre Dame, Ind.: Univ. of Notre Dame Press, 2007).
Sayes, José Antonio. *La presencia real de Cristo en la Eucaristia*. BAC 386. Madrid: EDICA, 1976.

Chapter II.5

As always, the handbooks of liturgiology mentioned above should be consulted. On the question of Sunday, see also my own book *A New Song for the Lord*.

In addition, see:

Fedalto, Giorgio. *Quando festeggiare il 2000? Problemi di cronologia cristiana*. Milan: Edizioni San Paolo, 1998.
Rahner, Hugo. *Griechische Mythen in christlicher Deutung*. Darmstadt, 1957; 3rd ed., Basel: Herder, 1989; new ed., Freiburg: Herder, 1993. Translated by Brian Battershaw as *Greek Myths and Christian Mystery* (New York: Harper and Row, 1963). My references to the Fathers are taken from this book.

Schade, Herbert. *Lamm Gottes und Zeichen des Widders: Zur kosmologisch-psychologischen Hermeneutik der Ikonographie des "Lammes Gottes".* Edited by Viktor H. Elbern. Freiburg, Basel, and Vienna: Herder, 1998.

Voss, Gerhard. "Christen auf der Suche nach einem gemeinsamen Osterdatum", parts 1 and 2, especially 2. In KNA. *Ökumenische Information* 24 (June 9, 1998): 5–10.

Weigl, Eduard. "Die Oration *Gratiam tuam, quaesumus, Domine:* Zur Geschichte des 25 März in der Liturgie". In *Passauer Studien: Festschrift für Bischof Simon Konrad Landersdorfer*, ed. by Josef Oswald, Anton Mayer, and Joseph Blinzler, 57–73. Passau, 1953.

Chapter III.1

Evdokimov, Paul. *L'Art de l'icône: Théologie de la beauté.* Paris: Desclée, 1970. Translated by Steven Bigham as *The Art of the Icon: A Theology of Beauty* (Redondo Beach, Calif.: Oakwood Pub., 1990). The page numbers given refer to the English edition of this book.

Onasch, Konrad. *Kunst und Liturgie der Ostkirche in Stichworten unter Berücksichtigung der Alten Kirche.* Vienna, Cologne, and Graz: Böhlau, 1981.

Van der Meer, Frederik. *Die Ursprünge christlicher Kunst.* Freiburg, Basel, and Vienna: Herder, 1982.

Various authors. *Arte e liturgia: L'arte sacra a trent'anni dal Concilio.* Milan: Edizioni San Paolo, 1983.

Chapter III.2

Fellerer, Karl Gustaf, ed. *Geschichte der katholischen Kirchenmusik.* 2 vols. Kassel: Bärenreiter, 1972–1976. Translated by Francis A. Brunner as *The History of Catholic Church Music* (Westport, Conn.: Greenwood Press, 1979).

Forte, Bruno. *La porta della bellezza: Per un'estetica teologica.* Especially 85–108. Brescia: Morcelliana, 1999.

Jaschinski, Eckhard. *Musica sacra oder Musik im Gottesdienst? Die Entstehung der Aussaagen über die Kirchenmusik in der Liturgiekonstitution "Sacrosanctum concilium" (1963) und bis zur Instruktion "Musicam sacram" (1967),* Studien zur Pastoralliturgie 8. Regensburg: Pustet, 1990.

Bibliography

Ravasi, Gianfranco. *Il canto della rana: Musica et teologia nella Bibbia.* Casale Monferrato: Piemme, 1990.

I should also like to refer especially to the relevant chapters in *Feast of Faith* and *A New Song for the Lord* [see editorial notes on parts C and D in the appendices of JRCW11].

Chapter IV.1

A good survey of the Eastern rites can be found in:

Bux, Nicola. *Il quinto sigillo: L'unità dei cristiani verso il terzo millennio.* Vatican City: Libreria editrice Vaticana, 1997.
Vazheeparampil, Prasanna. *The Making and Unmaking of Tradition: Towards a Theology of the Liturgical Renewal in the Syro-Malabar Church.* Especially the diagram of the rites on 57. Rome: Mar Thoma Yogam, 1998.

For information about the large world of the non-Byzantine Eastern Churches, the great work by Mahmoud Zibawi is very important: *Orienti cristiani: Senso e storia di un'arte tra Bisanzio e l'Islam.* Milan: Jaca Book, 1995.
I should also like to refer to the article "Liturgien", in LThK, 3rd ed. 6:972–87 (authors: Andreas Heinz, Hans-Jürgen Feulner, Karl-Heinrich Bieritz, and Teresa Berger).

Chapter IV.2

Cordes, Paul Josef. *Actuosa participatio—tätige Teilnahme: Pastorale Annäherung an die Eucharistiefeier in kleinen Gemeinschaften.* Paderborn: Bonifatius, 1995.
Dinkler, Erich. *Signum crucis: Aufsätze zum Neuen Testament und zur christlichen Archäologie.* Especially 1–76. Tübingen: Mohr, 1967.
Rahner, Hugo. *Griechische Mythen in christlicher Deutung.* Darmstadt, 1957; 3rd ed., Basel: Herder, 1989; new ed., Freiburg: Herder, 1993. Translated by Brian Battershaw as *Greek Myths and Christian Mystery* (New York: Harper and Row, 1963).

A helpful synthesis of the patristic testimonies is provided by Vinzenz Pfnür, "Das Kreuz: Lebensbaum in der Mitte des Paradiesgartens", in *Garten des Lebens: Festschrift für Winfrid Cramer*, ed. Maria Barbara von Stritzky and Christian Uhrig, 203–22. Altenberge: Oros, 1999.

The section on kneeling is to a large extent dependent on:

Sinoir, Michel. *La Prière à genoux dans l'Écriture Sainte*. Paris: Téqui, ca. 1997.

Many references relevant to the various sections of this chapter can be found in the book mentioned above, *Arte e liturgia: L'arte sacra a trent'anni dal Concilio* (Milan: Edizioni San Paolo, 1983), especially 139–209.

Kapellari, Egon. *Heilige Zeichen in Liturgie und Alltag*. Graz, Vienna, and Cologne: Styria, 1997.

PART B

TYPOS—MYSTERIUM—SACRAMENTUM

I. The Sacramental Foundation
of Christian Existence

*1. Preliminary Considerations: The Crisis of the Sacramental
Idea in Modern Consciousness*

In the present intellectual situation, whoever attempts to reflect on
the sacramental basis of Christian existence will immediately run into
a remarkable paradox of contemporary intellectual life: on the one
hand, our age has been called the century of the Church; it could just
as well be called the century of the liturgical and sacramental movement, for the discovery of the Church that took place in the time
between the two world wars is based on the rediscovery of the spiritual riches of ancient Christian liturgy and on the discovery of the
sacramental principle. Perhaps the most fruitful theological idea of our
century, the mystery theology of Odo Casel, belongs to the field of
sacramental theology, and one can probably say without exaggeration
that not since the end of the patristic era has the theology of the
sacraments experienced such a flowering as was granted to it in this
century in connection with Casel's ideas, which in turn can be understood only against the background of the Liturgical Movement and its
rediscovery of ancient Christian liturgy.

But all of this is still only one side of the facts of the case. For our
century of the Liturgical Movement and the renewal of sacramental theology is experiencing at the same time a crisis of sacramentality, an alienation from the reality of the sacrament that can scarcely have existed
with such severity and intensity within Christianity before. In a time
when we have grown accustomed to seeing in the substance of things
nothing but the material for human labor—when, in short, the world is
regarded as matter and matter as material—initially there is no room left
for that symbolic transparency of reality toward the eternal on which the

Translated by Kenneth Baker, S.J., and Michael J. Miller.

sacramental principle is based. Oversimplifying somewhat, one could indeed say that the sacramental idea presupposes a symbolist understanding of the world, whereas the contemporary understanding of the world is functionalist: it sees things *merely* as things, as a function of human labor and accomplishment, and given such a starting point, it is no longer possible to understand how a "thing" can become a "sacrament". Let us put it in even more practical terms: the man of today is certainly interested in the question of God, and he is even concerned about the problem of Christ; but the sacraments are something altogether too religious for him, all too bound up with a past stage of faith for him to see any practical reason even to begin discussing them. Is it not an unwarranted assumption to imagine that pouring a little water on a person should be existentially decisive for him? Or the imposition of hands by a bishop, which we call Confirmation? Or the anointing with a bit of consecrated oil that is given by the Church to a sick person to accompany him on the last stretch of his journey? And here and there even priests are starting to ask whether the laying on of hands by the bishop, which is called Holy Orders, really can signify an irrevocable commitment of a man's life down to his final hour and whether in this case the significance of the rite has not been overrated, since—they say—ultimately one cannot subordinate to it each day's experience as it occurs, with its ever-open future, with its imponderable circumstances, and with its ever new and urgent situations. The idea of the indelible character that such sacraments imprint on the soul seems to contemporary man an exceedingly strange, mystical philosophy: for him the existence of man is something that remains perpetually open, that grows through making decisions and cannot be sealed forever through a single ritual act. Similar ideas, of course, are then proposed against the sacramental view of marriage as well, and even the Eucharist is not spared such questions: the concept of substance, with which the idea of transubstantiation appears closely connected, seems to have become completely irrelevant, especially since bread, considered chemically and physically, is a mixture of heterogeneous materials that consist of an immense number of atoms, which in turn break down into a multiplicity of elementary particles, to which, finally, given the interplay of their corpuscular and wave-like character, no fixed substantial being can be attributed. Therefore what is "transubstantiation" supposed to mean? How and where can Christ's flesh and blood be present here? And what are we then to make of the fact that man eats and drinks the flesh and blood of Christ? Is this not a resurgence of the mythological idea that man can be influenced spiritually by earthly nourishment—a magical-mystical notion, therefore, that runs entirely counter to our knowledge of psychology and physiology? And eventually all this is inevitably condensed into the question about the meaning of Christian worship in the first place. Why, really, do I have to go to church in order to encounter God? Is God then bound to a rite and to a place? Can what is spiritual be mediated or even bound by ritual and material means? If anyone wants to and does or perhaps even needs to live on this level, let him do so, modern man will say, confident that he dwells on the heights of contemporary consciousness and is fully cognizant, moreover, of the fact that even today there are still people on a medieval or ancient or utterly primitive level of consciousness. But he himself will not be bound to levels of consciousness that he is convinced are relics of the past that the future will gradually eliminate, even if it will never be able to remove completely the undercurrent of primitive thinking, so that mankind in practice will always consist of a coexistence of different levels of consciousness.

Therefore, what should we say? Is the continued existence of the sacraments in our time nothing more than a concession to the past, to the invincibly primitive character of one part of mankind? Is it an aesthetic embellishment from the spirit of a long-gone world that modern man, too, tolerates with critical awareness, or is it an abiding claim and a reality that is still an existentially foundational reality today? A liturgical renewal that did not ask these basic questions would necessarily remain superficial and could hardly avoid the danger of becoming a merely aesthetic business. In order to attempt an answer to the question about the relation between sacrament and Christian existence, we must ask two questions that are announced in the two topics of this lecture: What is a sacrament? And: What is human existence? The two questions, however, overlap so much that it may suffice to analyze the question about sacrament so as to listen at the same time within it to the question about man's existence and thus to provide an answer to both questions.

2. The Sacramental Idea in Human History

What is a sacrament? The question is very far-reaching; the scope of it changes depending upon whether the question is posed in terms of the history of religion or theologically, and within theology it makes a difference whether one approaches the question historically or dogmatically, for in different periods of Christian history the word "sacrament" meant different things. Let us not hesitate to reflect on all three aspects of the question, for in a certain sense they all belong to the theme of the sacraments and the less exclusively we proceed with the questioning, the more comprehensive the answer can be. First of all, concerning human history on the whole, we will thus be able to establish that there is in it something like primeval sacraments, which appear with a sort of inherent necessity wherever men live together, and that in many metamorphoses they even extend into the de-sacramentalized technological world. One could call them creation sacraments, which develop at the important junctures of human existence and reveal both a picture of the essence of man and also the nature of his relation to God. Such important junctures are birth and death, a meal, and sexual relations. Obviously we are dealing with realities that do not actually proceed from the spiritual dimension of man but, rather, proceed from his biological nature, the junctures of his biological life, which is constantly realized and renewed in the taking of nourishment and in sexual relations, but in birth and death mysteriously experiences its limits, its contact with what is uncontrollable, greater, and other, out of which it perpetually rises but which also seems to swallow it up again immediately. These biological givens, the real actualizations of the stream of life in which man participates, acquire of course in man, as an entity that extends beyond the biological, a new dimension; they become—to use Schleiermacher's words—the fissures through which the eternal looks into the uniformity of the human routine. Precisely because these events are biological and not spiritual, man has in them an experience of being overwhelmed by a power that he can neither summon nor control, that already embraces and carries him along even before his decisions. This already suggests a further point: what is biological in man, as an entity that exists spiritually, acquires a new meaning and a new depth. Human eating is something different from the food intake of an animal: eating attains its human dimension by becoming a meal. Having a meal, however, means experiencing the delightfulness of those things whereby men are supplied with the gift of the earth's fertility, and having a meal means to experience also, in such a reception of the choice things of the earth, the company of other men: a meal creates community, eating is complete only when it happens in company, and human coexistence achieves its fullness in the community of nourishment that unites everyone in the common interest of receiving the gifts of this earth. But in this way the meal becomes a very penetrating interpretation of what it means to be a man, of human existence, for which we wanted to be on the lookout along with the question about the sacraments. In a meal man discovers that he is not the founder of his own being but lives his existence in receptivity. He experiences himself as someone who has been endowed, who lives on the unmerited gift of a fruitfulness that seems always to be waiting for him, as it were. And what is more: he experiences the fact that his existence, his "being-there" [*Dasein*], is grounded in communion with, or "being-with" [*Mitsein mit*], the world, in whose stream of life he is immersed, and that it is founded on communion with men, without which his humanity would lose the ground under its feet. Man is not founded on himself; rather, he is founded through a twofold "with": communion with things, communion with people; man can exist only in the plural, so to speak. But in this double "with" is concealed a third, no less fundamental thing: his mind *is* only by communion with the body, just as, of course, his body too, his biological being, consists only of being in terms of his rational dimension.

The communion of the mind with the body, however, includes being immersed into the unity of the cosmic stream of life and thus expresses a fundamental interconnectedness of all those beings who are privileged to be called human: this is the starting point of that deep-seated community which the Bible suggests when it calls all mankind a single Adam. Of course in the connection to one another that is produced by a common biological life, there is still at the same time the reason for a deep-seated separation of men from one another that ultimately keeps them from being of one mind and from finding their way to full community: we will have to reflect more on this.

The phenomenon of the meal led us unexpectedly to an initial outline of an answer to the question "what is man?", although our actual purpose in taking it up had been to get a view of one of the primeval sacraments identified by the history of religions. But the two things do overlap, and the interpretation of being human that just now forced itself on us is the interpretation on which the sacramental idea is based. For we can say now, in a first attempt at formulating it, that in the transformation of mere eating into the meal the original formation of the sacramental principle is accomplished: eating that has become a meal already bears sacramental traits in and of itself. The man who in a meal not only attempts the unspiritual biological act of food intake but also performs this biological act rationally, spiritually—the man, therefore, who considers human nature to be indivisible and thus considers what is biological to be human also—this man experiences in a meal the transparency of the sensible toward the spiritual; he experiences that interpenetration of *bios* and spirit which is his inmost essence. He discovers that things are more than things: that they are signs whose meaning extends beyond their immediate sensorial power. And when he experiences the foundation of his existence in a meal, then he knows that things give him more than they themselves have and are. In this way, however, the meal becomes for him a sign of the divine and the eternal that supports him and all things and men and is the real foundation of his existence. But at the same time he knows that since he himself is spirit only as body and body only from spirit, this divine element can meet him in no other way than in the sphere in which he has his humanity, namely, through the medium of common humanity and corporeality, without which he would necessarily cease to be a man. The sacrament in its universal form in the history of religion is therefore at first simply the expression of the experience that God encounters man in a human way: in the signs of common humanity and in the change of the merely biological into the human, which when accomplished in the context of religion undergoes a transformation into a third dimension—the authentication of the divine in the human.

Right at this point it would not be difficult to formulate an initial answer to the crisis of sacramental thinking, the starting point of our reflections, and to expose the truncated anthropology on which it is based. But it is probably better to set aside this thought for now and to continue developing the sacramental concept as we intended. Upon closer inspection, the facts of the case that we have encountered so far contain something remarkable in themselves: the primordial sacramental forms found in human history are connected, not with specific spiritual and religious events, but with intensifications of the biological dimension of human existence; indeed, they are, as it were, the experience of the "transparency" of the biological, through which man can glimpse the spiritual and the eternal. Then, over the course of history, the specifically human and spiritual domain developed its sacramental junctures, two of which especially stand out here. The first one arises from the primordial human experience of guilt. Man, who does not fashion his own existence but lives on an ontological endowment, experiences at the same time a sense of being obligated, of being governed by a predetermined form; failure to conform to it makes him guilty. Consequently, there is something like a sacrament of penance from the very beginning of human history, and St. Bonaventure, the great medieval Franciscan theologian, was not completely wrong when he said that two sacraments had already been instituted at the beginning of history and that they are as old as man himself: the sacraments of marriage and penance. In the religions of many nations, this has degenerated into the strangest external observances: it became a cult of washing or rituals of purification, of transferring guilt to animals or slaves, but in all of these somewhat repulsive, somewhat foolish rites, one still hears something like the stammering of an awareness that man experiences the nearness of his god by bowing down under the truth about his guilt; and when an attempt is made to cleanse the spiritual by corporeal methods, however absurd one may consider such a procedure, such rites still contain a moving cry for purification.

A second pattern of sacrament-like structure is found in the office of kings and priests: these decisive ministries in the community point again to the very basis of what is human, and their importance is not exhaustively defined by their social purposefulness; they are, rather, the expression of the transparency of the human toward the divine and at the same time the expression of the awareness that the human community is firmly anchored only when it does not depend merely on itself but, rather, is founded on what is greater than itself. Here of course we must add another remark that at the same time leads to the Christian formulation of the question. While the first group of sacramental patterns that we encountered is based on the relation of *bios* and spirit and, hence, causes the perpetual character of the connection between man and cosmos to become a sign for the connection between the divine and the human, the second group starts with the specifically human dimension of man, from which his individual and collective history accrues to him—a history that represents what is special and unique about him, as opposed to the everlasting sameness of cosmic death and becoming. In this respect, another basic type of sacrament could have arisen here, as we observed previously, which would have understood history as existentially fundamental for man and would have seen in historical events the mediation of the eternal. On the whole, however, that did not happen in non-Christian lands. Rather, the historical community is perceived as a copy of the cosmos, and the mediation of the divine that occurs within it is ultimately reduced to the cosmic-natural idea.

3. The Christian Sacraments

At this point we can now finally raise the question that is unavoidably suggested by the previous considerations: What is distinctive about Christianity? What is special about it in a world that at one time was influenced everywhere by the sacramental idea? Karl Barth protested, but—to say it at the outset—I do not think he is correct in seeing a strict opposition between religion and faith, so that the [Christian] faith would only be something totally other, completely discontinuous with all the religious history of mankind; nor do I think that the oversimplifications entailed in the notion of anonymous Christianity are right in suddenly trying now to declare the whole world always to have been anonymously Christian anyway. The reality is more complicated than such oversimplifications may admit.

What is a Christian sacrament? As already noted at the start, this word did not have from the beginning the clearly defined meaning that we attach to it today. In the early Church, sacraments were understood to include historical events, words of Holy Scripture, realities of Christian worship that have a transparency to the salvific act of Jesus Christ and, thus, make the eternal shine through into the temporal, indeed, cause it to become present as the truly fundamental reality. For example, in patristic language the story of the deluge can be called a "sacrament", because in it we glimpse something of the mystery of that new beginning which is accomplished in destruction—this structure is continued in the death of Jesus Christ on the Cross, in which the tides of death, as it were, crash down on him, yet the sinking of the old clears the way for the Resurrection, for his definitive presence in the midst of all those who believe in him; the same structure then reaches farther into history in the rite of Baptism, in which man lets the waters of death pass over him so as to enter into the new beginning that started with Christ. Another example: the wedding feast at

Cana is called a sacrament, because in that change of water into wine shines forth the mystery of the new wine with which Christ desired to fill the jugs of mankind by his Passion. And so many other examples could be given.

If we reflect on what has been said thus far, we can ascertain various similarities with the general "anthropological" idea of sacrament, but we can also clearly recognize already traces of what is distinctively Christian; this distinction initially and necessarily results simply through the clarification of the concept of God: who God is no longer remains in dark secrecy; no more does he appear as the unfathomable mystery of the cosmos in general, but, rather, he appears as the God of Abraham, Isaac, and Jacob; more precisely, as the God of Jesus Christ: as the God who is here for men and is defined precisely by his being with people. In a word: he appears as the personal God who is knowledge and love and who therefore is word and love with respect to us. Word that calls us, and the love that unites us.

With that presupposition, our previous findings certainly come into play in this new context: if historical events, words of Scripture, and cultic realities can be called sacraments, then this means that the early Christian concept of sacrament included an interpretation of the world, of man, and of God that is convinced of the fact that things are not just things and material for our labor; rather, they are at the same time signs pointing beyond themselves of that divine love toward which they become transparent for someone who has sight. "Water" is not just H_2O, a chemical compound that one can change by an appropriate method into other compounds and use for all sorts of purposes—in the water from a spring that the thirsty traveler encounters in the desert, something becomes visible of the mystery of refreshment that creates new life in the midst of despair; in the powerful waves of a river, on whose crests the brightness of the sun is reflected, something becomes visible of the might of the glory of creative love and also of the deadly force with which it can hit the man who gets in its way; in the majesty of the sea glimmers something of the mystery that we designate with the word "eternity". That is just one example to suggest what is meant when we say: Things are more than things. They are not known exhaustively when one has understood their chemical and physical properties, because then another whole dimension of their reality still eludes one: their transparency toward the creative power of the God from which they come and toward which they try to lead. The sacramental idea of the early Church is the expression of a symbolic understanding of the world that does not in the least dispute the earthly reality of things but at the same time points to a content that remains inaccessible to chemical analysis and yet does not cease to be real—to the dimension of the eternal, which is perceptible and present in the midst of the temporal.

Again it is clear that with that we have said something decisive about man: just as things are not merely things, material for human labor, so man is not merely a functionary who manipulates things; rather, only by examining the world with respect to its eternal first cause does man learn who he himself is: someone called by God and to God. Only the call of the eternal constitutes man as man. One could actually define him as the being capable of God: what theology tries to designate with the term "soul" is of course nothing other than the fact that man is known and loved by God in another way than all the other beings below him—known in order to know in return, loved in order to love in return. This sort of staying in God's memory is what makes man live forever—for God's memory never ends; it is what makes a human being man and distinguishes him from animals; if this is ruled out, then, instead of man, only a more highly developed animal is left. But in this way it has become a bit clearer in what sense we may speak about the sacramental foundation of human existence: If being called by God not only brings about man's humanity but constitutes it, then the transparency of the world toward the eternal, which is the basis of the sacramental principle, belongs to the foundation of his existence. Then sacramental communication with the eternal establishes man himself.

We must, however, take yet another step. For the Christian sacraments mean not only insertion into the God-permeated cosmos—in a certain sense, as we have seen, this could be shown absolutely even in the pre-Christian world—they mean at the same time insertion into the history that originates in Christ. Indeed, this addition of the historical dimension represents the distinctively Christian transformation of the sacramental idea, which for the first time gives to natural symbolism its binding force and its concrete claim, cleanses it of all ambiguity and makes it into a more certain guarantee for the nearness of the one true God, who is not just (for example) the mysterious abyss of the cosmos but, rather, its Lord and Creator. This truly Christian element, which we are thus beginning to track down, is of course simultaneously the real stumbling block for contemporary man, who at any event is still ready to attribute some divine mystery to the cosmos but is not quite capable of seeing how the fortuitousness of a series of historical events could possibly contain the decisive factor of his human destiny. And yet that should not be so impossible to understand. For indeed, man is historically determined, from the ground up; it is precisely his *essence* to be *historical*: one cannot contrast a timeless enduring essence with the change and chance of history without misunderstanding man fundamentally, for in him history and essence coincide and the one is real only in the other.

Let us say it more concretely: my humanity is realized in the word, in the language that shapes my thought and initiates me into the neighborly community that influences my own humanity. Language, however, which we may describe as the essential medium for realizing human existence, is not something that I myself create; indeed, it fulfills its purpose precisely through and in the fact that it unites me with the men around me and with the men before me: language is the expression of the continuity of the human mind in the historical development of its nature. But in this way it becomes evident that being human excludes all autonomy of the bare ego that tries to be self-sufficient: my humanity initially receives its foundation as well as the sphere of its possibilities and accomplishments through history, out of which and in which alone it is able to be. What is seemingly fortuitous in history is the essential thing for man (to repeat this once again); certainly, to the collective model into which he enters, he can add his own personal initiatives to a greater or lesser extent and, thus, become guilty or saved, but he cannot break loose from history and abandon it for a supposedly pure nature, which is a utopia wherein he misunderstands himself.

With that we can return again to the Christian sacraments, whose meaning is none other than the insertion of man into the historical context that comes from Christ. To receive the Christian sacraments means to enter into the history proceeding from Christ with the belief that this is the saving history that opens up to man the historical context that truly allows him to live and leads him into his true uniqueness—into the unity with God that is his eternal future. So now, recapitulating, we can determine in what sense the sacraments are fundamental for Christian existence: first of all, they express the vertical dimension of human existence; they refer to the call of God that makes a man human in the first place. But they also point beyond that to the horizontal dimension of the history of faith that comes to us from Christ, for human existence in its concrete form rests on this horizontal dimension—it is historically mediated and comes into its own only in this historical mediation. In the confusion of human history that initially seems to ensnare man in the inescapability of guilt, the sacraments lead him into the historical context with that man who was at the same time God; they thus provide for him, in the midst of the insurmountable connection with history and precisely through it, a liberating union with God's eternal love, which has fit itself into this horizontal dimension and thereby has broken into his prison: the chain of the horizontal that binds man has become in Christ the guide rope of salvation that pulls us to the shore of God's eternity.

Let us consider another point: without noticing it, we have already arrived, with this analysis of the sacramental dimension of Christian life, at the narrower dogmatic concept of sacrament in contemporary theology, whose chief characteristics we duly learned from our catechism: institution by Christ—outward sign—interior grace. Why these three belong together and why they constitute the reality called "sacrament" should now have become clear to some extent: the visible realities that (already in terms of their creaturely definition) display, as it were, a certain permeability for the Creator-God have acquired a new, existentially decisive meaning by the fact that they are inserted into the context of the history of Christ and have become means of mediating this new historical context. Because they have now taken over the function of directing man into this historical sphere, they have become carriers of his historical significance and his spiritual might and thus, in truth, salvific forces and a pledge of the coming glory.

4. The Meaning of the Sacraments Today

Perhaps the preceding considerations were a bit laborious. That could not be helped, but still it had the advantage of clearing away the rubble of prejudices that separates us men of today from those insights that are expressed, indeed, embodied in the Christian sacraments. Now it would not be difficult to investigate the meaning of the individual sacraments and thereby to make concrete the general insights to which the preceding considerations have led us. Let us refrain from doing that and simply make clear once again in a summary fashion what limitations of perspective separate contemporary man—that is, us—from the sacraments and what the Christian truly seeks when he celebrates his divine liturgy in the form of receiving the sacraments and, thus, in the manner of the Church of Jesus Christ. I believe that the hostile attitude toward the sacraments that is part of the average mentality today is based on a twofold anthropological error that originates in the presuppositions of our time (that is, in the historical form that precedes and receives us) and has sunk deep into the universal consciousness. The first influence still at work is the idealistic misreading of human nature that reached its extreme exaggeration in the writings of Fichte, as though each man were an autonomous spirit who constructs himself wholly out of his own decision-making ability and is entirely the product of his own choices—nothing but will and freedom, which tolerates nothing unspiritual but, rather, forms himself completely by himself. Fichte's creative ego rests, to put it mildly, on a confusion of man with God, and the identification of the two that he in fact makes is an altogether logical expression of his approach and of course at the same time its categorical condemnation, for man is not God: all it takes to know that, basically, is to be a human being oneself. As absurd as this idealism is in the final analysis, it is still has deep roots in the European (at least in the German) consciousness.

When Bultmann says that spirit cannot be nourished by material things and with that thinks he has dispensed with the sacramental principle, ultimately the same naïve notion about man's spiritual autonomy is still at work. Actually it strikes us as a bit odd that precisely in the period that believes it has rediscovered man's corporeality and also thinks it knows that man can be spirit only by way of corporeality, a spiritual metaphysics based on the denial of these connections continues to operate or has even just reached the apogee of its influence. To be fair, we will of course have to admit that Christian metaphysics, long before Fichte, ingested an all-too-strong dose of Greek idealism and in this way did a considerable amount to prepare the way for this misunderstanding. It, too, already regarded human souls to a great extent as isolated atoms, constructing themselves in ahistorical freedom; thus it could scarcely explain any more the historically determined articles of the Christian faith concerning original sin and redemption; instead of the sacraments, which are the expression of the historical inter-twining of men, we find the soul food of the self-sufficient individual spirit, in which case one can of course wonder why God did not choose a simpler path and present himself as spirit to man's spirit so as to impart his grace to him. If it were only a question of the individual soul being addressed as an individual by its God and receiving grace, then indeed it would not be clear what significance the interference of the Church and the material means of the sacraments are supposed to have in this very intimate, altogether interior and spiritual process. If, however, there is no such thing as the autonomy of the human spirit, if it is not a spiritual atom without relations to others but, rather, can live as a man only corporeally, with his fellow men and histori-cally, then the question is fundamentally different. Then his relation-ship to God, if it is to be a human relationship to God, must be just as man is: corporeal, fraternal, and historical. Or there is no such thing. The error of anti-sacramental idealism consists in the fact that it wants to make man into a pure spirit in God's sight. Instead of a man, the only thing remaining is a ghost that does not exist, and any religiosity that tried to build on such foundations has built on shifting sand.

Connected today in a peculiar way with the idealistic heresy (if we wish to call it that) is the Marxist heresy, about which Heidegger wit-tily said that materialism consists, not really in the fact that it inter-prets all being as matter but, rather in the fact that it classifies all matter as mere material for human labor. Indeed, here in the anthro-pological extension of the ontological approach lies the real heart of the heresy: in the reduction of man to *homo faber*, who does not deal with things in themselves but considers them only as functions of work, whose functionary he himself has become. With that, the symbolic perspective and man's ability to see the eternal fall by the wayside; he is now imprisoned in his world of work, and his only hope is that later generations will be able to have better working conditions than he did, if he has toiled sufficiently for the creation of such conditions. A truly paltry consolation for an existence that has become miserably confined!

With these perspectives we have automatically returned once again to the starting point of our considerations. We can now ask the ques-tion again in this way: What does a man actually do when he cel-ebrates the divine liturgy of the Church, the sacraments of Jesus Christ? He does not resign himself to the naïve notion that the omnipresent

God would dwell only in this precise place that is designated by the tabernacle in the church. That would contradict even the most superficial knowledge of the Church's dogmatic teaching, for the specific feature of the Eucharist is not the presence of God in general but rather the presence of the man Jesus Christ, which points to the horizontal, historically bound character of man's encounter with God. Someone who goes to church and receives the sacraments does this, if he understands the whole situation correctly, not because he thinks the spiritual God needs material means in order to touch man's spirit. He does this, on the contrary, because he knows that he, being a man, can encounter God only in a human way; but in a human way means: in the form of fraternal solidarity, corporeality, and historicity. And he does this because he knows that he, as a man, cannot personally control when and how and where God has to manifest himself to him, that he is, on the contrary, the one receiving, the one dependent on the fullness of power that is simply given and not to be produced on his own authority. That power is the sign of the sovereign freedom of God, who himself determines the mode of his presence.

No doubt, our piety in this regard has often proceeded somewhat superficially and has been the occasion for various misunderstandings. In this respect, the critical question of modern consciousness can provoke a salutary purification in the self-understanding of faith. In conclusion, it may suffice to offer another example, in which the crisis becomes particularly clear and in which the basic idea of the purification that is needed can come to light once again by way of summary. Eucharistic adoration or a quiet visit in church, if it is to make sense, cannot simply be a conversation with the God who is thought to be present in a circumscribed locality. Statements such as "God dwells here" and conversations with the "local" God that are justified in this way manifest a misunderstanding of both the Christian mystery and the concept of God that is necessarily repellent to a thinking man who knows about God's omnipresence. If someone wished to justify going to church on the grounds that one must pay a visit to the God who is present only there, then that would in fact be a reason that made no sense and would rightly be rejected by modern man. Eucharistic adoration is in truth related to the Lord, who through his historical life and suffering has become "Bread" for us; in other words, through his Incarnation and self-abandonment to death he has become the One who is open for us. Such prayer is therefore related to the historical mystery of Jesus Christ, to God's history with men that moves toward us in the sacrament. And it is related to the mystery of the Church: since it is related to the history of God with men, it is related to the whole "Body of Christ", to the community of believers, in which and through which God comes to us. In this way praying in church and before the Blessed Sacrament is the "classification" of our relation to God under the mystery of the Church as the specific locality where God meets us. And finally, this is the purpose of our going to church at all: so that I in an orderly fashion may take my place in God's history with men—the only setting in which I as a man have my true human existence and which alone therefore also opens up for me the true space of my encounter with God's eternal love. For this love does not seek merely an isolated spirit, which (as we have already said) would be only a ghost compared with man's reality; rather, it seeks man utterly and entirely, in the body of his historicity, and it gives him in the holy signs of the sacraments the guarantee of a divine answer in which the open question of being human arrives at its goal and comes to its fulfillment.

II. On the Concept of Sacrament

Christians today are still very familiar with the concept of "sacrament"; they encounter it continually in the Christian life. Yet it is very far removed from contemporary man's consciousness and life experience. To him a sacrament seems to be something strange that he is inclined to relegate to a magical or mythical age of mankind; he cannot quite figure out where it belongs in a rational and technological world. Therefore we are faced with the dilemma that this reality is central for the Christian consciousness but marginal for the normal awareness of everyday life today; this dilemma illustrates, indeed is emblematic of, the breach in Christian consciousness today. If we want to attempt, under these conditions, to recover the concept of sacrament, it is necessary to ascertain, first, what common human presuppositions and points of reference it contains within itself, so that from there we can arrive at what is specifically Christian about it.

If we do this, we run into two problems. On the one hand, we encounter a basic form of human understanding and human communication that has found its characteristically Christian expression in the sacrament: the symbol. In order to understand the nature of the sacrament—its lasting validity and the manner in which it reveals reality—one would therefore have to inquire about what a symbol is, how it can establish fellowship and communion in a common perception of reality, and to what extent it is possible to gain access to reality in the first place.[1] If one does this, the second step is

---

Translated by Kenneth Baker, S.J., and Michael J. Miller.

[1] The pertinent discussion of Jean Daniélou with René Guénon is important. It is to their credit that they have worked out the meaning of symbolic (as opposed to scientific) knowledge in its uniqueness and made it respectable. See Jean Daniélou, *Vom Geheimnis der Geschichte* (Stuttgart, 1955), 144–70. Important for the development of the concept of Christian symbol and sacrament are the studies written by Hans Urs von Balthasar in 1936 and 1937 on Origen's idea of mystery, which are found in a revised form in his book: *Parole et*

obvious. Whoever investigates the nature and "functioning" of symbols necessarily encounters the specific habitat in which this primordial human phenomenon is at home. For symbols do not simply *exist* autonomously—available, so to speak, for any use whatever; they *occur*, and they are effective only in the occurrence that is supported by the authority of the community, which the individual cannot simply bring about by himself. This communal happening is the feast. The feast, being an extraordinary event, is the place that supports the symbol and brings it to life; the two together form the human horizon within which the sacrament is to be understood. The Christian sacrament, too, is essentially a symbol-event. In this sense each sacrament, of course in a very different way, has something of the character of a feast. The common event of the feast is the reference point on which it builds.

This look at the common human roots of the sacrament opens up the possibility of presenting in more widely comprehensible terms this seemingly purely internal Christian phenomenon, which is quite alien to today's rationalism, and of forming a concept of sacrament that allows us to understand what is specifically Christian about it as the adoption and development of what is human and universal. Accordingly, although the methodological course of our considerations seems initially to be clearly defined, we now face an objection that might prove that we are on the wrong track after all. Karl Barth regarded the insertion of what is Christian into the common analogy of what is human as the essence of the Catholic decline that shifts what is unique, unprecedented, and unpredictable in God's new activity in Jesus down to our own level; as he sees it, the divine is now deduced from what is ours, from the human, and thus misses precisely what is uniquely Christian.[2] Now this objection no longer strikes us as

---

Mystère chez Origène (Paris, 1957). Of the more recent literature we should mention: Horst Jürgen Helle, "Symbol und Gottesdienst", in *Zum Gottesdienst morgen*, ed. Heinz G. Schmidt (Wuppertal, 1969), 24–32; Helle, "Symboltheorie und religiöse Praxis", in *Religion in Umbruch*, ed. Jakobus Wössner, 200–214 (Stuttgart, 1972); Helle, *Soziologie und Symbol: Ein Beitrag zur Handlungstheorie und zur Theorie des sozialen Wandels* (Cologne and Opladen, 1969). Also, Ingrid Jorissen and Hans Bernhard Meyer, *Zeichen und Symbole im Gottesdienst* (Innsbruck, 1977).

[2] On this subject cf. especially Hans Urs von Balthasar, *Karl Barth: Darstellung und Deutung seiner Theologie* (Cologne, 1951), 15–181 [trans. by Edward T. Oakes as *The Theology of Karl Barth* (Communio Books; San Francisco: Ignatius Press, 1992), 30–199]; Gottlieb Söhngen, *Die Einheit in der Theologie* (Munich, 1952), 235–64.

dramatically as it did thirty years ago, for we are living today, unlike then, in an anthropological phase of theology, too, and have long since grown tired of Barth's purism. But because confronting what is not self-evident, what is unpleasant, and what appears to be off the beaten track is also part of the search for truth, we will do well to remember this objection and to spend some time reflecting on it.

In fact this objection may have assumed a new form, one that is also immediately troubling to us, in two short lectures by the Lutheran systematic theologian at the University of Tübingen Eberhard Jüngel.[3] To his mind, Barth's idea seems to be no longer merely a protest of the strictly theological against the purely human but, rather, a necessary critique of dogmatic theology by exegesis, which for him is at the same time a critique of the Catholic Church (which includes Scripture as part of tradition) by the Reformation (which thinks in terms of Scripture). No doubt we are very alert today to such an objection (by both historical reason and the Reformation) to tradition and the Church of tradition. In his reflections, Jüngel starts out from the indisputable fact that the word *sacramentum* in the Church Fathers is the translation of the Greek word *mysterion*. From this he concludes very judiciously that one can verify the legitimacy of the concept of sacrament by examining the lexical meaning of the word *mysterion* in the New Testament. This endeavor leads him to an upsetting conclusion. In the New Testament, so he maintains (and historically it is quite incontestable), the word *mysterion* seldom appears in the first place; but secondly—and more importantly—where it does appear, it has christological and eschatological connotations. Nowhere, however, does it show any relation to cult or liturgy, much less to the mystery cults, the sacramental actions of the non-Christian world. It is perhaps interesting here to add parenthetically that Odo Casel, the great theologian of the Liturgical Movement in the period between the two world wars, was of the opinion that the pagan mystery cults were the vessel prepared by providence for the Christian concept of sacrament, which had no precursors in the Old Testament.[4] Now Jüngel would probably not dispute this connection for the early Church but would see precisely therein her falling away from the New Testament and from

---

[3] Eberhard Jüngel and Karl Rahner, *Was ist ein Sakrament?* (Freiburg, 1971).

[4] Cf. Theodor Filthaut, *Die Kontroverse über die Mysterienlehre* (Warendorf, 1947), 73–80; Odo Casel, *Das christliche Kultmysterium*, 2nd ed. (Regensburg, 1948), 60ff.

the Bible as a whole—the Hellenization of what is Christian. For his observation that the word *mysterion* in the New Testament has nothing to do with the mystery cults, nothing to do with sacramental actions, is expanded by his further statement that, conversely, this word is absent in those New Testament passages that deal with liturgical actions, such as Baptism and Eucharist. Jüngel formulates his thesis accordingly: "Where such relations are discernible (for example, in the sacramental texts) the term *mysterion* is not found; but where the term does appear, they (the liturgical references) are absent."[5] When he goes on to say that the early Church established this very connection—one not created by the New Testament—and developed the sacraments in competition with and in imitation of the pagan mysteries, the purpose of his thesis is clear (and apparently indisputable, since everything he says up to this point is historically correct): while he does not want to do away with the concept of sacrament as such, he views the Catholic understanding of sacrament that developed in the early Church as so dubious that a fundamental reinterpretation (such as he finds in Luther) seems to him unavoidable.

A thesis of this magnitude requires verification. At issue along with it is the correctness of the anthropological connection from which we started out earlier without challenging it in principle; but also at issue is the question regarding the relationship between the human and the Christian, in other words, the question about the nature of Christian universality as such. In this thesis we see the difference between the Catholic and the Lutheran concept of sacrament as the fundamental question about tradition and its interpretation of Scripture; consequently, this thesis also raises the question about Christian worship as such. It is advisable in this debate to follow Jüngel's methodology at first and to go a bit farther in examining the lexical history of the term *mysterion-sacramentum*. But then we will have to see whether it is right to frame the whole question in terms of the semantic analysis of one word or whether it is not essential to present another factual context as the original locus of the historical development.

The first thing involved in framing any New Testament question is to take a good look at its roots in the Old Testament. If we do that, we see that the word "mystery" does not occur in the classical writings of the Old Testament. It first appears in the later writings, in

---

[5] Jüngel, *Was ist ein Sakrament?* 30.

each of the three groups into which they are divided: in apocalyptic with Daniel, in wisdom literature (Wisdom and Sirach), and in pious edifying narratives, that is, in Tobit, Judith, and Second Maccabees. These instances confirm that there are no cultic connections there, either; the word *mysterion* simply means something secret. To be sure, in apocalyptic writings, which are concerned with the unveiling of the future, something more comes to light: there it means something like a revelation concealed beneath symbols, a veiled proclamation of future mysteries determined by God.[6] These ideas then undergo a significant modification in the theology of the rabbis, that is, in the theology that was developing in Jesus' time, even though our evidence for it is more recent. Here there is talk about the "mysteries of the Torah" (the five books of Moses). The Torah appears as the verbal clothing of "God's mystery of creation, which is at the foundation of all being and to which one can penetrate in a mystical interpretation".[7] According to the rabbis, therefore, the many words of the law have a secret center, a secret meaning that does not lie on the surface in plain view but, rather, is actually an unveiling of reality.

We are reminded of this by a saying of Jesus that we find in Mark 4:11. In the previous verses we read that the disciples do not understand the parables that Jesus tells, and they ask him what they mean. Jesus answers them: "To you has been given the secret (*mysterion*) of the kingdom of God, but for those outside everything is in parables." This sentence is very difficult to explain, yet this much is clear about its content: Behind the narrative parable with which Jesus faces the people dwells a hidden argument that leads down into the depths of reality. What this argument is, is not expressed, and obviously this is not at all possible in the form of normal discursive speech. Obviously, one cannot make this deep argument as perceptible as the narrative parable can. It can be conveyed only as a *reality* through which the discourse strides. It means becoming aware of the reality itself; it has to do with the person of the one addressed and of the speaker, namely, with Jesus Christ.

Let us leave this insight at that for now and turn our attention to the rest of the New Testament. Then we see that the word *mysterion* is used extensively only in the Pauline literature, where it appears twenty-one

---

[6] Günther Bornkamm, article μυστήριον in ThWNT 4:809–34, reference at 821.
[7] Ibid., 823.

times, but even here it is concentrated in three texts: 1 Corinthians, Ephesians, and Colossians. This concentration shows that the term is still by no means one of Paul's own words but, rather, was called for by the dialogue with those to whom he was writing. This means that it was still in an open-ended process of developing, so that we can only attempt to explore the outlines of the development insofar as they are visible in the New Testament. We find, then, that the rabbi Paul of Tarsus adopts the rabbinic interpretation. Indeed, the rabbinic question about the mysteries of the Torah was his question also. Now he knows that it is answered. He has come to know "the *mysterion*". The *mysterion* of the Torah and of all the parables has become visible for him in the crucified Christ. *He* is the hitherto hidden content that stands behind the manifold words and events of Scripture, the mystery of God that is at the foundation of everything that exists. In him the whence, why, and whither of creation and of man become evident. In him is revealed the central point of the parables that Scripture paces off; in him God has explained himself and given the authentic hermeneutic of Scripture— the authentic entrance into it. For this reason, Christ can then simply be named "the mystery of God" (1 Cor 2:1; see 2:7 in connection with 1:23; Col 2:2; see 1:27 and 4:3).

In this respect, the term *mysterion* appertains—an important finding!— to the question about the correct interpretation of Scripture: it is a hermeneutical concept. But at the same time this enables Paul to respond also to the mystery cults in Corinth; he accepts this new word from their vocabulary in order to raise it, of course, to a completely new level. He counters the mysticism of an elitist wisdom, of a Christianity of the initiates for whom the normal ecclesial Christianity is too lowly and who therefore wish to go beyond it hermeneutically, with the fact that the foolish scandal of the crucified Christ is itself *the* mystery, the most intrinsic, most profound, most hidden, and most elevated of all; no initiation can lead deeper than that, and no hermeneutic can go higher. This is not an intellectual formula that one can derive by interpreting the text; rather, it is the banal event itself: the Crucified One whom the unadorned kerygma proclaims—he himself is the *mysterion*.

In this context Paul goes into the structure and language of the mystery religions. Of course, part of the *mysterion* of the mystery religions is secrecy; it is elitist: Not everyone can see it—one must first go through initiations. To that Paul says: This *mysterion*, too, has its secrecy, and it is precisely that of *sophia*, that is, of elite wisdom that is hidden from hermeneutical know-it-alls and is made known precisely to those who know no better, the uninitiated, the naïve: to the *moros* or "fool", he says, namely, to someone who is considered an "idiot" by the hermeneutically enlightened elite.

The *mysterion* draws its boundary in a way that is exactly the reverse of the way in which men set limits. It sweeps aside all the "mysteries" by delivering what they promise but do not have: access to the innermost thoughts of God, who at the same time opens up the innermost foundation of the world and man's reason for living. This is disclosed precisely when one abides in simplicity, and to that extent it is ordered in a special way to simple souls and not to elite minds. We should consider it remarkable, therefore, that Paul adopts terminology and a world of ideas from the mystery religions but turns them on their head from the Christian perspective. The naïve kerygma, uncritically accepted; the accomplished historical reality of the death and Resurrection of Jesus Christ: *this* is the most profound wisdom, and the probing critic, someone who fancies himself to be an initiate, is instead the one who sinks to the level of "psychic" and unspiritual concerns. The one who stays and lives in the simplicity of the unity of the universal Church is the adept, the initiate. The fact that the new wise ones are torn apart in quarreling factions shows that, although they suppose that they are becoming wholly spiritual, they are actually "fleshly"—devoid of wisdom.

The expansion beyond a narrowly conceived view, purely in terms of salvation history, into one that takes the theology of creation and anthropology into account also has already been presented with the rabbinic component of the Pauline approach; for the Torah (of which Jesus proves to be the meaning and fulfillment) is at the same time and in its most profound sense a word of creation. This view is developed quite explicitly in the Letter to the Ephesians; the concept of *mysterion* here can perhaps be briefly paraphrased in this way: In speaking about Jesus, the Bible of the Jews speaks about the salvation of the Gentiles, and this is its true meaning. Whoever reads the book of the Jews correctly finds that it speaks about the salvation of the Gentiles *and* of the Jews, because it speaks about Jesus, who is the salvation of all, the uniting principle of creation. The meaning of creation, which comes to light in Jesus as the unveiling of the Scriptures, is unity, in which the fullness of God shines forth and illumines.

Now, however, we must also pay special attention to one text that seems to be incidental but can provide us with an opening for a significant step forward. I am thinking of the famous passage in Ephesians 5:31–32. It takes up again the conclusion of the creation account, which says about Adam and Eve: "For this reason a man shall leave his father and mother and be joined to his wife, and the two shall become one." To this Old Testament citation the author of the Letter to the Ephesians adds the comment: "This is a great *mysterion*, and I mean in reference to Christ and the church."

What does this verse mean for our inquiry? First of all, it is completely in keeping with the previous considerations. The author applies to a particular text the basic idea that Jesus is the *mysterium* of the Torah. Since, in the final analysis, Jesus is the meaning of all the words of Scripture, then of course one can demonstrate this in the case of particular texts. The quoted sentence points to the same center as all sentences: it speaks about Christ and the Church, in which now not only Israel but all mankind is drawn into the unity of love that leads to an indissoluble fusion into a single life. So far, that is still simply the application of the general basic idea of the *mysterium* of the Torah. But it goes farther, inasmuch as it is here no longer simply a *word* of the Bible interpreted "typologically", that is, in a christological sense; rather, it is a *reality* of creation: marriage—the union of man and woman in a marital community. This creation event is included in Scripture, and it has, as Scripture shows, its own *mysterium* and bears within itself a christological transparency. Accordingly, the *"mysterium"* is no longer merely the literal meaning of a biblical *text*, as we have come to know it until now; rather, it is the meaning of an event. It dwells in the event, which reaches down to the center of creation and reaches up to the innermost and definitive will of God. Thus we are faced with two factors that are very important for the formation of the concept of sacrament:

1. The *mysterium* of the Torah, of the Bible as a whole, is, as we have heard, in Paul's view Christ. But that makes the individual words *mysteria*, refractions of the great in the small, so that Christ becomes visible behind every one of them. This in turn implies that not only the words but also the realities described by them are *mysteria*—symbolic references to Christ. And this can apply to the realities of creation as well as to the realities of Israel's history. Translated into Latin, this means: Scripture as a whole is *sacramentum*. Therefore in

every single part it is full of *sacramenta*, which can be the literal meaning or the meaning of events in creation or salvation history. Accordingly, we can now say (somewhat schematically): Within the horizon of Paul's interpretation of Scripture, three types of *sacramenta* appear, namely, word sacraments, event sacraments, and creation sacraments. With this observation we are already right in the middle of the early Church's concept of sacrament, although the basic exegetical principle thereof becomes completely clear only when we add the second factor, which becomes discernible and comprehensible [*einsichtig und ansichtig*] to us from the perspective of the Letter to the Ephesians.

2. Since the conviction that the individual words of Scripture, being reflections and realizations of its overall meaning, are *mysteria*, scriptural words are explained as references pointing beyond themselves to Christ. They become, as Paul puts it, *typoi tou mellontos*, types of the One who is to come. They are types. In Latin, that means *sacramentum futuri*, sacrament (type) of what is to come. The word *typos* is used in the New Testament and especially in patristic writings almost synonymously with *mysterion*, with *sacramentum*.

To regard Scripture as mystery, as the rabbis had already done, means within the horizon of Paul's thought to regard it christologically, as a complex ensemble of references to Christ. Now if *mysterium*, *sacramentum*, and *typus* all mean the same thing, then "christological" interpretation is the same as "typological" interpretation: what is said in Scripture is a type, a sign pointing to the One who is coming.

Accordingly, we can now state that the Christian concept of *sacramentum*, as it took shape in the early Church based on Paul's writings, is the result of the linguistic interference of the terms *mysterium* and *typus* in the New Testament. The word *sacramentum* translates the blending of these two concepts that came about through St. Paul's christological understanding of Scripture. In this respect, this word *sacramentum* in the early Church is entirely the product of New Testament thinking, a new word formation that arose out of this early history. Of course this also means that the Catholic concept of *sacramentum* is based on the "typological" interpretation of Scripture—an interpretation in terms of parallels to Christ. This concept loses its mainstay when this interpretation is completely lost. When that happens, however, the way in which the New Testament itself understands Scripture is abandoned also; for all that the New Testament says is by no means intended to produce a new Scripture; rather, it means to give directions on how to understand the Christic content of the Old Testament. Whoever thinks that this way of dealing with the Bible is not allowed may perhaps gain a literal understanding of the Old Testament, but he thereby radically rejects the New Testament and its understanding of the Old.[8]

This central thesis of mine now clarifies the reason for the crisis of Catholicism in the modern era; for one of its intellectual components is the replacement of typological thinking—that is, an interpretation that reads the texts from the perspective of their future and with a view to their future—by literary-historical thinking, that is, an interpretation that reads the texts by looking back in time and tries to pin them down to their oldest original meaning. That is exactly the revolution to which the modern era leads with its new understanding of history and historical texts: an interpretation of texts with a view to what comes out of them, while rejecting any future set forth in them; this mentality thinks that a text is correctly interpreted only if it is put back into its past, fixed in that past, and spelled out in its most ancient form. With this thesis, however, the double knot of Jüngel's objection, which was our starting point, is loosed in principle. The assertion that the early Church's concept of sacrament is contrary to Scripture falls by the wayside, because with the fusion of *mysterium* and *typus* the way of the New Testament is adopted. The obstacle to a connection of the sacrament with the larger context of what is universally human or creation-oriented disappears, because the sacrament of the word is always a sacrament of creation as well—a creation, of course, that is purified and restored in the Word.

That still leaves us, however, at the early Church with a finding formulated in very general terms. There are still two considerable difficulties that stand in the way of a definitive solution to the dilemma formulated at the beginning of this essay. We will address these now in a final series of considerations. Here is the first question: How did we get from the early Church's concept of sacrament, which was very broadly compartmentalized and yet at the same time quite simple, to

---

[8] On this topic, cf. especially Henri de Lubac, *History and Spirit: The Understanding of Scripture according to Origen*, trans. Anne Englund Nash and Juvenal Merriell (San Francisco: Ignatius Press, 2007 [originally published in French 1950, German edition, 1968]); de Lubac, *Der geistige Sinn der Schrift*, Christ heute 5/2 (Einsiedeln, 1952); Jean Daniélou, *Sacramentum futuri: Études sur les origines de la typologie biblique* (Paris, 1950); Maximino Arias-Reyero, *Thomas von Aquin als Exeget: Die Prinzipien seiner Schriftdeutung und seine Lehre von den Schriftsinnen*, Sammlung Horizonte, n.s. 3 (Einsiedeln, 1971).

our current specific understanding of sacrament in the sense of the seven sacraments? In other words: How did it happen that suddenly one day in the twelfth or thirteenth century the distinction was made in this spacious and simple field between sacraments in the strict sense and what were from then on called sacramentals? Is that not a rupture, after all? The second question is: If the concept of sacrament is inseparably connected with an interpretation of Scripture that looks forward, with the christological or typological interpretation of Scripture, then has it not lost its foundation in the historical era, in an era of strictly literal interpretation?

These two questions are fundamental and once again show, I think, the far-reaching importance of the theme. But that also means that it is impossible to answer them comprehensively; still, some indication of the route is necessary. Regarding the first question, we must now take a closer look at a reality that so far has been alluded to only incidentally. We have said that scriptural words are *sacramenta futuri*, symbolic outlines foretelling the One who will come, an advance toward what is coming. Events are *sacramenta* of what is to come. This includes the fact that the liturgical rites of the Old Covenant, too, for someone with eyes to see, speak about the future, about Christ, and consequently are *sacramenta*—this theme is extensively developed in the Letter to the Hebrews, but it is by no means foreign to Paul's thought.[9] This leads to a new step. For if we establish that, together with words and events, the liturgical actions of the Old Covenant are also references to Christ, that they are *sacramenta*, then we discover a "refraction" in the concept of sacrament that is identical with the difference between promise and fulfillment, between preparation and present reality, between Old and New Covenant. The things that are accomplished in the New Testament are no longer simply *sacramenta futuri*, outlines of what is to come, but are, rather, representations of the present, the expression and fruit of the actual life, death, and Resurrection of Jesus Christ.

The Old Testament *sacramenta* are, from beginning to end, a movement toward what is as yet undisclosed; they are an invitation to a

---

[9] Cf. Rom 3:25f.; 1 Cor 5:7; Rom 15:16; Phil 2:17; 1 Cor 1:30; Col 1:14, etc. In addition we should refer to the most liturgically shaped book of the New Testament, the book of Revelation. On the question of interpreting Jesus' death in terms of cultist "types", see: Gerhard Delling, *Der Kreuzestod Jesu in der urchristlichen Verkündigung* (Göttingen, 1972); Karl Kertelge, *Der Tod Jesu: Deutungen im Neuen Testament*, QD 74 (Freiburg, 1976); Heinz Schürmann, *Jesu ureigener Tod: Exegetische Besinnungen und Ausblick*, 2nd ed. (Freiburg, 1976).

way. One celebrates [*begeht*] them correctly only by walking [*geht*] along them, by proceeding with them on the way toward what is coming, which they themselves are not yet. But as of that moment when Christ suffered and, having come from the Father, remains now with us forever, something new happened: the reality to which everything was still pending is now here. Therefore a sacrament now is the representation of the given, a transfer to what has already happened. Medieval theology later explained this by the contrast—since then so often misunderstood—between *ex opere operato* and *ex opere operantis*. Originally this distinction pertained to the contrast between the Old and the New Testament, between promise and fulfillment. Originally the formula was not just *ex opere operato*, but *ex opere operato Christi*.[10] This means: the sacraments now no longer work by foreshadowing and asking; rather, they are effective as a result of what has already happened, and therein is manifest the act of liberation accomplished by Christ. Man no longer has to rely on his own doing and going toward some undisclosed thing that is yet to come; instead, he can entrust himself to the reality that is already waiting for him and approaches him as something that has already happened.

This idea that the concept of sacrament is fractured by the difference between promise and fulfillment was joined together, logically and very early on, with the theme of liberation. Liberation means at the same time simplification, purification, and deepening. Instead of the complicated cultic system of yore, there is now the pure simplicity of the Eucharist of the Risen One. This unburdening, this release from the oppressive multiplicity of what is not yet comprehensible into the liberating simplicity of Christianity proves to be a release in a second sense, also, inasmuch as the rites that formerly were performed in front of the closed curtain of what was to come now become transparent, *rationabilia*, that is, accessible to reason, as the Fathers say. No longer is there mere duty whose meaning remains to be seen—that constitutes legalism; with the disclosure of the previously hidden *mysterion*, insight and its freedom have replaced legal obligation. It was plain to the Fathers that simplicity, freedom, and intelligibility— which is what necessarily comes to pass at the moment of fulfillment,

---

[10] Cf. Venicio Marcolino, *Das Alte Testament in der Heilsgeschichte: Untersuchung zum dogmatischen Verständnis des Alten Testaments als heilsgeschichtliche Periode nach Alexander von Hales*, Beiträge zur Geschichte der Philosophie und der Theologie des Mittelalters, n.s. 2 (Münster, 1970), 201–8.

of the lifting of the veil—also imply concentration and streamlining [*Raffung und Straffung*]. Therefore, the multiple requirements that necessarily accumulated in the time of expectation, in which new steps, so to speak, were always being tried out, stand in contrast to the few *sacramenta* of the New Covenant, the simplicity of the fulfillment. Of course no systematization took place. Yet this fundamental way of looking at it clearly prepared the way for the medieval delimitation of the Christian concept of sacrament. It is clear, moreover, that the number seven, a limitation fixed and agreed upon, was due in turn to typological considerations. It results from an a priori theological construct and does not arise from an a posteriori counting up of the phenomena observed.[11] But that surely corresponds to the structure of the whole and objectively conforms to the rudiments of the whole. That should answer the first question: How did the broad patristic concept of sacrament develop into the specific concept of Tridentine dogma? On that point we can now say that even for the Church Fathers the concept of sacrament was subdivided into the Old Testament multiplicity and its terminus—the simplicity of the New Testament. In that respect, the medieval limitation merely represents a systematization of the initial approach of the early Church.

At the same time this brings us to the second question, namely, the one about the legitimacy and permanent possibility of such a continuous interpretation of Scripture as *sacramentum futuri*. This is the question that Luther first posed in all its distinctness. In his treatment we can clearly recognize two dimensions of the problem, which are materially the same ones with which we are still dealing. First there is the process in which the Church as institution and the Church as a theological, spiritual entity become separated. But if that is the case, then the divine worship of the Church as such can no longer guarantee the continuity of salvation history; the institutional Church can no longer support the derivation of the whole from Jesus Christ. The necessary consequence is a naked confrontation between the individual and the scriptural word; instead of the unity of the typological account, we then have historical reconstruction and whatever it can find. The sacrament is no longer secure in the *institutio* of the Church but is

---

[11] Cf. the enlightening investigation by Michael Seybold, "Die Siebenzahl der Sakramente", MThZ 27 (1976): 113–38; Josef Finkenzeller, "Die Zählung und die Zahl der Sakramente", in *Wahrheit und Verkündigung*, Festschrift Michael Schmaus, ed. Leo Scheffczyk, Werner Dettloff, and Richard Heinzmann (Munich, 1967), 2:1005–33.

dependent on history. This means, secondly, that the typological-sacramental interpretation of Scripture now appears to be the ecclesiastical alienation of it and that this ecclesiastical expropriation of Scripture leading to a typological-sacramental interpretation now stands in opposition to the text alone in isolation from the Church, to the purely historical sense, which is considered the only original one. Viewed historically, this process, too, had the character of a liberation movement. Although formerly the transition from the law to the faith and liturgy of the Church was a great act of liberation—made possible and mediated by typology—whereby one could keep the whole Old Testament without being bound to each letter of it, so now this recourse to the letter, as opposed to the Church, becomes an act of liberation from the burden of the Church and her liturgy. This is, so to speak, the historical intelligibility that this event has.

Yet the further question inevitably arises: How can one bring the content of the old liberation into the new? For now an entirely new problem comes up: if the Bible is only literally true, then the Old Testament becomes a problem. To the Fathers this was clear: I can embrace the entire Old Testament without being bound to each letter because every word is a precursor of Christ, and naturally the precursor is surpassed yet is my own if I am with Christ himself. But if I am no longer allowed to think in this typological-sacramental way, if only strictly historical exegesis is valid, which means taking the letter without the Church as the unity of the past, present, and future, then this liberation from the demands of the law is no longer effective.

Incidentally, this had consequences for the whole history of exegesis; for example, the fact that the creation texts in Genesis suddenly became problematic and in their literal sense quarreled with the natural sciences is due to the fact that texts are considered valid, no longer in a dynamic exegetical system, but only in the literal sense from the past. Such a contradiction could not possibly come about as long as it was clear that everything should be read, above and beyond the letter, as leading to Christ, so that from this perspective freedom from the letter was provided. But that is only a digression.

Our question is this: After the abolition of ecclesial-sacramental, that is to say, "typological" exegesis, what about the Old Testament? There are really only two possibilities: either to continue to recognize the Old Testament as the Bible and then to abide by it literally or else to exclude it from the canon. The early Church battled over this question with Marcion and other strains of Gnosticism, which did not approve of typology, did not want to be bound by the law, and then saw no other alternative but to view the Old Testament as the bible of an Anti-God.[12] Luther was very much concerned about this problem and tried to resolve it by saying that he saw at work in Scripture a dialectic of law and gospel. Instead of the analogy of faith, then, there is the dialectic of law and gospel: the gospel as the power of salvation and the law as accusation and condemnation.[13]

To discuss this in detail would take us far beyond our topic. But there is no need to do that, because the crucial point here has basically already come into view. Indeed, we can now say that even Luther could not adhere to the purely literal character of the historical elements as the last word. He, too, needs a center of comprehension that goes beyond the mere letter of the text, just like anyone who tries to find in this text a possible way of living today and more than findings about the past. There is no such thing as reconstructing the faith out of mere history, however important the historical method may be. But someone who wants to receive the present from Scripture, in other words, faith, cannot remain stuck in mere historiography, which observes only the past. Faith is a form of understanding, and understanding always transcends pure facticity.

The historical method, therefore, does not exclude a hermeneutical center; it even demands it. In this sense a *sola scriptura* consisting merely of self-contained historical facts would be an oxymoron. By its own intrinsic design, the word refers to the *sacramentum*. It points to the living community of those who live it. It is so structured that it goes beyond itself and carries the dimension of the *sacramentum* within itself. Word and sacrament are not opposed to each other; rather, they are mutually dependent and productive. And the two of them are not opposed to creation and to anthropological elements; rather, they are the unification, purification, and fulfillment thereof.

What are the results to which our considerations have led us? I will try to summarize them in four points.

---

[12] Cf. Réal Tremblay, *La Manifestation et la Vision de Dieu selon St. Irenée de Lyon*, Münsterische Beiträge zur Theologie 41 (Münster, 1978), 49–65; Kurt Rudolph, ed., *Gnosis und Gnostizismus*, WdF 262 (Darmstadt, 1975).

[13] Cf. Wilfried Joest, *Ontologie der Person bei Luther* (Göttingen, 1967); Theobald Beer, *Der Fröhliche Wechsel und Streit: Grundzüge der Theologie Martin Luthers*, 2 vols. (Leipzig, 1974).

1. Understanding the sacraments presupposes a definite relationship to Scripture. It presupposes not only that we learn again how to read Scripture "backward", looking to the past so as to pin a given text down to its earliest stage—which is an important process—but also that we learn at the same time how to read it "forward", in terms of the dimension of the future, with a view to its totality and unity, in the discrepancy and unity of promise and fulfillment. I believe that here the decision is ultimately made as to whether or not Catholic theology is possible, based on the idea of the unity of Scripture.

2. Understanding the sacraments therefore presupposes the historical continuity of God's activity and, as its specific locus, the living community of the Church, which is the sacrament in the sacraments. This means: the biblical word can bear fruit and yield the present only when it is not merely a word but also has a living subject; when it belongs to a living context that is defined by it and that it in turn sustains.

3. Sacraments are liturgical acts of the Church in which the Church is involved as Church, that is, in which she not only functions as an association but takes action on the basis of that which she herself has not made and in which she gives more than she herself can give: the inclusion of man in the gift that she herself receives. This means that in the sacrament, the entire continuum of history is present—past, present, and future. As *memoria*, it must reach down into the roots of universal human history and thus meet man in his present moment and give him a *praesens*, a presence of salvation, whose essence is that it opens up a future extending beyond death.

4. Thus the sacraments are at the same time a Christian novelty and a primordially human thing. The newness of Christianity and the oneness of the human element do not contradict each other. In Jesus Christ, creation is taken up and purified, and in just this way he proves to be the One who gives man an answer and is his salvation. The symbols of creation are signs pointing to Christ, and Christ is the fulfillment not only of history but also of creation: In him who is the *mysterium* of God, everything attains its unity.

PART C

THE CELEBRATION OF THE EUCHARIST—
SOURCE AND SUMMIT OF CHRISTIAN LIFE

I. The Resurrection as the Foundation of Christian Liturgy—On the Meaning of Sunday for Christian Prayer and Christian Life

> We live under the observance of the Lord's Day,
> the day on which our life has also risen
> —Ignatius of Antioch

1. What Is the Issue Here?

It was the year 304, during the Diocletian persecution in North Africa, when Roman officials surprised a group of about fifty Christians who were attending the Sunday Eucharist to take them into custody. The transcript of the interrogations has been preserved. The proconsul said to the presbyter Saturninus: "By gathering all these together here you have acted against the orders of the emperors and the caesars." The Christian redactor adds at this point that the presbyter's response was inspired by the Holy Spirit. He said: "Unconcerned about that (*securi*, 'completely secure'), we have been celebrating what is the Lord's." "What the Lord's is"—that is how I translate the Latin word *dominicus*. Its complex meaning can hardly be translated at all. First of all it denotes the Lord's Day, but at the same time it refers to the content of this day, to the sacrament of the Lord, to his Resurrection and his presence in the eucharistic event. Let us return to the transcript: The proconsul insists on knowing why; the composed, superb response of the presbyter follows: "We have done this because that which is the Lord's cannot cease." Here the realization is unambiguously expressed that *the* Lord stands above *the* lords. Such knowledge lent the presbyter "security" (as he himself expressed it) precisely at the moment when it had become evident that the little Christian community was externally completely insecure and at the mercy of others.

Emeritus, the owner of the house where the Sunday celebration of the Eucharist had taken place, answered perhaps even more impressively. In response to the question of why he had permitted the forbidden gathering in his house, he said first of all that those gathered

Reprinted with permission from *A New Song for the Lord: Faith in Christ and Liturgy Today*, trans. Martha M. Matesich, 2nd ed. (1996; New York: Crossroad, 2005), 59–77.

187

were his brothers and he could not show them the door. Once again the proconsul was insistent. And there, in the second response, the real ground and motive come to light. "You had to forbid them entry", the proconsul had said. "I couldn't", answered Emeritus: "*Quoniam sine dominico non possumus*—for without the Day of the Lord, the mystery of the Lord, we cannot exist." The clear and decisive "we cannot" of the Christian conscience stands opposite the will of the caesars.[1] This phrase adopts the "we cannot be silent", the must of Christian preaching, used by Peter and John in response to the order of the Sanhedrin not to speak (Acts 4:20).

"Without the Day of the Lord we cannot exist." That is not arduous obedience toward a law of the Church felt to be external to oneself, but an expression of both interior necessity and desire. It points to that which has become the sustaining center of one's own existence, of one's entire being. It indicates something that has become so important that it must be done out of a feeling of great inner security and freedom, even at the risk of one's own life. For those speaking in this way it would obviously have appeared senseless to buy survival and outer peace by renouncing this foundation of life. They did not consider a casuistry that would have let worship appear to be dispensable as the lesser value when weighing the alternatives of Sunday obligation or a citizen's obligation, of Church law or the impending death sentence. For them it was a case, not of choosing between *one* law and *another*, but of choosing between the meaning that sustains life and a meaningless life. At this point we can also understand the words of St. Ignatius of Antioch that appear as a motto at the beginning of this chapter. "We live according to the Lord's Day on which our life has also risen. How could we ever live without it?"[2]

Such a witness from the dawn of Church history could easily give rise to nostalgic reflections if one contrasts it with the lack of enthusiasm for Sunday service typical of the middle-European Christian. Granted, the Sunday crisis did not just start in our time. It already becomes apparent at the point when the *inner necessity* of Sunday is no

---

[1] The patristic texts on the subject of the Sabbath and Sunday have been collected by Willy Rordorf, *Sabbat und Sonntag in der Alten Kirche*, Traditio christiana 2 (Zurich, 1972). The text quoted here is from the *Acta ss Saturnini, Datiui et aliorum plurimorum martyrum in Africa* (304), no. 109, pp. 176f.

[2] IgnMagn. 9:1, 2, in Rordorf, *Sabbat*, no. 78, p. 134 [translated into English from the German].

longer felt: Instead of "without Sunday we cannot exist", Sunday obligation appears only as an imposed Church law, an *external necessity*. Then, like all duties coming from the outside, it is cropped more and more until only the requirement remains to have to attend a half-hour ritual that is becoming ever more remote. Asking when and why one can be excused from it ultimately becomes more important than asking why one should regularly celebrate it. Consequently, in the end it does not take much for one to stay away without any excuse at all.

Since the meaning of Sunday has so completely degenerated into a positivistic façade, the question of whether the Lord's Day is still really such an important topic in our age arises for us as well, the question of whether there are not really much more important themes for Christians, and especially for Christians in a world rent by the danger of war and social problems. In private we also sometimes ask ourselves if we are not simply pursuing the survival of our "club", the justification of our own profession by insisting on the Lord's Day.

The more profound question lying behind this is whether the Church is really only "our club" or God's original idea whose realization determines the fate of the world. On the other hand, with nostalgic comparisons between the past and today we would be doing justice neither to the witness of the martyrs nor to reality today. Even while being aware of all the necessary self-criticism, we should not overlook the fact that there are still very many Christians today who would respond from a feeling of innermost security just like the early Christians. Without the Lord's Day we cannot exist; that which is the Lord's must not cease. On the other side of the issue we know that already during the New Testament period there was cause for complaining about poor church attendance (Heb 10:25); this complaint appears again and again in the works of the Church Fathers. It seems to me that the real, albeit misunderstood and for the most part unrecognized, driving force behind the restlessness of today's leisure-time activities, behind the escape from everyday life and the pursuit of something completely different, is the yearning for that which the martyrs called *dominicus*, that is, the longing for an encounter that makes life arise in us; it is the pursuit of what Christians received and are receiving on Sunday. Our question is: How can we show this to the people who seek it, and how can we find it again ourselves? Before we look for solutions and applications, which are without doubt also very necessary, I think that we ourselves must again arrive at an inner understanding of what the Lord's Day is.

2. The Theology of the Lord's Day

Let us begin with the simplest matter. First, Sunday is a particular day of the week, the first day according to Jewish numbering, which was adopted by the Christians. Here we immediately run into something that seems to us to be positivistic and external, so we ask: Why should we not celebrate on Friday in Islamic countries, on Saturday where the majority are Jewish, and then on some other day somewhere else? Why should each person not be able to pick his day according to the rhythm of his work or way of life? What led to specifying this day anyway? Is it just an agreement to make it possible for us at least to celebrate together? Or is there more to it than that?

To begin with, behind Sunday, the first day, there is another New Testament formula for the date that has also been adopted in the Credo of the Church: "He was raised on the third day in accordance with the scriptures" (1 Cor 15:4). In the earliest scriptural tradition the *third* day was recorded and hence the memory of the discovery of the empty tomb and the first appearances of the Risen One preserved.[3]

---

[3] Cf. Josef Blank, "Paulus und Jesus", StANT 18 (Munich, 1968): 154–56. Blank summarizes the result of his very careful analysis on p. 156 as follows: "'On the third day' is the specification of a day in agreement with the earliest Christian tradition in the Gospels and refers to the discovery of the empty tomb; as with the statement about his death, the 'in accordance with the scriptures' refers to Isaiah 53:10ff." For this reason it is exegetically and theologically completely groundless when Richard Heinzmann accuses the *Catechism* of a "naïve scriptural fundamentalism" because it also considers the third day to be—first and foremost—a historical measure of time from the burial of Jesus to the discovery of the empty tomb; see "Was ist der Mensch? Anfragen an das Menschenbild des *Katechismus der katholischen Kirche*", in *Ein Katechismus für die Welt*, ed. E. Schulz (Düsseldorf, 1994), 97–98. In his polemic against the *Catechism*, Heinzmann wrongly refers to Karl Lehmann, *Auferweckt am dritten Tag nach der Schrift*, QD 38, 2nd ed. (Freiburg, 1969). Lehmann tried to clarify the theological significance of the third day from the sources, which is what Paul is asking for when he says that the third day was the time of the Resurrection "in accordance with the scriptures"; with that he is expressly making two claims: this is a real day, and this day has theological significance. Such a concurrence between factuality and meaning is contradictory only for a person who can see no meaning in the fact and nothing actually realized in the meaning, that is, who sees history as simple, empirical fact deprived of God's direction. Furthermore, although written in completely different linguistic styles and from a different starting point, the Resurrection accounts in all four Gospels uniformly give the third day as the point in time for the discovery of the empty tomb and the first appearances of the Risen One—in spite of all their other differences. They all say that Friday, the eve of the great Sabbath, is the day of Jesus' death; they all mention the rest period of the Sabbath (taken for granted in Jewish areas); and they all say that on the first day of the week the walk to the grave took place and the discovery of the empty tomb and the first encounters with Christ, the Risen One, occurred. Whereas Jesus' prophecies of his Passion (cf. Mk 8:31;

At the same time—and this is why "in accordance with the scriptures" is added—we are reminded that the third day was the day specified by the Scriptures, that is, by the Old Testament itself, for this fundamental event of world history—or, rather, not of world history, but marking the escape from world history, the escape from the history of death and killing, the breakthrough and onset of a new life.

The concrete memory of the day is likewise interpreted by the designation "third day". In the Old Testament accounts describing the making of the covenant on Sinai, the third day is each time the day of theophany, that is, the day on which God reveals himself and speaks.[4] Accordingly, the time description "on the third day" marks Jesus' Resurrection as the definitive event of the covenant, as the ultimate and real entry into history of God, who lets himself be touched in the middle of our world—a "God you can put your hands on", as we would say today. The Resurrection means that God has retained power in history, that he has not relinquished it to the laws of nature. It means that he has not become powerless in the world of matter and matter-determined life. It means that the law of all laws, the universal law of death, is not the world's final power after all and that it does not have the last word. The last one is and remains he who is also the first one.

There is real theophany in the world. This is what the phrase "the third day" says. And it has occurred in such a way that God himself has restored the disturbed nature of justice and has established justice, justice not only for the living or for a still uncertain future generation, but justice extending beyond death, justice for *the* Dead One and for the dead, justice for all. Hence theophany has occurred in this event in which one has come back from death or, better put, gone beyond death. It has occurred through the reception of the body into eternity,

---

9:31; 10:34; Lk 9:22; 24:7) and 1 Cor 15:4 use the formula of the third day, these accounts of the Resurrection mention the first day of the week. From this specification of the day, the Sunday gathering for the Lord's Supper developed in apostolic times. Whoever blocks out the facts here and withdraws into the mere "theological" not only undermines Sunday for Christians, but also takes the body from the Resurrection and thus destroys the foundation of Christian faith as a whole.

[4] Cf. especially Ex 19:11, 16. I have tried to describe the contexts in more detail in my little book *Der Gott Jesu Christi* (Munich, 1976), 76–84 [trans. by Robert J. Cunningham as *The God of Jesus Christ* (Franciscan Herald Press, 1978)]; cf. also Joseph Ratzinger, *Suchen, was droben ist* (Freiburg, 1985), 40–47 [trans. by Graham Harrison as: *Seek That Which Is Above* (San Francisco: Ignatius Press, 1986)].

proving that it, too, is capable of the eternal, capable of divinity. Jesus has not died and somehow or other gone to God, as people now and then say today, expressing indirectly their despair of God's actual power and of Jesus' actual Resurrection in only a feigned demonstration of devotion. For behind this phrase is in truth their fear that they would be stepping on the toes of the natural sciences if they were to include the real body of Jesus in God's powerful actions and consider real time to be affected by God's might.

If this were the case, however, we would be denying that matter has the capacity to be saved. We would also be denying that men have this capacity since they are, after all, a combination of matter and spirit. It seems to me that the theories that emphasize the wholeness of man in a seemingly superb way and thus speak of the whole death and the wholly new corporeal life are in fact barely disguised dualistic theories that invent unknown matter in order to remove reality itself from the sphere of theology, that is, from the sphere of God's speaking and acting. Resurrection means, however, that God says Yes to *the whole* and that he *can* do this. In the Resurrection God brings the approval of the seventh day of creation, his saying that all is good, to completion. The sin of man has tried to make God into a liar. It has concluded that his creation is not good at all or that it is really only good for dying. Resurrection means that through the twisted paths of sin and more powerfully than sin God ultimately says: "It *is* good." God speaks his definitive "good" to creation by taking it up into himself and thus changing it into a permanence beyond all transience.

At this point the connection between Sunday and the Eucharist becomes apparent. If the situation is as described, then the Resurrection is not one event in a flood of others, an event that is followed by another and gradually slips back farther and farther into the past. Resurrection is the start of a present, a now that will never end. We often live at a great distance from this present. We separate ourselves all the more the more we stick to the merely transient, the more we turn our lives away from that which has proved itself on the Cross and in the Resurrection to be the real present in the midst of what passes by: the love that finds itself in losing itself. *It* remains present. The Eucharist is the present, the now of the Risen One who continually gives himself in the signs of the sacrifice and is our life in this way. For this reason the Eucharist is itself and as such the Day of the Lord: *dominicus*, as the martyrs of North Africa put it in one single word.

At the same time, the connection between Sunday and creational faith becomes evident here. The third day after Jesus' death is the first day of the week, the day of creation on which God said: "Let there be light!" Where belief in the Resurrection keeps its New Testament wholeness and concreteness, Sunday and the meaning of Sunday can never be locked into mere history, into the history of the Christian community and its paschal celebration. Matter is involved here; creation is involved; the first day is involved, which Christians also call the eighth day: the restoration of all things. The Old and New Testaments cannot be separated, especially not in the interpretation of Sunday. Creation and faith cannot be detached from each other, least of all at the core of the Christian profession.[5]

For a variety of reasons theologians often have a kind of phobia about treating the topic of creation. This, however, leads to the degeneration of faith into a kind of parochial ideology, to the worldlessness of faith and the godlessness of the world, which is life-threatening for both. Where creation shrinks to the world around us, men and the world are out of kilter. But there is a complaint resounding ever more audibly out of this creation which has degenerated into mere environment, and precisely this complaint should tell us once more that the creature is in fact reaching out for the appearance of the children of God.

3. Sabbath and Sunday

a. The Problem

At this point the question about the relationship between the Sabbath and Sunday appears. It is a disputed question for which there is no uniform answer in the New Testament. Only in the course of the fourth century and at the beginning of the fifth did a solution

---

[5] Concerning the patristic symbolism of the first, third, seventh, and eighth days, cf. Jean Daniélou, *Liturgie und Bibel* (Munich, 1963), 225–305 [trans. as *The Bible and the Liturgy* (London, 1956)]; Karl-Heinz Schwarte, *Die Vorgeschichte der augustinischen Weltalterlehre*, Antiquitas, vol. 1, pt. 12 (Bonn, 1966; very instructive on the patristic view of the connection between creation and salvation history); brief information can also be found in Hansjörg Auf der Maur, *Feiern im Rhythmus der Zeit*, vol. 1, GdK 5 (Regensburg, 1983), 26–49; interesting comments can also be found in Willy Rordorf, "Le Dimanche—source et plénitude du temps liturgique chrétien", *Cristianesimo nella storia* 5 (1984): 1–9.

gradually begin to take shape that was then generally accepted but that is once more being vehemently challenged today. According to the unanimous witness of the Synoptic tradition, Jesus himself repeatedly came into conflict with the Jewish Sabbath observance of his time. He opposed it vigorously as a misunderstanding of God's law. Paul took up this line of argument; his battle for freedom from the law was also a battle against the constraints of the Jewish calendar of feasts, including the Sabbath obligations. We encounter an echo of this confrontation in the text of St. Ignatius of Antioch that is guiding us: "Whoever has gone from life under the old rules to the new, to hope, is no longer a follower of the Sabbath, but lives according to the Day of the Lord." The rhythm of the Sabbath and this "living-by-the-Day-of-the-Lord" confront each other as two fundamentally different life-styles, the former as a state of being lodged in particular sets of ordinances and the latter as life from what is to come, from hope.

But how did the transition from the observance of the Sabbath to the celebration of Sunday actually take place? We may accept as certain that already in the apostolic age the day of the resurrection had established itself entirely on its own merit as the day of Christian gathering. This was the "Lord's Day" (Rev 1:10), on which he appeared among his followers and they went to meet him. To assemble around the Risen One meant that he was once again breaking bread for his followers (Lk 24:30, 35). It was an encounter with Christ here and now, a moving toward his Second Coming, and simultaneously the presence of the Cross as his true exaltation, as the occasion on which his love spreads. The New Testament as well as the earliest manuscripts from the second century confirm this beyond all doubt: Sunday is the day of worship for Christians.[6] It has assimilated the ritualistic meaning of the Sabbath and at the same time represents the transformation of the old cult into the new, which is precisely what has occurred through the Cross and the Resurrection. But also the connection with the theme of creation, which is fundamental for the Sabbath, was explicit in a changed form through the designation of the first day of the week, that is, the day creation began. The Resurrection connects the beginning and the end, creation and restoration. In the magnificent hymn to Christ in Colossians, Christ is presented as the firstborn of

---

[6] For the documentary evidence, cf. Rordorf, *Sabbat*, 27–87.

all creation (1:15) as well as the firstborn from the dead (1:18), through whom God wanted to reconcile all things to himself. It is precisely here that we find the synthesis that lay hidden in the designation of the first day and that should shape the theology of Sunday in the future. In this respect it was possible for the whole theological content of the Sabbath to pass into the Sunday celebration of Christians in a renewed way; indeed, the passage from the Sabbath to Sunday reflects precisely the continuity and innovation of what is Christian.

Admittedly, the most important practical characteristic of the Sabbath could not at first be transferred to Sunday—its social function as a day of rest and freedom from servile work. Since Christianity was classified by state law in the first three centuries as an unauthorized religion, open celebration of Sunday was not possible. In the Jewish-Christian milieu this role of the Sabbath remained, and it certainly continued to be kept there in this sense. We do not know in detail what the situation in the pagan world was in this regard. It is notable that after the conversion of Constantine, that is, in the fourth century, we do encounter the celebration of both days (Sunday and Sabbath) in various sources. As examples I would like to quote two texts from the so-called *Apostolic Constitutions*. One text states: "Spend the Sabbath and the Lord's Day in festive joy since the one is the commemoration of creation, the other the commemoration of the resurrection!" [7] Somewhat later it says: "I Paul and I Peter order: Slaves should work five days, but on the Sabbath and the Lord's Day they should have time for instruction in the faith of the Church. For the Sabbath has its foundation in creation, the Lord's Day in the Resurrection." [8] Perhaps the same author who speaks here under the pseudonym "I Paul and I Peter" also put himself in the shoes of St. Ignatius of Antioch and created a longer version of the *Letter to the Magnesians*, from which we have taken our motto. In this longer version he is concerned with toning down the fierce attack against the "followers of the Sabbath". So he writes under the name of the renowned bishop of Antioch as follows:

---

[7] *Apostolic Constitutions* 7, 23, 3, in Rordorf, *Sabbat*, no. 58, p. 100. [This and all the following quotations from Rordorf have been translated into English from the German.] The *Apostolic Constitutions* are a collection of Church legislation dating from the fourth century; cf. Hugo Rahner, "Apostolische Konstitutionen", LThK, 2nd ed. (1957), 1:759.

[8] *Apostolic Constitutions* 8, 33.; cf. Rordorf, *Sabbat*.

Let us therefore not observe the Sabbath in the Jewish manner any more, deriving pleasure from idleness, for "whoever does not work should not eat" (2 Thess 3:10).... Rather, each of you should observe the Sabbath in a spiritual way. You should derive pleasure from studying the law and not from resting the body. You should marvel at God's creation and not eat stale food, drink tepid liquids, walk a marked path, and delight in dancing and senseless racket![9]

The extent to which such texts are representative of the situation of Christianity at large is an open question. In any case, after the early clashes about differentiating the specifically Christian and about its uniqueness and importance, there emerge an effort to emphasize what is special about both days—the Sabbath and Sunday—and also an effort to show the compatibility of both traditions and make room for both of them in the life of a Christian. We find the same basic orientation in Gregory of Nyssa when he says that the two days "have become siblings".[10] Granted, he draws different conclusions from the related meaning of the two days than the *Apostolic Constitutions* does: there is no longer a compelling reason for dividing the spiritual content shared by the brothers between two days. It can be put into one single day, but the day of Jesus Christ must then necessarily take precedence. This day is simultaneously the third, the first, and the eighth day, the expression of Christian uniqueness and the expression of the Christian synthesis of all realities.[11]

Also crucial for working out this synthesis had been the fact that the Sabbath is part of the Decalogue. In Paul, even with all the polemic against the law, it had always remained clear that the Decalogue stays in full force as the form of the double commandment to love and that through it Christians retain the law and the prophets in their entirety,

---

[9] Pseudo-Ignatius, *Ad Magn.* 9; cf. Rordorf, *Sabbat*, no. 59, p. 102.

[10] Gregory of Nyssa, *Adversus eos qui castigationes aegre ferunt* (PG 46:309B–C; cf. Rordorf, *Sabbat*, no. 52, pp. 92–93): "You who did not cherish the Sabbath, with what kind of eyes do you regard the Lord's Day? Or do you not know that these days are siblings (ἀδελφαί)?"

[11] On this point, see the superb turn of phrase with which an anonymous homily (ascribed to Athanasius) probably from the close of the fourth century summarizes and definitively expresses in a more precise way the outcome of the struggle of the patristic period to state the relationship between the Sabbath and Sunday: μετέθηκε δὲ ὁ κύρις τὴν τοῦ σαββάτου ἡμέραν εἰς κυριακήν ("the Lord has transferred the Sabbath to his day"), in Rordorf, *Sabbat*, no. 64, pp. 110–11.

in their true depth.[12] On the other hand, it was also clear that the Decalogue had to be read in a new way, from Christ's perspective, and that it had to be understood in the Holy Spirit. This made it possible to give Christians the freedom of dropping the Sabbath as a specific day and including it in the Day of the Lord. This also had to give them the freedom to understand the meaning and the form of the Sabbath in a deeper way than the casuistry fought by Jesus and Paul had done. But it also had to entail the imperative to grasp and to fulfill the true meaning of the Sabbath.

b. The Theology of the Sabbath

The question therefore also arises for us with a certain degree of urgency: What is this real and valid content of the Sabbath? To answer this question in a suitable way we would have to interpret the fundamental texts on the Sabbath in the Old Testament with care, that is, not only the creation account (Gen 2:1ff.) but also the legal texts from Exodus (e.g., 20:8–11; 31:12–17) and Deuteronomy (e.g., 5:15; 12:9) as well as the texts of the prophetic tradition (e.g., Ezek 20:12). To do all this cannot be my aim here; instead I would like to try to focus briefly on three main points.

1. To start with, it is fundamental that the Sabbath is part of the story of creation. One could actually say that the metaphor of the seven-day week was selected for the creation account because of the Sabbath. By culminating in the sign of the covenant, the Sabbath, the creation account clearly shows that creation and covenant belong together from the start, that the Creator and the Redeemer can only be one and the same God. It shows that the world is not a neutral receptacle where men then accidentally became involved, but that right from the start creation came to be so that there would be a place for the covenant. But it also shows that the covenant can exist only if it conforms to the yardstick of creation. From this starting point a merely historical religion or simple salvation history without metaphysics is just as unthinkable as a worldless piety that contents itself with private happiness, the

---

[12] Cf. Hartmut Gese, *Zur biblischen Theologie: Alttestamentliche Vorträge* (Munich, 1977), 54–84; here one finds important information concerning the genuine meaning of the Sabbath in the Old Testament and its adoption by Jesus. Cf. also Rordorf, *Sabbat*, xiif.

private salvation of one's soul or the escape into an amiably active parish community.

Thus, the Sabbath calls first of all for deep respect and gratitude toward the Creator and his creation. If the creation story somehow describes the establishment of a cult as well, then this means in any case that the cult in both its form and matter is necessarily connected to creation. It means that the things of creation are at God's disposal and that we can and must ask him for them. On the other hand, it means that we must not forget God's right of ownership when we use the things of the world. It means that these things were not handed over to us for arbitrary domination but were given to us from the measure of the true ruler and owner for a dominion of service. Wherever the Sabbath or Sunday is cherished, creation is cherished as well.

2. A second aspect is connected to this. The Sabbath is the day of God's freedom and the day of man's participation in God's freedom. Reflecting on Israel's liberation from slavery is central to the Sabbath theme, which is, however, much more than commemoration. The Sabbath is not simply remembrance of what has passed but an active exercise of freedom. This fundamental content is the reason why the Sabbath should be a day of rest to an equal degree for men and animals, for masters and servants. The legislation for the Jubilee Year shows that we are concerned with more than just a regulation of free time. In the Jubilee Year all the proprietary relationships return to their origin and all the forms of subjugation that have been built up through time come to an end.[13]

The great Sabbath of the festival year thus reveals what the objective of every Sabbath is: anticipation of the society free of domination, a foretaste of the city to come. On the Sabbath there are no masters and no servants; there is only the freedom of all the children of God and creation's release from anxiety. What the social theorist regards as the utopia of a world that can never be formed is a concrete demand on the Sabbath: the reciprocal freedom and equality of all creatures. For this reason the Sabbath is the heart of social legislation. If all social subordinations are suspended on the first or the seventh day, and if all social arrangements are revised in the rhythm of seven times seven

---

[13] Cf. Thierry Maertens, *Heidnisch-jüdische Wurzeln christlicher Feste* (Mainz, 1965), 114–47, 150–59. Maertens, however, does give one-sided prominence to the aspect of "spiritualization" in the transition from the Old Testament to the New Testament and overlooks the fact that Christian "spiritualization" is incarnation and christological concentration.

years, then they will always be relative to the mutual freedom and common ownership of all. The book of Chronicles even teaches us that Israel's exile occurred because she ignored the regulations of the Jubilee Year, the great Sabbath, and hence disregarded the basic law of creation and of the Creator. Looking back, all other sins seem secondary in the face of this fundamental unfaithfulness, in the face of this locking oneself into the self-made world of work that negates God's sovereignty.[14]

3. The third element of the theology of the Sabbath is revealed here, its eschatological dimension. The Sabbath is the anticipation of the messianic hour, not only in thoughts and desires but in concrete action. Only by living according to the form of the Messianic age do we open up the doors of the world for the time of the Messiah. We also become practiced in the way of life of the world to come. Irenaeus would say: We are getting used to God's way of life just as he got used to us during his life as a man.

Thus, cultic, social, and eschatological dimensions permeate one another. The cult rooted in biblical faith is not an imitation of the course of the world in miniature—as is the case for the basic form of all cults of nature. It is an imitation of God himself and therefore a preliminary exercise in the world to come. Only in this way does one correctly understand the singularity of the biblical creation account. The pagan creation accounts on which the biblical story is in part based end without exception in the establishment of a cult, but the cult in this case is situated in the cycle of *do ut des*. The gods create men in order to be fed by them; men need the gods to keep the course of the world in order. As I have already said, the biblical creation account, too, must definitely be seen, at least in a certain sense, as the establishment of a cult. But here cult means the liberation of men through their participation in the freedom of God and thus the liberation of creation itself, its release into the freedom of the children of God.

c. The Christian Synthesis

If you read the dispute Jesus had concerning the Sabbath or St. Paul's polemic on the same subject in the light of this knowledge, then it

---

[14] Cf. 2 Chron 36:21.

becomes perfectly clear that in both cases the real significance of the Sabbath is not at issue. The point is instead to defend the essential meaning of the Sabbath as a feast of freedom over against a practice that has turned it into a day of non-freedom. If Jesus, however, wanted not to abolish the real substance of the Sabbath but to save it, then a Christian theology that would like to remove it from Sunday is not on the right path. In his foundational investigations on the Sabbath and Sunday, W. Rordorf supports the view that combining the Sabbath and Sunday was a work of the period following Constantine's conversion; by saying this he has already passed judgment on this synthesis. He thinks that, apart from a few exceptions, the Christian churches have hitherto been stuck in the spell of this post-Constantinian synthesis and adds: "Since they must, for better or for worse, break with the old traditions of the Constantinian age, they will now be faced with the question of whether they can summon up the courage to rid themselves of the yoke of the Sabbath/Sunday synthesis."[15] More recent Catholic statements sound even more radical. L. Brandolini, for example, maintains that the emergence of Sunday came about in strict opposition to the Jewish Sabbath but that in the fourth century a countermovement arose that gradually resulted in making a Sabbath out of Sunday and thus led to a naturalistic, legalistic, and individualistic concept of cult.[16] As a result, reform is difficult today, especially since the Church is stuck in the Middle Ages and hardly seems capable of change in spite of Vatican II's efforts at renewal.[17]

Such reflections are correct insofar as the Christian Sunday is not tied to the state's exempting this day from work. Under no circumstances does Sunday correspond to a sociopolitical phenomenon that is attainable only under very special social conditions. In this respect the struggle to understand the deeper meaning of Sunday is justified since it exists independently of the fluctuations in external situations. But whoever deduces from this fact that the spiritual meaning of the Sabbath is completely opposed to that of Sunday has radically misunderstood both the Old Testament *and* the New Testament. The spiritualization of the Old Testament, which is part of the essence of

---

[15] Rordorf, *Sabbat*, xx.

[16] Cf. Luca Brandolini, "Domenica", in *Nuovo dizionario di liturgia*, ed. Domenico Sartore and Achille M. Triacca (Rome, 1984), 377–95 (quotation from 385f.).

[17] Cf. ibid., 379 and 386.

the New, is at the same time an incarnation that is always new. It is not a retreat from society and not a retreat from creation, but a new and more profound way of penetrating them. As with all the major themes of theology, the issue of correctly determining the relationship between the Old and the New Testament proves to be fundamental here.

Today's theology often fluctuates between a Marcionism that would like to rid itself completely of the burden of the Old Testament and withdraw into the particularity of what is only inner-Christian and a return to a merely political and social interpretation of the biblical tradition lying behind the transition to the New Testament.[18] The synthesis of the Testaments worked out in the early Church corresponds solely to the fundamental intention of the New Testament message, and it alone can give Christianity its own historical force. If one rejects the aspect of creation and the social components along with the Old Testament—that is, in this case along with the Sabbath—then Christianity becomes a clublike pastime and liturgy turns into entertainment that still appears old-fashioned even when it is presented with all sorts of progressive decorations. By eliminating the world in such a way one loses the starting point for the Christian doctrine of freedom and consequently falsifies the Christian notion of worship, whose essential and basic pattern is seen in the creation account's structure of the week, a pattern that admittedly has received its dramatic content through the Pascha of Christ. This Passover of Christ, however, does not do away with the vision of the creation account but lends it its entire concreteness. Christian worship is the anticipation of communal freedom in which man imitates God, becomes the "image of God". It is possible to anticipate such freedom only because creation has been fashioned for its sake right from the beginning.

4. Applications

Finally, practical questions once more make their voices heard with great urgency. At the same time, however, we should never lose sight

---

[18] On this point, cf. what is said about the inversion of symbols in the *Instructio* of the Congregation for the Doctrine of the Faith *de quibusdam rationibus "Theologiae Liberationis"* from August 6, 1984, 10:14–16, in *Congregatio pro Doctrina Fidei, Documenta inde a Concilio Vaticano secundo expleto edita (1966–1985)* (Vatican City: Libreria Editrice Vaticana, 1985), 279.

of the fact that reflecting on theological truth is itself something quite practical. In his recently published autobiographical sketches, Romano Guardini movingly described how making the truth present seemed to him to be the most concrete and therefore the most pressing task of his age.[19] Because of this attitude he came into conflict with important figures who shared his moment during those years in Berlin, with Dr. Münch, at that time the chair of the Association of Academics, and with Dr. Sonnenschein, the distinguished Berlin university chaplain. Looking back, we have to say that each of these men attended to a necessary task and thus represented a necessary aspect of pastoral work. But if from the distance of half a century we could now reconcile what at that time clashed, we still have to recognize without excluding anyone that Guardini's passionate and unpremeditated effort simply to let the truth speak in the midst of the reign of lies had the most far-reaching effect and rapidly proved itself to be completely practical right up to the decisions of the Second Vatican Council. In the long run we will be able to have the greatest effect if we at first rely not on our own deeds but on the inner strength of truth, which we must learn to see and then let speak.

In conclusion I would like to tackle two of the most pressing practical issues from the perspective of the theological insights that have just been developed.

a. Priestless Sunday Services

As a consequence of these considerations, our actions in practice have to be guided by two principles.

1. The sacrament must take precedence over psychology. The Church must take precedence over the group.

---

[19] Romano Guardini, *Berichte über mein Leben: Autobiographische Aufzeichnungen* (Düsseldorf, 1984), 109–13. Cf. especially 109: "At the same time, the longer I worked, the less I was concerned about the immediate effect. Right from the start, at first instinctively, but then more and more consciously, I wanted to make the truth shine. Truth is a power; but only if you do not demand an immediate effect from it." Also moving is the statement on 114ff.: "Here [at the talks in St. Canisius Church in Charlottenburg] I experienced perhaps most intensely what I said above about the power of truth. I have rarely been so conscious of how great and how fundamentally true and in control of life the message of Catholic Christianity is as on those evenings. At times it was as if the truth were standing in the room like a living being." Similarly expressed on 110.

2. Operating under the proviso of this hierarchy, the local churches must seek the right answer for each situation respectively, knowing that the salvation of all men (the *salus animarum*) is their real mission. In this orientation of all their work both their obligation and their freedom are to be found.

Let us look at the two principles a little more closely. In mission countries, in the diaspora, and in situations of persecution, it is not new that people cannot get to the celebration of the Eucharist on Sunday and that they must then try to take part in the Sunday of the Church to the degree that this is possible. In our part of the world, the decline of priestly vocations has noticeably given rise to such situations, to which we were largely unaccustomed until now. Unfortunately people have often covered up the search for the right answer with ideological theories on communality that stand in the way of the real concern rather than being of service to it. For example, it has been said: Every church that once had a pastor or at least regular Sunday worship should continue to be the place of assembly for the parish of that locality. Only in this way would the church remain the focal point of the village; only in this way would the parish stay alive as a parish. For this reason it is more important for the parish community to gather here and hear and celebrate the Word of God than to take advantage of the actually given possibility of participating in the eucharistic celebration in a church close by.

There is much here that is plausible and undoubtedly also well meant. But the fundamental evaluations of faith have been forgotten. In this way of looking at things the experience of togetherness and the fostering of the village community rank higher than the gift of the sacrament. The experience of community is, without doubt, more immediately accessible and more easily explained than the sacrament. So it seems reasonable to switch from the objectivity of the Eucharist to the subjectivity of experience, from the theological to the sociological and the psychological. But the results of placing the experience of community above sacramental reality in such a way are momentous. The congregation is now celebrating itself; the Church becomes a vehicle for social purposes; and at the same time she is promoting a romanticism that is somewhat anachronistic in our mobile society. To be sure, at the outset people are elated because they feel confirmed by the fact that they themselves are celebrating in their church, that they can "do it alone". But soon they notice that there is *only* the entity of their own making—that they no longer receive but merely present themselves. Then, however, the whole thing becomes superfluous because the Sunday service basically goes no farther than what they normally and always do anyway. It no longer touches any other order; it, too, is just their own thing. For this reason, that unconditional "must" about which the Church had always spoken cannot be inherent to this service. But then, according to an inner logic, this evaluation expands to include the real celebration of the Eucharist as well. For if the Church herself seems to be saying that assembly is more important than Eucharist, then the Eucharist is also just "assembly"—otherwise it would not be possible to treat them as equivalents. The whole Church then sinks into what is self-made and Durkheim's sad vision is proven right, namely, that religion and cult in general are only forms of social stabilization through the self-portrayal of a society. But once you know this, this stabilization no longer functions since it only works when you think there is more at stake. Whoever elevates the community to the level of an end in itself is precisely the one who dissolves its foundations. What seems to be so pious and reasonable at the beginning is actually a radical inversion of the important concerns and categories in which we eventually achieve the opposite of what was intended. Only when the sacrament retains its unconditional character and its absolute priority over all communal purposes and all spiritually edifying intentions does it build community and "edify" men. Even if a sacramental liturgy had fewer psychological trappings and were subjectively more lackluster and duller (if one may speak in such a purpose-oriented way), it is still "socially" more effective in the long run than the self-edification of a parish community performed with psychological and sociological expertise. We are concerned, namely, with the fundamental question of whether something happens here that does not come from us or whether we alone plan and shape the community ourselves. If there is not the higher "must" of the sacrament, the freedom that we claim for ourselves becomes empty since it has been robbed of its content.

Things are completely different when there is a real emergency. If we have a priestless Sunday service in this situation, we are no longer turning to something that is simply of our own making; this service is rather the collective gesture with which we reach out for *dominicus*, the Sunday of the Church. With this action we are holding on to the shared "must" and "want to" of the Church and thus holding on to the Lord himself. The crucial question is: Where is the boundary between what we merely want and what is real necessity? Certainly this boundary cannot be clearly drawn in the abstract, and even in each case it will be fluid again and again. In separate situations it must be set in agreement with the bishop on the basis of the pastoral sensitivity of those affected. There are rules that can help. It is not an explicit precept of canon law that a priest may not celebrate Mass more than three times on Sunday, but it does correspond to the limits of what he can possibly do. This arrangement has to do with the celebrant; on behalf of the faithful the questions to ask are whether the distance to travel is reasonable and whether the services are available at suitable times. We should not create too much prefabricated casuistry out of this, but leave room for conscientious decision making in view of what each situation requires. It is important that the weights remain correctly distributed and that the Church is not celebrating herself but the Lord whom she receives in the Eucharist and toward whom she moves in those situations in which the priestless parish reaches out for his gift.

b. Weekend Culture and the Christian Sunday

In my opinion it is far more realistic in our part of the world to turn the question around: What do we do when our parish communities leave their places of residence on Friday evening or Saturday in great haste only to show up again after the last Sunday service is long since over? How can we reconcile weekend culture and Sunday with each other? How can we again relate leisure time to the greater freedom we should be practicing on the Day of the Lord? I think we will have to have more ideas on this subject than we have had up till now—on the one hand, concerning the mobility of pastoral work and the mutual openness of the parishes to one another; on the other hand, concerning ways to make the parish community an inner home prior to what goes on in worship, a home that absorbs industrial society's compulsion to get away and gives it another goal. I am of the opinion that all the getaways we witness may be directed at diversion, relaxation, encounter, and liberation from the toils of everyday life, but that behind these totally legitimate desires there is still a deeper yearning: the longing to find a real home in brotherly communion and to experience a real contrast, that is, the longing for something "totally other" in the face of the glut caused by the immense scale of all we have made.

The Sunday liturgy should be responding to this. It will come off badly if it wants to enter the competition of show business. A pastor is not an emcee, and the liturgy is not a variety show. It will also come off badly if it wants to be a sort of engaging circle of friends. That can perhaps develop subsequent to the liturgy and out of encounters that have evolved there. But the liturgy itself must be more. It must become clear that a dimension of existence opens up here that we are all secretly seeking: the presence of that which cannot be made—theophany, mystery, and in it God saying that all is good, his approval, which reigns over being and is alone capable of making it good so that it can be accepted by us in the midst of all the tensions and suffering.[20]

We have to find the happy medium between a ritualism in which the liturgical action is performed in an unintelligible and nonrelational manner by the priest and a craze for understandability that in the end dissolves the whole into the work of men and robs it of its Catholic dimension and of the objectivity of mystery. Through the community that believes and believingly understands, the liturgy must have its own luminosity, which then becomes a call and hope for those who do not believe and therefore do not understand. As *opus dei* it must be the place where all *opera hominum* come to an end and are transcended and thus the place where a new freedom dawns, which we seek in vain in the liberties of the entertainment industry.

In such a way the liturgy, in accordance with the essential meaning of Sunday, could again become a place of freedom that is more than free time and permissiveness. This true freedom, however, is the one for which we are all on the lookout.

---

[20] For this reason the theory propagated on several occasions that the liturgy can only be celebrated with a priest one knows and in a parish where the parishioners know one another is wrong. Here the liturgy quite clearly sinks to the level of a social ritual. The wonderful thing about Catholicism, after all, is that believers are not strangers to one another and that wherever faith is present each one of the faithful is at home.

II. Is the Eucharist a Sacrifice?

1. Framing the Question: Luther's Concern

Although the question about the sacrificial character of the Eucharist is not in the foreground of the Catholic-Protestant theological dialogue today, it is nevertheless one of the decisive differences that gave the schism during the century of the Reformation its distinctive character, its spiritual and theological depth. The problem of justification, in which Luther had found himself obliged to rediscover the question of the nature of Christian faith and to regard the Catholic way of faith as a deviation from its real center, takes on here its full acuteness and specificity: as long as it is a matter of discussing faith and works, the meaning of the question becomes difficult to grasp for the individual Christian, who one way or the other has to live by faith, that is, can carry out God's call only in faith but also *must* carry it out in faith. In this context, however, where the form of Christian worship is decided, things become immediately tangible. For Luther, the Mass, that is, the Eucharist understood as a sacrifice, is idolatry, an abomination, because it is a regression from the newness of Christianity back into pagan sacrificial practices; for a Catholic, it is the Christian way of glorifying God together through Christ in the Church.

In fact for Luther, the dispute about the Mass is only one illustration of the basic problem of justification; although he sees in it a perversion of the true nature of Christian faith and thinks that the center of Christianity is thereby destroyed and turned upside down, ultimately what is expressed therein is the struggle over the fundamental understanding of the faith around which his theology repeatedly revolves. In the final analysis, for him there are only two opposing ways of relating to God: the way of the law and the way of faith. The way of

Translated by Michael J. Miller.

the law says that man seeks on his own to placate God by offering God works and accomplishments, with which he tries to satisfy him and obtain salvation. The Christ-event, to which the New Testament bears witness, means, on the contrary, that God puts an end to all these ultimately unholy attempts, that through Christ he spontaneously grants salvation, which man can never earn by his works and sacrifices. Thus the direction of faith is diametrically opposite to that of the law: it is receiving divine favor, not offering gifts. Consequently, Christian worship by its very nature can be receiving only, not giving; it is the acceptance of God's saving deed in Christ Jesus, which suffices once for all. This means then, conversely, that Christian worship is by its very nature distorted, indeed, is turned into its very opposite, when offering is reintroduced instead of thanksgiving. For then the law has replaced grace again, the sufficiency of the saving deed of Jesus Christ is denied, and man has gone back again to an attempt at self-redemption, achievement, and autonomy. From this vantage point, it is understandable that Luther saw in the idea of the Sacrifice of the Mass a denial of grace, a revolt of human autonomy, the backsliding from faith into the law that Paul fought so keenly.[1]

The serious theological importance of these reflections is unmistakable, especially since it would be possible to develop similar thoughts, apart from Luther, directly from the New Testament itself, especially from the Letter to the Hebrews, which presents with the most pointed emphasis the unrepeatable uniqueness of the priesthood and sacrifice of Jesus Christ and contrasts it with the repeated sacrifices of the Old Covenant. For this reason, a theology of the Sacrifice of the Mass should never bypass these questions carelessly; of course it does no good either to shove the matter sheepishly into a corner by limiting

---

[1] There is no need here to give detailed references to the extensive scholarly literature on Luther. Compare the summary presentation of the question in Reinhold Seeberg, *Lehrbuch der Dogmengeschichte*, vol. 4, pt. 1, 5th ed. (Darmstadt, 1953), 396–407, especially 405–7; Paul Althaus, *Die Theologie Martin Luthers* (Gütersloh, 1962). The recent study by Hans Bernhard Meyer, *Luther und die Messe*, KKTS 11 (Paderborn, 1965), deals exclusively with the history of the liturgy. On the present state of the Protestant-Catholic dialogue about the sacrificial character of the Eucharist, see Erwin Iserloh and Peter Meinhold, *Abendmahl und Opfer* (Stuttgart, 1960); and especially the large-scale study by Wilhelm Averbeck, *Der Opfercharakter des Abendmahls in der neueren evangelischen Theologie*, KKTS 19 (Paderborn, 1966); also, on the Catholic side, Wilhelm Breuning, "Die Eucharistie in Dogma und Kerygma", TThZ 74 (1965): 129–50; on the Protestant side, Gottfried Voigt, "Christus sacerdos: Zum ökumenischen Gespräch über das Altarsakrament", ThLZ 90 (1965): 482–90; and the fine work by Max Thurian referenced in n. 9.

oneself to an emphasis on the meal-character of the Eucharist: simply saying nothing about certain questions cannot advance theology or help believers put their faith into practice. What should we say then? Certainly it is not easy to find an answer, and much more honest controversy will be necessary in order to move closer to it from both sides.

I think that we start out on the path toward it when we first realize that Luther's passionate polemic, the content of which I have just tried to indicate, includes not only negations but also positive decisions, which can perhaps be formulated in these two theses:

a. The saving deed of Christ is the once and for all sufficient sacrifice in which God himself gives us, instead of the futility of our worship, the true, propitiatory sacrifice: this great keynote of the Letter to the Hebrews is also at the basis of Luther's theses.

b. Hence Christian worship can no longer consist in the offering of one's own gifts but, rather, is by its very nature reception of the saving deed of Jesus Christ that was bestowed once and, therefore, thanksgiving: *Eucharistia*.

Without any false apologetics, it is now possible to maintain that lying hidden in these two theses, correctly understood, is simultaneously a twofold starting point for a genuinely Christian concept of sacrifice and for a theologically legitimate understanding of the Eucharist as sacrifice that is realized within New Testament faith.

a. This does rule out entirely the notion of the Mass as an independent, self-contained sacrifice, yet it makes even more insistent the consideration whether the Mass, being the grant of the Christ-gift to his followers, must not also mean somehow the presence of this gift, the presence of Jesus Christ's salvific deed. Precisely Luther's theology—which gives so much prominence to the "for me" as the content of faith and which by no means understands the saving deed merely as a completed historical event but, rather, understands it only in its relation to me, as an appropriated reality that only in this way finds its meaning—actually had to hit upon this idea. In fact, Luther says: ". . . as long as it is not distributed to me, it is the same as if it had not yet happened for me. . . . For it is poured out for me when it is distributed to me."[2] Here the insight stands out quite clearly after all: that

---

[2] WA 18, 205; cf. Seeberg, *Lehrbuch der Dogmengeschichte*, 404; Meinhold and Iserloh, *Abendmahl und Opfer*, 53.

what once happened becomes present in the sacramental celebration with a view to me; that the act of receiving does not refer to something absolutely past but, rather, receives the past as something present.

b. This strongly suggests the thought that grateful reception is the Christian manner of sacrifice, inasmuch as it means the presence of the Christ-sacrifice and our being filled by it. Indeed, Melanchthon attempted an approach toward such ideas but framed it in such narrowly polemical terms that Trent found in it no usable starting point for an adequate formulation of the sacrificial character of the Mass.[3]

At this point let us interrupt our reflections for a moment so as to turn directly to the testimony of Sacred Scripture.

2. The New Testament Witness

a. The Texts

Every theology of the Last Supper has its immovable standard in the Lord's words of institution, which must remain forever the center of all that is said and thought about this matter. Its unfathomable richness has already provided material for countless learned monographs, so that it must seem almost presumptuous to try to interpret this passage in a few lines for our question. Consequently the comprehensive exegetical work, which would require a thoroughgoing examination, can only be presupposed here; we intend to try to meet it at its latest stage, so to speak, and to take up in telescoped form the core of its implications for the question of Last Supper and sacrifice.[4]

The starting point will have to be a reminder that the four accounts of the Last Supper handed down to us by the New Testament

---

[3] *Apologie der Augsburger Konfession* 24, 19, in *Die Bekenntnisschriften der evangelisch-lutherischen Kirche* (Göttingen, 1952), 354. The whole Article 24 "On the Mass" could be consulted for our topic. The Tridentine rejection of the idea of a mere sacrifice of thanksgiving can be found in DS 1753.

[4] From the exceedingly rich secondary literature I shall mention only: Joachim Jeremias, *Die Abendmahlsworte Jesu* (Göttingen, 1960); Paul Neuenzeit, *Das Herrenmahl* (Munich, 1960); Johannes Betz, *Die Eucharistie in der Zeit der griechischen Väter*, vol. 2, pt. 1 (Freiburg, 1961); Heinz Schürmann, *Der Abendmahlsbericht Lukas 22,7–38*, 3rd ed. (Leipzig, 1960; summary of several larger studies by the same author); Franz-Jehan Leenhardt, *Le Sacrement de la Sainte Cène* (Neuchâtel and Paris, 1948); Pierre Benoît, "Le Récit de la cène dans Luc XXII, 15–20", RB 48 (1939): 357–93.

(Mk 26:26–29; Mk 14:22–25; Lk 22:15–20; 1 Cor 11:23–26) are sub-divided into two types, the one represented by Matthew/Mark and the one offered by Luke/Paul. The main differences between these two forms of tradition consist, on the one hand, in the absence in Mt/Mk of the command to repeat the sacred action and, on the other hand, in the different ways of naming the offering of the chalice. The relevant interpretive expression in Mt/Mk reads, "This is my blood of the covenant", whereas in Lk/Pl it says "This cup . . . is the new covenant in my blood." If we analyze these two formulas, we will once again be able to note two salient differences whereby they differ in a not insignificant way, despite all the external similarity. In the one case (Mt/Mk), the offering is referred to directly as "blood"; in the other case, however, the offering as such is "the covenant" (Lk/Pl). Furthermore, Mt/Mk mentions "covenant" without a modifier, whereas the Pauline type speaks about the "new covenant".

b. The Marcan Type: Old Testament Theology of Sacrifice

The actual depth of these distinctions, which at first seem purely for-malistic, becomes apparent when one recognizes that each group of texts in this way brings an entirely different Old Testament background into play and, so to speak, offers a different New Testament theology of the Old Testament. After all, the astonishing wealth of the words at the Last Supper is due to the fact that they resonate with an extensive area of Old Testament tradition: while striking their one chord, they call to mind a whole symphony, as it were, and simultaneously set before it a new key signature that for the first time gives it its decisive form. Behind the expression "blood of the covenant" taken from Exodus 24:8 stands the whole covenantal theology of Exodus and with it also the theology of sacrifice, the concept of worship found in the Books of Moses. The juxtaposition of "body" and "blood" contained in the words at the Last Supper in this version takes up the sacrificial terminology of the Old Testament. The real heart of the Torah, the idea of covenant and its actualization in worship, thus extends into these words at the Last Supper and from it receives a new meaning. The Last Supper appears in parallel with the covenantal event on Sinai and with the ongoing cultic confirmation of it throughout Israel's history, in such a way, of course, that the new Moses himself—Jesus—at the same time offers the blood of the covenant in this new covenantal liturgy. Here we do not need to dwell on the far-reaching perspectives resulting from this parallel between the event on Sinai and the Last Supper, which thereby appears as the conclusion of a covenant and, thus, as the founding of the People of God; the important thing for us is that the idea of sacrifice unquestionably enters into the Last Supper event through the concept of "blood of the covenant": the liturgy of the life and death of Jesus Christ is interpreted as a covenantal sacrifice, which adopts the Mosaic first step at a higher level and directs it to its authentic meaning.

c. The Pauline Type: Prophetic Critique of Worship

A completely different atmosphere results at first if we look at the Old Testament background of the Pauline type of Last Supper. Although we were just able to establish that the essential Old Testament root of the Mt/Mk text is found in the Torah, in other words, in the books of the law, Lk/Pl harkens back to the other great stream of Old Testament tradition: the theology of the prophets. The mention of the "New Covenant" initially recalls the promise recorded by Jeremiah: "Behold, the days are coming, says the LORD, when I will make a new covenant with the house of Israel and the house of Judah, not like the covenant which I made with their fathers. . . . I will put my law within them, and I will write it upon their hearts" (Jer 31:31–33). The backdrop for these words of promise, however, is the prophetic theology of covenant and its conflict with the priestly understanding of covenant that is reflected in the Torah. If for the Torah covenant and worship belong together, the concept of covenant is understood liturgically and vice versa, so the covenantal theology of the prophets is based on a cultic critique of unprecedented severity, which radically calls into question the self-sufficiency of the cultic function: "For I desire steadfast love and not sacrifice" (Hos 6:6; cf. 1 Sam 15:22; also Mt 9:13). A life of faith in Yahweh and love for one's brethren is depicted as the true worship, without which external worship becomes an empty, indeed, repulsive farce (cf. Ps 40[39]:6ff.; 50[49]:7ff.; 51[50]:16f.; Is 1:11ff.; Jer 6:20; 7:22f.). With the formula "new covenant", in which the Word of God is supposed to be fulfilled (and cold, empty pomp is not supposed to be promoted), this whole line of Old Testament thought begins to resound, and the weighty antithesis that it offers to the cultic theology of the

Torah enters into the words of the Last Supper and causes their meaning to appear in a completely new light: the Last Supper of the Lord now stands as the fulfillment of this spiritual line, just as it previously was understood as the fulfillment of the law. It appears as the overcoming of the cult and the sacrificial practice by the one who offers no bulls or rams but truly offers himself: "Sacrifice and offering you do not desire; but you have given me an open ear" (Ps 40[39]:6), or, as the Letter to the Hebrews quotes the verse: "Sacrifices and offerings you have not desired, but a body have you prepared for me" (10:5). Sacrificial objects have been replaced by the self-giving I of Jesus Christ; the cultic critique has arrived at its destination; the temple has become superfluous.

d. The Common Center: The Idea of Vicarious Substitution

Now does this mean that there is an unbridgeable opposition between the cultic aspect of Mt/Mk and the prophetic aspect of Lk/Pl? The answer emerges if we look at a further bit of Old Testament theology that—in varying forms—is again common to all four texts. According to Mt/Mk, Jesus says that the covenantal blood of the Last Supper will be poured out "for many"; Lk updates the fundamentally unlimited universality included in the Old Testament concept of "the many" to the cultic community that is present: based on the certainty implied by this universality, he has Jesus say specifically to the community, "for you". As we said, this does not abolish the universality but, rather, means applying it in practice, fastening it to its *hic et nunc* [here and now]. Paul mentions the "for you" only in connection with the words over the bread (where it is found also in Lk, who says it twice), whereas he omits it in the words over the chalice. This saying about service "for many" incorporates the centerpiece of the Suffering Servant songs of Deutero-Isaiah into the words of the Last Supper; indeed, the prophet says that the Servant of God has borne the sins of many (53:12) and thus has freed them from guilt (53:11). The Suffering Servant theme, which we encounter in this way in the theology of the Last Supper, is furthermore closely connected in Isaiah with the theme of covenant (42:6; 49:8). Through this connection, the prophetic idea of covenant acquires a new depth: the future covenant appears to be based, no longer merely on internalization of the law, but, rather, on the substitutionary love of him who bears the burden for all; the idea of this "for" gives the prophetic message a new center, which of course was never again conceived and contemplated with the same depth as in the Suffering Servant songs. Let us go one step farther and ask how this totality goes together with the duality of cult and cultic critique that we just encountered. Then we may determine that the figure of the Suffering Servant expresses a theology that Israel developed during the time of banishment into exile, when it no longer had a temple or worship. During that time when God seemed to have forgotten his people and worship had expired and, so, the cultic critique had become pointless, an insight matured: Israel *itself*, in its rejection, in its fate of being expelled and shattered, is the sacrifice of mankind before the face of God; the people's history of suffering itself, and not some ritual or another, is worship and sacrifice in God's sight. Israel becomes acquainted with a new and more central form of sacrifice than the Temple was able to offer: martyrdom, in which ritual sacrifice is overcome by the self-offering of man.[5] Heinz Schürmann has pointed out that formulas like "to give up one's body" and "to lay down one's life" are technical terms for the death of a martyr. "Therefore Jesus here is probably characterizing his impending death as a martyr's death."[6] He takes up the Suffering Servant theme and interprets in these terms the meaning of his life and death and thereby gives the idea of worship its definitive meaning. He depicts himself as the Suffering Servant, in whom that visionary destiny is summed up and definitively comes to pass; this means, however, that all ritual theories of sacrifice become obsolete and that the New Covenant also is accomplished and concluded by a truly new sacrifice: it becomes evident that Jesus, the man who lays down his life, is the real worship and the true glorification of God. All four accounts of the Last Supper agree in professing a kind of worship that consists not in rituals but in the total self-surrender of the one who delivers himself up to the Father for mankind: the Suffering Servant theme is the unifying center that combines the two and thus makes the law and the prophets one. With Johannes Betz we can summarize our findings along these lines by saying that Jesus' self-offering is "primarily

---

[5] Cf. Joseph Ratzinger, article "Stellvertretung", in *Handbuch theologischer Grundbegriffe*, ed. Heinrich Fries, vol. 2 (Munich, 1963), 566–75.

[6] Schürmann, *Abendmahlsbericht Lukas 22,7–38*, 35.

to be understood, not technically in terms of sacrificial worship . . . , but, rather, in terms of martyrdom and the complete self-giving of the person." [7]

Thus we have found the real heart of the New Testament concept of sacrifice implicit in the words of institution at the Last Supper. In this idea the law and the prophets, the worship and the cultic critique have all arrived at their destination, so to speak, and have been "ful-filled". Once again the Letter to the Hebrews probably contains the deepest reflections and theological development of this magnificent synthesis, which is achieved here, not through ideas, but, rather, through the reality of Jesus' Passion. The witness of Jesus' life and death takes up again the real intention of Old Testament worship, which—like all worship in general—is based on the idea of substitution: human sac-rifice is abolished as undignified and is declared to be not in keeping with God's will; now man tries to replace himself with offerings and yet must constantly acknowledge that nothing is sufficient to com-pensate for himself; that he can sacrifice hecatombs of animals and produce and it will always amount to too little: he cannot pay his own ransom (cf. Mk 8:37 and parallel passages). Man cannot give himself and cannot replace himself, and so his situation seems hopeless. Wor-ship as a whole seems to be one great exercise in futility. In the man Jesus, who truly throws himself into the balance, the meaning of wor-ship is fulfilled, and, so, the former worship is simultaneously abol-ished: He himself is worship, and, according to this understanding, the Last Supper is a sacrifice that we receive with thanksgiving, a sacrifice that in our memorial truly enters into our midst.

e. Making the Sacrifice Present

This brings us to a final step: the question about the character of the Last Supper as something present. Unfortunately a very brief note on this subject must suffice here. This question, too, is touched on in the biblical words at the Last Supper, namely, in the command to repeat the sacred action: "Do this in remembrance of me" (Lk 22:19; 1 Cor 11:24, 25, 26). Hans Lietzmann once thought that he had found in these words the key to the Hellenistic origin of the sacramental

---

[7] Betz, *Eucharistie in der Zeit der griechischen Väter*, 40.

Lord's Supper, and starting from this premise he believed that he could prove that it was a Pauline institution analogous to the Hellenistic memorial meal for the dead.[8] Today it is clear to us, above all thanks to research by Joachim Jeremias, which Max Thurian has comprehensively elaborated, that we are dealing in this very instance with a fundamental term of Old Testament theology.[9] "Remembrance" is a central category of the Old Testament sacrificial practice; it anchors the Last Supper again in the same spiritual contexts that we have previously investigated and further clarifies it. "Remembrance", however, is above all also (and not separately from the previous remark) a type of making-present: when Israel commemorates salvation history, it receives it as something present, enters into that history, and becomes a participant in its reality. One could even say that the idea of commemorating and the classification of all worship under the heading of remembrance constitute the decisive difference between the cult of Israel and the cult of the Gentile world all around it: while the surrounding cults are related to the perpetually recurring "death and rebirth" of the cosmos and thus translate the myth of the eternal return into ritual form,[10] the worship of Israel is related to the historical action of God with the patriarchs and with Israel, is inclusion in this history, and, thus, is essentially a "remembrance" that creates presence. Cosmic worship and historical faith are separated from each other in the concept of remembrance. One more thing should be added in conclusion: "remembrance" has to do not only with past and present but above all with future also: it is man's recollection of God's saving acts but, precisely thus, also God's recollection of what is still outstanding: a call of hope and trust in what is yet to come.[11]

The passage in Paul's account that supplements and interprets the command in the words of institution points in the same direction: "For as often as you eat this bread and drink the cup, you proclaim the Lord's death until he comes" (1 Cor 11:26). The "proclamation"

---

[8] Hans Lietzmann, *Messe und Herrenmahl* (Bonn, 1926), 223; cf. his commentary on the First Letter to the Corinthians.

[9] Jeremias, *Abendmahlsworte Jesu*, 229–46 (detailed response to Lietzmann); Max Thurian, *Eucharistie: Einheit am Tisch des Herrn* (Mainz and Stuttgart, 1963), especially 15–26 and 125–67. Translated from *Eucharistie* (Neuchâtel, 1959).

[10] Cf. Mircea Eliade, *Cosmos and History: The Myth of the Eternal Return*, trans. Willard R. Trask (New York: Harper, 1959).

[11] The future orientation of the "remembrance" has been studied in detail particularly by Jeremias, *Abendmahlsworte*.

spoken about here is more than mere speech or a theoretical communication with no content of reality; it is an announcement that creates reality in the word of remembering and proclaiming.[12] This is so important because it shows how closely connected the verbal event and the sacrifice are here, how much Christian sacrifice as "remembrance" comes to pass precisely in proclamation, which is at the same time thanksgiving and a profession of hope; how little opposition there is between word and sacrament (unfortunately with this antithesis we later distorted the nature of both too much). At the same time, the Church Fathers had initially latched on to this precise state of affairs and, starting from the idea of "rational [or word-like] sacrifice", had developed the idea of Eucharistic sacrifice that initially is connected more to the word than to the sacramental elements. With that, by the way, we have automatically arrived again at our point of departure, and to some extent at least it must have become evident how little opposition there is, from the New Testament perspective, between thanksgiving and sacrifice: rather, they mutually define each other. Obviously an explicit dogmatic theory of the Eucharist as sacrifice has by no means been offered in all these remarks, but perhaps nevertheless the starting point has become visible from which such a theory must and can be developed, a point at which separated Christians, too, could try to find and to understand one another.

---

[12] Cf. Heinrich Schlier, *Die Zeit der Kirche*, 2nd ed. (Freiburg, 1958), 249; Schlier, *Wort Gottes* (Würzburg, 1958), 65ff.; Julius Schniewind, art. καταγγέλλω, in ThWNT 1:68–71, reference at 70f.

III. The Problem of Transubstantiation and the Question about the Meaning of the Eucharist

Just a few years ago it seemed as if the theme of "transubstantiation", even in Catholic theology, had been pretty much laid to rest. One did not challenge the Tridentine dogma, but in theological discussions one respectfully steered clear of it, for several reasons. The word itself seemed all too reminiscent of a sort of theology that tends to turn into mere philosophy and, caught in the squabble of hairsplitting debates, to forget its real task: the understanding appropriation of the word issued in service to the proclamation of the Good News of salvation. Moreover, the word "transubstantiation" recalls the self-alienation of eucharistic doctrine that was largely dominant well into our century: the emphasis in teaching about the sacrament shifted from active association with the risen Lord, who grants us table fellowship with himself, to a static, ontological perspective that, in a mentality strongly tinged with Monophysitism, skips over the humanity of Jesus Christ and simply considers the Host as the locus of God's presence, as God's earthly throne before which one adores, while almost forgetting the invitation to table fellowship, contrary to the original reason for the institution of the sacrament.

Besides these reservations within theology itself about the theme of "transubstantiation", however, there was (and is) another further difficulty for us today, being children of an age that thinks scientifically: apart from those specific connotations that come from the faith itself, does the word transubstantiation really still have any meaning at all today? Or with the disintegration of the medieval concept of substance—as a result of which bread is for us no longer a uniform "substance" but exhibits a complicated, artificial, chemical structure—has the original statement become at the same time a glaring anachronism? The concurrence of these two groups of questions seems to produce a situation

---

Translated by Kenneth Baker, S.J., and Michael J. Miller.

that not at all infrequently confronts those who work today in theology: the protest arising from the simplicity of a faith that remains true to its origin and opposes the dilution thereof by worldly spirituality encounters questions posed by critical reason about a theology that became involved too early with some kind of science or philosophy and thereby endangered the candor of the faith.

If one reflects on what has been said, one will have to admit that there are plenty of reasons not to put too much emphasis on the word "transubstantiation" in contemporary theology; that it is right to push it aside from the central position that it wrongly acquired in a theology excessively oriented to philosophy. But one will have to add that there are likewise plenty of reasons to treat the topic in its more modest present position and to address the questions that it poses. For to pass over them in silence or to suppress them would necessarily contradict the intellectual integrity that is vitally important for the faith. Thus, after years of silence, of restoring balance in eucharistic doctrine and centering it anew on the act of celebrating the Eucharist, it was completely consistent with the logic of the matter, for the theme of transubstantiation to increase again in significance in recent years. The present lecture was drafted independently of the debate that has started up again and was essentially completed before that discussion began. Hence it does not try to respond to the attempted solutions that have emerged in the meantime; instead, the lecture has been left in its original form with its independent line of argumentation.[1]

Its purpose and point of departure are therefore by all means intrinsically related to the new debate but with a somewhat different slant: the new approaches that have been developed, especially in Holland, essentially start with the scientific and philosophical problem of the concept of substance and attempt to respond to it by striving to explain the question of transubstantiation—not philosophically, but, rather, within the context of the liturgical event and of the way in which it defines the direction of the Eucharist. The weakness of this effort may lie in the fact that it telescopes two levels that simply do

---

[1] On this point, cf. the essay by Wolfgang Beinert, "Die Enzyklika 'Mysterium fidei' und neuere Auffassungen über die Eucharistie", ThQ 147 (1967): 159–78. In a later work I hope to be able to complete a detailed comparison of my interpretation with the new attempts to explain transubstantiation that have appeared in recent years. It seemed to me inappropriate to discuss them in this lecture, which is not directly related to them.

not fit together; a philosophical question (and transubstantiation is such a question) cannot be cleared up in terms of liturgical thinking, however much liturgical thinking necessarily determines and limits the possible areas of philosophical inquiry. It seems to me that the real weakness in the efforts that have come to light thus far is due to this incongruity of question and answer and to the underlying confusion of the levels of the problem. But, as we said, that will not be discussed here. Instead, we should just indicate the entirely different point of departure of the thoughts proposed here. They find their initial impetus in the intramural theological conflict that the doctrine of transubstantiation stirred up during the Reformation; the protest in that era was by its very nature related also specifically to the Catholic development of eucharistic devotion and eucharistic faith, and in this respect the polarization was focused on two main points: the idea of sacrifice and, precisely, the doctrine of transubstantiation. If one keeps that in mind, one will realize that here Catholic theology simply has a historical debt to pay: the two questions of the Reformers are with us now as before, and although they have lost much of their severity, given the developments on both sides, they still continue to be problems. Accordingly, I would like to try first of all to sketch briefly the Reformation conflict in its two figures—Luther and Calvin—so as to investigate from that perspective the original meaning of the doctrine of transubstantiation and to indicate its true place in the overall eucharistic reality. The answer to the philosophical question (which must be made in a philosophical manner and in precisely that way can of course be of service to theology) will thereby result automatically.

1. The Background to the Formulation of the Question: The Protestant Objection[2]

It does not have to be mentioned expressly that a detailed historical analysis of statements by Calvin and Luther on the subject of transubstantiation cannot be attempted here; instead, we will merely note

---

[2] The following presentation, which is concerned, not with an overview of the historical phenomenon, but solely with marking out the scope of the problem, agrees rather closely with the material and to some extent also with the evaluation in Peter Pfeiffer, "Die Thesen der Konfessionen zur Anbetung des Altarsakramentes", US 17 (1962): 225–26.

the central thing that brings them to protest against the Catholic doctrine of transubstantiation and the basic approach with which they counter it.

a. Calvin

While Zwingli demoted the sacraments almost to pure symbols and then, later, when he had learned to speak more cautiously, conceded that there is in the Eucharist only a "praesentia in mente" (presence in the mind), Calvin endeavored to restore Augustine's eucharistic teaching as faithfully as possible. Of course, upon closer inspection *his* attempt shows that there is no such thing as a simple renewal of the past: one cannot undo a thousand years of history; there is no going back behind the formulations of questions once they have been broached. Two facts of the case clearly distinguish Calvin's teaching on the Eucharist in advance from that of Augustine:

a. Calvin transformed Augustine's open, non-systematic teaching about the Eucharist into a closed system. It is thus robbed of its richness and multiple facets.

b. Calvin gives explicit answers to questions that were not yet posed by Augustine and thereby necessarily produces extended arguments not found in Augustine's teaching.

Calvin's starting point is a strong emphasis on the real humanity of Jesus that manifests itself in his writings as a *theology of the Ascension* understood very emphatically and quite essentially in a local sense as well. Christ sits at the right hand of the Father and nowhere else; because he is true man, he cannot be everywhere at the same time. Since Calvin obviously had learned about the Real Presence primarily in its Lutheran form as a doctrine about the ubiquity of the man Jesus, he felt obligated just by his stance on the humanity of Jesus to reject this doctrine: Christ is seated at the right hand of the Father and *not* on our altars. Nevertheless, even according to Calvin, there is a real union with Christ in the genus of the Eucharistic Gifts, namely, insofar as Christ *draws us up to himself* by the power of the Holy Spirit.

In this concept of the Sacrament of the Eucharist two things deserve a positive evaluation:

1. The pneumatological character of Christian worship and of the eucharistic celebration is again seen clearly in Calvin's writings. Christian

worship is something that happens in the Holy Spirit. The Holy Spirit is the space in which Christian worship of God is enacted.

2. As for the theological structure at work here, one could speak about a dialectic between a theology of the Incarnation of the Lord, who gives himself completely into our hands, and a theology of the Ascension of the Lord, who nonetheless remains the completely-Other in his superior power, which nothing and no one can bind or obligate. The mysterious "simultaneity" of Christ's "being here" and "not being here", of his being a servant and being Lord, becomes visible in this dialectic in an astonishing way.

From the basic approach just outlined, Calvin concludes that Christian worship is directed *upward*. For him, as it is for Augustine, the decisive word in the eucharistic liturgy is *Sursum cor* (lift up your heart): the purpose of the liturgy is to raise us up to the Lord who is not here but is above. The central content of the eucharistic celebration is having one's heart on high, being lifted up and allowing oneself to be lifted up to the Lord.

At this point, of course, the dangerous side of this interpretation of sacrament also becomes clear. The sacrament is reduced to an act of being lifted up by the Holy Spirit. It has no reality here *below*, in our midst. It is only *dynamis*, an upward movement of transition. This means that in the dialectic between the theology of the Ascension and the theology of the Incarnation the former has won a one-sided victory: there is no longer any real entrance of the Lord into earthly reality; in the dialectical interplay of "being here" and "not being here", the "being here" runs the risk of being abolished in practice; the "here" becomes meaningless in contrast with the "there". This state of affairs comes to light with the utmost clarity in two statements by Calvin:

a. In Holy Communion, real union with Christ does take place through the Holy Spirit who lifts us up on high, but something similar takes place in every other encounter with the Lord: in reading Sacred Scripture, in hearing a sermon, as well as generally in the daily practice of the faith. In this complete reduction of the sacrament to a dynamic, there is no longer anything unequivocally unique or distinctive about the Eucharist. "Christ is the substance and the matter of preaching and of prayer just as he is of Baptism and of Holy Communion."[3] Certainly one should not make too much of

---

[3] Ibid., 240.

these statements; other assurances of real sacramental faith contrast with them, but neither should one underestimate them: the completely and utterly pneumatic-dynamic understanding of worship necessarily produces such thoughts, and while they do not negate a certain form of eucharistic Real Presence, they tend nevertheless to make it synonymous with the general real presence found in the faith.

b. This is corroborated by the fact that Calvin (relying on Augustine) very emphatically asserts that the pious men of the Old Covenant received the Body and Blood of Christ just as really as we do and, conversely, that Christ is no more present *in* the bread and wine of the Lord's Supper than he was *in* the sacrificial animals of the Old Covenant.[4]

Based on this completely upward-oriented understanding of sacrament, Calvin decisively draws a line in the sand against the most far-reaching consequence that the medieval Church logically drew from the Real Presence in the area of devotion, namely, adoration of the Eucharistic Species and of the Lord who is believed to be present in them. In his system, doing such a thing becomes impossible. For Calvin, it is idolatry, because the meaning of the sacrament lies solely in the *actio* of the sacramental celebration, which points us strictly upward.

If one surveys the whole matter, one will have to say that the chief tendencies of Calvin's eucharistic doctrine can be understood very well against the background of the shift in eucharistic faith that occurred in the High Middle Ages and became to a large extent dubious and in the context of the pious practices ordered to that faith; from this perspective, they must be seriously reconsidered as a question and problem for the contemporary reflection of Catholic theology.

a. In contrast to the drawing down of God and Christ completely into earthly things that can be observed in the late Middle Ages, Calvin sets up a radical theology of the Ascension; in opposition to the undialectical "here" (in the tabernacle, in the monstrance), he sets up a decisive "not here", in which, of course, the "here" now almost completely disappears.

b. The medieval understanding of the Eucharist that became totally static (the Host "is" Christ, hence exposition, contemplation, and adoration as the real center of the Eucharist) is confronted by a radicalized

---

[4] Ibid., 241. Cf. Wilhelm Niesel, "Vom Abendmahl Jesu Christi", in *Abendmahlsgemeinschaft?* Beiheft zu *Evangelischer Theologie* (1937), 52.

dynamic understanding, which holds that Christ's approach to man, or man's being drawn upward to Christ, occurs only in the *actio sacramentalis* that is sustained by the Holy Spirit.

c. The Monophysite tendency of the medieval doctrine of the Eucharist, which continued in another way in Luther's position, is countered by a radical emphasis on the humanity of the glorified Lord as well.

d. In contrast to the undialectically localized devotion of adoration, we find the dynamic understanding of adoration as well, which is seen as an elevation of the heart that one could thus describe as the counterpart to focusing the eucharistic celebration on the elevation of the Host and as the antithesis of the concentration on the static understanding of adoration: over against that, the *Sursum cor* appears here as the markedly pneumatic center of the sacramental celebration. In spite of such legitimate concerns, in which Calvin brings the great heritage of Augustine to bear in a time far removed from it and in a lasting way for every Christian age, one cannot deny that he himself becomes the victim of his characteristic tendency to systematize, in which the mystery falls victim to the airtight logical consistency of the system and ultimately the Eucharist no longer has anything proper or distinctive vis-à-vis other ways of encountering the glorified Lord. This, however, also entails the loss of the basic attitude that for Augustine is the real breathing space of his speaking and thinking about the Eucharist—that attitude in which he is at the same time simply a witness of the unbroken power of the origin: the central connection between "corpus Christi verum" (the true body of Christ) and "corpus Christi mysticum" (the mystical body of Christ) that with all the changes in terminology from Paul to the early Middle Ages defined the essential place of the Eucharist and that is most capable of making its irreplaceable and proper character manifest. Here Calvin pays his tribute to the Middle Ages, which he attacked and whose basically individualistic attitude to the Sacrament he unwittingly adopts in his own eucharistic doctrine while carrying it to its logical extreme. Thus, despite all the important initial steps, the *sacramentum ecclesiae* has finally slipped from his grasp after all along with the *ecclesia*.

b. Luther

The Lutheran confessional writings start, like Luther himself, from faith in the Real Presence, which along with him they understand as *substantial* presence—in contrast to the completely dynamic-actual and, thus, anti-substantialist thinking of Calvin. This recognition of the category of substance in defining the specific form of the eucharistic reality, of course, goes hand in hand with the simultaneous rejection of the category of transubstantiation. This separation of concepts appears to be purely philosophical yet has an incisive theological significance: it means that while admitting that *"cum* pane et vino substantialiter *adesse* exhiberi et sumi corpus et sanguinem Christi"[5] (the Body and Blood of Christ are shown and reckoned *to be present with* the bread and wine), on the other hand, a lasting connection of the species with Christ's Body and Blood and consequently a presence of the Lord *extra usum* are rejected.[6] With that, the real motive for rejecting transubstantiation already becomes apparent at the same time: the mere concept of substance, as a more precise description of what is meant by Real Presence, can still be connected dynamically by a *"cum"* with bread and wine and thus be enclosed within the dynamic context of *exhiberi* and *sumi*. To affirm transubstantiation, on the other hand, means to have recourse to ontology in much more radical way; it necessarily includes a lasting event and thus entails the extension of the Eucharist and of its reality beyond the moment of the sacramental celebration. The unavoidable conclusion seems to be that ontology imposes its law on the sacrament and becomes the norm of devotion instead of Christ's command in instituting the sacrament or Church tradition. For from the idea of the enduring eucharistic presence, which is necessarily supposed in the concept of transubstantiation, necessarily follows the adoration of the Lord who is present even outside of the celebration, in other words, a new dimension of the Eucharist unknown in Christian antiquity, which now exists no longer merely as a celebration of the assembled community, but also in a second dimension as a reference point for forms of worship independent of the celebration.

---

[5] *Solida Declaratio* VII, 14, in *Bekenntnisschriften der evangelisch-lutherischen Kirche*, 2nd ed. (Göttingen, 1952), 977.

[6] Ibid., VII, 15, p. 977: "Nam extra usum, cum reponitur aut asservatur in pixide aut ostenditur in processionibus, ut fit apud Papistas, sentiunt non adesse corpus Christi." (For apart from reception/apart from accepted usage, when it is reposed or reserved in a pyx or displayed in processions, as is the custom among the Papists, they [Protestant theologians] say that the Body of Christ is not present.) See the condemnation of eucharistic adoration found in *Konkordienformel, Epitome* VII, ibid., 803 §40. Further documentation is given in Pfeiffer, "Thesen", 246f.

But we are getting ahead of ourselves. First of all, there is still the question about the exact delimitation of eucharistic "substantial presence" in Luther's view, which we find indicated by the words "extra usum". What does that mean? In the *Solida declaratio*, the word *usus* is translated *Niessung* (usufruct, use), that is, limited to the moment of reception. This notion in fact made a decisive impression on the consciousness of Lutheran Christianity. It appears, however, that we find here already a certain adaptation to Calvinist thought that distances itself a bit from Luther's original intention. His concept of *usus* seems to have been broader and did not simply coincide with the moment of the *sumptio*, the reception: there are texts that show that Luther recognized a Real Presence beyond the immediate moment of the *sumptio* and by no means called into question the possibility of reserving Communion for the sick. Thus one could more correctly say (with Peter Pfeiffer) that *extra usum* for Luther is synonymous with *extra institutionem Christi* (apart from Christ's institution). That would mean that the Real Presence in his view is extinguished when the framework instituted by Christ is abandoned, that is, when the Eucharist is taken out of the context of "take and eat" and made autonomous. Then for Luther *usus* becomes *abusus*, use becomes abuse, and adoration becomes idolatry. "He did not institute the sacrament in order that we might adore it but in order that we might eat it." [7] *That is why* Luther condemns the elevation of the Host and Chalice at the consecration. That is why he acrimoniously rejects the Feast of Corpus Christi and throws out the tabernacle and the monstrance: in all that, in his view, the Eucharist stands *extra usum*, and so for him what takes place then is not worship of God but idolatry.

The driving force behind Luther's doctrine of the Eucharist is not difficult to recognize: by setting aside all philosophy and arbitrary attempts to systematize and to explain, he intends to return to the plain simplicity of the Bible, to the original purity of the Lord's institution, to restore its full value as opposed to all later excesses. With that we have arrived again at the rejection of the doctrine of transubstantiation: it should be understood from this perspective and can be traced back more particularly to two supporting points of view:

---

[7] "Non ideo instituit sacramentum ut adoretur, sed ut vesceremur." WA 11:449. Pfeiffer, "Thesen", 253.

a. First of all, the No to the term and idea of transubstantiation is a part of Luther's general polemic against the dominance of philosophy in theology, against the overrunning of the faith by the supposed authority of human reason for which he always reproached the Scholastics.

b. As we saw earlier, the denial of philosophy in this case receives additional nourishment from the consequences that philosophical thinking itself set loose, so that the question of transubstantiation could actually become concrete proof of the dangers that spring from the improper dominance of philosophy in theology. For transubstantiation means enduring presence; if one affirms it, then it would require a new miracle to terminate the substantial presence of the Lord again once it had become a fact. This makes the logical consistency of eucharistic adoration quite plain; yet in this way it appears that philosophical thinking has been set up as the standard for faith: although the concept of "substance" can still be deemed a means of understanding that does not detract from the faith but, rather, helps to convey it, so that philosophy accordingly stays within its limits, yet in the case of transubstantiation it appears that there has been a transition from understanding to standardization and, thus, a reversal of the relationship [between faith and philosophy]. It is not necessary to demonstrate here that the concept of transubstantiation did not give rise to the possibility of eucharistic adoration and that it was never based on that concept alone. Nonetheless, for Luther the close connection of the two facts was obvious and a compelling reason to reject the idea of transubstantiation decisively.

c. The studies by Erwin Iserloh[8] have made it clear that of course even Luther could not escape the inevitability of philosophical thinking and that in fact besides these strictly theological reasons he had an important philosophical motive as well: in the philosophical development of late Scholasticism, the Thomistic concept of transubstantiation had become intellectually untenable and inherently contradictory as a result of the extensive recasting of the Aristotelian categories

---

[8] Erwin Iserloh, *Die Eucharistie in der Darstellung des Johannes Eck: Ein Beitrag zur vortridentinischen Kontroverstheologie über das Messopfer*, RGST 73/74 (Münster, 1950); Iserloh, *Der Kampf um die Messe in den ersten Jahren der Auseinandersetzung mit Luther*, KLK 10 (Münster, 1952); Iserloh, *Gnade und Eucharistie in der philosophischen Theologie des Wilhelm von Ockham: Ihre Bedeutung für die Ursachen der Reformation*, VIEG 8 (Wiesbaden, 1956); Erwin Iserloh and Peter Meinhold, *Abendmahl und Opfer* (Stuttgart, 1960).

that had taken place almost unnoticed in the leading schools. This process, on which the development of modern physics is based, had already started immediately after Thomas: the identification of substance and quantity, of substance and "mass", as we would say today. However, since in the celebration of the Eucharist nothing about the quantities changes perceptibly, the concept of transubstantiation had lost its meaning vis-à-vis the prevalent understanding of substance. In a procedure typical of late Scholasticism and nominalism, theologians continued nevertheless to adhere to transubstantiation in a purely verbal way: whereas it is absurd, naturally considered, it must however be accepted in faith even contrary to this insight. This double-entry bookkeeping, in which the faith was no longer elaborated rationally and thought went its own way independent from it, while the formulas of theology were adhered to externally although they had become intrinsically absurd or meaningless— this double-entry bookkeeping is characteristic of that inner fragility which the situation of faith and Church in the late Middle Ages increasingly exacerbated. Given this intellectual situation, individual theologians had abandoned the concept of transubstantiation and replaced it with that of consubstantiation; Luther, who philosophically belonged entirely to the nominalism of the late Middle Ages, merely drew in this regard the logical conclusion from the intellectual climate when he decided to take the same step, which of course in his case became something totally new because of the determination with which he carried out the further consequences for the ecclesial form of the sacrament and for the limits of Church teaching: here the limits of theological doctrine were abandoned, and the Church herself, which had become deeply committed to this doctrine as well as to its application as the basis of devotion, was called into question.

Of course at this point we see clearly also the limits of Luther's procedure; there is something deeply moving about its uncompromising quest for the original form. But precisely in this it is not without an odd sense of tragedy as well. For, the wheel of history—as we saw earlier with Calvin's allegedly pure Augustinianism—cannot be reversed. Once a question has made its appearance, it cannot be taken back; the previous situation is irrevocably gone. After the question of transubstantiation has been raised, one can no longer speak about the Eucharist as if this question did not yet exist. Even if one tries to get behind it, one is no longer simply doing the same thing, as if the question did not yet exist. So also Luther—as we just saw briefly—in his own way spoke and had to speak about the Eucharist within the context of the problem of transubstantiation; from that vantage point, he did in fact say some new things about the Eucharist and did not simply restore the original as he wished to do. Two facts will make this clear.

a. As previously indicated, Luther adopted the theory of consubstantiation, following Peter of Ailly, who for his part stands in a line of tradition going back to early Scholasticism, although it was interrupted in the thirteenth century: bread and wine remain in existence entirely as before; they are neither changed nor elevated by the sacramental words. Instead, the Body and Blood of Christ become present "in, with, and under" the bread and wine.

b. After the beginning of the debates with Karlstadt and the Symbolists around the year 1525, another line of thought connected with Occam makes its appearance. Occam, in keeping with his voluntaristic world view, had attempted to explain the Real Presence of the Lord in the Eucharist in terms of the idea of multivoli-presence: although the Body of Christ is not omnipresent, the divine will has the power to make it present wherever he wills. Luther radicalized this thought to absolute omnipresence, to the "ubiquity" of the man Jesus, also, and therefore of his Body, too. For him such a way of looking at it—diametrically opposed to Calvin's strict theology of the Ascension—results from his understanding of the communication of idioms—that grammar of Christology which had definitively developed in the Middle Ages but very soon ran the risk of leading to the vicinity of Monophysite patterns of thought. "When you can say: God is here, then you must also say: Christ the man is here also. And if you were to point to a place where God was and not the man, then the person would already be divided."[9] Therefore, the right hand of God, where Christ is, should not—the contrast to Calvin again comes to mind—be thought of in a local sense as a "golden chair" at the Father's side; rather, God's right hand is the "almighty power of God", which is everywhere, in the "smallest tree leaf", in "the most interior place", and in "the most external

---

[9] WA 26:332f.; cf. Reinhold Seeberg, *Lehrbuch der Dogmengeschichte*, vol. 4, pt. 1 (Darmstadt, 1953), 466f.

place". In this respect, the Body of Christ is *everywhere*, even in every stone, in fire and water. Indeed: *we* can find and grasp him only in places where he instructs us to do so through his word: "It is one thing when God is there, and another when he is there *for you*." [10] Thus the word of institution teaches us to seek and find in a particular piece of bread the Christ-Body that in and of itself is present everywhere and, therefore, also in *every* piece of bread.

This constitutes a critical modification of the understanding of Holy Communion that departs considerably from the understanding of Holy Communion in the early Church. A new, twofold polarization of the Eucharist results: the accent moves away from the gifts to the word as the only really distinctive feature, and it shifts decisively to the ego of the believer: here the presence of Christ is allocated *to me*. "Now while all those who still have sins are in need of the Body and Blood of Christ, it is nevertheless true that it is given for them; for although an event may have happened, as long as it is not communicated to me, it is for me as though it had not yet happened.... For it is poured out for me if it is distributed and assigned to me." [11] In this view, the meaning of Holy Communion is identified to a large extent with the meaning of the preached word: to seek consolation in the sacrament means to seek consolation, not in the Cross, not in the bread and wine, not in the Body and Blood "but in the *word* that in the sacrament presents, entrusts, and gives to me the Body and Blood of Christ as something given and poured out for me". Eating becomes secondary to hearing; the purpose of the sacrament is to strengthen faith and to assure the troubled ego of the forgiveness of its sins.

However, this triple reduction of the eucharistic event to the word, to the *pro me*, [12] and to the certainty of the forgiveness of sins is linked, albeit unintentionally, with a far-reaching questioning of the sacrament in general. And it becomes obvious that it is problematic to attempt to return to biblical simplicity at a moment when the human mind has irrevocably abandoned this simplicity and is able to preserve the old and the original articles of faith only by articulating them in

---

[10] WA 23:151; 19:492. Seeberg, *Lehrbuch*, 469f.

[11] WA 18:205. Seeberg, *Lehrbuch*, 404.

[12] This broaches the fundamental problem of Lutheran theology; cf. Paul Hacker, *Das Ich im Glauben bei Martin Luther* (Graz, 1966); on the question of the Eucharist, see 219–33.

something new. History allows no return, and this becomes particularly clear in Luther's eucharistic teaching as well.

Thus there is no denying a remarkable conflict in Luther's understanding of the Eucharist: On the one hand, it presents itself as a simple repetition of the biblical faith with a plain and undivided Yes to the Real Presence, which, moreover, is described in keeping with medieval Church teaching as substantial presence; it appears as an emphatic reference back to the original sense, to the pure *institutio*, as opposed to the varied excrescences of the Middle Ages. On the other hand, it is unmistakably supported and defined by a new way of thinking, by a new relation to reality that does not negate the first insight, yet modifies it in very essential ways.

2. The Present State of the Question

All the previous discussion was supposed to clarify the *theological* problem that is concealed behind what seems to be a purely *philosophical* concept of transubstantiation and, thus, at the same time to make clear the limits of the philosophical question as well as its inescapability as a question that has been formulated. This could be said to mark off, to some extent, the area in which efforts to deal with the question of transubstantiation must move and, at the same time, to clarify the larger contexts that must be kept in mind if one wishes to address our topic in an objective and meaningful way. Of course, conversely, if we seek now to determine the meaning of transubstantiation positively, we will not be able to avoid concentrating on the second front along which this idea must justify itself: philosophical thinking and our scientific knowledge about the structure of reality. For the thesis that bread and wine undergo a "substantial change" is the philosophical formulation of an article of faith that in turn borders immediately on statements from the field of physics. Thus the thesis not only involves serious theological consequences (as we noted earlier), but it must also prove its worth and its meaningfulness in light of philosophical thinking. Any attempt to do so runs into a difficulty: the teaching about substantial change was developed in terms of twelfth- and thirteenth-century thought, out of its world view, so that the question unavoidably arises whether perhaps this teaching may be valid as a meaningful explanation of the sacrament within the framework of that world view but has passed away along with that world view as far as we are concerned.

a. The Philosophical Problem of Transubstantiation

On the History of the Concepts of Substance and Transubstantiation

The intellectual situation in which the discussion about substance finds itself today can perhaps best be visualized through a formulation by Bernhard Bavink, who explains that modern physics, whether in the theory of relativity or in quantum physics, is no longer willing to make, with regard to substance, the "distinction between substance, which per se only fills space, and process, which fills time". Similarly, for this mindset, that "something" which distinguishes the world from nothingness is being *and* happening, matter *and* energy, so that the difference between substance and accident loses its meaning, as far as fundamental principles are concerned.[13] Recall the mutual convertibility of matter and energy; the duality of particle and wave as the two manifestations of material being.

Now of course at this point anyone acquainted with thirteenth-century thought will immediately have to object that these considerations affect only the concept of substance found in classical physics or, at any rate, going back to the Middle Ages. For classical physics, as everyone knows, substance was the last indivisible unit of corpuscular being; at first atoms were regarded as those units and, later, the elemental particles found in atoms. They appeared to be the things ultimately responsible for material reality, the "building blocks of reality" out of which the world is constructed. Thus they were considered the substances in which the different dynamic processes occurred accidentally. The demonstration that matter in principle can be transformed into energy demolished this notion of substance. Matter is not something that exists as solid clumps of reality. The ultimate particles are not some "mass" in rigid contrast to energy. Consequently, the concept of substance in classical physics and the late Middle Ages is in fact abolished.

---

[13] Bernhard Bavink, *Ergebnisse und Probleme der Naturwissenschaften*, 9th ed. (Zurich, 1949), 210; cf. the whole chapter "Der Substanzbegriff in der heutigen Physik", 194–218.

The thirteenth-century concept of substance, however, as it was classically formulated by Thomas Aquinas, is completely different. For High Scholasticism, not only the "when" but also the "where" is an accident; that is to say, not only the process unfolding over the course of time but also the structure existing in space is an accident. In still other words: not just the quality but also the *quantity* is considered an accident. That is an important observation. For with that we have caught sight of the subject matter peculiar to the field of metaphysics, as the High Middle Ages understood it; at the same time, this makes evident the central element in the rearrangement of our understanding of reality that became the presupposition of the classical physics of the modern era. For the High Middle Ages, "matter" as *materia prima* is a pre-physical, precisely meta-physical entity; it is pure potentiality, and as such it does not become intelligible anywhere; it can only be grasped speculatively, metaphysically as the one root of physically observable material being. The same is true of "substance", which refers to the metaphysical reality of the subsistence of an existing thing, but not to the appearing thing as phenomenon. Starting in the late Middle Ages, there was an identification, which became definitive with Descartes, of *materia* with *quantitas*, of substance with *quantitas*; matter was now equated with the appearing, physically tangible, and measurable material quantity. Of course this process was produced mainly by the lack of clarity inherent in the metaphysical statements even of High Scholasticism, in which the fundamentally intended separation of the metaphysical concept from the physical phenomenon was never consistently maintained. But in terms of the speculative intention we can say: In understanding quantity as an accident, High Scholasticism assigns the *entire* subject matter of physics to the realm of what the metaphysician calls "accident"—to the sphere of the phenomenal, of "appearances", and not to that of the noumenal [what is knowable]. It should not be that difficult for us to see how completely this arrangement agrees with the contemporary positivistic-nonmetaphysical self-understanding of physics, which at this point in a more profound sense also becomes comprehensible as something metaphysically relevant. But then that also means that the "substance" about which the metaphysician speaks refers altogether to a pre-physical and unphysical entity; it means that it would be foolish and methodically absurd to try to make substance physically intelligible somewhere in atoms or in the elementary particles. But then that also means that *no* physical phenomenon can represent a substantial change in the metaphysical sense.

Attempt at a New View of the Problem

At this point, of course, it now becomes evident that our question includes the whole problem of the foundations of philosophy and categorically subjects all philosophical thinking to the fundamental question: What is "metaphysics", really? About what kind of reality does it actually speak, and with what right can it do so? Confronted with this question, surely, Scholastic thinking, which we just found to be in many respects more critical, that is, more discriminating in comparison with the thinking of modern philosophy and its accompanying physics, will appear precritical to us in three ways: precritical, first of all, because in fact it was not able to carry through consistently the fundamentally intended critical separation of physics and metaphysics, of phenomenon and noumenon. Precritical, next, because it has not yet clearly taken up the Kantian critical reflection on the limits of human cognition. Precritical, finally, because it has not yet considered the crisis, announced by Luther, of the role of philosophy in theology. In this respect, a fundamental question becomes evident here that concerns theology, philosophy, and physics equally; we are standing at one of those junctions where the three essential ways in which man perceives reality, and takes a stance toward it, collide with each other and must give an account of their respective limits and their possible mutual relations. Although one may be inclined today, starting from a theology of unobjectifiability, to regard such a meeting a priori as proof of the presence of a theological blind alley, we must decisively reject that conclusion from the perspective of faith's claim to totality. If the faith really concerns the whole life of man, then there must be such points of intersection; the fact that the theology of nonobjectivity tries to set them aside completely demonstrates instead the dangerous loss of reality by which it is threatened. Admittedly we should not overlook the contrary danger of faith overstepping its limits, and we should fight against that also at such points.

It goes without saying that we cannot expatiate and elaborate fully here on the fundamental problem we have encountered: that would require a complete course in fundamental theology, the necessity of which becomes apparent here once again. So we can only attempt to state summarily, from the perspective of our special problem, where such a reflection would necessarily lead. On that point we can return to our previous finding, which led us to the recognition that substantial change cannot mean a physical event, if one assumes the metaphysical concept of substance that was prevalent as the concept of transubstantiation was being developed. That means, then, specifically in reference to our case: the eucharistic essential change is not a physical event, because the "essence", "the substance" that is spoken about here, lies outside of the realm of physics and physical phenomena. Physics is by its very nature "positive", that is, it is related to the level of appearances, which can be made comprehensible by experience as a sense impression. In other words: the physicist *qua* physicist is a positivist and must be one within his own discipline. He concerns himself, not with the essence of things, but, rather, with the impression they present to our perception and observation. He deals with and can only deal with the impression things make on us, their appearance for us; that is his level. But the eucharistic transformation relates *per definitionem*, not to that which appears, but to that which never *can* appear. It takes place outside of the physical realm. But that means, to put it quite clearly: viewed from the perspective of physics and chemistry, absolutely nothing takes place in the gifts—not even somewhere in a microscopic realm; considered physically and chemically, after the transformation, they are exactly the same as they were before it. Only great speculative naïveté and a complete misunderstanding of what faithful Catholic thinking means by transubstantiation could contest this statement.[14]

With that, of course, the question arises even more categorically: What actually happens in an event in which nothing happens physically or chemically? And surely this highlights the fate of the modern age, for which positivism has developed from a—justified—method into a standpoint that cannot be transgressed, by dint of which only the physical, the phenomenon, appears to it as real at all, although in

---

[14] Cf. Carlo Colombo, "Teologia, filosofia e fisica nella dottrina della transustaziazione", *La Scuola Cattolica* 83 (1955): 89–124 (against Filippo Selvaggi, "Realtà fisica e sostanza sensibile nella dottrina eucaristica", *Gregorianum* 37 [1956]: 16–33); see also Jakob Fellermeier, "Das Dogma der Transsubstantiation und die Krise des Substanzbegriffes in der modernen Naturwissenschaft", *Die Neue Ordnung* 3 (1949): 163–68; Hermann Lais, *Probleme einer zeitgemäßen Apologetik* (Vienna, 1956), 68.

principle it must admit that what appears cannot already signify being itself. At the same time, of course, it becomes evident that, as in the patristic era, the faith today must construct its own philosophy, because reaching back behind appearance to being cannot be accomplished without a decision in favor of being that will never follow from the scientific method of observation alone. Let us again skip over the questions of principle that once more confront us here so as to say with regard to our question: Physically and chemically nothing happens in the Eucharist. That is not its level of reality. But a faith-filled approach to reality includes at the same time the conviction that physics and chemistry do not exhaust the totality of being; therefore it cannot be said that where nothing happens in the physical order nothing at all has happened. On the contrary: the reality lies behind the physical.

But what is this reality? Clearly this question can be tackled only by applying a concept of substance that has been critically refined. The concept of substance in High Scholasticism relies too much on the dualistic world view of Aristotle, on the composition of all being out of matter and form, and he also presupposes an interweaving of metaphysics and physics that is too close to provide an adequate solution. But if the Aristotelian concept of substance is constructed out of the fundamental vision of the world that Aristotle intuited, that is, out of the dualism of matter and form, what else could anyone use to construct an understanding of substance that is in keeping with the faith other than the belief in creation? From this perspective, however, one can assert a twofold substantiality of created being: the general substantiality of the creature based on the fact that, while it is "being from elsewhere", it is nevertheless "being in its own right"; as something created, it is not God but, rather, is posited in the autonomy of an independent, non-divine being that exists for itself. Alongside this general substantiality of created being there is the special way of being oneself that is proper to a being endowed with intellect, the person.

If we apply to our question this concept of substance, which has been derived here in very broad strokes from the basic Christian understanding of reality, then we will be able to say: bread and wine participate first of all in the general autonomy of created being; they share in the fundamental "substantiality" that belongs to the created thing as an independent being beside divine Being. Transubstantiation, however, signifies that these things lose their creaturely independence, that they cease to exist simply in themselves in the manner befitting a creature, and instead they become *pure* signs of his presence.[15] The sacramental word does not produce a physical transformation (that would have to be brought about through physical operations), but, rather, through God's mighty benevolence it causes things to be changed from autonomously existing things into mere signs that have lost their creaturely peculiarity and exist no longer for themselves but only for him, through him, in him.[16] Thus they are now in their *essence*, in their being, *signs*, as they were previously in their essence *things*. And they are in this regard truly "trans-substantiated", affected at the deepest and most intimate level, in their being, in what they truly are in themselves. What has happened here does not affect the physical phenomenon as such, but it reveals the provisional character of the merely physical as "accident" and points to the distinctive reality that is encountered here and that now of course lends an entirely new meaning and a new value to the physical elements. The potential that in principle lies hidden in all creatures—the fact that they can and should be signs of His Presence—becomes here through the sacramental word a reality in the highest degree.

These considerations lead now immediately to an insight that could be of some importance for interconfessional theological dialogue: it becomes clear that "transubstantiation" forms no antithesis at all to "consubstantiation", if the latter is simply supposed to mean that bread and wine as physical-chemical entities continue to exist unchanged. Of course, if one regards that as self-evident, one will have to say frankly that the model of consubstantiation—that is, two substances next to each other, both of which can and must be called "substance" in the same sense—remains philosophically and theologically too superficial. The reality of the flesh and blood of Christ does not mean an additional substance of the same sort as bread and wine that would accompany the first as a second thing more or less on the same level.

---

[15] This solution has elements in common with the suggestion given by Bernhard Welte in 1960 (reprinted with the new title "Zum Verständnis der Eucharistie", in Welte, *Auf der Spur des Ewigen* [Freiburg, 1965], 459–67), however it was developed independently of it and is different from it, especially on account of the ontological elaboration of the idea that is attempted here.

[16] The real article of faith here consists in the fact that it is not just a matter of men agreeing to revaluate a thing into a symbol—a reassessment that could also be revoked by men (Welte's speculative suggestion perhaps gets bogged down with that approach)—but rather that God's Word dwells in man's word, and so the revaluation that has taken place is not merely one of human estimation but is one of being itself.

The presence of Jesus Christ means something by its very nature different from the presence of physical entities and hence does not compete with them. It means the incorporation of bread and wine into the mighty presence of the Lord, which touches things at the foundation of their being and so renews and transforms them in their hidden, truly meta-physical depth.

b. The Theological Meaning of the Assertion

Consequently, the philosophical analysis leads directly back to the theological question and now makes possible a more suitable discourse about the manner of Christ's presence. Thomas Aquinas says that it is a presence "secundum substantiam".[17] According to what has been said thus far, that means: Christ is present according to his essential selfhood, into which he incorporates the creature through the fact that he makes it a sign of his presence. Present also is his love, which has endured the Cross, the love in which he grants to us his very self (the "substance" of his self): his Thou, bearing the marks of his death and Resurrection, given to us as a salvific reality.

In this way we have gained a position from which we can overcome both the one-sidedness of the ubiquity doctrine and Calvin's doctrine about the local presence at God's right hand as well as an exaggerated Counter-Reformation position, and at the same time we can come to grips with their essential intentions.

Omnipresence of Christ?

As opposed to the bald notion of ubiquity, we will establish that the new mode of existence of the risen Lord cannot be a simple natural ubiquity, indeed, that it cannot be understood "secundum modum naturae" at all, according to the mode of natural things, but, rather, must be understood "secundum modum personae": the Lord is present, not like a natural thing, but in a personal way that is ordered to persons. Something like that should already be involved in our thinking about divine omnipresence per se. God is Person; the nearness of his

---

[17] S.Th. III, q. 76, art. 5.

presence depends on the nearness in which he allows himself to be perceived and in which he is perceived. Someone who speaks about God's nearness and remoteness knows that God is not present like a stone that is simply there but, rather, that the nearness and remoteness of God are actualities of the personal order. Such an insight applies all the more to the sphere of salvation history and the sacraments. Christ the Lord is present to history, not in a natural ubiquity, but, rather, through the offer of his nearness, his *agape* [love] for us. The fact that such "being there" does not have a self-evident, natural character means positively that it must be understood in terms of the manner in which love alone can be present: as the free self-grant and self-gift of an I to a Thou; this process of giving, however, is performed by Christ in the *sacramentum ecclesiae*, just as, conversely, what a sacrament actually is could actually be defined only from this perspective.

Because it is important, let us try once again to understand the whole matter by the analogy of our daily life. Here we run into a similar situation, if we observe that two people in a crowded streetcar can be pressed against each other and yet be infinitely far away from each other. And, on the other hand, two people can be thousands of kilometers distant from each other and yet be very close to each other: deep within their personal core they touch each other across all that distance. Thus what we can observe in the limitations of our flesh-world [*Sarx-Welt*] comes to pass in a radical and total sense concerning the Risen One, who has burst the confines of the "sarx", of historical delimitations, and has the power to impart himself in all places, to be really present with his complete fullness for the Thou of mankind: precisely this openness of self-giving beyond all places is the essence of his Resurrection existence that has now passed through death. Through his Resurrection, Christ has entered into the freedom that allows him to grant his Thou where he wishes; and he imparts himself in and through the thanksgiving prayer of the Church gathered together in his name. In this respect, a correct intention hidden in the ubiquity doctrine becomes manifest here: the Lord, who as the Risen One has overcome the limit of historical existence, can impart himself when and where he wishes. But contrary to the naturalistic understanding of this idea, which tends toward Monophysitism, it becomes manifest that his presence in history is not simply a "being there" but, rather, is realized wherever the freedom of his love has chosen for itself the place of its presence—preeminently and most profoundly in the sacrament of his Body and Blood.

When we have understood this new definiteness of resurrected being and its freedom vis-à-vis natural dimensions, then many complicated philosophical distinctions become superfluous. There is no longer any need to ask how accidents can exist without substance and substance without accidents; no need to wonder whether it is a question of "production" or "adduction" when the Real Presence comes about; no need to inquire about the quantity of Christ's Body, how one body can be present in many places and then again be there in each host, and so forth. All that is condensed into the simple statement: In the sacramental signs the living Lord gives himself to men, the incorporation into the reality of his love.

Natural-Local Presence of Christ?

Our reflections thus far, however, lead also now to the correction of Calvin's local understanding of the Lord's being, just as on the other hand we can preserve the element that correctly kept him back from a simple agreement with Luther's ubiquity doctrine. So we will now say that certainly no natural ubiquity is to be attributed to Christ, and on this point Calvin is right as opposed to Luther. But no local limitation to an imaginary heavenly place should be attributed to him, either. Nowhere does the Risen One have a physically restricted place that can be designated. As the Risen One, he has entered into a new mode of existence and participates in God's might, by virtue of which he can give himself to his own whenever and wherever he wishes.

Theological Classification of the Doctrine of Transubstantiation

In conclusion, this now opens up a view of the definite place to be assigned in theology to what is meant by transubstantiation generally speaking. We had characterized Calvin's understanding as a theology of the Ascension, which however, in spite of several attempts along these lines, lacks the necessary dialectical reinforcement with Incarnation theology, so that Christianity has no more Here, but is referred completely to the There, namely, to heaven, to the afterlife. In connection with the position of van de Pols, Peter Pfeiffer has tried to explain Catholic eucharistic doctrine as Incarnation theology taken seriously and radically: as a Yes to God's decision to tie himself to earthly realities: God not only became involved in history, but actually handed himself over to it, having been bound to earthly things. Jesus' being nailed to the Cross appears as the sign for the fact that God bound himself in and to our history. The Incarnation would thus really be affirmed, in its permanent structural significance for Christianity, which goes beyond the Christmas event.[18]

One can agree by and large with this idea. But it needs to be supplemented. The Incarnate One is the One who passed through the Cross and Resurrection, who only in this way became the One who is open to us and the One who wins salvation for us. That is why Incarnation as a theological statement is not separable from Cross and Resurrection, just as, conversely, the Easter events can retain their true meaning only on the basis of the Incarnation. I maintain the position that in this sense (of explicitly including the Incarnation) one can assert that the understanding of the Real Presence just sketched in the final analysis simply expresses a theology of the Resurrection in which faith in the Incarnation finally reaches its goal. The Resurrection and Ascension of the Lord, after all, means, not a translation from one definite place in Palestine to another definite place, heaven, but, rather, entrance into the new mode of existence of God-given openness toward men: "By virtue of the Ascension, Christ is not the One Absent from the world; rather, he is the One Present in it in a new way; in him the kingdom of God over the world is actualized."[19] Consequently, faith in the transformation of the gifts [during Mass] is, on the one hand, coordinated no doubt with the reality of the Incarnation: with the incorporation of what is created into the hidden presence of the Lord and with the Lord's self-giving into earthly, human history. But this Yes to the Incarnation is fulfilled in the sphere of the Resurrection, by virtue of which the Lord can and does grant his nearness to his own. At the same time, he thereby elevates the Eucharistic Gifts to an eschatological sign, to an indication of the world to come in which the whole universe will become the "praeclarus calix", the precious chalice of his nearness. In this respect, one may in fact speak here about a dialectic between Here and Not Here, between Already and Not

---

[18] Cf. Willem Hendrik van de Pol, *Das reformatorische Christentum in phänomenologischer Betrachtung* (Einsiedeln, 1956), 259–312.

[19] Joseph Ratzinger, "Himmelfahrt", in LThK, 2nd ed., 5:361 (there the presuppositions of the Resurrection theology sketched here are developed in more detail).

Yet, between Below and Above: Christ is here, and yet he is the Hidden One; he is near and yet the completely Other, the One who gives himself and yet the One whom we cannot control, who instead controls us. So at the conclusion of these reflections, however fragmentary and insufficient they may have been in the details, perhaps it may have become apparent that "transubstantiation", precisely in terms of the original meaning of the concept, can be understood in a way that is neither intellectually indefensible nor ecclesially divisive. To be sure: no one can deny that in the name of this concept not a few sins were committed, that it quite often became the term for an almost intolerable confusion of faith, philosophy, and physics. Correctly understood, however, "transubstantiation" is the straightforward expression of the critical refinement of limits and, in this limitation, of an opening to the breadth of real understanding—*fides quaerens intellectum*—and, consequently, the expression of a movement that is just as irrevocable as it is interminable.[20]

---

[20] The question of eucharistic adoration, which is closely connected with the problem of transubstantiation, is so vast that it did not seem appropriate to address it in the context of this essay. I hope to be able to give it special consideration on another occasion.

Book Reviews

a. Of: Edward Schillebeeckx. *Die eucharistische Gegenwart: Zur Diskussion über die Realpräsenz* (The eucharistic presence: A discussion about the Real Presence), translated from Dutch by Hugo Zulauf. Theologische Perspektiven Düsseldorf, 1967.

After many secondhand descriptions of the Dutch conversation about transubstantiation, one is glad to possess now a book on this question by one of the leading theologians of the Dutch-speaking world and, thus, finally to have firsthand information. In the discussion until now, of course, Schillebeeckx has not been in the forefront: the endeavors by Piet Schoonenberg, L. Smits, and Stephanus Trooster have drawn the most attention. But that is exactly what makes Schillebeeckx the right person to go beyond the experimental, trial-balloon stage and to lead the way back to an examination of the question according to the stricter rules of the scientific method. What is impressive about Schillebeeckx's book is, first of all, the spirit of responsibility with which he does his work and his consciousness of the extent to which the publicity that theology is getting nowadays increases this responsibility and makes it more difficult. This situation perhaps should make us realize again that less publicity would serve to promote the objectivity of theological work, which can only suffer harm when it tries too hard to set itself up as "theologia publica". Impressive also, however, is the common sense and patience with which the various aspects of the matter—the historical as well as the philosophical—are examined in turn and illuminated. One of the best parts of the book, certainly, is the thoroughgoing presentation of the Tridentine discussion, which

---

Translated by Kenneth Baker, S.J., and Michael J. Miller.

contains a series of valuable observations; in particular, the reference on page 46 to the possible origin of the eucharistic concept of substance in the wording of the Our Father in the Latin Bible ("panis supersubstantialis") calls for further study. Very useful also is the survey (pp. 58–81) of the development that led to the new approaches in the Dutch-speaking world, whose continuity with the work of recent decades becomes quite clear. In this connection one misses somewhat a reference to the progress of theology in German, which—unlike theology in the Romance languages—scarcely discussed transubstantiation between the two world wars and right up to the eve of Vatican II, while at the same time it experienced an intense renewal of eucharistic doctrine, in which an understanding of this sacrament was developed entirely from the act of liturgical celebration and ontological considerations, while not denied, were put in second place and, therefore, almost completely excluded from the discussion. Perhaps another reason for the specific situation of the Dutch debate over the Eucharist was that the impetus of this sacramental-liturgical theology, with too little reflection, became connected with the more philosophical discussions in the Romance languages. The far too summary biblical section (81–84) leaves the reader somewhat unsatisfied, especially since, as Schillebeeckx himself clearly sees, "the guiding principle" must be sought here and not "in an unmediated way" in phenomenology (84). Schillebeeckx's own answer, which is based on the distinction of three levels—the level of faith, the ontological level, and the level of natural philosophy—is carefully prepared; he takes pains to consider and to assimilate all the factors in the discussion. He proves convincingly that a merely phenomenological understanding does not suffice, since the ontological level is involved. The significance of this fundamental statement is weakened, though, by the twilight in which the relationship between ontology and phenomenology ultimately remains. At the same time, Schillebeeckx's own solution leaves this relationship in a certain obscurity, even though previously his investigation, especially in the discussion about transcendence through interiority (53ff.), pushed forward to convincing new insights.

The reader may allow the reviewer to pose a few more particular questions, as is almost necessarily demanded by a book that is so dense and contains such a wealth of ideas and materials. The relegation of the concept of substance to the field of natural philosophy seems problematic (41; 90: "nature-ontological"); should it not be stated more correctly that this concept expresses a metaphysical intention in a notion having the color of natural philosophy? Also problematic, in my view, is the distinction between "metaphysical" and "sacramental" that appears on page 63 and elsewhere; after all, does one not also have to ask what the sacrament "is"? Does the refusal to ask this question (which Schillebeeckx, by the way, does not keep up) not imply a flight from ontology into phenomenology, which Schillebeeckx correctly resists? What does it mean when he says on page 72 about Baciocchi that he has spoken "at least objectively" about transfunctionalization, transfinalization, and transsignification? Is he speaking now only objectively or also terminologically about it? It seems to me that the expression "at least" here does not make any sense. The description of Schoonenberg and Smits (79ff.) remains unclear, and an argument against Smits, without naming him, is not forthcoming until page 92. The position of Schillebeeckx would have achieved more clarity if he had dealt more directly with opposing views. The concept of anamnesis recalled on page 85 is insufficient and fails to appreciate the all-important function of the *Word* in the *eucharistia*, which, after all, took its name from a prayer and not from the meal. The omission of this factor (already in the exegetical analysis, especially on page 83) is one of the chief weaknesses of most works of recent eucharistic theology. The colloquial notion of mystery makes me uncomfortable; from page 86 on, it appears again and again and contrasts oddly with the concurrent talk about the "worldly world" (54f.). It is completely unintelligible to me what the assertion found on page 90 in note 52 is supposed to mean, namely, that the bread that Jesus used every day has, according to historians, little to do with the wheat bread "with which the Western world became familiar only since the sixteenth century". I do not know which historians could be meant here: the voluminous material compiled, for example, in the article "Brot" in RAC (2:611–20: Klauser/Haussleiter/Stuiber) presents a completely different state of affairs. The idea developed on pages 94–95 of the reciprocal presence of Christ for the Church *and of the Church* for Christ is untenable in its present form; it precariously misconstrues the absolute priority of Christology over ecclesiology, of Christ over his Church. It is a misunderstanding of Augustine's thought if one concludes from his drastically pointed homiletic expressions, for example, "you receive yourself", and so on, that there is a real presence of Christ and of the Church in the Eucharist. The texts in question are meant in an emphatically christological sense; they mean to say that the community has already turned completely into Christ, so that basically only Christ remains there. The danger of such expressions lies in a Christo-Monism; the tendency here is certainly not toward a simultaneous presence of Christ and of the Church. The reduction of knowledge to perception seems to me very problematic; it is proposed in practice on pages 98–99 (in the wake of the telescoping of phenomenology and ontology)—especially when it is stated (albeit not carried through afterward) that what is perceived is "not an objective quality of reality" (95). Putting it that way misses several important distinctions. If one subsequently hopes that the special character of ontology as opposed to mere phenomenology will now become clear, then one is all the more disappointed to find that on page 103 everything becomes blurred again: "Therefore I am saying, not that this (= eucharistic) reality lies behind the phenomenal, but, rather, that it appears for believing consciousness precisely *in* the phenomenal." If one remains true to the philosophical concept of the phenomenal (and does not perhaps underhandedly substitute for it the idea of the cultic epiphany), then one can only decisively deny this proposition.

All of these remarks are intended merely to further the discussion; they in no way change our fundamental agreement with the guiding intentions of Schillebeeckx, much less diminish our gratitude for the painstaking work that he has done.

b. Of: Wilhelm Averbeck, *Der Opfercharakter des Abendmahls in der neueren evangelischen Theologie* (The sacrificial character of the Last Supper in recent Protestant theology). Konfessionskundliche und kontroverstheologische Studien 19. Paderborn, 1967.

The question of the Last Supper became considerably more consequential at the end of the liberal era, during the associated renewal of attention to the Church and liturgy in Protestant thinking in recent decades, and in this connection there was also a lively debate about the problem posed by Catholic teaching on the sacrificial character of the Eucharist. Averbeck has taken upon himself the laborious task of surveying and describing the many strands in the complex discussion of this theme among German Lutheran theologians in the period between 1917 and 1958. The year 1917—which Peter Brunner called a "major turning point" because of the appearance of Rudolf Otto's book *Das Heilige* (*The Idea of the Holy*), because of the publication of Heinrich Hansen's *Stimuli et clavi* then, and because of other events (3)—can indicate only an approximate boundary, just like the year in which the Arnoldshain Theses were published (1958); likewise, it was not possible to limit the topic strictly to German theologians throughout the volume. Nevertheless, the indicated field of inquiry does designate a whole. An epoch that had started around 1917/1918 and had assumed a very specific form in German-speaking countries came to an end with the 1950s; only today, as we look back at this period as something past, do we fully realize what a pronounced change was taking place. Therefore a survey of the exceedingly rich and fruitful discussion over those four decades necessarily seems very desirable, especially today; widely scattered pieces thus become accessible as a whole and could become fruitful in a new way.

The strength of this analysis lies in its wealth of particulars and in the impressive care taken with the detailed work, which overlooks no phase of the intricate process and listens with inexhaustible patience to statements by the individual authors so as to make them intelligible in their place in the fabric of the whole. Averbeck did not make it easy for himself, either, inasmuch as he actually understood the flexible parameters of his study to be as wide as the subject matter demanded. Moreover, in his introduction he has given an excellent, concise presentation of the subject matter in the writings of the Reformers themselves and traced the subsequent history in broad strokes down to the actual start of his own topic. By this method, he has produced a work with a truly impressive wealth of information that will render an irreplaceable service to every future study in this field. The attention to detail by no means causes the reader to lose sight of the whole. Although Averbeck (legitimately, in my opinion) renounced any attempt to distill something like a line of development from the particular materials, the thought process becomes clear simply through the orderly, condensed presentation of the course of the discussion, which sets out energetically toward liturgical renewal but then turns back again to the Lutheran starting points and seems increasingly to relegate those who opt in favor of the sacrificial character to minor circles that are readily suspected of "Catholicizing" the faith.

The account necessarily involved self-denial, since it left no room for Averbeck's own theological reflections, but this silence is broken in the conclusion, in which the author subtly elaborates the real heart of the debate: the question of a purely katabatic [top-down] Christology, and thus, in retrospect, finally gives to the whole a perspicuity that lends itself to further systematic work on the topic. This assures the book a reputation of being, not just a historical report, but beyond that an independent work of theological scholarship. Naturally, in reading a study like this, which had to sort out intricately interwoven material and organize it in an orderly fashion, one will also be able to pose questions. Thus (to mention one example) one could perhaps have presented the struggle for a liturgical ritual in an even more concentrated form, so that the connections and contrasts between the work of the Berneuchener Movement, of the Michaelsbruderschaft, and that of the VELKD would have been more evident. It probably would have made sense in this regard to include also a synopsis of the texts, which would have made them more perspicuous and research less laborious. The work can easily frighten the reader off by its extraordinary size, and the author himself, as I happen to know, repeatedly wondered whether an abridgment of the study might still be possible; if the book was to retain its wealth of information, its thoroughness, and its reliability, however, significant cuts were in fact hardly possible.

On the whole, one can say that in six years of painstaking work, Averbeck has created a rich mine of information, for which we can only be grateful to him.

IV. The Eucharist—Heart of the Church

Foreword

In the crisis of faith through which we are going, again and again the focal point proves to be the correct celebration and the correct understanding of the Eucharist. That is why I was glad to use the four Lenten sermons that P. Wagner, S.J., from St. Michael's Church in Munich invited me to give [in 1978] to develop a basic catechesis on this sacrament, which was meant to consider carefully the main problems of the liturgical form and reform as well as the central dogmatic questions. In this regard, the emphases are certainly a reflection of that time; nevertheless, I hope that none of the basic themes of a Catholic catechesis on the Eucharist has been entirely overlooked.

The text presented here is based on the transcription of the audio tape recording of the sermons, and I cordially thank the press office of the Archbishop's chancery in Munich for their care in making it available. For publication I smoothed the style and also sparingly supplemented the text here and there but deliberately left the basic spoken character of the discourse unaltered. So it goes without saying that this is not a scholarly treatment but just an adult catechesis, which of course is based on a repeated scholarly handling of the material. The notes therefore limit themselves to documenting what is cited directly in the text; they do not try to introduce references to the broader scholarly discussion. Thus the sole purpose of this little book remains to show the standards for faith instruction and for our own faith consciousness that are set for us by the faith of the Church of all ages. I

The Foreword translated by Michael J. Miller. The remainder of the chapter reprinted from *God Is Near Us: The Eucharist, the Heart of Life*, trans. Henry Taylor (San Francisco: Ignatius Press, 2003), 27–93.

hope to perform thereby a modest service to all those who are struggling to present the faith vividly in our time.

1. The Origin of the Eucharist in the Paschal Mystery

Some years ago, Gonsalv Mainberger—who was at that time still a member of the Order of Preachers—shocked his audience in Zürich, and soon after that his readers right across Europe, with the assertion: "Christ died for nothing." Exactly what he meant by that remained to some extent obscure; he was probably trying to translate into a striking slogan what we can read in Bultmann's writings in the cautious phrasing of the scholar. Bultmann says: We do not know how Jesus met his death, how he endured it. We must leave open the possibility of his having failed.[1] To understand this, we must have in mind how Bultmann himself portrays Jesus. On the basis of the supposition that everywhere and always only normal and probable things can actually happen, that the miracle of something wholly other is historically impossible, he strips away from Jesus all that is unusual, extraordinary, or even divine.[2] What is left in the end is an average sort of rabbi, such as might have lived in any age. Then it certainly does become incomprehensible for this rabbi suddenly to end up on the Cross, since people do not crucify the average professor. So it is not actually the real Jesus who breaks down on the Cross, but this notional Jesus does come to grief there. Seen from the viewpoint of the Cross, it becomes clear that Jesus was the kind of person who transcends all normal standards and who cannot be explained in normal terms. It would otherwise be incomprehensible for groups hostile to one another, Jews and Romans, believers and atheists, to join together to rid themselves of this remarkable prophet. He just did not fit into any of the ready-made categories people use, and therefore they had to clear him out of the way. There, again, it becomes clear that we cannot get to know

---

[1] Rudolf Bultmann, *Das Verhältnis der urchristlichen Christusbotschaft zum historischen Jesus* (Heidelberg, 1960). For the contemporary discussion among exegetes, see: Karl Kertelge, ed., *Der Tod Jesu: Deutungen im Neuen Testament*, QD 74 (Freiburg, 1976); and Heinz Schürmann, *Jesu ureigener Tod* (Freiburg, 1975).

[2] Cf. on this point the important essay of Heinrich Schlier, which may mark a turning point in the treatment of this subject: "Zur Frage: Wer ist Jesus?", in *Neues Testament und Kirche*, Festschrift für Rudolf Schnackenburg, ed. Joachim Gnilka (Freiburg, 1974), 359–70.

the real Jesus by trimming him to fit our normal standards. Only the Jesus of the witnesses is the real Jesus. There is no better way of learning about him than to listen to the word of those who lived with him, who accompanied him along the paths of this earthly life.

If we question these witnesses, then we see—and this is in fact self-evident—that it was by no means a surprise to Jesus, something quite unforeseen, when he ended up on the Cross. He could hardly have been blind to the storm brewing up, to the force of the contradiction, enmity, and rejection that was gathering round him. It was of no less significance for his walking on toward the Cross with his eyes open that he lived from the heart of the faith of Israel, that he prayed the prayer of his people with them: the Psalms, which were inspired by the prophets and expressed the religion of Israel, are deeply marked by the figure of the righteous man who suffers, who for the sake of God can no longer find any place in this world, who for the sake of his faith endures suffering. Jesus appropriated this prayer, which we can see springing ever new, with ever deeper tones, both in the Psalms and in the prophets, from the Servant of Second Isaiah right up to Job and to the three young men in the fiery furnace; he made it intimately his own, filled it out, offered his own self for its sake, and thereby finally gave the key that opened up this prayer.[3]

Thus, in his preaching all paths lead into the mystery of him who proves the truth of his love and his message in suffering. The words he spoke at the Last Supper then represent the final shaping of this. They offer nothing entirely unexpected but, rather, what has already been shaped and adumbrated in all these paths, and yet they reveal anew what was signified throughout: the institution of the Eucharist is an anticipation of his death; it is the undergoing of a spiritual death. For Jesus shares himself out, he shares himself as the one who has been split up and torn apart into body and blood. Thus, the *eucharistic words* of Jesus are the answer to Bultmann's question about how Jesus underwent his death; in these words he undergoes a spiritual death, or, to put it more accurately, *in these words Jesus transforms*

---

[3] There is much valuable material on this in Hans-Joachim Kraus, *Psalmen*, vols. 1 and 2, Biblischer Kommentar zum Alten Testament 15 (Neukirchen, 1960) [trans. by Hilton C. Oswald as *Psalms 1–59* and *Psalms 60–150* (Fortress Press, 1988–1989)]; and in Hans Urs von Balthasar, *Herrlichkeit*, vol. 3, pt. 2, *Alter Bund* (Einsiedeln, 1967) [trans. by Brian McNeil and Erasmo Leiva-Merikakis as *The Glory of the Lord*, vol. 6, *Theology: The Old Covenant* (San Francisco: Ignatius Press, 1991)].

death into the spiritual act of affirmation, into the act of self-sharing love; into the act of adoration, which is offered to God, then from God is made available to men. Both are essentially interdependent: the words at the Last Supper without the death would be, so to speak, an issue of unsecured currency; and again, the death without these words would be a mere execution without any discernible point to it. Yet the two together constitute this new event, in which the senselessness of death is given meaning; in which what is irrational is transformed and made rational and articulate; in which the destruction of love, which is what death means in itself, becomes in fact the means of verifying and establishing it, of its enduring constancy. If, then, we want to know how Jesus himself intended his death to be understood, how he accepted it, what it means, then we must reflect on these words; and, contrariwise, we must regard them as being constantly guaranteed by the pledge of the blood that was his witness.

Before we look at them more closely, let us just cast a glance at the great drama that St. John has unfolded in the thirteenth chapter of his Gospel—in the story of the *washing of the disciples' feet*. In this scene, the evangelist sums up, as it were, the whole of Jesus' message, his life, and his Passion. As if in a vision, we see what this whole really is.[4] In the washing of the disciples' feet is represented for us what Jesus does and what he is. He, who is Lord, comes down to us; he lays aside the garments of glory and becomes a slave, one who stands at the door and who does for us the slave's service of washing our feet. This is the meaning of his whole life and Passion: that he bends down to our dirty feet, to the dirt of humanity, and that in his greater love he washes us clean. The slave's service of washing the feet was performed in order to prepare a person suitably for sitting at table, to make him ready for company, so that all could sit down together for a meal. Jesus Christ prepares us, as it were, for God's presence and for each other's company, so that we can sit down together at table. We, who repeatedly find we cannot stand one another, who are quite unfit to be with God, are welcomed and accepted by him. He clothes himself, so to speak, in the garment of our poverty, and in being taken up by him, we are able to be with God, we have gained access to God. We are washed through our

---

[4] Cf. Heinz Schürmann, *Der Geist macht lebendig* (Freiburg, 1972), 116–25, and similarly the commentaries on the Gospel of John by Rudof Bultmann and Rudolf Schnackenburg.

willingness to yield to his love. The meaning of this love is that God accepts us without preconditions, even if we are unworthy of his love, incapable of relating to him, because he, Jesus Christ, transforms us and becomes a brother to us.

Certainly, John's account shows us that even where God sets no limits, man can sometimes do so. Two such instances appear here. The first becomes apparent in the figure of Judas: There is the No stemming from greed and lust, from vainglory, which refuses to accept God. This is the No given because we want to make the world for ourselves and are not ready to accept it as a gift from God. "Sooner remain in debt than pay with a coin that does not bear our own portrait—that is what our sovereignty demands", as Nietzsche once said.[5] The camel will not go through the eye of the needle; it sticks its proud hump up, so to speak, and is thus unable to get through the gate of merciful kindness. I think we all ought to ask ourselves, right now, whether we are not just like those people whose pride and vainglory will not let them be cleansed, let them accept the gift of Jesus Christ's healing love. Besides this refusal, which arises from the greed and the pride of man, there is, however, also the danger of piety, represented by Peter: the false humility that does not want anything so great as God bending down to us; the false humility in which pride is concealed, which dislikes forgiveness and would rather achieve its own purity; the false pride and the false modesty that will not accept God's mercy. But God does not wish for false modesty that refuses his kindness; rather, he desires that humility which allows itself to be cleansed and thus becomes pure. This is the manner in which he gives himself to us.

Let us now turn again to Jesus' words at the Last Supper, as they are recounted to us in the first three Gospels, and let us ask what we find there. We have in the first place these two immeasurably profound sayings, which stand for all time at the heart of the Church, at the heart of the eucharistic celebration, the sayings from which we draw our life, because these words are the presence of the living God, the presence of Jesus Christ in our midst, and thereby they tear the world free from its unbearable boredom, indifference, sadness, and evil. *"This is my Body, this is my Blood"*: these are expressions taken from the Israelite language

---

[5] *Fröhliche Wissenschaft* 3:252; quoted from Josef Pieper, *Über den Begriff der Sünde* (Munich, 1977), 120.

of sacrifice, which designated the gifts offered in sacrifice to God in the Temple.[6] If Jesus makes use of these words, then he is designating *himself* as *the true and ultimate sacrifice*, in whom all these unsuccessful strivings of the Old Testament are fulfilled. What had always been intended and could never be achieved in the Old Testament sacrifices is incorporated in him. God does not desire the sacrifice of animals; everything belongs to him. And he does not desire human sacrifice, for he has created man for living. God desires something more: he desires love, which transforms man and through which he becomes capable of relating to God, giving himself up to God. Now, all those thousands of sacrifices that were always presented to God in the Temple at Jerusalem and all the sacrifices performed in the whole course of history, all this vain and eternal striving to bring ourselves up to God, can be seen as unnecessary and yet, at the same time, as being like windows that allow us, so to speak, a glimpse of the real thing, like preliminary attempts at what has now been achieved. What they signified—giving to God, union with God—comes to pass in Jesus Christ, in him who gives God nothing but himself and, thereby, us in him.

But we now have to ask: How does that happen, and what does that mean, more precisely? Here we meet with a second factor. To each of the phrases under consideration, which derive from the Temple theology of Israel or, alternatively, from the Sinai covenant, Jesus adds a saying that is taken from the book of Isaiah: "This is my body, *which is given for you*; my blood, *which is shed for you and for many*." This phrase is taken from the Songs of the *Suffering Servant*, which we find in Isaiah (chap. 53).[7] We need briefly to cast a glance over their background in order to grasp their content. With the Babylonian Exile, Israel had lost its Temple. It could no longer worship God; it could no longer offer up its praises; it could no longer present the sacrifices of atonement; and it was bound to ask what should happen now, how its relationship with God could be kept alive, how order could be maintained in the world's affairs. For that was what the cult was about, in the final analysis: maintaining the correct relationship between God

---

[6] Joachim Jeremias, *Die Abendmahlsworte Jesu*, 3rd ed. (Göttingen, 1960); Johannes Betz, *Die Eucharistie in der Zeit der griechischen Väter*, vol. 2, pt. 1: *Die Realpräsenz des Leibes und Blutes Jesu im Abendmahl nach dem Neuen Testament* (Freiburg, 1961).

[7] Cf. Josef Scharbert, "Stellvertretendes Sühneleiden in den Ebed-Jahwe-Liedern und in altorientalischen Ritualtexten", BZ 2 (1958): 190–213; Scharbert, "Die Rettung der 'Vielen' durch die 'Wenigen' im Alten Testament", TThZ 68 (1959): 146–61.

and man, since only thus can the axis around which reality turns be kept true. Through these questionings, which necessarily arose in this period of the absence of the cult, Israel came to a new experience. It could no longer celebrate the Temple worship; it could only suffer for the sake of its God. The great minds of Israel, the prophets, were enlightened by God so as to understand that this suffering of Israel is the true sacrifice, the great new form of worship, with which it could come before the living God on behalf of mankind, on behalf of the whole world. But there is still one point at which this remains incomplete: Israel is the suffering servant of God, who accepts God in his suffering and stands before God on behalf of the world, and yet it is at the same time stained and guilty and selfish and lost. It cannot play the part of the servant of God properly and completely. Thus, these great songs, in a remarkable fashion, remain indeterminate; on the one hand, they speak of the fate of the suffering people and offer an interpretation of this; they help people to accept their suffering as a positive response to the God who loves and who judges. But at the same time they open up an expectation of the one in whom this will all be entirely true, the one who will truly be the undefiled witness to God in this world and who cannot yet be named. At the Last Supper, Jesus takes this saying into his own mouth: He is suffering for the many, and he shows, thereby, that in him this expectation is fulfilled: that this great act of worship on the part of mankind comes to pass in his suffering. He himself is, so to speak, the pure representative, the one who does not stand on his own behalf, but stands before God on behalf of all.

At this point I should like to include a question about which some people argue in extremely heated fashion: The German translation no longer says, "for many", but "for all", and this takes into account that in the Latin Missal and in the Greek New Testament, that is to say, in the original text that is being translated, we find "for many". This disparity has given rise to some disquiet; the question is raised as to whether the text of the Bible is not being misrepresented, whether perhaps an element of untruth has been brought into the most sacred place in our worship. In this connection, I would like to make three points.

1. In the New Testament as a whole, and in the whole of the tradition of the Church, it has always been clear that God desires that everyone should be saved and that Jesus died, not just for a part of

mankind, but for everyone; that God himself—as we were just saying—does not draw the line anywhere. He does not make any distinction between people he dislikes, people he does not want to have saved, and others whom he prefers; he loves everyone because he has created everyone. That is why the Lord died for all. That is what we find in St. Paul's Letter to the Romans: God "did not spare his own Son but gave him up for us all" (8:32); and in the fifth chapter of the Second Letter to the Corinthians: "One has died for all" (2 Cor 5:14). The first Letter to Timothy speaks of "Christ Jesus, who gave himself as a ransom for all" (1 Tim 2:6). This sentence is particularly important in that we can see, by the context and by the way it is formulated, that a eucharistic text is being quoted here. Thus we know that at that time, in a certain part of the Church, the formula that speaks of a sacrifice "for all" was being used in the Eucharist. The insight that was thus preserved has never been lost from the tradition of the Church. On Maundy Thursday, in the old missal, the account of the Last Supper was introduced with the words: "On the evening before he died, for the salvation of all he...." It was on the basis of this knowledge that in the seventeenth century there was an explicit condemnation of a Jansenist proposition that asserted that Christ did not die for everyone.[8] This limitation of salvation was thus explicitly rejected as an erroneous teaching that contradicted the faith of the whole Church. The teaching of the Church says exactly the opposite: Christ died for all.

We cannot start to set limits on God's behalf; the very heart of the faith has been lost to anyone who supposes that it is only worthwhile if it is, so to say, made worthwhile by the damnation of others. Such a way of thinking, which finds the punishment of other people necessary, springs from not having inwardly accepted the faith; from loving only oneself and not God the Creator, to whom his creatures belong. That way of thinking would be like the attitude of those people who could not bear the workers who came last being paid a denarius like the rest; like the attitude of people who feel properly rewarded only if others have received less. This would be the attitude of the son who stayed at home, who could not bear the reconciling kindness of his father. It would be a hardening of our hearts, in which it would become clear that we were only looking out for ourselves and not looking for God; in which it would be clear that we did not love our

---

[8] DS 2005.

faith, but merely bore it like a burden. We must finally come to the point where we no longer believe it to be better to live without faith, standing around in the marketplace, so to speak, unemployed, along with the workers who were only taken on at the eleventh hour; we must be freed from the delusion that spiritual unemployment is better than living with the Word of God. We have to learn once more so to live our faith, so to assent to it, that we can discover in it that joy which we do not simply carry around with us because others are at a disadvantage but with which we are filled, for which we are thankful, and which we would like to share with others. This, then, is the first point: It is a basic element of the biblical message that the Lord died for all—being jealous of salvation is not Christian.[9]

2. A second point to add to this is that God never, in any case, forces anyone to be saved. God accepts man's freedom. He is no magician who will in the end wipe out everything that has happened and wheel out his happy ending. He is a true father; a creator who assents to freedom, even when it is used to reject him. That is why God's all-embracing desire to save people does not involve the actual salvation of all men. He allows us the power to refuse. God loves us; we need only to summon up the humility to allow ourselves to be loved. But we do have to ask ourselves, again and again, whether we are not possessed of the pride of wanting to do it for ourselves; whether we do not rob man, as a creature, along with the Creator-God, of all his dignity and stature by removing all element of seriousness from the life of man and degrading God to a kind of magician or grandfather who is unmoved by anything. Even on account of the unconditional greatness of God's love—indeed, because of that very quality—the freedom to refuse, and thus the possibility of perdition, is not removed.

3. What, then, should we make of the new translation? Both formulations, "for all" and "for many", are found in Scripture and in tradition. Each expresses one aspect of the matter: on one hand, the all-embracing salvation inherent in the death of Christ, which he suffered for all men; on the other hand, the freedom to refuse, as setting a limit to salvation. Neither of the two formulae can express the whole of this; each needs correct interpretation, which sets it in the context of the Christian gospel as a whole. I leave open the question of whether

---

[9] I have fully developed this idea in my little book *Vom Sinn des Christseins* (Munich, 1965), 39–41.

it was sensible to choose the translation "for all" here and, thus, to confuse translation with interpretation, at a point at which the process of interpretation remains in any case indispensable.[10] There can be no question of misrepresentation here, since whichever of the formulations is allowed to stand, we must in any case listen to the whole of the gospel message: that the Lord truly loves everyone and that he died for all. And the other aspect: that he does not, by some magic trick, set aside our freedom but allows us to choose to enter into his great mercy.

Now let us turn back to look at yet a third saying in the Last Supper accounts: "This is the *new covenant* in my blood." We saw just now how Jesus, in accepting his death, gathers together and condenses in his person the whole of the Old Testament; first the theology of sacrifice, that is, everything that went on in the Temple and everything to do with the Temple, then the theology of the Exile, of the Suffering Servant. Now a third element is added, a passage from Jeremiah (31:31) in which the prophet predicts the New Covenant, which will no longer be limited to physical descendants of Abraham, no longer to the strict keeping of the law, but will spring from out of the new love of God that gives us a new heart. This is what Jesus takes up here. In his suffering and death this long-awaited hope becomes reality; his death seals the Covenant. It signifies something like a blood brotherhood between God and man. That was the idea underlying the way the Covenant had been depicted on Sinai. There, Moses had set up the altar to represent God and, over against it, twelve stones to represent the twelve tribes of Israel and had sprinkled them with blood, so as to associate God and man in the one communion of this sacrifice. What was there only a hesitant attempt is here achieved. He who is the Son of God, he who is man, gives himself to the Father in dying and thus shows himself to be the one who *brings us all into the Father*. He now institutes true blood brotherhood, *a communion of God and man*; he opens the door that we could not open for ourselves. We can do no more than give a little tentative thought to God, and it is

---

[10] The fact that in Hebrew the expression "many" would mean the same thing as "all" is not relevant to the question under consideration inasmuch as it is a question of translating, not a Hebrew text here, but a Latin text (from the Roman liturgy), which is directly related to a Greek text (the New Testament). The institution narratives in the New Testament are by no means simply a translation (still less, a mistaken translation) of Isaiah; rather, they constitute an independent source.

not in our power to know whether or not he responds. This remains the tragic element, the shadow hovering over so many religions, that they are simply a cry to which the response remains uncertain. Only God himself can hear the cry. Jesus Christ, both Son of God and man, who carries on his love right through death, who transforms death into an act of love and truth, he is the response; the Covenant is founded in him.

Thus we see how the Eucharist had its origin, what its true source is. The words of institution alone are not sufficient; the death alone is not sufficient; and even both together are still insufficient but have to be complemented by the Resurrection, in which God accepts this death and makes it the door into a new life. From out of this whole matrix—that he transforms his death, that irrational event, into an affirmation, into an act of love and of adoration—emerges his acceptance by God and the possibility of his being able to share himself in this way. On the Cross, Christ saw love through to the end. For all the differences there may be between the accounts in the various Gospels, there is one point in common: Jesus died praying, and in the abyss of death he upheld the First Commandment and held on to the presence of God.[11] Out of such a death springs this sacrament, the Eucharist.

We finally have to return to the question with which we started. Did Jesus fail? Well, he certainly was not successful in the same sense as Caesar or Alexander the Great. From the worldly point of view, he did fail in the first instance: he died almost abandoned; he was condemned on account of his preaching. The response to his message was not the great Yes of his people, but the Cross. From such an end as that, we should conclude that Success is definitely not one of the names of God and that it is not Christian to have an eye to outward success or numbers. God's paths are other than that: his success comes about through the Cross and is always found under that sign. The true witnesses to his authenticity, down through the centuries, are those who have accepted this sign as their emblem. When, today, we look at past history, then we have to say that it is not the Church of the successful people that we find impressive; the Church of those popes who were universal monarchs; the Church of those leaders who knew

---

[11] This reflection was adumbrated by Ernst Käsemann in 1967, in an address at the Congress of the German Evangelical Church (published under the title: "Die Gegenwart des Gekreuzigten", in Käsemann, *Kirchliche Konflikte*, vol. 1 [Göttingen, 1982], 76–91, especially 77, 80f.).

how to get on well with the world. Rather, what strengthens our faith, what remains constant, what gives us hope, is the Church of the suffering. She stands, to the present day, as a sign that God exists and that man is not just a cesspit, but that he can be saved. This is true of the martyrs of the first three centuries and, then, right up to Maximilian Kolbe and the many unnamed witnesses who gave their lives for the Lord under the dictatorships of our own day; whether they had to die for their faith or whether they had to let themselves be trampled on, day after day and year after year, for his sake. The Church of the suffering gives credibility to Christ: she is God's success in the world; the sign that gives us hope and courage; the sign from which still flows the power of life, which reaches beyond mere thoughts of success and which thereby purifies men and opens up for God a door into this world. So let us be ready to hear the call of Jesus Christ, who achieved the great success of God on the Cross; he who, as the grain of wheat that died, has become fruitful down through all the centuries; the Tree of Life, in whom even today men may put their hope.

2. The Eucharist: Heart of the Church

John the evangelist has set his account of the Passion of Jesus Christ between two marvelous pictures, providing a kind of framework in which, in each case, he portrays the whole meaning of Jesus' life and suffering, so that he can then expound the origin of the Christian life, the origin and meaning of the sacraments. At the beginning of the Passion story stands the account of washing the disciples' feet; at the end, the solemn and moving account of the *opening of Jesus' side* (Jn 19:30–37). In constructing his narrative thus, John takes great care to establish which day it was that Jesus died.[12] It is clear in his Gospel that Jesus died at exactly the time when the paschal lambs were being sacrificed in the Temple for the feast of Passover. Thus, through the exact time of his death it becomes clear that he is the true Paschal Lamb, that the business with the lambs is finished, because the Lamb is come. For the side of Jesus, when it is pierced, John has chosen exactly the same word as is used in

---

[12] We do not intend to reopen here the dispute about the historical accuracy of the Synoptic or the Johannine chronology of the Passion; cf. on this point Rudolf Pesch, *Das Markusevangelium*, vol. 2, HThKNT, vol. 2, pt. 2 (Freiburg, 1977), 323–28.

the creation story to tell of the creation of Eve, where we normally translate it as Adam's "rib".[13] In this fashion John makes it clear that Jesus is the New Adam, who goes down into the darkness of death's sleep and opens within it the beginning of a new humanity. From his side, that side which has been opened up in loving sacrifice, comes a spring of water that brings to fruition the whole of history. From the ultimate self-sacrifice of Jesus spring forth blood and water, Eucharist and Baptism, as the source of a new community.

The Lord's opened side is the source from which spring forth both the Church and the sacraments that build up the Church. Thus what we were trying to comprehend in our first meditation is once more portrayed in this picture offered to us by the evangelist. The Last Supper alone is not sufficient for the institution of the Eucharist. For the words that Jesus spoke then are an anticipation of his death, a transformation of his death into an event of love, a transformation of what is meaningless into something that is significant, significant for us. But that also means that these words carry weight and have creative power for all time only in that they did not remain mere words but were given content by his actual death. And then again, this death would remain empty of meaning, his words would remain mere empty claims and unredeemed promises, were it not shown to be true that his love is stronger than death, that meaning is stronger than meaninglessness. The death would remain empty of meaning, and would also render the words meaningless, if the Resurrection had not come about, whereby it is made clear that these words were spoken with divine authority, that his love is indeed strong enough to reach out beyond death. Thus the three belong together: the word, the death, and the Resurrection. And this trinity of word, death, and Resurrection, which gives us an inkling of the mystery of the triune God himself, this is what Christian tradition calls the "Paschal Mystery", the mystery of Easter. Only the three together make up a whole, only these three together constitute a veritable reality, and this single mystery of Easter is the source and origin of the Eucharist.

But that means that the Eucharist is far more than just a meal; it has cost a death to provide it, and the majesty of death is present in it.

---

[13] Cf. on this point Hugo Rahner, *Symbole der Kirche: Die Ekklesiologie der Väter* (Salzburg, 1964), 177–205; and on the Jewish background, A. Tossato, *Il matrimonio nel Giudaismo Antico e nel Nuovo Testamento* (Rome, 1976), 49–80.

Whenever we hold it, we should be filled with reverence in the face of this mystery, with awe in the face of this mysterious death that becomes a present reality in our midst. Certainly, the overcoming of this death in the Resurrection is present at the same time, and we can therefore celebrate this death as the feast of life, as the transformation of the world. In all ages, and among all peoples, the ultimate aim of men in their festivals has been to open the door of death. For as long as it does not touch on this question, a festival remains superficial, mere entertainment to anaesthetize oneself. Death is the ultimate question, and wherever it is bracketed out there can be no real answer. Only when this question is answered can men truly celebrate and be free. The Christian feast, the Eucharist, plumbs the very depths of death. It is not just a matter of pious discourse and entertainment, of some kind of religious beautification, spreading a pious gloss on the world; it plumbs the very depths of existence, which it calls death, and strikes out an upward path to life, the life that overcomes death. And in this way the meaning of what we are trying to reflect on, in this meditation, becomes clear, what the tradition sums up in this sentence: *The Eucharist is a sacrifice, the presentation of Jesus Christ's sacrifice on the Cross.*

Whenever we hear these words, inhibitions arise within us, and in all ages it has always been so. The question arises: When we talk about sacrifice, do we not do so on the basis of an unworthy picture of God, or at least a naïve one? Does this not assume that we men should and could give something to God? Does this not show that we think of ourselves as equal partners with God, so to speak, who could barter one thing for another with him: we give him something so that he will give us something? Is this not to misapprehend the greatness of God, who has no need of our gifts, because he himself is the giver of all gifts? But, on the other hand, the question certainly does remain: Are we not all of us in debt to God, indeed, not merely debtors to him but offenders against him, since we are no longer simply in the position of owing him our life and our existence but have now become guilty of offenses against him? We cannot give him anything, and in spite of that we cannot even simply assume that he will regard our guilt as being of no weight, that he will not take it seriously, that he will look on man as just a game, a toy.

It is to this very question that the Eucharist offers us an answer.

First of all, it says this to us: *God himself gives to us, that we may give in turn.* The initiative in the sacrifice of Jesus Christ comes from God.

In the first place it is he himself who comes down to us: "God so loved the world that he gave his only-begotten Son" (Jn 3:16). Christ is not in the first instance a gift *we* men bring to an angry God; rather, the fact that he is there at all, living, suffering, loving, is the work of God's love. He is the condescension of merciful love, who bows down to us; for us the Lord becomes a slave, as we saw in the previous meditation. It is in this sense that, in the Second Letter to the Corinthians, we find the words in which grace calls out to us: "Be reconciled to God" (2 Cor 5:20). Although *we* started the quarrel, although it is not God who owes us anything, but we him, he comes to meet us, and in Christ he begs, as it were, for reconciliation. He brings to be in reality what the Lord is talking about in the story of the gifts in the Temple, where he says: "If you are offering your gift at the altar, and there remember that your brother has something against you, leave your gift there before the altar and go; first be reconciled to your brother, and then come and offer your gift" (Mt 5:23f.). God, in Christ, has trodden this path before us; he has set out to meet us, his unreconciled children—he has left the temple of his glory and has gone out to reconcile us.

Yet we can already see the same thing if we look back to the beginning of the history of faith. Abraham, in the end, does not sacrifice anything he has prepared himself but offers the ram (the lamb) that has been offered to him by God. Thus, through this original sacrifice of Abraham a perspective opens up down the millennia; this lamb in the brambles that God gives him, so that he may offer it, is the first herald of that Lamb, Jesus Christ, who carries the crown of thorns of our guilt, who has come into the thorn bush of world history in order to give us something that we may give. Anyone who correctly comprehends the story of Abraham cannot come to the same conclusion as Tilmann Moser in his strange and dreadful book *Poisoned by God*; Moser reads here the evidence for a God who is as dreadful as poison, making our whole life bitter.[14] Even when Abraham was still on his way, and as yet knew nothing of the mystery of the ram, he was able to say to Isaac, with trust in his heart: *Deus providebit*—God will take care of us. Because he knew this God, therefore, even in the dark

---

[14] Cf., on the subject of Tilmann Moser, the lovely contribution by Odil Hannes Steck, "Ist Gott grausam?" in *Ist Gott grausam? Eine Stellungnahme zu Tilmann Mosers "Gottesvergiftung"*, ed. Wolfgang Böhme (Stuttgart, 1977), 75–95.

night of his incomprehension he knew that he is a loving God; therefore, even then, when he found he could understand nothing, he could put his trust in him and could know that the very one who seemed to be oppressing him truly loved him even then. Only in thus going onward, so that his heart was opened up, so that he entered the abyss of trust and, in the dark night of the uncomprehended God, dared keep company with him, did he thereby become capable of accepting the ram, of understanding the God who gives to us that we may give. This Abraham, in any case, has something to say to all of us. If we are only looking on from outside, if we only let God's action wash over us from without and only insofar as it is directed toward us, then we will soon come to see God as a tyrant who plays about with the world. But the more we keep him company, the more we trust in him in the dark night of the uncomprehended God, the more we will become aware that that very God who seems to be tormenting us is the one who truly loves us, the one we can trust without reserve. The deeper we go down into the dark night of the uncomprehended God and trust in him, the more we will discover him and will find the love and the freedom that will carry us through any and every night. God gives that we may give. This is the essence of the Eucharistic Sacrifice, of the sacrifice of Jesus Christ; from the earliest times, the Roman Canon has expressed it thus: "De tuis donis ac datis offerimus tibi"—from your gifts and offerings we offer you.

Even the second element—*we* offer—is absolutely true, not a mere fiction. So we must now ask: How can this come about—that, on the one hand, since we have nothing to give, God gives to us and that, on the other hand, we are not thereby reduced to mere passive objects of his action, who can only stand there in shame, but are on the contrary genuinely permitted to give him something? In order to understand that, we have to turn back again to the history of the people of Israel, whose faithful members engaged in a profound and passionate debate about what really constitutes a sacrifice and how it can be performed in a manner appropriate to God and to man. Out of this debate an insight gradually emerged, developed, and consolidated in the religion of the prophets and of the psalmists, which might be expressed roughly in these words: A contrite spirit is the true sacrifice to offer you. May our prayers ascend to you like the smoke of incense. May our prayers to you carry more weight than the sacrifice of thousands of fat rams.

Israel was beginning to grasp that the sacrifice pleasing to God is a man pleasing to God and that prayer, the grateful praise of God, is thus the true sacrifice in which we give ourselves back to him, thereby renewing ourselves and the world. The heart of Israel's worship had always been what we express in the Latin word *memoriale: remembrance*. Whenever the Passover is celebrated, before the lamb is eaten, the head of the household recites the Passover Haggadah, that is to say, an account praising the great works God has done for Israel. The head of the house gives praise for the history God has made with his people, so that the next generation may hear it. But he does not recount this like mere past history; rather, he gives praise for the presence of God who supports us and who leads us, whose activity is thus present for us and in us. In the period in which Jesus lived, there was a growing consciousness of the Passover Haggadah as being at the real heart of Israel's worship, as being the true offering to God. The religion of Israel was at one here with the new religious outlook of the pagan world, in which the idea was emerging that the true sacrifice was the word or, rather, the man who in thanksgiving gave a spiritual dimension both to things and to himself, purified them, and thereby rendered them fit for God.

Now, it was into the texture of the Passover Haggadah, this thanksgiving prayer, that Jesus wove his sayings at the Last Supper, and it thereby acquired, over and above the shape it had developed in Israel, a new heart and center. It had hitherto remained merely verbal, in danger of turning into a mere form of words; it remained a verbal assertion in the midst of a history in which the victory of God is far from obvious, despite all his great works. Jesus Christ now gave to this prayer a heart that opens the locked door; this heart is his love, in which God is victorious and conquers death. The Canon of the Roman Mass developed directly from these Jewish prayers of thanksgiving; it is the direct descendant and continuation of this prayer of Jesus at the Last Supper and is thereby the heart of the Eucharist. It is the genuine vehicle of the sacrifice, since thereby Jesus Christ transformed his death into verbal form—into a prayer—and, in so doing, changed the world.[15]

---

[15] I have given a more complete account of the relations between these various elements in the article "Gestalt und Gehalt der eucharistischen Feier", in IKaZ 6 (1977): 385–96; reprinted, with two appendices, in Joseph Ratzinger, *Das Fest des Glaubens: Versuche zur Theologie des Gottesdienstes*, 3rd ed. (Einsiedeln, 1993), 31–54 [trans. by Graham Harrison as *The Feast of Faith: Approaches to a Theology of the Liturgy* (San Francisco: Ignatius Press, 1986), 33–60; JRCW 11:299–318].

As a result, this death is able to be present for us, because it continues to live in the prayer, and the prayer runs right down through the centuries. A further consequence is that we can share in this death, because we can participate in this transforming prayer, can join in praying it. This, then, is the new sacrifice he has given us, in which he includes us all: Because he turned death into a proclamation of thanksgiving and love, he is now able to be present down through all ages as the wellspring of life, and we can enter into him by praying with him. He gathers up, so to speak, the pitiful fragments of our suffering, our loving, our hoping, and our waiting into this prayer, into a great flood in which it shares in his life, so that thereby we truly share in the sacrifice.

Christ does not stand facing us alone. It was alone that he died, as the grain of wheat, but he does not arise alone, but as a whole ear of corn, taking with him the communion of the saints. Since the Resurrection, Christ no longer stands alone but is—as the Church Fathers say—always *caput et corpus*: head and body, open to us all. Thus he makes his word come true: "I, when I am lifted up from the earth, will draw all men to myself" (Jn 12:32). That is why we do not need to harbor the fear that motivated Luther to protest against the Catholic idea of the Mass as sacrifice, that thereby the glory of Christ might be diminished, or that the "sacrifice of the Mass" is founded on the idea that Christ's sacrifice was not enough and that we ought to, or could, add something to it. Such mistaken ideas may well have been current, but they have nothing to do with the real meaning of the concept of the sacrificial character of the Mass. The magnitude of Christ's achievement consists precisely in his not remaining someone else, over and against us, who might thus relegate us once more to a merely passive role; he does not merely bear with us; rather, he bears us up; he identifies himself with us to such an extent that our sins belong to him and his being to us: *he truly accepts us and takes us up, so that we ourselves become active with his support and alongside him, so that we ourselves cooperate and join in the sacrifice with him, participating in the mystery ourselves.* Thus our own life and suffering, our own hoping and loving, can also become fruitful, in the new heart he has given us.

Let us summarize what we have said so far. As a continuation of the Passover Haggadah, the Canon, as *eucharistia* (that is, as the transformation of existence into thanksgiving), is the true heart of the Mass. The liturgy itself calls it *rationabile obsequium*, an offering in verbal form.

It presupposes in the first place the spiritual struggle of the prophets, of the suffering men of righteousness in Israel, but equally the mature religion of the Hellenistic world, which was increasingly close to Judaism. But above all it shows an awareness that human words can become true worship and sacrifice only if they are given substance by the life and suffering of him who is himself the Word. The transforming of death into love, which is achieved in his word of almighty power, thereby combines human words with the Word of eternal love, which is what the Son is, as he ceaselessly gives himself up in love to the Father. That is why this word can do what human love merely longs to do: open the door, in death, to resurrection. Thus the Canon, the "true sacrifice", is the word of the Word; in it speaks the one who, as Word, is life. By putting these words into our mouths, letting us pronounce them with him, he permits us and enables us to make the offering with him: his words become our words, his worship our worship, his sacrifice our sacrifice.

Following this farther, we now have to look at the structure of the Canon. In doing so we should note that the new Eucharistic Prayers share the same structure as the traditional Roman Canon; so that our reflections in respect of this one instance are relevant in essentials to the others. So, when we look at the so-called Roman Canon, we notice first of all something quite remarkable: it does not talk only about God and about Christ, his death and his Resurrection. It mentions people by name: Sixtus, Clement, Cyprian; it allows us to insert names, the names of people we have loved and who have gone before us into the other world; the names of people whom we would like to thank or whose burden we would like to be able to share. Indeed, the Canon goes beyond this to speak of the whole creation, for when it says at the close: "Through him you bless all these good gifts", then it is envisaging everything we have received from God's good hands; every one of our meals is, as it were, offered up in this new feast that is Christ's gift to us and bears within it something of the new feast's thanksgiving to God the Creator. We ought—I would add—to renew our awareness of this fact that all our meals are alive with the goodness of God the Creator, and all thereby point toward this greatest feast of all, in which we receive no longer just earthly things, but the incarnate act of God's mercy. We should resolve to make our meals once more holy times, to open and to close them with prayer. Doing this will introduce a new atmosphere into our homes; wherever we pray together, where we receive God's gifts with thankfulness, a new heart comes into being, which also changes us ourselves.

We were saying that people are mentioned in the Canon; there is a very simple reason for this. There is only *one* Christ. Wherever the Eucharist is celebrated, he is wholly and fully present. Because of that, even in the most humble village church, when the Eucharist is celebrated, the whole mystery of the Church, her living heart, the Lord, is present. But this Christ, fully present, is yet at the same time one. That is why we can only receive him together with everyone else. He is the same, here or in Rome, in America or in Australia or in Africa. Because he is one, we can only receive him in unity. If ever we were opposed to unity, we would be unable to meet with him. For that reason, every celebration of the Eucharist has the structure we find in the *Communicantes*, that of communion not only with the Lord but also with creation and with men of all places and all times. This, too, is something we ought to take to heart anew, that we cannot have communion with the Lord if we are not in communion with each other; that when we go to meet him in the Mass, we necessarily go to meet each other, to be at one with each other. Therefore the mentioning of the bishop and the pope by name, in the celebration of the Eucharist, is not merely an external matter, but an inner necessity of that celebration. For *the celebration of the Eucharist* is not just *a meeting of heaven and earth*; rather, it is also *a meeting of the Church then and now* and *a meeting of the Church here and there*; it assumes that we visibly enter into a visible unity, one that can be described. The names of the bishop and the pope stand for the fact that we are truly celebrating the *one* Eucharist of Jesus Christ, which we can receive only in the *one* Church.

Thus a final point becomes evident: at the heart of the Canon is the narrative of the evening before Jesus' Passion. When this is spoken, then the priest is not recounting the story of something that is past, just recalling what happened then, but something is taking place in the present. "This *is* my Body" is what is said now, today. But these words are the words of Jesus Christ. No man can pronounce them for himself. No one can, for his own part, declare his body to be the Body of Christ, declare this bread to be his Body, speaking in the first person, the "I" of Jesus Christ. This saying in the first person—"*my* Body"—only he himself can say. If anyone were to dare to say, on his own behalf, that he saw himself as the self of Christ, this would surely be blasphemy. No one can endow himself with such authority; no one else can give it to him; no congregation or community can give it to him. It can only be the gift of the Church as a whole, the one whole Church, to whom the Lord has communicated himself. *For this reason the Mass needs the person who does not speak in his own name, who does not come on his own authority, but who represents the whole Church, the Church of all places and all ages, which has passed on to him what was communicated to her.* The fact that the celebration of the Eucharist is tied to ordination as a priest is not, as we sometimes hear, something that the Church has invented, by means of which she arrogates to herself all kinds of privileges and restricts the activity of the Spirit. It follows from the essential significance of these words, which no one has the right to pronounce on his own behalf; it follows that these words can be pronounced only in the sacrament of the Church as a whole, with the authority that she alone, in her unity and her fullness, possesses. Being entrusted with the mission that the whole Church in her unity has herself received is what we call ordination to the priesthood. On the basis of all this we ought to try to discover a new reverence for the eucharistic mystery. Something is happening there that is greater than anything we can do. The magnitude of what is happening is not dependent on the way we perform it, but all our efforts to perform it aright can always be only at the service of the great act that precedes our own and that we cannot achieve for ourselves. We should learn anew that the Eucharist is never merely what a congregation does, but that we receive from the Lord what he has granted to the entirety of the Church. I am always moved by those stories of what happened in concentration camps or Russian prison camps, where people had to do without the Eucharist for a period of weeks or months and yet did not turn to the arbitrary action of celebrating it themselves; rather, they made a eucharistic celebration of their longing, waiting with yearning upon the Lord, who alone can give of himself. In such a Eucharist of longing and yearning they were made ready for his gift in a new way, and they received it as something new, when somewhere or other a priest found a bit of bread and some wine.

On this basis, we should likewise accept the question of intercommunion with appropriate humility and patience. It is not for us to act as if there were unity where this is not the case. The Eucharist is never the means we can use to any end; it is the gift of the Lord, the heart of the Church herself, and not within our control. It is not a matter of personal friendship here, of the strength of subjective faith, which in any case we have no means of measuring, but of standing within the unity of the one Church and of our humbly waiting for God to grant this unity himself. Instead of conducting experiments in this area and robbing the mystery of its greatness and degrading it to an instrument in our hands, we too should learn to celebrate a Eucharist of longing and yearning and in shared prayer and shared hope to walk together with the Lord toward new ways of finding unity.

St. John's account of the Lord's death closes with the words: "They shall look on him whom they have pierced" (Jn 19:37 = Zech 12:10). He begins his Revelation with these words, which in that place constitute the opening of the Day of Judgment, that day on which the one who was pierced will rise over the world as its judgment and its life. But he commands us to look upon him now, so that the judgment may be turned to salvation. "They shall look on him whom they have pierced." This might be a description of the inner direction of our Christian life, our learning ever more truly to look upon him, to keep the eyes of our heart turned upon him, to see him, and thereby to grow more humble; to recognize our sins, to recognize how we have struck him, how we have wounded our brethren and thereby wounded him; to look upon him and, at the same time, to take hope, because he whom we have wounded is he who loves us; to look upon him and to receive the way of life. Lord, grant to us to look upon you and, in so doing, to find true life!

3. The Proper Celebration of the Holy Eucharist

When you assemble as a church, I hear that there are divisions among you; and I partly believe it, for there must be factions among you in order that those who are genuine among you may be recognized. When you meet together, it is not the Lord's supper that you eat. For in eating, each one goes ahead with his own meal, and one is hungry and another is drunk. What! Do you not have houses to eat and drink in? Or do you despise the church of God and humiliate those who have nothing? What shall I say to you? Shall I commend you in this? No, I will not.

For I received from the Lord what I also delivered to you, that the Lord Jesus on the night when he was betrayed took bread, and when he had given thanks, he broke it, and said, "This is my body which is for you. Do this in remembrance of me." In the same way also the cup, after the supper, saying, "This cup is the new covenant in my blood. Do this, as often as you drink it, in remembrance of me." For as often as you eat this bread and drink the cup, you proclaim the Lord's death until he comes.

Whoever, therefore, eats the bread or drinks the cup of the Lord in an unworthy manner will be guilty of profaning the body and blood of the Lord. Let a man examine himself, and so eat of the bread and drink of the cup. For any one who eats and drinks without discerning the body eats and drinks judgment upon himself.

1 Corinthians 11:18–29

Paul's rebuke to the congregation at Corinth applies to us, for among us, too, a dispute has broken out concerning the Eucharist; among us, too, the opposition of one party to another threatens to obscure the central mystery of the Church. In this dispute about the holy Eucharist there are two parties opposed to each other: the one, let us call them the progressives, says that with the traditional form of celebrating the Mass the Church has strayed far from the original intentions of the Lord. The Lord, they say, held a simple meal of fellowship with his disciples, and he said: "Do this in remembrance of me!" But it is precisely this that the Church does not do, they say; rather, she has made of it yet another sacral cultic ritual; she has reworked the whole thing into the Mass, has surrounded it with richly decorated cathedrals and with an imposing and sublime liturgy, and has thus altered beyond recognition the simple nature of what Jesus commanded us to do. The watchword that emerges from such reflections is: desacralization. The Lord's Supper should once more become a simple, human, everyday meal. And from that there followed, for instance, the conclusion that it is not really right to have a church building, but we should have a multipurpose area, so that the Lord's Supper can truly be held in an everyday setting and not be elevated into a cultic ritual. In the same way the demand emerged to do away with liturgical forms and vestments and the call to get back to the way we look in ordinary daily life. The louder these voices became, and the more such things were actually put into practice, the more strongly there arose an objection to the contrary, directed against the liturgical reform as a whole. The reshaped liturgy was accused of puritanism, poverty, iconoclasm. It was said that the Mass had been made completely Protestant and that the real Catholic element in it had been destroyed. Thus, it was said, the Catholic Church, at this point in her very heart, had ceased to be catholic. The Eucharist would have to be celebrated outside her and despite her, since there was no longer a valid Eucharist within her. With these things in mind, let us try to look at these two questions.

And now the first question: Jesus did not, it is said, call for any kind of cult or liturgy, but just an everyday meal of fellowship, when he said: "Do *this!*" Plausible though this objection may seem, as soon as we listen more carefully to Holy Scripture and refuse to be satisfied with superficialities, it becomes clear to us that it is untrue. For Jesus did not command his disciples to repeat the Last Supper as such and as a whole; this would in any case not have been possible, as it was a Passover meal.[16] But Passover is an annual festival, with a quite specific date in the lunar calendar, which comes around just once a year. No more than I can keep Christmas whenever I feel like it can the Passover just be continually repeated. Jesus did not give the command to repeat, as a whole, this Jewish liturgy that he had kept with his people—this, as we said, would have been impossible. His command to repeat something referred to the new element he was presenting them, to his gift of himself, which he had instituted within the old setting of the worship of Israel. We are thus presented with the *essential element*, but it has not yet found a new Christian form. Not until the moment when, through the Cross and the Resurrection and the story that followed, the Church emerged from within Israel as an independent community could this new gift find its own new form. And that gives rise to the question: From what source did the Mass actually derive its shape, if it was not possible to repeat the entire Last Supper as such? What could the disciples build upon to develop this new shape?

Nowadays New Testament scholars essentially give one of two answers. Some of them say that the Eucharist of the early Church built upon meals that Jesus shared with his disciples day after day.

---

[16] The difference between the Johannine and the Synoptic Christology supports this; cf. Rudolf Pesch, *Das Markusevangelium*, vol. 2, HThKNT, vol. 2, pt. 2 (Freiburg, 1977), 323–28; Rudolf Schnackenburg, *Das Johannesevangelium*, vol. 3, HThKNT, vol. 4, pt. 3 (Freiburg, 1975), 38–53. Besides this, John assumes the presence of the ritual elements of the Passover meal (Pesch, *Markusevangelium*, 2:326), so that the fact of this being something that could not simply be repeated in the Christian community applies likewise, indeed especially, in his case.

Others say that the Eucharist is the *continuation of the meals with sinners that Jesus had held.*[17] This second idea has become for many people a fascinating notion with far-reaching consequences. For it would mean that the Eucharist is the sinners' banquet, where Jesus sits at the table; the Eucharist is the public gesture by which he invites everyone without exception. The logic of this is expressed in a far-reaching criticism of the Church's Eucharist, since it implies that the Eucharist cannot be conditional on anything, not dependent on denomination or even on baptism. It is necessarily an open table to which all may come to encounter the universal God, without any limit or denominational preconditions. But then, again—however tempting the idea may be—it contradicts what we find in the Bible. Jesus' Last Supper was not one of those meals he held with "publicans and sinners". He made it subject to the basic form of the Passover, which implies that this meal was held in a family setting. Thus he kept it with his new family, with the Twelve; with those whose feet he washed, whom he had prepared, by his Word and by this cleansing of absolution (Jn 13:10), to receive a blood relationship with him, to become one body with him.[18] The Eucharist is not itself the sacrament of reconciliation, but in fact it presupposes that sacrament. It is the *sacrament of the reconciled,* to which the Lord invites all those who have become one with him; who certainly still remain weak sinners, but yet have given their hand to him and have become part of his family. That is why, from the beginning, the Eucharist has been preceded by a discernment. We have just heard this, in very dramatic form, from Paul: Whoever eats unworthily, eats and drinks judgment on himself, because he does not distinguish the Body of the Lord (1 Cor 11:27ff.). The *Teaching of the Twelve Apostles,* one of the oldest writings outside the New Testament, from the beginning of the second century, takes up this apostolic tradition and

---

[17] There are more details on this in my essay "Gestalt und Gehalt der eucharistischen Feier", in my *Fest des Glaubens,* 31–54 [*Feast of Faith,* 33–60; JRCW 11:299–318].

[18] Cf. on this point especially John 13:8, which speaks of "having a part" in Jesus, where, on the one hand, we hear an echo of eucharistic terminology, while, on the other, there is a recognizable application to the depths of our being. Cf. Rudolf Schnackenburg, *Johannesevangelium,* vol. 2, HThKNT, vol. 4, pt. 2 (Freiburg, 1971), 21; Rudolf Bultmann, *Das Evangelium des Johannes,* 15th ed., Kritisch-exegetische Kommentar über das Neue Testament, sec. 2 (Göttingen, 1957), 357, n. 3; and there is important material on this subject in Kenneth Hein, *Eucharist and Excommunication: A Study in Early Christian Doctrine and Discipline,* Europäische Hochschulschriften, series 23, Theologie 19 (Frankfurt, 1973).

has the priest, just before distributing the Sacrament, saying: "Whoever is holy, let him approach—whoever is not, let him do penance!" [19] The Eucharist is—let us repeat it—the sacrament of those who have let themselves be reconciled by God, who have thus become members of his family and put themselves into his hands. That is why there are conditions for participating in it; it presupposes that we have voluntarily entered into the mystery of Jesus Christ.

Yet even the second line of inquiry to which we referred—supposing that the Eucharist was built upon the *daily fellowship meals Jesus held* with his disciples—is unconvincing, since we know that in the first place the Eucharist was celebrated every Sunday; so that it was in fact something apart from ordinary everyday life and thus apart from everyday table fellowship. It was the Resurrection that offered the actual starting point for the Christian shaping of the legacy of Jesus. It was this, basically, that opened up the possibility of his being present beyond the limitations of earthly corporeal existence and of sharing himself out. But the Resurrection took place on the first day of the week. The Jews saw this as the day on which the world was created. For Jesus' disciples, it became the day on which a new world began, the day when, with the breaking of the bonds of death, the new creation had its beginning. It was the day on which Jesus Christ entered the world anew as the Risen One. Thereby he had made this day, the first day of creation, his day, the "Day of the Lord". It is already called that in the first century; that is the name given in the book of Revelation (1:10). And both in the Acts of the Apostles (20:7) and in the First Letter to the Corinthians (16:2) we find evidence that this was the day of the Eucharist. The Lord had risen on the first day of the week; and this day, his day, was kept week after week as the day of remembrance of the new thing that had happened. In doing this, the disciples had no need to look back on the Resurrection as something in the past: the Risen One is alive; that is why the day of Resurrection was, of its very nature, the day of his presence, the day he gathered them together, when they gathered around him. Sunday, as the day of the Resurrection, became the inner basis, the inner point of location, for the eucharistic celebration of the developing Church. It was on this basis that its shape was developed.

---

[19] *Didache* X, 6.

It was now, as it were, transplanted out of the soil of the Jewish Passover into the context of the Resurrection: its essential characteristic was now that of being the *celebration of the Resurrection*. As early as the beginning of the second century, Ignatius of Antioch refers to Christians as those who "live consistently with Sunday",[20] that is to say, people who live on the basis of the Resurrection, of its presence in the eucharistic celebration. Thus the basis for the reshaping of the eucharistic celebration was established. *After* the earthly meal that satisfied the hunger of the assembled believers, they celebrated with praise and thanksgiving the presence of the death and Resurrection of the Lord. Thus, by an inner logic, the Last Supper developed into a celebration in which joy has its place. It is the Acts of the Apostles, again, that tells us that Christians celebrated the Eucharist with songs of praise, and we know from the fifth chapter of the Letter to the Ephesians (5:19; cf. Col 3:16), and from many other passages, that they praised the Lord with psalms and hymns and songs.[21] By its being transplanted into the context of the Resurrection, without which the Eucharist would be merely the remembrance of a departure with no return, there arose two natural developments: worship and praise, that is to say, its cultic characteristics, and also the joy over the glory of the Risen One.

But the shaping of the Eucharist, the developed form of the Church's liturgy, was still not completed. We have to bear in mind that Jewish worship had two elements. One was the sacrificial worship in the Temple, where in accordance with what the law prescribed the various sacrifices were offered. Side by side with this Temple worship, which took place, and could only take place, in Jerusalem, a second element was steadily developing: the synagogue, which could be set up anywhere. Here the service of the word was celebrated, the Holy Scriptures were read, the Psalms were sung, people joined in praising God, hearing the Word of God interpreted, and making petitions to God. After the Resurrection of Jesus, his followers ceased to take part in the sacrificial cult in the Temple. They could no longer do so, for the curtain in the Temple was torn, that is, the Temple was

---

[20] IgnMagn. 9, 1.

[21] Cf. Erik Peterson, "Von den Engeln", in his *Theologische Traktate* (Munich, 1951), 323–407; Joseph Ratzinger, *Theologische Probleme der Kirchenmusik* (Rottenburg, 1978) [trans. as "The Artistic Transposition of the Faith: Theological Problems of Church Music", in *Crux et cithara*, ed. Robert A. Skeris (Altötting, 1983), 214–22; JRCW 11:480–93].

empty.[22] It was no longer that stone building that was the Temple, but the Lord, who had opened himself to the Father as the living Temple and had opened a way for the Father, from himself, into humanity. In place of the Temple there is the Eucharist, since Christ is the true Paschal Lamb; everything that ever took place in the Temple has been fulfilled in him.

But while, for this reason, the disciples no longer shared in the bloody sacrifices of the Temple but celebrated the *new* Paschal Lamb in their stead, they continued to take part in the synagogue worship just as before. The Bible of Israel was, after all, the Bible of Jesus Christ. They knew that the whole of the Holy Scriptures, law and prophets, was talking about him; they therefore tried to read this holy book of their fathers, together with Israel, as referring to Jesus and thus to open Israel's heart to Jesus. They continued to sing the Psalms with Israel, so as thus to sing them with Jesus, and from within the New Covenant to open up a way to understanding them from the standpoint of Christ. Yet at the same time we can follow, in the texts of the New Testament, that tragic path which was to lead eventually to the breakdown of what remained of unity with Israel. Christians were unable to persuade Israel to read the Bible as the word of Jesus Christ and for Jesus Christ. The synagogue rapidly closed itself against such an interpretation of Holy Scripture, and toward the end of the first century the break was complete. It was no longer possible to understand Scripture in company with Jesus within the synagogue. Thus Israel and the Church stood separate, side by side. The Church had become an independent entity. Since she could now no longer share in Israel's service of the word, she had to perform her own. This meant necessarily that the two halves of the liturgy, hitherto separate, came together: the service of the Word became united with the eucharistic worship; and now that this had taken on the shape of fully developed Christian worship, and the Church was thus fully the Church, the whole thing was relocated to Sunday morning, the time of the Resurrection; the logic of the Resurrection had worked itself out.

The basic Christian form of worship, as we keep it up to the present day in the Church's Eucharist, was thereby completed. It looks like

---

[22] Cf. Wolfgang Trilling, *Christusverkündigung in den synoptischen Evangelien*, Biblische Handbibliothek 4 (Munich, 1969), 191–211; Yves Congar, *Le Mystère du temple* (Paris, 1957), 158–80.

this: at the beginning is the service of the Word, consisting of readings from the Old and New Testaments, songs from the Psalms, new prayers, and the joyous greeting of the Lord, the Kyrie, which is the transformation of the ancient cry in homage to the emperor into the cry in homage to Christ as the true Lord of the world.[23] There follows the eucharistic worship itself, and in our earlier reflections we saw that the Canon, as an inclusive "Sacrifice of the Word", grew directly out of the prayer of Israel and of Jesus, given substance now with the narrative and action from the Last Supper as its new heart and also with Holy Communion. Thus, out of the inner logic of Jesus' giving of himself, the shape of the Mass sprang. It developed without any break, as the fulfillment of the original command; and now that it had completed this development, it stood open to receive the wealth of the Temple, the wealth of the nations. Naturally it is always in need of purification. That is the task in every century. And a part of that great process is what we have seen happening, certainly not for the first time, in the middle of our own century. It is always a matter of allowing the wealth of prayers and hopes and faith of all the peoples to find a way in, on one hand, but, on the other, of clearing things away so that its heart is not obscured, so that the mystery of Jesus Christ itself remains visible in its sublime purity. Anyone who has understood that knows that the historical development of the Church's Eucharist is not a decline from its origins but the true fruit of those origins. Those attempts to tell us that we should "get back" to a simple profane meal, to multipurpose areas and so on, are only in appearance a return to the origins. In reality, they are a step back behind the *turning point of the Cross and the Resurrection*, that is, behind the essentials that are the basis for Christianity in all its novelty. This is not restoring the original state, but abandoning the mystery of Easter and, thereby, the very center of the mystery of Christ.

And now we can turn to the second question, which is voiced ever more loudly. Has the fruit of this growth not been destroyed in the reform of the liturgy? We do not wish to concern ourselves here with particular cases of abuse, which have no doubt occurred and probably are still occurring. On that point I would wish to say only this: We all need to be quite clear that the Eucharist is not at the disposal of any individual priest or that of any particular congregation but is the gift

---

[23] Theodor Schnitzler, *Was die Messe bedeutet: Hilfen zur Mitfeier* (Freiburg, 1976), 73–78.

of Jesus Christ to the whole Church and that it retains its sublime quality only if we accept it as being exempt from arbitrary change. All those apparent successes we are aiming for, if instead we give free rein to our own creations, remain mere show and a pottage of lentils, because they obscure the fact that there is more happening, in the true Eucharist of the Church, than we can ever organize ourselves. So let us talk no more about abuses for which individuals are responsible and which we have to try to overcome through our common faith. Let us talk about the attacks that are made upon the authorized form of the liturgy. We have already mentioned the dispute about "for many" or "for all", in the first of these reflections.

There are three further substantial objections. One says that with the changes to the Offertory the sacrificial aspect of the Mass has been destroyed and that the Mass has thus ceased to be Catholic. A second is directed against the manner of receiving Communion: standing, in the hand. And of course the question of the language is also still a matter of dispute.

Let us start with the first. A sociologist who teaches at Saarbrücken has tried to show, with a great display of learning, that it is of the essence of any religion, and especially the Catholic religion, that a *sacrifice* be offered.[24] But instead of that, he says, hymns of praise have now been introduced. Thus there is no longer any sacrifice, and since the Council the Eucharist, he suggests, is no longer the Mass of the Catholic Church. Well, even a modest acquaintance with the *Little Catechism* would be enough for us to realize that the sacrificial dimension was never located in the Offertory; rather, it is in the Eucharistic Prayer, the Canon. For we do not offer God this or that thing; the new element in the Eucharist is the presence of the sacrifice of *Christ*. Therefore the sacrifice is effective where his word is heard, the word of the Word, by which he transformed his death into an event of meaning and of love, in order that we, through being able to take up his words for ourselves, are led onward into his love, onward into the love of the Trinity, in which he eternally hands himself over to the Father. There, where the words of the Word ring forth, and our gifts thus become his gifts, through which he gives himself, *that* is the sacrificial element that has ever and always been characteristic of the Eucharist.

---

[24] Wigand Siebel, *Freiheit und Herrschaftsstruktur in der Kirche: Eine soziologische Studie,* Religionssoziologische Schriften 1 (Berlin, 1971), 20–52.

What we call the "Offertory" has another significance.* The German word *Opferung*, and likewise the English word "offertory", comes either from the Latin *offerre* or, more probably, from *operare*.[25] *Offerre* does not mean to sacrifice (that is *immolare* in Latin); it is rather to provide, prepare, make available.[26] And *operari* means to effect; in this case it, too, means to prepare. The idea was simply that at this point the eucharistic altar had to be made ready and that to this end *operari*, that is, various activity, was necessary, so that the candles, the gifts, bread and wine, should be standing ready for the Eucharist, as was befitting. This was therefore in the first instance simply an external preparation for what was to happen. But people very soon came to understand it in a deeper sense. They borrowed the action of the head of the household in Judaism, who holds the bread up before the face of God, so as to receive it anew from him. By lifting up the gifts to God, by entering together into Israel's manner of preparing itself for God, the outward acts of preparation were increasingly understood as an inward preparation for the approach of God, who seeks us out himself through our gifts. Right up to the ninth or tenth century this act of preparation, which had been taken over from Israel, happened without any words. Then there arose a feeling that every action in the Christian sphere also required words. Thus in about the tenth century those offertory prayers were composed that the older ones among us know and love from the old missal and perhaps even miss in the new form of Mass. These prayers were beautiful and profound. But we have to admit that they carried within them the seeds of a certain misunderstanding. The way they were formulated always looked forward to the actual matter of the Canon. Both elements, the preparation and the actual sacrifice of Christ, were intertwined in these words. Something that made good sense within the world of faith and within the faith can be understood—that is, that in our approach to Christ we are always carried onward by his coming to find us—was also liable, for those looking on from outside or those who came seeking the

---

*There is a widespread misunderstanding among many German speakers, who have been misled by the verbal similarity between *Opfer* (= "sacrifice") and *Opferung* (= "offertory"); Cardinal Ratzinger is here trying to unravel this confusion.—TRANS.

[25] Schnitzler, *Was die Messe bedeutet*, 117ff.

[26] Concerning the semantic field of *offerre*, see the important study of Rupert Berger, *Die Wendung "offerre pro" in der römischen Liturgie*, LWQF 41 (Münster, 1965); cf. also on this point Josef Andreas Jungmann, *Messe im Gottesvolk: Eine nachkonziliarer Durchblick durch Missarum Sollemnia* (Freiburg, 1970), 60–67.

truth, to lead to misunderstanding. That it did have this effect is shown by the reactions we were just talking about.

For this reason, those who were reforming the liturgy wished first of all to return to the situation before the ninth century and to leave the ritual of offering the gifts without any words. The Holy Father, Pope Paul VI, decided personally, and with some emphasis, that some words of prayer would have to remain here. He himself took part in the formulation of these prayers. In their main outlines they are derived from the table prayers of Israel. We must also bear in mind that all these prayers over meals of Israel, these blessings, as they are called, are related to the Paschal Mystery; they look toward the Passover of Israel, are thought out on that basis and draw their life from it. That means that they are implicitly looking forward to the Paschal Mystery of Jesus Christ, that we may call them at the same time both Advent and Easter prayers. Above all, we will recall that the Holy Family, Jesus, Mary, and Joseph, prayed in this way—on their flight into Egypt, in the strange land, and then at home in Nazareth, and again that Jesus prayed in this way with his disciples. At that time the Jewish rule was probably already in force that in the evening the mother lights the candles and that she is then the leader of family prayers. Thus, in these prayers we may hear the voice of Mary and pray with her. The whole secret life of Nazareth, this Advent progression toward the Easter event, is present in them. Thus, a new treasure has entered the liturgy. We start, as it were, with Nazareth, in the act of preparation, and from there we move—in the middle of the Canon—toward Golgotha, and finally on into the Resurrection event of Communion.[27] I think if we hear these new old prayers in this way, then they can become for us a wonderful treasure in uniting us with the earthly life of Jesus, uniting us with the waiting prayer of Israel, and in our sharing the journey from Nazareth to Golgotha and up to the hour of the Resurrection.

The second objection we wanted to consider was directed against the act of receiving Communion: *kneeling—standing, hand—mouth.* Well, first of all, I would like to say that both attitudes are possible, and I would like therefore to ask all priests to exercise tolerance and to

---

[27] Cf. on this whole matter the fine expositions in Schnitzler, *Was die Messe bedeutet,* 117–29, especially 122f.; and in Louis Bouyer, *Woman in the Church,* trans. Marilyn Teichert (San Francisco: Ignatius Press, 1979), 19.

recognize the decision of each person; and I would further like to ask you all to exercise the same tolerance and not to cast aspersions on anyone who may have opted for this or that way of doing it. But you will ask: Is tolerance the proper answer here? Or is it not misplaced with respect to this most holy thing? Well, here again we know that until the ninth century Communion was received in the hand, standing. That does not of course mean that it should always be so. For what is fine, sublime, about the Church is that she is growing, maturing, understanding the mystery more profoundly. In that sense the new development that began after the ninth century is quite justified, as an expression of reverence, and is well-founded. But, on the other hand, we have to say that the Church could not possibly have been celebrating the Eucharist unworthily for nine hundred years.

If we read what the Fathers say, we can see in what a spirit of reverence they received Communion. We find a particularly fine passage in the writings of Cyril of Jerusalem, from the fourth century. In his catechetical homilies he tells the candidates for baptism what they should do at Communion. They should make a throne of their hands, laying the right upon the left to form a throne for the King, forming at the same time a cross. This symbolic gesture, so fine and so profound, is what concerns him: the hands of man form a cross, which becomes a throne, down into which the King inclines himself. The open, outstretched hand can thus become a sign of the way that a man offers himself to the Lord, opens his hands for him, that they may become an instrument of his presence and a throne of his mercies in this world.[28] Anyone who reflects on this will recognize that on this point it is quite wrong to argue about this or that form of behavior. We should be concerned only to argue in favor of what the Church's efforts were directed toward, both before and after the ninth century, that is, a reverence in the heart, an inner submission before the mystery of God that puts himself into our hands. Thus we should not forget that not only our hands are impure but also our tongue and also our heart and that we often sin more with the tongue than with the hands. God takes an enormous risk—and at the same time this is

---

[28] *Mystagogical Catechesis* V, 21, ed. Auguste Piédagnel, SChr 126 (1966), 170ff.; revised and introduced by Georg Röwekamp, FC 7 (Freiburg, 1992), 162f.; cf. Josef Andreas Jungmann, *Missarum Sollemnia*, vol. 2 (Freiburg, 1952), 469, and, regarding the ritual form of the Communion of the faithful in history, 463–86.

an expression of his merciful goodness—in allowing not only our hand and our tongue but even our heart to come into contact with him. We see this in the Lord's willingness to enter into us and live with us, within us, and to become from within the heart of our life and the agent of its transformation.

And finally allow me to say just a few words about *language*. Here again there are two points to consider, which between them open the possibility of a whole range of varying decisions and practice. On one hand, using the magnificent terminology of Hellenistic culture, the Roman Canon calls the action of the Mass *rationabile obsequium*—an action of the word, an action in which spirit and reason play their part. The Word of God wants to speak to man, wants to be understood and answered by him. That is why in Rome, in about the third century, when Greek was no longer generally understood, they made the transition from Greek, which had hitherto been used in the Eucharist, to Latin.[29] But there is also a second point. The Church later hesitated to make use of the developing national languages of Europe in the liturgy, first of all, because for a long time they had not attained the literary level or the unity of usage that would have permitted a common celebration of the Eucharist over a wide area; but then also because she was opposed to anything that would give a national identity to this mystery, because she wanted to express in the language, too, the inclusive character that reaches out beyond the boundaries of place and time. She was able to keep on with Latin as the common liturgical language because she knew that, while it is, in the Eucharist, *also* a matter of comprehensibility, yet it is more than comprehensibility—that this demands a greater, more mature, and more inclusive understanding than that of mere comprehension: she knew that, here, the heart must also understand.

After what we have said, use of the vernacular is in principle justified. It would be a danger only if it were to drag the Eucharist back into the realm of national culture. It would be a danger only if we were to push our translation to the point where only what was immediately comprehensible or, even, obvious in everyday terms remained. In any such translation you would have to omit more and more, until the essential meaning disappeared. Because things are as they are, we should gratefully accept both: the normal form of Eucharist is in the

---

[29] Cf. Theodor Klauser, *Kleine abendländische Liturgiegeschichte* (Bonn, 1965), 23–28.

vernacular, but we should not on that account forget to pray it, to love it, in the common language of the Church over the centuries, so that in this unsettled and changeable world, in which the nations are forever meeting and mingling with each other, we are still able ever and again to worship together and, in that language, to praise the living God together. Here too, we should rise above a fruitless dispute and become one in the multiplicity the Lord has given us; one in recognizing and in loving the understanding and comprehensibility but also the inclusiveness that transcends the rationality of what is immediately understood.

Let me now, to finish, tell you a little story about Martin Buber. The value of understanding things clearly is apparent in it; but at the same time it is marvelously persuasive for the greater possibilities of an understanding heart. Martin Buber tells how Rabbi Levi Yitzhak of Berdichev came one day to an inn where many merchants were staying overnight. In the morning they said morning prayers. It turned out that there was only one phylactery, which is what one must put on, according to Jewish tradition, to say the morning prayers. So this was handed from one to the other, and because that was taking so much time, each one, out of consideration for his neighbor, said the prayers so quickly that you could hardly catch a single distinct word of them. The rabbi, watching this, felt increasingly uncomfortable; and when the whole thing was over, he turned to two young people and just said to them, "Ma-ma-ma, wa-wa-wa." They looked at him in amazement and said, "What is it you want?" In reply, he said again just "Ma-ma-ma, wa-wa-wa." At this, they took him—quite understandably—for an idiot. But he said to them, "Do you really not understand that language, when you've just been talking to the Lord God in it?" After a moment of confusion, one of them said, "Have you never seen a child lying in a cradle, who doesn't yet know how to talk properly? Haven't you heard how he makes all sorts of noises with his mouth: Ma-ma-ma, wa-wa-wa? All the wise men and scholars together cannot understand what he says; but when his mother comes, she knows straight away what the noises mean." [30] This story is not an argument in favor of baby talk. But it does make us aware that there is an understanding of the heart that reaches

---

[30] Martin Buber, *Werke*, vol. 3, *Schriften zum Chassidismus* (Munich and Freiburg, 1963), 334.

beyond a literal understanding. We should seek above all for this understanding of the heart, so that our words may be filled with life and we may worthily praise the living God.

4. The Real Presence of Christ in the Eucharistic Sacrament

Jesus said: "I am the bread of life. Your fathers ate the manna in the wilderness, and they died. This is the bread which comes down from heaven, that a man may eat of it and not die. I am the living bread which came down from heaven; if any one eats of this bread, he will live for ever; and the bread which I shall give for the life of the world is my flesh."

The Jews then disputed among themselves, saying, "How can this man give us his flesh to eat?" So Jesus said to them, "Truly, truly, I say to you, unless you eat the flesh of the Son of man and drink his blood, you have no life in you; he who eats my flesh and drinks my blood has eternal life, and I will raise him up at the last day. For my flesh is food indeed, and my blood is drink indeed. He who eats my flesh and drinks my blood abides in me, and I in him. As the living Father sent me, and I live because of the Father, so he who eats me will live because of me. This is the bread which came down from heaven, not such as the Fathers ate and died; he who eats this bread will live for ever." Jesus said this in the synagogue, as he taught at Capernaum.

—John 6:48–59

St. Thomas Aquinas, in his sermon for Corpus Christi, picked up the saying from the fifth book of Moses, which expresses Israel's joy over its election, over the mystery of the covenant. The saying goes: "What great nation is there that has a god so near to it as the Lord our God is to us?" (Deut 4:7).* We can sense, in Thomas' words, a tone of triumphant joy at the way this saying from the Old Testament had acquired its true sublimity only in the Church, in God's new people. For if, in Israel, God had humbled himself in his speaking to Moses, and had thus drawn near to his people, now he himself has taken flesh, has become a man among men, and has remained, so far remained

---

*Thomas Aquinas, *Officium de festo Corporis Christi*, in *Sanctae Thomae Aquinatis Opera Omnia*, ed. R. Busa, S.J., vol. 6 (Stuttgart and Bad Cannstatt, 1980), 581 (DSG, ps. 3, n. 3; ps. 5, n. 3).

that he places himself, in the mystery of transubstantiated bread, in our hands and in our hearts. This joy at the way that a "people of God" has truly come into being, that God is so near that he could be no closer, was the origin in the thirteenth century of the Feast of Corpus Christi, as one great hymn of thanksgiving that such a thing could be.

But we all know that something that is in fact a cause for rejoicing, and rightly so, is at the same time a stumbling block, a crisis point, and was so from the beginning. For we have heard, in the reading from the Gospel of John, how at the very first advance notice concerning the Eucharist people murmured and revolted against it. Since that time, the murmurs have run down through the centuries, and in particular the Church of our own generation has been deeply hurt by them. We do not want God as near as that; we do not want him so small, humbling himself; we want him to be great and far away. Thus questions arise, which are intended to show that his coming so near is impossible. If, in this meditation, we reflect on a couple of these questions, it is not a matter of indulging a taste for difficulties, but in order to learn anew and more profoundly the Yes of faith, to receive anew its joy and thus to learn anew once more to pray and to know the Eucharist itself. There are three questions above all that are opposed to the belief in the Real Presence of the Lord. The first: Does the Bible actually say anything like that? Does it present us with this, or is it just the naïve misunderstanding of a later age, which transposed the exalted and spiritual reality of Christianity down to a lesser ecclesiastical version? The second question is this: Is it truly possible for a body to share itself out into all places and all times? Does this not simply contradict the limitations that are of the essence of a body? The third question is: Has modern science, with everything it says about "substance" and material being, not so obviously rendered obsolete those dogmas of the Church that relate to this that in the world of science we just finally have to throw them on the scrap heap, since we are unable to reconcile them with contemporary thought?

Let us turn to the first question: Does the Bible say anything like that? We know that in the sixteenth century this dispute was passionately pursued as a dispute about one word, about "is": "This is my Body, this is my Blood." Does this "is" really signify the full force of bodily presence? Or does it not merely indicate an image, so that it should be understood: "This stands for my Body and my Blood"? In the meantime, scholars have disputed about this word until they were weary of it and have realized that an argument about a single word, removed from its context, can only lead up a blind alley. For just as in music a note derives its significance from the interrelating whole, and can only be understood within the whole, so also we can only understand the words in a sentence by the meaning of the whole within which they have their place. We must ask about the whole context. If we do that, the Bible gives a perfectly clear answer. We have just heard the dramatic and incomparably explicit words of Jesus from John's Gospel: "Unless you eat the flesh of the Son of man and drink his blood, you have no life in you.... My flesh is food indeed" (6:53, 55). When the murmuring of the Jews arose, the controversy could easily have been quieted by the assurance: Friends, do not be disturbed; this was only metaphorical language; the flesh only signifies food, it isn't actually that!—But there is nothing of that in the Gospel. Jesus renounces any such toning down; he just says with renewed emphasis that this bread has to be literally, physically eaten. He says that faith in the God who became man is believing in a God with a body and that this faith is real and fulfilled; it brings full union only if it is itself corporeal, if it is a sacramental event in which the corporeal Lord seizes hold of our bodily existence. In order to express fully the intensity and reality of this fusion, Paul compares what happens in Holy Communion with the physical union between man and woman. To help us understand the Eucharist, he refers us to the words in the creation story: "The two [= man and wife] shall become one" (Gen 2:24). And he adds: "He who is united to the Lord becomes one spirit [that is, shares a single new existence in the Holy Spirit] with him" (1 Cor 6:17).

When we hear this, we at once have some notion of how the presence of Jesus Christ is to be understood. It is not something at rest but is a power that catches us up and works to draw us within itself.[31] Augustine had a profound grasp of this in his teaching on Communion. In the period before his conversion, when he was struggling

---

[31] Most insistent on the Real Presence in Paul's writings is Ernst Käsemann, "Anliegen und Eigenart der paulinischen Abendmahlslehre", in his *Exegetische Versuche und Besinnungen*, vol. 1 (Göttingen, 1960), 11–34; on 28, as a summary of the preceding analysis: "The expression 'Real Presence', therefore, whatever objection may be raised against it, exactly expresses what Paul means." On John 6, see: Heinrich Schlier, "Johannes 6 und das johanneische Verständnis der Eucharistie", in his *Das Ende der Zeit* (Freiburg, 1971), 102–23.

with the incarnational aspect of Christian belief, which he found impossible to approach from the point of view of Platonic idealism, he had a sort of vision, in which he heard a voice saying to him: "I am the bread of the strong, eat me! But you will not transform me and make me part of you; rather, I will transform you and make you part of me."[32] In the normal process of eating, man is the stronger being. He takes things in, and they are assimilated into him, so that they become part of his own substance. They are transformed within him and go to build up his bodily life. But in the mutual relation with Christ, it is the other way around; he is the heart, the truly existent being. When we truly communicate, this means that we are taken out of ourselves, that we are assimilated into him, that we become one with him and, through him, with the fellowship of our brethren.

And now we have already arrived at our second question: Is it really possible for a body to share itself out so that it is many hosts, so that beyond the limits of place and time this body is always there? Now, we certainly have to be quite aware, first of all, that we will never wholly understand something like that, since what is happening is part of God's sphere, the sphere of the Resurrection. We, however, do not live in the sphere of the Resurrection. We live on the hither side of death's boundary. If we could perhaps imagine some creature that did not have three dimensions, height, length, and breadth, but only two, in a flat plane, then such a being would never be able to imagine a third dimension, simply because it does not have such a dimension itself. It would only be able to try to think beyond its own limitations, but without ever really being able to picture this other thing or fully to comprehend it. That is just how it is with us. We live in the sphere of death; we can reach out in thought into the sphere of the Resurrection, try to make approximations. But it remains something different that we never quite comprehend. This is because of the boundary of death, which closes us in and within which we live.

But we can look for approximations. One of these becomes apparent when we reflect that in the language of the Bible the word "body"—"This is my Body"—does not mean just a body, in contradistinction to the spirit, for instance. Body, in the language of the Bible, denotes rather the whole person, in whom body and spirit are indivisibly one. "This is my Body" therefore means: This is my whole

---

[32] Augustine, *Confessions* VII, 10, 16.

person, existent in bodily form. What the nature of this person is, however, we learn from what is said next: "which is given up for you". That means: This person is: existing-for-others. It is in its most intimate being a sharing with others. But that is why, since it is a matter of this person and because it is from its heart an opening up, a self-giving person, it can then be shared out.

We can understand that a little bit, just from the experience of our own bodily existence. When we reflect on what the body means for us, we will notice that it carries within it a certain contradiction. On the one hand, the body is the boundary that separates us from others. Where this body is, no other body can be. When I am in this place, I am not at the same time elsewhere. Thus the body is the boundary that separates us from each other; and it thus involves our being some-how strangers to each other. We cannot look inside the other person; corporeal existence hides his inner self; he remains hidden from us; on that account, indeed, we are strangers even to ourselves. We cannot even see into ourselves, into our own depths. That is one thing, then: The body is a boundary that makes us opaque, impermeable for each other, which sets us beside each other and prevents our being able to see or to touch each other's intimate selves. But there is a second thing: The body is also a bridge. For we meet each other through the body; through it we communicate in the common material of cre-ation; through it we can see ourselves, feel ourselves, come close to one another. In the gestures of the body are revealed who and what the other person is. We see ourselves in the way the body sees, looks, acts, offers itself; it leads us to each other: it is both boundary and means of communion in one.

That is why anyone can live out his bodily existence in different ways: we can live it out more inclined toward shutting off or more inclined toward communion. A person can live his bodily existence, and within it the existence of himself, so much directed toward shut-ting off, toward selfishness, that it becomes hardly more than a bound-ary and no longer opens up meetings with others. Then comes about what Albert Camus once depicted as the tragic situation of men in relation to each other: It is as if two people are separated by the glass wall of a telephone box. They can see each other; they are quite close; and yet there is this wall that keeps them apart. Indeed, it seems like frosted glass, which only allows us to see outlines. Man can therefore live in the direction of "body"; he can so shut himself up in selfishness that the body is nothing more than a division, a limit, preventing any communion, and he no longer really encounters anyone in it, lets no one touch his closed-up inner self.

But bodily existence can also be lived in the opposite way: as opening oneself up, as the developing freedom of a person who shares himself. We all know that this happens, too; that transcending the limits we touch one another intimately, are close to each other. What people call telepathy is only an extreme case of what to a lesser extent happens among us all: a hidden movement from the heart, being close to each other even at a distance. Resurrection means quite simply that the body ceases to be a limit and that its capacity for communion remains. Jesus could rise from the dead, and did rise from the dead, because he had become, as the Son and as the One who loved on the Cross, the One who shares himself wholly with others. To have risen from the dead means to be communicable; it signifies being the one who is open, who gives himself. And on that basis we can understand that Jesus, in the speech about the Eucharist that John has handed down to us, puts the Resurrection and the Eucharist together and that the Fathers say that the Eucharist is the medicine of immortality.[33] Receiving Communion means entering into communion with Jesus Christ; it signifies moving into the open through him who alone could overcome the limits and thus, with him and on the basis of his existence, becoming capable of resurrection oneself.

Yet, a further point follows from this. What is given us here is not a piece of a body, not a thing, but him, the Resurrected One himself—the person who shares himself with us in his love, which runs right through the Cross. This means that receiving Communion is always a personal act. It is never merely a ritual performed in common, which we can just pass off as we do with other social routines. In Communion I enter into the Lord, who is communicating himself to me. Sacramental Communion must therefore always be also spiritual Communion. That is why the liturgy changes over, before Communion, from the liturgical "we" to "I".[34] This makes demands on me personally. At this point I have to move out, go toward him, call to him.

---

[33] IgnEph. 20, 2.

[34] Cf. on this point the fine article by Karl Lehmann, "Persönliches Gebet in der Eucharistiefeier", IKaZ 6 (1977): 401–6.

The eucharistic fellowship of the Church is not a collectivity, in which fellowship is achieved by leveling down to the lowest common denominator, but fellowship is created precisely by our each being ourself. It does not rest on the suppression of the self, on collectivization, but arises through our truly setting out, with our whole self, and entering into this new fellowship of the Lord. That is the only way that something other than collectivization can come about; the only way that a true attitude of turning toward each other, one that reaches down to the roots and into the heart and up to the highest level of a person, can develop. Because this is so, the personal approach to Christ, the "I" prayer, is the first part of Communion; that is why we need a time of silence afterward, in which we converse quite personally with the Lord, who is with us. In recent decades, perhaps, we have all far too much lost the habit of this. We have discovered anew the congregation, liturgy as a communal celebration, and this is a great thing. But we also have to discover anew that fellowship requires the person. We must learn anew this quiet prayer before Communion and the silent time at one with the Lord, abandoning ourselves to him.

And finally a further point becomes obvious: What we receive is—as we were just saying—a person. But this Person is the Lord Jesus Christ, both God and man. The previous devotional understanding of Communion, in earlier centuries, perhaps forgot the man Jesus too much and thought too much about God. But we are in danger of the opposite, of only seeing the man Jesus and forgetting that in him, as he gives himself to us in bodily form, we are at the same time coming into contact with the living God. Yet because this is so, Communion is therefore always simultaneously adoration. In any genuine human love there is an element of bowing down before the God-given dignity of the other person, who is in the image of God. Even genuine human love cannot mean that we have the other person all to ourselves and possess him; it includes our reverential recognition of something sublime and unique in this other person, whom we can never entirely possess, our bowing down and thus becoming one with him. In our Communion with Jesus Christ, this attains a new level, since it inevitably goes beyond any human partnership. The Word of the Lord as our "partner" explains a great deal but leaves much else undisclosed. We are not on the same footing. He is the wholly other; it is the majesty of the living God that comes to us with him. Uniting ourselves with him means submitting and opening ourselves up to his greatness. That has found expression in the devotional approach to Communion in every age. Augustine says in one place, in a sermon to his new communicants: No one can receive Communion without first adoring. Theodore of Mopsuestia, a contemporary of his who was active in Syria, tells us that every communicant, before receiving the holy gift, spoke a word of adoration. What we are told about the monks of Cluny, around the year one thousand, is particularly striking. Whenever they went to receive Communion, they took their shoes off. They knew that the burning bush was here, the mystery before which Moses, in the desert, sank to his knees.[35] The form may change, but what has to remain is the spirit of adoration, which signifies a genuine act of stepping outside ourselves, communication, freeing ourselves from our own selves and thereby in fact discovering human fellowship.

Let us come to the third and last question: Has the teaching about the Real Presence of Christ in the Eucharistic Gifts not long been refuted, rendered obsolete, by science? Has the Church not, with her concept of substance—for she speaks of "transubstantiation"—fettered herself, to far too great an extent, to a science that is basically primitive and obsolete? Do we not know precisely how material is constituted: made up of atoms, and these of elementary particles? That bread is not a "substance", and, in consequence, none of the rest of it can possibly be true? Well, objections like that are in the end very superficial. We cannot consider them in detail now, and it certainly is not necessary for each person always to think through every intellectual point that is grappled with in the Church. What matters is that the framework of thought is still intact, for it helps us to live out joyfully, without anxiety, the real heart of the faith that it supports. So let me just point out a couple of things. First: the word "substance" was used by the Church precisely to avoid the naïveté associated with what we can touch or measure. In the twelfth century the mystery of the Eucharist was on the point of being torn apart by two groups, who each in its own way failed to grasp the heart of it. There were those filled with the thought: Jesus is really there. But "reality", for them, was simply physical, bodily. Consequently, they arrived at the conclusion: In the Eucharist we chew on the flesh of the Lord; but therein they were under the sway of a serious misapprehension. For

---

[35] These texts are to be found in: Jungmann, *Missarum Sollemnia*, 2:467f.

Jesus has risen. We do not eat flesh, as cannibals would do. That is why others quite rightly opposed them, arguing against such primitive "realism". But they, too, had fallen into the same fundamental error of regarding only what is material, tangible, visible as reality. They said: Since Christ cannot be there in a body we can bite on, the Eucharist can only be a symbol of Christ; the bread can only signify the body, but not be the body. A dispute such as that has helped the Church to develop a more profound understanding of reality.

After wrestling with the difficulty, the insight was made explicit: "Reality" is not just what we can measure. It is not only "quantums", quantifiable entities, that are real; on the contrary, these are always only manifestations of the hidden mystery of true being. But here, where Christ meets us, we have to do with this true being. This is what was being expressed with the word "substance".[36] This does not refer to the quantums, but to the profound and fundamental basis of being. Jesus is not there like a piece of meat, not in the realm of what can be measured and quantified. Anyone who conceives of reality as being like that is deceiving himself about it and about himself. He is living his life all wrong. That is why this is no scholarly dispute but something that affects us ourselves: How should we relate to reality? What is "real"? What should we be like, so as to correspond to what is true? Concerning the Eucharist it is said to us: The substance is transformed, that is to say, the fundamental basis of its being. That is what is at stake, and not the superficial category, to which everything we can measure or touch belongs. Having thought that out, we have taken a good step forward but have still not yet got there. For we now know what is not meant, but the question remains: How is this to be understood, in a positive sense? Again, we will just point out a couple of things, for the limitations of our perception will only allow us hesitant ventures toward this mystery.

a. First. What has always mattered to the Church is that a real transformation takes place here. Something genuinely happens in the Eucharist. There is something new there that was not before. Knowing about

---

[36] On transubstantiation, see Jose Antonio Sayes, *La presencía real de Christo en la Eucharistia*, BAC 386 (Madrid, 1976); Eduard Schillebeeckx, *Die eucharistische Gegenwart* (Düsseldorf, 1967); Alexander Gerken, *Theologie der Eucharistie* (Munich, 1973); Johannes Betz, "Eucharistie als zentrales Mysterium", in *Mysterium Salutis*, vol. 4, pt. 2, ed. Johannes Feiner and Magnus Löhrer (Einsiedeln, 1973), 185–311, especially 289–311; Josef Wohlmuth, *Realpräsenz und Transsubstantiation im Konzil von Trient*, 2 vols., Europäische Hochschulschriften, series 23, Theologie 37 (Frankfurt, 1975).

a transformation is part of the most basic eucharistic faith. Therefore it cannot be the case that the Body of Christ comes to add itself to the bread, as if bread and Body were two similar things that could exist as two "substances", in the same way, side by side. Whenever the Body of Christ, that is, the risen and bodily Christ, comes, he is greater than the bread, other, not of the same order. The transformation happens, which affects the gifts we bring by taking them up into a higher order and changes them, even if we cannot measure what happens. When material things are taken into our body as nourishment, or for that matter whenever any material becomes part of a living organism, it remains the same, and yet as part of a new whole it is itself changed.[37] Something similar happens here. The Lord takes possession of the bread and the wine; he lifts them up, as it were, out of the setting of their normal existence into a new order; even if, from a purely physical point of view, they remain the same, they have become profoundly different.

That has an important consequence, which at the same time demonstrates more clearly what is meant here: Wherever Christ has been present, afterward it cannot be just as if nothing had happened. There, where he has laid his hand, something new has come to be. This points us back again to the fact that being a Christian as such is to be transformed, that it must involve repentance and not just some embellishment added onto the rest of one's life. It reaches down into our depths and renews us from those very depths. The more we ourselves as Christians are renewed from the root up, the better we can understand the mystery of transformation. Finally, this capacity things have for being transformed makes us more aware that the world itself can be transformed, that it will one day as a whole be the New Jerusalem, the Temple, vessel of the presence of God.

b. The second thing is this: What is going on in the Eucharist is an event happening to the thing itself and not just something agreed among ourselves. If the latter were true, then the Eucharist would be merely something arranged among us, a fiction by which we agreed to regard "this" as "something else". Then it would be only a game, not reality. The celebration would be only a kind of game. The gifts would be only temporarily, for cultic purposes, subject to

---

[37] Cf. Jacques Monod, *Zufall und Notwendigkeit: Philosophische Fragen der modernen Biologie*, 5th ed. (Munich, 1973), 79–123.

a "change of use". On the contrary: what is happening here is not a "change of use" but a genuine transformation; the Church calls it transubstantiation. Here we are touching on a dispute that raised great waves in the sixties. Then, it was said that we should understand the Eucharist roughly like this: Let us suppose we had a piece of cloth that is made into a national flag or perhaps a regimental flag. It has remained the same cloth, but because this piece of cloth has now become the symbol of a nation or the symbol of a regiment, I have to take my hat off to it. It is not a different thing, but it means something different. Later it will be preserved in a museum and will represent, will carry within it, the whole history of that period. People called the alteration in the cloth transignification, in English, a change of meaning, "change of use". Well, an example like that can certainly help us to understand to a certain extent how being taken into a new context can effect a change.[38] But that example is inadequate. What happens to bread and wine in the Eucharist is more profound; it is more than a change of use. The Eucharist transcends the realm of functionality.

That is in fact the poverty of our age, that we now think and live only in terms of function, that man himself is classified according to his function, and that we can all be no more than functions and officials, where being is denied. The significance of the Eucharist as a sacrament of faith consists precisely in that it takes us out of functionality and reaches the basis of reality. The world of the Eucharist is no game; it does not rest on conventions, to which we agree and which we can also renounce; but here it is a matter of reality, of its fundamental basis. That is the crucial point, when the Church rejects mere "change of use" ("transignification") as inadequate and insists on "change of substance": The Eucharist is more real than the things we have to do with every day. Here is the genuine reality. This is the yardstick, the heart of things; here we encounter that reality against which we need to learn to measure every other reality.

---

[38] On the theories concerning transfinalization and transignification, see Sayes, *Presencia,* 192–274; Wohlmuth, *Realpräsenz,* especially 1:4–52 and 453–61; Wolfgang Beinert, "Die Enzyklika 'Mysterium Fidei' und neue Auffassungen über die Eucharistie", TQ 147 (1967): 159–77. The comparison with a piece of cloth made into a flag had first been formulated by Bernhard Welte (in Michael Schmaus, *Aktuelle Fragen der Eucharistie* [Munich, 1960]), but for the purposes of an argument that went well beyond questions of function and was ontological in its aim.

c. Consequent on that is a third thing. If that is how it is, that is, if we do not just change the use of the bread and wine, but through the faithful prayer of the Church the Lord himself is acting and doing a new thing, then that means that his presence remains. It is because it remains that we adore the Lord in the Host. There are many objections to that. It is said that this was not done during the first thousand years. On that point we must first say simply that the Church grows and matures in the course of history. And we must add that she did already reserve the holy elements, to take them to the sick. This was done on account of knowing that the presence of the Lord remains. That is why she has always surrounded the elements with holy reverence.

A second objection goes: The Lord gave himself in bread and wine. Those are things we eat. He showed thereby clearly enough what he meant to happen and what he did not. Accordingly, it was said that the bread is there, not to be gazed upon, but to be eaten. This is essentially right: even the Council of Trent says so.[39] But let us just recall: What does that mean, to receive the Lord? That is never just a physical, bodily act, as when I eat a slice of bread. So it can therefore never be something that happens just in a moment. To receive Christ means: to move toward him, to adore him. For that reason, the reception can stretch out beyond the time of the eucharistic celebration; indeed, it has to do so. The more the Church grew into the eucharistic mystery, the more she understood that she could not consummate the celebration of Communion within the limited time available in the Mass. When, thus, the eternal light was lit in the Church, and the tabernacle installed beside the altar, then it was as if the bud of the mystery had opened and the Church had welcomed the fullness of the eucharistic mystery. The Lord is always there. The church is not just a space in which something sometimes happens early in the morning, while for the rest of the day it stands empty, "unused". There is always the "Church" in the church building, because the Lord is always giving himself, because the eucharistic mystery remains present, and because we, in approaching it, are always included in the worship of the whole believing, praying, and loving Church.

We all know what a difference there is between a church that is always prayed in and one that has become a museum. There is a great danger today of our churches becoming museums and suffering the

---

[39] DS 1643.

fate of museums: if they are not locked, they are looted. They are no longer alive. The measure of life in the Church, the measure of her inner openness, will be seen in that she will be able to keep her doors open, because she is a praying Church. I ask you all therefore from the heart, let us make a new start at this. Let us again recollect that the Church is always alive, that within her evermore the Lord comes to meet us. The Eucharist, and its fellowship, will be all the more complete, the more we prepare ourselves for him in silent prayer before the eucharistic presence of the Lord, the more we truly receive Communion. Adoration such as that is always more than just talking with God in a general way. But against that could then rightly be voiced the objection that is always to be heard: I can just as well pray in the forest, in the freedom of nature. Certainly, anyone can. But if it were only a matter of that, then the initiative in prayer would lie entirely with us; then God would be a mental hypothesis—whether he answers, whether he can answer or wants to, would remain open. The Eucharist means, God has answered: The Eucharist is God as an answer, as an answering presence. Now the initiative no longer lies with us, in the God–man relationship, but with him, and it now becomes really serious. That is why, in the sphere of eucharistic adoration, prayer attains a new level; now it is two-way, and so now it really is a serious business. Indeed, it is now not just two-way, but all-inclusive: whenever we pray in the eucharistic presence, we are never alone. Then the whole of the Church, which celebrates the Eucharist, is praying with us. Then we are praying within the sphere of God's gracious hearing, because we are praying within the sphere of death and resurrection, that is, where the real petition in all our petitions has been heard: the petition for the victory over death; the petition for the love that is stronger than death.[40]

In this prayer we no longer stand before an imagined God but before the God who has truly given himself to us; before the God who has become for us Communion and who thus frees us and draws us from the margin into communion and leads us on to resurrection. We have

---

[40] I had already tried to expound the same basic idea in the little booklet *Sakramentale Begründung christlicher Existenz* (Meitingen and Freising, 1966), 26f. [JRCW 11:153–68] This text, giving a mere outline, was written before the development of the dispute about the Eucharist in the years since the Council and had in the meantime given rise to the misapprehension that I intended thereby to deny the Real Presence and to oppose adoration. I hope that the exposition given here will leave no room for this misunderstanding.

to seek again this kind of prayer. The fruit of Lent should be that we become once more a praying Church and, thereby, an open Church. Only the praying Church is open. Only she is alive and invites people in; she offers them fellowship and at the same time a place of silence.

From all these reflections there naturally follows one last consideration. The Lord gives himself to us in bodily form. That is why we must likewise respond to him bodily. That means above all that the Eucharist must reach out beyond the limits of the church itself in the manifold forms of service to men and to the world. But it also means that our religion, our prayer, demands bodily expression. Because the Lord, the Risen One, gives himself in the Body, we have to respond in soul and body. All the spiritual possibilities of our body are necessarily included in celebrating the Eucharist: singing, speaking, keeping silence, sitting, standing, kneeling. Perhaps in the past we too much neglected singing and speaking and simply kept silence side by side; today, on the contrary, we run the risk of forgetting about keeping silence. But only all three together—singing, speaking, keeping silence—constitute the response in which the full capacity of our spiritual body opens up for the Lord. The same is true of the three bodily attitudes: sitting, standing, kneeling. Again, perhaps in the past we too far forgot standing and, to some extent, sitting, as an expression of relaxed listening, and practiced kneeling too exclusively; there, too, we find ourselves today running the opposite risk. And yet here, too, we need the particular mode of expression of all three. Sitting to concentrate on listening to the word of God is part of the liturgy. Standing, as a sign of readiness, is part of it, just as Israel ate the paschal lamb standing to manifest its readiness to depart and be led by the word of God. Besides that, standing is the expression of the victory of Christ: at the end of a duel it is the victor who is standing. That is what it means when Stephen, before his martyrdom, sees Christ standing at the right hand of God (Acts 7:56). Thus our standing for the Gospel is, over and beyond the Exodus attitude, which we share with Israel, standing in the presence of the Risen One, a recognition of victory.

Finally, kneeling is also essential: as the bodily expression of adoration, in which we remain upright, ready, available, but at the same time bow before the greatness of the living God and of his Name. Jesus Christ himself, according to St. Luke's account, in the last hours before his Passion, prayed on his knees on the Mount of Olives (Lk 22:41). Stephen fell on his knees when just before his martyrdom he saw the heavens open and Christ standing there (Acts 7:60). Before him who was standing, he knelt. Peter prayed kneeling to beseech God to raise up Tabitha (Acts 9:40). After his great farewell speech before the elders of Ephesus (before he went off to Jerusalem and to his captivity), Paul knelt and prayed with them (Acts 20:36). The most profound teaching is in the hymn to Christ in the Letter to the Philippians (Phil 2:6–11), which refers the promise in Isaiah, of people paying homage on their knees to the God of Israel, to Jesus Christ: He is the "name, that at the name . . . every knee should bow, in heaven and on earth and under the earth" (Phil 2:10). From this text we learn, not only the fact that the primitive Church knelt down before Jesus, but also her reason: She thereby rendered homage to him—to the Crucified One— publicly, as the ruler of the world, in whom the promise of the world-wide rule of the God of Israel has been fulfilled. She thereby gave witness to her faith, over against the Jews, that the law and the prophets are speaking about Jesus when they mention the "Name" of God; as against the Caesar worship—the totalitarian claims of politics—she insisted on the new worldwide dominion of Jesus, which sets limits to political power. She expressed her affirmation of the divinity of Jesus. We kneel with Jesus; we kneel with his witnesses—from Stephen, Peter, and Paul onward—before Jesus, and this is an expression of faith, which was from the beginning the requisite visible witness of the relationship of faith to God and to Christ in this world. Kneeling in this way is the bodily expression of our positive response to the Real Presence of Jesus Christ, who as God and man, with body and soul, flesh and blood is present among us.

"What great nation is there, that has a god so near to it as the Lord our God is to us?" Let us beseech the Lord to reawaken in us the joy at his presence and that we may once more adore him. Without adoration, there is no transformation of the world.

V. Form and Content of the Eucharistic Celebration

1. Problematic: The Category of "Form"

If we want to understand the current problems of liturgical reform, we shall need to recall a largely forgotten debate that took place between the two World Wars and that is at the center of these issues. In his book on the Mass, which gave classic expression to the inner experiences and demands of the preceding two decades, Romano Guardini had concentrated on the question of the essential form or structure of the Mass.[1] This development reflected the new liturgical awareness that had been growing in these years. At that time, young people were interested not so much in the inherited dogmatic problems of eucharistic doctrine as in the liturgical celebration as a living form [*Gestalt*]. They found that this form, or structure, was a theological and spiritual entity with an integrity of its own. What previously had been the rubricist's sphere of operations, mere ceremonial, having no apparent connection with dogma, now seemed to be an integral part of the action. It was its actual manifestation, apart from which the reality itself would remain invisible. Some years later Joseph Pascher put it like this: as far as the structure is concerned, up to now people had only paid attention to the rubrics, to what was printed in red; now it was time to give equal attention to the red *and* the black print. "There is far more in the form and structure of the texts and the whole celebration than in the rubrics."[2]

Now the structure of the Mass, the form in which it manifests itself, no longer appeared to be a more or less fortuitous collection of ceremonies governed by laws of performance, enveloping a dogmatic core

---

From *The Feast of Faith: Approaches to a Theology of the Liturgy*, trans. Graham Harrison (San Francisco: Ignatius Press, 1986), 33–60.

[1] Romano Guardini, *Besinnung vor der Feier der heiligen Messe*, 2 vols. (Mainz, 1939).

[2] Joseph Pascher, *Eucharistia: Gestalt und Vollzug* (Münster and Krailling, 1947), 8.

but having no effect upon it. It was seen as the inner expression of the spiritual reality that takes place within the Mass. So it became essential to go behind the contingent individual rites to appreciate the total form that "in-forms" them and that, as such, is the key to what takes place in the Eucharist. Next, this total form or structure could also provide the lever of the reform; it could be used to decide which prayers and gestures were secondary accretions, obscuring rather than revealing the structure. It could be used to determine whether particular aspects were to be heightened or lightened. Thus the concept of form or structure, a hitherto unknown category, entered the theological dialogue, clearly recognizable as a power for reform. Indeed, it can be said that it was this category that gave birth to liturgical scholarship in the modern sense. For the first time, liturgy appeared as a specific field beside that of dogmatics and canon law, with the result that the issue here was one of theology and a theologically based reform without dogmatics being directly involved. To see the full implications of this development, we need to ask in what terms this fundamental structure was described. There was a very simple way of discovering the structure: the New Testament contains a relatively full account of the blueprint of the celebration in the institution of the Eucharist by Jesus himself; it took place on Holy Thursday in the context of the Last Supper. It seemed therefore that the Eucharist's basic structure was unequivocally that of a meal. No one disputed the fact that Jesus celebrated it as a meal; this, surely, was enough to silence all the critics. "The determining structure is that of the meal", said Joseph Pascher;[3] Guardini and others had already said as much. Protagonists of the liturgical reform were explicitly applying the Lord's "Do this" to the meal structure. People were fond of remarking sarcastically that, after all, Jesus had said, "Do this", and not, "Do what you like."

This kind of talk was bound to stimulate great interest among dogmatic theologians. Was this not the same as Luther's position, which was condemned by Trent? Did it not reduce the sacrificial character of the Mass in favor of a meal-oriented theory? Liturgists replied to these accusations by saying that their critics had not appreciated the level of the discussion. To describe the Mass as a sacrifice was a dogmatic statement referring to the hidden theological essence of what takes place in it; to speak of the meal structure, on the other hand,

---

[3] Ibid., 27.

was to direct attention to the visible liturgical per-formance, in no way denying the theological content defined by Trent. What was presented liturgically in the structure of the meal could without difficulty mediate what, dogmatically speaking, was a sacrifice. Such a simple juxtaposition, of course, could not provide a satisfactory answer in the long run. Particularly if the structure is not merely a ceremonial form but is at its core an indispensable manifestation of its essential content, it makes no sense absolutely to separate the one from the other. The lack of clarity that has prevailed in this area, even during the Council, regarding the relation between the dogmatic and liturgical levels must be regarded as the central problem of the liturgical reform. Failure to deal with it has resulted in a great many of the individual problems that have since preoccupied us.

We must therefore see it as our task to work toward a clarification here—not in purely formal deliberation, but by critically analyzing what is meant by the basic thesis that the Eucharist is fundamentally a meal. This thesis involves a total separation between dogmatic content and liturgical structure, if, indeed, it actually concedes the dogmatic view that the Mass is a sacrifice. But if it should appear that a separation of the two fields cannot be maintained, the thesis itself becomes highly questionable. This became clear at an early stage. In what follows we shall endeavor to trace the stages of the dispute and bring some light to bear on the problem.

We find a first attempt at a reconciliation in Joseph Pascher, who speaks of sacrificial symbolism being introduced into the meal structure. The separation of the gifts of bread and wine, symbolically indicating the fatal spilling of Jesus' blood, introduces the mark of sacrifice into the basic structure of the meal. Of more far-reaching significance, although presented in a restrained vein, was the qualification made by the liturgist Josef Andreas Jungmann. On the basis of the liturgical texts themselves, Jungmann shows that, even in the most ancient forms, the *eucharistia*—the prayer of anamnesis in the shape of a thanksgiving—is more prominent than the meal aspect. According to Jungmann, the basic structure, at least from the end of the first century, is not the meal but the *eucharistia;* even in Ignatius of Antioch this is the term given to the whole action.[4] In a subsequent study, Jungmann has gone on to

---

[4] Josef Andreas Jungmann, *Missarum Sollemnia*, 2 vols. (Freiburg 1948–), here, 1:327ff. [trans. Francis A. Brunner as *The Mass of the Roman Rite*, 2 vols. (New York, 1951 and 1955)].

show that, linguistically speaking, Luther's use of the word "Supper" was a complete innovation. After 1 Corinthians 11:20 the designation of the Eucharist as a "meal" does not occur again until the sixteenth century, apart from direct quotations of 1 Corinthians 11:20 and references to the satisfaction of hunger (in deliberate contrast to the Eucharist).[5] Thus the *eucharistia* thesis is able to put the dogmatic and liturgical levels in touch with each other. Late antiquity had formulated the concept of the verbal sacrifice, which even found its way into the Roman canon under the term *oblatio rationabilis*: sacrifice to the Divinity does not take place by the transfer of property but in the self-offering of mind and heart, expressed in word. This concept was adopted into Christianity without any difficulty. The Eucharistic Prayer is an entering into the prayer of Jesus Christ himself; hence it is the Church's entering into the Logos, the Father's Word, into the Logos' self-surrender to the Father, which, in the Cross, has also become the surrender of mankind to him.[6] So, on the one hand, *eucharistia* made a bridge to Jesus' words of blessing at the Last Supper, in which he actually underwent, in an inward and anticipatory manner, his death on the Cross;[7] and, on the other hand, it built a bridge to the theology of the Logos and hence to a trinitarian deepening of the theology of Eucharist and of the Cross. Ultimately it facilitated the transition to a spiritual concept of sacrifice that was ideally suited to interpret what is special in Jesus' sacrifice. For what we have here is death transformed into a word of

---

[5] Josef Andreas Jungmann, "'Abendmahl' als Name der Eucharistie", ZKTh 93 (1971): 91–94; here, 93: "Thus it is clear that the term 'Supper' was a complete innovation in the sixteenth century."

[6] Cf. Odo Casel, "Die Λογικὴ θυσία der antiken Mystik in christlich-liturgischer Umdeutung", JLW 4 (1924): 37–47; Pascher, *Eucharistia*, 94–98. Enriching new insights in Louis Bouyer, *Eucharistie: Théologie et spiritualité de la prière eucharistique* (Tournai, 1966) [trans. Charles Underhill Quinn as *Eucharist: Theology and Spirituality of the Eucharistic Prayer* (Notre Dame, Ind., and London: Univ. of Notre Dame Press, 1968)]. Bouyer shows the Jewish roots of the idea of a verbal sacrifice and thus presents a convincing picture of the inner unity between Jesus and Church in terms of *eucharistia*. Cf. also Hans Urs von Balthasar, "Die Messe, ein Opfer der Kirche?" in his *Spiritus Creator* (Einsiedeln, 1967), 166–217 [trans. Brian McNeil, C.R.V., as "The Mass, a Sacrifice of the Church?" in von Balthasar, *Explorations in Theology*, vol. 3: *Creator Spirit* (San Francisco: Ignatius Press, 1993), 185–243].

[7] Cf. especially Heinz Schürmann, *Jesu ureigener Tod: Exegetische Besinnungen und Ausblick* (Freiburg, 1975); Karl Kertelge, ed., *Der Tod Jesu: Deutungen im Neuen Testament*, QD 74 (Freiburg, 1976); especially in ibid., the essay by Rudolf Pesch, "Das Abendmahl und Jesu Todesverständnis", 137–87.

acceptance and self-surrender. The il-logical fact of death had become the concern of the Logos: the Logos had died; and as a result, death had become life.

This much should be clear at this stage: if the basic structure of the Mass is not the "meal" but *eucharistia*, there remains a necessary and fruitful difference between the liturgical (structural) and the dogmatic level; but they are not estranged: each seeks and determines the other. Moreover, the meal element is not simply excluded, for *eucharistia* is *also* (but not solely) the grace said before the sacred meal. But the meal symbolism is subordinated to a larger whole and integrated into it. At this point, however, a serious objection arises: it could be said that, once the Church's liturgy has become something tangible, it does not exhibit primarily a meal structure but is subordinated to the "word" dimension of *eucharistia*—as in 1 Corinthians 11, for instance. But does this change the fact that the Last Supper of Jesus was precisely that, a supper? Does this not simply mean that the decline from the pristine form occurred in the very first generation? Can there ever be any other standard than that given by Jesus himself, however ancient be contrary Church traditions? As we see, this question leads us into the fundamental problem of current theology, which is marked by the dispute between history and dogma, namely, the issue of Jesus versus the Church. To that extent it shares in the fundamental difficulties of Catholic Christianity; it would be surprising if it did not exemplify them in this way. It need hardly be said that the more recent exegesis tends largely to make an increasingly radical separation of the Supper of Jesus and the Church's sacrament and to cut the knot of the Lord's "institution"; this is only a symptom of the same basic problem.[8]

---

[8] Characteristic of the present situation is, e.g., Rupert Feneberg, *Christliche Passafeier und Abendmahl: Eine biblisch-hermeneutische Untersuchung der neutestamentlichen Einsetzungsberichte*, StANT 27 (Munich, 1971). The current state of research is summarized in the articles "Abendmahl II" (Gerhard Delling) and "Abendmahl III/1" (Georg Kretschmar), in TRE 1:47–89, clearly indicating a return to continuity between Jesus and the Church's Eucharist; cf. also Georg Kretschmar, "Abendmahlsfeier I", in TRE 1:229–78. Notable exegetical works in the same direction are Hermann Patsch, *Abendmahl und historischer Jesus*, Calwer Theologische Monographien A1 (Stuttgart, 1972), and Rudolf Pesch, *Wie Jesus das Abendmahl hielt: Der Grund der Eucharistie* (Freiburg, 1977). For a systematic presentation of the subject in an ecumenical perspective, cf. the magnificent article "Abendmahl IV" by Ulrich Kühn, in TRE 1:145–212.

2. The Growth of the Church and the Development of the Eucharist

The work of Heinz Schürmann has been of decisive importance in shedding light on the transition from the Last Supper of Jesus to the Church's Eucharist. Here we cannot enter into the endless controversies that surround the eucharistic tradition: we are deliberately restricting our enquiry to the structure and its development, and in this regard Schürmann has identified three stages: 1. the Eucharist at the Last Supper of Jesus; 2. the Eucharist in connection with the apostolic community meal; 3. the celebration of the Eucharist in postapostolic times, separated from the community meal.[9] Unfortunately there is not space here to reproduce the details of the process; we can only mention the critical transitions and examine their inner significance. As far as the Eucharist at the Last Supper of Jesus is concerned, it is possible to reconstruct the locus of Jesus' eucharistic actions fairly precisely through recourse to the Gospels and Jewish meal customs. Assuming that the meal in question was a Passover supper, it had a fourfold structure encompassing a small preliminary meal, the Passover liturgy, the main meal, and the concluding rites. The breaking of bread took place therefore before the main meal itself; the giving of the cup follows the main meal, as Luke expressly says: "*after* supper" (22:20). Schürmann concludes two things from this: "1. At the Last Supper the eucharistic action was an *integral and constitutive part of a meal-structure.... 2.* At the Last Supper the eucharistic action had a *relatively autonomous existence and significance* in contrast to the meal event."[10] What the Lord is doing here is something new. It is woven into an old context—that of the Jewish ritual meal—but it is clearly recognizable as an independent entity. He commanded it to be repeated, which implies that it was separable from the immediate context in which it took place.

There is nothing fortuitous in this interplay of old and new. It is the exact and necessary expression of the existing situation in salvation history. Jesus prays his new prayer within the Jewish liturgy. The crucifixion has not yet taken place, even though, in a way, it has begun. Jesus has not yet become separated from the Jewish community, that is, the Church as Church has not yet come into being; "Church" in

[9] Heinz Schürmann, "Die Gestalt der urchristlichen Eucharistiefeier", in his *Ursprung und Gestalt: Erörterungen und Besinnungen zum Neuen Testament*, Kommentare und Beiträge zum Alten und Neuen Testament 27 (Düsseldorf, 1970), 77–99.
[10] Ibid., 83 and 84.

the narrower historical sense does not come about until the attempt to win the whole of Israel has failed. Since, as yet, there is no independent Christian reality, but only an open-ended form within Judaism, there cannot be an independent and specifically Christian form of liturgy. The real mistake of those who attempt uncritically to deduce the Christian liturgy directly from the Last Supper lies in their failing to see this fundamental point: the Last Supper of Jesus is certainly the basis of all Christian liturgy, but in itself it is not yet Christian. The act constituting the Christian reality takes place *within* the Jewish framework, but it has not yet attained a form, a structure of its own as Christian liturgy. Salvation history is still open-ended; no definitive decision has been made as to whether the Christian phenomenon will or will not have to separate itself from its Jewish matrix as a distinct reality. Indeed, we could make the issue clearer by taking the earlier suggestions of the Liturgical Movement and turning them upside down: the Last Supper is the foundation of the dogmatic content of the Christian Eucharist, not of its liturgical form. The latter does not yet exist. As her separation from Israel became unavoidable, the Church had to discover an appropriate form of her own in which to express the reality bequeathed to her. This is a necessity arising out of the situation, not a decline. This seems to me to be a crucial point, not only for the debate about the liturgical form, but for a genuine understanding of the Christian reality. The idea that, after Jesus, there was an immediate decline in primitive Christianity, resulting in the hiatus between Jesus and the Church that still persists today,[11] rests on a failure to take these facts into account. If this is the case, there *can* be no direct continuity between Jesus and the Church; this is also why the proclamation of the word has moved its center of gravity from the "Kingdom of God" to Christology.[12] In this situation, unity with Jesus has to be sought in that discontinuity which is manifested where the proclamation of the Kingdom to Israel is left behind and the Church of the Gentiles is embraced.

Now let us turn to the second phase of the development traced by Schürmann, the apostolic Eucharist connected with the community

---

[11] The picture of Jesus given in Hans Küng's *Christ sein* (Munich, 1975) [trans. Edward Quinn as *On Being a Christian* (Garden City, N.Y.: Doubleday, 1976)] is in many respects symptomatic of this. Cf. my observations in the collection *Diskussion über Hans Küngs "Christ sein"* (Mainz, 1976), 7–18.

[12] Further details in Joseph Ratzinger, *Eschatologie*, KKD 9 (Regensburg, 1977), 30–42.

meal. For the sake of brevity I go straight to the core of Schürmann's description of this phase: "The primitive Christian community meal was not a repetition of the Last Supper of Jesus (which is not what Jesus commanded to be repeated); it was the continuation of Jesus' everyday table fellowship with his disciples. . . . Faced with the issue of incorporating Jesus' twofold eucharistic action into this community meal, the more obvious course was to insert the two actions together rather than to place them before and after their usual meal." [13] Two things here are important for our present consideration: first of all, it is clear that Jesus' command to repeat the action does not refer to the Last Supper as a whole at all, but to the specifically eucharistic action. Thus the Last Supper was not repeated, and this in itself caused a change in the overall structure and gave birth to a specifically Christian form. An ordinary meal precedes the eucharistic celebration; the eucharistic acts, now joined together, follow in the form of a distinct action, framed and heightened by the prayer of thanksgiving, *eucharistia*. This sequence is clearly visible in 1 Corinthians 11:17–34, but it is also perceptible in the way Matthew and Mark "match" the words spoken at the giving of the bread and of the cup. At one point, however, we must disagree with Schürmann. His thesis, that the apostolic Eucharist is a continuation of Jesus' daily table fellowship with his disciples, was limited to the question of the structural origin of the celebration, but it is used by many people who wish to deny that anything was "instituted" at the Last Supper and who assume that the Eucharist originated more or less exclusively in Jesus' meals with sinners. This view identifies the Eucharist of Jesus with a strictly Lutheran doctrine of justification, namely, the pardoning of the sinner; ultimately, among those who see Jesus' eating with sinners as the only solid fact about the historical Jesus that has come down to us, the whole of Christology and theology is reduced to this one factor.[14] It

---

[13] Schürmann, "Gestalt", 85.

[14] This is the tendency of several studies by Ernst Fuchs, e.g., *Das urchristliche Sakramentsverständnis*, Schriftenreihe der Kirchlich-Theologischen Sozietät in Württemberg, no. 8, 2nd ed. (Bad Cannstatt, 1958); cf. the remarks of James McConkey Robinson on this issue in his *New Quest of the Historical Jesus* (London, 1969). The conception of the Eucharist in Wolfhart Pannenberg tends somewhat in the same direction; cf. his (otherwise most helpful) study "Die Problematik der Abendmahlslehre aus evangelischer Sicht", in *Evangelischkatholische Abendmahlsgemeinschaft?* ed. Gerhard Krems and Reinhard Mumm (Regensburg and Göttingen 1971), 9–45; Wolfhart Pannenberg, *Thesen zur Theologie der Kirche* (Munich, 1970), especially theses 77 and 85, pp. 34 and 36.

results in a view of the Eucharist that has nothing in common with primitive Christianity. Whereas Paul says that those who approach the Eucharist in sin "eat and drink judgment" upon themselves (1 Cor 11:29) and pronounces an anathema to protect the Eucharist from abuse (1 Cor 16:22), proponents of this view see it as the essence of the Eucharist that it is available to all without distinction and without conditions. It is interpreted as the sign of the unconditional grace of God, offered directly to sinners and even to unbelievers—but at this point it certainly has little in common with Luther's understanding of the Eucharist. The fact that this thesis contradicts the entire eucharistic inheritance of the New Testament indicates the wrong-headedness of its basic assumption: the Christian Eucharist was not understood in the context of Jesus' eating with sinners, nor can it be seen simply as a continuation of his daily table fellowship with the disciples. There are two reasons for this:

a. First, as Schürmann himself observes, there is the festal quality of the Eucharist. Through the provision of wine, it was lifted from everyday ordinariness and shown to be a festal celebration. There is no evidence that the Eucharist was celebrated daily in apostolic times, as Schürmann's thesis would suggest. We must assume a weekly celebration; indeed, as Revelation 1:10 (cf. Acts 20:7; 1 Cor 16:2) indicates, a Sunday Eucharist.[15]

b. The second reason against this interpretation is the firm outline of the Eucharist, based on the Passover ritual. Just as the Passover meal was celebrated in a clearly defined household, the Eucharist too, from the beginning, had definite conditions for admission. From the start, Eucharist was celebrated in what one might call the household of Jesus Christ, and thus it built the "Church".

The situation, then, is highly nuanced. As such, the Christian Eucharist is not a repetition of the Last Supper (which was in fact unique). If the latter was a Passover meal, for which there is much evidence, it cannot have been repeated, for Passover occurs once a year according to the lunar calendar, whereas the Eucharist is celebrated weekly. On the other hand, the Eucharist does take over substantial elements from the Passover tradition, not least the festal atmosphere and the precise

---

[15] This does not impugn the Western custom of daily Eucharist, which can certainly be traced back to the third century. This development could easily take place once the Christian liturgy had discovered its own special form.

admission conditions. Right from the apostolic period it clearly begins to construct its own special form. We might put it like this: the eucharistic actions are taken out of the context of the Passover and are placed within the new context of the "Lord's Day", that is, the day that marked the first meeting with the Risen Lord. The appearance of the Risen Lord to those who are his is the new beginning, causing the Jewish calendar of feasts to be left behind as obsolete and situating the gift of the Eucharist in its new setting. In this respect, Sunday, the first day of the week (also regarded as the first day of creation and now marking the new creation) is the real inner locus of the Eucharist as a Christian form. Sunday and Eucharist belong together right from the beginning; the day of the Resurrection is the matrix of the Eucharist.[16]

3. The Definitive Form

This is the situation, therefore, in the second phase: the new, Christian elements are taken out of the context of the Last Supper, joined together, and placed after the disciples' fellowship meal. Meal and Eucharist are linked by the fundamental Christian idea of agape. The mutual agape of the community provides the context for the transforming agape of the Lord. However, the actual development of the communities cannot match this ideal vision. What in fact happened was that the community agape, which had been meant to open the door to the Lord, became an occasion for egoism. Thus it proved unsuitable as a preparation for the meeting with Christ. This resulted in the separation of meal and Eucharist, as documented in 1 Corinthians 11:22: "Have you not houses to eat and drink in?" This development will have taken place at a different speed in different places, but it signifies the start of the third phase, resulting in the final ecclesial form of the sacrament.[17] We find the first witness to this form in the letter of Pliny to Trajan that speaks of the morning celebration of the Eucharist.[18] Justin Martyr (d. ca. 165) gives us the first full description of the new form. Sunday morning proves to be the Christians' time for

---

[16] Very important observations on the connection between Eucharist and Sunday are to be found in Jean-Jacques von Allmen, *Ökumene im Herrenmahl* (Kassel, 1968), 20f.

[17] Cf. Schürmann, "Gestalt", 92, especially n. 77; on the theological problems connected with the agape, cf. von Allmen, *Ökumene*, 69–75.

[18] Cf. Schürmann, "Gestalt", 92.

worship, underlining the connection between the service of worship and the event of the Resurrection. Separation from the Jewish matrix and the independent existence of the Christian reality, which began with the Christians' commitment to assemble on the Lord's Day, have become definitive by the fixing of the time for worship. But there is a further consequence: as long as the Eucharist immediately followed a community meal, participation in the synagogue's service of the word was presupposed. Very early on (though not from the beginning), Christians had withdrawn from the Temple sacrifice; but they did assemble in Solomon's Portico, continuing to share, there and in the synagogues, in the service of readings and prayer of the people of Israel. Within this service they had tried to explain their interpretation of Scripture, that is, the Old Testament, by reference to Christ, hoping to make the entire Bible, without loss, the Lord's.[19] John's Gospel belongs to a period when a complete and final break had occurred.[20] Now a distinct, Christian service of the word had to be created, and this was joined to the eucharistic celebration, resulting in the growth of a coherent Christian liturgy. The inner rationale of the resultant liturgical pattern is presented in the account of the disciples on the road to Emmaus (Lk 24:25–31). First we have the searching of the Scriptures, explained and made present by the Risen Lord; their minds enlightened, the disciples are moved to invite the Lord to stay with them, and he responds by breaking the bread for his disciples, giving them his presence, and then withdrawing again, sending them out as his messengers. This coherent and integrated form arose quite naturally when the Church was no longer able to participate in synagogue worship and thus acquired an identity and a form of her own, as the community of believers in Christ.

One can hardly allot a single term to a reality that has grown in this way to become the norm for all liturgical development in Christendom—and the whole thrust of this liturgy means that it must

---

[19] Cf. Franz Mussner, "Die *Una Sancta* nach Apg 2, 42", in his *Praesentia salutis* (Düsseldorf, 1967), 212–22, especially 221; Joseph Ratzinger, "Auferbaut aus lebendigen Steinen", in *Kirche aus lebendigen Steinen*, ed. Walter Seidel (Mainz, 1975), 30–48, especially 39f. and 43, n. 12 [trans. Martha M. Matesich as "Built from Living Stones", in *A New Song for the Lord: Faith in Christ and Liturgy Today* (New York: Crossroad, 1996), 78–93; JRCW 11:371–87].

[20] Cf. on this issue, Reinhold Leistner, *Antijudaismus im Johannesevangelium? Darstellung des Problems in der neueren Auslegungsgeschichte und Untersuchung der Leidensgeschichte*, Theologie und Wirklichkeit 3 (Frankfurt, 1974).

remain normative. Schürmann, too, comes to this conclusion, although, as far as the question of form and structure is concerned, he feels obliged to separate the Liturgy of the Word from eucharistic liturgy in the narrower sense. Initially he speaks of a meal structure in course of development. But even when he has kept the Liturgy of the Word out of the discussion—a questionable decision—his concept of meal structure is subject to so many qualifications that it disintegrates. First of all he says, "We are somewhat uneasy about applying the term 'meal structure' to the eucharistic action described by Justin",[21] and he defines the outer limits of the term: in the first place, the meal structure is so strongly stylized that one can only speak of a "symbolic" meal. This fact is evident in the posture of those celebrating the Eucharist: whereas they sit for the service of the word, they *stand* for the eucharistic action, which certainly does not indicate the transition to a normal meal situation. Furthermore, the prayer, the *eucharistia*, has become so dominant that Schürmann feels obliged to describe the "symbolic" meal structure as "impaired".[22] It would show greater objectivity, under these conditions, simply to abandon the inappropriate term "meal structure". The determining element is the *eucharistia*. Since this is a participation in the thanksgiving of Jesus, which includes the prayer of gratitude for the gifts of the earth, it already expresses whatever element of the "meal" the liturgical action actually contains.

The analysis of the historical development thus confirms and deepens the thesis cautiously put forward by Jungmann on the basis of the liturgical sources. At the same time, it has become clear that, while we must reject the idea that the Christian liturgy originates simply in the Last Supper, there is no hiatus between Jesus and the Church. The Lord's gift is not some rigid formula but a living reality. It was open to historical development, and only where this development is accepted can there be continuity with Jesus. Here, as so often, "progressive" reformers exhibit a fundamentally narrow view

---

[21] Schürmann, "Gestalt", 95.

[22] Ibid., 92–95. Schürmann makes a useful comparison (96): "A great number of the parables of Jesus share a distinctive feature: at a certain point the image does not fit; it is exaggerated, becomes paradoxical, grotesque, improbable. And this is the very point of contact between the image and what lies behind it; it is where the reality shines through the image and bursts it. Similarly, the overemphasis on the Eucharistic Prayer at the eucharistic meal causes what lies behind the meal to shine through." Once again, it is objectively clear that the concept of the "meal structure" is in reality inappropriate.

of Christian beginnings, seeing history piecemeal, whereas the sacramental view of the Church rests upon an inner developmental unity. It is precisely by pressing forward that this unity keeps faith and brings into one, by the power and gift of the one Lord, all the changing times of history. This formal aspect, as well as the actual content, can be of great importance for the Church in her contemporary struggles. Once the concept of the "meal" is seen to be historically a crass oversimplification, once the Lord's testament is correctly seen in terms of *eucharistia*, many of the current theories just fade away. And above all it puts an end to the baneful isolation of the liturgical and dogmatic levels without confusing what is specific to each level. Thus *eucharistia* is the gift of *communio* in which the Lord becomes our food; it also signifies the self-offering of Jesus Christ, perfecting his trinitarian Yes to the Father by his consent to the Cross and reconciling us all to the Father in this "sacrifice". There is no opposition between "meal" and "sacrifice"; they belong inseparably together in the new sacrifice of the Lord.

Postscript 1

The issues raised in the foregoing brief study have since been taken up and extended by Lothar Lies in "Eulogia—Überlegungen zur formalen Sinngestalt der Eucharistie", ZKTh 100 (1978): 69–97, including an appendix of relevant reviews (98–126). What I have called form, structure [*Gestalt, Grundgestalt*] in common with liturgical scholars of the interwar and postwar period, Lies refers to as the "material structure" [*Materialgestalt*], going on to inquire as to the formal structure [*Formalgestalt*], which he defines thus: "By the formal structure of the Eucharist we mean that structure which is able to embrace the ideas of anamnesis, sacramental Real Presence, sacrifice, and meal, imparting to all aspects of the Eucharist their formal meaning" (69). Lies discovers this formal structure in the concept *of eulogia*.

> As the auto-eulogia of God, Jesus enters into the form of the Old Testament Passover-eulogia; he presents himself as this Passover-eulogia. This is the essential vehicle of meaning [*Sinngestalt*] of the Church's Eucharist. Thus the idea of *eulogia* is able to embrace that christological concentration which systematic theologians require in

the doctrine of the Eucharist. Since the Lord's Supper is something that takes place here and now, under the sign of blessing, it embraces both the Real Presence aspect and the aspect of eulogic anamnesis. The Eucharist exhibits a sacrificial structure in a twofold sense. . . . The concept of *eulogia* can provide an integrated model for the Christian Eucharist, expressing both its theological and its liturgical meaning. (96)

I am in full agreement with Lies' remarks: I find they confirm and enrich my own conclusions. My own enquiry was concerned, however, with an earlier stage of the argument. Whereas he presupposes the developed structure of anamnesis, sacramental Real Presence, sacrifice, and meal, my own concern was to establish the legitimacy of the transition from the Last Supper to the Mass, from Jesus to the Church's Eucharist. For this is the salient point of the whole discussion in contemporary theology. It determines the view of Jesus and the Church, the relation of pre-Easter to post-Easter kerygma, and the concept of tradition and Church development.

Because of our distinct approaches, therefore, our fundamental agreement as to results seems all the more significant. People should no longer be able to speak of the Eucharist's "meal structure" *tout court*, since such a view is based on a misunderstanding of the Eucharist's origins and leads to a false view of the sacrament. There is even less excuse for the Eucharist being referred to simply as a "meal" (or even as a "sacrificial meal"). In this regard there is an urgent need to revise the German translation of the Missal of Paul VI, where, in the post-communion prayers, contrary to the Latin original, the word "meal" [*Mahl*] is almost used as a regular term for the Eucharist.

Postscript 2

A whole new perspective has been opened up by the seminal study by Hartmut Gese entitled "Die Herkunft des Herrenmahls" [The origin of the Lord's Supper] in his book *Zur biblischen Theologie* (Munich, 1977), 107–27. This most stimulating article not only confirms the basic thesis presented here but extends its scope in a totally unforeseen manner. Gese begins by taking issue with the still current hypothesis that there were two forms of the Lord's Supper: a sacramental, Hellenistic form and a non-sacramental, Jewish form associated with

Jerusalem—a hypothesis in no way supported by the texts themselves. "Behind this hypothesis is a further problem: for it is held that the sacramental view cannot have evolved from the Jewish view" (109). It is this contradiction which causes Gese to take up the question of origins again, as a result of which he comes down in favor of the eucharistic view.

First he discusses the various origins proposed, such as the Jewish meal, the Passover, the Qumran meals, Jesus' meals, the miraculous feedings, the meals of the Risen Jesus. He is able to show that none of these proposed solutions does justice to the evidence of the New Testament. Thus, for instance, the miracles of feeding and the (anti-Docetic) meals of the Risen Lord, "far from explaining the Lord's Supper, in fact presuppose it" (117). In the Passion narratives the death of Jesus is already presented as a Passover sacrifice, as a "saving Passover-event of liberation and new birth out of the chaos of the old world" (114); but this by no means implies that the Lord's Supper is identified with the Passover or can be traced back to it. The results show that, while the Passover came to be very important for an understanding of Christ's Passion and hence acquired a fundamental significance in the theology of the Eucharist, it is impossible, all the same, to deduce the Eucharist from it.

The Passover meal is a specific form of the Jewish ritual meal. Before going on to examine the various alternative forms, therefore, we must establish the theological content of the Jewish ritual meal in general and see what kinds of bridges exist between it and the Eucharist. At this point Gese brings to light a number of striking facts.

> The Jewish meal exhibits several basic characteristics, arising from the fact that the celebratory meal was associated in ancient times with a primary form of sacrifice, the *zēbaḥ*. In pre-Deuteronomic times, the slaughter of animals could only take place at the altar. Therefore the eating of meat presupposed a sacrificial context.... Bread and wine were, however, basic constituents, and these unbloody elements did not of themselves presuppose an altar. The sacrificial character of this meal has a twofold significance: it expresses communion with God, in whose sacrifice people are permitted to share, and communion among the participants; these two things correspond to the saving fact that *shalom* reigns among those who share in the sacrificial meal (which is why these sacrifices, celebrated as a public, liturgical feast, are called *šᵉlamim*, "peace offerings") (109f.).

One is reminded of the ancient Church's designation of the Eucharist as *pax*, continuing the tradition of Israel, which itself reflects a fundamental human tradition. There is another important fact: the ancient ritual meal—which always begins with the *berakah*, the blessing pronounced over bread and wine—"inaugurates . . . a being-in-peace". Thus the raising of the cup acquires a special meaning, for it is associated with the ritual proclamation initiating this particular mode of being. "Thus the sacrificial meal is given its particular meaning from the particular circumstances in which it is celebrated. In Exodus 24:11 it inaugurates the covenant between Yahweh and Israel on Sinai; in Isaiah 25:1–10 the new covenant on Sion is established by the meal— here in the special form of the thanksgiving sacrifice. A great variety of ritual meals can be envisaged" (110).

Here we are faced once more with the question: What was the special meal that was able to develop into the Lord's Eucharist? Gese observes:

> Strangely enough, one particular form of the ritual meal that is deeply rooted in the Old Testament and that also played a prominent part in Judaism at the time of Jesus (according to the Mishnah) has been neglected by scholars: the *tōda*, "thanksgiving sacrifice". This sacrifice is in the category of *zēbah*, it is a sacrificial meal in the wider sense, but it differs considerably from the general sacrificial meal as far as the ritual and the theological significance are concerned. We have been looking for a link with the death and saving activity of the offerer. Here it is. (117)

As to the influence of this kind of sacrificial meal, we can say "that *the tōda* formed the cultic basis of the major part of the Psalter*" (119). As examples of *tōda* psalms (psalms that have their *sitz im leben* in a celebration of *tōda*), Gese analyzes Psalms 69; 51; 40:1–12, and 22—the great christological psalms of the New Testament. (Indeed, for the evangelists, Psalm 22 became a textbook on the Passion of Christ.) From the context revealed by Gese, it is clear that what we have here is not some retrospective application of Old Testament words to an event, transforming and "theologizing" it: the Passion and Resurrection of Jesus *is tōda*. It is the real fulfillment of the words of these psalms at a new depth. Indeed, it is as if the words had been waiting for their profound fulfillment in Jesus, a fulfillment that surpasses every individual destiny, whether of death or of deliverance, and that also surpasses the merely collective destiny of Israel, expanding both individual and collective destinies into something far greater and hitherto unknown.

What is *tōda*? Gese describes it like this:

> The thanksgiving sacrifice presupposes a particular *situation*. If a man is saved from death, from fatal illness, or from those who seek his life, he celebrates this divine deliverance in a service of thanksgiving that marks an existential new start in his life. In it, he "confesses" (*jd[h]*) God to be his deliverer by celebrating a thankoffering (*tōda*). He invites his friends and associates, provides the sacrificial animal, ... and celebrates, ... together with his invited guests, the inauguration of his new existence.... In order to recall God's deliverance and give thanks for it, it is necessary to reflect on one's pilgrimage through suffering, to bring to mind the process of redemption.... It is not a mere sacrificial rite; it is a sacrifice in which one professes one's involvement.... Here we have a unity that embraces a service of the word and a ritual meal, praise, and sacrifice. The sacrifice cannot be misunderstood as a "gift" to God; rather it is a way of "honoring" the Deliverer. And the fact that the rescued man is able to celebrate "life restored" in the sacred meal is itself the gift of God. (117f.)

As regards the formal elements, two factors are particularly important in the present context. As we have already noted, this type of sacrifice is a "confession of thanksgiving". "Once the confession of divine deliverance had become a constitutive part of the sacrifice, this rite could be seen as complementing the sacrifice itself. The cup corresponds to the proclamatory aspect of the *tōda*, the sacrifice corresponds to its meal aspect" (118). Here we come across the Hellenistic idea of verbal sacrifice, to which we have already referred where we spoke of the Eucharist as the structural element and vehicle of the sacrifice concept. It is an idea we find deeply rooted in the Old Testament, bursting forth from the inner dynamism of Old Testament faith. It is a bridge, already in existence, linking the Old Testament and Jesus to the "nations", to the Greek world. Here distinct developments of the human mind are in touch with one another; it is as if both the Jewish and the Hellenistic traditions are awaiting him who is himself the Word, the crucified Logos, and the Righteous One who has been rescued from the abyss of death. The second important formal element concerns what nowadays we call the "matter" of the sacrament: "The *tōda* is not restricted to a bloody sacrifice of flesh but also embraces the unbloody offering of bread; *tōda* is the only form of sacrifice that is concerned with unleavened bread. Thus in the context of *tōda*, bread and wine acquire a special significance; the one becomes part of the sacrifice itself, the other plays a constitutive role in proclamation" (119).

I would like to draw attention to just two points from Gese's analysis of the *tōda* psalms. First, from Psalm 51: "The sacrifice acceptable to God is a broken spirit; a broken and contrite heart, O God, thou wilt not despise" (v. 17). Here we find "the external sacrifice of the *tōda* interiorized: it has become the sacrificial suffering of one's own life" (120). We can see how "the understanding of sacrifice and the understanding of life have influenced one another through the *tōda* spirituality". In Psalm 40:1–12 the same idea is present in an intensified form: "In connection with the idea of the New Covenant (Jer 31:33; Ezek 36:27), the goal is now the total interiorizing of the Torah. What we find in the Psalms is not a kind of rationalistic criticism of sacrifice; it is a view of man's total involvement in the very nature of the sacrifice, arising from a deeply rooted spirituality of the thankoffering" (121).

The second point is connected especially with Psalms 22 and 69. Here the mortal suffering of the praying worshipper seems to be "heightened to an ultimate of suffering"; correspondingly, "the experienced deliverance also bursts all historical bounds.... It became the sign of the eschatological inauguration of the *basileia*. In the apocalyptic perspective, the fundamental experience of *tōda* spirituality, namely, death and redemption, was lifted to the level of an absolute. Deliverance from death led to the world being converted, the dead partaking of life, and salvation being preached to all nations (Ps 22:28ff.)" (121).

Anyone who takes account of these factors will not find it difficult to understand the origins of the Eucharist of Jesus Christ. Structurally speaking, the whole of Christology, indeed the whole of eucharistic Christology, is present in the *tōda* spirituality of the Old Testament. As Gese sums it up: "The Lord's Supper is the *tōda* of the Risen One" (122). We need not go into every detail of this transposition here. But it is important to point out the crucial deepening of the Old Testament *tōda* sacrifice, a development that is entirely consonant with its inner intentionality and that thus transforms the Old Covenant into the New:

In the old *tōda* the man who had experienced deliverance provided a sacrificial animal as a sacrifice for himself and the community. However, the Risen Lord has given himself; the sacrifice is *his* sacrifice, his physical, earthly existence, offered up for us.... Because of its sacredness as a sacrifice, the food of the sacred meal represented by the sacrificial bread is the body of Jesus.... The bread does not signify the body of Jesus in a metaphorical sense; in its very nature, as the substance of the meal eaten in *tōda* sacrifice, it is the sacrifice of Jesus. (123)

The *tōda* of Jesus vindicates the rabbinic dictum: "In the coming (Messianic) time, all sacrifices will cease except the *tōda* sacrifice. This will never cease in all eternity. All (religious) song will cease too, but the songs *of tōda* will never cease in all eternity" (quoted by Gese, 122).

I have reproduced the context of Gese's study in some detail because I feel that its importance cannot be overestimated. It puts the dispute over the question of sacrifice, which has separated Christendom for more than four centuries, in an entirely different light. Surely there are new possibilities here for the ecumenical dialogue between Catholics and Protestants? For it gives us a genuinely New Testament concept of sacrifice that both preserves the complete Catholic inheritance (and imparts to it a new profundity) and, on the other hand, is receptive to Luther's central intentions. Such a synthesis is possible because the inner unity of both Testaments has been brought to light, a unity of which modern theology had increasingly lost sight, whereas the New Testament itself wished to be no more than the complete and full understanding of the Old Testament, now made possible in Christ. The whole Old Testament is a movement of transition to Christ, a waiting for the One in whom all its words would come true, in whom the "Covenant" would attain fulfillment as the New Covenant. Here too, finally, we can see the meaning of the Real Presence and the entire theology of the Easter worship of Christianity against the biblical background of salvation history. Just as this analysis has shown us the unity of the Old and New Testament, of the Catholic and the Protestant inheritance, so too it reveals the unity of the Bible and the faith of the Church, of theology and pastoral practice. Thus I would also like to quote the warning that Gese addresses to those engaged in pastoral practice: "Let no one imagine that we can help modern man by cutting down on the sacramental dimension. The reverse is the case. People have been cutting down for a long time now, and this is what has caused so many misunderstandings. The only way really to help is to expound this central service of worship fully and in a positive spirit. And as for experimentation, it is *least* appropriate where the liturgy of the Lord's Supper is concerned" (127).

The conclusion that *eucharistia*, or *eulogia*, is the determining "form" of the Eucharist has been confirmed in a startling way by Gese's study. For the first time we can see clearly the full content of the Eucharist and what follows from it. For the moment we can leave aside the question of the various corrections and additions that may prove necessary as a result of scholarly response to Gese's work.[23] It seems to me that his central insight, that is, the close connection between *tōda* sacrifice and Eucharist, *tōda* spirituality and Christology, is completely sound. The close connection made, in the New Testament tradition, between the *tōda* psalms and Christology, the structural unity between these psalms and the content of the Eucharist—these things are so obvious that, on the basis of the New Testament texts, they cannot be disputed.

---

[23] Shortly before his death Joachim Jeremias took up a decidedly negative position in his short article "Ist das Dankopfermahl der Ursprung des Herrenmahls?" in *Donum Gentilicium: New Testament Studies in Honour of David Daube*, ed. Charles Kingsley Barrett, Ernst Bammel, and William David Davies (Oxford, 1977), 64–67. Unfortunately Jeremias was dealing, not with the study by Gese that we have presented here, but Gese's earlier study "Psalm 22 und das Neue Testament: Der älteste Bericht vom Tode Jesu und die Entstehung des Herrenmahls", ZThK 65 (1968): 1–22. This earlier study manifested neither the full content of Gese's theses nor his full reasons substantiating them. In a letter to me, Professor Gese has kindly indicated, in considerable detail, his response to the objections of Jeremias and has disposed of them convincingly. In particular, Gese clearly refutes Jeremias' suggestion that the location of the *tōda* psalms in the institution of *tōda* sacrifice is Gese's own (unproven) theory. On the contrary, it is a "view common in Old Testament scholarship ever since Gunkel's study of literary types". And whereas Jeremias had adduced a Mishnah rule to the effect that "thankofferings were most strictly forbidden during the week of Easter", Gese replies with a contrary text, showing that the rule admitted of exceptions.

If I were to question Gese, I should do so on the following lines: the *tōda* sacrifice is the thanksgiving of the man who has already been delivered; in a real sense, surely, it cannot take place until after the Resurrection. This would fit perfectly with the thesis I have presented, namely, that Eucharist is only possible at the Last Supper in an anticipatory form and that therefore it cannot be a simple development of the Last Supper alone. The Last Supper looks to the Cross, where Jesus' words of self-offering will be fulfilled, and to the hope of the Resurrection. Apart from them it would be incomplete and, indeed, unreal. Again, this means that the form of the Last Supper is not complete in itself. If we trace the Eucharist back to the institution of *tōda*, it becomes impossible to see it as a development of the Last Supper alone. In view of *tōda*, the form of the Last Supper must be an "open" form, since *tōda* does not become a reality until it is complemented by Cross and Resurrection.

VI. On the Structure of the Liturgical Celebration

The crisis in the liturgy (and hence in the Church) in which we find ourselves has very little to do with the change from the old to the new liturgical books. More and more clearly we can see that, behind all the conflicting views, there is a profound disagreement about the very nature of the liturgical celebration, its antecedents, its proper form, and about those who are responsible for it. The issue concerns the basic structure of all liturgy, and, whether we are aware of it or not, two fundamentally different views are involved. The basic concepts of the new view are creativity, freedom, celebration, and community. It sees things like rite, obligation, interiority, and church order as negative factors, belonging to the "old" liturgy that is to be superseded. Here is an illustration, chosen at random, of this "new" view of liturgy:

> Liturgy is not some officially prescribed ritual but a concrete celebration, fashioned as an authentic expression of the celebrating community, with the minimum of external control. Liturgy is not a specifically ecclesiastical cult with its own spirituality, to be performed in an objective manner. . . . The priest's missal is his guidebook for his particular role . . . and in a similar way, *Gotteslob* [the congregational music book] is the congregation's guidebook. Liturgy is created in a particular place at a particular time; this emphasizes the role of the community. . . . Since the Council, a higher value has been placed on the congregation's singing. No longer does the reality exist *behind* the singing: what is sung *is* the reality.[1]

The fundamental idea here is that liturgy is a community celebration, an act in which the community forms and experiences itself as

From *The Feast of Faith: Approaches to a Theology of the Liturgy*, trans. Graham Harrison (San Francisco: Ignatius Press, 1986), 61–78.

[1] Elisabeth Bickl, "Zur Rezeption des 'Gotteslob': Einführungsschwierigkeiten und Lösungsvorschläge", *Singende Kirche* 25 (1977/1978): 115–18.

such. In fact this means that the liturgy more and more acquires a "party" character and atmosphere, as we see for instance in the increased importance attached to the words of greeting and dismissal and in the search for elements with "entertainment" value. A "successful" liturgical celebration is judged by the effects achieved in this way. Liturgy is thus dependent on the "creativity", the "ideas" of those who organize it.

1. The Nature of the Liturgical Celebration

The fact that this approach, consistently carried out, would destroy liturgy, that is, the common public worship of the Church, must not obscure the fact that it is right about *one* fundamental element, namely, the "celebratory" character of liturgy. Here is common ground for a discussion of the structure of liturgy. Strictly speaking we should say that liturgy, of its nature, has a festal character.[2] If we can agree on this starting point, the issue then becomes: What makes a feast a feast? Evidently, for the view in question, the festal quality is guaranteed by the concrete "community" experience of a group of people who have grown together into this community. What facilitates this experience of community, what it expresses, in this view, is spontaneity and free expression, that is, the departure from the fixed routine of everyday life, the creativity expressing what animates the community as community. Here liturgy means "playing" with the various roles, with everyone "playing" together and creating the "celebration". Again it seems to me that there *is* an element of truth in this, namely, the idea that central to the "feast" is the freedom whereby we extract ourselves from the constraints of everyday life and that in this way the feast creates a foundation for community. However, if we are really to be made free, we need also to break out of the restrictions of "roles"; we need to lay them aside and allow our real selves to come to light. Otherwise it all remains a game, a more or less beautiful veneer, holding us at a superficial level and, far from facilitating freedom and community, obstructing them.

This being so, all civilizations have found that those who celebrate a feast need some external motive empowering them to do so. They cannot

---

[2] Cf. Joseph Ratzinger, *Eucharistie—Mitte der Kirche* (Munich, 1978), 37f. [trans. Henry Taylor as *God Is Near Us: The Eucharist, the Heart of Life* (San Francisco: Ignatius Press, 2003), 60–62; JRCW 11:274–76]. On the subject of the feast, cf. again Josef Pieper, *Zustimmung zur Welt: Eine Theorie des Festes*, 2nd ed. (Munich, 1964).

do it of themselves. There needs to be a reason for the feast, an objective reason prior to the individual's will. In other words, I can only celebrate freedom if I *am* free; otherwise it is tragic self-delusion. I can only celebrate joy if the world and human existence really give me reason to rejoice. *Am* I free? *Is* there cause for joy? Where these questions are excluded, the "party"—the post-religious world's attempt to rediscover the feast—is soon revealed as a tragic masquerade. It is no coincidence that, wherever people go to parties looking for "redemption", that is, the experience of liberation from self-alienation, from the constraints of everyday life, from a society that represses the self, such parties burst the bounds of middle-class entertainment and become bacchanalia. The taking of drugs is "celebrated" together,[3] a way of journeying into a realm that is completely "other", a liberating excursion from the daily round into a world of freedom and beauty. But in the background there is the number one question concerning the power of suffering and death that no freedom can resist. To avoid these questions is to inhabit a dream world, artificial and insubstantial. It takes more than emotional declamations about the suffering of oppressed peoples—which have become the stock in trade of so many of these homemade "liturgies"—to conceal their fundamental lack of grip. In other words, when "celebration" is equated with the congregation's group dynamics, when "creativity" and "ideas" are mistaken for freedom, the fact is that human nature is being soft-pedaled; its authentic reality is being bypassed. It does not take a prophet to predict that experiments of this kind will not last long; but they can result in a widespread destruction of liturgy.

Now let us turn to the positive side. We have said that liturgy is festal, and the feast is about freedom, the *freedom of being* that is there beneath the role-playing. But where we speak of being, we also raise the question of death. Therefore the festal celebration, above all else, must address itself to the question of death. Conversely, the feast presupposes joy, but this is only possible if it is able to face up to death. That is why, in the history of religions, the feast has always displayed a cosmic and universal character. It attempts to answer the question of death by establishing a connection with the universal vital power of

---

[3] Instructive details in Erwin K. Scheuch, *Haschisch und LSD als Modedrogen* (Osnabrück, 1970).

the cosmos. At this point some may object that, if we are trying to identify what is specifically Christian, we cannot infer the nature of Christian liturgy from the manifestations of religion in general. This is quite right as far as the *positive* form and message of the Christian feast is concerned; but at the same time the fact is that the new and unique Christian reality answers the questions of *all* men. To that extent there must be a fundamental anthropological connection, otherwise what is new and specifically Christian would be unintelligible.

The novel Christian reality is this: Christ's Resurrection enables man genuinely to rejoice. All history until Christ has been a fruitless search for this joy. That is why the Christian liturgy—Eucharist—is, of its essence, the Feast of the Resurrection, *Mysterium Paschae*. As such it bears within it the mystery of the Cross, which is the inner presupposition of the Resurrection. To speak of the Eucharist as the community meal is to cheapen it, for its price was the death of Christ. And as for the joy it heralds, it presupposes that we have entered into this mystery of death. Eucharist is ordered to eschatology, and hence it is at the heart of the theology of the Cross. This is why the Church holds fast to the sacrificial character of the Mass; she does so lest we fail to realize the magnitude of what is involved and thus miss both the real depth of what it means to be human and the real depth of God's liberating power. The freedom with which we are concerned in the Christian feast—the feast of the Eucharist—is not the freedom to devise new texts but the liberation of the world and ourselves from death. Only this can make us free, enabling us to accept truth and to love one another in truth.

This basic insight automatically yields two further structures essential to the Eucharist. One is the Eucharist's worship dimension, which is hardly mentioned in the "roles" approach. Christ died praying; his consent to his Father took precedence over political advantage, thus he was brought to the Cross. On the Cross, therefore, he held aloft his Yes to the Father, glorifying the Father in the Cross, and it was this manner of his dying which led, by an inner logic, to the Resurrection. This means that worship is the context in which we can discover joy, the liberating, victorious Yes to life. The Cross is worship, "exaltation"; Resurrection is made present in it. To celebrate the Feast of the Resurrection is to enter into worship. If we can describe the central meaning of Christian liturgy as the "Feast of the Resurrection", its formative core is "worship". In worship, death is overcome and love is made possible. Worship is truth.

Secondly, it follows that liturgy has a cosmic and universal dimension. The community does not become a community by mutual interaction. It receives its being as a gift from an already existing completeness, totality, and in return it gives itself back to this totality. We cannot go into detail here, but this is why liturgy cannot be "made". This is why it has to be simply received as a given reality and continually revitalized. This is why its universality is expressed in a form binding on the whole Church, committed to the local congregation in the form of the "rite". As "feast", liturgy goes beyond the realm of what can be made and manipulated; it introduces us to the realm of given, living reality, which communicates itself to us. That is why, at all times and in all religions, the fundamental law of liturgy has been the law of organic growth within the universality of the common tradition. Even in the huge transition from the Old to the New Testament, this rule was not breached, the continuity of liturgical development was not interrupted: Jesus introduced his words at the Last Supper organically into the Jewish liturgy at the point where it was open to them, as it were, waiting for them. The growing Church carefully continued this process of inwardly deepening, purifying, and expanding the Old Testament inheritance. Neither the apostles nor their successors "made" a Christian liturgy; it grew organically as a result of the Christian reading of the Jewish inheritance, fashioning its own form as it did so.[4] In this process there was a filtering of the individual communities' experiences of prayer, within the basic proportions of the one Church, gradually developing into the distinctive forms of the major regional churches. In this sense liturgy *always* imposed an obligatory form on the individual congregation and the individual celebrant. It is a guarantee, testifying to the fact that something greater is taking place here than can be brought about by any individual community or group of people. It expresses the gift of joy, the gift of participation in the cosmic drama of Christ's Resurrection, by which liturgy stands or falls. Moreover, the obligatory character of the essential parts of the liturgy

---

[4] Cf. Louis Bouyer, *Eucharistie: Théologie et spiritualité de la prière eucharistique* (Tournai, 1966) [trans. Charles Underhill Quinn as *Eucharist: Theology and Spirituality of the Eucharistic Prayer* (Notre Dame, Ind., and London: Univ. of Notre Dame Press, 1968)]. Cf. also the interview with the author "Liturgie—wandelbar oder unwandelbar?" [trans. Graham Harrison as "Change and Permanence in Liturgy", in Joseph Ratzinger, *The Feast of Faith: Approaches to a Theology of the Liturgy* (San Francisco: Ignatius Press, 1986), 79–95; JRCW 11:519–30] as well as my *Eucharistie—Mitte der Kirche*, 34–41 [*God Is Near Us*, 57–65; JRCW 11:371–77].

also guarantees the true freedom of the faithful: it makes sure that they are not victims of something fabricated by an individual or a group, that they are sharing in the same liturgy that binds the priest, the bishop, and the pope. In the liturgy, we are all given the freedom to appropriate, in our own personal way, the mystery that addresses us.

It is also worth observing here that the "creativity" involved in manufactured liturgies has a very restricted scope. It is poor indeed compared with the wealth of the received liturgy in its hundreds and thousands of years of history. Unfortunately, the originators of homemade liturgies are slower to become aware of this than the participants. Furthermore, those able to draw up such liturgies are necessarily few in number, with the result that what is "freedom" for them means "domination" as it affects others. In the Church's received liturgy, however, there are plenty of opportunities calling for the application of creativity. There is the artistic area, particularly that of music; the organization of the liturgical ministries and the preparation of the liturgical space in ways appropriate to the particular celebration; there is the area of the intercessions. Creativity is needed above all in the proclamation of the word, which is committed to the priest, where the common message is translated into the here and now of the participants. The man who seriously faces up to this task will be continually and painfully aware of the limits of his "creativity": he will hardly want further demands to be placed on it!

2. The Subjective Response to the Objective Nature of the Liturgy

So far we have tried to make plain the objective basic structure of the liturgy, provisionally applying the concept "feast" to it, that is, it is the Feast of the Lord's Resurrection. This in turn showed us the primacy of worship and the objective motive for joy, which presupposes that the individual and the community are bound to the universal Church and her history as well as to the form that she prescribes. This liturgical form is shown to be the realm of freedom and genuine community. This naturally brings us to consider in more depth the position of the individual and the congregation in worship. As is well known, the Second Vatican Council referred to this aspect in terms of *participatio actuosa*, active participation. We find ourselves continually returning to this point because it is a basic problem in the theology of worship.

In our present context we need to analyze the anthropological substance of this concept. Such an analysis will also be essential when it
comes to a discussion of the practical measures to be taken.

In order to do justice to our humanness, "participation" and "activity" must be seen in the perspective of the individual and the community, of inwardness and external expression. For community to exist,
there must be some common *expression*; but, lest this expression be
merely external, there must be also a common movement of *internalization*, a shared path inward (and upward). Where man operates *only*
at the level of expression, at the level of "roles", he is only "playing"
at community. This "acted" community only lasts as long as the playing of the roles. We can see this in the writings of Sartre, Simone de
Beauvoir, and Camus. As representatives of a whole generation they
have described the feeling of isolation, the sense of man's essential
loneliness, and the impossibility of communication between separate
selves. To a large extent this lies behind the disgust with human existence that we see around us. And the feeling itself comes from the
experience that the interior path only leads to the isolation of separate
selves and the outer path can only cover over the total impossibility of
real relationship. Christian liturgy could and should take up this very
point. But it cannot do so by exhausting itself in external activity. The
only way is to open up these separate selves through the process of
interiorization, by an entering into the liturgical word and the liturgical reality—which is the presence of the Lord—and by enabling them
inwardly to communicate with him who first communicated himself
to us all, in his self-surrender on the Cross. It becomes genuinely
possible for people to share in a common expression once this interiorization has taken place under the guidance of the common prayers
of the Church and the experience of the Body of Christ that they
contain. Then people are no longer merely juxtaposed in role-playing
but actually touch one another at the level of being. Only in this way
can "community" come about.

For this reason I am less than happy with the idea of liturgical "roles".
Where a liturgical prayer book is used by the congregation, it certainly does enable people to fit into the common liturgical movement, and to that extent it can be seen as a "script". But it only
fulfills its purpose if it enables men to stand in prayer before God in a
personal way, unconcealed, stripped of "roles". Only then can we be
opened up and put genuinely in touch with one another. Though it

is a community prayer, the liturgy must have *real* prayer as its goal, that is, we must speak to God, not merely to one another; then we shall be better able to speak to one another at the deepest level. This means that, in the area of liturgical participation—which is, at its most profound, a *participatio Dei*, a participation in God and hence in life and freedom—the process of interiorization is of prime importance. In turn it follows that this participation must not cease once the liturgical action is over; liturgy is not some kind of "happening", externally applied to man: it needs education and practice. Lamentably, the magnificent work done in this field by men like Romano Guardini and Pius Parsch has been thrown into the wastepaper basket with the advent of the new books. Thank God there are signs that the inheritance bequeathed by these great liturgical teachers is being rediscovered and carried forward.[5] True liturgical formation cannot be achieved by a continual stream of new ideas and new forms. We need to be led from the form to the content. In other words, we need an education that will help us to grow into an inner appropriation of the Church's common liturgy. This is the only way to get beyond the profusion of words and explanations that tear the liturgy to pieces and ultimately explain nothing.

The question of the relationship between the individual and the community has thus brought us to the question of liturgical expression. The theology of creation and the theology of the Resurrection (which includes and ratifies Incarnation) demand that prayer should be expressed in a bodily form, involving all the dimensions of bodily expression. The spiritualization of the body calls for the embodiment of the Spirit, and vice versa. Only in this way can man and the world be "humanized", which means that matter is brought to its spiritual capacity and that the Spirit is expressed in the wealth of creation. Criticism must be applied to the one-sided dominance of the word, which is unfortunately evident even in the official liturgical books. Recently, however, there are indications that liturgical science has once again taken up the idea of sacred signs and their meaning, along the lines of Romano Guardini's unforgettable little book. To liturgy belong

---

[5] I see this indicated in two volumes that give a picture of the personalities and aims of two pioneers of liturgical renewal: Norbert Höslinger and Theodor Maas-Ewerd, *Mit sanfter Zähigkeit: Pius Parsch und die biblisch-liturgische Erneuerung*, Schriften des Pius-Parsch-Instituts 4 (Klosterneuburg, 1979); Balthasar Fischer and Hans Bernhard Meyer, eds., *J. A. Jungmann: Ein Leben für Liturgie und Kerygma* (Innsbruck, 1975).

both speech *and* silence, singing, the praise of instruments, the visual image, the symbol, and the gesture that corresponds to the word.[6]

In conclusion I would like briefly to examine two of these elements. If there is to be a real *participatio actuosa*, there must be silence. In this silence, together, we journey inward, becoming aware of word and sign, leaving behind the roles that conceal our real selves. In silence man "bides" and "abides"; he becomes aware of "abiding" reality. Liturgy's tension, tautness, comes, not from "variety", as Bruno Kleinheyer has correctly observed,[7] but from the fact that it creates a space in which we can encounter what is truly great and inexhaustible, something that does not need "Variety" because it *suffices*, namely, truth and love. If silence is of such great importance, the few seconds' pause between the "Let us pray" and the prayer itself is totally inadequate—and indeed, it often seems artificial in any case. There is scope for silence at the Preparation of the Gifts, as well as before and after Communion. Regrettably, the silence before Communion is very rarely observed, contrary to the intention of the Missal. I must add, though it conflicts with the accepted view, that it is not essential for the entire Canon of the Mass to be recited aloud on every occasion. The idea that it *must* rests on a misunderstanding of its nature as proclamation. Where a community has undergone the requisite process of liturgical education, the congregation is well acquainted with the component parts of the Church's Eucharistic Prayer. In such a case it is only necessary to pray aloud the first few words of each section of the prayer—the headings, as it were; in this way the congregation's participation (and hence the quality of proclamation) will be often far greater than when its internal appropriation of the words is stifled by an uninterrupted loud recitation. The unhappy multiplication of Eucharistic Prayers that we see in other countries and that has long been underway here too [in Germany] is symptomatic of a very serious situation, quite apart from the fact that the quality and the theological content of some of these productions are hardly bearable. The continual recitation of the Canon aloud results in the demand for "variety", but the

---

[6] Cf., e.g., Ingrid Jorissen and Hans Bernhard Meyer, *Zeichen und Symbole im Gottesdienst* (Innsbruck, 1977); Bruno Kleinheyer, *Heil erfahren in Zeichen* (Munich, 1980). Sociology, too, has turned toward the symbol. Cf. Horst Jürgen Helle, *Soziologie und Symbol* (Cologne and Opladen, 1969). Cf. also Karl-Heinrich Bieritz, "Chancen einer ökumenischen Liturgik", ZKTh 100 (1978): 470–83.

[7] Bruno Kleinheyer, *Erneuerung des Hochgebetes* (Regensburg, 1969), 24.

demand is insatiable, however much these Eucharistic Prayers may proliferate. There is only one solution: we must address ourselves once again to the *intrinsic tension of the reality itself*. In the end even variety becomes boring. This is why, here especially, we are in such urgent need of an education toward inwardness. We need to be taught to enter into the heart of things. As far as liturgy is concerned, this is a matter of life or death. The only way we can be saved from succumbing to the inflation of words is if we have the courage to face silence and in it learn to listen afresh to the Word. Otherwise we shall be overwhelmed by "mere words" at the very point where we should be encountering *the Word*, the Logos, the Word of love, crucified and risen, who brings us life and joy.

My second observation concerns the significance of gestures. Standing, kneeling, sitting, bowing, beating one's breast, the sign of the Cross—all these have an irreplaceable anthropological significance as the way the Spirit is expressed in the body. Josef Pieper has shown convincingly that such gestures bring together the "outside" and the "inside" in a reciprocal relationship that is equally important for both.[8] Here I would like to refer to the gesture that is central to worship, and one that is threatening to disappear, namely, the practice of kneeling.[9] We know that the Lord knelt to pray (Lk 22:41), that Stephen (Acts 7:60), Peter (Acts 9:40), and Paul (Acts 20:36) did so too. The hymn to Christ in Philippians 2:6–11 speaks of the cosmic liturgy as a bending of the knee at the name of Jesus, seeing in it a fulfillment of the Isaian prophecy (Is 45:23) of the sovereignty of the God of Israel. In bending the knee at the name of Jesus, the Church is acting in all

---

[8] Josef Pieper, "Das Gedächtnis des Leibes: Von der erinnernden Kraft des Geschichtlich-Konkreten", in *Kirche aus lebendigen Steinen*, ed. Walter Seidel (Mainz, 1975), 68–83.

[9] From what I have said it should be clear that those who try to hang on to a form of liturgical development that the whole Church has found obsolete are also retreating into a small-group situation; in distancing themselves from the Church's common approach, they are in fact constructing a homemade liturgy of their own. It is quite a different question whether—as in the reform of 1570—the Church should show her magnanimity by allowing people to continue to use the old Missal for the time being, under certain conditions. There is the further, and distinct, question as to the particular weaknesses of the new liturgical books as compared with the old and how one might succeed in integrating some of the advantages of the old into the new. But it is of prime importance to make it clear that the real contrast is not between the old and new books but between a liturgy of the whole Church and homemade liturgies. The greatest obstacle to the calm and orderly appropriation of the renewed liturgical forms lies in the impression so often given that liturgy is now a matter of individual experiment.

truth; she is entering into the cosmic gesture, paying homage to the Victor and thereby going over to the Victor's side. For in bending the knee, we signify that we are imitating and adopting the attitude of him who, though he was "in the form of God", yet "humbled himself unto death". In this way, by combining the prophetic word of the Old Covenant and the manner of life of Jesus Christ, the Letter to the Philippians has taken up the sign of kneeling, which it regards as the appropriate posture for Christians to adopt at the name of Jesus, and has given it a cosmic significance in salvation history. Here, the bodily gesture attains the status of a confession of faith in Christ: words could not replace such a confession.

This brings us back to the concept with which we started: Christian liturgy is cosmic liturgy, as St. Paul tells us in the Letter to the Philippians. It must never renounce this dignity, however attractive it may seem to work with small groups and construct homemade liturgies. What is exciting about Christian liturgy is that it lifts us up out of our narrow sphere and lets us share in the truth. The aim of all liturgical renewal must be to bring to light this liberating greatness.[10]

---

[10] On the question of "creativity", cf. also Guy-Marie Oury, *La Créativité liturgique* (Quebec, 1977).

VII. Eucharist and Mission

1. Preliminary Thoughts about Eucharist and Mission

An old legend about the origin of Christianity in Russia tells how a series of people presented themselves before Prince Vladimir of Kiev, who was seeking to find the right religion for his people: each in turn, representatives of Islam from Bulgaria, representatives of Judaism, and then emissaries of the pope from Germany, offered him their faith as being the right one and the best. Yet the prince remained unsatisfied by any of these things being offered. The decision was made, it is said, when his ambassadors returned from a solemn liturgical celebration in which they had taken part in the Church of Hagia Sophia in Constantinople. Filled with enthusiasm, they told the prince: "Then we came to the Greeks, and we were taken to the place where they worship their God.... We do not know whether we have been in heaven or on earth.... We have experienced how God dwells there among men." [1]

This story, as such, is certainly not historical. The way the "Rus" turned to Christianity and the final decision in favor of the link with Byzantium constitute a long and complicated process, and historians now believe they can trace its main outlines.[2] Yet as is always the case, there is also a kernel of profound truth within this legend. For the inner power of the liturgy has without doubt played an essential role in the spread of Christianity. The legend of the liturgical origin of

---

From *Pilgrim Fellowship of Faith: The Church as Communion*, trans. Henry Taylor (San Francisco: Ignatius Press, 2005), 90–122.

[1] Cf. Petro Borys T. Bilaniuk, *The Apostolic Origin of the Ukrainian Church* (Parmo, Ohio, 1988).

[2] Cf. Friedrich Kempf, "Die Missionierung der Slawen und Ungarn im 10. und 11. Jahrhundert", in *Handbuch der Kirchengeschichte*, vol. 3, pt. 1, *Die mittelalterliche Kirche: Vom Frühmittelalter bis zur gregorianischen Reform*, ed. Hubert Jedin (Freiburg, 1966), 267–82; on the "Rus" kingdom: 275–78, and the detailed bibliography given there, 268f.

Russian Christianity, however, above and beyond this general connection between worship and mission, tells us something particular about their inner relationship. For the Byzantine liturgy, which transported to heaven the foreign visitors in search of God, was not of itself missionary in character. It did not advertise the faith with an interpretation for outsiders, for nonbelievers, but dwelt entirely within the inner home of faith. The report in Acts 20:7 of how Paul celebrated the Eucharist with the Christians of Troas "in the upper room" was, in the early Church, as a matter of course, connected with the story according to which, after the Lord's Ascension into heaven, the disciples together with Mary waited in prayer for the Holy Spirit in the upper room and received him there (Acts 1:3). This upper room, in turn, was identified—historically, this was probably correct—with the room in which the Last Supper was held, where Jesus had celebrated the first Eucharist with the Twelve. The upper room became a symbol of the inner recollection of the faithful, for the way the Eucharist is removed from ordinary everyday life. It became an expression for the "mystery of faith" (1 Tim 3:9; cf. 3:16), in the inmost heart of which stands the Eucharist. If the Roman liturgy has inserted this acclamation, "The mystery of faith", into the institution narrative and has thus made it a part of the central action of the Eucharist, then its interpretation here of the heritage from primitive Christianity is entirely correct—the eucharistic liturgy is not, as such, directed toward nonbelievers; rather, it presupposes, as a mystery, that worshippers are "initiated": only those who have entered into the mystery with their whole life, who know Christ no longer just from the outside—like "the people" whose opinions Peter recounts to the Lord before his confession of faith at Caesarea Philippi (Mk 8:28)—only these can come to the Eucharist. Only someone who, in the communion of faith, has arrived at the point of an inner agreement and an understanding with him can communicate with Christ in the Sacrament.

Let us turn back to our legend: What persuaded the emissaries of the Russian prince of the truth of the faith celebrated in the Orthodox liturgy was not a kind of missionary persuasiveness, with arguments that seemed to them clearer than those of the other religions. What moved them was in fact the mystery as such, which demonstrated the power of the truth actually in transcending the arguments of reason. To put it again another way: The Byzantine liturgy was not, and is not, concerned to indoctrinate other people or to show them how pleasing and entertaining it might be. What was impressive about it was particularly its sheer lack of a practical purpose, the fact that it was being done for God and not for spectators; it was simply striving to be εὐάρεστος—εὐπρόσδεκτος (Rom 12:1; 15:16) before God and for God: to be pleasing to God, as the sacrifice of Abel had been pleasing to God. The very selflessness of this standing before God and turning the gaze toward God was what allowed God's light to stream down into what was happening and for it to be detected even by outsiders.

With this we have established in advance one first important result for our investigation. The way of talking about "missionary liturgy" that became widespread in the fifties is, at the least, ambiguous and problematical.[3] In many circles, among people concerned with liturgy, it led, in a quite inappropriate fashion, to turning a didactic element in the liturgy, and its comprehensibility even for outsiders, into the primary standard for shaping liturgical celebrations. Likewise, the saying that the choice of liturgical forms must be made with respect to "pastoral" points of view betrays the same anthropocentric error. The liturgy is then being constructed entirely for men; it is either serving to convey certain contents or—after people are tired of the rationalism that arises that way and of its banality—to build up community in a way that is related, no longer necessarily to any comprehensible content, but to processes in which people draw close to one another and experience community. Thus, suggestions for styling the liturgy became—and are still becoming—more one-sided and more dependent upon profane models, drawn, for instance, from the way meetings are held or from ancient or even modern socialization rituals. God does not actually play any role there; it is all concerned with winning people over or keeping them happy and satisfying their demands.

No faith is aroused that way, of course, since faith has to do with God, and it is only where his closeness is felt, where human intentions take second place to reverence before him, that the credibility comes about that creates belief. We have no need to discuss here the various paths to be pursued and opportunities that open up in mission, which no doubt often have to begin with very simple human

---

[3] The main representative of the idea of "missionary liturgy" in German-speaking countries in the fifties was Johannes Hofinger; cf. Johannes Hofinger, ed., *Mission und Liturgie: Der Kongreß von Nimwegen 1959* (Mainz, 1960); Johannes Hofinger and Joseph Kellner, *Liturgische Erneuerung in der Weltmission* (Innsbruck, 1957).

contacts, yet contacts that are illuminated by love for God. For us it is sufficient to note that the Eucharist, as such, is not directly oriented toward the awakening of people's faith in a missionary sense. It stands, rather, at the heart of faith and nourishes it; its gaze is primarily directed toward God, and it draws men into this point of view, draws them into the descent of God to us, which becomes their ascent into fellowship with God. It aims at being pleasing to God and at leading men to see this as being likewise the measure of their lives. And to that extent it is, of course, in a more profound sense, the origin of mission.

2. The Theology of the Cross as the Presupposition and Basis of Eucharistic Theology

Following this anticipation of the answer to our question, which has been provided by the old legend of the conversion of Russia, we now have to try to work our way farther into the network of relationships we have thus far glimpsed in a few suggestions. In doing this, I would like to concentrate on the witness of Holy Scripture and, in it, on some central passages from St. Paul, so as to put some boundaries to the subject. If, accordingly, we try to grasp what Paul says about the connection between the Eucharist and faith, then the first thing we see is that there are three very different levels at which this subject is presented—which are, of course, nonetheless closely interlinked, both in their roots and in their intentions. The first thing is the interpretation of Christ's death on the Cross in terms of the cult, which represents the inner presupposition of all eucharistic theology. We are still hardly able to grasp the enormous importance of this step. An event that was in itself profane, the execution of a man by the most cruel and horrible method available, is described as a cosmic liturgy, as tearing open the closed-up heavens—as the act by which everything that had hitherto been ultimately intended, which had been sought in vain, by all forms of worship, now in the end actually comes about.

In Romans 3:24–26, making use of older, pre-Pauline formulas, Paul has put together the fundamental text for this interpretation.[4] Yet, possibly, this was only because Jesus himself, at the Last Supper, had

---

[4] Cf. Heinrich Schlier, *Der Römerbrief*, HThKNT 6 (Freiburg, 1977), 106–16.

anticipated his own death, had gone through it in advance and transformed it from within into an event of self-sacrifice and love. On that basis, Paul could describe Christ as *hilasterion*, which in the cultic terminology of the Old Testament meant the center of the Temple, the cover that lay upon the ark. It was called *kapporeth*, which was translated into Greek with *hilasterion*, and was seen as the place above which Yahweh appeared in a cloud. This *kapporeth* used to be sprinkled with the blood from expiatory sacrifices, in order that God might thus come as close as possible.[5] If, then, Paul says that Christ is the heart of the Temple, which has been lost ever since the Exile, the real place of atonement, the true *kapporeth*, then modern exegesis has represented this as a spiritualizing reinterpretation of the old cult and, thus, in fact as the abolition of the cult, as its replacement by spiritual and ethical elements. Yet the contrary is the truth: for Paul, it is not the Temple that is the true reality of worship, and the other thing a kind of allegory, but vice versa. Human cults, including that of the Old Testament, are mere "images", foreshadowing the real worship of God, which is what does not happen in the animal sacrifices. When the tabernacle of the covenant, which is the model for the Temple, is portrayed in the book of Exodus, and it is said that Moses arranged everything in accordance with the image he saw when he was with God, then the Fathers saw in this an expression of the fact that the worship of the Temple was a mere copy.[6] And indeed, the sacrifices of animals and other things are only ever helpless attempts to substitute for man, who ought to be giving himself—not in the horrible form of human sacrifices, but in the entire wholeness of his being. Yet this is precisely what he is incapable of.

Thus for Paul, as for the whole Christian tradition, it is clear that the voluntary self-sacrifice of Jesus is not an allegorical abolition of the concept of worship; rather, here the intent and purpose of the Feast of Atonement become reality, just as the Letter to the Hebrews has portrayed in detail. It is not the killers of Christ who are offering a sacrifice—it would be a perversion to think that. Christ gives glory to God by sacrificing himself and thus bringing human existence within God's own being. Hartmut Gese has interpreted the meaning of Romans 3:25 like this:

[5] Cf. Hartmut Gese, *Zur biblischen Theologie: Alttestamentliche Vorträge* (Munich, 1977), 85–106, especially 105f.; Bernhard Lang, "kippaer-kapporaet", etc., in ThWAT 4:303–18.

[6] Cf. Ex 25:8, 40; 26:30; 27:8; cf. also Ex 39:43; 40:23, 29; further, Heb 8:5. Cf. Irenaeus, *Adversus haereses* IV, 14, 3 (SChr 100:548).

He who is crucified represents God on his throne and unites us with him through the sacrifice of the human blood that is his life. God becomes accessible to us and appears to us in him who is crucified. The reconciliation is effected, not from man's side in a rite of substitutionary shedding of blood or giving of life, but from God's. God sets up the link between us.... The curtain in front of the Holy of Holies is torn asunder; God is very close to us; he is present for us in death, in suffering, in dying.[7]

Yet the question then arises: How could it ever occur to anyone to interpret the Cross of Jesus in such a way as to see it as actually effecting what had been intended by the cults of the world, especially by that of the Old Testament, by what had often been dreadfully distorted in them and had never truly been achieved? What opened up the possibility at all of such a tremendous reworking of this event, of transferring the whole of the Old Testament's theology of worship and the cult to this apparently most profane occurrence? I have already hinted at the answer: Jesus himself had told the disciples about his death and had interpreted it in terms of prophetic categories, which were available to him above all in the Servant Songs of Deutero-Isaiah. Thus the theme of atonement and of substitution, which belongs to the broad sphere of cultic thought, had already been introduced. At the Last Supper, he developed this more profoundly by welding together Sinaitic covenant theology and prophetic theology, which go to shape the sacrament in which he accepts and anticipates his death and, at the same time, makes it capable of becoming present as the holy cult for all ages.[8] Without this kind of essential foundation in the life and activity of Jesus himself, the new understanding of the Cross is unthinkable—no one would have been able, as it were, to overlay the Cross with this understanding at a later stage. Thus the Cross also becomes the synthesis of the Old Testament festivals, the Day of Atonement, and the Pascha in one, the point of passage into a New Covenant.[9]

---

[7] Gese, *Zur biblischen Theologie*, 105.

[8] I have described the interrelationship of all this somewhat more fully in my little book *Die Vielfalt der Religionen und der eine Bund* (Hagen and Urfeld, 1998), 47–49 [trans. Graham Harrison as *Many Religions—One Covenant: Israel, the Church, and the World* (San Francisco: Ignatius Press, 1999), 57–60].

[9] In his important book *Le Sacerdoce du Christ et ses ministres* (Paris, 1972), André Feuillet has shown that John 17 is rooted in the Jewish liturgy of the Day of Atonement; see especially 39–63. From this point of view, the Gospel of John is close to the Letter to the Hebrews, which also understands the Cross of Christ entirely on the basis of the liturgy of

Because this is the state of affairs, we can say that the theology of the Cross is eucharistic theology, and vice versa. Without the Cross, the Eucharist would remain mere ritual; without the Eucharist, the Cross would be merely a horrible profane event.[10] Thus something else becomes clear: the close connection between life as it is lived and experienced and sacral actions in worship. From that then develops the third level of eucharistic theology we have to discuss: Just as the Cross of Christ provides the eucharistic liturgy with its reality and content and lifts it above what is merely ritual and symbolic, making it into the real worship for all the world, so the Eucharist must ever and again press out beyond the sphere of mere cult, must become reality over and beyond that sphere, precisely in order that it may wholly become what it is and remain what it is. We shall have to consider a series of Pauline texts in which martyrdom, the Christian life, and finally the special apostolic service of preaching the faith are described in terms of strictly cultic concepts, so that they are thus brought into line with the Cross of Christ himself, so that they appear as the continuing realization of what is portrayed in the Eucharist and thus hold fast, throughout the epoch of the Church, that close connection between sacrament and life which stands at the origin of the Sacrament and is what alone constitutes the Sacrament as such. Thus the three dimensions, of theology of the Cross, theology of the Eucharist as a sacrament, and also theology of martyrdom and of preaching, belong together inseparably. Only in their

Yom Kippur. On the other hand, John—like the Synoptic Gospels—links the Cross with the Jewish liturgy and theology of the Pascha. Thierry Maertens, in *Heidnisch-jüdische Wurzeln der christlichen Feste* (Mainz, 1965; translated from French), shows on 59–72 that elements from the theology and the liturgy of the Feast of Booths have also found their way into the Christian theology of Easter.

[10] That is why we must inevitably level criticism at any accounts by liturgical specialists of the development of the liturgy that—quite rightly—do make use of preliminary reflections from the history of religions and in which the roots of the Eucharist in the Old Testament and in Judaism are investigated but in which the *Cross*—because it cannot be classed as a liturgical action—is left to one side. Thereby we fail from the start to do justice to the realism proper to the Christian liturgy, to what is new in Christian liturgy, although this is what links it, in a quite unexpected way, with the worship of the other world religions. Would it ever occur to anyone to describe the Jewish Passover liturgy without starting from the fundamental event described in Exodus 12, which the liturgy is meant to make present? This objection unfortunately has to be raised even against the account given by Hans Bernhard Meyer—which is in many respects a model one—in *Eucharistie*, GdK 4 (Regensburg, 1989), where even in the little section "Sign of Giving His Life" the word "Cross" does not occur (70f.).

interplay and interconnection can we learn to understand what the Eucharist means.

3. Eucharistic Theology in the First Letter to the Corinthians

With respect to the theology of the Cross, I should be happy to make do with those references we have already made; let us now look at the other two dimensions. Again, we shall have to stay with a selection of passages; for eucharistic theology in the narrower sense—the second dimension—I should like to restrict my attention to the First Letter to the Corinthians, which is of course particularly productive for this theme. There are four passages here that have something more or less detailed and explicit to say about the Sacrament of the Body and Blood of the Lord, and we shall look at them each in turn.

a. 1 Corinthians 5:6: The Christian Pascha

First there is 1 Corinthians 5:6–8:

> Do you not know that a little leaven leavens all the dough? Cleanse out the old leaven that you may be new dough, as you really are unleavened. For Christ, our Paschal Lamb, has been sacrificed. Let us, therefore, celebrate the festival, not with the old leaven, the leaven of malice and evil, but with the unleavened bread of sincerity and truth.

Here are seen the two essential elements of the Old Testament Pascha: the lamb that is sacrificed and the unleavened bread; thus the christological basis and the anthropological consequence, the application in life of the sacrifice of Christ, are apparent. If the lamb represents Christ in anticipation, then the bread becomes the symbol of the Christian life. The absence of leaven becomes a sign of the new start: being a Christian is portrayed as a continuing celebration on the basis of the new life. We might talk about an interpretation of the Old Testament Pascha that is at the same time christological and existential and in which the themes associated with the Exodus are probably to be heard in the background: the sacrifice of Christ becomes a breakthrough, a setting out into a new life, a life whose simplicity and sincerity are represented in the symbol of the unleavened bread. In any case, the German ecumenical translation unfortunately obscures one aspect of the whole thing: where it gives "Get rid of the old leaven", the Greek has "Purify the old leaven away." The old cultic concept of purity is now becoming a category of everyday life: this does not refer to ritual purifications but to the breakthrough to a new way of life.

The Eucharist itself is not mentioned in the text, but we are still aware of it as the constant basis of life for Christians, as the motive force that shapes their existence. The whole passage makes it impressively clear that the Eucharist is much more than a liturgy and a rite, yet it also makes clear, on the other hand, that Christian life is more than just moral striving—that at a profound level it draws life from him who, for our sake, became a lamb and sacrificed himself.

b. 1 Corinthians 6:12–19: Uniting Oneself to the Lord

The second text, 1 Corinthians 6:12–19, is of some importance for our question, and I would like just to concentrate on verses 15–17:

> Do you not know that your bodies are members of Christ? Shall I therefore take the members of Christ and make them members of a prostitute? Never! Do you not know that he who joins himself to a prostitute becomes one body with her? For, as it is written, "The two shall become one." But he who is united to the Lord becomes one spirit with him.

Here, the most profound content of Christian eucharistic piety is formulated as a standard of conduct, and at the same time the heart of Christian mysticism is presented: this does not rely on human techniques of self-elevation or self-emptying, useful though these well may be; it is based on the *mysterion*, that is, on the descent and self-giving of God, received by us in the Sacrament. We should bear in mind here that "sacrament" is the translation of *mysterion* and that the word "mysticism" is linguistically connected to this. According to this text, receiving the Eucharist means blending one's existence, closely analogical, spiritually, to what happens when man and wife become one on the physical-mental-spiritual plane. The dream of blending divinity with humanity, of breaking out of the limitations of a creature—this dream, which persists through all the history of mankind and in hidden ways, in profane versions, is dreamed anew even within the atheistic ideologies of our time, just as it is in the drunken excesses of a world without God—this dream is here fulfilled. Man's promethean attempts to break out of his limitations himself, to build with his own capacities the tower by which he may mount up to divinity, always necessarily end in collapse and disappointment—indeed, in despair. This blending, this union, has become possible because God came down in Christ, took upon himself the limitations of human existence, suffering them to the end, and in the infinite love of the Crucified One opened up the door to infinity. The real end of creation, its underlying purpose—and conversely that of human existence as willed by the Creator—is this very union, "that God may be all in all". The eros-love of the created being is taken up into the agape-love of the Creator and, thus, into that fulfilling and holy embrace of which Augustine speaks. The Letter to the Ephesians took up the theme of this passage in 1 Corinthians and developed it; it quotes in full the prophecy connected with Adam, about husband and wife "becoming one", and quotes it as the vision, at the very beginning of mankind, of the mystery of which the eros-love of man and woman constitutes the fundamental analogy in concrete reality, a vision that is, as it were, ever driving mankind onward.[11]

There is something else in this passage from 1 Corinthians that is important for the question we are raising: here we have also come upon the starting point for referring to the Church as the body of Christ, upon the inner interlacing of the Eucharist and ecclesiology. This way of talking of the Church as the body of Christ is more than just some term that might be taken from the social pattern of the ancient world to compare a concrete body with a body consisting of many people. This expression takes as its starting point the Sacrament of the Body and Blood of Christ and is therefore more than just an image: it is the expression of the true nature of the Church. In the Eucharist we receive the Body of the Lord and, thus, become one body with him; we all receive the same Body and, thus, ourselves become "all one in Christ Jesus" (Gal 3:28). The Eucharist takes us out of ourselves and into him, so that we can say, with Paul, "It is no longer I who live, but Christ who lives in me" (Gal 2:20). I, yet no

---

[11] Cf. Heinrich Schlier, *Der Brief an die Epheser: Ein Kommentar*, 2nd ed. (Düsseldorf, 1958), 252–80; especially the considerable excursus "Hieros Gamos", 264–76.

longer I—a new and greater self is growing, which is called the one body of the Lord, the Church. The Church is built up in the Eucharist; indeed, the Church *is* the Eucharist. To receive Communion means becoming the Church, because it means becoming one body with him. Of course, this "being one body" has to be thought of along the lines of husband and wife being one: one flesh, and yet two; two, and yet one. The difference is not abolished but is swallowed up in a greater unity.

c. 1 Corinthians 10:1–22: One Body with Christ, but without Any Magical Guarantee of Salvation

The same ideas recur in the third eucharistic text in the First Letter to the Corinthians, in 10:1–22, and here they are further developed and added to. In the second part of this passage, the Eucharist is contrasted to sacrificing to idols: anyone who makes sacrifices to idols makes common cause with them, gives himself up to them, and ultimately belongs in their sphere and is under their power. There are of course no gods as such, but there are forces that we make into gods this way and to which, in doing so, we give power over us, allowing ourselves to be guided and shaped by these forces. Just as idolatry draws us into the sphere of power of these false idols and shapes us in their image, something analogous to this—and yet quite different—happens in connection with the sacrifice of Christ: "The bread which we break, is it not a participation in the body of Christ? Because there is one bread, we who are many are one body, for we all partake of the one bread" (10:16–17).

Once more, the religious attitude toward Communion and that toward the Church blend into one another: the one bread makes us into one body; the Church is simply that unity created by eucharistic Communion, the unity of the many in and through the one Christ.

This section of Paul's letter, which shows the hope and the magnitude of the Christian life, is preceded by a little catechism, which emphasizes the risks run by the person in Christ. We can deal with this briefly, because the essential point of this passage can be seen as part of the interpretation of the fourth passage about the Eucharist in this letter. Paul compares the Christians with the generation of Israel wandering in the wilderness and says about these latter that they all enjoyed the same spiritual food and drank the same spiritual drink, which came from the spiritual Rock that was following them. "And the Rock was Christ" (10:4). Nevertheless (Paul continues), with most of them God was not pleased, and in fact they came to grief in the wilderness. Paul applies this to Christians: If they, like the generation of Israel in the wilderness, tempt God or murmur against him, then they run the same risk. Three things are important here. First, Paul talks about the universal presence of Christ: he, too, was wandering in the wilderness, along with Israel, and in mysterious fashion he was feeding them and giving them to drink with the Holy Spirit; he gave himself to them sacramentally, that is, in a secret fashion, through external food and drink. The second important point is that the life of the Christian, and that of the Church, is interpreted as a wandering. The theology of the Wandering People of God, who have "no lasting city" here but are simply on their way to the Promised Land, to their inheritance, has here one of its basic starting points. The Eucharist is nourishment for pilgrims; Christ is the spiritual Rock, who is wandering along with us. And finally a third point follows: The Eucharist does not grant us any quasi-magical assurance of salvation. It always demands and involves our freedom. And therefore the risk of losing our salvation always remains; our gaze remains fixed on the judgment to come.

d. 1 Corinthians 11:17–33: The Institution of the Eucharist and the Right Way to Celebrate It

And that brings us to the final and most important passage about the Eucharist in the First Letter to the Corinthians, which also includes Paul's version of the institution narrative: 11:17–33. First of all, the connection between the Eucharist and the congregation is important here, and we may recall that the word *Ecclesia*, "Church", comes from the Old Testament, where it is the classic expression for the assembly of the People of God, the prototype and pattern for which was the assembly at Sinai, the people congregating at the feet of the God who spoke, whose word called people together and united them. Yet the assembly at Sinai goes beyond the word: in the covenant, it unites God and man in a kind of community of blood, as blood relations, symbolically represented there, which is the heart of the "covenant". Because the Eucharist is the New Covenant, it is the renewal of the assembly at Sinai, and that is why, on the basis of the word and the Body and the Blood of Christ, it brings into being the People of God.

But let us take things in order. The Eucharist gathers people together; it creates for human beings a blood relationship, a sharing of blood, with Jesus Christ and, thus, with God, and of people with one another. Yet in order for this, the coming together on the highest level, to come about, there must first be a simpler level of getting together, so to speak, and people have to step outside their own private worlds and meet together. The coming together of people in response to the Lord's call is the necessary condition for the Lord's being able to make them into an assembly in a new way. Respecting all this, the Apostle's gaze is directed in the first place at the local congregation of Corinth, who lack any true sense of coming together, in that when they meet the various groups still remain apart. But the horizon of this perspective lies far beyond the particular place and includes the Church as a whole: all eucharistic assemblies taken together are still just *one* assembly, because the body of Christ is just *one*, and hence the People of God can only be *one*. Thus, an exhortation directed to one local congregation is relevant to all congregations in the Church as a whole: they must celebrate the Eucharist in such a way that they all come together, on the basis of Christ and through him. Anyone who does not celebrate the Eucharist with everyone is merely creating a caricature of it. The Eucharist is celebrated with the one Christ, and thus with the whole Church, or it is not being celebrated at all. Anyone who is only looking for his own group or clique in the Eucharist, who is not, in the Eucharist—and through it—plunging himself into the whole Church, moving beyond his own realm, is doing exactly what is being criticized in the Corinthians' behavior. He is, so to say, sitting down with his back to the others and is thus annihilating the Eucharist for himself and spoiling it for the others. He is then just holding his own meal and is despising the Churches of God (1 Cor 11:21f.). If the eucharistic assembly first brings us out of the world and into the "upper room", into the inner chamber of faith (as we have seen), this very upper room is yet the place of meeting, a universal meeting of everyone who believes in Christ, beyond all boundaries and divisions; and it thus becomes the point from which a universal love is bound to shine forth, overcoming all boundaries and divisions: if others are going hungry, we cannot live in opulence. On the one hand, the Eucharist is a turning inward and upward; yet only from the depths within, and from the heights of what is truly above, can come the power that overcomes boundaries and divisions and changes the world.

We shall have to come back to that point. Let us first take another look at the implications of the congregational assembly. Coming together in the fellowship of Christian worship does not yet, in Paul's writings, presume the existence of any sacred place in an external sense; in the situation in which the Christians found themselves as the Church came into being, that would have been impossible. Yet it nonetheless involves making a distinction between the sacred and the profane. The Eucharist and the profane meal are sharply separated. "Do you not have houses to eat and drink in?" (v. 22). "If anyone is hungry, let him eat at home—lest you come together to be condemned" (v. 34). In the Eucharist, God's holiness enters in among us. Thus it creates a sacred sphere of itself and demands of us reverence before the Lord's mystery. At the beginning of the second century, in the *Didache*, the sharing out of the sacred gifts is preceded by the cry: "Let anyone who is holy draw near! Let anyone who is not holy do penance" (10:6).* Taking as its starting point Jesus' command to be reconciled before bringing a gift to the altar [Mt 5:23–24], the text expresses it thus:

> On the Lord's Day come together, break bread, and hold Eucharist, after confessing your transgressions, that *your offering may be pure*; but let none who has a quarrel with his fellow join in your meeting until he be reconciled, *that your sacrifice be not defiled.* For this is that which was spoken by the Lord, *"in every place and time offer me a pure sacrifice, for I am a great king,"* says the Lord, *"and my name is wonderful among the heathen."* (14:1–3)**

These directions for worship breathe the spirit of Paul himself. Coming together for worship means being reconciled with men and with God.

The consciousness that this is a holy place, because the Lord is coming in among us, should come over us ever anew—that consciousness by which Jacob was so shaken when he awoke from his vision, which had shown him that from the stone on which he had been sleeping, a ladder was set up on which the angels of God were passing up and

---

The Didache, or Teaching of the Twelve Apostles, Apostolic Fathers, vol. 1, Loeb Classical Library (1912; Cambridge, Mass., and London, 1977), 303–33.
**Ibid., 330–31.

down: "And he was afraid, and said, 'How awesome is this place! This is none other than the house of God, and this is the gate of heaven'" (Gen 28:17). Awe is a fundamental condition for celebrating the Eucharist correctly, and the very fact that God becomes so small, so humble, puts himself at our mercy, and puts himself into our hands should magnify our awe and ought not to tempt us to thoughtlessness and vainglory. If we recognize that God is there and we behave accordingly, then other people will be able to see this in us, as did the ambassadors of the Prince of Kiev, who experienced heaven in the midst of the earth.

The actual account of the Lord's Supper is introduced by Paul with almost exactly the same words as he uses to present the message of the Resurrection (1 Cor 15:1ff.): "For I received from the Lord what I also delivered to you." The structure and process of receiving, handing over, and passing on are very strictly formulated in this area at the heart of Paul's faith. Where the teaching about the Eucharist is concerned, and the message about the Resurrection, he sets himself most decidedly in obedience to the tradition, which is binding to the very last word, because in this tradition what is most holy, and thus most fundamental, comes down to us. Paul, that impetuous creative spirit who opened up new horizons for Christianity, starting from his meeting with the Risen One and from his experience of faith and service, is nonetheless, in the central area of Christian faith, the faithful steward who does not "peddle" God's word (2 Cor 2:17) but hands it on as the precious gift of God, which is beyond our arbitrary will and thereby enriches us all. The Eucharist unites us with the Lord and does it in fact by limiting us, binding us to him. Only thus are we freed from ourselves. If nowadays people say to us that the gifts of the Mediterranean world were wheaten bread and wine, and in other spheres of culture we have to use as materials for the sacrament whatever is characteristic for that given culture, those speculations are therefore wrong and in profound opposition to the biblical message. For the Incarnation, which is claimed as a basis for this, is not just some general philosophical principle, in accordance with which we should always have to embody what is spiritual and express it in a way corresponding to the situation at the time. The Incarnation is not a philosophical idea but a historical event, which in its very uniqueness and truth is the point at which God breaks into history and the place at which we come into contact with him. If we deal with it, as is appropriate on the basis of the Bible, not as a principle but as an event, then our conclusion is necessarily the opposite one: God has associated himself with a quite specific point in history, with all its limitations, and wishes us to share in his humility. Allowing oneself to be associated with the Incarnation means accepting this self-limitation of God: these very gifts, which for other spheres of culture—including German culture—are strange and foreign, become for us the sign of his unparalleled and unique action, of his unique historical figure. They are the symbols of God's coming to us, he who is a stranger to us and who makes us his neighbors through his gifts. The response to God's descent can only be one of humble obedience, an obedience that in receiving the tradition and remaining faithful to it is granted as a gift the certainty of his close presence.

I have no wish to embark upon an exegesis of the institution narrative at this point; that would go beyond the limits of this lecture. We have already seen how the words of institution are a theology of the Cross and a theology of the Resurrection—they reach right down into the heart of the historical event, and in the inwardness of Jesus that transcends time they rise up so that this essential core of the event now reaches into every age: this inner core now becomes the point at which time opens up to God's eternity. That is why the "memorial" constituted by the Eucharist is more than a remembrance of something in the past: it is the act of entering into that inner core which can no longer pass away. And that is why the "preaching" of Christ's death is more than mere words: it is a proclamation that bears the truth within it. In the words of Jesus, as we have seen, all the streams of the Old Testament—law and prophets—flow together into a new unity that could not have been foreseen. Those words that had simply been waiting for their real speaker, such as the song of the Suffering Servant, now become reality. We could even go farther and say that ultimately this is where all the great streams of the history of religions meet together, for the most profound knowledge of the myths had been that of the world's being built up on sacrifice, and in some sense, beneath shadowy forms that were often dark, it was being taught that, in the end, God himself must become a sacrifice so that love might prevail over hatred and lies.[12] With its vision of the cosmic liturgy, in

---

[12] Cf. in this context the Vedic Purusa myth: the creation arises from the sacrifice of the primeval giant Purusa: the world is based on sacrifice. See Jan Gonda, *Die Religionen Indiens*, vol. 1, *Veda und älterer Hinduismus* (Stuttgart, 1960), 187, etc.

the midst of which stands the Lamb who was sacrificed, the Apocalypse has presented the essential contents of the eucharistic sacrament in an impressive form that sets a standard for every local liturgy. From the point of view of the Apocalypse, the essential matter of all eucharistic liturgy is its participation in the heavenly liturgy; it is from thence that it necessarily derives its unity, its catholicity, and its universality.[13]

Paul returns once more to the theme of Christian worship not being profane, being sacred, after the institution narrative, when he emphatically demands that each of the communicants should examine himself: "Any one who eats and drinks without discerning the body eats and drinks judgment upon himself" (v. 29). Anyone who wants Christianity to be just a joyful message in which there can be no threat of the judgment is distorting it. Faith does not reinforce the pride of a sleeping conscience, the vainglory of people who make their own wishes the norm for their life, and who thus refashion grace so as to devalue both God and man, because God can then in any case only approve, and is only allowed to approve, everything. Yet any one of us who is suffering and struggling can be certain that "God is greater than our hearts" (1 Jn 3:20) and that whatever my failures, I may be full of confident trust, because Christ suffered for me, too, and has already paid the price for me.

4. Martyrdom, Christian Life, and Apostolic Service as Ways of Living out the Eucharist

Following this attempt to look at the broad outlines of eucharistic theology in the New Testament at a genuinely sacramental level, as we find it in the First Letter to the Corinthians, we will have at least to look briefly at the third level, which I should like to call "existential", before we then try to draw some conclusions about the theme of Eucharist and mission. I should like to present for your consideration three texts: Philippians 2:17, to which 2 Timothy 4:6 again makes brief reference; Romans 12:1; and Romans 15:16.

---

[13] Cf. Joseph Ratzinger, *Ein neues Lied für den Herrn: Christusglaube und Liturgie in der Gegenwart* (Freiburg, 1995), 165–86 [trans. Martha M. Matesich as *A New Song for the Lord: Faith in Christ and Liturgy Today* (New York: Crossroad, 1997), 128–46; JRCW 11:461–79].

a. Martyrdom as a Way in Which the Christian
Can Become a Eucharist

In the Letter to the Philippians, Paul, who is sitting in prison awaiting trial, talks about the possibility of becoming a martyr, and he
does so, surprisingly, in liturgical terminology: "Even if I am to be
poured as a libation upon the sacrificial offering of your faith, I am
glad." The witness of the Apostle's death is liturgical in character; it
is a matter of his life being spilled out as a sacrificial gift, of his
letting himself be spilled out for men.[14] What happens in this is a
becoming one with the self-giving of Jesus Christ, with his great act
of love, which is as such the true worship of God. The Apostle's
martyrdom shares in the mystery of the Cross of Christ and in its
theological status. It is worship being lived out in life, which is recognized as such by faith, and thus it is serving faith. Because this is
true liturgy, it achieves the end toward which all liturgy is directed:
joy—that joy which can arise only from the encounter between man
and God, from the removal of the barriers and limitations of earthly
existence.

What Paul briefly hints at here in a single short sentence has been
fully thought out in the account of the martyrdom of St. Polycarp.
The entire martyrdom is depicted as liturgy—indeed, as the process of
the martyr's becoming a Eucharist, as he enters into full fellowship
with the Pascha of Jesus Christ and thus becomes a Eucharist with
him. First we are told how the great bishop is fettered and his hands
are tied behind his back. Thus he appeared "as a noble *ram* (*lamb!*) out
of a great flock, for an oblation, *a whole burnt offering made ready and
acceptable to God*". The martyr, who has meanwhile been brought to
the ready-laid fire and bound there, now utters a kind of eucharistic
prayer: he gives thanks for the knowledge of God that has been imparted
to him through his beloved Son Jesus Christ. He praises God that he
has been found worthy to come to share in the cup of Jesus Christ in
the prospect of resurrection. Finally, using words from the book of
Daniel that were probably included in the Christian liturgy at an early
stage, he asks "may I, today, be received ... before thee as *a rich and
acceptable sacrifice*." This passage ends with a great doxology, just like

---

[14] Cf. Pierre Bonnard, "Mourir et vivre avec Jésus-Christ selon Saint Paul", RHPhR
36 (1956): 101–12.

Eucharistic Prayers in the liturgy. After Polycarp has said "Amen", the servants set fire to the woodpile, and now we are told of a triple miracle in which the liturgical character of the event is manifested in all its diversity. First, the fire swells out in the shape of a sail, which enfolds the saint all around. The blazing pile of wood appears like a ship with billowing sails, carrying the martyr beyond the bounds of earth and into the hands of God. But his burned-up body, so it is said, looked, not like burned flesh, but like *baked bread*. And then finally there is no smell of burned flesh arising, but those who were present became aware of a sweet odor "like that of incense or of costly spices". The *sweet smell*, in the Old Testament just as in the New, is an essential element in the theology of sacrifice. In the writings of Paul it is an expression for a life that has been made pure, giving forth, no longer the stench of lies and corruption or death's smell of decay, but the refreshing air of life and love, the atmosphere appropriate for God and one that heals people. Thus, the image of the sweet odor goes along with that of being changed into bread: the martyr has become like Christ; his life has become a gift. From him comes, not that poison of the power of death which undermines living things, but the dynamic force of life; he builds life up, just as good bread helps us live. The self-giving into the body of Christ has overcome the power of death: the martyr lives, and gives life, above all through his death, and thus he has himself entered into the eucharistic mystery. Martyrdom is the source of faith.[15]

This theology of martyrdom is found in its most popularized version in the story of St. Lawrence being roasted on the grill, which was seen at a very early stage as an image of Christian life as such: the troubles of life may turn into that purifying fire which gradually remolds us so that our life becomes a gift for God and for other people. In our own time, the martyrdom of St. Maximilian Kolbe is perhaps the most impressive demonstration of all this. He dies for someone else; he dies amid songs of praise; he is burned, and his ashes are scattered—his whole life is destroyed, and in that very way the radical self-giving, the giving away of himself, is consummated: whoever would save his life will lose it; and whoever loses his life will save it.

---

[15] The text in Greek and German is found in Andreas Lindemann and Henning Paulsen, *Die Apostolischen Väter* (Tübingen, 1992), 258–85; Greek and English text in *The Apostolic Fathers*, vol. 2, Loeb Classical Library (1913; Cambridge, Mass., and London, 1976), 307–45.

b. Worship Consistent with the Logos— Christian Living as a Eucharist

Let us end by listening to those two marvelous passages from the Letter to the Romans that I mentioned earlier. In 12:1 the Apostle exhorts the Romans to "present" their bodies—that is, themselves—"as a living sacrifice, holy and acceptable to God, which is your spiritual worship". Let us first look a little more closely at that last phrase, which is really impossible to translate. In the Greek it is λογικὴ λατρεία— worship characterized by logos. That is an expression that had developed in the sphere of the encounter of Jewish with Greek religion at around the time of Christ.[16] In contrast to the worship involving external sacrifices such as animals and things—and building on perceptions from Israel's time in exile—it is now being said that the true sacrifice to God is that of man's inmost being, which is itself transformed into worship. The word is the sacrifice; the sacrifice must be wordlike (*logikon*), but the word meant here is of course the "word" in which the whole of man's spirit sums itself up and expresses itself.

In Greek mysticism of the first centuries A.D., that was then developed into the notion that the divine logos itself is praying within man and is thus drawing man into its own participation in the Divine Being.[17] We find the same word, too, in the Roman Canon, where we ask, immediately before the Consecration, that our sacrifice may be made *rationabilis*. It is not enough—indeed, it is quite wrong—to translate

---

[16] The classic article by Odo Casel, "Die Λογικὴ φυσία der antiken Mystik in der christlichen Umdeutung", in JLW 4 (1924): 37–47, takes into account—as is consistent with the basic orientation of Casel's thought, with its somewhat negative stance toward the Old Testament—merely the Hellenistic Greek roots of this concept. It is certainly no accident that the idea and the term make their first appearance in the realm in which Judaism, Hellenism, and Christianity are in contact, such as in Philo, in the Odes of Solomon, and in the Jewish prayers of the seventh and eighth books of the Apostolic Constitutions. The idea, as such, had in fact fully developed within the Old Testament; we need only think of Hosea 14:3; Psalm 50 (49):8–14, "I will accept no bull from your house.... If I were hungry, I would not tell you.... Do I eat the flesh of bulls, or drink the blood of goats? Offer to God a sacrifice of thanksgiving"; Psalm 51 (50):16–17, "Were I to give a burnt offering, you would not be pleased. The sacrifice acceptable to God is a broken spirit"; Psalm 68 (67):31f.; Psalm 119 (118):108, "Accept my offerings of praise [lit., the offerings of my mouth], O Lord." We are justified in saying that the concept of the sacrifice of words derives from the Old Testament and that the door had thus been opened for the Christian concept of sacrifice and also for new developments arising from the encounter with Greek thought.

[17] Cf. the relevant passages and their interpretation in Schlier, *Römerbrief*, 356ff.

this as saying that it should become rational. We are asking rather that it may become a logos-sacrifice. In this sense we are asking for the gifts to be transformed—and then, again, not just for that; rather, this petition is going in the same direction as suggested by the Letter to the Romans: We ask that the Logos, Christ, who *is* the true sacrifice, may himself draw us into his act of sacrifice, may "logify" us, make us "more consistent with the word", "more truly rational", so that his sacrifice may become ours and may be accepted by God as ours, may be able to be accounted as ours. We pray that his presence might pick us up, so that we become "one body and one spirit" with him.[18] We ask that his sacrifice might become present not just in an exterior sense, standing over against us and appearing, so to speak, like a material sacrifice, that we might then gaze upon and regard as men once did the physical sacrifices of old. We would not in that case have entered into the New Covenant at all. We are asking rather that we ourselves might become a Eucharist with Christ and, thus, become acceptable and pleasing to God. What Paul is saying in the First Letter to the Corinthians about cleaving to the Lord, that we might become one with him in a single spiritual life— that is exactly what is meant.

I am persuaded that the Roman Canon has in its petition hit upon the real intention of Paul in his exhortation in Romans 12. The application of liturgical language to Christian life is not a moralizing allegory; it does not bypass the Cross and the Eucharist; on the contrary, it is correctly understood only when it is read in the context of the Eucharist and of the theology of the Cross. The corrections that are being made here to the ideas of Hellenistic mysticism are important ones, and they help us to see the true nature of Christian mysticism. The mysticism of identity, in which the Logos and the inner dimension of man blend together, is transcended by a christological mysticism: the Logos, who is the Son, makes us sons in the sacramental fellowship in which we are living. And if we become sacrifices, if we ourselves become conformed to the Logos, then this is not a process confined to the spirit, which leaves the body behind it as something distanced from God. The Logos himself has become a body and gives himself to us in his Body. That is why we are being urged to present our bodies as a form of worship consistent with the Logos, that is to

---

[18] Cf. Josef Andreas Jungmann, *Missarum Sollemnia*, vol. 2 (Freiburg, 1952), 236f.

say, to be drawn into the fellowship of love with God in our entire bodily existence, in bodily fellowship with Christ.[19]

Paul tells us in the following verses what that looks like: it signifies our "metamorphosis", our being reshaped in a way that takes us beyond this world's scheme of things, beyond sharing in what "people" think and say and do, and into the will of God—thus we enter into what is good and pleasing to God and perfect. The transformation of the gifts, which is to be extended to us—thus the Roman Canon, following the Letter to the Romans—has to become, for us ourselves, a process of remolding: bringing us out of our restricted self-will, out into union with the will of God. Self-will, however, is in reality a subordination to the schemes and systems of a given time, and, despite appearances, it is slavery; the will of God is truth, and entering into it is thus breaking out into freedom. It seems to me no accident that the following verses, 4 and 5, talk about the way we should become all of us one body in Christ. The bodies—that is, the bodily persons—that become a Eucharist no longer stand alongside each other but become one with and one in the one Body and in the one living Christ. Thus, the ecclesiological and eucharistic background of the whole train of thought clearly comes to light here.

c. Mission as Service in the Cosmic Liturgy

Still more important for our question about Eucharist and mission is the final passage we have to look at, Romans 15:16. Paul is here justifying his boldness in writing a letter to the Romans, whose congregation he neither founded nor knows at all well. The reason for the Letter to the Romans that Paul offers here is quite profound: his understanding of the office of apostle, of the task with which he has been charged, is manifested here in a depth that, despite all the great declarations

---

[19] Cf. Schlier, *Römerbrief*, 355f. The interpretation of Romans 12:1–2 in the commentary by Erik Peterson, which has now finally been edited from his posthumous papers by Barbara Nichtweiß and Ferdinand Hahn: *Der Brief an die Römer*, in *Schriften*, vol. 6 (Würzburg, 1997), 331f., is most profound. Peterson shows with great emphasis the connection with Christ's death on the Cross, understood as a cultic action, as likewise the cultic significance of these verses as a whole. He also underlines the silent polemic directed against animal sacrifice: "Anyone who sacrifices his body is making sacrifice more in conformity with the λόγος than anyone who presents animals to God" (332). On that basis, finally, he emphasizes the Logos nature of Christian worship: "The Logos nature of Christian faith, in contrast to all irrational beliefs and attitudes, can be recognized in it."

about the apostolate, appears nowhere else with such clarity. Paul says that he has written the letter "to be a minister of Jesus Christ to the Gentiles in the priestly service of the gospel of God, so that the offering of the Gentiles may be acceptable, sanctified by the Holy Spirit" (15:16). The Letter to the Romans, this word that has been written that it may then be proclaimed, is an apostolic action; more, it is a liturgical—even a cultic—event. This it is because it helps the world of the pagans to change so as to be a renewal of mankind and, as such, a cosmic liturgy in which mankind shall become adoration, become the radiance of the glory of God. If the Apostle is handing on the gospel by means of this letter, this is not a matter of religious or philosophical propaganda, nor is it a social mission or even a personal and charismatic enterprise, but (as Heinrich Schlier puts it) "the accomplishing of a mandate authorized by God, legitimized by him, and delegated by him to the Apostle". This is a priestly sacrificial action, an eschatological service of ministry: the fulfillment and the perfecting of the Old Testament sacrificial services. In this verse Paul presents himself—again, it is Schlier who says it—"as sacrificial priest of the eschatological cosmos".[20]

If, in the Letter to the Philippians, we found martyrdom being presented as a liturgical event, associated with the theology of the Cross and with eucharistic theology; if, in Romans 12, the same was being said to us about the Christian life as such; now it is the specifically apostolic service of preaching the faith that appears as a priestly activity, as actually performing the new liturgy, open to all the world and likewise worldwide, which has been founded by Christ. The connection with the Pascha of Jesus Christ and with his presence in the Church through the Eucharist is not immediately evident here. And yet we cannot disregard it. Here, too, the "cleaving to the Lord" that unites us with him in a life of body and soul is ultimately indispensable as a spiritual foundation. For without this concrete christological cohesion, the whole thing would just simply decline into a mere fellowship in thought, will, and activity—that is, it would be reduced to what relates

---

[20] Schlier, *Römerbrief*, 430f. Peterson, *Brief an die Römer*, 367, points out the connection between this passage and Isaiah 66:20: "And they shall bring all your brethren from all the nations as an offering [*minchah*] to the LORD." Peterson comments, "Paul feels himself to be the one who is carrying out this promise that was envisaged as being part of the end." There is also a reference to Isaiah 66:20 in Joseph A. Fitzmyer, *Romans*, Anchor Bible 33 (Doubleday, 1993), 712. Fitzmyer likewise emphasizes the connection with Philippians 2:17 and Romans 12:1.

to morality and rational considerations. That, however, is exactly what Paul is trying to counter by talking about liturgy, which he uses to show that mission is more than that: that it has a sacramental basis, that it involves being united in a concrete sense with the Body of Christ, which was sacrificed and is living eternally in the Resurrection. So the ideas that came to us in considering Romans 12 are after all being taken up and further developed. The Eucharist, if it continued to exist over against us, would be relegated to the status of a thing, and the true Christian plane of existence would not be attained at all. Conversely, a Christian life that did not involve being drawn into the Pascha of the Lord, that was not itself becoming a Eucharist, would remain locked in the moralism of our activity and would thus again fail to live up to the new liturgy that has been founded by the Cross. Thus, the missionary work of the Apostle does not exist alongside the liturgy; rather, both constitute a living whole with several dimensions.

5. Concluding Reflections: The Eucharist as the Source of Mission

What does that ultimately mean for the connection between the Eucharist and mission? In what sense can we say that the Eucharist is the source of mission? We cannot, as we have seen, talk as if the Eucharist were some kind of publicity project through which we try to win over people for Christianity. If we do so, then we are damaging both the Eucharist and mission. We might rather understand the Eucharist as being (if the term is correctly understood) the mystical heart of Christianity, in which God mysteriously comes forth, time and again, from within himself and draws us into his embrace. The Eucharist is the fulfillment of the promise made on the first day of Jesus' great week of climax: "I, when I am lifted up from the earth, will draw all men to myself" (Jn 12:32). In order for mission to be more than propaganda for certain ideas or trying to win people over for a given community—in order for it to come from God and lead to God, it must spring from a more profound source than that which gives rise to resource planning and the operational strategies that are shaped in that way. It must spring from a source both deeper and higher than advertising and persuasion. "Christianity is not the result of persuading people; rather, it is something truly great", as Ignatius of Antioch so beautifully puts it in one place (*Epistle to the Romans* 3:3).

The sense in which Thérèse of Lisieux is patroness of missions may help us to understand in what way that is meant. Thérèse never set foot in a missionary territory and was never able to practice any missionary activity directly. Yet she did grasp that the Church has a heart, and she grasped that love is this heart. She understood that the apostles can no longer preach and the martyrs no longer shed their blood if this heart is no longer burning. She grasped that love is all, that it reaches beyond times and places. And she understood that she herself, the little nun hidden behind the grille of a Carmel in a provincial town in France, could be present everywhere, because as a loving person she was there with Christ in the heart of the Church.[21] Is not the exhaustion of the missionary impulse in the last thirty years the result of our thinking only of external activities while having almost forgotten that all this activity must constantly be nourished from a deeper center? This center, which Thérèse calls simply "heart" and "love", is the Eucharist. For the Eucharist is not only the enduring presence of the divine and human love of Jesus Christ, which is always the source and origin of the Church and without which she would founder, would be overcome by the gates of hell. As the presence of the divine and human love of Christ, it is also always the channel open from the man Jesus to the people who are his "members", themselves becoming a Eucharist and thereby themselves a "heart" and a "love" for the Church. As Thérèse says, if this heart is not beating, then the apostles can no longer preach, the sisters can no longer console and heal, the laymen no longer lead the world toward the Kingdom of God. The heart must remain the heart, that through the heart the other organs may serve aright. It is at that point, when the Eucharist is being celebrated aright "in the upper room", in the inner sphere of reverent faith, and without any aim or purpose beyond that of pleasing God, that faith springs forth from it: that faith which is the dynamic origin of mission, in which the world becomes a living sacrificial gift, a holy city in which there is no longer any temple, because God the ruler of all is himself her temple, as is the Lamb. "And the city has no need of sun or moon to shine upon it, for the glory of God is its light, and its lamp is the Lamb" (Rev 21:22f.).

---

[21] Thérèse of Lisieux, "Manuscrit B (Lettre à soeur Marie du Sacré-Coeur)", in *Oeuvres complètes* (Cerf and Desclée, 1992), 225f. A profound interpretation of this text is to be found in Ulrich Wickert, *Leben aus Liebe: Thérèse von Lisieux* (Vallendar and Schönstatt, 1997), 15–40.

VIII. Eucharist—Communio—Solidarity

In this talk, which was presented during the Eucharistic Congress celebrated in the year 2002 in the Diocese of Benevento, the author explores in greater depth the relationship between the central mystery of the Church—the Sacrament of the Holy Eucharist—and the Church's most practical task: her work of sharing, reconciling, and unifying. These reflections were meant to help the participants in the Eucharistic Congress to celebrate the sacrament more worthily and to live more effectively Christ's new commandment: "Love one another."

In the early Church, the Eucharist was often called *agape*, "love", or simply *pax*, "peace". The Christians of that time thus expressed in a remarkable way the inseparable connection between the *mysterium* of the hidden presence of the Lord and the *praxis* of serving the cause of peace, of Christians *being* peace. No distinctions were made then between orthodoxy and orthopraxis, between right doctrine and right action, which some people are fond of contrasting today, whereby there is usually a hint of disdain for the word "orthodoxy": anyone who insists on right doctrine is seen as narrow-minded, rigid, potentially intolerant. In the final analysis, everything is supposed to depend on right action, whereas one can always argue about doctrine. The important thing, they say, is the fruit that doctrine produces, whereas it does not matter by what paths one arrives at just deeds.

Such a contrast would have been incomprehensible and unacceptable to the early Church, because the word "orthodoxy" does not mean "right doctrine" at all; rather, it means "the right way of worshipping and glorifying God". The early Christians were convinced that everything depends on being in the right relationship with God, on knowing what pleases him and what one can do to respond to him

From *On the Way to Jesus Christ*, trans. Michael J. Miller, 2nd ed. (San Francisco: Ignatius Press, 2005), 107–30.

in the right way. That is why Israel loved the law: from it, they knew what God's will is; they knew how to live righteously and how to worship God properly: by doing his will, which brings order into the world, by opening it to the transcendent. This was the new joy of the Christians: that they finally knew now, from Christ, how God should be glorified and how, precisely through that glorification, the world is set right. The fact that these two things belong together had been proclaimed by the angels on Christmas night: "Glory to God in the highest, and on earth peace among men with whom he is pleased", they said (Lk 2:14). God's glory and peace on earth are inseparable. Where God is shut out, peace on earth breaks down, and no godless orthopraxis can save us. For there is no such thing as right action without a knowledge of what is right. The will without knowledge is blind, and so action, orthopraxis, without knowledge is blind and leads into the abyss. The great deception of Marxism was to tell us that we had thought long enough about the world, that it was finally time to change it. But if we do not know what we should change it into, if we do not understand its intrinsic meaning and inner purpose, then change alone becomes destruction—as we have seen and continue to see. But the inverse is also true: doctrine alone, which does not become life and action, becomes idle chatter and thus becomes equally empty. The truth is concrete. Knowledge and action should go together, as faith and life belong together. This is precisely what is meant by combining the words Eucharist—Communio—Solidarity as the motto for the Eucharistic Congress in Benevento. Accordingly in the following remarks I will try to elaborate on the meaning of these three terms.

1. Eucharist

"Eucharist" is today—and rightly so—the most common name for the Sacrament of the Body and Blood of Christ, which the Lord instituted on the night before his Passion. In the early Church there was a series of other names for it—we have already mentioned *agape* and *pax*. Besides these there was, for example, also *synaxis*—an assembly, a gathering of individuals. Among the Protestants the sacrament is called "Supper", which is meant to be a return to the biblical origin, in keeping with Luther's claim that only Scripture has validity. In fact, in the letters of Paul this sacrament is called the "Supper of the Lord".

But it is significant that this title very soon disappeared and, by the second century, was no longer used. Why? Was this perhaps a departure from the New Testament, as Luther thought, or did it have some other significance?

No doubt, the Lord had instituted his sacrament within the context of a meal, specifically, as part of the Jewish Passover meal, and so at first it, too, was connected with a gathering at table. But the Lord had not ordered his disciples to repeat the Passover meal, which constituted the framework but was not *his* sacrament, not his new gift. Besides, the Passover meal could be celebrated only once a year. Furthermore, the celebration of the Eucharist was itself actually separated from the gathering at table as the separation from the law took place and the transition was made to a Church consisting of Jews and Gentiles, but mainly of former pagans. The connection with a supper thus proved to be extrinsic, indeed, as an occasion for misunderstandings and abuses, as Paul emphatically demonstrated in his First Letter to the Corinthians.

So it was part of the essential development of the Church that she slowly detached the Lord's own gift, that which was new and everlasting, from the old context and gave it a distinctive form. This happened, on the one hand, because it was combined with the liturgy of the word, which has its model in the synagogue, and, on the other hand, because the Lord's words of institution formed the climax of the great prayer of thanksgiving and blessing (*berakha*) that was derived from the synagogue traditions and so ultimately from the Lord, who had rendered thanks and praise to God in the Jewish tradition and lent new depth to this very thanksgiving through the sacrifice of his Body and Blood.[1]

The early Christians recognized that the essential thing that took place at the Last Supper was not the eating of the lamb and the other traditional dishes; rather, it was the great prayer of praise that now contained Jesus' words of institution as its centerpiece. With these words he had transformed his death into the gift of himself, so that we can now give thanks for this death. Yes, only now is it possible to render thanks to God unconditionally, because the most horrible thing—the

---

[1] The connection between the *berakha* (Greek: *eucharistia*, thanksgiving prayer) of the Last Supper and the Eucharistic Prayers of the Mass has been demonstrated in detail by Louis Bouyer, *Eucharistie: Théologie et spiritualité de la prière eucharistique* (Desclée, 1990) [trans. Charles Underhill Quinn as *Eucharist: Theology and Spirituality of the Eucharistic Prayer* (Notre Dame, Ind., and London: Univ. of Notre Dame Press, 1968)].

death of the Redeemer and the death of us all—has been transformed by an act of love into the gift of life.

So it was recognized that the essential element of the Last Supper was the *eucharistia*, what we call today the Eucharistic Prayer. *Eucharistia* is the translation of *berakha* and therefore means praise as well as thanksgiving and blessing. The *berakha* was the essential and central element of the Last Supper of Jesus; the Eucharistic Prayer, then, which incorporates this centerpiece, is derived immediately from the prayer of Jesus on the eve of his suffering and is the heart of the new spiritual sacrifice. That is why some of the Church Fathers described the Eucharist simply as "prayer", as the "sacrifice" of praise, as a spiritual sacrifice, which, however, also becomes material and transforms matter: bread and wine become the Body and Blood of Christ, the new food that nourishes us until the resurrection, for eternal life.

Thus the whole complex of words and material elements becomes a prefiguration of the eternal wedding feast. We will have to return again at the conclusion to these connections. Here we are concerned only with understanding better why we as Catholic Christians do not call this sacrament "Supper" but rather "Eucharist". The infant Church gradually gave to the sacrament its specific configuration, and precisely in this way, under the guidance of the Holy Spirit, she clearly identified and correctly represented in signs what is truly essential to it, what the Lord actually "instituted" on that night. It is precisely by examining this process in which the Sacrament of the Eucharist gradually took form that we can understand in a very beautiful way the profound connection between Scripture and tradition. Resorting to the Bible in isolation as a mere historical document does not sufficiently communicate to us an insight into what is essential. That appears only when the Bible is read in the living context of the Church, which has lived the Scriptures and so has understood their deepest aspirations and has made them accessible to us.

2. Communio

The second word in the motto of your Eucharistic Congress—Communio—has by now become quite a fashionable word. It is, in fact, one of the most profound and essential words of Christian tradition, but for this very reason it is extremely important to understand it in all its profundity and breadth. Perhaps I may interject here a rather personal observation. When together with a few friends—in particular, Henri de Lubac, Hans Urs von Balthasar, Louis Bouyer, Jorge Medina—I went about founding a periodical, in which we intended to set forth and develop the legacy of the Council, we looked for a name that would express as comprehensively as possible the purpose of this publication in *one* word. Already in 1965, the last year of Vatican II, a review had been founded that was supposed to be the permanent voice, so to speak, of the Council and its spirit, which therefore was called *Concilium*.

Hans Küng's book *Structures of the Church* may have played a role in this decision. Küng believed that he had discovered an equivalence between the words *ekklesia* (Church) and *concilium*. He argued that hidden beneath the surface of both terms was the Greek word *kalein* (to call); the one word, *ekklesia*, therefore meant "to call out", while the other word, *concilium*, meant "to call together": the same thing in either case, then. From these etymological notes he reasoned that the concepts of Church and council were in some way identical. He saw the Church as being by her very nature the ongoing Council of God in the world. The Church therefore was to be thought of as conciliar and actualized in the manner of a council; conversely, the Council was viewed as the fullest possible presence of "Church", the Church *in actu* [in act], so to speak.[2]

Over the next few years I occasionally pursued this idea, extremely enlightening at first, that the Church manifests herself in the world as the permanent assembly of God's councilors. The practical consequences of this idea are considerable, and its attractiveness is immediate. I eventually came to the conclusion that the vision of Hans Küng certainly contained some truth and was to be taken seriously, but that it was also in need of substantial revision.

I would like to summarize very briefly here the result of my studies at that time. Both philological studies and research into the practical understanding of church and council during the foundational period of the Church showed that a council can certainly be an important, vital manifestation of the Church, but that the Church herself is something more than that and her nature is more deeply rooted. A council

---

[2] Hans Küng, *Strukturen der Kirche*, QD 17 (Freiburg, 1962), especially 19–23 [trans. Salvator Attanasio as *Structures of the Church* (New York: T. Nelson, 1964), especially 9–15].

is something that the Church does, but the Church *is* not a council. The Church does not exist primarily to deliberate; rather, she exists to live the Word that has been given to us.

The word *koinonia*—in Latin, *communio*—occurred to me as the fundamental concept that expresses the very essence of the Church. The Church holds councils, but she *is* communion; that is more or less how I summarized my findings at that time.[3] The structure of the Church, therefore, should be described, not with the word "conciliar", but rather with the word "communional".

When I proposed these ideas publicly in 1969 in my book *Das neue Volk Gottes* [The new people of God], the concept of *communio* did not yet play an important part in theological and ecclesiastical circles; my thoughts on this subject, therefore, received scarcely any attention. They gave me a head start, however, in searching for a title for the new journal, which we did in fact call *Communio*.

The concept did not receive wide public recognition until the Synod of Bishops in 1985. Until then it had been thought that the new expression "people of God" held the key position in the terminology for the Church, since it was believed to have summed up the intentions of Vatican II. That might have been acceptable, too, if the expression had been understood in the fullness of its biblical meaning and in the broad context in which the Council had used it.

When a grand expression becomes a slogan, though, its meaning is inevitably diminished—indeed, trivialized. And so the Synod of 1985 sought a new beginning by focusing on the word *communio*, which refers first of all to the eucharistic center of the Church and thus anchors our understanding of the Church in the most intimate encounter between Jesus and mankind, in his act of giving himself to us.

It was unavoidable that this great fundamental concept of the New Testament, taken in isolation and used as a slogan, should also become shallow, indeed, positively trivialized. Those who speak today of an "ecclesiology of communion" generally mean two things: (1) they intend to contrast a pluralist, or "federalist", ecclesiology, so to speak, with a centralist conception of the Church; and (2) they want to emphasize

---

[3] Joseph Ratzinger, *Das neue Volk Gottes: Entwürfe zur Ekklesiologie* (Düsseldorf, 1969), 147–70. Cf. also Joseph Ratzinger, *Kirche, Ökumene und Politik* (Einsiedeln, 1987) [trans. Michael J. Miller et al. as *Church, Ecumenism, and Politics* (San Francisco: Ignatius Press, 2008)], in which I tried to sketch the main lines of an ecclesiology of communion (16–19 [English trans.: 17–20]).

the interconnectedness of the local Churches in the give-and-take of their exchanges as well as the pluralism of their cultural forms of expression in worship, discipline, and doctrine.[4]

Even when these tendencies are not elaborated in detail, *communio* is still generally understood in a horizontal sense—as a complex network of correlations. This concept of the *communio*-structure of the Church is barely distinguishable, then, from the conciliar vision mentioned above. The horizontal dominates. The emphasis is on the idea of self-determination within a community on a wide scale. Now in all this, naturally, there is much that is quite true. However, the basic approach is not correct, and thus its proponents lose sight of the true depth of what the New Testament and Vatican II, as well as the Synod of 1985, wanted to say.

To clarify the central meaning of the term *communio*, I would like to refer briefly to two great *communio* passages in the New Testament. The first is found in 1 Corinthians 10:16ff., where Paul tells us: "The cup of blessing which we bless, is it not a participation [in Greek, *koinonia*; in Latin, *communicatio*] in the blood of Christ? The bread which we break, is it not a participation in the body of Christ? Because there is *one* bread, we who are many are *one* body, for we all partake of the one bread" (emphasis added).

The concept of *communio* is anchored first and foremost in the most Blessed Sacrament of the Eucharist, which is why, in the language of the Church, we still describe the reception of this sacrament today, and rightly so, simply as "going to communion". The very practical social significance of this sacramental event thereby becomes immediately clear as well, and this in a radical way that is unattainable in merely horizontal perspectives. Here we are told that through this sacrament we enter, as it were, into a blood relationship with Jesus Christ, whereby blood, according to the Hebrew way of thinking, stands for "life". Thus the passage declares an interpenetration of Christ's life with ours.

Of course, "blood" in connection with the Eucharist also stands for self-giving [*Hingabe*], for a life that pours itself out, so to speak, gives itself away for us and to us. Thus the blood relationship is also involvement in the dynamic of this life, of this "blood poured out". Our

---

[4] A model for this type of *communio* ecclesiology—which admittedly has become coarsened in common usage—is provided in the book by Jean-Marie-Roger Tillard, *Église d'églises: L'Ecclésiologie de communion*, Cogitatio fidei 143 (Paris: Cerf, 1987).

existence is energized in such a way that life itself should become a "being for others", as we can see right before our eyes in the pierced heart of Christ.

In many respects the words about bread are even more striking. Bread stands for a bodily communion with Christ, which Paul compares to the union of husband and wife (cf. 1 Cor 6:17–18; Eph 5:26–32). Paul illuminates this from another perspective when he says that it is one and the same bread that we all receive in the sacrament. This is quite literally true: The "bread"—the new manna that God gives to us—is one and the same Christ for all. It is truly the one Lord himself whom we receive in the Eucharist, or better: the Lord who receives us and makes us part of him.

St. Augustine declared this in a saying that he had heard in a sort of vision: "Eat the bread of the strong, and yet you will not change me into yourself; rather, I will transform you into me." [5] In other words, the bodily nourishment that we consume is assimilated by the body and itself becomes a structural component of our body. But this bread is of another sort. It is greater and more substantial than we are. We do not assimilate it into ourselves, but rather it assimilates us into itself, so that we are conformed to Christ—in Paul's words, as members of his body, one in him.

We all "eat" *the same man*, not only the same thing; in this way we all are wrested from our self-enclosed individuality and drawn into a greater one. We all are assimilated into Christ, and so through communion with Christ we are also identified with one another, identical and one in him, members of one another. To be in communion with Christ is by its very nature to be in communion with one another as well. No more are we alongside one another, each for himself; rather, everyone else who goes to communion is for me, so to speak, "bone of my bone and flesh of my flesh" (cf. Gen 2:23).

A true spirituality of communion, therefore, together with its christological depth, necessarily has a social character also, as Henri de Lubac argued magnificently more than a half-century ago in his book *Catholicism*. For this reason, in my prayers at communion I must, on the one hand, look totally toward Christ, allowing myself to be transformed by him and, as needed, to be consumed in the fire of his love. But precisely for this reason I must always realize also that he joins me

---

[5] *Confessions* VII, 10, 16.

in this way with every other communicant—with the one next to me, whom I may not like very much; but also with those who are far away, whether in Asia, Africa, America, or some other place. By becoming one with them, I must learn to open myself toward them and to become involved in their situations. This is the test of the authenticity of my love for Christ.

Whenever I am united with Christ, I am also united with my neighbor, and this unity does not end at the communion rail; rather, it is just beginning there. It comes alive, becomes flesh and blood, in the everyday experience of being with others and standing by others. Thus the individual element in my going to communion is inseparably interwoven with my membership in the Church and my dependence upon her life.

Church does not arise from a loose federation of communities. She originates in the one bread, in the one Lord, and thanks to him she is first and foremost and everywhere the one and only Church, the one body that comes from the one bread. She does not become one through a centralist form of government; instead, one common center for all is possible because she is always derived from the one Lord, who in the one bread makes her to be one body. That is why her unity goes deeper than any human union could ever go. It is when the Eucharist is understood in the full intimacy of the union of each individual with the Lord that it automatically becomes also a social sacrament in the highest degree.

The great socially committed saints, therefore, were always great eucharistic saints as well. I would like to mention just two examples, selected entirely at random. First, the beloved figure of St. Martin de Porres, who was born in 1569 in Lima, Peru, the son of a black mother from Panama and a Spanish nobleman. Martin lived on adoration of the Lord present in the Eucharist and spent entire nights in prayer before the crucifix, whereas by day he tirelessly cared for the sick and assisted the socially disadvantaged, to whom he, a mulatto, felt close by reason of his ethnic descent as well. The encounter with the Lord, who gives himself to us from the Cross and makes all of us members of one body through the one bread, was converted logically into service rendered to the suffering, into care for the weak and the forgotten.

In our time, the image of Mother Teresa of Calcutta is right before our eyes. Wherever she opened houses of her sisters in order to serve the dying and outcast, the first thing she asked for was a place for the tabernacle, because she knew that the strength for such service could only come from there. Whoever recognizes the Lord in the tabernacle recognizes him in the suffering and the needy; he is among those to whom the Judge of the world will say: "I was hungry and you gave me food, I was thirsty and you gave me drink, ... I was naked and you clothed me, I was sick and you visited me, I was in prison and you came to me" (Mt 25:35–36).

Very briefly I would like to refer to a second important New Testament text under the heading of *communio* (*koinonia*). It is found right at the beginning of the First Letter of John (1:3–7). The author of the letter speaks initially about the encounter with the Word-made-flesh that was granted to him. John can say that he is passing on what he has seen with his own eyes and touched with his own hands. This encounter has given him the gift of *koinonia*—*communio*—with the Father and his Son, Jesus Christ. It has become a true communication and participation. This communion with the living God, he tells us, brings man into the light. He can now see and lives in the light, that is, in the truth of God, which is expressed in the one, new, all-encompassing commandment—the commandment to love.

And so communion with the "Word of life" automatically becomes righteous living; it becomes love; furthermore it becomes communion with one another: "If we walk in the light, as he is in the light, we have fellowship [*koinonian, communionem*] with one another" (1 Jn 1:7). The text demonstrates to us the same logic of *communio* that we have already found in Paul: communicating with Jesus becomes communion with God himself, communion with light and with love; it becomes in this way righteous living, and all of this unites us with one another in truth. Only when we see the depth and breadth of *communio* in this way do we have something to say to the world.

3. Solidarity

Finally, let us examine the third key word, "solidarity". Whereas the first two words, "Eucharist" and "*communio*", are taken from the Bible and from Christian tradition, this word comes to us from outside. The concept of "solidarity"—as Archbishop Paul Cordes has shown—was first developed in the context of early socialist thought by Pierre Leroux

(d. 1871) as a counterpart to the idea of Christian charity, to be the new, reasonable, and effective response to social problems.[6]

Karl Marx declared that Christianity had had a millennium and a half to demonstrate its capabilities and was now sufficiently convinced of its own ineffectiveness; now new measures had to be taken. For decades many believed that the socialist model summed up in the concept of solidarity was at last the way to achieve equality for all, to eliminate poverty, and to bring about peace in the world. Today, we can survey the rubble in a landscape ruined by a godless social theory and praxis.

It is undeniable that the liberal model of the market economy produced great achievements in some parts of the world, especially in places where it was tempered and corrected by the influence of Christian social thought. The legacy left behind by the confrontation of world powers and of economic interests, especially in Africa, is all the more tragic because of this.[7] Behind the superficial solidarity of the developing-nations model has sometimes been hidden the desire to expand the reach of one's own power, one's own ideology, one's own market share. In the process, old social structures have been destroyed, and spiritual and moral forces have been wasted, with consequences that should ring in our ears as an unprecedented indictment.

No, without God it just does not work. And since God has shown us his face, spoken his name, and entered into communion with us only in Christ, ultimately it will not work without Christ.

There is no question that Christians, too, during the centuries of the modern period, have incurred a heavy debt. Slavery and the slave trade remain a bleak chapter in our history; these practices show how un-Christian the Christians were, how far they were from the faith and love of the gospel, from true communion with Jesus Christ. On the other hand, the faith-filled charity and humble self-sacrifice of so many priests and nuns provided a counterbalance and left a testament of love that mitigated the horror of exploitation, even if it could not abolish it. We must build upon this witness and continue along this path.

---

[6] Paul Josef Cordes, *Communio: Utopie oder Programm?* QD 148 (Freiburg: Herder, 1993), 29–32.

[7] A disturbing insight into this tragic legacy and into the cruelty of the liberal capitalist system is offered by Peter Scholl-Latour, *Afrikanische Totenklage: Der Ausverkauf des Schwarzen Kontinents* (Munich, 2001).

Along these lines the concept of solidarity has slowly been transformed and Christianized in recent decades, especially in the Holy Father's writings on social justice, so that today we can rightly combine it with the themes of "Eucharist" and "*communio*". Solidarity in this sense means standing up for one another, the healthy for the sick, the rich for the poor, the countries of the North for those of the South, in the knowledge that we have a mutual responsibility and with the awareness that it is in giving that we receive, that we can only give that which has been given to us, which therefore never simply belongs to us for our own sake.

Today we see that it is not enough to pass on technical know-how, intellectual knowledge, and the theory or even the practice of particular political structures. All that is no help—it is even harmful—unless there is also an awakening of the spiritual forces that give meaning to these technologies and structures and make it possible to apply them responsibly. It was easy for the Enlightenment to destroy to a great extent the traditional religions, which now—deprived of their best elements—live on as subcultures and can harm people, body and soul, as systems of superstition. It would have been necessary to salvage the core of these religions and to open them up to Christ and thus to bring to fulfillment the quiet expectation that is within them. Through such a process of purification and development, continuity and progress would be fruitfully united. Where the missions were successful, they followed this path in practice and thus helped to develop the forces of faith that we need so urgently. During the crisis of the 1960s and 1970s, many missionaries were of the opinion that mission work, that is, the proclamation of the gospel of Jesus Christ, was no longer opportune; now it was simply a matter of providing services for the sake of social development. But how can positive social development be achieved if we become illiterate in relation to God?

The tacit assumption that peoples and tribes should keep their own religions and not be bothered with ours only shows that the faith had grown cold in the hearts of such men, despite a considerable measure of goodwill; it demonstrates that their communion with the Lord was no longer alive. How else could they have thought that it was a good thing to exclude other people from it?

The basis for this—often unrecognized—is a disdain for religion in general and by no means a respect for the other religions, as it would appear. Religion is viewed as an archaic vestige in mankind that has to be left in place but that ultimately has nothing to do with the real aim of development. It seems that what religions say and do is basically irrelevant; they are thought to be excluded from the rational sphere, and their contents are ultimately unimportant. The orthopraxis that is anticipated on the basis of this disdain is truly built on sand.

It is high time to abandon this misguided way of thinking. We need faith in Jesus Christ, if for no other reason than because it joins together reason and religion. Thus it provides us with standards of responsibility and unbinds the force needed to live according to this responsibility. Sharing on all levels, in both the material and the spiritual realm, in the ethical as well as the religious sphere, is part of solidarity between peoples and continents. It is clear that we must further develop our economy in such a way that the bottom line is, no longer merely the interests of a particular country or group of countries, but the welfare of the whole world. This is difficult and is never fully achieved. It requires that we cut back and do without. But once there is a spirit of solidarity that is truly nourished by the faith, this does become possible, although always in an imperfect way.

The theme of globalization would be pertinent to this discussion, but I cannot go into it here. It is clear that nowadays we all depend on one another. But there is a sort of globalization that is conceived of unilaterally in terms of special interests, whereas there ought to be a kind of globalization in which all parties take real responsibility for one another and each one carries someone else's burden. All this cannot be put into practice in a value-neutral way, relying solely upon marketplace mechanisms. Preexisting values are always determinants in making market decisions.

In this regard our religious and moral horizon is always decisive, as well. If globalization in technology and economy is not accompanied by a new openness to an awareness of the God to whom we will all render an account, then it will end in catastrophe. This is the great responsibility imposed on us Christians today.

Christianity has always had its origins in the one Lord, the one bread, which seeks to make us one body, with a view to the unification of mankind. If we, precisely at the moment when a hitherto unimaginable external unification of humanity comes about, fail as Christians and suppose that we cannot or should not give anything more, we will be incurring a heavy responsibility. For any unity that is created without God, or even in opposition to him, ends like the experiment of Babylon: in total confusion and destruction, in the hatred and violence of universal conflict.

4. Perspective: The Eucharist as the Sacrament of Transformations

Let us return to the Most Holy Eucharist. What actually happened on the night when Christ was betrayed? Let us listen to the Roman Canon—the heart of the *Eucharistia* [Eucharistic Prayer] of the Church at Rome:

> The day before he suffered, [Jesus] took bread in his sacred hands, and looking up to heaven, to you, his almighty Father, he gave you thanks and praise. He broke the bread, gave it to his disciples, and said: "Take this, all of you, and eat it: this is my body, which will be given up for you."
>
> When supper was ended, he took the cup. Again he gave you thanks and praise, gave the cup to his disciples, and said: "Take this, all of you, and drink from it: this is the cup of my blood, the blood of the new and everlasting covenant. It will be shed for you and for all so that sins may be forgiven. Do this in memory of me."

What is happening in these words? First of all the word "transformation" comes to mind. Bread becomes body, his body. The bread of the earth becomes the bread of God, the "manna" from heaven, with which God nourishes man in a way that transcends earthly life and looks ahead to the Resurrection—which prepares for the Resurrection, indeed, initiates it. The Lord, who could have changed stones into bread, who was capable of raising up children to Abraham from stones, willed to transform bread into body, his body. Is that possible? How can it be? The questions that the people in the synagogue of Capernaum asked are inevitable for us as well. He is standing there, in the presence of his disciples, with his body; how can he say over the bread: "This is my body"? Now it is important to pay close attention to what the Lord really says. He does not simply say: "This is my body"; rather, he says: "This is my body, which is given up for you." It can become gift, because it is given up. Through the act of self-giving it becomes capable of communicating and is itself changed into a gift. We can observe the same thing in the words spoken over the cup. Christ does not simply say: "This is my blood"; rather, he says:

"This is my blood, which will be shed for you." Because it is shed, inasmuch as it is poured out, it can be given.

But now a new question arises: What does this mean, "given up" and "shed"? What is going on here? Well, Jesus is killed; he is nailed to a cross and dies there amid torments. His blood is shed, first on the Mount of Olives when he agonizes over his mission, then in the scourging, in the crowning with thorns, at the crucifixion, and after his death in the piercing of his heart. What is happening here is first of all an act of violence, of hatred, that tortures and destroys.

At this point we run into a second, deeper level of transformation: he transforms, from within, men's act of violence against him into an act of self-giving for these men—into an act of love. This becomes dramatically evident in his struggle in Gethsemane on the Mount of Olives. What he says in the Sermon on the Mount he now puts into action: he does not counter violence with new violence, as he could have done, but rather he puts an end to violence by transforming it into love. The act of killing, of death, is changed into love; violence is conquered by love.

This is the fundamental transformation upon which all the rest is based. It is the genuine transformation that the world needs and that alone is capable of redeeming the world. Because Christ from within transforms violence into an act of love and thus conquers it, death itself is transformed: love is stronger than death. It lasts. And so within this transformation is contained the further transformation of death into resurrection, of the dead body into the risen body. Although the first man was a living being, as St. Paul says, the new Adam, Christ, becomes through this process a life-giving spirit (1 Cor 15:45). The Risen One *is* self-gift, is life-giving spirit, and as such is communicable, indeed, communication.

This does not mean farewell to matter; rather, in this way material existence reaches its goal: without the material process of death and the interior victory over it, all of this would not be possible. And so, in the transformation of the Resurrection, the whole Christ continues to exist but is transformed now in such a way that bodily existence and self-giving are no longer mutually exclusive but complementary.

Before taking the next step, let us try to survey all this again and to understand it. During the Last Supper Jesus anticipates and already accomplishes the Calvary event. He accepts death through the Cross and by his acceptance transforms the act of violence into an act of self-giving, of pouring himself out—"I am to be poured [out] as a libation", St. Paul says from this perspective about his own imminent martyrdom (Phil 2:17). At the Last Supper the Cross is already present, accepted by Jesus and transformed.

This first and fundamental transformation draws the subsequent ones after it—the mortal body is transformed into the resurrected body: into "life-giving spirit". From there the third transformation becomes possible: the gifts of bread and wine, which are gifts of creation and at the same time the product of human acceptance and "transformation" of creation, are changed, so that in them the Lord who gives himself— his gift, he himself—becomes present, because he *is* self-giving. It is not a trait of his; rather, it is he himself.

From there the prospect opens onto two further transformations, which are involved in the Eucharist from the moment of its institution: the transformed bread, the transformed wine, in which the Lord gives himself as a life-giving spirit, are there in order to transform us men, so that we become one bread with him and then one body with him. The transformation of the gifts, which only continues the fundamental transformations of the Cross and Resurrection, is not the point of arrival; rather, it is in turn a beginning. The goal of the Eucharist is the transformation of those who receive it in authentic communion with his [Christ's] transformation. And so the goal is unity, that we, instead of being separated individuals who live alongside or in conflict with one another, might become, with Christ and in him, one organism of self-giving and might live unto the resurrection and the new world.

With that, the fifth and final transformation involved in this sacrament becomes visible: through us, who have been transformed and have become one body, a life-giving spirit, all creation must be transformed. All of creation must become a "new city", a new paradise, the living dwelling place of God: "that God may be everything to every one" (1 Cor 15:28)—so Paul describes the goal of creation, which is supposed to come about starting from the Eucharist.

Thus the Eucharist is a process of transformations in which we become involved, God's power to transform hatred and violence, God's power to transform the world. Therefore we pray that the Lord will help us to celebrate the Eucharist in this way and to live it. Therefore we pray that he will transform us, and the world together with us, into the new Jerusalem.

IX. "Built from Living Stones": The House of God and the Christian Way of Worshipping God

1. The Biblical Message about the Temple Made from Living Stones

The phrase "living stones" is taken from the First Letter of Peter; its meaning, however, pervades the entire New Testament—it is characteristic of the way the hope of the Old Covenant is transformed and intensified in the face of the crucified and risen Jesus Christ. The verses in the Letter of Peter referring to the spiritual house built from living stones belong to a textual unit that may be regarded as an early baptismal catechesis, as an introduction to the Christian faith in which the inner claim of the process experienced by a person in baptism is interpreted.[1] According to these verses, it belongs to the fundamental content of this process that baptized Christians are fitted into a growing edifice that has Christ as its foundational stone. Various motifs run together here. The words from the Psalter about the stone that was rejected by the builders (Ps 118:22) are incorporated. In the prayer of Israel this was a message of comfort and hope during the trying experiences of her history. The rejected stone that became the cornerstone was Israel herself—the people who counted for nothing in the game of the powers who created history, the people who were thoughtlessly cast aside

---

Reprinted with permission from *A New Song for the Lord: Faith in Christ and Liturgy Today*, trans. Martha M. Matesich, 2nd ed. (New York: Crossroad, 2005), 78–93.

[1] For the exegesis, cf. Karl Hermann Schelkle, *Die Petrusbriefe: Der Judasbrief*, HThKNT, vol. 13, pt. 2 (Freiburg, 1961), 57–63; the following are also recommended from the wealth of literature available: Joseph Coppens, "Le Sacerdoce royal des fidèles: Un Commentaire de I Petri II,4–10", in *Au service de la parole de Dieu: Mélanges offerts à Mgr. A. M. Charue* (Gembloux, 1969), 61–75; John Hall Elliott, *The Elect and the Holy: An Exegetical Examination of 1 Peter 2:4–10*, Novum Testamentum Supplements 12 (Leiden, 1966). On the parallel text, Eph 2:19–22, see Joachim Gnilka, *Der Epheserbrief*, HThKNT, vol. 10, pt. 3 (Freiburg, 1971), 152–60; on the stone motif in the New Testament in general, see Johannes Betz, "Christus—petra—Petrus", in *Kirche und Überlieferung*, ed. Johannes Betz and Heinrich Fries (Freiburg, 1960), 1–21.

and did not seem to belong anywhere except to the building rubble of world history. Standing before their God they knew that the mystery of election reigned over them and that they were in reality the cornerstone. But in the fate of Jesus Christ, these words were then fulfilled in a completely unexpected way. Oddly enough, the psalm from which they are taken, Psalm 118, had also been messianically interpreted in early Judaism, but it had not occurred to anyone to deduce from this that the Messiah would suffer. On the contrary, according to this exegesis the coming of the Messiah spelled the realization of the triumphant message found in these verses: through him Israel would finally arise from the rubble and become the cornerstone. But when the Bible is read anew in a dialogue with the risen Christ, the phrase about the rejected stone appears as a prophecy of suffering, a prediction of the crucified Christ who became the cornerstone from the Cross and *in this way* made Israel the cornerstone. Two phrases from Isaiah (28:16 and 8:14) that were also integrated into the early Christian catechesis reinforce this view. All these texts, however, ultimately say the same thing: Becoming a Christian means becoming part of the building erected on the rejected stone. They speak of the passion and the glory of the Church, which is always subject to the law of the castaway stone. Precisely in this way the Church fulfills the dream of hope, which ultimately supports all human construction. The building done by humans aims at the construction of a place to stay; it seeks security, a home, freedom. It is a declaration of war against death, against insecurity, against fear, against loneliness. For this reason the desire of men to build is fulfilled in the Temple, in that building into which they invite God. The Temple is the expression of the human longing to have God as a fellow occupant, the longing to be able to reside with God and thus to experience the perfect way of living, the consummate community, which banishes loneliness and fear once and for all. The idea of the Temple is really the cohesive motif in the various verses about the stone that are found in the First Letter of Peter and in related New Testament texts. After the horrible catastrophe of Jerusalem in which the people, in a terrible misunderstanding of the Promise and under the impression that God would ultimately defend his residence, had turned the Temple into the site of a vicious battle right up into the Holy of Holies—after this catastrophe Christianity really knew what it had actually known since the Cross and Resurrection anyway: that the true temple of God is built from living stones. It knows that the true temple of God has not been destroyed and that it is in fact indestructible. It knows that God himself erects this temple and that the primordial dream of God dwelling among his people is fulfilled in those who trust in the rejected stone—they themselves are the temple.

a. Old Testament Roots

The few sentences that mention the living stones in 1 Peter therefore include an account that has come a long way, and they show the new slant Christian faith has given this account. In order to clarify what is audible here—the understanding of God's presence in the world, of his dwelling among men, and the understanding of Church and Christian existence that this entails, I would like to examine to some extent at least two stages of the path taken for granted in this text. First of all we must look back at the beginning of the Temple in Israel. After fighting many battles, David has finally been able to secure the realm. His monarchy is unchallenged; he lives in a palace built of cedar. Israel has overcome the period of her unsettledness, her wandering, and her homelessness and is now permanently housed in the Promised Land. Her God, however, continues to dwell in the tabernacle, as he did during the time Israel wandered in the desert—he has remained a homeless, a wandering God, so to speak. David senses the contradiction here, the anachronistic nature of this state of affairs in which two stages of civilization exist side by side—in which God has been left behind in the nomadic phase and should now be brought into that which has been newly attained. He wants to build God an appropriate house, and at first he finds himself encouraged by the prophet Nathan. But then, before long, the word of God comes to Nathan with a new directive, which states: "Are you the one to build me a house to live in? ... The Lord declares to you that the Lord will make *you* a house" (2 Sam 7:5, 11). In these verses a breakthrough and radical change in the religious history of mankind appear on the scene, whose dimensions would become clear only centuries later. In principle the change has already occurred here but admittedly still required the Passion of Jesus the Son. Men do not build a house for God; God builds a house for men. God himself executes God's building. What the house built by God consists of becomes clear in the subsequent verses of Nathan's prophecy: it consists of people. It consists in the kingdom remaining in the house of David forever. It consists in God's grace being more powerful than all the sins of this house. The house of David will be punished for its sins, but it will not be destroyed. Through all the decline and decay it stands; God builds it up. Here it is predicted that David's kingdom and his house, which will become God's own building, will last forever. For the first time the features emerge of that son of David who endures all the sin of the world and in whom the greater power of grace is living presence. David does not build; God builds. Through all the destruction of sin and guilt, God, in indestructible graciousness, builds a kingdom by means of which he himself reigns and dwells among his people. God remains the homeless one for whom every building of stone is too small and who in spite of this finds room in men, especially in men. His indwelling transpires in grace that builds. It is perhaps seldom that one can grasp the inner unity of the Testaments as palpably as in this bold scene of the prophecy of Nathan. Compared with this central point of view, the Temple of Solomon along with its successors has only "come in in-between", to adopt a phrase of St. Paul. A verse in the Nathan prophecy definitely refers to it as well; here we can leave the question aside whether this verse has come from a later theological redaction, as prominent Old Testament exegetes assume, or whether it is original.[2] With regard to the real issue, it is in any case peripheral to the main drift of the prophecy, referring to an intermediate solution that was unavoidable, but which must remain an intermediate solution and not become the goal of the Promise. God cannot simply be housed like a man on a new cultural level as if he also had to go through the stages of human development. The homelessness of the nomadic years has made him known more accurately than the housing of the advanced civilization that wanted to hold him captive in the human dimensions.

b. New Testament Fulfillment

Only against this background can the New Testament scene of the cleansing of the Temple be understood correctly, which, according to what the evangelists imply, became the definitive starting point of Jesus'

---

[2] On the problem of interpreting the text of 2 Sam 7:1–29, cf. Hans Wilhelm Hertzberg, *Die Samuelbücher*, ATD 10, 3rd ed. (Göttingen, 1965). On the entire complex of the theology of the temple, see Yves Congar, *Le Mystère du temple* (Paris, 1957).

Passion but which at the same time also decisively helped to bring to light the true depth of his mission. Without this incident, the different sayings about the building and the living stones would not have arisen.[3] In general the account of the expulsion of the money changers and sheep and cattle dealers from the holy precinct is understood much too innocuously. We have the impression that Jesus acted in holy anger much like someone who would pounce on the sellers of devotional objects and denounce their improper linking of faith and business. But it is not quite that simple. In the Temple district the Roman currency with its images of pagan gods or deified emperors could not be used; exchange bureaus were therefore needed to convert the secular currency into the currency of the Temple. This was a completely legitimate practice just like the one of providing animals that were needed for worship in the Temple and were sacrificed there. What Jesus does is of a very fundamental nature. It follows along the lines of the momentous words to the Samaritan woman: the true worshippers will worship in spirit and truth (Jn 4:23)—not on Mount Gerizim or on Mount Zion. The action of Jesus is an assault on the existing form of the Temple in general, a prophetic action that symbolically anticipates the demolition of the Temple. From the Messiah one expected a reform of the cult (see Mal 3:1–5; 1:11)—the cleansing of the Temple is its prophetic-symbolic execution.

But what is it aiming at? What do the new cult and the new temple that Jesus seeks to achieve with his prophetic gesture look like? According to the Synoptic Gospels Jesus explained the meaning of this gesture with a saying that combines Isaiah 56:7 and Jeremiah 7:11. In Isaiah 56:7 we find the statement: "My house shall be called a house of prayer for all peoples." Here we must pay attention to the fact that the cleansing of the Temple took place in the so-called *hieron*, the court of the Gentiles. Whereas only members of the chosen people could participate in the sacrificial worship of Israel in the Temple court—the so-called *naos*—there was supposed to be room in the large court surrounding it

---

[3] On the theme of Jesus and the Temple, see Yves Congar, *Le Mystère*, 133–80, as well as the substantial material in Rudolf Bultmann, *Das Evangelium des Johannes* (Göttingen, 1957), 85–91; and Rudolf Schnackenburg, *Das Johannesevangelium*, vol. 1, HThKNT, vol. 4, pt. 1 (Freiburg, 1965), 359–71 [trans. Cecily Hastings et al. as *The Gospel according to St. John* (New York, 1980)]. The reader will readily note that in what follows I am not trying to enter into the debate about the *ipsissima facta et verba* of Jesus, but simply trying to describe the Jesus of the Gospels—certainly a worthwhile and largely neglected undertaking after so many depictions of the "historical Jesus".

for all peoples to pray with Israel to the God of the whole world. In the intervening period, however, this place of prayer had long since become a livestock market and an exchange bank; the cult of the law had crushed the broad reach of the words that called all men. In the false positivism of obedience to the law one had taken away the prayer space kept open for all the people. The cleansing of the Temple is in fact a gesture of opening the Temple for all people; it is a prophetic anticipation of the promised pilgrimage of all people to the God of Israel. In the explanation Jesus gives for his action, however, God's words from Jeremiah 7:11 are also discernible: "Has this house, which is called by my name, become a den of robbers in your sight? You know, I too am watching, says the Lord." This saying in Jeremiah was directed against that blind policy which, in a foolish overestimation of its own strengths, did not keep to the relationship of subjugation under Babylon and risked war since it was thought that the Lord of heaven and earth would defend his Temple regardless of the circumstances. After all, he cannot be deprived either of his dwelling place in the world or of his worship. God becomes a factor in a foolish political calculation, and the Temple becomes a "den of robbers" in which the people imagine themselves to be safe in an earthly fashion. This leads to the first destruction of the Temple and to the first dispersal of Israel. Jesus repeats Jeremiah's warning at a time when similar political ventures are already clearly in the offing, and, like Jeremiah, he becomes a martyr because he defends the true dwelling of God against its earthly confiscation.

From this perspective we can now understand the puzzling words Jesus speaks to the Jews in John's Gospel in response to their question about the sign through which he shows his authorization for reforming the cult: "Destroy (*lysate*) this temple, and in three days I will raise it up" (2:19). In a disguised way Jesus is prophesying the end of the Temple and with it the end of the law, the end of the present form of the covenant. But in a way that is no less mysterious he weaves his own fate into this. The cleansing of the Temple becomes a prophecy of his death and a promise of his Resurrection. Regardless of what its precise formulation may have been, this saying was so bold and so unprecedented that the first three Gospels did not dare to recount it directly. They quote it only indirectly, on the lips of the false witnesses at Jesus' trial and on the lips of those mocking Jesus at the foot of the Cross (Mk 14:58 and Mt 26:61; Mk 15:29 and Mt 27:40). From this we know that the crime against the cult—the attack on the Temple and thus on the very center of religion, the worship of God—played a major role in Jesus' martyrdom. The fact that the first martyr in the history of the Church, Stephen, was also killed because he had attacked the Temple shows how sensitive this issue was. In this context it is also understandable why the Synoptics shied away from placing these words directly in the mouth of Jesus: that would have caused the failure of the attempt to unite all Israel in the faith in Jesus, an attempt that would still continue for a long time. The power of the words is weakened for the sake of peace. John, seeing that the separation has irreparably happened, is the first to come to the fore in an uninhibited way with the sharp clarity of the beginning. But what is actually being said here? It is prophesied that a living body that has gone through death will take the place of the stone Temple. It is prophesied that the period of sacrifice according to the law is over and that he who is raised from the dead to new life takes its place. It is prophesied that he, the rejected stone, will become the cornerstone of God's new house. The crucified body of Jesus Christ who stretches his hands out over the whole world (cf. John 12:32) is the site where God and men meet. The Risen One is the perpetual abiding of men in God and of God in men; he is the truth that replaces the images; he is the fount of the Spirit through whom worship in spirit and truth becomes possible. Through him God builds his house. If we look back from here to the starting point, the prophecy of Nathan, we can see that Jesus indeed does not destroy the Old Covenant, but only pushes aside that which has "come in in-between" and lays bare the core—fulfills the essence of the promise. But something else becomes clear as well: to be fitted into the new house as a living stone means to undergo the fate of the Passion. The fate of the cornerstone reveals the plan of the entire building. One had to suffer and die for the breakthrough out of the narrowness of legal positivism and its national particularism. The new dimension will not be achieved without the passion of transformation. When describing the congregation or the Church as the new temple, as God's building, as God's house, or as the body of Christ, early Christian preaching could draw its concepts from already existing rough drafts, for instance, from Qumran, which was also familiar with the designation temple for the congregation.[4] But only through

---

[4] Cf. Schnackenburg, *Das Johannesevangelium*, 1:365. The ideas touched on here concerning the unity of the Testaments and the "must" of the Passion I tried to expand and explain further in a lecture on Israel, the Church, and the world given in Jerusalem in

the death of Jesus Christ did this insight acquire real meaning. From a spiritualized way of speaking it had become the most concentrated of all reality. The spiritual temple was no longer a spiritual cliché, but a reality paid for in body and blood whose vitality was able to permeate the centuries.

2. What Prompted the Building of Christian Churches?

But now it is time to ask: Does all this not stand in crass opposition to what we are doing here? After all, are we not honoring the stone building in which we are again trying to pull God into the world, as was done before?[5]

Since Constantine, have we not regressed into that interim period again, that in-between time which Christ overcame through his Passion and Resurrection? Has not the Church with the magnificence of her cathedrals strayed from the simplicity of Jesus and retreated down the path away from the direction in which Jesus pointed? Are we not passing off as Christian what in truth is a sign of its loss? Indeed, rather than celebrating the anniversary of a stone building, should we not be striding away from the fossilized past in a bold and resolute manner? Should we not instead be building a new community that worships God by taking care of men in a radical way? Did not that author point out the right path who quite consciously entitled his religious instruction *The House of Man* in order to steer people away from the houses of God and to that house of man whose construction would be a real imitation of Jesus? Even if we want to be less radical in our formulations, we must at least ask: What are we celebrating when we celebrate the millennium of a cathedral? How should we celebrate in order to remain on that path which leads from Nathan to the temple prophecy of Jesus, the rejected cornerstone?

Before we try to answer these questions it will be helpful to consider the following: What did the situation really look like in the emerging Church? What conclusions did the Church draw from the words and action of Jesus? How did it come about that by the time

---

1994; it has been published in my little book *Evangelium, Katechese und Katechismus* (Munich, 1995), 63–83.

[5] This essay was written as a speech for the celebration of the millennium of the Cathedral of Mainz.

of Constantine's triumph a type of church construction was already fully developed? How did one perceive it? How were spirit and stone related to each other? There is scholarly research on all these questions whose results are very complex and also in part still very controversial. From these I would like to select just three basic themes:

1. Like Jesus himself, the apostles loved the Temple as a place of prayer. From the Acts of the Apostles (3:1) we know that Peter and John went "up to the temple at the hour of prayer, at three o'clock in the afternoon", but of course not to take part in the afternoon Tamid offering "but because it is the hour at which the true Tamid and Passover sacrifice bleeds to death; with the community they praise the Father for this with an 'offering of the lips'."[6] Continuity and discontinuity are visible here at one and the same time. Unlike the Qumran sect, the disciples of Jesus pray with Israel in its temple; they remain within the prayer community of God's covenant. But in contrast to the old and obsolete form of the law, they go to Solomon's Portico to pray without taking part in the sacrificial service. For them the Temple is a house of prayer; they move in that part of the Temple which may be described as a kind of synagogue—indeed, as the starting point of synagogues in general.[7] The sacrificial cult was bound to Jerusalem, but the house of prayer could be everywhere. They kept that part of the Temple which has a promising future: the place of congregation, the place of proclamation, the place of prayer. As a result, they did away with the exclusivity of the Temple, on the one hand, and preserved that which is universal and can be repeated everywhere, on the other. The Temple is thus fundamentally nothing other than the synagogue, the space that brings people together before the God of the covenant, the God of Jesus Christ. It still has a special significance as the primordial cell of all assembly, as a sign of the unity of God's history throughout the centuries, but wherever else an assembly occurs, that is essentially the same as in the Temple, that is, there is temple. Thus all the exclusivity of this building had disappeared without any disloyalty toward the history of faith expressed in the Jerusalem shrine. It was understood to be the house of prayer for all peoples; with that the precondition for the universality of the Church was created at the same time.

---

[6] Franz Mussner, "Die UNA SANCTA nach Apg 2,42", in Mussner, *Praesentia salutis: Gesammelte Studien zu Fragen und Themen des Neuen Testaments* (Düsseldorf, 1967), 212–22 (quotation from 221).

[7] Cf. ibid., 220–21.

Externally this shift is most obvious in the change of direction for prayer: no matter where they are, Jews pray facing Jerusalem—the Temple is the point of reference for all religion so that the connection to God, the prayer relationship, always has to go through the Temple, even if only through the direction one faces at prayer. Christians pray, not in the direction of the Temple, but toward the east. The rising sun, which triumphs over the night, symbolizes the risen Christ and is simultaneously understood to be a sign of his Second Coming. Through their position at prayer Christians show that the direction toward the Risen One is the true point of reference of their life with God.[8] For this reason eastward orientation has become the governing principle for Christian churches over the centuries; it is an expression of the omnipresence of the Lord's power to assemble, the Lord who reigns throughout the whole world like the rising sun. This shows clearly that the emerging Church by no means rejects the room of prayer, the place where people are gathered into the word and into the transpired history of faith; it universalizes the Temple and thereby creates new possibilities for structuring it. Concentration on Solomon's Portico and opening up to the expanse of the world do not spell the end of holy places. Just the opposite is the case: since the living house, which is the issue here, is supposed to gather all men together, houses of assembly and places of prayer are now growing all over the world.

2. By the time Constantine promulgated his Edict of Tolerance for Christians, the church building had already found its definitive form. Eusebius recounts that the places that had been destroyed by the tyrant "rose anew from a long and deadly fall" and that "the churches rose up to immeasurable heights from scratch and became much more magnificent than the destroyed ones had been."[9] Previously the "jealous fiend ... like a rabid dog" had turned "his brutish insanity first of all against the stones of our temples" and made "the churches into barren sites, or so he thought".[10] Thus, what happens under Constantine is reconstruction, not the transition from a religion of the spirit to a religion of stones. But we must ask: What idea had lent those early

---

[8] Cf. Erik Peterson, "Die geschichtliche Bedeutung der jüdischen Gebetsrichtung", in Peterson, *Frühkirche, Judentum und Gnosis: Studien und Untersuchungen* (Freiburg, 1959), 1–14.

[9] Eusebius, *Hist. Eccl.* X, 2; I am following Philipp Haeuser's translation (Kempten, 1932) in the new edition by Heinrich Kraft (Munich, 1967), 412 [translated into English from the German].

[10] Ibid., X, 14; quoted in Kraft, 416 [translated into English from the German].

buildings their shape? What justifies them and brings them into harmony with the tradition of the origin? In the face of only very fragmentary traces of circumstantial evidence, these questions are being
disputed up to the present moment and will probably always be disputed. The most plausible theory is the one that explains the earliest
form of the Christian basilica from the theology of the martyrs.[11] In
its essential design the basilica corresponds to the audience hall in which
the god-emperor presented himself in a spectacle that was to be interpreted as the epiphany, the appearance of the divine. For the Christians this self-portrayal of the Caesar was a blasphemous event; over
against the emperor's divine claim they placed the kingdom of God in
the crucified and risen Christ. He alone was really that which the
Caesars only claimed to be. Thus, the assembly room of Christians
where the Lord continued to give himself to his own in the broken
bread and the poured-out wine became the site of *their* cult of the
emperor—the audience hall of the true king. For this antithesis they
died; martyrdom has been set into the design of this room, as it were.
Following Solomon's Portico and the synagogue, one had first emphasized in a special way the promise from the sayings of Jesus that the
house of prayer is for all peoples; but now the emphasis is on God's
building a living house for himself through the passion of his own
people and on his also taking the stones into his service precisely for
this reason. This brings to light at the same time the motif that distinguishes the Christian ecclesia from the Jewish synagogue: its axis is
not the Torah scroll but the living Lord; he builds it, and it is built in
response to him. The christological factor through which the Church
is more and other than the synagogue enters into the shape of the
room, as it were, translating the inner essence of the Church into
something visible.

3. In the course of history the motives and patterns are multiplied.
There is no doubt that less valuable, remote, even negative aspects
find their way in as well. Two basic ideas seem to me to dominate in
a positive way. One is the motif of the Incarnation. John has described

---

[11] Cf. Bernhard Kötting, "Die Gestaltung des Kultraumes in der frühen Kirche", in
Kötting, *Ecclesia peregrinans*, vol. 2 (Münster, 1988), 186–98. Recent clarifications concerning the essence and development of the Christian church can be found in the important
little book by Louis Bouyer, *Architecture et liturgie* (Paris, 1991) [trans. as *Liturgy and Architecture* (Notre Dame, Ind.: Univ. of Notre Dame Press, 1967)].

Jesus' flesh as the tent of the Word (1:14).[12] The flesh of Jesus is the temple; it is the tent, the *shekinah*. For John the flesh of Jesus is paradoxically the truth and the spirit, which take the place of the old buildings. But now the idea awakens in Christianity that precisely God's Incarnation was his entry into matter, the beginning of a momentous movement in which all matter is to become a vessel for the Word, but also in which the Word consistently has to make a statement about itself in matter, has to surrender itself to matter in order to be in a position to transform it. As a consequence, Christians are now deriving pleasure from making faith visible, from constructing its symbol in the world of matter. The other basic idea is connected to this: the idea of glorification, the attempt to turn the earth into praise, right down to the stones themselves, and thus to anticipate the world to come. The buildings in which faith is expressed are, as it were, a visualized hope and a confident statement of what can come to be, projected into the present.

3. Consequences for Today

After this discussion, let us now return to our questions from above: What is the relationship between the stone building and the building of living stones? Is it Christian to celebrate the building of a cathedral? If so, what are we celebrating when we do this? How should we celebrate so that we truly celebrate in a Christian way? I would like to respond in four steps.

1. The spirit builds the stones, not vice versa. The spirit cannot be replaced with money or with history. Where the spirit does not build, the stones become silent. Where the spirit is not alive, where it is not effective and does not reign, cathedrals become museums, memorials to the past whose beauty makes you sad because it is dead. That is the warning, as it were, that emanates from this cathedral celebration. Our history's greatness and our financial potency do not save us; both can turn into debris that smothers us. If the spirit does not build, money

---

[12] Furthermore, it is probably not irrelevant that the word *shekinah* was discernible in the Greek word *skēnē*, and thus it identified Jesus as the place of God's presence; cf. Bultmann, *Evangelium des Johannes*, 43; Schnackenburg, *Johannesevangelium*, 245; Wilhelm Michaelis, art. "skēnē", in *Theological Dictionary of the New Testament*, 7:378–79; Paul van Imschoot, art. "Schekina", in *Bibel-lexikon*, ed. Herbert Haag, 2nd ed. (Einsiedeln, 1968), 1536.

builds in vain. Faith alone can keep cathedrals alive, and the question the one-thousand-year-old cathedral is asking us is whether we have the strength of faith to give it a present and a future. In the end, organizations for the protection of historical monuments do not preserve the cathedral, as important and commendable as they are—only the spirit that created it can do this.

2. The spirit builds the stones, not vice versa—this also denotes the essential replaceability and the fundamental equivalence of all church buildings, whether we like it or not. Wherever people let the Lord gather them together, wherever he grants them his presence in Word and sacrament, there the saying about the house of prayer being for all peoples is present; there the promise of the "upper room", the room of the Last Supper, is fulfilled.[13] The hierarchical differences between the individual church buildings exist only on a second level, but they are for this reason by no means unimportant. Apart from the considerations of art history, a church building can receive a particular rank in principally two ways. It can first of all result from the history of faith and prayer that has taken root there. That we pray in the same churches in which our predecessors have been bringing their petitions and hopes before God over the centuries is not irrelevant. In St. Ludger's Church in Münster it has always moved me deeply to know that this was the place where Edith Stein struggled with her vocation. And this is just a tiny excerpt from the history of faith and prayer and the history of sinners and saints preserved in our great old churches. Thus they are also an expression of the identity of faith throughout history, an expression of the faithfulness of God which reveals itself in the unity of the Church. Or should it not move us to know that a thousand years ago the bishop of Mainz spoke the same words of consecration and used basically the same missal in his cathedral as his successors today? The other thing that can distinguish a church building is its position in the organization of the living assembly that is the Church.

---

[13] With this remark I would like to suggest that in addition to Solomon's Portico the room of the Last Supper and of the Pentecost event must be seen as a second early Christian precursor of the church building. Only half of the Christian religious service, the Liturgy of the Word, transpires in Solomon's Portico. The feature most interiorly proper to and characteristic of the new community, the Lord's Supper, which replaces and fulfills the old sacrifices, cannot find space there. Only when the cenacle and Solomon's Portico come together in one room is "church" realized in the specific sense. If you overlook this, you arrive at a purely "synagogal" construction not only of the church building but of Christianity as a whole and so miss the central point in the end.

The special rank of the bishop's church is derived from this; it directs our attention to the bishop as the focus of the Church community. The cathedral expresses in stone that the Church is not an amorphous mass of parishes but exists in an interconnection that binds each individual parish beyond its own borders to the whole through the cohesion of the episcopal system. For this very reason the Second Vatican Council, which called to mind the episcopal organization of the Church with such vigor, also quite emphatically stressed the rank of the cathedral church. The individual churches refer to it—are built around it, so to speak—and precisely in this cohesion and in this organization individual churches effect the assembly and oneness of the Church. For the same reason the cathedral churches of the common bishop of all Christianity, the Lateran and St. Peter's in Rome, mean a great deal to us. Not as if God were more present there than in any village church, but because they express the assembly and the uniqueness of God's house in the many places of worship on earth. If one would reject this connection and negate this visible ordering of the churches to each other, one would be renouncing precisely the promise that the house of prayer is for *all* peoples. This promise is fulfilled in particular when the apostolic ordering of the assembly is reflected in the classification of the places of assembly that thus become one single house.

3. This signifies the basic openness of all places of worship that are either a part of the whole Church or are not really Church at all. In order to maintain its Christian legitimacy the church building must be "catholic" in the original sense of the word: home of the faithful everywhere. A number of years ago a book of pictures was published with the title *You Are at Home Everywhere*. These words articulate in fact a task for the Church that began her journey under the dictum that the house of prayer is for all peoples. In one of his early works describing a trip to Prague, Albert Camus writes in a distressing way about the experience of being in a foreign place, of being isolated. In a city whose language he does not understand he is like an exile; even the magnificence of the churches remains silent and offers no comfort.[14] For those who believe, it should not be possible for this to happen:

---

[14] Cf. Albert Camus, "L'Envers et l'endroit: La Mort dans l'âme", in Camus, *Essais*, Bibl. de la Pléiade (Paris, 1965), 31–39. Cf. Gisela Linde, *Das Problem der Gottesvorstellungen im Werk von Albert Camus*, MBTh 39 (Münster, 1975), especially 10–11.

where there is Church, where there is the eucharistic presence of the Lord, they experience home. But before this can occur, something just the opposite of this is required: faith must be experienced as assembly, as oneness; people entering the realm of faith must leave behind what is merely their own and let catholicity, the turning of themselves over to the whole, happen to them as an ongoing process. In the face of the *Zeitgeist* and the many forms of chauvinism, it is imperative that the faithful take upon themselves the condition of being foreign, which is necessary so that there be a home for the whole in all places, so that the same home, as it were, is encountered everywhere. This again raises questions for us: How does this actually work? Can legal immigrants find a home in our churches? Can foreigners find people there who understand them? When viewed correctly, this transcending of what is one's own which is under discussion here definitely has something to do with the theology of passion found at the start of the Christian way. Only those who have set out on the path to become free of themselves, only those who have taken at least a few steps can meet foreigners and offer them a home. The Church Fathers were acquainted with the beautiful metaphor that the stones have to be hewn and matched to become a building and that people who are to become one house are not spared this either.

4. Let us once again return to the fundamental question about spirit and stone, about the living house and the stone church. The direction in which Christ's words point and in which the early Church continues to go can with good reason be described as "spiritualization". But if it were only that, then Christianity would not stand out from a trend that we come across in the entire Mediterranean region at the time of Jesus, in Judaism as well as in the Hellenistic world. The particularity of the Christian way consists of the fact that the Christian spiritualization is simultaneously an incarnation.[15] Paul has splendidly formulated its motto: "Now the Lord is the Spirit" (2 Cor 3:17). This distinguishes it from all other kinds of spiritualization, whether philosophical or merely mystical. The Spirit into which it transforms all that has come to pass is the

---

[15] I tried to describe the problem of spiritualization and incarnation in somewhat more detail in the essay "Zur theologischen Grundlegung der Kirchenmusik", in my book *Das Fest des Glaubens* (Einsiedeln, 1981), 86–111 [trans. Graham Harrison as "On the Theological Basis of Church Music", in *The Feast of Faith: Approaches to a Theology of the Liturgy* (San Francisco: Ignatius Press, 1986), 97–126]; cf. also the relevant essays of this volume [JRCW 11, Part D, 421–515].

body of Christ. Accordingly, an authentic development of the Christian beginning has to turn against a vapid sort of spiritualizing propaganda that seeks the spirit without the body and thereby destroys the spirit as well. The opposite misunderstanding must of course also be rejected that sees in the word "incarnation" the justification for every kind of secularization as well as an institutional ossification of the faith. During the golden age of incarnational theology one liked to say that the things of the earth had to be baptized. All right, but one must not forget that baptism is a sacrament of death, that we are baptized into the death of Christ, that to be baptized means to go through or rather to go into the transformation of death in order to move toward the risen Christ. To spiritualize means to incarnate in a Christian way, but to incarnate means to spiritualize, to bring the things of the world to the coming Christ, to prepare them for their future form and thus to prepare God's future in the world. In St. Irenaeus' work we find the lovely thought that the meaning of the Incarnation was for the Spirit—the Holy Spirit—to get used to the flesh, as it were, in Jesus.[16] Turning this around we could say: The meaning of ongoing incarnation can only be the reverse, to get the flesh used to the Spirit, to God, to make it *capax spiritus* and in this way to prepare its future.

But what does all this mean in terms of our question? Well, to begin with, I think it takes us back to what is completely elementary, which is fundamental for all New Testament statements, namely, that in fact God himself first builds his house, or, to express it in a more accessible way for us, that we cannot do it alone, on our own. Such a statement is directed against those who believe that with a certain number of walled-in square meters the task is done as well as against those who want to create the Church anew in a chemically pure way in the retort of their pastoral strategies. God builds his house; that is, it does not take shape where people only want to plan, achieve, and produce by themselves. It does not appear where only success counts and where all the "strategies" are measured by success. It does not materialize where people are not prepared to make space and time in their lives for him; it does not get constructed where people only build by themselves and for themselves. But where people let them-

---

[16] *Adversus haereses* V, 12, 4, (SChr 153, 154). Cf. Hans Jochen Jaschke, *Der Heilige Geist im Bekenntnis der Kirche: Ein Studie zur Pneumatologie des Irenaeus von Lyon im Ausgang vom altchristlichen Glaubensbekenntnis*, MBTh 40 (Münster, 1976).

selves be claimed for God, there they have time for him and there space is available for him. There they can dare to represent in the present what is to come: the dwelling of God with us and our gathering together through him, which make us sisters and brothers of one house. Being open to simplicity is just as natural here as recognizing the right to beauty, to the beautiful. Indeed, the beautiful only becomes evident in its transforming and comforting power in such spiritualization of the world toward the coming Christ. Something unusual is revealed here as well: the house of God is the true house of man. It becomes the house of man even more the less it tries to be this and the more it is simply put up for him. We only have to think for a moment what Europe would really look like if we took all the churches away from it. It would be a desert of utility in which the heart would probably stop beating. Where people just want to inhabit the earth by themselves it becomes uninhabitable. Nothing more is built up where men only want to build by themselves and for themselves. But where they pull back and part with their time and their space, there the house of the community is built, there a piece of utopia, of the impossible on earth, becomes a present reality. The beauty of the cathedral does not stand in opposition to the theology of the Cross but is its fruit: it was born from the willingness not to build one's city by oneself and for oneself. The misuse of something just for oneself is of course not excluded by this. No church building possesses the promise of eternity; none is irreplaceable; each can be taken from us when the power justifying it crumbles.

"Built from living stones"—if there had not been living stones at the beginning, these stones would not be standing here. Now, however, they speak to us. They call upon us to build the living cathedral, to be the living cathedral so that the cathedral of stone remains a present reality and heralds the future.

X. On the Question of the Orientation of the Celebration

Eastward- or Westward-Facing Position? A Correction

1. Note on the Question of the Orientation of the Celebration

Nowadays the question of eastward- or westward-facing position is hardly mentioned anymore. Nor would it be right, after the upheavals of past years, to press for further external changes. Therefore it seems all the more important to promote the kind of liturgical education that will enable people to participate in a proper inward manner, involving them in that movement, that direction, which is of the essence of the Eucharist. In doing so we must be aware of the mistaken approaches that can easily arise out of a misunderstanding of the liturgical reform.

In an impressive article in the International Catholic Review *Communio* 5, no. 4 (1978): 326–43, Everett A. Diederich, S.J., spoke of "The Unfolding Presence of Christ in the Celebration of Mass", giving a sensitive treatment of the liturgy's inner dynamism as it proceeds step by step to make Christ present. Apropos he observed that in the old rite the Mass was celebrated facing the altar, that is, toward the holy of holies, an observation that caused me to make the following correction:

The eastward-facing position of the celebrant in the old Mass was never intended as a celebration toward the holy of holies, nor can it really be described as "facing the altar". In fact it would be contrary to all theological reason, since the Lord is present in the Eucharistic Gifts during the Mass in the same way as he is in the Gifts of the tabernacle that come from the Mass. Thus the Eucharist would be celebrated "from" the Host "to" the Host, which is plainly meaningless. There is only one inner direction of the Eucharist, namely, from Christ in the Holy Spirit to the Father. The only question is how this can be best expressed in liturgical form.

From *The Feast of Faith: Approaches to a Theology of the Liturgy*, trans. Graham Harrison (San Francisco: Ignatius Press, 1986), 139–46.

Thus the positive content of the old eastward-facing direction lay not in its orientation to the tabernacle. It was twofold. The original meaning of what nowadays is called "the priest turning his back on the people" is, in fact—as Josef Andreas Jungmann has consistently shown—the priest and people together facing the same way[1] in a common act of trinitarian worship, such as Augustine introduced, following the sermon, by the prayer "*Conversi ad Dominum*". Priest and people were united in facing eastward; that is, a cosmic symbolism was drawn into the community celebration—a factor of considerable importance. For the true location and the true context of the eucharistic celebration is the whole cosmos. "Facing east" makes this cosmic dimension of the Eucharist present through liturgical gesture. Because of the rising sun, the east—*oriens*—was naturally both a symbol of the Resurrection (and to that extent it was not merely a christological statement but also a reminder of the Father's power and the influence of the Holy Spirit) and a presentation of the hope of the parousia. Where priest and people together face the same way, what we have is a cosmic orientation and also an interpretation of the Eucharist in terms of Resurrection and trinitarian theology. Hence it is also an interpretation in terms of parousia, a theology of hope, in which every Mass is an approach to the return of Christ. In short, what Fr. Diederich calls "facing the altar" was in reality expressing a view of the eucharistic celebration in the context of cosmos and parousia.

It must be added that, according to Erik Peterson,[2] this eastward-facing position for prayer, making the cosmos a sign of Christ and thus defining the cosmos as the locus of prayer, was underlined very early on by the custom of placing a cross on the east wall of Christian meeting-houses. First this was seen as a sign of the returning Christ; later it became more and more a reminder of the Lord's historical Passion, and finally the eschatological idea disappeared almost entirely from the image of the cross. This primitive Christian tradition is behind

---

[1] Cf. the review by Josef Andreas Jungmann of Otto Nussbaum's work *Der Standort des Liturgen am christlichen Altar vor dem Jahre 1000*, 2 vols. (Bonn, 1965), in ZKTh 88 (1966): 445–50.

[2] Erik Peterson, "Die geschichtliche Bedeutung der jüdischen Gebetsrichtung", in Peterson, *Frühkirche, Judentum und Gnosis* (Freiburg, 1959), 1–14; Peterson, "Das Kreuz und die Gebetsrichtung nach Osten", ibid., 15–35. For the development of the image of the cross, cf. Erich Dinkler, *Signum crucis: Aufsätze zum Neuen Testament und zur christlichen Archäologie* (Tübingen, 1967); Dinkler, *Das Apsismosaik von S. Apollinare in Classe* (Opladen, 1964); Peter Stockmeier, *Theologie und Kult des Kreuzes bei Johannes Chrysostomos*, TThS 18 (Trier, 1966).

the old rubric that ordered that there must be a cross on the altar. So what has come down to us in the altar cross is a relic of the ancient eastward orientation. It maintained the ancient tradition of praying to the Lord who is to come under the sign of the Cross, a tradition with strong associations, in former times, with the cosmic symbol of the "east". So, with regard to the eastward-facing position of the celebration prior to the Council, one cannot talk of celebrating "toward" the altar, let alone "toward the holy of holies", but it can be said that the Mass was celebrated facing the image of the cross, which embodied in itself the whole theology of the *oriens*. In this sense there was a continuity going right back to the threshold of the apostolic era.

Now it must be admitted that, at least since the nineteenth century, not only had the awareness of the liturgy's cosmic orientation been lost, but there was also little understanding of the significance of the image of the cross as a point of reference for the Christian liturgy. Hence the ancient eastward orientation of the celebration became meaningless, and people could begin to speak of the priest celebrating "facing the wall" or imagine that he was celebrating toward the tabernacle. This misunderstanding alone can explain the sweeping triumph of the new celebration facing the people, a change that has taken place with amazing unanimity and speed, without any mandate (and perhaps for that very reason!). All this would be inconceivable if it had not been preceded by a prior loss of meaning from within.

The best results of liturgical scholarship, such as Fr. Diederich's article, explain the new orientation by referring to the inner dynamism of the liturgical action, as the community's progressive approach to the Lord. In this way the attempt is made to fuse the present direction of the celebration with the nature of the ancient Christian inheritance. Generally, however, this view is not shared by many people. The general view is totally determined by the strongly felt community character of the eucharistic celebration, in which priest and people face each other in a dialogue relationship. This does express *one* aspect of the Eucharist. But the danger is that it can make the congregation into a closed circle that is no longer aware of the explosive trinitarian dynamism that gives the Eucharist its greatness. A truly liturgical education will have to use all its resources to counter this idea of an autonomous, complacent community. The community does not carry on a dialogue with itself; it is engaged on a common journey toward the returning Lord. Here are three suggestions for this kind of education:

1. Today we are in the midst of a crisis in the anthropocentric view of the world, a crisis that pervades the whole of man's self-made world. At such a time we need to rediscover (and indeed we are rediscovering) the significance of creation. We also need to be reminded that liturgy involves the cosmos—that Christian liturgy is cosmic liturgy. In it we pray and sing in concert with everything "in heaven and earth and under the earth" (Phil 2:10), we join in with the praise rendered by the sun and the stars. Thus in church architecture, for instance, we should see to it that churches are not designed merely with human utility in mind, but that they stand in the cosmos, inviting the sun to be a sign of the praise of God and a sign of the mystery of Christ for the assembled community. A rediscovery of the value of the church building's eastward orientation would help, it seems to me, in recovering a spirituality that embraces the dimension of creation.

2. Traditionally, the "east" and the image of the cross (that is, the cosmic and the soteriological aspects of spirituality) were fused; the cross itself, which may originally have had a purely eschatological significance, called to mind the Lord's suffering, faith in the Resurrection, and the hope of the parousia, that is, it signified the whole tension of the Christian concept of time. It is this tension which has transformed star time into human time and into God's time—for God *is not* time, but he *has* time for us. In so many ways the cross embodies the theology of the icon, which is a theology of incarnation and transfiguration; as against the proscription of images in the Old Testament (and in Islam), it indicates a new feature in the view of God as a result of the Son's Incarnation: God presents himself to our senses. Now, in the man who is his Son, he is depictable.[3] There are many reasons for the loss of the image that has occurred in the wake of the Council, but it is not something we can accept with equanimity. Surely we must regard it as a priority to reestablish the meaning of the image of the cross, which has been a constant shaping factor on the whole tradition of faith. Even now, when the priest faces the people, the cross could be placed on the altar in such a way that both priest and people can see it. At the Eucharistic Prayer they should not look at one another; together they ought to behold him, the Pierced Savior (Zech 12:10; Rev 1:7).

---

[3] Cf. Christoph von Schönborn, *L'Icône du Christ: Fondements théologiques élaborés entre le Ier et le IIe Concile de Nicée (325–787)*, Paradosis 24 (Fribourg, 1976).

3. It always impresses me that our Protestant brethren, in transforming the medieval liturgical forms, have achieved a real balance between, on the one hand, the relationship of the community to its leader and, on the other, their common relationship to the cross. Their whole basic approach laid great weight on the community character of worship and the interplay of leader and congregation, whereas in the Catholic liturgy of former times this only consisted in the priest's turning round for a brief *"Dominus vobiscum"* or to invite the people to pray. But when it is a question of praying together, Protestants, people and leader, together turn to the image of the Crucified. I think we should seriously try to learn from this. When we pray it is not necessary, indeed it is not even appropriate, to look at one another; the same is true when we receive Holy Communion. Local conditions will determine how best we can do justice to these points. In many cases our second suggestion may be a practical way forward. Even in St. Peter's in Rome, as a result of the exaggerated and misconceived idea of "celebrating facing the people", the altar cross has been removed from the center of the altar, so that it does not obstruct the view between celebrant and congregation. But the cross on the altar is not obstructing the view; it is a common point of reference. It is an open "iconostasis" that, far from hindering unity, actually facilitates it: it is the image that draws and unites the attention of everyone. I would even be so bold as to suggest that the cross on the altar is actually a necessary precondition for celebrating toward the people. It would help in clarifying the distinction between the Liturgy of the Word and the Liturgy of the Eucharist. The first is concerned with proclamation and, hence, with a direct, face-to-face situation, whereas the second is a matter of all of us worshipping together in response to the call *"Conversi ad Dominum"*—"Let us turn to the Lord; let us be converted to the Lord!" [4]

---

[4] I would also like to mention the valuable remarks made by Franz Josef Nüss, in IKaZ 8 (1979): 573–75, in response to my presentation of the issue. Then, despite the criticism that can be leveled against it, mention should be made of the relevant research of Klaus Gamber, e.g., *Gemeinsames Erbe: Liturgische Neubesinnung aus dem Geist der frühen Kirche*, 1. Beiheft zu den Studia patristica et liturgica (Regensburg, 1980), 82–89; *Liturgie und Kirchenbau: Studien zur Geschichte der Messfeier und des Gotteshauses in der Frühzeit*, Studia patristica et liturgica 6 (Regensburg, 1976); *Die Reform der römischen Liturgie: Vorgeschichte und Problematik* (Regensburg, 1979), 46–52.

2. Foreword to Uwe Michael Lang, Turning towards the Lord: Orientation in Liturgical Prayer, 2004

To the ordinary churchgoer, the two most obvious effects of the liturgical reform of the Second Vatican Council seem to be the disappearance of Latin and the turning of the altars toward the people. Those who read the relevant texts will be astonished to learn that neither is in fact found in the decrees of the Council. The use of the vernacular is certainly permitted, especially for the Liturgy of the Word, but the preceding general rule of the Council text says, "Particular law remaining in force, the use of the Latin language is to be preserved in the Latin rites" (*Sacrosanctum Concilium*, 36.1). There is nothing in the Council text about turning altars toward the people; that point is raised only in postconciliar instructions. The most important directive is found in paragraph 262 of the *Institutio Generalis Missalis Romani*, the General Instruction of the new Roman Missal, issued in 1969. That says, "It is better for the main altar to be constructed away from the wall so that one can easily walk around the altar and celebrate facing the people (*versus populum*)." The General Instruction of the Missal issued in 2002 retained this text unaltered except for the addition of the subordinate clause, "which is desirable wherever possible". This was taken in many quarters as hardening the 1969 text to mean that there was now a general obligation to set up altars facing the people "wherever possible". This interpretation, however, was rejected by the Congregation for Divine Worship on September 25, 2000, when it declared that the word *expedit* ("is desirable") did not imply an obligation but only made a suggestion. The physical orientation, the Congregation says, must be distinguished from the spiritual. Even if a priest celebrates *versus populum*, he should always be oriented *versus Deum per Iesum Christum* (toward God through Jesus Christ). Rites, signs, symbols, and words can never exhaust the inner reality of the mystery of salvation. For this reason the Congregation warns against one-sided and rigid positions in this debate.

This is an important clarification. It sheds light on what is relative in the external symbolic forms of the liturgy and resists the fanaticisms that, unfortunately, have not been uncommon in the controversies of

---

Foreword to U. M. Lang, *Turning towards the Lord: Orientation in Liturgical Prayer*, 2nd ed. (San Francisco: Ignatius Press, 2009), 9–12.

the last forty years. At the same time it highlights the internal direction of liturgical action, which can never be expressed in its totality by external forms. This internal direction is the same for priest and people, toward the Lord—toward the Father through Christ in the Holy Spirit. The Congregation's response should thus make for a new, more relaxed discussion, in which we can search for the best ways of putting into practice the mystery of salvation. The quest is to be achieved, not by condemning one another, but by carefully listening to each other and, even more importantly, listening to the internal guidance of the liturgy itself. The labelling of positions as "preconciliar", "reactionary", and "conservative", or as "progressive" and "alien to the faith" achieves nothing; what is needed is a new mutual openness in the search for the best realization of the memorial of Christ.

This small book by Uwe Michael Lang, a member of the London Oratory, studies the direction of liturgical prayer from a historical, theological, and pastoral point of view. At a propitious moment, as it seems to me, this book resumes a debate that, despite appearances to the contrary, has never really gone away, not even after the Second Vatican Council. The Innsbruck liturgist Josef Andreas Jungmann, one of the architects of the Council's Constitution on the Sacred Liturgy, was from the very beginning resolutely opposed to the polemical catch-phrase that previously the priest celebrated "with his back to the people"; he emphasized that what was at issue was not the priest turning away from the people, but, on the contrary, his facing the same direction as the people. The Liturgy of the Word has the character of proclamation and dialogue, to which address and response can rightly belong. But in the Liturgy of the Eucharist the priest leads the people in prayer and is turned, together with the people, toward the Lord. For this reason, Jungmann argued, the common direction of priest and people is intrinsically fitting and proper to the liturgical action. Louis Bouyer (like Jungmann, one of the Council's leading liturgists) and Klaus Gamber have each in his own way taken up the same question. Despite their great reputations, they were unable to make their voices heard at first, so strong was the tendency to stress the communality of the liturgical celebration and to regard therefore the face-to-face position of priest and people as absolutely necessary.

More recently the atmosphere has become more relaxed so that it is possible to raise the kind of questions asked by Jungmann, Bouyer, and Gamber without at once being suspected of anti-conciliar sentiments.

Historical research has made the controversy less partisan, and among the faithful there is an increasing sense of the problems inherent in an arrangement that hardly shows the liturgy to be open to the things that are above and to the world to come. In this situation, Lang's delightfully objective and wholly unpolemical book is a valuable guide. Without claiming to offer major new insights, he carefully presents the results of recent research and provides the material necessary for making an informed judgment. The book is especially valuable in showing the contribution made by the Church of England to this question and in giving, also, due consideration to the part played by the Oxford Movement in the nineteenth century (in which the conversion of John Henry Newman matured). It is from such historical evidence that the author elicits the theological answers that he proposes, and I hope that the book, the work of a young scholar, will help the struggle—necessary in every generation—for the right understanding and worthy celebration of the sacred liturgy. I wish the book a wide and attentive readership.

Joseph Cardinal Ratzinger
Rome, Laetare Sunday 2003

XI. Homilies

1. On the Question of the Adoration of the Eucharist and Its Sacredness

The liturgy for this evening before Maundy Thursday includes the consecration of holy oil for Baptism, Confirmation, the ordination of priests, and the Anointing of the Sick. All these sacraments, whenever they are celebrated in our diocese, thus stem from what happens in this paschal moment. It should thus be clear to us that all sacramental acts have their origin in the Paschal Mystery of the Lord's Cross and Resurrection. At the same time, however, the sacraments are thereby united in this one place, our cathedral church, and set with this church in the unity of the Catholic Church, the unity of all bishops, in the unity of that chain of laying-on of hands which takes us back to the calling of the first apostles, to that hour by the Lake of Genesareth, to the Last Supper and that time after the Resurrection of the Lord. We are all anointed at Baptism and Confirmation. So today we are going to try to enter likewise from within into the great unity of the Body of Christ, into the Paschal Mystery from which our healing comes; to ask the Lord that we may live out ever more truly our Baptism and Confirmation and may thus become worthy also of his eucharistic presence.

The Chrism Mass that we are celebrating today gives particular emphasis, from amid the Paschal Mystery as a whole, to the mission of a priest, which like all sacraments has its origin and its continuing basis in the Cross and Resurrection of Jesus Christ. Again this year the Holy Father has sent a letter to all priests to help us understand our task anew in the light of the Paschal Mystery and, thus, in unity

From *God Is Near Us: The Eucharist, the Heart of Life*, trans. Henry Taylor (San Francisco: Ignatius Press, 2003), 94–101.

with the whole Church, to live it more fully.[1] On that account we make our recollection this day in fellowship with all the faithful, because our service is to them: even when we are talking about the priesthood, precisely then we are not proclaiming ourselves but Christ crucified, in whose service we are here.

In his letter the Holy Father has turned this year to questions concerning the eucharistic sacrament and has quite deliberately addressed those points on which we risk becoming in some sense one-sided. It is a matter, as people would say nowadays, of a sort of "révision de vie", an examination of our common path at a certain point, so as to find our course again and clarify it. This evening I would like to take two main points out of the Pope's letter and reflect on them with you before the Lord: the question of the adoration of the most holy Eucharist, and that of its sacredness.

First, there is *eucharistic adoration*. We had rediscovered with renewed clarity in the Council that the heart of the eucharistic sacrament is the celebration of the holy mystery in which the Lord assembles his people, unites them, and builds them up by taking them into his sacrifice and giving himself to them, letting himself be received by us. The Eucharist, as we had rediscovered, is an assembly in which the Lord acts upon us and brings us together. All this is correct and remains correct. But in the meantime this idea of assembly had become flattened and separated from the idea of sacrifice, and thus the Eucharist had shrunk to a mere sign of brotherly fellowship. At the same time the concentration on the eucharistic celebration was causing faith and sacrament to lose something of their place among us. This has become quite visible in many churches—the place of adoration hides away somewhere on the edge of things, like a bit of the past. What was more far-reaching was the way the Eucharist itself was shrinking to the space of a brief half-hour, so that it could no longer breathe life into the building, no longer be the pulse of time. Confined to the space of the sacred rite, it was becoming a tiny island of time on the edge of the day, which as a whole was given over to the profane and hectic business of our worldly activity. If, today, we look back on this development, we realize that the adoration of the Sacrament was not in competition with the living

[1] John Paul II, Letter *Dominicae Cenae*, subtitled "The Eucharistic Mystery in the Life of the Church and of the Priest" (1980).

celebration of the community, but its condition, its indispensable environment. Only within the breathing space of adoration can the eucharistic celebration indeed be alive; only if the church and thus the whole congregation is constantly imbued with the waiting presence of the Lord, and with our silent readiness to respond, can the invitation to come together bring us into the hospitality of Jesus Christ and of the Church, which is the precondition of the invitation.

The Pope has further clarified these interconnections with a series of reflections. A first of these has been touched on in what was just said: Eucharistic adoration is, as it were, the vertical dimension in which universal and special priesthood coincide. If the distinction of the two callings over against each other is expressed in the Mass, in adoration we see how they are joined together: of this sacrament we all receive. All of us can only stand before him and adore. Even the authority of the priest must in the end be adoration, must spring from adoration and culminate in adoration. And thereby something else becomes clear: Communion and adoration do not stand side by side, or even in opposition, but are indivisibly one. For communicating means entering into fellowship. Communicating with Christ means having fellowship with him. That is why Communion and contemplation belong together: a person cannot communicate with another person without knowing him. He must be open for him, see him, and hear him. Love or friendship always carries within it an impulse of reverence, of adoration. Communicating with Christ therefore demands that we gaze on him, allow him to gaze on us, listen to him, get to know him. Adoration is simply the personal aspect of Communion.

We cannot communicate sacramentally without doing it personally. Sacramental Communion becomes empty, and finally a judgment for us, unless it is repeatedly completed by us personally. The saying of the Lord in the book of Revelation is valid not only for the end times: "Behold, I stand at the door and knock; if any one hears my voice and opens the door, I will come in to him and eat with him, and he with me" (3:20). This is at the same time a description of the most profound content of eucharistic piety. True Communion can happen only if we hear the voice of the Lord, if we answer and open the door. Then he will enter in with us and eat with us. Because this is so, I would like to underline and emphasize two thoughts in the papal letter: "Let us be generous with our time in going to meet him in adoration and ... [let] our adoration never cease." [2] And the other is connected with this: the Pope heavily emphasizes the intimate personal relationship with Christ as the heart of eucharistic piety.[3] In the death of Jesus Christ, says the Pope, each one of us has been loved to the end.[4] Too narrow a conception of the humanity of Jesus Christ has meanwhile sometimes prevented our being aware of this: The Lord knows me, too, and did know me; he suffered for me as well.

And a further aspect expounded in the papal letter is connected with this: the adoration of the Lord in the Sacrament is also an education in sensitizing our conscience. "Christ comes into the hearts of our brothers and sisters and visits their consciences." [5] When the conscience becomes dulled, this lets in the violence that lays waste the world. Anyone who gazes upon the face of the Lord, which the servants of the Sanhedrin and Pilate's servants have spat upon, which they have slapped and covered with spittle, will see in his face the mirror of our violence, a reflection of what sin is, and their conscience will be purified in the way that is the precondition for every social reform, for every improvement in human affairs. For the reform of human relationships rests in the first place on a reinforcement of moral strength. Only morality can set limits to violence and selfishness, and wherever it becomes insignificant it is man who is the loser every time, and the weak first of all.

Thus the Pope also tells us that eucharistic adoration "is an education in active love of one's neighbor".[6] It is not just God whom we venerate in eucharistic adoration: "Eucharistic worship is not so much worship of the inaccessible transcendence as worship of the divine condescension." [7] Jesus Christ's sacrifice of his life meets us here and, within this, love itself. But we can only understand love by sharing in it, by loving. "Let all pastoral activity be nourished by it, and may it also be food for ourselves and for all the priests who collaborate with us and, likewise, for the whole of the communities entrusted to us. In this practice there should thus be revealed, almost at every step, that close relationship between the Church's spiritual and apostolic vitality

---

[2] Ibid., no. 3, last paragraph.
[3] Ibid., no. 4, second paragraph.
[4] Ibid., no. 3, third paragraph.
[5] Ibid., no. 6, second paragraph.
[6] Ibid., first paragraph.
[7] Ibid., no. 7, last paragraph but one.

and the Eucharist, understood in its profound significance and from all points of view." [8]

Let us now turn to the second aspect, the *sacred nature* of the Eucharist. Our thinking over the last fifteen years has been influenced rather by the notion of "desacralization". We had been struck by the saying in the Letter to the Hebrews that Christ suffered outside the gate (13:12). This, again, chimed in with the other saying, that at the death of the Lord the veil of the Temple was torn in two. Now the Temple is empty. The true holiness, the holy presence of God, is no longer dwelling there; it is outside the city gate. The cult has been transposed out of the holy building into the life, suffering, and death of Jesus Christ. That is where its true presence was already, in his lifetime. When the Temple veil was torn across, so we had thought, the boundary between sacred and profane was torn apart. The cult is no longer something set apart from ordinary life, but holiness dwells in everyday things. What is holy is no longer a special, separate sphere but has chosen to be everywhere, has chosen to make itself felt even in worldly things. Entirely practical conclusions have been drawn from this, right down to some concerning priestly dress, concerning Christian worship and church buildings. This razing of the bastions should be carried out everywhere; nowhere should cult and life be any longer distinguishable one from the other. But thereby the message of the New Testament had ultimately been subject to substantial misunderstanding, albeit on the basis of an idea that was itself correct. For God is not withdrawing from the world so as to leave it to its worldliness, any more than he is affirming it in its worldliness, as if this were in itself holy. For as long as the world is imperfect, the distinction within it between sacred and profane will remain, for God is not withdrawing from it the presence of his holiness, and yet his holiness still does not comprehend the whole.

The suffering of Jesus outside the city wall and the tearing in two of the Temple veil does not mean that the Temple is now either everywhere or nowhere at all. That will not be the case until the New Jerusalem. Rather, these things mean that with the death of Jesus Christ the wall between Israel and the world of the nations has been broken down. They mean that God's promise has stepped out of the narrow framework of the Old Covenant and its Temple into the wide world

---

[8] Ibid., no. 4, last paragraph.

of the nations. They mean that the place of the merely symbolic holiness of the Old Testament images has been taken by the true holiness, the holy Lord in his love become man. Finally, they mean that henceforth the holy tent of God and the cloud of his presence are found wherever the mystery of his Body and Blood is celebrated, wherever men leave off their own activity to enter into fellowship with him. That means that the holiness is more concentrated and powerful than it used to be in the Old Covenant, because it is more true; it also means that that has become more vulnerable and demands of us still greater respect and reverence: not only ritual purity, but the comprehensive preparation of the heart. It demands that we lead lives directed toward the New Jerusalem, that we bring the world into the presence of Jesus Christ, and that we purify it for this; that we take the presence of Jesus Christ into everyday life and thereby transform it. Reverence has become, not superfluous, but more demanding. And because man is made up of body and soul and is, further, a social animal, that is why, now and for the future, we need a visible expression of reverence, the rules of play for its social form, for its visible sign in this sick and unholy world. People are not shaped merely from within outward; another line of influence runs from without inward, and to overlook this or to deny its existence is a kind of spiritualism that soon takes its toll. Holiness, the Holy One, is there in this world, and whenever the educative effect of his visible expression disappears, this leads both people and the world to become more superficial and more barbarous.

In his letter to priests the Holy Father reminds us of a particularly striking sign of reverence in the Roman liturgy: the hands of the priest are anointed. There is perhaps no organ as much as the hand that so clearly shows the special place of man in the world: parted from the ground, it shows how man walks upright. We give and we take with our hands; we heal and we hit with our hands. Among all peoples, men lift up their hands whenever they turn in prayer to him who is above them. Our hands are anointed. Our hands are bound in duty to the Lord. We are allowed to touch him. What a holy obligation for our whole will and being, what a change it might bring, and would necessarily bring, if we felt the demands made upon us and the direction given us by this sign, day after day. Let us ask the Lord that this sign of the anointing of our hands may more and more be made real in our lives, that our hands may more and more be instruments of blessing, that through his mercy we ourselves may become a blessing and, thus, receive blessing.

2. The Lord Is Near Us in Our Conscience, in His Word, in His Personal Presence in the Eucharist, on Deuteronomy 4:7

In today's reading there is a marvelous saying, in which we can sense all the joy of Israel at its redemption: "What great nation is there that has a god so near to it as the LORD our God is to us, whenever we call upon him?" (Deut 4:7).

St. Thomas Aquinas took up this saying in his reflections for the Feast of Corpus Christi.[9] In doing so, he showed how we Christians in the Church of the New Covenant can pronounce these words with yet more reason and more joy and with thankfulness than Israel could; in doing so, he showed how this saying, in the Church of Jesus Christ, has acquired a depth of meaning hitherto unsuspected: God has truly come to dwell among us in the Eucharist. He became flesh so that he might become bread. He gave himself to enter into the "fruit of the earth and the work of human hands"; thus he puts himself in our hands and into our hearts. God is not the great unknown, whom we can but dimly conceive. We need not fear, as heathen do, that he might be capricious and bloodthirsty or too far away and too great to hear men. He is there, and we always know where we can find him, where he allows himself to be found and is waiting for us. Today this should once more sink into our hearts: God is near. God knows us. God is waiting for us in Jesus Christ in the Blessed Sacrament. Let us not leave him waiting in vain! Let us not, through distraction and lethargy, pass by the greatest and most important thing life offers us. We should let ourselves be reminded, by today's reading, of the wonderful mystery kept close within the walls of our churches. Let us not pass it heedlessly by. Let us take time, in the course of the week, in passing, to go in and spend a moment with the Lord who is so near. During the day our churches should not be allowed to be dead houses,

---

From *God Is Near Us: The Eucharist, the Heart of Life*, trans. Henry Taylor (San Francisco: Ignatius Press, 2003), 102–6.

[9] Thomas Aquinas, *Officium de festo Corporis Christi*, in *Sanctae Thomae Aquinatis Opera Omnia*, ed. Roberto Busa, S.J., vol. 6 (Stuttgart and Bad Cannstatt, 1980), 581 (DSG ps. 3, n. 3; ps. 5, n. 3).

standing empty and seemingly useless. Jesus Christ's invitation is always being proffered from them. This sacred proximity to us is always alive in them. It is always calling us and inviting us in. This is what is lovely about Catholic churches, that within them there is, as it were, always worship, because the eucharistic presence of the Lord dwells always within them.

And a second thing: let us never forget that Sunday is the Lord's Day. It is not an arbitrary decision of the Church, requiring us to attend Mass on Sunday. This is never a duty laid upon us from without; it is the royal privilege of the Christian to share in paschal fellowship with the Lord, in the Paschal Mystery. The Lord has made the first day of the week his own day, on which he comes to us, on which he spreads the table for us and invites us to share with him. We can see, in the Old Testament passage at which we are looking, that the Israelites saw in the presence of God, not a burden, but the basis of their pride and their joy. And indeed the Sunday fellowship with the Lord is not a burden, but a grace, a gift, which lights up the whole week, and we would be cheating ourselves if we withdrew from it.

"What great nation is there that has a god so near to it as the LORD our God is to us, whenever we call upon him?" This passage from the Old Testament has found its ultimate depth of meaning in the eucharistic presence of the Lord. But its earlier meaning is not thereby abolished, but merely purified and exalted. We must now investigate that, in order to understand what the Lord is saying to us here. In the chapter of the book of Deuteronomy from which this passage is taken, the marvelous closeness of God is seen above all in the law he has given to Israel through Moses. Through the law he makes himself permanently available, as it were, for the questions of his people. Through the law he can always be spoken with by Israel; she can call on him, and he answers. Through the law he offers Israel the opportunity to build a social and political order that breaks new ground. Through the law he makes Israel wise and shows her the way a man should live, so as to live aright. In the law Israel experiences the close presence of God; he has, as it were, drawn back the veil from the riddles of human life and replied to the obscure questionings of men of all ages: Where do we come from? Where are we going? What must we do?

This joy in the law astounds us. We have become used to regarding it as a burden that oppresses man. At its best periods, Israel saw in the law in fact something that set them free for the truth, free from the burden of uncertainty, the gracious gift of the way. And, indeed, we do know today that man collapses if he has constantly to reinvent himself, if he has to create anew human existence. For man, the will of God is not a foreign force of exterior origin, but the actual orientation of his own being. Thus the revelation of God's will is the revelation of what our own being truly wishes—it is a gift. So we should learn anew to be grateful that in the word of God the will of God and the meaning of our own existence have been communicated to us. God's presence in the word and his presence in the Eucharist belong together, inseparably. The eucharistic Lord is himself the living Word. Only if we are living in the sphere of God's Word can we properly comprehend and properly receive the gift of the Eucharist.

Today's Gospel reading[10] makes us aware, besides this, of a third aspect. The law became a burden the moment it was no longer being lived out from within but was broken down into a series of obligations external in their origin and their nature. Thus the Lord tells us emphatically: The true law of God is not an external matter. It dwells within us. It is the inner direction of our lives, which is brought into being and established by the will of God. It speaks to us in our conscience. The conscience is the inner aspect of the Lord's presence, which alone can render us capable of receiving the eucharistic presence. That is why that same book of Deuteronomy, from which our reading today was taken, says elsewhere: "The word is very near you; it is in your mouth and in your heart, so that you can do it" (Deut 30:14; cf. Rom 10:8). Faith in Christ simply renders the inmost part of our being, our conscience, once more articulate. The Holy Father, John Paul II, says on this point: "Man's obedience to his conscience is the key to his moral grandeur and the basis of his 'kingliness', his 'dominion'.... Obedience to conscience is ... the Christian's share in the 'munere regali Christi'. Obedience to conscience ... is what equates 'serving Christ in others' reigning'."[11]

The Lord is near us in our conscience, in his word, in his personal presence in the Eucharist: this constitutes the dignity of the Christian and is the reason for his joy. We rejoice therefore, and this joy is expressed

---

[10] Gospel for the 22nd Sunday in Ordinary Time, Year B: Mark 7:1–8, 14–15, 21–23.

[11] John Paul II, *Zeichen des Widerspruchs: Besinnung auf Christus* (Zürich, 1979), 162f. [trans. from the Italian original as *Sign of Contradiction* (New York: Crossroad; Seabury Press, 1979), 141].

in praising God. Today we can see how the closeness of the Lord also brings people together and brings them close to each other: it is because we have the same Lord Jesus Christ in Munich and in Rome that we form one single People of God, across all frontiers, united in the call of conscience, united by the word of God, united through communion with Jesus Christ, united in the praise of God, who is our joy and our redemption.

3. Standing before the Lord—Walking with the Lord— Kneeling before the Lord: Celebrating Corpus Christi

If we want to understand the meaning of Corpus Christi, the best thing to do is simply to look at the liturgical form in which the Church celebrates and expounds the significance of this feast. Over and above the elements common to all Christian feasts, there are three components especially that constitute the distinctive shape of the way we celebrate this day.

First there is what we are doing right now, meeting together around the Lord, *standing before the Lord*, for the Lord, and thus standing side by side together. Next there is *walking with the Lord*, the procession. And finally there is the heart and the climax of it, *kneeling before the Lord*, the adoration, glorifying him and rejoicing in his presence. Standing before the Lord, walking with the Lord, and kneeling before the Lord, these three therefore are the constituent elements of this day, and we are now going to reflect on them a little.

Standing before the Lord

In the early Church there was an expression for this: *statio*. And when I mention that term, we touch on the oldest roots of what happens on Corpus Christi and what Corpus Christi is about. At the time when Christianity was spreading out across the world, from the beginning its representatives laid great emphasis on having in each city just one bishop, only one altar. This was supposed to express the unity

From *God Is Near Us: The Eucharist, the Heart of Life*, trans. Henry Taylor (San Francisco: Ignatius Press, 2003), 107–13.

brought by the one Lord, who embraces us in his arms outstretched on the Cross, transcending all the barriers and limits traced by earthly life, and makes us one Body. And this is the inmost meaning of the Eucharist, that we, receiving the *one* bread, enter into this *one* heart and thus become a living organism, the *one* Body of the Lord.

The Eucharist is not a private business, carried on in a circle of friends, in a club of like-minded people, who seek out and get together with those who already suit them; but just as the Lord allowed himself to be crucified outside the city wall, before all the world, and stretches out his hands to everyone, thus the Eucharist is the public worship of all those whom the Lord calls, irrespective of their personal make-up. It is particularly characteristic of him, as he demonstrated in his earthly life, to have men of the most diverse groupings, social backgrounds, and personal views brought together in the greater whole of his word and his love. It was characteristic of the Eucharist, then, in the Mediterranean world in which Christianity first developed, for an aristocrat who had found his way into Christianity to sit there side by side with a Corinthian dock worker, a miserable slave, who under Roman law was not even regarded as a man but was treated as chattel. It was characteristic of the Eucharist for the philosopher to sit next to the illiterate man, the converted prostitute and the converted tax collector next to the religious ascetic who had found his way to Jesus Christ. And we can see in the writings of the New Testament how people resisted this again and again, wanted to stay in their own circle, and yet this very thing remained the point of the Eucharist: gathering together, crossing the boundaries, and leading men through the Lord into a new unity.

When Christianity grew in numbers, this exterior form could no longer be maintained in the cities. As early as the time of persecutions, the titular churches in Rome, for instance, were already developing as precursors of the later parishes. Even here, of course, the public nature and the given structure of worship remained, so that people who would otherwise never meet were brought together. But this opening up of relationships within a single space was no longer sufficiently visible. That is why they developed the custom of the *statio*. That means that the pope, as the one bishop of Rome, especially in the course of Lent, leads the worship for the whole of Rome and goes right through each of the titular churches. The Christians meet together, go to the church together, and thus in each particular church the whole becomes visible and touches each individual. This basic idea is taken up by Corpus Christi. It is a *statio urbis*: we open up the parish churches; we open up for ourselves all the odd corners and farthest reaches of this city to be brought together to the Lord, so as to be at one through him. Here, too, we are together irrespective of party or class, rulers and ruled, men who work with their hands and those who do mental work, men of this tendency or that. And this is the essential thing, that we have been brought together by the Lord, that he leads us to meet each other. This moment should issue a call to us to accept one another inwardly, open ourselves up, go to meet each other, that even in the distraction of everyday life we should maintain this state of being brought together by the Lord.

Our cities, as we all know, have become places of solitude of a kind never known before. And nowhere are people so lonely and abandoned as perhaps in apartment complexes, where they are packed together most closely. A friend told me how once, when he had moved into a big city in the north, he was on his way out of the apartment complex, and he greeted someone else who lived in that complex, but the person just stared at him in amazement and said, "You've mistaken me for someone else!" Where people are just masses, a greeting turns into a mistake. But the Lord brings us together and opens us up, so that we can accept one another, belong to one another, so that in standing before him we can learn again to stand next to each other. Thus, the Marienplatz itself comes into its own true role. How often we hurry past each other here. Today this is the setting for our being together, which, as a duty and a gift, will continue. There are of course many big gatherings, yet so often it is what we are against that unites us, more than what we are for. And it is almost always the case that we are brought together by something we want, and this interest is directed against other such interests. But what unites us today is not the private interest of this group or that, but the interest that God takes in us, to which we can calmly confide all our own interests and wishes. We are standing for the Lord. And the more we stand for the Lord and before the Lord, the more we stand with one another, and our capacity to understand one another grows again, the capacity to recognize each other as people, as brothers and sisters, and thus, in being together, to build the basis and to open up the possibilities of humanity and of life.

Walking with the Lord

Standing together in the Lord's presence, and with the Lord, has resulted from the beginning in what it has indeed at its heart presupposed, *walking to the Lord*. For we are not automatically side by side. That is why a *statio* could happen only if people gathered beforehand and went to each other in the *processio*. That is the second call issued by Corpus Christi. We can stand side by side only if, first of all, under the guidance of the Lord, we go to each other. We can come to the Lord only in this *procedere*, in this moving out and moving forward, by transcending our own prejudices, our limits, and our barriers, going forward, going toward him, and moving to the point at which we can meet each other. This also is as true in the realm of the Church as in the world. Even in the Church—let us lament before God—there are conflict, opposition, and mistrust. *Processio, procedere*, should challenge us to move forward again, to go ahead toward him, and to subject ourselves to his measure and in our common belief in him who became man, who gives himself to us as bread, once more trusting each other, opening up to each other, and together letting ourselves be led by him.

The procession, which from an early period was a part of the stational worship in Rome, certainly did acquire a new dimension, a new depth, in Corpus Christi. For the Corpus Christi procession is no longer just walking to the Lord, to the eucharistic celebration; it is walking with the Lord; it is itself an element of eucharistic celebration, one dimension of the eucharistic event. The Lord who has become our bread is thus showing us the way, is in fact our way, as he leads us. In this fashion the Church offered a new interpretation of the Exodus story, of Israel's wandering in the wilderness, about which we heard in the reading. Israel travels through the wilderness. And it is able to find a path in the pathless wilderness, because the Lord is leading it in the guise of cloud and of light. It can live in the pathless and lifeless wilderness because man does not live by bread alone but by every word that proceeds from the mouth of God. And so in this story of Israel's journey through the wilderness the underlying meaning of all human history is revealed. This Israel was able to find a country and was able to survive after the loss of that country because it did not live from bread alone, but found in the Word the strength to live on through all the pathless and homeless wilderness of the centuries. And this is thus an enduring sign set up for us all. Man finds his way only if he will let himself be led by him who is Word and bread in one.

Only in walking with the Lord can we endure the peregrinations of our history. Thus Corpus Christi expounds the meaning of our whole life, of the whole history of the world: marching toward the Promised Land, a march that can keep on in the right direction only if we are walking with him who came among us as bread and Word. Today we know better than earlier ages that indeed the whole life of this world and the history of mankind is in movement, an incessant transformation, and moving onward. The word *progress* has acquired an almost magical ring. Yet we know, at the same time, that progress can be a meaningful term only if we know where we want to go. Mere movement in itself is not progress. It can just as well represent a rapid descent into the abyss. So if there is to be progress, we must ask how to measure it and what we are aiming at, certainly not merely an increase in material production. Corpus Christi expounds the meaning of history. It offers the measure, for our wandering through this world, of Jesus Christ, who became man, the eucharistic Lord who shows us the way. Not every problem, of course, is solved thereby. That just is not the way God goes about things. He gives us our freedom and our capacities so that we can make efforts, discover things, and struggle with things. But the basic yardstick has been laid down. And whenever we look to him as the measure and the goal of our path, then a criterion has been given that makes it possible to distinguish the right path from the wrong: walking with the Lord, as the sign and as the duty of this day.

Kneeling before the Lord

And finally there is *kneeling before the Lord*: adoration. Because he himself is present in the Eucharist, adoration has always been an essential part of it. Even if it was not developed in this form of a great feast until the Middle Ages, nonetheless it is not a change or a form of decadence; it is nothing essentially different, but merely the complete emergence of what was already there. For if the Lord gives himself to us, then receiving him can only mean to bow before him, to glorify him, to adore him. And even today it is not contrary to the dignity and freedom and status of man to bend his knee, to be obedient to him, to worship him and glorify him. For if we deny him, so as not to have to adore him, then what remains is merely the eternal necessity of physical material. Then we are truly bereft of freedom, a mere speck of dust that is flung around among the mill wheels of the universe and that vainly tries to persuade itself of having freedom. Only if he is the Creator is freedom the basis of all things; only then can we be free. And when our freedom bows before him, it is not abrogated but is at that moment truly accepted and rendered definitive.

But today there is one additional thing. The One whom we adore—as I was saying—is not some distant power. He has himself knelt down before us to wash our feet. And that gives to our adoration the quality of being unforced, adoration in joy and in hope, because we are bowing down before him who himself bowed down, because we bow down to enter into a love that does not make slaves of us but transforms us. So let us ask the Lord that he may grant us to understand this and to rejoice in it and that this understanding and this joy may spread out from this day far and wide into our country and our everyday life.

4. What Corpus Christi Means to Me: Three Meditations

I

What does Corpus Christi mean to me? Well, first of all it brings back memories of special feast days when we took quite literally what Thomas Aquinas put so well in one of his Corpus Christi hymns: *Quantum potes tantum aude*—dare to do as much as you can, giving him due praise.... In fact these words also recall something Justin Martyr said as early as the second century. In his description of the Christian liturgy he writes that the one who presides at the eucharistic celebration, that is, the priest, is to offer up prayers and thanksgivings "as much as he is able".[12] This is what the entire community feels called to do at Corpus Christi: Dare to do what you can. I can still smell those carpets of flowers and the freshness of the birch trees;

From *The Feast of Faith: Approaches to a Theology of the Liturgy*, trans. Graham Harrison (San Francisco: Ignatius Press, 1986), 127–38.

[12] *Apol.* I, 67, 5.

I can see all the houses decorated, the banners, the singing; I can still hear the village band, which indeed sometimes dared more, on this occasion, than it was able! I remember the *joie de vivre* of the local lads, firing their gun salutes—which was their way of welcoming Christ as a head of state, as *the* Head of State, the Lord of the world, present on their streets and in their village. On this day people celebrated the perpetual presence of Christ as if it were a state visit in which not even the smallest village was neglected.

Corpus Christi also brings to mind the issues raised by the liturgical renewal with all its theological insights. Is it right, we had to ask ourselves, to have this annual celebration of the Eucharist in the form of a state visit of the Lord of the world, with all the outward signs of triumphal joy? We were reminded that the Eucharist was instituted in the upper room—and somehow this must be a normative factor. The signs of bread and wine, chosen deliberately by the Lord, show that the Eucharist is meant to be received as food. Therefore the correct way of showing gratitude for the institution of the sacrament is actually to celebrate the Eucharist; here we celebrate his death and Resurrection and are built up by him into the living Church. Anything else seemed to be a misunderstanding of the Eucharist. Then we had a horror of everything that looked like triumphalism: it seemed irreconcilable with the Christian awareness of sin and with the tragic situation of the world. So it was that Corpus Christi became an embarrassment. The standard textbook on liturgy that appeared between 1963 and 1965 does not even refer to Corpus Christi in its treatment of the Church's year. Somewhat shamefacedly it offers us a page under the heading "Eucharistic Devotions"; in its embarrassment it makes the curious suggestion that the Corpus Christi procession should conclude with communion of the sick, this being the only functional rationale for a procession with the Host.[13]

The Council of Trent had been far less inhibited. It said that the purpose of Corpus Christi was to arouse gratitude in the hearts of men and to remind them of their common Lord.[14] Here, in a nutshell, we have in fact three purposes: Corpus Christi is to counter

---

[13] Aimé Georges Martimort, ed., *The Church at Prayer*, 2 vols. (New York, 1968 and 1973).

[14] "Aequissimum est enim, sacros aliquos statutos esse dies, cum Christiani omnes singulari ac rara quadam significatione gratos et memores testentur animos erga communem Dominum et Redemptorem pro tam ineffabili et plane divino beneficio, quo mortis eius

man's forgetfulness, to elicit his thankfulness, and it has something to do with fellowship, with that unifying power which is at work where people are looking to the one Lord. A great deal could be said about this; for with our computers, meetings, and appointments we have become appallingly thoughtless and forgetful.

Psychologists tell us that our rational, everyday consciousness is only the surface of what makes up the totality of our soul. But we are so hounded by this surface awareness that what lies in the depths can no longer find expression. Ultimately man becomes sick for sheer lack of authenticity; he no longer lives as a subject: he exists as the plaything of chance and superficiality. This is connected with our relationship to time. Our relationship to time is marked by forgetting. We live for the moment. We actually *want* to forget, for we do not want to face old age and death. But in reality this desire for oblivion is a lie: suddenly it changes into the aggressive demand for the future, as a way of destroying time. However, this romanticism of the future, this refusal to submit to time, is also a lie, a lie that destroys both man and the world. The only way to master time, in fact, is the way of forgiveness and thankfulness whereby we receive time as a gift and, in a spirit of gratitude, transform it.

Let us consider Trent again for a moment. There we find the unqualified statement that Corpus Christi celebrates Christ's triumph, his victory over death. Just as, according to our Bavarian custom, Christ was honored in the terms of a great state visit, Trent harks back to the practice of the ancient Romans who honored their victorious generals by holding triumphal processions on their return. The purpose of Christ's campaign was to eliminate death, that death which devours time and makes us cultivate the lie in order to forget or "kill" time. Nothing can make man laugh unless there is an answer to the question of death. And conversely, if there *is* an answer to death, it will make genuine joy possible—and joy is the basis for every feast. At its very heart the Eucharist is the answer to the question of death, for it is the encounter with that love which is stronger than death. Corpus Christi is the response to this central eucharistic mystery. Once a year it gives demonstrative expression to the triumphal joy in Christ's victory, as we accompany the Victor on his triumphal procession through the streets. So,

---

victoria et triumphus repraesentatur." *Decr. de sc. Eucharistia* (session 13, October 11, 1551) cap. 5; DS 1644.

far from detracting from the primacy of reception that is expressed in the gifts of bread and wine, it actually reveals fully and for the first time what "receiving" really means, namely, giving the Lord the reception due to the Victor. To receive him means to worship him; to receive him means, precisely, *Quantum potes tantum aude*—dare to do as much as you can.

The Council of Trent concludes its remarks on Corpus Christi with something that offends our ecumenical ears and has doubtless contributed not a little toward discrediting this feast in the opinion of our Protestant brethren. But if we purge its formulation of the passionate tone of the sixteenth century, we shall be surprised by something great and positive. First of all let us simply listen to what Trent says. Corpus Christi must show forth the triumph of the truth in such a way that, "in the face of such magnificence and such joy on the part of the whole Church, the enemies of the truth will either fade away or, stricken with shame, attain to insight." [15] If we remove the polemical element, what we have left is this: the power in virtue of which truth carries the day can be none other than *its own joy*. Unity does not come about by polemics or by academic argument but by the radiance of Easter joy; this is what leads to the core of the Christian profession, namely: Jesus is risen. This leads, too, to the core of our humanity, which yearns for this joy with its every fiber. So it is this Easter joy which is fundamental to all ecumenical and missionary activity; this is where Christians should vie with each other; this is what they should show forth to the world. This too is the purpose of Corpus Christi. In its deepest sense what our dictum means (*quantum potes tantum aude*) is this: Let beauty shine out in all its radiance when you come to express this joy of all joys. Love is stronger than death; in Jesus Christ God is among us.

II

When we think of Corpus Christi, we think first of all of the procession that marks this day. When the feast was instituted in 1246, there was no procession. It is first attested in Cologne in 1277, and

---

[15] ". . . ut eius adversarii, in conspectu tanti splendoris et in tanta Ecclesiae laetitia positi, vel debilitati et fracti tabescant, vel pudore affecti et confusi aliquando resipiscant." Ibid.

nine years later it is also found in Benediktbeuren. Since the fourteenth century, therefore, it has been a permanent part of the day's
celebration on German soil; indeed, the procession has become a feature of the feast. But after Trent it was precisely the *procession* that
presented difficulties. Why—so people said—carry the Host around?
People could only imagine one meaningful kind of procession, a procession or pilgrimage *from* a place or places *to* a common celebration
of the Eucharist somewhere else, that is, a procession *to* the Eucharist,
not *with* it. This is to exclude what is specific to the Corpus Christi
procession. Behind this approach lay the idea that the only authentic
liturgy was the old Roman liturgy, developed in the area of Rome in
the first centuries. What had arisen in the Middle Ages and north of
the Alps could only be regarded as the result of decadence and ignorance. Nowadays we have to learn all over again that the Church is
always alive, in every period, and that therefore her development cannot be thought complete at any particular time, as if thereafter nothing of original value could be produced. Of course a preeminence
attaches to the period of the founding of Christianity, when the permanent marks of its identity were being established. But the inner
wealth contained in this identity was not exhausted then; it can develop
and prove to be fruitful through all centuries.

How then are we to understand the Corpus Christi procession? I
have found it helpful to take a look at its roots. First of all there is a
general human factor that has caused processions to arise in all religious circles. Our relationship to God needs not only the inward aspect;
it also needs to be expressed. And as well as speech, singing and silence,
standing, sitting, and kneeling, expression also calls for this celebratory walking along together in the community of the faithful, together
with the God in whom we believe. In the Christian liturgy itself we
can identify two elements that gave rise to the Corpus Christi procession.[16] The liturgy of the "Great Week", in which the Church
reenacts the drama of the last week of Jesus' life, presents two "pro-
cessional" paths found in the sacred events themselves, namely, the
procession of palms and Jesus' ascent to the Mount of Olives after the
institution of the Eucharist. In the one he enters the Holy City in
triumph; in the other he goes from it in prayer, into the darkness of
night, into betrayal and death. There is a close relationship between

---

[16] Cf. Joseph Pascher, *Das liturgische Jahr* (Munich, 1963), 269–72.

these two processions: Jesus enters the city to cleanse the Temple, symbolically destroying it and thus incurring his death. This in turn is the inner precondition for his giving of himself in instituting the Eucharist and thus opening the new Temple of his love. Again, in sharing himself in the Eucharist, he is anticipating his death and looking forward to the Resurrection. But his departure from the city into the Passover night is a departure from the peaceful and protected sphere of salvation into the realm of death.[17] Very early on, the liturgy began to enact these processions in a solemn manner. In certain parts of France in the eleventh century the Blessed Sacrament was carried along in the procession of palms: it was a case of going beyond mere historical remembrance and of accompanying *Christus Victor* on his triumphal entry into his house to take possession of it once again. Essentially, the Holy Thursday procession is an accompanying of the Host, a walking with the Lord as he goes to deliver himself up for us. All this must be peripheral in Holy Week, but Corpus Christi brings these partial elements of the Easter mystery into the center and makes them into a special great feast. What was ambivalent on Palm Sunday, overshadowed by the darkness of the Cross, takes place publicly and on a grand scale at Corpus Christi in the joy of the Resurrection; the triumphal procession of the Lord, whom we publicly recognize as Lord, inviting him to take possession of our streets and squares.

There is a second root, namely, the "rogation" processions. We can see this connection in the custom [in Bavaria] of having four altars, from which in former times the four Gospels were sung. Throughout the whole history of religion, and thus here too, the number four symbolizes the four corners of the earth, that is, the whole universe, the world in which we live. The blessing was imparted in four directions, with the intention of putting them under the protection of the eucharistic Lord. The four Gospels express the same thing. For they are inspired, they are the breath of the Holy Spirit, and their fourfold number expresses the world-embracing power of God's word and God's Spirit. The beginning of the Gospel stands for the whole; uttering it, one is as it were sending out the breath of the Holy Spirit to engage the four winds, pervading them and turning them to good. The world

---

[17] Hartmut Gese, *Zur biblischen Theologie* (Munich, 1977), 111, where this leaving behind of "the houses of Jerusalem, the only area of salvation and protection against . . . all evil" is interpreted against the background of the Passover tradition.

is thus declared to be the realm of God's creative word; matter is sub-ordinated to the power of his Spirit. For matter too is his creation and hence the sphere of his gracious power. Ultimately we receive the very bread of the earth from his hands. How beautifully the new eucha-ristic bread is thus related to our daily bread! The eucharistic bread imparts its blessing to the daily bread, and each loaf of the latter silently points to him who wished to be the bread of us all. So the liturgy opens out into everyday life, into our earthly life and cares; it goes beyond the church precincts because it actually embraces heaven and earth, present and future. How we need this sign! Liturgy is not the private hobby of a particular group; it is about the bond that holds heaven and earth together, it is about the human race and the entire created world. In the Corpus Christi procession, faith's link with the earth, with the whole of reality, is represented "in bodily form", by the act of walking, of treading the ground, our ground; Joseph Pas-cher puts it well when he observes that this treading of the ground is related to the simple and eloquent rite of the imposition of hands.[18] The difference is that on this day we do not lay *our* hands on the earth, hands that so often exploit and violate it: we carry the Lord himself, the Creator, over the ground—the Lord who willed to give himself in the grain of the wheat and the fruit of the vine. So there is no contradiction between the rogation procession and the procession with the Blessed Sacrament that developed out of the liturgy of Holy Week; they come together on Corpus Christi in a single solemn pro-fession of faith in the world-embracing power of Jesus Christ's redeem-ing love. Therefore when we walk our streets with the Lord on Corpus Christi, we do not need to look anxiously over our shoulders at our theological theories to see if everything is in order and can be accounted for, but we can open ourselves wide to the joy of the redeemed: *sacris sollemniis iuncta sint gaudia*—in joy let us celebrate the holy feasts.

III

What does Corpus Christi mean to me? It does not only bring the liturgy to mind; for me, it is a day on which heaven and earth work together. In my mind's eye it is the time when spring is turning into

---

[18] Pascher, *Liturgische Jahr*, 286.

summer; the sun is high in the sky, and crops are ripening in field and meadow. The Church's feasts make present the mystery of Christ, but Jesus Christ was immersed in the faith of the people of Israel and so, arising from this background in Israel's life, the Christian feasts are also involved with the rhythm of the year, the rhythm of seedtime and harvest. How could it be otherwise in a liturgy that has at its center the sign of bread, fruit of earth and heaven? Here this fruit of the earth, bread, is privileged to be the bearer of him in whom heaven and earth, God and man have become one. The way the Church's feasts fit in with the seasons of the year is therefore not an accident. Consequently we must go on to discover the inner rhythm of the Church's year and see the place Corpus Christi has within it.

First of all, clearly, it grows out of the mystery of Easter and Pentecost: it presupposes the Resurrection and the sending of the Spirit. But it is also in close proximity to the Feast of the Trinity, which reveals the inner logic in the connection between Easter and Pentecost. It is only because God himself is the eternal dialogue of love that he can speak and be spoken to. Only because he himself is relationship can we relate to him; only because he is love can he love and be loved in return. Only because he is threefold can he be the grain of wheat that dies and the bread of eternal life. Ultimately, then, Corpus Christi is an expression of faith in God, in love, in the fact that God is love. All that is said and done on Corpus Christi is in fact a single variation on the theme of love, what it is and what it does. In one of his Corpus Christi hymns Thomas Aquinas puts it beautifully: *nec sumptus consumitur*—love does not consume: it gives and, in giving, receives. And in giving it is not used up but renews itself. Since Corpus Christi is a confession of faith in love, it is totally appropriate that the day should focus on the mystery of transubstantiation. Love is transubstantiation, transformation. Corpus Christi tells us: Yes, there is such a thing as love, and therefore there is transformation, therefore there is hope. And hope gives us the strength to live and face the world. Perhaps it was good to have experienced doubts about the meaning of celebrating Corpus Christi, for it has led us to the rediscovery of a feast that, today, we need more than ever.

PART D

THEOLOGY OF CHURCH MUSIC

I. On the Theological Basis of Church Music

*1. Introduction: Some Aspects of the Postconciliar Dispute
with Regard to Church Music*

It is astonishing to find that in the German edition of the documents of Vatican II, edited by Karl Rahner and Herbert Vorgrimler, the brief commentary that introduces the chapter on Sacred Music in the Constitution on the Liturgy begins with the observation that genuine art, as found in church music, is "of its very nature—which is esoteric in the best sense—hardly to be reconciled with the nature of the liturgy and the basic principle of liturgical reform".[1] It is astonishing, because the Constitution on the Liturgy, on which it is supposed to be commenting, does not see music as "merely an addition and ornamentation of the liturgy" but as itself liturgy, an integrating part of the complete liturgical action.[2] Of course neither Rahner nor Vorgrimler wants to banish all music from the worship of God; but what they do find alien to its nature is art music, that is, the musical heritage of the Western Church. Consequently they feel that the Council, in recommending that "the treasury of sacred music is to be preserved and cultivated with great care",[3] does not mean "that this is to be done within the framework of the liturgy".[4] In a similar vein our commentators lay stress on the Council's recommendation that choirs should be cultivated "especially in cathedral churches", and in context the

From *The Feast of Faith: Approaches to a Theology of the Liturgy*, trans. Graham Harrison (San Francisco: Ignatius Press, 1986), 97–126.

[1] Karl Rahner and Herbert Vorgrimler, *Kleines Konzilskompendium*, 2nd ed. (Freiburg, 1967), 48.

[2] Cf. Josef Andreas Jungmann, "Einleutung und Kommentar zur Konstitution über die Heilige Liturgie 'Sacrosanctum Concilium'", in *Das zweite Vatikanische Konzil: Dokumente und Kommentare*, vol. 1, LThK, 2nd ed., Supplement 1, 10–109, here, 95f.

[3] SC 114.

[4] Rahner and Vorgrimler, *Kleines Konzilskompendium*, 48.

impression is given that the Council really wanted to limit them to cathedrals, and even then provided they did not obstruct the people's participation.[5] For Rahner and Vorgrimler, the normal musical component of liturgy is hence not "actual church music" but "so-called utility music".[6]

Now we can grant the fact that there is a definite tension within the Council document; it reflects the tension between the various approaches represented in the Council itself, but it may also reflect a tension inherent in the subject. This document contains a very clear recommendation of what Rahner and Vorgrimler call "actual church music": in addition to what we have already seen, there is particular emphasis on the teaching of church music in seminaries and on the training of church musicians and singers, especially boys. Special mention is made of the desirability of establishing "higher institutes of sacred music".[7] Gregorian chant is particularly recommended, but there is also an express affirmation of polyphony.[8] There is also a positively enthusiastic panegyric upon the pipe organ, causing Josef Andreas Jungmann to remark that this most ancient instrument of church music is praised here in terms "markedly different from the usually sober, juridical language".[9] But other instruments too are encouraged in church music, under the conditions formulated by tradition.[10] On the other hand, we must acknowledge that, together with the affirmation of this rich inheritance with its high technical demands, there is a desire to see the liturgy completely open to all, a desire for the common participation of all in the liturgical action, including liturgical singing, and this, inevitably, must put a curb on artistic requirements.

Comparing the Council document itself with the commentary by Rahner and Vorgrimler, we find a contrast that is characteristic of the difference, in general, between what the Council said and how it has

---

[5] Ibid.; cf. SC 114: "The treasury of sacred music is to be preserved and cultivated with great care. Choirs must be assiduously developed, especially in cathedral churches. Bishops and other pastors of souls must take great care to ensure that whenever the sacred action is to be accompanied by chant, the whole body of the faithful may be able to contribute that active participation which is rightly theirs", *Vatican Council II: The Conciliar and Post Conciliar Documents*, ed. Austin Flannery (Dublin, 1975).

[6] Rahner and Vorgrimler, *Kleines Konzilskompendium*, 48.

[7] Cf. SC 115.

[8] SC 116.

[9] Jungmann, "Kommentar", 99; also SC 120.

[10] SC 120.

been taken up by the postconciliar Church. During the Council the Fathers became aware of a problem that had not arisen in such a pointed form before—the tension between the demands of art and the simplicity of the liturgy; but when experts and pastors meet together, the pastoral issues predominate, with the result that the view of the whole starts to get out of focus. In its struggle for unanimity, the Council document maintains a difficult balance; what happens then is that it is read one-sidedly in the interests of a particular concern, and the original balance becomes a useful rule of thumb: the liturgy needs utility music, and "actual church music" must be cultivated elsewhere—it is no longer suitable for the liturgy. People are prepared to overlook the fact that, in this view, "actual church music" is no longer actually music for the Church, that the Church no longer has "actual church music". The years that followed witnessed the increasingly grim impoverishment that follows when beauty for its own sake is banished from the Church and all is subordinated to the principle of "utility". One shudders at the lackluster face of the postconciliar liturgy as it has become, or one is bored with its banality and its lack of artistic standards; all the same, this development has at least created a situation in which one can begin to ask questions.

So let us take up this problem: genuine art is "esoteric in the best sense", say Rahner and Vorgrimler; liturgy is simple; it must be possible for everyone, particularly the simple, to participate. Can liturgy accommodate real church music? Does it in fact demand it, or does it exclude it? In looking for an answer to these questions, we will not find much help in our theological inheritance. It seems that relations between theology and church music have always been somewhat cool. Yet if there is to be a meaningful answer, it must lie within historical Christian experience, that is, within the compass of tradition; for this is where the problem is worked over, this is where we discover the response to issues at stake and a view of liturgy and of church music as they have developed throughout a common history.

There can be no doubt that these problems have been seen differently over the course of time. With Rahner and Vorgrimler the issue is that of the "esoteric" versus "utility", and they opt for the latter. It would probably be a mistake to look for some deep philosophical factor behind this attitude; largely it is the average pastoral reaction, recalling the perennial dispute between the pragmatic, practical man and the specialist. Certainly there are underlying attitudes at work here:

the Baroque period with its manifest delight in music was succeeded by the Enlightenment's pedagogic interest, its concern with rationality and reason; the Cecilian movement was followed by the Liturgical Movement, initially exaggerating the importance of Gregorian chant, which appealed to the romantic nostalgia characteristic of large parts of the movement; then came the craze for utility, for the catchy melody, for the participation of everyone in everything. A related factor may be seen in the way modern art has taken refuge more and more in specialism, in the high pitch of virtuosity, in the abstruse and abstract, leaving nothing but schmaltz for the general public. It may also be symptomatic of the divisive tendency of the present age: its rationalism has erected the dilemma of specialism versus banality, while its functionalism ruins any sense of the integrity and vitality, the wholeness, of the artistic utterance. Ultimately it goes back to a conception of activity, community, and equality that no longer knows the unity-creating power of shared listening, shared wonder, the shared experience of being moved at a level deeper than words. At all events, one thing has become clear in recent years: the retreat into utility has not made the liturgy more open; it has only impoverished it. This is not the way to create the required simplicity.

2. Church Music as a Theological Problem in the Work of Thomas Aquinas and in the Authorities He Cites

As we have already said, the antithesis of the esoteric versus utility formulated by Rahner and Vorgrimler is only a contemporary variation of a problem that goes back to the dawn of Christianity. If we are to get to the bottom of it, we must at least take a look at another, earlier form of the same problem. Some years ago Winfried Kurzschenkel produced a historical treatment of music in theology; but while it did open up our present topic, it by no means presented a complete answer.[11] Here I would like to give a glimpse of the debate in history by analyzing the relevant *quaestiones* of St. Thomas Aquinas. This will be particularly valuable because it is part of the greatness of his work

---

[11] Winfried Kurzschenkel, *Die theologische Bestimmung der Musik* (Trier, 1971). Important material also in Karl Gustav Fellerer, ed., *Geschichte der katholischen Kirchenmusik*, 2 vols. (Kassel, 1972–1976); all the following references are to vol. 1.

that it mirrors all the substantial elements of tradition. Thomas discusses the question in his analysis of the concept and nature of "religio", by which he does not mean "religion" in the modern sense but the whole context of the cult, of the worship of God.[12] Here *one* question is devoted to the problem of "the praise of God with the external voice". The introductory article asks whether the vocal praise of God is meaningful at all, and a second article enquires "whether singing can be brought into the praise of God".[13] Now the Church has been singing since the time of Jesus and the apostles, for they sang in the synagogue and brought that singing into the Church.[14] To that extent the principle is established. All the same, weighty arguments were adduced, not against singing entirely, but for limiting it very severely, by those people whose conception of the nature of Christianity allowed only a restricted significance to singing in church.

a. Theology's *Auctoritates* Question the Value of Church Music

Thomas was confronted primarily with three influential traditional authorities critical of church music. Two of these had gained admission into the "Decretum" of Gratian and had thus more or less acquired the status of customary law. First there is the somewhat coarse asceticism of Jerome, which Gratian had adopted into his handbook. Commenting on the words in Ephesians that speak of Christians singing hymns and psalms to God in their hearts (5:19), he wrote: "This applies particularly to the young people who perform the ministry of psalmist

---

[12] Cf. Hermann Josef Burbach, *Studien zur Musikanschauung des Thomas von Aquin*, Kölner Beiträge zur Musikforschung 34 (Regensburg, 1966); Burbach, "Thomas von Aquin und die Musik", *Musica sacra* 94 (1974): 80–82. There is an analysis of Thomas' treatise on worship in Erich Heck, *Der Begriff religio bei Thomas von Aquin*, Abhandlungen zur Philosophie, Psychologie, Soziologie der Religion und Ökumenik, n.s., 21 and 22 (Paderborn, 1971). A useful commentary on questions 81–200 of S.Th. IIa–IIae is that of Ignace Mennessier: St. Thomas d'Aquin, *La Religion*, vols. 1 and 2 (Paris, 1953).

[13] S.Th. II–II, q. 91, a. 1 and 2, in Mennessier, *St. Thomas d'Aquin*, 2:136–48; commentary, 391–93. A full, though in my view too subjective, interpretation of this text is found in Dalmace Sertillanges, "Prière et Musique", *Vie Intellectuelle* 7 (1930): 130–64.

[14] Cf. Karl Gustav Fellerer, "Die katholische Kirchenmusik in Geschichte und Gegenwart", in Fellerer, *Geschichte*, 1–7, especially 1: "The great Hallel (Ps 113–18) at the Last Supper (Mt 26:30; Mk 14:26) signifies the beginning of Christian cultic song." For an extremely instructive article, cf. Eric Werner, "Die jüdischen Wurzeln der christlichen Kirchenmusik", ibid., 22–30, especially 26.

in the church: they should sing to God with their hearts, not with their voices, not plastering neck and throat with ointments like stage-players, churning out theatrical tunes and songs in church."[15] Whatever one thinks of this outburst of the controversial exegete, it is clear that at his time there was an artistically developed church music.

Next to Jerome there is Pope Gregory the Great. In the context of a local Roman synod he prohibited clerics, once they had been ordained to the diaconate, from functioning as cantors (and even added an anathema to the decree), lest they should be distracted from their proper task, namely, the proclamation of the word and the service of the poor. Moreover, Gregory is aware of moral danger too: a fateful contradiction could easily develop between the beautiful voice and the manner of life, between the admiration of the listeners and the verdict of God. So the higher clergy must restrict their musical activity to the singing of the Gospel at Mass; all other musical tasks—the singing of the psalms and the other readings—are to be performed by the lower clergy, by subdeacons or, in case of necessity, by those in minor orders.[16] Evidently, fanatics found support in this canon for their enmity toward church music. But the most important argument comes from the tradition of interpretation of the New Testament itself, which we have already seen in a particularly angular form in Jerome. Colossians 3:16 speaks of praising God with "spiritual songs", and exegesis generally took this as a clear authority for the maxim *"Deus mente colitur magis quam ore"*—God is honored more by the spirit than by the mouth.[17]

Finally we should note an observation that Thomas makes almost as an aside: "In the praise of God the Church does not employ musical instruments ... lest she appear to be falling back into Jewish ways."[18]

---

[15] Jerome, *Comm in ep ad Eph* III 5, PL 26:528C–D; *Decr. Gratiani* I, dist. 92, c. 1; Thomas Aquinas, S.Th. II–II, q. 91, a. 2 opp. 2. The passage is also quoted in Heinrich Hüschen, "Musik der 'Anbetung im Geiste'", in Fellerer, *Geschichte*, 31–36, here, 36. I follow Hüschen in translating the (technical) term "moduli" as "tunes" ("melodies").

[16] Gratian, *Decr.* I, d. 92, c. 2; Thomas, S.Th., II–II, q. 91, a. 2 opp. 3; cf. PL 77:1335A–B (Appendix, V, *Decreta sancti Gregorii Papae I*).

[17] S.Th. II–II, q. 91, a. 1 opp. 2. Cf. the detailed presentation of this line of tradition in Hüschen, "Musik", 31–36.

[18] S.Th. II–II, q. 91, a. 2 opp. 4. Thomas would probably have made use of the eighth book of Aristotle's *Politics* to go into this question more deeply, but unfortunately he did not write the commentary on this book that is attributed to him. In fact the latter was written by his pupil Peter of Auvergne (cf. Burbach, *Studien*, 14) and restricts itself to a paraphrase of the text without dealing with the problem. In his commentary on Psalm 32:2, Thomas does attempt to adapt Aristotle's political approach to music to the new

Instrumental music, understood as a "judaizing element", simply disappeared from the liturgy without any discussion; the instrumental music of the Jewish Temple is dismissed as a mere concession to the hardness of heart and sensuality of the people at the time. What the Old Testament said about music in worship could no longer be applied directly; it had to be read allegorically, it had to be spiritualized. Thomas could not have known that, precisely by banning instrumental music and severely restricting church music to the vocal sphere, the Church was expressing her continuity with early Judaism, linking up with the musical practice of the synagogue and also with the puritanism of the Pharisees, who utterly discountenanced instrumental music.[19] As far as the Church was concerned, the decision had a certain consistency since there was no direct connection with the Temple worship; the liturgy of the Church could only be developed initially along the lines of synagogue worship, not of the Temple cult. In Thomas (or rather in the tradition received by him), this practical reason does in fact acquire the status of a principle: instrumental music is put under the category of "the law", which is not to be understood literally but spiritually. Thus the problem of church music is seen as part of the problem of law and gospel. In the patristic, Platonic tradition of exegesis, the opposition of law and gospel is largely identified with the philosophical opposition of the sensual and the spiritual; in concrete terms this means that music (and particularly instrumental music) falls under the heading of the sensual; the "spiritual" movement of the gospel must therefore be seen more or less as the renunciation of the sensual reality of musical sound in favor of the solely spiritual, that is, the word alone.

b. Issues Underlying the Theological Critique of Music

Thus we have already gone beyond the question of "authorities" to consider intrinsic reasons, and this will enable us to assess the meaning

---

musical situation created by the medieval Church but without taking into account the changed significance of the modes (Doric—Phrygian—and, as he calls it, "Hippolydian"), with the result that the problem is not substantially advanced. Cf. Burbach, *Studien*, 50–58; Mennessier, *St. Thomas d'Aquin*, 2:393; on Aristotle in the present study, cf. nn. 27 and 44 below.

[19] Cf. Werner, "Jüdischen Wurzeln", 25ff.

and scope of the positive theology of church music that Aquinas erects in order to counter the negative position of the traditional authorities. Analyzing the texts—not infrequent in the Fathers—that are critical of music or even openly hostile to it, one can clearly identify two constant and governing factors:

a. In the first place there is a one-sidedly "spiritual" understanding of the relationship between the Old and New Testaments, between law and gospel. It is a fact that, in the transition from Israel to the Gentile Church, a highly influential part was played (in terms of the preparation of a climate of thought) by the spiritual currents that had long been a medium for the encounter of Jewish faith and philosophical piety. This philosophical piety had enabled Greek thought to abandon polytheism and its cults; in its monotheistic yearnings and its interiority it could influence and combine with the Jewish spirit. For its part, the Jewish diaspora had been obliged to ask serious questions about its own universal form, and even in Palestine itself, with the increasing importance of the synagogue and the advance of ideas critical of the Temple, there was a strong tendency toward spiritualizing its historical inheritance of faith.[20] No doubt it is this spiritualizing tendency which lies behind the "allegory" in which Paul expressed the freedom from law (Gal 4:24); for Paul, to read the Old Testament with a view to Christ is to read it in a "spiritual" sense.[21] All the same, to christianize the Old Testament is not simply to spiritualize it: it also implies incarnation.[22] In principle the Church

---

[20] Cf. the material selected by Charles K. Barrett, *The New Testament Background: Selected Documents* (London, 1956). A survey of the Jewish area is available in Marcel Simon, *Die jüdischen Sekten zur Zeit Christi* (Einsiedeln, 1964); on the whole problem, cf. also Harry Austryn Wolfson, *The Philosophy of the Church Fathers*, vol. 1 (Cambridge, Mass., 1956); Olof Gigon, *Die antike Kultur und das Christentum* (Gütersloh, 1966), and the wealth of material in Hüschen, "Musik", 31–36.

[21] Cf. Henri de Lubac, *Exégèse médiévale: Les Quatre sens de l'Écriture* (Paris, 1959–1960), where there is also an analysis of the concepts of allegory, typology, and the spiritual sense [trans. Mark Sebanc (vol. 1) and E. M. Macierowski (vol. 2) as *Medieval Exegesis: The Four Senses of Scripture* (Grand Rapids, Mich.: Eerdmans; Edinburgh: T. & T. Clark, 1998–2009)]; also de Lubac, *Histoire et Esprit: L'Intelligence de l'Écriture d'après Origène* (Paris, 1950) [trans. Anne Englund Nash and Juvenal Merriell as *History and Spirit: The Understanding of Scripture according to Origen* (San Francisco: Ignatius Press, 2007)]. On Thomas' handling of the issue: Maximino Arias-Reyero, *Thomas von Aquin als Exeget* (Einsiedeln, 1971). See also my remarks in Internationale Theologenkommission, *Die Einheit des Glaubens und der theologische Pluralismus*, Sammlung Horizonte, n.s. 7 (Einsiedeln, 1973), 22–29.

[22] Internationale Theologenkommission, *Einheit des Glaubens*, 26, with further refs. I am not entirely satisfied with the otherwise valuable book by Thierry Maertens, *Heidnisch-jüdische*

Fathers were aware of this; the fight against Gnosticism, as that against Arius, is a fight against a merely "spiritual" understanding of Christianity that would have changed it from a concrete faith into a religious philosophy.

In retrospect it must be said, however, that the Fathers could not simply step out of the intellectual climate of their time; they were obliged to make concessions to it that went beyond what was permissible and appropriate from the point of view of Christianity. Once again we must assert that there is and can be a genuine communion of interest between Christianity and Platonism. The "allegory" of the Old Testament, on which Christianity is founded, is closely related to the "allegory" that arises from Platonic thought; or rather, put more exactly: as spiritual paths, Christianity and Platonism pursue parallel courses for quite a distance. But in Christian terms, "spiritualization" is not simply opposition to the world of the senses, as in Platonic mysticism, but a drawing near to the Lord who "is the Spirit" (2 Cor 3:17; cf. 1 Cor 15:45). Therefore the body is included in this spiritualization: the Lord is "the Spirit" precisely in that his body does not experience corruption (Ps 15:9f. LXX = Acts 2:26) but is seized by the life-giving power of the Spirit. Christology reveals the central divergence from the Platonic teaching on spiritualization; its background is the theology of creation, whose inner unity is not destroyed but ratified by Christology.

But there is something more. As we have seen, the Christian liturgy linked up as a matter of historical necessity with the synagogue, not the Temple. In doing so it took on a more or less puritan form. Initially this was unavoidable, in order to express the fundamental gulf between it and the Old Law, which was focused in the Temple cult. If it was to be made clear that the Christian liturgy was not a mere multiplication of the Temple but a complete break leading to a new level, this break had to be consistently manifested in institutional terms. In fact, during the first decades of the Christian movement, the Temple and its ordinances still existed, and Jewish Christians continued to participate legitimately in its life; hence in any case there could be no question of imitating Temple worship. In spite of

---

Wurzeln der christlichen Feste (Mainz, 1965) [trans. as *A Feast in honor of Yahweh* (Notre Dame, Ind., 1965)], since it puts forward the "spiritualization" view one-sidedly. By contrast, the specifically Christian perspective is very well demonstrated in Jean Daniélou, *Bible et Liturgie* (Paris: Cerf, 1951) [trans. as *The Bible and the Liturgy* (London, 1956)].

this we cannot avoid wondering how far such a central text as John 2:13–22, with its promise of a new Temple "in three days", affected the way Christianity saw itself and influenced it to take over the reality signified by the Temple.[23] This question is of great importance for the problem of the priestly office: Does the primitive Church's connection solely with the synagogue, as a matter of necessity, imply a definitive and fundamental break with the idea of priesthood, or must the Temple's authentic inheritance be continued, once it has undergone a christological transformation? This is only one of the instances that show plainly how intractable, so far, the problem of the relationship of the Testaments to one another has proved. Another instance is the question of the legitimacy of the church building, the "sacral" edifice—nowadays an increasingly pressing question. Then, out of this same melting pot, there comes the issue of images that has been so traumatic in Church history.

In fact, patristic theology did incorporate the idea of the Temple into Christianity; it was elevated to the level of a category in the understanding of the Christian reality.[24] For the most part, however, it was used "allegorically", in a strictly applied, spiritualizing theology; it was not until the iconoclastic controversy that the Greek Church's passion for the image led to a breakthrough in which Christianity's historical development—with complete justification—succeeded in moving in the opposite direction: from the absence of images in the Old Testament to the glorification of God in the image.[25] This decision has been largely called into question in the postconciliar Catholic Church, and the only possible course, people have felt, is to abandon images. This results from the same approach that wants to remove "actual church music" from worship; it shows how close today's issues are to those of yesterday, once one penetrates below the surface.

---

[23] On this, cf. the thorough study by Yves Congar, *Le Mystère du temple* (Paris, 1957) [trans. as *The Mystery of the Temple* (London, 1962)]. Valuable insights into the related question of the priesthood in André Feuillet, *Le Sacerdoce du Christ et de ses ministers* (Paris, 1972) [trans. as *The Priesthood of Christ and His Ministers* (Doubleday, 1975)].

[24] Cf. my remarks in Joseph Ratzinger, *Volk und Haus Gottes in Augustins Lehre von der Kirche*, MThS.S 7 (Munich, 1954).

[25] Cf. Paul Evdokimov, *L'Art de l'icône: Théologie de la beauté* (Paris: Desclée, 1970); Christoph Schönborn, *L'Icône du Christ: Fondements théologiques élaborés entre le Ier et le IIe Concile de Nicée (325–787)*, Paradosis 24 (Fribourg, 1976) [trans. Lothar Krauth as *God's Human Face: The Christ-Icon* (San Francisco: Ignatius Press, 1994)]; valuable too is Stylianos Harkianakis, *Orthodoxe Kirche und Katholizismus* (Munich, 1975), 75–88.

The results are surprisingly similar. The idea that God can only really be praised in the heart means that no status can be accorded to music, to the audible form of this praise, within the act of praise itself in Christian worship. Yet, as a matter of fact, the worship of God *has* a vocal form; there *is* singing in worship. As a way of getting around this, music must be relegated to a secondary level. Augustine is a splendid example of this. His sensitivity to music causes him much torment because his mind is dominated by a spiritualizing theology that ascribes the senses to the Old Testament, the "old man", the old world: he is afraid of "sinning grievously" when he is "moved more by the music than by the reality to which the singing refers"—and would prefer "not to hear singing at all". Fortunately his rigorism is dampened when he recalls the profound stirring his soul experienced when he first heard church music in Milan, and although he does not risk a final decision, he is "more inclined to value the use of singing in church: by means of the delight of the ears, the soul that is still weak is encouraged to rise to the world of piety".[26] Thomas was justified in seeing here a confirmation of Boethius' theory of music and could sum up his reasons for church music by saying that "thus the minds of the weak are more effectively summoned to piety." [27] So church music

---

[26] *Confessions* X, 33, 50; Thomas, S.Th. II-II, q. 91, a. 2 resp.

[27] Thomas, S.Th. II-II, q. 91, a. 2 resp.; cf. Boethius, *De institutione musica*, prol. PL 63:1168. With a certain justification, Thomas supports his argument by reference to the eighth book of Aristotle's *Politics*, although he by no means exhausts the richness it contains. If one recalls that Aristotle devotes almost this entire eighth book to music, it becomes clear just how important a place he assigns to music in his philosophy of community. Among the four disciplines that according to Aristotle form the rootstock of education—writing (γράμματα), gymnastics, music, and drawing (γραφική) (VIII, 3, Bekker II, 1337b, 24f.)—music is given a special place. Unlike the other three, it is not oriented to a trade and a purpose but instructs man in true leisure, which needs no extrinsic justification but has an intrinsic purpose: ταύτας τὰς μαθήσεις ἑαυῶν χάρινν, τὰς δὲ πρὸς τὴν ἀσχολίαν ... χάριν ἄλλων (VIII, 3; 1338a, 12f.). Cf. also the splendid verdict: "The lofty mind, the free man is not always asking what use a thing is" (1338b, 2ff.). In the philosophy of music of Aristotle's *Politics*, we become aware of a side of Greek thought that is largely forgotten, as Henri-Irénée Marrou emphasizes: "As we see the Greeks through the medium of our own classical culture, they seem to us to be primarily poets, philosophers, and mathematicians; if we honor them as artists, we think of them primarily as architects and sculptors; as a result of our education we give less attention to their music than to their ceramics! Yet, in fact and in intention, they were musicians first and foremost" (*Geschichte der Erziehung im klassischen Altertum* [Freiburg and Munich, 1957], 68 [*Histoire de l'éducation dans l'antiquité* (Paris, 1955); trans. as *History of Education in Antiquity* (London, 1956)]). Certainly, Plato's purism (*Politeia* III, 398a–400a) pursues a different line, which, in late classical times, could without difficulty be combined with the puritanism of the synagogue, cf. n. 44. It is a pity

is put at the level of what is pedagogically useful; in practice, therefore, it is subject to the criterion of "utility".

We shall show that both Thomas and Augustine can go much farther than this, in fact, on the basis of their experience and understanding. But the "spiritualization" framework that had become part of the question of the relation of the two Testaments (and hence of what is specifically Christian) stops them from carrying their insight through consistently.

b. First, however, we must bring to light a second group of ideas that stood in the way of a positive evaluation of church music. Only by understanding the reasons for the denial of church music can we show forth the positive rationale in a convincing manner. The matter is put in a nutshell in Thomas' fundamental article on the praise of God, where he says that "vocal worship is necessary, not for God's sake, but for the sake of the worshipper." [28] Here we see how much the ancient world's concept of God's absolute immutability and impassibility had entered into Christian thought through Greek philosophy, creating a barrier to any satisfactory theology, not only of church music, but of all prayer whatever. In Aristotle this concept of God had led logically to the identification of piety with self-culture, that is, the cultivation of what is most pleasing to the gods, namely, reason. [29] Only with great difficulty has Christian theology, dominated by the

---

that in this issue Thomas was inhibited by the patristic authorities and hence was not able to follow Aristotle's lead into a Christian context, with the result that, as yet, we have no "Christian Aristotle" in the theory of church music. Considering that, as far as the Christian is concerned, the Church, by virtue of her locus in the structure of existence, has taken over the place of the *polis* of the ancient world, the Aristotelian connection of *polis* and music could have yielded an ideal starting point in the question of church music. A brief summary of the form and development of Greek music can be found in *Der kleine Pauly* 3:1485–96.

[28] S.Th. II-II, q. 91, a. 1 resp.

[29] *Nichomachean Ethics* X, 9 (Bekker 1179a, 24ff.). Cf. the commentary by Franz Dirlmeier (*Aristoteles, Nikomachische Ethik* [Darmstadt, 1956], 598f.), where he shows that the philosophical achievement of this passage lies in the way it sublimates the *do ut des*, so that, in spite of the axiomatic self-love of the gods, Aristotle is able to present an impressive picture of the friendship with the gods enjoyed by the man of insight. On the problem of immutability in Christian theology, cf. Wilhelm Maas, *Unveränderlichkeit Gottes: Zum Verhältnis von griechisch-philosophischer und christlicher Gotteslehre*, Paderborner theologische Studien 1 (Paderborn, 1974). Cf. also on the whole question: Joseph Ratzinger, "Zur theologischen Grundlegung von Gebet und Liturgie", in Ratzinger, *Das Fest des Glaubens*, 2nd ed. (Einsiedeln, 1981), 11–30 [trans. Graham Harrison as "On the Theological Basis of Prayer and Liturgy", in *The Feast of Faith: Approaches to a Theology of the Liturgy* (San Francisco: Ignatius Press, 1986), 11–32].

idea of immutability, been able to shake free from these notions; indeed, the regression today into a theory in which prayer is simply the activation of those of man's powers which are felt to be "the best" has assumed frightening proportions. No doubt classical theology is far removed from this kind of rationalism; liberated by Christ, who is the Word of God, it knows that it is enabled to speak with God; but in the philosophical superstructure the influence of the old ideas of God still makes itself felt; hence a shadow of rationalism is cast over the theory of liturgy.

c. The Theological Basis of Church Music

We have spoken of the commitment to the "spiritualization" framework, and to the ancient concept of God, as the burden of the theological tradition; on the other hand, the latter's freedom and breadth spring from two sources internal to Christianity: the living experience of liturgy and the theology of the psalms. With the transition from the synagogue to the church, singing in worship had increased; at a very early date "hymns" had been added to the psalms.[30] In contrast to theology, the psalms manifested an utterly unpuritanical delight in music, which, in spite of allegorical exegesis, was bound to have an influence. The fact that these songs of Israel continued to be prayed and sung as hymns of the Church meant that the whole wealth of feeling of Israel's prayer was present in the Church. Thus Thomas too concludes his reflections on the vocal quality of prayer with a quotation from the psalms that goes far beyond the considerations that precede it: "... his praise shall continually be in my mouth.... Let the afflicted hear and be glad. O magnify the Lord with me...."[31] Here, delight in the Lord is felt to be meaningful and beautiful in itself; joy in shared praise of him, the awareness, through celebratory music-making, that

---

[30] Hymns of this kind are indicated in 1 Cor 14:25–26; Col 3:16; Eph 5:19ff. The New Testament contains quite a number of early Christian hymns, e.g., Phil 2:5–11; Eph 2:14–16; 2 Tim 2:11–13. They are collected in Heinrich Schlier, *Das Ende der Zeit* (Freiburg, 1971), 212f.; cf. also Solange Corbin, "Grundlagen und erste Entwicklung der christlichen Kultmusik", in Fellerer, *Geschichte*, 16–21. I have endeavored to show these connections in more detail in my article "Theologische Probleme der Kirchenmusik", IKaZ 9 (1980): 148–57 [JRCW 11:480–93].

[31] Ps 33:2–4; Thomas, S.Th. II-II, q. 91, a. 1 resp. Cf. also St. Thomas' commentary on Ps 33 (1–4), which develops these ideas a little further.

God is worthy of worship—this is self-evident, it needs no theories. By quoting from the psalms, Thomas is in fact saying Yes to that joy which *expresses* itself and in doing so unites those who participate (and this includes particularly those who "listen"); this expressed joy manifests itself as the presence of the glory that is God: in responding to this glory, it actually *shares* in it. It would not be difficult to take this theme of "glorification", found in the Old Testament in the context of the theology of creation, and fill it out in terms of Christology (Christ as the glory of God now accessible to us) and pneumatology (the Spirit speaks, sighs, and gives thanks in us).[32] As opposed to a narrow, rationalistic theory of proclamation, we would need to point to that cosmic proclamation which finds expression in Psalm 19: The heavens are telling the glory of God. The Creator's glory cannot be manifested in word only: it needs to be expressed in the music of creation, too, and in its creative transformation by the mind of the believing and beholding man. At the same time we would need to remind ourselves that the psalms are also the prayers of the poor, the prayer of the crucified Righteous One, and as such they are to a large extent laments; but here too they are to be seen as the lament of the whole creation, which goes beyond words, transforming them into a music in which the lament becomes both a beseeching of God and a sign of hope: glory, too, but in the mode of suffering.

"Glorification" is the central reason why Christian liturgy must be cosmic liturgy, why it must as it were orchestrate the mystery of Christ with all the voices of creation.[33]

The other themes found in the tradition represented by Thomas can be fitted into this basic context and fill it out. Thus, for instance, Thomas says that through the praise of God man ascends to God.[34] Praise itself is a movement, a path; it is more than understanding,

---

[32] The trinitarian dimension of church music is very well described in the important article by Ferdinand Haberl entitled "Zur Theologie der Kirchenmusik", *Musica sacra* 91 (1971): 213–19; cf. Haberl, "Die humane und sakrale Bedeutung der Musik", in *In caritate et veritate: Festschrift für Johannes Overath*, ed. Hans Lonnendonker (Saarbrücken, 1973), 17–23.

[33] Cf. the magnificent outline of a theological aesthetics by Hans Urs von Balthasar, *Herrlichkeit*, 7 vols. (Einsiedeln, 1967–1969) [trans. Erasmo Leiva-Merikakis et al. as *The Glory of the Lord*, 7 vols. (San Francisco: Ignatius Press, 1982–1989)]; von Balthasar, *Kosmische Liturgie: Das Weltbild Maximus' des Bekenners*, 2nd ed. (Einsiedeln, 1961) [trans. Brian E. Daley as *Cosmic Liturgy: The Universe according to Maximus the Confessor* (Communio; San Francisco: Ignatius Press, 2003).

[34] "Homo per divinam laudem affectu ascendit in Deum": S.Th., q. 91, a. 1 resp.

knowing, and doing—it is an "ascent", a way of reaching him who dwells amid the praises of the angels. Thomas mentioned another factor: this ascent draws man away from what is opposed to God. Anyone who has ever experienced the transforming power of great liturgy, great art, great music, will know this. Thomas adds that the sound of musical praise leads us and others to a sense of reverence.[35] It awakens the inner man,[36] as Augustine had discovered in Milan. With Augustine the academic, a man who had come to appreciate Christianity as a philosophy but was uneasy about the Church herself, which seemed to have a lot of vulgarity about her, it was the singing Church that gave him a shattering experience, penetrating the whole man, and that led him forward on the way to the Church.[37] From this point of view, the other, pedagogical aspect, the "stimulating of others to praise God",[38] becomes meaningful and

---

[35] "Ut nos ipsos et alios audientes ad eius reverentiam inducamus": ibid.

[36] "Valet tamen exterior laus oris ad excitandum interiorem affectum laudantis": ibid., q. 91, a. 1 ad 2.

[37] Cf. the beautiful description in *Confessions* IX, 6, 14: "How I wept to hear Your hymns and songs, deeply moved by the voices of Your sweetly (suave) singing Church! Their voices penetrated my ears, and with them truth found its way into my heart; my frozen feeling for God began to thaw, tears flowed and I experienced joy and relief." On the idea of *suave* ("sweetly"), cf. Werner, "Jüdischen Wurzeln", in Fellerer, *Geschichte*, 26: the cantor was required to sing with a "sweet" voice, i.e., a high, lyrical voice of tenor quality. Augustine's other statements on church music do not match up, however, to this testimony to direct experience because of the influence of his theory of spiritualization. Apart from *Conf.* X, 33, 50, mention should be made of his *Epist.* 55 to Januarius. Here he says that, with regard to following the custom of the particular church, it is praiseworthy if she ministers to the weakness of the little ones, a principle that is based on the use of hymns and psalms and spiritual songs, authorized by the Lord and the apostles. It is interesting that the Donatists criticized the musical puritanism of the African Catholics, which made many Catholics even more sceptical with regard to church music: XVIII, 34 [CSEL 34, 2, p. 208f.]. This leads us to conclude that the Donatist liturgy adopted large elements of indigenous musical tradition (which would correspond to the markedly African and nationalist quality of Donatism). Hence Augustine's reserve in the matter of church music may be traceable not only to his spiritualization philosophy but also to the Catholic-Donatist controversy. In *Enarr. II in Ps 18,1* (C.Chr 38:105), Augustine distinguishes human singing from birdsong: the birds sing what they do not understand. "But we who have learned in the Church how to sing the divine words must recall what is written: blessed the people that sings praises with understanding. Therefore, my beloved, what we have sung with united voices we must understand and appreciate with perceptive hearts." On Augustine and the Milan liturgy, cf. Bonifazio Baroffio, "Ambrosianische Liturgie", in Fellerer, *Geschichte*, 191–204, here, 192; on Augustine's path from intellectual to ecclesial Christianity, cf. Frederik van der Meer, *Augustinus der Seelsorger* (Cologne, 1951), 25ff.; Ratzinger, *Volk und Haus Gottes in Augustins Lehre von der Kirche*, 1–12.

[38] Thomas, S.Th., q. 91, a. 1 ad 2: "ad provocandum alios ad laudem Dei".

intelligible, particularly when we recall what "pedagogy" meant for the ancients, namely, a leading to one's real nature, a process of redemption and liberation.[39]

d. The Positive Significance of the Theological Critique of Music

In undertaking to identify and develop the positive elements of the tradition, we must face the question of to what extent its critical stance may be justified. The very breadth of this aspect of the tradition, with the substantial reasons given (however qualified), oblige us to do so. We found that the basic reason underlying all particular criticisms is the idea of "spiritualization", which expresses the transition from the Old to the New Testament and hence the special orientation of Christianity. We discovered that this element is misunderstood if it is simply equated with the denial of the "senses", of man's bodily nature, and with the renunciation of the fullness of creation. The movement of spiritualization in creation is understood properly as bringing creation into the mode of being of the Holy Spirit and its consequent transformation, exemplified in the crucified and resurrected Christ. In this sense, the taking up of music into the liturgy must be its taking up into the Spirit, a transformation that implies both death and resurrection. That is why the Church has had to be critical of all ethnic music; it could not be allowed untransformed into the sanctuary. The cultic music of pagan religions has a different status in human existence from the music that glorifies God in creation. Through rhythm and melody themselves, pagan music often endeavors to elicit an ecstasy of the senses, but without elevating the senses into the spirit; on the contrary, it attempts to swallow up the spirit in the senses as a means of release. This imbalance toward the senses recurs in modern popular music: the "God" found

---

[39] Gisbert Greshake emphasized the religious depth of the concept of *paideia* in "Der Wandel der Erlösungsvorstellungen in der Theologiegeschichte", in L. Scheffczyk, *Erlösung und Emanzipation*, QD 61 (Freiburg, 1973), 69–101, here, 76ff. In fact the theory of music that Aristotle develops in book 8 of the *Politics* is governed by the idea of *paideia*. In musical education *paideia* goes far beyond a training in what is useful and necessary: it facilitates authentic leisure and hence is an education for freedom, for beauty: "... ἐστὶ παιδεία τις ὧν οὐχ ὡς χρησίμην παιδευτέον ... ἀλλ' ὡς ἐλευθέριον καὶ καλήν" (VIII, 3, Bekker 1338a, 30ff.).

here, the salvation of man identified here, is quite different from the God of the Christian faith. Quite different coordinates of existence are applied, quite a contrary view of the cosmos as a whole is exhibited. Here music can indeed become a "seduction" leading men astray. Here music does not purify but becomes a drug, an anesthetic. Superficially, the reason why elements of African pagan music are taken up with such facility into post-Christian pagan music may seem to have to do with a similarity of formal components; but the deeper reason lies in their basically sympathetic attitudes, their understanding of reality, for, at heart, the "enlightened" technological world can be both pagan and primitive. If music is to be the medium of worship, it needs purifying; only then can it in turn have a purifying and "elevating" effect.

The whole of Church history can be seen as the struggle to achieve the proper kind of spiritualization; and although, musically speaking, the theologians' puritanism was frequently unenlightened, the fruit of this struggle has been the great church music of the West—indeed, Western music as a whole. The work of a Palestrina or a Mozart would be unthinkable apart from this dramatic interplay in which creation becomes the instrument of the spirit, and the spirit, too, becomes organized sound in the material creation, thus attaining a height inaccessible to "pure" spirit. Spiritualization of the senses is the true spiritualization of the spirit. No one could have foreseen, at the outset of this process, the fruits it would yield. To that extent it is impossible to lay down a priori musical criteria for this spiritualization process, although it is certainly easier to say what is excluded than what is included. Vatican II was well advised, therefore, only to indicate very general standards: music must "accord with the spirit of the liturgical action";[40] it must be "suitable", or be capable of being "made suitable, for sacred use";[41] it must "accord with the dignity of the temple" and "truly contribute to the edification of the faithful".[42]

At this point the tradition embodied by Thomas is clearer. The text we have analyzed presents us with two clear limits: following an

---

[40] SC 116, par. 2.
[41] SC 120, par. 2.
[42] Ibid.

apparently undisputed tradition, he insists on the strictly vocal character of church music. Behind Jerome's rasping criticisms we can see the bitter dispute between the early Church and the ancient theatre that exercised such a fascination; it is the music of the theatre that Jerome wishes to exclude, not because it exemplifies the ecstatic character of earlier cultic music, but because of the vanity and affectation in which it involves the artist concerned. Here we can agree unreservedly with him: liturgical music must be humble, for its aim is not applause but "edification". It is appropriate that in church, unlike the concert hall, the musician is for the most part not seen. But what shall we say of the express option in favor of vocal music? It should be clear from what we have already said that Thomas' exclusive espousal of it is based historically and in fact on a misunderstanding. All the same I would hesitate to dismiss such a deeply rooted tradition as completely mistaken. We must surely admit that the liturgy of the incarnate Word is necessarily and specifically word-oriented. To say this is not to be a party to the banal rationalism of the postconciliar period, which held that only what everyone could follow intellectually was suitable for liturgy, a view that led to the exclusion of art and the increasingly banal treatment of the "word". These false conceptions are parried at the conclusion of Aquinas' *quaestio* on music: he is dealing with the objection that when something is sung it is harder for the hearers to understand than when it is said. He replies: "Even if those who listen sometimes do not understand the words being sung, they do understand the reason for the singing, namely, the praise of God. And that is sufficient to arouse men to worship." [43] A relation to the word, then, is fundamental all the same. Perhaps it should be said that, where an instrument is concerned, there is a greater possibility of alienation from the spirit than in the case of the voice; music can slip away from or turn against the spirit, the more remote it is from the human being. Conversely this would mean that, with instruments, the process of purification, of elevation to the spirit, must be considered with special care. But here again it is this essential purification which has resulted in the development of the instruments of Western music, endowing mankind with its most precious gifts. Man fails to measure up to this inheritance to the extent that he rejects the claim that the spirit of

---

[43] S.Th. II-II, q. 91, a. 2 opp. 5 and ad 5.

faith makes upon the senses. The struggle between faith and the world's music has been most fruitful.[44]

3. Conclusion: Governing Principles in This Time of Crisis

To conclude these observations I would like to put forward a number of basic principles, applying what we have discovered from history to the current problems that formed our starting point.

1. Liturgy is for all. It must be "catholic", that is, communicable to all the faithful without distinction of place, origin, and education. Thus it must be "simple". But that is not the same as being cheap. There is a banal simplism, and there is the simplicity that is the expression of maturity. It is this second, true simplicity which applies in the Church. The greatest efforts of the spirit, the greatest purification, the greatest maturity—all these are needed to produce genuine simplicity. The requirement of simplicity, properly speaking, is identical with the requirement of purity and maturity. Certainly there are many stages on the way to it, but each one makes demands on the soul without which nothing is achieved.

2. Catholicity does not mean uniformity. Vatican II had a purpose in making special mention of the cathedral church in its Constitution on the Liturgy. The cathedral can and should be more ambitious than the normal parish church in terms of the solemnity and beauty of the worship of God, and here too art will be involved at different levels

---

[44] A related debate can already be found in Aristotle, where he distinguishes Doric music as "ethical" music from the "orgiastic and pathetic" Phrygian music and excludes the latter from education (*Politeia* VIII, 7, Bekker 1341f.); characteristically he adduces the myth of Athene's rejection of the flute: for him such music contradicts the spiritualized humanity symbolized in Athene (VIII, 6, Bekker 1341b, 2ff.). Here we clearly see the continuing influence of ancient cultic and cultural oppositions. For Aristotle, Lydian music is suitable for education, however, because it combines a sense of beauty with an educative content (VIII, 7, Bekker 1342b, 31f.). But, in his magnanimous and open approach, he allows Phrygian music for relief (catharsis). He deliberately adopts this tolerant attitude in opposition to Plato in the *Politeia*, who excluded Mixolydian, Hyperlydian ("syntonoly-disti"), Ionic, and Lydian music from his ideal state, only permitting Doric and Phrygian music; and as for instruments, Plato wanted to allow nothing but the lyre and cithara in the city and a kind of reed-pipe in the country. Here too, behind the philosophical deduction one can perceive a mythico-religious substratum: "For we are doing nothing new ... by giving the preeminence to Apollo and his instruments before Marsyas and his" (*Republic* III, 399e, cf. III, 398d–400a).

depending on the occasion and the prevailing conditions. Together we make up the whole; we do not all have to be doing everything. It is strange that the postconciliar pluralism has created uniformity in one respect at least: it will not tolerate a high standard of expression. We need to counter this by reinstating the whole range of possibilities within the unity of the Catholic liturgy.

3. One of the principles of the Council's liturgical reform was, with good reason, the *participatio actuosa*, the active participation of the whole "People of God" in the liturgy. Subsequently, however, this idea has been fatally narrowed down, giving the impression that active participation is only present where there is evidence of external activity—speaking, singing, preaching, liturgical action. It may be that articles 28 and 30 of the Constitution on the Liturgy, which define active participation, have encouraged this narrow view by speaking largely of external activities. Yet article 30 also speaks of silence as a mode of active participation. We must go on to say that listening, the receptive employment of the senses and the mind, spiritual participation, are surely just as much "activity" as speaking is. Are receptivity, perception, being moved, not "active" things too? What we have here, surely, is a diminished view of man that reduces him to what is verbally intelligible, and this at a time when we are aware that what comes to the surface in rationality is only the tip of the iceberg compared with the totality of man. In more concrete terms, there are a good number of people who can sing better "with the heart" than "with the mouth"; but their hearts are really stimulated to sing through the singing of those who *have* the gift of singing "with their mouths". It is as if they themselves actually sing in the others; their thankful listening is united with the voices of the singers in the one worship of God. Are we to compel people to sing when they cannot and, by doing so, silence not only their hearts but the hearts of others too? This is not to impugn the singing of the whole faithful people, which has its inalienable place in the Church, but it *is* opposed to a one-sidedness that is founded neither on tradition nor on the nature of the case.

4. A Church that only makes use of "utility" music has fallen for what is, in fact, useless. She too becomes ineffectual. For her mission is a far higher one. As the Old Testament speaks of the Temple, the Church is to be the place of "glory" and, as such, too, the place where mankind's cry of distress is brought to the ear of God. The Church must not settle down with what is merely comfortable and serviceable

at the parish level; she must arouse the voice of the cosmos and, by glorifying the Creator, elicit the glory of the cosmos itself, making it also glorious, beautiful, habitable, and beloved. Next to the saints, the art that the Church has produced is the only real "apologia" for her history. It is this glory which witnesses to the Lord, not theology's clever explanations for all the terrible things that, lamentably, fill the pages of her history. The Church is to transform, improve, "humanize" the world—but how can she do that if at the same time she turns her back on beauty, which is so closely allied to love? For together, beauty and love form the true consolation in this world, bringing it as near as possible to the world of the resurrection. The Church must maintain high standards; she must be a place where beauty can be at home; she must lead the struggle for that "spiritualization" without which the world becomes the "first circle of hell". Thus to ask what is "suitable" must always be the same as asking what is "worthy"; it must constantly challenge us to seek what is "worthy" of the Church's worship.

5. The Constitution on the Liturgy observes that "in certain countries, especially in mission lands, there are people who have their own musical tradition, and this plays a great part in their religious and social life. For this reason their music should be held in proper esteem and a suitable place is to be given to it."[45] This corresponds to the Council's idea of catholicity, according to which "whatever goodness is found in the minds and hearts of men, or in the particular customs and cultures of peoples, far from being lost is purified, raised to a higher level, and reaches its perfection...."[46] These expressions have been rightly welcomed in theology and pastoral care, even if on occasion the element of "purification" has been neglected. It is strange however that, in their legitimate delight in the new openness to other cultures, many people seem to have forgotten that the countries of Europe also have a musical inheritance that "plays a great part in their religious and social life"! Indeed, here we have a musical tradition that has sprung from the very heart of the Church and her faith. One cannot, of course, simply equate the great treasury of European church music with the music of the Church or, on account of its stature, consider that its history has come to an end; it would

---

[45] SC 119.
[46] Cf. AG 9.

be equally impossible simply to identify the great figures of Latin theology with the teaching of the Church or to see in them some ultimate theological perfection. All the same it is just as clear that the Church must not lose this rich inheritance which was developed in her own matrix and yet belongs to the whole of mankind.[47] Or does this "esteem" and a "suitable place" in the liturgy (art. 119) apply only to non-Christian tradition? Fortunately the Council itself clearly opposes any such absurd conclusion, insisting that "the treasury of sacred music is to be preserved and cultivated with great care" (art. 114). Music such as this can only be preserved and cultivated, however, if it continues to be sung and played as prayer, as a gesture glorifying God, in the place where it was born—in the Church's worship.

---

[47] Haberl puts it splendidly in "Zur Theologie der Kirchenmusik", 218: "Church music must be both a traditional and a progressive art." On this whole issue, cf. also the valuable contribution by Josef Friedrich Doppelbauer, "Kompositorische Fragen und Aufgaben", in *Magna gloria Domini*, ed. Johannes Overath (Altötting, 1972), 148–56, where, from a musical point of view, he arrives at the same conclusions as we have reached through examining the theological sources.

II. The Image of the World and of Man in the Liturgy and Its Expression in Church Music

Right from the beginning liturgy and music have been closely related. Wherever people praise God, words alone do not suffice. Conversation with God transcends the boundaries of human speech; everywhere it has, according to its nature, called on music for help, on singing and on the voices of creation in the sound of the instruments. Not only man has a role in the praise of God. Worship is singing in unison with that which all things bespeak.

As closely as liturgy and music are related by their very natures, their relationship has been difficult time and again, especially during the transition periods of history and culture. It is therefore no surprise that the question about the right form of music in worship has again become controversial today. In the disputes of the Second Vatican Council and immediately thereafter it seemed to be merely a question of the difference between pastoral practitioners, on the one hand, and church musicians, on the other hand. The musicians did not want to let themselves be subjected to mere pastoral expediency, but tried to show the inner dignity of music as a pastoral and liturgical standard in its own right.[1] The controversy seemed to be taking place essentially on the level of application alone, but the rift goes deeper. The second wave of liturgical reform is pushing the questions forward, as far as the foundations themselves. Here the issue is the essence of liturgical action as such, its anthropological and theological foundations. The controversy about church music has become symptomatic for the deeper question about what liturgical worship is.

Reprinted with permission from *A New Song for the Lord: Faith in Christ and Liturgy Today*, 2nd ed. (1996; New York: Crossroad, 2005), 111–27.

[1] Cf. Joseph Ratzinger, *Das Fest des Glaubens* (Einsiedeln, 1981), 86–111 [trans. Graham Harrison as *The Feast of Faith: Approaches to a Theology of the Liturgy* (San Francisco: Ignatius Press, 1986), 97–126; JRCW 11:421–42].

1. Surpassing the Council? A New Conception of Liturgy

The new phase of the will to reform liturgically no longer sees its foundation explicitly in the words of the Second Vatican Council, but in its "spirit". As a symptomatic text I shall use the learned and clearly drafted article on song and music in the Church in the *Nuovo Dizionario di Liturgia*. The superior artistic quality of Gregorian chant or of classical polyphony is in no way denied here. It is not even a question of playing off congregational activity against elitist art. Nor is the point the rejection of historical rigidity that only copies the past and thus remains without a present and a future. We are rather concerned with a new, fundamental understanding of liturgy with which one hopes to overtake the Council, whose Constitution on the Sacred Liturgy is seen to be of two minds.[2]

Let us briefly try to become acquainted with this conception in its essential features. It states that the starting point for the liturgy is the gathering of two or three who come together in the name of Christ.[3] This reference to the Lord's words of promise in Matthew 18:20 sounds harmless and traditional at first hearing. It receives revolutionary momentum, however, when one isolates this one biblical text and contrasts it with the entire liturgical tradition. For the two or three are then brought into conflict with an institution having institutional roles and with every "codified program". This definition therefore means that the Church does not come before the group, but the group before the Church. It is not the Church as an integral whole that carries the liturgy of the individual group or parish; rather, the group is itself the place of origin for the liturgy. Hence, liturgy does not grow out of a common given either, a "rite" (which now, as a "codified program", has acquired the negative image of lack of freedom); it originates on the spot from the creativity of those gathered. In this specialized language of sociologists, the Sacrament of Holy Orders appears as an institutional role that has created a monopoly for itself and dissolves the original unity and community of the group by means of the institution (= the Church).[4] We

---

[2] Felice Rainoldi and Eugenio Costa, Jr., "Canto e musica", in *Nuovo Dizionario di Liturgia*, ed. Domenico Sartore und Achille M. Triacca (Rome, 1984), 198–219; especially 211a: "i documenti del Vaticano II rivelano l'esistenza di due anime"; and 212a: "Queste serie di spunti, dedotti dallo spirito più che dalla lettera del Vaticano II."

[3] Cf. ibid., 199a.

[4] Cf. ibid., 206b.

are told that in this configuration music (just like Latin) then becomes a language of the initiates, "a language of another Church, namely, of the institution and its clergy".[5]

Isolating Matthew 18:20 from the entire biblical and ecclesial tradition of the common prayer of the Church has, as one can see, far-reaching consequences. The Lord's promise to all those praying everywhere is turned into the dogmatization of the autonomous group. The communality of praying is raised to the level of an egalitarianism that sees in the development of the priestly office the emergence of another Church. In such a view, any directive from the whole is a fetter that one must resist for the sake of the originality and freedom of the liturgical celebration. It is not obedience toward the whole but the creativity of the moment that becomes the determining form.

It is evident that with the adoption of sociological language the prior adoption of its evaluations has also occurred. The system of values that sociological language has formed constructs a new view of the past and the present, the one negative, the other positive. Thus, traditional concepts (also conciliar ones!) such as "the wealth of the *musica sacra*", the "organ as queen of the instruments", and the "universality of Gregorian chant" now appear as "mystifications" for the purpose of "preserving a particular form of power."[6] A certain administration of power, we are told, feels threatened by the cultural processes of change and reacts by masking its effort to preserve itself as love for the tradition. Gregorian chant and Palestrina are said to be tutelary gods of a mythicized, ancient repertoire,[7] components of a Catholic counterculture that is based on remythicized and supersacralized archetypes,[8] just as in the historical liturgy of the Church it is generally more a question of representing a cultic bureaucracy than showing concern for the singing

---

[5] Ibid., 204a: "La celebrazione si configura come splendido 'opus' cui assistere e ai suoi protagonisti si riconoscono poteri misteriosi: così lo stacco culturale comincia a diventare stacco 'sacrale'.... La musica si avvia a diventare, come il latino, una 'lingua' colta: la lingua di un'altra chiesa, che è l'istituzione ed il suo clero."

[6] Ibid., 200a: "Si pensi ... alla ripetività di schemi mentali e giudizi preconfezionati; all'affabulazione-occultamento di dati per sostenere una determinata forma di potere e di visione ideologica. Si pensi ad espressioni mistificatorie correnti come: 'il grande patrimonio della musica sacra'; 'il pensiero della chiesa sul canto'; 'l'organo re degli strumenti'; 'l'universalità del canto gregoriano' ecc."; cf. 210b, 206b.

[7] Cf. ibid., 210b.

[8] Cf. ibid., 208a.

activity of the people.[9] Finally, the content of Pius X's *motu proprio* on sacred music is described as a "culturally near-sighted and theologically empty ideology of sacred music".[10] There is of course not only an idolization of sociology at work here but also a complete separation of the New Testament from the history of the Church that is connected to a theory of decline typical of many Enlightenment situations. Purity is found only in the original beginnings with Jesus; all the rest of history appears as a "musical adventure with disoriented and unsuccessful experiences", which we now "must bring to an end" so that we can finally begin again with what is right.[11]

But what do these new and better ideas look like? The leading concepts have already been touched on in passing; we must now pay attention to how they are concretized further. Two basic values are clearly formulated. The "primary value" of a renewed liturgy is, we are told, "the full and authentic action of all persons".[12] Accordingly, church music means first and foremost the following: the "People of God" represents its identity in song. As a result of this statement, the second value judgment operative here is also addressed: music proves to be the power that effects the cohesion of the group; the familiar songs are the identifying mark of a community, so to speak.[13] From this perspective the main categories of the musical structuring of worship ensue: the project, the program, the animation, the direction. We are told that the "how" is more important than the "what".[14] The ability to celebrate is above all "the ability to create"; before all else music must be "created".[15] To be fair I must add that the authors do show a sensitivity for different cultural situations and leave room for the adoption of historical material as well. And, more than anything else, they emphasize the paschal character of the Christian liturgy: the singing of this liturgy not only represents the identity of the People of God but should also give account of our hope and proclaim to all the countenance of the Father of Jesus Christ.[16]

---

[9] Cf. ibid., 206a.

[10] Ibid., 211a.

[11] Ibid., 212a.

[12] Ibid., 211b.

[13] Cf. ibid., 217b.

[14] Cf. ibid., 217b.

[15] Ibid., 218b: "i membri dell'assemblea credente, e soprattutto gli animatori del rito ... sapranno acquistare ... quella capacità fondamentale, che è il 'saper celebrare,' ossia un saper fare."

[16] Cf. ibid., 212a.

Thus, elements of continuity remain in the deep split. They make discourse possible and instill hope that we can again achieve unity in the basic understanding of the liturgy, although it threatens to disappear through the derivation of the liturgy from the group instead of from the Church—not only theoretically but in concrete liturgical praxis. I would not be speaking of all this in so much detail if I thought that such ideas were attributable to only a few theoreticians. But the belief that the spirit of the Council points in this direction has been able to gain acceptance in many a liturgical office and its agencies, although it is indisputable that these ideas cannot be supported by the text of the Second Vatican Council. In the sense just described, the opinion is all too widely held today that so-called creativity, the active participation of all present, and the relationship to a group in which everyone is acquainted with and speaks to everyone else are the real categories of the conciliar understanding of liturgy. Not only assistant pastors but even some bishops think they are not being faithful to the Council if they pray everything just the way it is found in the Roman Missal; at least *one* "creative" formulation must be inserted, regardless of how trite it may be. And the conventional greeting of the congregation at the beginning along with friendly wishes at the dismissal have already become obligatory elements of the sacred action, which hardly anyone would dare omit.

2. The Philosophical Basis of the Concept and Its Questionable Aspects

In considering all this, however, we have not yet touched the core of the change in values. All that has been said up to now results from placing the group before the Church. But why has this been done? The reason is that the Church is categorized under the general term "institution", and, in the type of sociology adopted here, an institution has a negative value in itself. It represents power, and power is regarded as the opposite of freedom. Since faith ("imitation of Christ") is held to be a positive value, it must stand on the side of freedom and thus be anti-institutional by its very nature. For this reason worship should be neither a mainstay nor a component of an institution, but should constitute a counterforce that contributes to dethroning the mighty. From such a starting point the paschal hope, to which the liturgy should be bearing witness, can take on a very earthly form. It turns into the hope that institutions will be overcome, and it itself becomes a means in the struggle against power. Whoever reads the texts of the *Missa Nicaraguensis*, for example, can get an idea of this shift in hope and of the new realism the liturgy acquires as an instrument of militant promise. One also sees the significance that music in fact accrues in the new conception. The stirring power of the revolutionary songs communicates an enthusiasm and a conviction that could not come from a simple spoken liturgy. Here there is no more opposition to liturgical music; it has received a new and irreplaceable role in arousing irrational forces and awakening the communal élan at which the whole thing is aiming. But at the same time it is shaping consciousness, since what is sung gradually communicates itself to the spirit much more effectively than anything that is only spoken or thought. Incidentally, via the liturgy of the group the boundary of the locally assembled parish is again passed over—on purpose: through the liturgical form and its music a new solidarity develops through which a new people is to come into being that calls itself the People of God. But by "God" it only means itself and the historical energies realized in the people.

Let us return once again to the analysis of the values that have become determinative in the new liturgical consciousness. For a start there is the negative quality of the concept "institution" and the fact that the Church is regarded exclusively under this sociological aspect, which is, moreover, not an aspect of empirical sociology, but a point of view that we owe to the so-called masters of suspicion. One sees that they have done their job thoroughly; they have achieved a formation of consciousness that is still effective even where people know nothing of this origin. Suspicion, however, could not have such stirring sway if it were not accompanied by a promise whose fascination is almost irresistible: the idea of freedom as the genuine claim of human dignity. In this respect the question about the right concept of freedom must represent the core of the debate. The controversy over the liturgy has thus moved away from all the superficial questions about its organization and come back to its core, for in the liturgy we are indeed concerned with the presence of redemption, with the access to true freedom. The positive feature of the new debate lies without doubt in its exposure of this as the central issue.

At the same time we can see what Catholicism is suffering from today. If the Church appears only as an institution, as a bearer of power and thus as an opponent of freedom and a hindrance to redemption, then faith is living in a self-contradictory state. For, on the one hand, it cannot dispense with the Church, but, on the other hand, it is completely opposed to her. The truly tragic paradox of this trend in liturgical reform lies here. For liturgy without the Church is a self-contradiction. Where all act so that all may themselves become subjects, the One who truly acts in the liturgy also disappears with the collective subject, the Church. Here it has been forgotten that the liturgy should be *opus Dei* in which God himself first acts and we become redeemed people precisely through his action. The group celebrates itself, and exactly for this reason it is celebrating nothing at all since it is no cause for celebration. This is why the general activity turns into boredom. Nothing happens if he is absent whom the world awaits. It is then only logical that one would move on to more concrete goals such as the ones reflected in the *Missa Nicaraguensis*.

We must therefore resolutely ask the proponents of this position: Is the Church really just an institution, a cultic bureaucracy, or an apparatus of power? Is priestly office only the monopolization of sacred privileges? Also, if we do not succeed in overcoming these ideas affectively, succeed in seeing the Church differently again from the heart, then the liturgy is not being renewed; on the contrary, the dead are burying the dead and calling it reform. Neither is there church music any more in this view, since its subject, the Church, has been lost. Indeed, you cannot even rightly speak of liturgy any more, which of course presupposes the Church; what remains are group rituals that make use of musical means of expression with more or less expertise. If liturgy is to survive or even be renewed, it is essential that the Church be rediscovered. I would like to add: If human alienation is to be overcome, if men are to find their identity again, it is indispensable that they again find the Church, which is not an institution hostile to men but that new "we" in which the "I" can first secure its foundation and a place to stay.

In this context it would be salutary to reread carefully the little book with which Romano Guardini, the great pioneer of liturgical renewal, concluded his literary endeavors in the last year of the Council.[17] He wrote this book, as he himself stressed, out of concern and

---

[17] Cf. Romano Guardini, *Die Kirche des Herrn: Meditationen* (Würzburg, 1965) [trans. Stella Lange as *The Church of the Lord: On the Nature and Mission of the Church* (Chicago:

love for the Church whose humanity and whose imperilment he knew very well. But he had learned to discover in the humanity of the Church the scandal of the Incarnation of God; he had learned to see in her the presence of the Lord who has made the Church his body. Only if this is the case is Jesus Christ contemporaneous with us. And only if there is this contemporaneity is there real liturgy, which is not just remembrance of the Paschal Mystery, but its true presence. And once again, only if this is the case is liturgy participation in the trinitarian dialogue of Father, Son, and Holy Spirit; only in this way is it not our "doing", but *opus Dei*—God's action in us and with us. For this reason Guardini emphatically stressed that the important thing in the liturgy is not to do something but to be. The idea that collective activity is the central merit of the liturgy is the most radical antithesis imaginable to Guardini's liturgical conception. In reality, the general activity of everybody is not only not the fundamental value of the liturgy, but as such is not a value at all.[18]

I shall refrain from expanding on these matters any further; we must concentrate on finding the starting point and norm for the right relation of liturgy and music to each other. In this respect the realization that the Church, to be precise, the *communio sanctorum* of all places and all times, is the true subject of the liturgy is really momentous. As Guardini has shown in detail in his earlier work *Liturgische Bildung*,[19] the elusiveness of the liturgy in the face of the willfulness of the group and of individuals (including clerics and specialists), a characteristic

---

Regnery, 1967)]. Guardini comments here on the "opening", which is just in progress; he welcomes it, but at the same time he also shows what its inner criterion is: "May the events of the present not lead to a trivialization or a softening of the Church, but may it ever stand clearly in our consciousness that the Church is a 'mystery' and a 'rock'" (18). He comments briefly on both concepts, tracing the concept "rock" back to that of truth; from the claim of truth follows that the Church must stand "unshakable in the distinction between true and false in spite of all her ties to the times ... since only the truth and the demand for the truth mean genuine respect, whereas compliance and accepting-anything-else-as-well is weakness, which does not dare to challenge man with the majesty of the self-revealing God; basically it is contempt of man" [translated into English from the German]. In this context one should also reread the *Méditation sur l'Église* by Henri de Lubac, which has appeared in a new French edition (Paris, 1985) [trans. Michael Mason as *The Splendor of the Church*, from the 2nd ed. (San Francisco: Ignatius Press, 1986)].

[18] I have tried to give more details about Guardini's understanding of the liturgy in the chapter "Von der Liturgie zur Christologie" of my book *Wege zur Wahrheit: Die bleibende Bedeutung von Romano Guardini* (Düsseldorf, 1985), 121–44.

[19] Cf. Romano Guardini, *Liturgische Bildung: Versuche* (Rothenfels, 1923); revised new edition under the title *Liturgie und liturgische Bildung* (Würzburg, 1966).

that he referred to as the objectivity and positivity of the liturgy, is not the only characteristic that follows from this; above all the three ontological dimensions in which the liturgy lives follow from this: cosmos, history, and mystery. The reference to history involves development, that is, belonging to a living entity that has a beginning that continues to have an effect and stays present but is not completed and lives only by being developed further. Some things die out; some are forgotten only to return later in a new way, but development always means participation in a beginning that is open to what lies ahead. Here we have already touched on a second category that acquires its special meaning through the connection to the cosmos: liturgy understood in this way lives in the basic form of participation. No one is its one and only creator, for each of us it is participation in something greater that transcends us all, yet just in this way each of us is also an agent precisely because each is a recipient. Finally, the relationship to mystery means that the beginning of the liturgical event never lies in us. It is a response to an initiative coming from above, to a call and an act of love that is mystery. Problems are there to be explained; mystery, however, is not open to explanation, but reveals itself only in acceptance, in the Yes that we, following the lead of the Bible, may confidently call, even today, obedience.

We have now arrived at a point that is of great importance for the beginnings of what is artistic. The liturgy of the group is not cosmic; it thrives on the autonomy of the group. It does not have a history; precisely the emancipation from history and autonomous creativity are characteristic for group liturgy, even when it works with historical settings in the process. And it does not know mystery because in it everything is and must be explained. For these reasons development and participation are just as foreign to group liturgy as that obedience within which a meaning that is greater than the explicable is revealed. Creativity in which the autonomy of the emancipated tries to prove itself now takes the place of all this. Such creativity, which would like to function as autonomy and emancipation, is for this very reason in strict opposition to all participation. Its characteristics are: arbitrariness as the necessary form of the rejection of each previously given form or norm; unrepeatability because in repetition there would already be dependence; and artificiality, since the result must be a pure creation of men. In this way, however, it becomes apparent that human creativity that does not want to be receptivity and participation is by its very nature absurd and untrue since men can only be themselves through receptivity and participation. Such creativity is a flight from the *conditio humana* and therefore untruth. This is the reason why cultural disintegration begins wherever faith in God disappears and a professed *ratio* of being [*Vernunft des Seins*] is automatically called into question.

Let us summarize what we have discovered up to now so that we can then deduce the consequences for the starting point and fundamental form of church music. It has become clear that the primacy of the group stems from an understanding of Church as institution. In turn, this understanding is based on a notion of freedom that does not fit with the idea or the reality of the institutional and is no longer capable of perceiving the dimension of mystery in the reality of the Church. Freedom is understood in terms of the key ideas of autonomy and emancipation. It becomes concrete in the idea of creativity, which in this context is the direct opposite of the objectivity and positivity that belong to the essence of church liturgy. The group is only free if it constantly reinvents itself. At the same time we have seen that a liturgy that deserves the name is radically opposed to this. It is against ahistorical willfulness, which ignores development and thus leads nowhere, and against unrepeatability, which is also exclusiveness and loss of communication despite all group formations. It is not opposed to the technical, but definitely to the artificial, in which men create a counterworld for themselves and do not see God's creation with their eyes and in their hearts. The oppositions are clear; also clear, at least incipiently, is the inner rationale of this group mentality, which is based on an autonomistically conceived idea of freedom. But now we must ask in a constructive way about the anthropological concept upon which the liturgy as understood by the faith of the Church is based.

3. The Anthropological Model of the Church's Liturgy

Two pivotal sayings from the Bible provide a key for answering our question. Paul coined the expression *logiké latreia* (Rom 12:1), which is quite difficult to translate into our modern languages because we do not have a real equivalent for the concept of logos.* One could

---

*The heading for pt. 2, "Worship in Accord with the Logos", is based on this verse. There Ratzinger renders *logiké latreia* as *logosgemäßer Gottesdienst*.—Trans.

translate it "spiritual worship" and so refer at the same time to the saying of Jesus about worshipping in spirit and truth (Jn 4:23). One could, however, translate it "divine worship shaped by the word", but would then of course have to add that "word" in the biblical sense (and also the Greek sense) is more than language and speech, namely, creative reality. It is also certainly more than mere thought and mere spirit. It is self-interpreting, self-communicating spirit. At all times the word-orientation, the rationality, the intelligibility, and the sobriety of the Christian liturgy have been derived from this spirit and given to liturgical music as its basic law. It would, however, be a narrow and false interpretation if one understood by this that all liturgical music should be referred to the text in a strict way, and if one would then exaggerate the intelligibility of the text so much that there would be no more room for what is proper to music. For "word" in the sense of the Bible is more than "text", and understanding reaches farther than the banal understandability of what is immediately clear to everyone and can be accommodated to the most superficial rationality. But it is correct that music that serves worship "in spirit and truth" cannot be rhythmic ecstasy, sensual intimation or anesthetization, subjective sentimentality, or superficial entertainment; instead it is ordered to a message, to a comprehensive, spiritual, and in the fullest sense rational statement. In other words, it is correct to say that music in a comprehensive sense and deep down inside must correspond to this "word", indeed must serve it.[20]

This leads us automatically to another biblical text, the truly foundational one concerning the question of cult or worship in which we are told more exactly what the "Word" means and how it relates to us. I am referring to the following sentence in John's prologue: "And the Word became flesh and lived [pitched his tent] among us, and we have seen his glory" (Jn 1:14). The "Word" to which Christian worship refers is first of all not a text, but a living reality: a God who is self-communicating meaning and who communicates himself by becoming a man. This incarnation is the sacred tent, the focal point of all worship that looks at the glory of God and gives him honor. These statements in John's prologue, however, do not convey everything yet. They have been misunderstood if they are not read together with the

---

[20] For a proper understanding of the Pauline *logiké latreia*, see especially Heinrich Schlier, *Der Römerbrief*, HThKNT 6 (Freiburg, 1977), 350–58, particularly 356–58.

farewell discourses in which Jesus tells his followers: I am going, and I will come again to you; by going I am returning; it is good that I go, for only in this way can you receive the Holy Spirit (Jn 14:2f.; 14:18f.; 16:5ff., and so on). The Incarnation is only the first part of the movement. It becomes meaningful and definitive only in the Cross and the Resurrection. From the Cross the Lord draws everything to himself and carries the flesh—that is, mankind and the entire created world— into God's eternity.

Liturgy is ordered to this line of movement, and this line of movement is the fundamental text, so to speak, to which all liturgical music refers, which must measure up to it from the inside. Liturgical music is a result of the claim and the dynamics of the Word's Incarnation. For incarnation means that also among us the Word cannot be just speech. To begin with, the sacramental signs themselves are certainly the central way in which the Incarnation continues to work. But they would be homeless if they were not immersed in a liturgy that as a whole follows this extension of the Word into the physical and into the sphere of all our senses. The right to have images—indeed their necessity—comes from this in contrast to the Jewish and Islamic types of worship.[21] And from this also comes the necessity to call on those deeper realms of understanding and response that reveal themselves in music. Faith becoming music is a part of the process of the Word becoming flesh. But in a completely unique way this "musification" is at the same time also ordered to that inner shift of the incarnational event that I tried to indicate before: in the Cross and the Resurrection the Incarnation of the Word [*Fleischwerdung des Wortes*] becomes the "verbalization" of the flesh [*Wortwerdung des Fleisches*]. These two pervade each other. The Incarnation is not taken back; it only becomes final, so to speak, at the moment the movement is reversed. The flesh becomes "logicized", but precisely this process of the flesh becoming word produces a new unity of all reality, which was obviously so important to God that he let it cost him his Son on the Cross. The Word becoming music is, on the one hand, sensualization, incarnation, the attraction of pre-rational and trans-rational forces, the attraction of the hidden sound of creation, and the uncovering of the song that lies

---

[21] Cf. the thorough work of Christoph Schönborn, *L'Icône du Christ: Fondements théologiques élaborés entre le Ier et le IIe Concile de Nicée (325–787)*, Paradosis 24 (Fribourg, 1976) [trans. Lothar Krauth as *God's Human Face: The Christ-Icon* (San Francisco: Ignatius Press, 1994)].

at the base of things. But this musification is also itself now the site of the shift in the movement: it is not only the Incarnation of the Word, but at the same time the spiritualization of the flesh. Wood and brass turn into tone; the unconscious and the unsolved become ordered and meaningful sound. An embodiment comes into play that is spiritualization, and a spiritualization occurs that is embodiment. The Christian embodiment is always simultaneously a spiritualization, and the Christian spiritualization is an embodiment into the body of the incarnate Logos.

4. Consequences for Liturgical Music

a. Fundamentals

Provided that this interpenetration of both movements occurs in music, it serves to the highest degree and in an indispensable way that inner exodus which liturgy always seeks to be and to become. But this means that the appropriateness of liturgical music is measured by its inner correspondence to this basic anthropological and theological form. At first glance such a statement seems to be very far removed from the concrete reality of music. It becomes concrete immediately, however, if we pay attention to the opposing models of ritual music to which I briefly referred above. For instance, let us think first of all of the Dionysian type of religion and its music, which Plato tackled from his own religious and philosophical point of view.[22] In many forms of religion music is ordered to stupor and to ecstasy. Freeing men from limitations, which is the goal of that hunger for the infinite proper to men, is supposed to be achieved through holy madness, through the delirium of the rhythm and the instruments. Such music pulls down the barriers of individuality and personality; in it men free themselves from the burden of consciousness. Music turns into ecstasy, liberation from the ego, becoming one with the universe. Today we experience the profane return of this type of music in a large part of the rock and pop music whose festivals are a countercult of the same orientation—the pleasure of destruction, the

---

[22] Cf. Ratzinger, *Fest des Glaubens*, 86–111 [*Feast of Faith*, 97–126; JRCW 11:421–42]. Albert Rivaud, "Platon et la musique", *Rev. d'histoire de la philosophie* (1929): 1–30.

removal of the barriers of everyday life, and the illusion of redemption in the liberation from oneself, in the wild ecstasy of noise and the masses. It is a question of redemptive practices whose form of redemption is related to drugs and diametrically opposed to the Christian faith in redemption. Hence it makes sense that in this area satanical cults and satanical types of music are constantly spreading today whose dangerous power intentionally to wreck and eradicate the person has not yet been taken seriously enough.[23] The dispute between Dionysian and Apollonian music with which Plato deals is not ours, since Apollo is not Christ. But the question Plato posed concerns us in a most meaningful way. In a form we could not have imagined a generation ago music has become today the decisive vehicle of a counterreligion and thus the showplace for the discerning of spirits. On the one hand, since rock music seeks redemption by way of liberation from the personality and its responsibility, it fits very precisely into the anarchistic ideas of freedom that are manifesting themselves more openly all over the world. But that is also exactly why such music is diametrically opposed to the Christian notions of redemption and freedom, indeed their true contradiction. Music of this type must be excluded from the Church, not for aesthetic reasons, not out of reactionary stubbornness, not because of historical rigidity, but because of its very nature.

We could concretize our question further if we go on to analyze the anthropological base of different types of music. There is music of provocation, which rouses people for various collective goals. There is sensual music, which drives people into the erotic or is in some other

---

[23] These connections, which have been much too little noticed, have been emphasized in the writings of Bob Larson, a former disc jockey and leader of a rock band: *Rock and Roll: The Devil's Diversion* (Carol Stream, Ill., 1967); *Rock and the Church* (Carol Stream, Ill., 1971); *Hippies, Hindus and Rock and Roll* (Carol Stream, Ill., 1972). Concerning music from the realm of jazz and pop, which is perhaps less harmful but opposed to the liturgy in essentially the same way, cf. Hermann-Josef Burbach, "Sacro-Pop", IKaZ 3 (1974): 91–94. "'Sacro-pop', posing here as avantgarde, is the product of a 'dirigiste mass culture' that reproduces the cheap taste of the lowbrow consumer public" (94). See also Burbach, "Aufgaben und Versuche", in *Geschichte der katholischen Kirchenmusik*, vol. 2, ed. Karl Gustav Fellerer (Kassel, 1976), 395–405. In sum, Burbach concludes: "It is a question of music that tends toward a constantly advancing liquidation of the individual, especially in its 'rhythm', and does this in a world that is moving toward total management by virtue of the concentration of ever larger power complexes. Music becomes an ideology. It steers, regulates, filters, and combines a stream of feelings that at first lacks direction. The music restricts this stream to stereotyped patterns of experience" (404).

way essentially intent on sensual feelings of pleasure. There is ordinary light music, which does not seek to make a statement, but only wants to break open the burden of silence. There is rationalistic music, in which the tones simply serve rational constructions but no real penetration of the mind and senses ensues. Here one would have to include a number of sterile catechetical songs and modern hymns that have been fabricated in committee. The music that corresponds to the worship of the incarnate One who was raised up on the Cross lives from another, greater, and broader synthesis of spirit, intuition, and sensuous sound. We can say that Western music, from Gregorian chant through the music of the cathedrals and great polyphonic music, through Renaissance and baroque music, right up to Bruckner and beyond, derives from the inner richness of this synthesis and has developed its possibilities abundantly. This magnificence exists only here because it was able to grow solely from the anthropological ground that combined the spiritual and the profane in an ultimate human unity. The unity disintegrates to the degree that this anthropology disappears. For me the greatness of this music is the most immediate and most evident verification that history has to offer of the Christian image of men and of Christian faith in redemption. Whoever is really touched by it knows somehow deep down inside that the faith is true even if this person still has far to go before comprehending this insight with the mind and will.

This means that the liturgical music of the Church must be subject to that integration of the human state which appears before us in incarnational faith. Such redemption is more arduous than that of rapture, but this struggle is the exertion of truth itself. On the one hand, it must integrate the senses into the spirit; it must correspond to the impulse of the *sursum corda*. On the other hand, however, this effort aims not at pure spiritualization but at an integration of sensuality and spirit so that in one another both become person. It does not debase the spirit when it takes the senses into itself; rather, it supplies the spirit with the whole wealth of creation. Nor does it make the senses less real when they are permeated by the spirit; rather, only in this way do they receive a share in its infinity. Every sensual pleasure is narrowly delimited and ultimately incapable of intensification because the sense act cannot go beyond a certain measure. Whoever expects redemption from it will be disappointed, "frustrated"—as we would say today. But by being integrated into the spirit the senses receive a new depth and reach into the infinity of the spiritual adventure. Only there do they come completely into their own. This, however, presupposes that the spirit as well does not remain closed. The music of faith looks for the integration of man in the *sursum corda*; man, however, does not find this integration in himself, but only in the self-transcendence into the incarnate Word. Sacred music that is in the framework of this movement thus becomes a purification of man, his ascent. But let us not forget that this music is not the work of a moment, but participation in a history. It is realized not by a single individual but only in cooperation. Hence, it is precisely in this music that the entry into the history of faith and the cooperation of all the members of the body of Christ also express themselves. This music leaves behind joy, a higher kind of ecstasy that does not wipe out the person, but unites and thus liberates. It lets us glimpse what freedom is, that freedom which does not destroy, but gathers and purifies.

b. Comments on the Present Situation

The question for the musician is now, of course: How does one do this? In principle, great works of church music can be bestowed only because the self-transcendence involved cannot be achieved by man alone, whereas a delirium of the senses is producible according to the known mechanisms of intoxication. Producing stops where the truly great begins. We must first of all see and accept this boundary. In this respect, at the beginning of great sacred music there is of necessity awe, receptivity, and a humility that is prepared to serve by participating in the greatness that has already gone forth. Only one who lives through and through from the inner structure of this image of man can create the music that belongs to this image.

The Church has put up two further road signs. Liturgical music must in its inner character meet the requirements of the great liturgical texts—the *Kyrie, Gloria, Credo, Sanctus, Agnus Dei*. As I have already said, this does not mean that it can only be text music, but it does find a guide for its own message in the inner orientation of these texts. The second road sign is the reference to Gregorian chant and to Palestrina. Once again, this does not mean that all church music has to be imitation of this music. On this point there was indeed a certain narrowness in the renewal of church music during the last century and probably also in the papal documents based on this renewal. Correctly understood, we are simply saying that models were given here that provide orientation. What can arise through the creative application of such an orientation cannot, however, be decided in advance.

The question remains: Humanly speaking can we hope that new creative possibilities are still open here? And how is this to happen? The first question is actually easy to answer. If this image of man is inexhaustible in contrast to every other image, then it also opens ever new possibilities to artistic expression. And the more the possibilities, the more vitally will it define the spirit of an age. But herein lies the difficulty for the second question. In our age faith has largely disappeared as a publicly formative force. How is it to become creative? Has it not been driven back everywhere into being a mere subculture? In response we could say that certainly in Africa, Asia, and Latin America we can hope for a new flowering of the faith from which new forms of culture could sprout. But even in the Western world the word "subculture" should not frighten us. In the crisis of culture we are experiencing, it is only from islands of spiritual concentration that a new cultural purification and unification can break out at all. Wherever faith reawakens in lively communities we also see how Christian culture develops anew, how the communal experience provides inspiration and opens new paths that we could not see before. Furthermore, Josef Friedrich Doppelbauer has correctly pointed out that often and not incidentally liturgical music actually has a mature quality about it and presupposes that a process of growth has already taken place.[24] Here it is important that there are the antechambers of popular piety and its music as well as spiritual music in the broader sense, which should always be involved in a fertile exchange with liturgical music. Popular spiritual music will be enriched and purified by liturgical music, on the one hand, but will also prepare new styles of liturgical music. From the freer popular forms there can then mature what can join the common ground of the universal worship of the Church. This is also the area in which the group can test its creativity

---

[24] Cf. Josef Friedrich Doppelbauer, "Die geistliche Musik und die Kirche", IKaZ 13 (1984): 457–66.

in the hope that what grows from this may one day belong to the whole.[25]

5. A Final Word: Liturgy, Music, and Cosmos

At the end of my reflections I would like to note a beautiful saying of Mahatma Gandhi that I recently found in a calendar. Gandhi refers to the three habitats of the cosmos and how each of these provides its own mode of being. The fish live in the sea, and they are silent. The animals of the earth scream and shout; but the birds, whose habitat is the heavens, sing. Silence is proper to the sea, shouting to the earth, and singing to the heavens. Man has a share in all three of them. He carries the depths of the sea, the burden of the earth, and the heights of the heavens in himself, and for this reason all three properties also belong to him: silence, shouting, and singing. Today—I would like to add—we see that only the shouting is left for the man without transcendence since he only wants to be earth and also try to make the heavens and the depths of the sea into his earth. The right liturgy, the liturgy of the communion of saints, restores totality to him. It teaches him silence and singing again by opening to him the depths of the sea and teaching him to fly, the angels' mode of being. It brings the song buried in him to sound once more by lifting up his heart. Indeed, we can now even turn this around and say: One recognizes right liturgy by the fact that it liberates us from ordinary, everyday activity and returns to us once more the depths and the heights, silence and song. One recognizes right liturgy in that it has a cosmic, not just a group, character. It sings with the angels. It is silent with the expectant depths of the universe. And that is how it redeems the earth.

---

[25] Important for the theological and musical foundations of church music, which have only been mentioned briefly here, is Johannes Overath, "Kirchenmusik im Dienst des Kultes", IKaZ 13 (1984): 355–68; a very extensive panorama of ideas can be found in Paul-Werner Scheele, "Die liturgische und apostolische Sendung der Musica sacra", *Musica sacra: Zeitschrift des allgemeinen Cäcilienverbandes für die Länder deutscher Sprache* 105 (1985): 187–207.

III. "In the Presence of the Angels I Will Sing Your Praise": The Regensburg Tradition and the Reform of the Liturgy*

1. Earthly and Heavenly Liturgy: The View of the Fathers

After an unforgettable helicopter flight over the mountains of South Tyrol in the fall of 1992, I was able to visit the monastery of Marienberg in the Vinschgau, which was founded there in magnificent scenery in praise of God, thus embracing in its own way the invitation of the three young men: "Mountains and hills, sing praise to him" (Dan 3*b*:53 [RSV-2CE Prayer of Azariah v. 53]). The real treasure of the monastery is the crypt, consecrated on July 13, 1160, with its marvelous frescoes, which have since been almost completely laid open to view.[1] As with all medieval art, the pictures were not just of aesthetic import. They can be seen as liturgy, as part of the great liturgy of creation and of the redeemed world; the monastery was founded to harmonize with this liturgy. The iconography therefore corresponds to the common fundamental understanding of liturgy still alive in the entire Church—East and West. It exhibits a strong Byzantine influence, but at its core it is quite simply biblical and, in another respect, considerably determined by the monastic tradition, specifically by the Rule of St. Benedict.

For this reason the real focal point is the *Majestas Domini*, the risen Lord lifted up on high, who is seen at the same time and above all as the one returning, the one already coming in the Eucharist. In the celebration of the liturgy the Church moves toward the Lord; liturgy

---

Reprinted with permission from *A New Song for the Lord: Faith in Christ and Liturgy Today*, trans. Martha M. Matesich, 2nd ed. (1996; New York: Crossroad, 2005), 128–46.

*I have deliberately kept the local flavor of this address, held at a celebration for my brother, who was leaving the position of cathedral choirmaster, because it seems to me that it is precisely in the concrete case that the fundamentals can best be examined and clarified.

[1] Cf. Helmut Stampfer and Hubert Walder, *Die Krypta von Marienberg im Vinschgau* (Bozen, 1982).

is virtually this act of approaching his coming. In the liturgy the Lord is already anticipating his promised coming. Liturgy is anticipated parousia, the "already" entering our "not yet", as John described it in the account of the wedding at Cana. The hour of the Lord has not yet come; all that must happen is not yet fulfilled; but at Mary's—the Church's—request Jesus does give the new wine now and already bestows in advance the gift of his hour.

The risen Lord is not alone. In the images of the heavenly liturgy given in the Apocalypse of John he is surrounded by the four creatures and above all by a host of singing angels. Their singing is an expression of a joy that cannot be taken away, of existence releasing itself into the jubilation of fulfilled freedom. From the beginning, monasticism was understood as living in the manner of the angels, and the manner of the angels is worshipping. To enter the angels' way of life means forming life into worship as far as human frailty allows.[2] Thus, the liturgy is the center of monasticism, but monasticism only makes visible for all what the point of Christian existence, indeed of human existence really is. When the monks of Marienberg saw these frescoes, they certainly thought of the nineteenth chapter of the Rule of St. Benedict—the discipline of singing the Psalms—where, among other things, the father of the monks reminds them of Psalm 138(137):1: "Before the angels I sing your praise" (RSV-2CE). Benedict goes on to say: "Let us reflect upon how we should be in the presence of God and the angels, and when we sing let us stand in such a way that our hearts are in tune with our voices—*mens nostra concordet voci nostrae.*" Hence, it is not the case that you think something up and then sing it; instead, the song comes to you from the angels, and you have to lift up your heart so that it may be in tune with the music coming to it. But above all else this is important: the liturgy is not a thing the monks create. It is already there before them. It is entering into the liturgy of the heavens that has always been taking place. Earthly liturgy is liturgy because and only because it joins what is already in process, the greater reality. Thus, the meaning of the frescoes becomes completely clear. Through them the true reality, the heavenly liturgy, looks into this space; they are the window, as it were, through which the monks look out and look into the great heavenly choir. To sing with this choir is the essence of their calling.

---

[2] Important for the theme of the *vita angelica* is Jean Leclerq, *Wissenschaft und Gottverlangen* (Düsseldorf, 1963), 70; cf. also Stampfer and Walder, *Krypta*, 20.

"In the presence of the angels I will sing your praise"—through the frescoes this ideal stands forever present before their eyes.

2. Highlighting the Postconciliar Dispute on the Liturgy

Let us climb down from Marienberg and the views and insights it affords into the plain of the ordinary life of liturgy today. The panorama here is far more confusing. Harald Schützeichel has described the situation today as an "already and not yet". This no longer describes the eschatological anticipation of the coming of Christ in a world still marked by death and its tribulations; rather, the new that is "already" present is now the reform of the liturgy, but the old—the Tridentine order—has "not yet" been overcome.[3] Thus, the question Where shall I turn? is no longer, as it once was, a search for the countenance of the living God, but a description of the helpless plight of church music that has resulted from the halfhearted realization of liturgical reform. A momentous change of perspectives has obviously occurred here. A chasm separates the history of the Church into two irreconcilable worlds: the preconciliar and the postconciliar. Indeed, in many circles there is no worse verdict than being able to say that a Church decision, a text, a particular structuring of the liturgy, or a person is "preconciliar". Accordingly, Catholicism must have been imprisoned in a truly dreadful situation until 1965.

Let us apply this to the practical case at hand. If this is the case, then a cathedral choirmaster who carried out his duties in the Regensburg cathedral from 1964 to 1994 found himself in a rather hopeless situation. When he began, the Constitution on the Sacred Liturgy of the Second Vatican Council had not yet been implemented. At the time he assumed office, he was still quite clearly subject to the standard of the Regensburg tradition that had been established with understandable pride, or, to put it more precisely, of the *motu proprio* "Tra le sollecitudini" on the question of sacred music, which was promulgated by Pius X on November 22, 1903.[4] Nowhere had this *motu proprio* been so joyfully received, so unconditionally accepted as norm

---

[3] Harald Schützeichel, "Wohin soll ich mich wenden? Zur Situation der Kirchenmusik im deutschen Sprachraum", StdZ 209 (1991): 363–74.

[4] Original text in Italian, *Acta Sanctae Sedis* 36 (1903–1904): 329–39; German translation in *Dokumente zur Kirchenmusik unter besonderer Berücksichtigung des deutschen Sprachgebietes,*

as in the Regensburg cathedral, which became with this stance exemplary for many cathedrals and parishes in Germany and beyond. In this reform of church music, Pius X had made use of his own knowledge and experience of the liturgy. As bishop of Mantua and patriarch of Venice he had fought against the operatic church music that was dominant in Italy at that time. Insisting on chant as the truly liturgical music was for him part of a larger reform program that was concerned with restoring to worship its purity and dignity and shaping it according to its own inner claim.[5] In his endeavors he had come to know the Regensburg tradition that represented one of the godparents for the *motu proprio*, although this did not lead to its being canonized as such and as a whole. In Germany today Pius X is seen only as the antimodernist pope. In his critical biography Gianpaolo Romanato has clearly shown how much this pope of pastoral care was a pope of reform.[6]

For someone who takes all this into consideration and looks at it a little more closely, the chasm between preconciliar and postconciliar already becomes narrower. The historian will add a further insight. The Constitution on the Sacred Liturgy did indeed lay the foundations for reform; the reform itself was then shaped by a postconciliar commission and cannot in its concrete details simply be credited to the Council. The Council was an ambitious beginning whose large framework permitted a variety of actualizations. If one considers all this properly, one would describe the poles of tension that developed

---

ed. Hans Bernhard Meyer and Rudolf Pacik (Regensburg, 1981), 23–34. One can find an implicit reference to Regensburg in the introduction (24).

[5] The introduction of the *motu proprio* (German trans., 25) and pt. 2, 3 (German trans., 27–28), explicitly speaks of the active participation of the faithful as a fundamental liturgical principle. Gianpaolo Romanato portrays the past history of the *motu proprio* in his biography of Pius X, *Pio X: La vita di Papa Sarto* (Milan, 1992): In the seminary in Padua, Sarto had directed the *schola cantorum* and jotted down notes about this in a notebook he still carried with him as patriarch of Venice. As bishop of Mantua he had expended much time and energy on the *scuola di musica* during the reorganization of the seminary. There he also met Lorenzo Perosi, who remained closely connected with him and who had received significant impulses for his path as church musician from his time of study in Regensburg. The relationship with Perosi continued in Venice. There Sarto published a pastoral letter in 1895 that was based on a memorandum he had sent to the Sacred Congregation of Rites in 1893 and that anticipates almost verbatim the *motu proprio* of 1913 (179ff.; 213–14.; 247–48; 330).

[6] Romanato, *Pio X*, 247, also refers here to the judgment expressed by Roger Aubert, who has described Pius X as the greatest reformer of inner-ecclesial life since the Council of Trent.

during these decades not as preconciliar tradition and conciliar reform but more accurately as the reform of Pius X and the reform initiated by the Council, that is, stages of reform, not a chasm between two worlds. If we expand this view even further, then we can say that the history of liturgy always stands in the tension between continuity and renewal. It is always growing into new todays, and it must constantly prune the today that has become yesterday, so that what is essential may appear vigorous and new. Liturgy needs growth as well as cleansing, and the preservation of its identity is crucial. Without this, liturgy would lose its very raison d'être, the ground of its being. But if this is the case, then the alternative between traditional forces and reformers is oversimplified. Those who think that we can choose only between the old and the new are barking up the wrong tree. The question is rather: What is liturgy by its very nature? Which standard does it establish on its own? Only when this is clarified can we go on to ask: What must remain? What can and what should perhaps be different?

3. On the Essence of Liturgy and the Criteria of Reform

In the frescoes of Marienberg we found an initial, preconceptual answer to the question of the essence of liturgy that must now be developed further. In this endeavor we run into one of the alternatives that stems from the dualistic historical view of a pre- and postconciliar world. According to this alternative, the priest alone was the celebrant of the liturgy before the Council, but since the Council it is the assembled congregation. Therefore—so the conclusion   the congregation as the true subject determines what happens in the liturgy.[7] The priest, of course, never had the right to determine by himself what was to be done in the liturgy. Liturgy was completely nonarbitrary for him. It preceded him as "rite", that is, as an objective form of the corporate prayer of the Church.

The polemical alternative "priest or congregation as celebrant of the liturgy" is absurd; it obstructs an understanding of the liturgy instead of promoting it, and it creates that false rift between preconciliar and postconciliar which rends the overarching coherence of the living history of the faith. It is based on a superficial kind of thinking in which the real issue no longer appears at all. In contrast, if we open the

[7] Cf. Schützeichel, "Wohin soll ich mich wenden?" 363–66.

Catechism of the Catholic Church, we find the sum of the best insights of the Liturgical Movement put in a masterly concise and clear way, and as a result we find the permanent and the valid things that this great tradition contains. First we are reminded that liturgy means "service in the name of/on behalf of the people".[8] When Christian theology adopted this word from the Greek Old Testament, a word that had been coined in the pagan world, it naturally thought of the People of God, whom Christians had become by Christ's having torn open the wall between Jews and pagans to unite them all in the peace of the one God. "Service on behalf of the people"—the theologians remembered that this people did not exist on its own at all, for instance, through a community of common descent, but that it only came into existence through the paschal service of Jesus Christ and is thus based on the service of another, the Son. The People of God is not simply there, as the Germans, French, Italians, or other peoples are; it comes into being again and again only through the service of the Son and by his lifting us into the community of God, which we cannot enter on our own. Accordingly, the *Catechism* continues: "In Christian tradition it [the word 'liturgy'] means the participation of the People of God in 'the work of God.'" The *Catechism* quotes the Constitution on the Sacred Liturgy, which states that every liturgical celebration is an action of Christ the priest and his Body which is the Church.[9]

Now the situation really looks quite different. The sociological reduction that can compare human protagonists only with each other has been done away with. Liturgy presupposes—as we have seen—that the heavens have been opened; only if this is the case is there liturgy at all. If the heavens are not open, then whatever liturgy was is reduced to role playing and, in the end, to a trivial pursuit of congregational self-fulfillment in which nothing really happens. The decisive factor, therefore, is the primacy of Christology. Liturgy is God's work, or it does not exist at all. With this "first" of God and of his action, which looks for us in earthly signs, the universality of all liturgy and its universal public nature are given; we cannot comprehend them from the category of congregation, but only from the categories of People of God and Body of Christ. Only in this large framework is the reciprocal relation of priest and congregation correctly understood. In the

---

[8] CCC 1069.
[9] Cf. CCC 1069, 1070.

liturgy the priest says and does what he cannot do and say on his own; he acts—as the tradition expresses it—*in persona Christi*, that is, from the sacrament that vouches for the presence of the other, of Christ. He does not represent himself, nor is he a delegate of the congregation that has assigned him a role, as it were. Rather, his standing in the sacrament of imitation, of following, expresses precisely that "first" of Christ which is the fundamental condition of all liturgy. Since the priest represents this "first" of Christ, he refers each gathering to a point beyond itself into the whole, for Christ is only one and, by opening up the heavens, he is also the one who does away with all earthly limitations.

The *Catechism* structures its theology of the liturgy in a trinitarian way. I think it is very important that the congregation, the assembly, appears in the chapter on the Holy Spirit; there it states:

> In the *liturgy of the New Covenant* every liturgical action, especially the celebration of the Eucharist and the sacraments, is an encounter between Christ and the Church. The liturgical assembly [*Gemeinde*, community] derives its unity from the "communion [*die Gemeinschaft*] of the Holy Spirit" who gathers the children of God into the one Body of Christ. This assembly transcends racial, cultural, social— indeed, all human affinities. The assembly should *prepare* itself to encounter its Lord and to become "a people well disposed." [10]

It should be recalled that the German word *Gemeinde*—which dates from the tradition of the Reformation [and is related to the Latin word *communio*]—cannot be translated into most languages. Its equivalent in the romance languages is *assemblée* ("assembly or gathering"), which already emphasizes a slightly different aspect. Two important features are indisputably addressed by both expressions (community, assembly): (1) that the participants of the liturgical celebration are not unrelated individuals but are joined together through the liturgical event into a concrete representation of the People of God; (2) that as the People of God assembled here they are by virtue of the Lord active co-celebrants of the liturgical event. But we must resolutely defend ourselves against the hypostatization of the community, which is common today. As the *Catechism* rightly states, the assembled derive their unity from the communion of the Holy Spirit; they are not such on

---

[10] CCC 1097, 1098.

their own, as a sociologically self-contained quantity. But when they stand in a unity derived from the Spirit, it is always an open unity whose transcendence of racial, cultural, and social barriers is expressed in concrete openness to those who do not belong to the core group. Today's talk about community presupposes to a large extent a homogeneous group that can plan and execute common activities. This "community" could probably be expected to accept only a priest who knows it and whom it knows. All this has nothing to do with theology. When, for example, people who definitely do not form a uniform group in the sociological sense and who can, for instance, only with difficulty join together in common song, when these people are gathered for solemn worship in a large cathedral, are they a community or not? Yes, they are because the common turning to the Lord in faith and the Lord's coming toward them unite these people inwardly much more deeply than a mere social sense of solidarity could effect. In sum we can say that neither the priest alone nor the community alone is the celebrant of the liturgy, but the whole Christ is the celebrant, head and members. The priest, the assembly, and the single individuals are all celebrant insofar as they are united with Christ and insofar as they represent him in the communion of head and body. In every liturgical celebration the whole Church—heaven and earth, God and man—is involved, not just theoretically but in a wholly real manner. The more the celebration is nourished from this knowledge and from this experience, the more concretely will the liturgy become meaningful.

With these reflections we have seemingly strayed quite far from the subject of the Regensburg tradition and postconciliar reform, but only seemingly. This large framework had to come into view since each reform is judged by it, and only from its perspective can we adequately describe the inner place and the right style of church music. Now we can say in brief what the essential tendency of the reform chosen by the Council was. In the face of modern individualism and the moralism connected with it, the dimension of mystery was supposed to reappear, that is, the cosmic character of liturgy that embraces heaven and earth. In its participation in the Paschal Mystery of Christ, liturgy transcends the boundaries of places and times in order to gather all into the hour of Christ that is anticipated in the liturgy and hence opens history to its goal.[11]

---

[11] Cf. SC 8; see also the following note.

Two further points are added in the liturgical constitution of Vatican II. In the Christian faith the concept of mystery is inseparable from that of Logos. In contrast to many pagan mystery cults, the Christian mysteries are Logos-mysteries. They go beyond human reason, but instead of leading to the formlessness of intoxication or to the dissolution of reason into an irrationally understood cosmos, they lead to Logos, that is, to the creative reason on which the meaning of all things is based. The ultimate sobriety, rationality, and verbal character of the liturgy come from this. A second element is connected to it: the Logos has become flesh in history; for Christians, therefore, orientation toward the Logos is also always orientation toward the historical origin of faith, toward the biblical word and its normative development in the Church of the Fathers. From looking at the mystery of a cosmic liturgy that is Logos-liturgy there arose the necessity to represent the character of worship as communion, its character as action, and its determination as word in a visible and concrete way; all the individual instructions for the revision of books and rites are to be understood on this basis. If this is kept in mind, then it turns out that the Regensburg tradition as well as the *motu proprio* of Pius X point in the same direction with the same intent in spite of external differences. Dismantling the orchestral apparatus, which had evolved into operatic dimensions particularly in Italy, was supposed to place music completely at the service of the liturgical word and at the service of worship again. Church music was no longer supposed to be a performance on the occasion of worship, but was to be liturgy itself, that is, a harmonizing with the choir of the angels and saints. Thus, it was supposed to become transparent that liturgical music leads the faithful straight to the glorification of God, into the sober intoxication of the faith. The emphasis on Gregorian chant and classical polyphonic music was therefore ordered to both the character of the liturgy as mystery and its character as Logos, as well as to its bond to the historical word. It was supposed to bring out the normativeness of the Fathers, so to speak, which had perhaps at times been interpreted in a too exclusive and too historicized way. Normativity, when properly understood, does not mean the exclusion of the new, but guidance that points one toward what lies on the horizon. Striding forth into new country is made possible here precisely by the fact that the right path has been found. Only when one understands that the reforms of Pius and the Council have this intention and this direction essentially in common can one correctly evaluate the differences in their practical instructions. Conversely, we can then say that viewing the liturgy while blind to its character as mystery and its cosmic dimension necessarily causes not reform but deformation of the liturgy to occur.

4. Foundation and Role of Music in Worship

The question concerning the essence of liturgy and the criteria of reform has automatically brought us back to the question concerning the place of music in liturgy. As a matter of fact, one cannot speak of liturgy without also talking about the music of worship. Where liturgy deteriorates, the *musica sacra* also deteriorates, and where liturgy is correctly understood and lived, there good church music also grows. We have already seen that the concept of "community", or "assembly", first appears in the *Catechism* where the Holy Spirit is spoken of as the one who gives the liturgy its shape; we said that thereby the inner place of the assembly is exactly delineated. It is no coincidence either that the phrase "to sing" first appears where the cosmic nature of the liturgy is under consideration—to be precise, in a quotation from the Constitution on the Sacred Liturgy of the Second Vatican Council: "In the earthly liturgy we share in a foretaste of that heavenly liturgy which is celebrated in the Holy City of Jerusalem toward which we journey as pilgrims. . . . With all the warriors of the heavenly army we sing a hymn of glory to the Lord." [12] Philipp Harnoncourt has expressed the same point very beautifully by adapting Wittgenstein's saying "What one cannot talk about one must remain silent about" as follows: "What one cannot talk about one can, indeed must, sing and make music about if one cannot be silenced." [13] Somewhat later he adds: "Jews and Christians agree with one another that their singing and music-making point to heaven, or rather that these come from heaven or are learned from heaven." [14] The fundamental principles of liturgical music are given already in these sentences. Faith comes from listening to God's word. But wherever God's word is translated into human words there remains a surplus of

---

[12] CCC 1090; SC 8. The *Catechism* points out that the same thought is also in the Dogmatic Constitution on the Church *Lumen gentium*, no. 50, last paragraph.

[13] Philipp Harnoncourt, "Gesang und Musik im Gottesdienst", in *Die Messe: Ein kirchenmusikalisches Handbuch*, ed. Harald Schützeichel (Düsseldorf, 1991), 9–25 (quotation from 13).

[14] Ibid.,17.

the unspoken and unspeakable that calls us to silence—into a silence that in the end lets the unspeakable become song and also calls on the voices of the cosmos for help so that the unspoken may become audible. This means that church music, coming from the Word and the silence perceived in it, always presupposes a new listening to the whole richness of the Logos.

Whereas Schützeichel maintains that in principle every kind of music could be used in religious service,[15] Harnoncourt refers to more profound and fundamental connections between particular actions in life and the musical expressions appropriate to them; he goes on to say: "For the encounter with the mystery of faith I am convinced that there is ... in a certain way appropriate, or also inappropriate, music."[16] As a matter of fact, music that is supposed to serve the Christian liturgy must correspond to the Logos, concretely. It must stand in a meaningful relation to the words in which the Logos has expressed himself. It cannot free itself, not even as instrumental music, from the inner orientation of these words, which open up endless space, but also draw distinctions. By its nature such music must be different from music that is supposed to lead to rhythmic ecstasy, stupefying anesthetization, sensual excitement, or dissolution of the ego in Nirvana, to name just a few possibilities. On this point there is a lovely saying in St. Cyprian's interpretation of the Our Father:

> Discipline, which includes tranquility and awe, belongs to the words and posture of praying. We should be mindful that we are standing before the eyes of God. One must please the divine eyes through the posture of the body and the implementation of its voice. Shame-lessness expresses itself in vulgar shouting; it is proper for the reverent one to pray in timid words. ... When we come together as one with our brothers and celebrate the divine sacrifice with the priest, we must not stir the air with formless sounds nor fling our petitions to God with extensive palaver, which should instead be humbly commended to him because God ... does not need to be reminded through our shouting.[17]

---

[15] Cf. Schützeichel, "Wohin soll ich mich wenden?" 366: "In principle every kind of music from Gregorian chant to jazz can be used in religious service. Naturally there is music that is more suitable and less suitable. The deciding factor is the quality."

[16] Harnoncourt, "Gesang und Musik", 24.

[17] St. Cyprian, *De oratione dominica*, 4, CSEL 3, 1 (ed. Hartel), 268–69 [translated into English from the German].

Naturally this internal norm of music in accord with the Logos must be grounded. It must show people here and now, at this time and in this place, as prayers into Christ's communion. It has to be accessible to them but at the same time lead them farther, and lead them farther exactly in that direction which the liturgy itself indicates in a matchlessly brief formula at the beginning of the Preface: *sursum corda*—the heart, that is, the inner person, the entirety of the self, lifted up into the height of God, to that height which is God and which in Christ touches the earth, draws it to itself, and pulls it up to itself.

5. Choir and Congregation: The Question of Language

Before I try to apply these principles to a few specific problems of church music in the Regensburg cathedral, there is still something to say about the subjects of liturgical music and the language of hymns. Where an exaggerated and, especially in our mobile society (as we were able to establish), completely unrealistic concept of congregation prevails, only the priest and congregation can be acknowledged as the legitimate singers of liturgical hymns. The primitive actionism and prosaic pedagogical rationalism of such a position have generally been seen through today and are therefore only rarely maintained. That a schola and choir can also contribute to the whole is seldom challenged, not even where one falsely interprets the conciliar phrase "active participation" in the sense of an external actionism. Admittedly, vetoes against the use of a choir remain, which we will consider in a moment. They are based on an inadequate interpretation of liturgical togetherness. In this togetherness the present congregation can never simply be the subject; rather, it must be understood as an assembly that is open upward and open synchronically and diachronically into the wide expanse of God's history. Once again Harnoncourt has brought an important point into play when he speaks of elevated forms that cannot be missing in the liturgy as God's celebration, but whose high demands cannot be satisfied by the congregation as a whole. He goes on to say: "The choir, therefore, is not standing before a community that is listening like an audience that lets itself be sung to, but is itself part of the community and sings for it in the sense of legitimately representing it or standing in for it." [18] The concept of representation, of standing in for another, which affects all levels of religious reality and is thus also important in the liturgical assembly in particular, is one of the fundamental categories of Christian faith as a whole.[19] The insight that this is a matter of representation does indeed eliminate the rivalry of the other side. The choir acts for the others and includes them in its own action in this "for". Through its singing everyone can be led into the great liturgy of the communion of saints and thus into that kind of praying which pulls our hearts upward and lets us join, above and beyond all earthly realizations, the heavenly Jerusalem.

But are we really allowed to sing in Latin if the people do not understand it? After the Council a fanaticism about vernacular appeared in a number of places, which is actually abstruse in a multicultural society, just as the hypostatization of the community in a mobile society has no logic to it. Let us first disregard the fact that a text is not yet understandable to everyone just because it has been translated into each person's mother tongue, even though we have touched on a question of no little importance here. Once again Philipp Harnoncourt has described in an excellent fashion an aspect that is essential for Christian liturgy in general:

This celebration is not interrupted as soon as something is sung or played by instruments ... ; on the contrary, it displays its "celebratory" character precisely in this. This requirement, however, demands neither uniformity in liturgical language nor uniformity in the style of the musical parts. The traditional, so-called "Latin Mass" always had Aramaic (*Amen, Alleluia, Hosanna, Maran atha*) and Greek (*Kyrie eleison, Trisagion*) parts, and the sermon was usually given in the vernacular. Real life is not acquainted with stylistic unity and perfection; on the contrary, where something is really alive formal and stylistic variety will occur ..., and the unity is an organic one.[20]

In the thirty years of theological and liturgical upheaval during which he was given the task of discharging his duties, the departing cathedral choirmaster has known, from the perspective of these insights, how to manage continuity in development and development in continuity, quite

---

[18] Harnoncourt, "Gesang und Musik", 17.

[19] Cf. the thorough work by Karl-Heinz Menke, *Stellvertretung: Schlüsselbegriff christlichen Lebens und theologische Grundkategorie*, Sammlung Horizonte, n.s. 29 (Freiburg, 1991).

[20] Harnoncourt, "Gesang und Musik", 21.

frequently in the headwind of tremendously pretentious trends. In this he was supported by the confidence of Bishop Graber as well as of his successor, Bishop Manfred Müller and the auxiliary bishops Flügel, Guggenberger, and Schraml. Thanks to this deep rapport with the responsible bishops and their staff he could contribute considerably and in a steadfast, yet open way so that the liturgy in the Regensburg cathedral kept its dignity and excellence and remained transparent to the cosmic liturgy of the Logos in the unity of the whole Church without taking on a museumlike character or turning into a nostalgic fossil in the shadows. In conclusion I would like to examine briefly, and also contrary to prevailing opinions, two characteristic examples of this struggle for continuity in development: the issue of the *Sanctus* and *Benedictus* and the question about the appropriate place for the *Agnus Dei*.

6. *Specific Questions:* Sanctus—Benedictus—Agnus Dei

My former Münster colleague and friend Emil Joseph Lengeling has said, if one understands the *Sanctus* as an authentic part for the congregation celebrating Mass, "then this not only leads to compelling conclusions for new musical settings, but also results in vetoes for most of the Gregorian and for all the polyphonic versions since they exclude the people from singing and do not take the character of acclamation into account."[21] With all due respect for the eminent liturgist, his opinion shows that even experts can be wide of the mark. First of all, mistrust is always in order when a large part of the living history has to be thrown onto the garbage dump of discarded misunderstandings. This is all the more true for the Christian liturgy, which lives from the continuity and inner unity of the history of religious prayer. In fact, the assertion that the acclamatory character can be attended to only by the congregation is completely unfounded. In the entire liturgical tradition of the East and the West, the Preface always closes with the reference to the heavenly liturgy and invites the assembled congregation to join in the acclamation of the heavenly choirs. The end of the

---

[21] Emil Joseph Lengeling, *Die neue Ordnung der Eucharistiefeier*, 2nd ed. (Münster, 1971), 234; cf. also Birgit Jeggle-Merz and Harald Schützeichel, "Eucharistiefeier", in *Messe*, 90–151, on this point, 109–10.

Preface in particular has had a decisive influence on the iconography of the *Majestas Domini*, which was the point of departure for my remarks.[22] Compared to the biblical basis of the *Sanctus* in Isaiah 6, there are three new accents in the liturgical text.[23] The scene is no longer the Temple in Jerusalem, as in Isaiah, but heaven, which opens itself up to the earth in mystery. For this reason it is no longer just the seraphim who are exulting, but all the hosts of heaven in whose acclamation the whole Church, redeemed mankind, can sing in unison because of Christ, who connects heaven and earth with each other. Finally, from there the *Sanctus* has been transferred from the "he"-form to the "you"-form: heaven and earth are full of your glory. The "Hosanna", originally a cry for help, thus becomes a song of praise. Whoever does not pay attention to the mystery character and cosmic character of the invitation to sing in unison with the praise of the heavenly choirs has already missed the point of the whole thing. This unison can occur in a variety of ways, and it always has to do with being representative of or standing in for others. The congregation assembled in one place opens into the whole. It also represents those who are absent and unites itself with those who are far and near. If the congregation has a choir that can draw it into cosmic praise and into the open expanse of heaven and earth more powerfully than its own stammering, then the representative function of the choir is at this moment particularly appropriate. Through the choir a greater transparency to the praise of the angels and therefore a more profound, interior joining in with their singing are bestowed than a congregation's own acclamation and song would be capable of doing in many places.

I suspect, though, that the real objection cannot consist of the acclamatory character or the *tutti*-demand; that would seem to me to be too shallow. Looming behind these is probably the fear that through a choral *Sanctus*, especially if it is also obligatory to connect it to the *Benedictus*, a kind of concert interlude and with that a pause in prayer would occur just at the start of the Eucharistic Prayer and so at a point where it is least justifiable. And indeed, this objection is correct—if one presupposes that there is neither the representative function of the

---

[22] Cf. Konrad Onasch, *Kunst und Liturgie der Ostkirche* (Vienna, Cologne, and Graz, 1984), 329.

[23] Cf. Josef Andreas Jungmann, *Missarum Sollemnia*, vol. 2 (Freiburg, 1952), 168ff. [trans. Francis A. Brunner as *The Mass of the Roman Rite*, vol. 2 (New York, 1955)].

choir nor an implicit singing and praying along with it in the outward silence of the congregation. If all those who are not singing during the *Sanctus* are only waiting for its end or can only focus themselves on a piece of religious music, then the performance by the choir is intolerable. But must this be the case? Have we not forgotten something here that we must urgently learn again? Perhaps it is helpful to remind the reader that the silent praying of the Canon by the priest did not arise because the singing of the *Sanctus* took so long that one had to start praying to save time. The sequence of events is just the other way around. Certainly since Carolingian times, but perhaps even earlier, the priest has proceeded into the Canon "silently"; the Canon is the time of pure silence as "preparation for the nearness of God".[24] Briefly an "office of accompanying petitions, comparable to the oriental intercessions (*Ektenien*)" settled "on the celebrant's silent praying of the Canon like an exterior cover".[25] Later it was the singing of the choir that continued in this way, as Jungmann formulated it, "to retain the old dominating feature of the Eucharistic Prayer, thanksgiving, and praise," and stretch it "over the entire Canon for the ears of the participants".[26] Even though we do not want to restore this state of affairs, it can still offer guidance for the way to go. Does it not do us good, before we set off into the center of the mystery, to encounter a short time of filled silence in which the choir calms us interiorly, leading each one of us into silent prayer and thus into a union that can occur only on the inside? Must we not relearn this silent, inner co-praying with each other and with the angels and saints, the living and the dead, and with Christ himself? This way the words of the Canon do not become worn-out expressions that we then in vain attempt to substitute with ever newly assembled phrases, phrases that conceal the absence of the real inner event of the liturgy, the departure from human speech into being touched by the eternal.

Lengeling's veto, which has been repeated by many others, is meaningless. The choral *Sanctus* has its justification even after the Second Vatican Council. But what about the *Benedictus*? The assertion that it may under no circumstances be separated from the *Sanctus* has been put so emphatically and with such apparent competence that only a

---

[24] Ibid., 174.
[25] Ibid., 175–76.
[26] Ibid., 172.

few brave souls have been able to refuse to comply with it. But this assertion cannot be justified—either historically, or theologically or liturgically. Of course it makes good sense to sing them together when a composition specifies this connection, which is ancient and very well founded. What has to be rejected here is again only the exclusion of their separation.

The *Sanctus* and *Benedictus* both have their own starting point in Scripture so that at first each one developed separately from the other. Whereas we find the *Sanctus* already in the first epistle of Clement (34:5–6)[27] and so definitely still in the apostolic age, we first encounter the *Benedictus*, as far as I can see, in the *Apostolic Constitutions*, that is, in the second half of the fourth century, and here as an acclamation before the distribution of Holy Communion, as a response to the phrase: "To the holy ones the Holy One". We find it again in the sixth century in Gaul, where it is connected to the *Sanctus*, as also happened in the tradition of the East.[28] Whereas the *Sanctus* evolved from Isaiah 6 and was then transferred from the earthly to the heavenly Jerusalem and so became the song of the Church, the *Benedictus* is based on a New Testament rereading of Psalm 118:26. In the Old Testament text this verse is a blessing at the arrival of the festive procession in the Temple; on Palm Sunday it received a new meaning, which, however, had already been prepared in the development of Jewish prayer, for the expression "he who comes" had become a name for the Messiah.[29] When the youths of Jerusalem shout this verse to Jesus, they are greeting him as the Messiah, as the king of the last days who enters the Holy City and the Temple to seize possession of them. The *Sanctus* is ordered to the eternal glory of God; in contrast, the *Benedictus* refers to the advent of the incarnate God in our midst. Christ, the one who has come, is also always the one coming. His eucharistic coming, the anticipation of his hour, makes a present occurrence out

---

[27] Cf. Onasch, *Kunst und Liturgie*, 329; Jungmann, *Missarum Sollemnia*, 2:166. In Clement's epistle (*1 Clem.* 34) we already find the connection of Isaiah 6 with Daniel 7:10, which is presupposed in the liturgical form of the *Sanctus*; it is precisely that version we found in the images of Marienberg: "Let us heed how the whole host of his angels stand by him." Concerning the dating of *1 Clement*, see Thomas J. Herron, *The Dating of the First Epistle of Clement to the Corinthians* (Rome, 1988). Herron tries to show that *1 Clement* is not to be dated ca. A.D. 96, as is usually done, but rather around A.D. 70.

[28] Jungmann, *Missarum Sollemnia*, 2:170–71, nn. 41 and 42.

[29] Ibid., 171 n. 42; cf. Rudolf Pesch, *Das Markusevangelium*, vol. 2, HThKNT, vol. 2, pt. 2 (Freiburg, 1977), 184.

of a promise and brings the future into the here and now. For this reason the *Benedictus* is meaningful both as an approach to the Consecration and as an acclamation to the Lord who has become present in the Eucharistic Species. The great moment of his coming, the immensity of his real presence in the elements of the earth, definitely call for a response. The elevation, genuflection, and ringing of the bells are such faltering attempts at a reply.[30] Following a parallel in the Byzantine rite, the reformers of the liturgy composed an acclamation of the people: "Christ has died, ..." But the question of other possible acclamations to welcome the Lord who is coming/has come has been posed. It is evident to me that there is no more appropriate or more profound acclamation, or one that is more rooted in tradition than precisely this one: Blessed is he who comes in the name of the Lord. It is true that splitting the *Sanctus* and the *Benedictus* is not necessary, but it makes a lot of sense. If the choir sings the *Sanctus* and the *Benedictus* together, then the break between the Preface and the Eucharistic Prayer can indeed be too lengthy. When this happens, it no longer serves the congregation's silent, yet cooperative entering into cosmic praise because the inner tension is not sustained. On the other hand, if a filled silence and an interior greeting of the Lord along with the choir take place after the Consecration event, it corresponds profoundly to the inner structure of the occasion. The pedantic proscription of such a split, which came about not without reason in the development, should be forgotten as quickly as possible.

Now just a word about the *Agnus Dei*. In the Regensburg cathedral it has become a tradition that after the Sign of Peace the *Agnus Dei* is first spoken three times by both the priest and the people and then continued by the choir as a communion hymn during the distribution of Communion. Over against this custom it has been asserted that the *Agnus Dei* belongs to the rite of the breaking of the bread. Only a completely fossilized archaism can draw the conclusion from its original purpose of accompanying the time of the breaking of the bread that it should be sung exclusively at this point. As a matter of fact, it became a communion song as early as the ninth and tenth centuries

---

[30] Cf. Jungmann, *Missarum Sollemnia*, 2:165. In this context it might be of interest to note that the *motu proprio* of Pius X from 1903 (pt. 3, 8, p. 29 of the German text) insisted that only liturgical texts were allowed to be used in the hymns at Mass; just *one* exception was permitted: following the custom of the Roman Church a motet could be sung after the *Benedictus* of a High Mass.

when the old rites of the breaking the bread were no longer necessary because of the new hosts. Jungmann points out that in many cases in the early Middle Ages only one *Agnus Dei* was sung after the Sign of Peace, while the second and third ones found their niche after Communion and thus accompanied the distribution of Communion where there was one.[31] And does the request for the mercy of Christ, the Lamb of God, not make sense at that exact moment when he defenselessly gives himself into our hands again as Lamb, the sacrificed, yet triumphant Lamb who holds the keys of history in his hands (Rev 5)? And is the request for peace made to him, the defenseless yet victorious One, not appropriate especially at the moment of receiving Communion since peace was, after all, one of the names of the Eucharist in the early Church because it tears down the boundaries between heaven and earth and between peoples and states and joins men to the unity of the Body of Christ?

At first glance, the Regensburg tradition and the conciliar as well as postconciliar reform seem to be two opposite worlds, which clash in harsh contradiction. Whoever stood right between them for three decades was able to experience the severity of the posed questions for himself. But where this tension is endured, it turns out that all this belongs to the stages of one single path. Only if one holds these stages together and holds out will they be correctly understood and will true reform flourish in the spirit of the Second Vatican Council—reform that is not discontinuity and destruction but purification and growth to a new maturation and a new fullness. The cathedral choirmaster who has borne the weight of this tension deserves thanks: This was not only a service for Regensburg and its cathedral, but a service for the entire Church.

---

[31] Jungmann, *Missarum Sollemnia*, 2:413–22.

IV. The Artistic Transposition of the Faith
Theological Problems of Church Music

The critical situation of church music today is part of a general crisis of the Church that has developed since Vatican II. We do not primarily intend to discuss the artistic crisis that is affecting church music along with all other forms of art at present. We shall rather discuss the crisis conditioned by the situation of theology, in other words, the properly theological and ecclesiastical crisis of church music. *Musica sacra* seems indeed to have fallen between two opposing theological millstones that of course work together harmoniously to grind it down.

On the one side stands the puritanical functionalism of a liturgy conceived in purely pragmatic terms: the liturgical event, it is claimed, should be made non-cultic and returned to its simple point of departure, a community meal. Everyone knows that the Second Vatican Council described the position of the individual in the liturgy with the phrase "*participatio actuosa*", active participation. This concept, in itself quite significant, has not infrequently led to the opinion that the ideal goal of liturgical renewal is the uniform activity of all present in the liturgy. Accordingly, we have witnessed the reduction of specially prominent tasks; in particular, festive church music was widely considered a sign of an inappropriate "cultic" understanding that appeared incompatible with general activity. On this view, church music can continue to exist only in the form of congregational singing, which in turn is not to be judged in terms of its artistic value but solely on the basis of its functionality, that is, its "community-building" and participatory function. The lengths to which the renunciation of musical quality can go are illustrated by the statement of a leading German liturgist. After the Council he declared that none of the traditional

From Robert A. Skeris, ed., *Crux et cithara* (Altötting, 1983), 214–22; or *Sacred Music* 135 (2008)—http://musicasacra.com/theological-problems/. Reprinted by permission of the editor of *Sacred Music*.

church music could satisfy the liturgical norms now in force; everything would have to be created anew. Obviously, from this perspective liturgical music is not regarded as art, but merely as a utilitarian object.

Now at this point the first millstone (which we called puritanical functionalism) makes contact with the second, which I would like to call the functionalism of accommodation. Again and again observers have described the remarkable and paradoxical phenomenon that, parallel to the disbanding of church choirs and orchestras, new ensembles often appeared in order to perform "religious" jazz. They made an impression but were certainly no less elitist than the old church choirs, yet they were not subjected to the same criticism. When such a takeover was enforced with passionate exclusivity, one could recognize an attitude that regarded all church music, indeed all previous Western culture, as no longer part of the present; hence it could not be part of a contemporary practice, such as liturgy intends to be and must be. Instead, traditional culture is pushed aside into a more or less museum-like state of preservation in the concert hall. This attitude has in common with the first one its exclusively functional way of thinking, which of course comes into play here no longer merely as a theory about liturgy but rather with its fundamental force: the contemporary world is understood so much in terms of functionality that the connection with history is broken, and history itself can retain any importance at all only as a function, namely, as an object in a museum. Thus history is completely relegated to the past and loses all power to shape life today.

These reflections make it clear that in the crisis described above we are dealing with a difficult and very deeply rooted phenomenon that cannot be remedied with mere polemics. We need to reflect on the roots of this attitude in order to be able to overcome it from within. Some of the tangled roots from which these contemporary problems have sprung are already clear from what has been said so far. When we attempt to arrange and complete our insights, it turns out that we can probably speak about four levels of the problem.

1. The Panorama of Problems

1. The first and relatively harmless, superficial level is located in the old dilemma of the pragmatism of parish priests versus art's absolute

claims. This dilemma has always existed and will always do so. Whether we think of St. Jerome's outbursts against the vanity of artists or recall the archbishop of Salzburg who prescribed to Mozart the maximum permissible length of his liturgical compositions—it is always the same friction between two different claims. Here, one must try to see where each side is right in order to find the common ground on which they can meet. Liturgy is something done in common, hence intelligibility and feasibility are among its essential requirements. In a certain sense, art is elitist activity; hence it resists being fit into a set of requirements that are not its own. In this respect there is a conflict rooted in the very nature of the matter, but it can be fruitful because the matter itself points toward an inner unity that of course must always be sought anew: the liturgy is not merely something done in common, but is by its very nature "feast". When exaggerated meal theories fail to take this fundamental character of the liturgy into account, they no longer explain the essence of the liturgy but rather conceal it. As feast, though, the liturgy thrives on splendor and thus calls for the transfiguring power of art. Indeed, the liturgy is the actual birthplace of art; from the liturgy art acquired its anthropological necessity and its religious legitimization. Conversely, though, we can now say that when there is no longer a genuine feast, art becomes a museum piece, precisely in its most magnificent manifestations. It then lives on the memory that the feast once existed, and it becomes past-tense. But there is no feast without liturgy, without a warrant to celebrate that surpasses man, and so art, too, is now referred to liturgy. For its part, art lives insofar as it repeatedly places itself at the service of the festive liturgy and is continually reborn therein.[1]

2. As we have seen, the tension between the pragmatism of parish priests and the absolutism of artists is a perpetual problem in practice, but at least it is not necessarily a problem at the level of basic principles. The question that we previously hinted at in passing with the word "puritanism" is more profound and far-reaching. In more precise theological and intellectual historical terms one would have to speak about the problem of iconoclasm. In his book *Where is the Vatican Heading?* Reinhard Raffalt impressively describes the revival

---

[1] On this subject, cf. Josef Pieper, *Zustimmung zur Welt: Eine Theorie des Festes*, 2nd ed. (Munich: Kösel, 1963); Walter Dürig, *Das christliche Fest und seine Feier* (St. Ottilien: EOS-Verlag, 1974), each book with further bibliography.

of iconoclastic currents in the postconciliar church and tries to find a common biblical denominator for this phenomenon. The Church as she used to be, the "old Church" (as he puts it) allowed her existential sense to be defined in terms of, say, the parables of the laborers in the vineyard or the lilies of the field; today, driving the merchants out of the Temple and the eye of the needle that makes it difficult for the rich to enter the Kingdom of Heaven have moved into the foreground.[2]

As a matter of fact, there were repeated outbreaks of iconoclastic riots in Church history. In the seventh and eight centuries the Church of Byzantium was roiled by this problem in a way that touched the very nerve of her existence; the Orthodox Church accordingly celebrates the Second Council of Nicaea as the "Feast of Orthodoxy", because it brought about the definitive victory of images and thus the vindication of art within faith in general. This means that the Orthodox Church sees in this question the salient point of ecclesial existence in general, where the fundamental decision about our understanding of God, the world, and man is ultimately at stake.[3]

Although the Western Church was convulsed by the question during the Carolingian age,[4] not until the Reformation did Europe play out the great iconoclastic tragedy in which Luther sided with the ancient Church against Calvin and the leftist Reformers, the so-called *Schwärmer* or Fanatics. The earthquake that we are experiencing in the Church today belongs in this historical context: this is the real sore point in the theological question about the justification for images and music in the Church. Hence the main part of our reflections should be devoted to the investigation of this question, which for now will be postponed. At any rate this much is clear: the problem of church music is not merely a problem for music but is also a vital question for the Church. And I would add that it is conversely a question for music as a whole and not just for church music, because when the religious basis for music is cut away, then in keeping with

---

[2] Reinhard Raffalt, *Wohin steuert der Vatikan?* (Munich and Zurich: Piper, 1973), especially 93 ff.; Raffalt, *Musica eterna: von Palestrina bis Mozart* (Munich: Piper, 1978), 221–39.

[3] Cf. Christoph von Schönborn, *L'Icône du Christ: Fondements théologiques élaborés entre le Ier et le IIe Concile de Nicée (325/787)* (Fribourg: Éditions Universitaires, 1976); [trans. Lothar Krauth as *God's Human Face: The Christ-Icon* (San Francisco: Ignatius Press, 1994].

[4] Cf. the presentation of Franz Schupp, *Glaube—Kultur—Symbol: Versuch einer kritischen Theorie sakramentaler Praxis* (Düsseldorf: Patmos-Verlag, 1974).

the foregoing considerations music and art itself are threatened, even though this may not be immediately apparent.

3. To be sure, this makes it quite clear that the *ecclesiastical crisis* of church music cannot be separated at all from the present crisis of art in which we find ourselves. I hear that Maurizio Kagel wrote an opera some years ago that depicts in reverse the history of the modern era, and thus ultimately world history, as a utopian myth: the America of the Incas, the Mayas, the Chibchas, and so on, is not discovered by the Christian Spaniards, but rather Spain and Europe are discovered by the Indians and liberated from their Christian "superstition". The myth is intended as a utopian project: this is the way that history should have unfolded; this would have been progress toward humanity and world unity: it could have and should have come about in Pre-Christian and Anti-Christian culture. Such images are not only an expression of protest against Christianity but are also intended as a cultural option, as a disowning of Christian culture and a search for new shores of cultural expression that are contrasted with the Christian world in protest.[5] Herein lies the symptomatic significance of such images: the demands of Christian culture and of the cultural manifestations that have developed within that sphere actually appear as a threat to the men of a world that has once again become pagan. And many aspects of the art industry in recent decades can at bottom be understood only as deliberate mockery of what previously had been art, as an attempt to liberate itself from the greatness of art through mockery and ridicule, an attempt to overtake and to supersede art and to regain the ascendancy vis-à-vis a demand that we simply cannot meet.

4. This in turn is connected with the phenomenon of functionalism described earlier, which is in fact the real name for the existential form of today's world. In their book *Opportunity and Risk of the Present*, Hugo Staudinger and Wolfgang Behler have examined in

---

[5] The most radical philosophical development of this position is found in Claude Lévi-Strauss, especially in *La Pensée sauvage* (Paris: Plon, 1962). Cf. for example the sentence on 326: "The ultimate aim of the anthropological sciences is not to construct man but to dissolve him." Cited here from Hans Urs von Balthasar, *Prolegomena*, vol. 1 of *Theodramatik* (Einsiedeln: Johannes-Verlag, 1973), 41 [trans. Graham Harrison as *Prolegomena*, vol. 1 of *Theo-Drama: Theological Dramatic Theory* (San Francisco: Ignatius Press, 1988), 44]. Instructive as to the intellectual background is Gustave Martelet, *L'Au-delà retrouvé: Christologie des fins dernières* (Paris: Desclée, 1974), 35ff.

great detail the comprehensive character of this functionalism.[6] Characteristic elements are that the machine ultimately becomes the universal pattern of life, for man as well, that all realities are reduced to quantitative dimensions, and that this reducibility applies in principle and everywhere. Here there is no longer any room for the uniqueness of artistic achievements; that must be replaced by what is calculable. Art falls under the laws of the marketplace and, hence, is abolished as art.[7]

All of this should have made it somewhat clear that the problems of church music today are only to a very small extent purely ecclesiastical problems; conversely, though, it should also be evident that problems of the present day and of its culture have something to do with the convulsions racking Christianity and, hence, are also decisively influenced by them. Accordingly, the task of the second part of our reflections must be to illuminate the genuinely theological core of the whole question: Is Christianity itself iconoclastic, perhaps from its very root, and did it become artistically creative only through a *"felix culpa"* (in the sense in which Gottlieb Söhngen called Salzburg a *felix culpa*, a princely-episcopal misunderstanding of apostolic succession, but a fortunate one)?[8] Or is iconoclasm perhaps un-Christian after all, so that art and particularly church music would actually be an intrinsic requirement of Christianity itself, and thus music in general along with church music could constantly draw new hope from this fact?

The inner crisis of Christianity today consists in the fact that Christianity can no longer recognize "orthodoxy" as it was formulated at

---

[6] Hugo Staudinger and Wolfgang Behler, *Chance und Risiko der Gegenwart* (Paderborn: Schöningh, 1976), especially 97–224.

[7] The attempt to escape this consequence through a "creativity" that frees itself from anything already established and drafts a totally new reality leads nowhere. The intellectual underpinnings of the attempt to find a new basis for art in this way by disconnecting it from its religious origin have been most impressively elaborated by Ernst Bloch, for whom the artist is "the absolute transgressor of boundaries", "the pioneer at the frontier of an advancing world, indeed a most important component of the world that is only now creating itself". Genius is "consciousness that has progressed the farthest". This does away with the qualitatively specific characteristic of art, which is mere anticipation of what is to come. Accordingly, Ernst Bloch's understanding of art quite logically leads to the prediction of a world in which "electric power plants and St. Mark's Churches" will be identical. For more details, see Friedrich Hartl, *Der Begriff des Schöpferischen: Deutungsversuche der Dialektik durch Ernst Bloch und Franz von Baader*, Regensburger Studien zur Theologie 18 (Frankfurt: Lang, 1979).

[8] Gottlieb Söhngen, *Der Weg der abendländischen Theologie: Grundgedanken zu einer Theologie des "Weges"*, Bücherei der Salzburger Hochschulwochen (Munich: Pustet, 1959), 61.

the Second Council of Nicaea and actually considers iconoclasm to be the original position. All that remains then is either the desperate schizophrenia of joy on account of the fortunate misunderstanding in history or a new revival of iconoclasm. Why is it that the experts today consider it a settled question that enmity toward art, Puritan functionalism, is the genuinely Christian attitude? As a matter of fact, this view has two roots. The first lies in the fact that the transition from the Old Testament to the community of Jesus Christ appears as an escape from the Temple into the liturgy of the commonplace. Jesus continues the criticism of Temple worship begun by the Israelite prophets and, indeed, intensifies it to the point of symbolically destroying the Temple when he cast out the money changers. The crucifixion of Jesus "outside the gate" (Heb 13:12) thus appears to his apostles as the new worship[9] and hence as the end of all worship in the previous sense. From this, people today conclude that Christianity as Jesus Christ understood it is opposed to Temple, cult, and priesthood; that Christianity recognizes no other sacredness and no other sacred space than that of everyday life; that consequently Christian worship too must be "profane"—a bit of the commonplace. And wherever cult and priesthood may have arisen once again, that is simply regression into a pre-Christian stage. Such a profane comprehension of Christianity then provokes the twofold reaction that we spoke about at the outset. On the one hand, the festive solemnity of Christian worship must be denied, and with it all previous church music is ushered out the door, since it appears "sacred". On the other hand, worship is supposed to be no different from everyday activity, and music can enter into worship, so to speak, on one condition: that it be profane.

Such ideas were unknown to the growing Church of the early centuries. Already from the New Testament letters we learn about a rich and by no means profane liturgical life in which the psalms of Israel were still sung, along with Christian additions in the form of hymns and chants. Erik Peterson has shown how in many respects the book of Revelation expands the Temple vision of Isaiah, which mentions the cries and utterances of the angels before God. Among other things,

---

[9] Cf. my article "Weltoffene Kirche", in *Umkehr und Erneuerung*, ed. Theodor Filthaut (Mainz: Matthias-Grünewald-Verlag, 1966), 273–91, here, 281ff. For more details on the entire subject of desacralization, see Heribert Mühlen, *Entsakralisierung* (Paderborn: Schöningh, 1971).

Revelation reports more than mere cries: singing, calling, giving glory.[10] The background for this is a differentiation in liturgical usage that opened a new dimension in cultic praise and glorification by supplementing psalmody with hymnody, speech, or recitation with song. In this context, Peterson refers to a noteworthy passage from Origen: "Singing psalms befits men, but singing hymns is for angels and for those who lead a life like that of the angels."[11] Note well: from the very beginning, Christian worship was the worship of *God* and clearly set apart from the everyday and the commonplace. Indeed, from the very beginning it was characterized by efforts to devise a new form of poetic and musical praise, and this for theological motives.

On the other hand, it is true that Christian worship presupposes a break with the Temple and to that extent is closer to the synagogue service than to the Temple liturgy, in terms of its outward form, at any rate. This means the omission of instruments; it does not signify a transition into the profane, but rather a sacrality accentuated by purism. The Church Fathers accordingly described the entire path from the Old Testament Temple cult to Christian worship, and the path from Old to New Testament in general, as a process of spiritualization. From this point of view they were devoted to a liturgy that was as purely logocentric as possible and, at first, generally opposed to liturgical splendor at all levels. This is especially true of the father of Western theology, St. Augustine, who furthermore in his realm adhered to a prohibition of images as an expression of his theology of spiritualization, thus leaving his mark in a special way on the development of the Church and of theology in the West.[12]

Of course the concept of spiritualization alone would not necessarily have produced such effects, since great art is after all precisely the result of a maximum of spiritualization. Here, instead, the Platonic root in patristic thought comes to the fore, giving its particular cast to the patristic idea of spiritualization and hence also to the patristic view of the relationship between Old and New Testament. In a certain respect

---

[10] Erik Peterson, "Von den Engeln", in his *Theologische Traktate* (Munich, 1951), 323–407, here, 356 [trans. Ronald Walls as *The Angels and the Liturgy* (New York: Herder & Herder, 1964), 26].

[11] Ibid., 357 [English trans., 27] (Origen, *Selecta in psalmos*, on Ps 119[118]:71).

[12] Cf. Frederik van der Meer, *Augustinus der Seelsorger* (Cologne: Bachem, 1951), 329–74, as well as my article "Zur theologischen Grundlegung der Kirchenmusik", in *Gloria Deo-Pax Hominibus*, ed. Franz Fleckenstein, Allgemeiner Cäcilien-Verband für die Länder des Deutschen Sprache 9 (Regensburg: Habbeldruck, 1974), 39–62 [JRCW 11:431–39].

Plato may be called the discoverer of the spirit in the West, and that is his lasting fame. He describes humanity as a passage from the sensory to the spiritual, as a process of de-materialization. His comprehensive pedagogical program is formulated starting with that. As a genuine Greek, he allots to music a central position in the education of men, but even his musical pedagogy is based on the concept of a dematerialization of music, through which he intends to achieve in general the victory of Greek humanity over the sensualizing music of inherited religions. The basic concept as such is important, but he who constructs a perfect world in a test tube actually does violence to reality.[13]

To the Fathers of the Church, these concepts seemed like an anticipated explanation of the Christian passage from Temple to Church. And thus they too regarded the musical riches of the Old Testament and Greco-Roman culture as a part of the sensible, material world that was to be overcome in the spiritual world of Christianity. They understood spiritualization to mean dematerialization and hence understood it in a manner that more or less borders on iconoclasm. This is theology's historical mortgage in the question of ecclesiastical art, which comes up over and over again.[14]

2. The Foundations of Church Music in the Nature of Liturgy

Nonetheless, with these reflections we have already come closer to an answer to our basic question: Is Christianity from its origin iconoclastic and hostile toward art, or is it—when it remains true to itself—precisely a summons to artistic expression? We have seen that genuine liturgical activity is essential to Christianity and that precisely in its earliest phase, the *novum* [new thing] that occurred with Christ appears as a summons to intensified expression and is presented as the transition from crying to singing. We must now examine this viewpoint in still greater depth in order to find the correct solution to our problem. Let us return to Peterson's analyses. He shows that the changes that the book of Revelation makes as compared with Isaiah include the appearance not only of the Seraphim but of articulated and ordered

---

[13] For evidence of this, see my article "Zur theologischen Grundlegung", 50ff., 58ff.

[14] Once again, cf. my article, ibid., as well as the book by Christoph von Schönborn, *L'Icône du Christ*, especially pages 77–85 [Eng. trans., 47–56, "Origen—An Iconoclastic Christology?"].

choirs of angels. This in turn is related to the fact that Isaiah's vision is strictly localized at the Temple in Jerusalem. Judaism has always maintained, even after the destruction of the Temple, that God's glory dwells only in the Temple of Jerusalem. Christians, in contrast, believe that during Christ's crucifixion, when the veil of the Temple was torn, God's glory departed from the Temple and now dwells where Jesus Christ is, namely, in heaven and in the Church that gathers with Jesus. Accordingly, heaven and earth are mentioned as the place where chants of praise are now sung.[15] But this means that the Church is after all something quite different from the synagogue that had remained in Judaism after the destruction of the Temple, although it would not and could not replace it. The synagogue is the site of a purely lay worship service, which as such is also a mere liturgy of the word. Anyone who would like to reduce the Church to a lay worship service, a liturgy of the word, is not pursuing what is new in Christianity, but rather is equating the Church with the synagogue and leaving out the path leading to Christ. The Church, as Church, accepts with Christ the heritage of the Temple in a modified way. This is expressed liturgically in the fact that the Church assembles not only for readings and prayers, but also to offer the Eucharistic Sacrifice. But then this also means that in the external form of her celebration she can and must lay claim to the heritage of the Temple. This means that the Church's liturgy, which now regards the whole cosmos as a temple, must itself have a cosmic character, must make the whole cosmos resound. On this point, Peterson's comment, although certainly somewhat exaggerated, is basically quite worth pondering:

And finally it is not by pure coincidence that the mediaeval music theorists begin their treatises by referring to the harmony of the spheres. Since the Church's hymn of praise tunes in to the praises of the cosmos, any consideration of the musical element in the Church's cult must also take into account the sort of praise offered by sun, moon, and stars.[16]

What this means *in concreto* becomes clearer when we recall the prayer in Pseudo-Cyprian that speaks of God as the One who is praised by angels, archangels, martyrs, apostles, and prophets,

---

[15] Cf. Peterson, *Angels*, 16ff.
[16] Ibid., 29.

to whom all the birds sing praises, whom the tongues of those in heaven, upon the earth and under the earth glorify: all the waters in heaven and under the heavens confess thee....[17]

This text is interesting because it discloses, so to speak, the theological principle according to which the "organon" was understood, for it was simply called "the" instrument as opposed to all the others. The organ is a theological instrument that originally had its place in the cult of the emperor. When the Emperor of Byzantium spoke, an organ played. The organ in turn was supposed to be the unison of all the voices of the cosmos. Accordingly, the organ music at an imperial speech meant that when the divine emperor spoke, the entire universe resounded. As a divine utterance, his statement is the resounding of all the voices in the cosmos. The "organon" is the cosmic instrument and as such the voice of the world's ruler, the *imperator*.[18] In contrast to this Byzantine custom, Rome stresses cosmic Christology and on that basis the cosmic function of the Vicar of Christ on earth: what was good enough for the emperor was quite good enough for the pope. Of course, this is a matter, not of superficial problems of prestige, but rather of the public, political, and cultic representation of the commissions received. Imperial theology increasingly entrusted the Church to the emperor and demoted the bishops to mere imperial officials;[19] Rome countered the exclusivity of that claim with the pope's cosmic claim and thus with the cosmic rank of belief in Christ, which is independent of and indeed superior to politics. Therefore the organ had to resound in the papal liturgy as well.

Such a borrowing from imperial theology is not regarded favorably by contemporary theological scholarship, which considers it as

---

[17] Ibid., 22–23.

[18] I gratefully acknowledge here the kindness of the Rt. Rev. Abbot Emeritus Urbanus Bomm of Maria Laach, who pointed out these facts and referred me to the pertinent literature: Dietrich Schuberth, *Kaiserliche Liturgie: Die Einbeziehung von Musikinstrumenten, insbesondere der Orgel, in den frühmittelalterlichen Gottesdienst*, Veröffentlichungen der Evangelischen Gesellschaft für Liturgieforschung, ed. Oskar Söhngen, 17 (Göttingen, Vandenhoeck & Ruprecht, 1968); Ewald Jammers, "Der gregorianische Choral und das byzantinische Kaisertum", in StdZ 86 (1960–1961): 445–52; Jammers, *Musik in Byzanz, im päpstlichen Rom und im Frankenreich: Der Choral als Musik der Textaussprache*, AHAW.PH 1962, 1 (Heidelberg: C. Winter, 1962); Egon Wellesz, *A History of Byzantine Music and Hymnography* (Oxford: Oxford Univ. Press, 1949; 2nd ed., 1961).

[19] Cf. Alois Grillmeier, "Auriga Mundi: Zum Reichskirchenbild der Briefe des sog. Codex Encyclicus (458)", in Grillmeier, *Mit ihm und in ihm: Christologische Forschungen und Perspektiven* (Freiburg im Breisgau: Herder, 1975), 386–419.

"Constantinian" or as "Romanization", which is naturally much worse than Hellenization. In reality, what has been said thus far may very well have made clear the compelling reasons for the process as well as its logic within the Christian context: by way of this detour the Church avoided turning into a synagogue and the true claim of faith in Christ was put into effect. This faith accepts the heritage of the Temple and surpasses it, embracing the whole world.

Furthermore, the history of the organ remained a theo-political history for quite a long time. The fact that an organ resounded at the Carolingian court was an expression of its claim to equality with Byzantium. Conversely, the Roman usage was transferred to the cathedrals and abbeys. Less than a generation ago it was still customary for the organ to accompany softly the abbot's recitation of the *Pater noster* in Benedictine abbeys, and this is to be understood as a direct inheritance from the ancient cosmic liturgy.[20]

We are now in a position to formulate our thesis: Church music with artistic pretensions is not contrary to the nature of Christian liturgy but, rather, is a necessary way of expressing belief in the universal glory of Jesus Christ. The Church's liturgy has a compelling task of disclosing in the glorification of God that lies hidden in the cosmos and causing it to resound. This, then, is the nature of the liturgy: to transpose the cosmos, to spiritualize it into the gesture of sung praise and thus to redeem it; to "humanize" the world.

One final question remains: the question of sacrality, the distinction between sacred and profane music. This distinction was very much present in the patristic Church but was almost completely buried beneath other problems. The problem was posed openly for the first time during the separation of profane from sacred culture in the fourteenth century and then was again aggravated in the Renaissance culture of the sixteenth century. Ever since the twelfth century and the appearance of polyphonic music the question has been posed with increasing urgency, although a full awareness of the problem was not attained until the exile of the popes in Avignon, "where the French *ars nova* appeared at the papal court; it must have seemed quite strange to Curia members who were familiar with Roman musical practice."[21] It was

---

[20] For this reference, too, I am grateful to Abbot Emeritus Urbanus Bomm.

[21] Karl Gustav Fellerer, "Die Constitutio Docta SS. Patrum Johannes XXII", in *Geschichte der katholischen Kirchenmusik*, ed. Fellerer, vol. 1 (Kassel: Bärenreiter, 1972), 379–80.

time to inquire anew into the meaning of Christian spiritualization. Once again the Church faced the dilemma between puritanical exclusion of the new development in principle and an accommodation that makes the Church lose face and simultaneously eliminates her as a separate source of human reality. The Constitution *Docta Sanctorum Patrum* promulgated by Pope John XXII in 1324–1325 found a path that was more than a compromise in the sense of the arithmetical mean:

> It was not polyphony per se that Pope John XXII rejected, but rather the suppression of the Gregorian melody by a polyphony that had a sensual effect, which in terms of its tone and rhythmic movement as well as its expressiveness was far removed from the liturgical function.[22]

The Holy Father put it this way: "the occasional use of certain consonant intervals superposed upon the simple ecclesiastical chant" was not forbidden, "but always on condition that the melodies themselves remain intact in the pure integrity of their form."[23] In other words a close relationship to the text, predominance of the melody, and reference to the formal structures of chant as the point of departure for ecclesiastical polyphony, as opposed to an understanding of structure that destroys the text or an emphasis on sensual sonorous effects.

The Council of Trent confirmed and elaborated on these provisions. In Masses celebrated with singing and organ music, "nothing profane should be intermingled, but only hymns and divine praises"; it should not be a matter of mere empty pleasure for the ear, but the words must remain comprehensible, so that the hearts of the listeners might be drawn (*rapiantur*) to a desire for heavenly harmonies, in the contemplation of the joys of the blessed.[24]

When the Council speaks about "*raptus*" and "*desiderium*" (longing) for heavenly harmonies, it is presupposing a power to enrapture that mere functional application can never produce; instead, it requires inspiration, which surpasses what is objective and rational. Incidentally, Hubert Jedin has recently shown that the well-known legend about

---

[22] Ibid., 379.

[23] Ibid., 380.

[24] Karl Gustav Fellerer, "Das Konzil von Trient und die Kirchenmusik", in *Geschichte der katholischen Kirchenmusik*, ed. Fellerer, vol. 2 (Kassel: Bärenreiter, 1976), 7–9, citation at 9.

the *Missa Papae Marcelli* influencing the Fathers of Trent is not just a legend but has a core of historical fact, which he admittedly does not explain in any greater detail: the *composition* must be convincing, and not the theory, which can only follow the composition.[25]

Of course, one cannot expect timeless prescriptions in these conciliar texts. Otherwise, further doctrinal statements, such as those made in our own century by Pius X, Pius XII, and Vatican II, would be superfluous. But the structure remains valid: the liturgy requires an artistic transposition, originating in the spirit of faith, of the music of the cosmos into human music that glorifies the Word made flesh. Such music obeys a stricter law than everyday music: such music is beholden to the Word and must lead to the Spirit.

Hence church music must find its way again and again in a struggle not to stray on either side: as opposed to puritanical pride it must justify the necessary incarnation of the spirit in the musical event, and in contrast to the commonplace it must seek to direct the spirit and the cosmos toward the Divine. When this succeeds, it is always a gift; but the gift is not given without the preparation that we make to the cause through our own effort. When this happens, then it is primarily a matter, not of pursuing an informal hobby, but rather of living out a necessary dimension of the Christian faith and, thereby, of capturing a necessary dimension of what it means to be human, without which culture and humanity inevitably decay from within.

---

[25] Hubert Jedin, *Geschichte des Konzils von Trient*, vol. 4, pt. 1 (Freiburg: Herder, 1975), 208 and 345, n. 47, where we read: "The widely publicized version of Agazzari, that the *Missa Papae Marcelli* changed the minds of the Council Fathers, was previously ... regarded as a legend. ... Otto Ursprung has shown that probably this 'legend' is not entirely lacking in foundation."

V. "Sing Artistically for God"

Biblical Directives for Church Music

1. Preliminary Remarks on the Situation of Church and Culture

Since church music is faith that has become a form of culture, it necessarily shares in the current problematic nature of the relationship between Church and culture. In this relationship there are problems on both sides. The inner connection of faith to culture is in the throes of a crisis. Since the end of the Enlightenment, faith and contemporary culture have drifted apart more and more. Up to that time culture had developed from the roots of religion in Christian Europe, as in all history, and had remained tied to this matrix even in its secular forms of expression. The Renaissance and the Reformation marked a first crisis for this blending of Church and culture. But not until the Enlightenment does a real cultural revolution, a decisive emancipation of culture from faith occur. The two go their separate ways, even if the nineteenth century was still marked by a lively exchange between them. In any case, whoever looks at a number of neo-gothic or neo-romanesque churches sees that the Church, although she was not able to disavow her epoch, was still being pushed back into a kind of subculture that was marginalized on the edge of the mainstream of cultural development. This situation is also apparent in the relationship between the Caecilian reform of church music and the general development of music during the second half of the nineteenth century as well as at the beginning of the twentieth century. It should not be denied, however, that within this "subcultural" movement great things were accomplished that can be placed beside the main trend in culture at that time since they are of completely equal rank. It should not be denied that the historicizing

Reprinted with permission from *A New Song for the Lord: Faith in Christ and Liturgy Today*, trans. Martha M. Matesich, 2nd ed. (1996; New York: Crossroad, 2005), 94–110.

tendency visible in the renewal of older styles and in the connection of faith to the cultural expression of earlier periods also corresponded to the spirit of the century. Finally we should not forget that such an important cultural event as the rediscovery and renewal of Gregorian chant and great polyphonic church music was the fruit of such orientations, which have thus displayed a significant intellectual productivity. But all in all the gap has become wider and wider, and in the confusing conflict between the cultural experiments and cultureless pragmatic activities of the Church today it is obvious that we are at a loss as to how faith can and should express itself culturally in the present age.

Even for modern culture, however, the separation from its religious matrix has not been without consequences. For this reason it, too, has been driven into a dead end in which it can say less and less about its own *quo vadis*. Culture somehow seems useless in the modern world, and, making a virtue out of necessity, it defines itself frankly as follows: Art is that which fulfills no function but is simply just there. There is some truth to this, but negation alone does not suffice to establish a meaningful space for any kind of phenomenon in the existential framework of man and the world. The difficulties that art has gotten into through the complete secularization of culture are becoming particularly clear in the area of music. Like any other cultural expression, music always had different levels, from the unsophisticated singing of simple people, which is nevertheless genuine in itself, to the highest artistic perfection. But now something completely new has occurred. Music has split into two worlds that hardly have anything to do with each other anymore. On the one hand, there is the music of the masses, which, with the label "pop" or popular music, would like to portray itself as the music of the people. Here music has become a product that can be industrially manufactured and is evaluated by how well it sells. On the other hand, there is a rationally construed, artificial music with the highest technical requirements that is hardly capable of reaching out beyond a small, elite circle. In the middle between the two extremes we find the recourse to history, a staying at home in the familiar music that preceded such divisions, touched the person as a whole, and is still capable of doing this even today. It is understandable that church music mostly settles in this middle ground. But since the Church, after all, is living in this age it was inevitable that she also try her hand at the two opposing spheres of today's cultural schizophrenia. When people rightly call for a new dialogue between Church and culture today, they must not forget in the process that this dialogue must necessarily be bilateral. It cannot consist in the Church finally subjecting herself to modern culture, which has been caught up to a large extent in a process of self-doubt since it lost its religious base. Just as the Church must expose herself to the problems of our age in a radically new way, so too must culture be questioned anew about its groundlessness and its ground and, in the process, be opened to a painful cure, that is, to a new reconciliation with religion since it can get its lifeblood only from there.

For this reason the issue of church music is really a very vital piece of a comprehensive task for our age that requires more than mere dialogue; it requires a process of rediscovering ourselves. When theologians try to contribute something in this struggle, they must make use of the means available to them. They cannot enter into the musical discussions per se, but they can nonetheless ask where the seams are, so to speak, that link faith and art. They can try to explain how faith prepares an interior place for art and which directives it gives for the path of art. This, too, would still be a very extensive undertaking if one wanted to explore the entire range of available theological sources. All the sources, however, ultimately depend on the original source, on the Bible; I would therefore like to limit myself to the question whether there are biblical directives for the path of church music. Because of the extent and complexity of the biblical witness it is necessary to narrow this down once more. I am asking concretely: Can we find one biblical text that sums up the way Holy Scripture sees the connection between music and faith?

2. A Psalm Verse as Mirror of the Biblical Directives for Music in Worship

A first approach to the topic presents itself if we recall that the Bible contains its own hymnal: the Psalter, which was not only born from the practice of singing and playing musical instruments during worship but also contains by itself—in the practice, the live performance—essential elements of a theory of music in faith and for faith. We must pay attention to the place of this book in the biblical canon in order to appreciate its significance properly. Within the Old Testament the Psalter is a bridge, as it were, between the law and the prophets. It has grown out of the requirements of the Temple cult, of the law, but by appropriating the law in prayer and song it has uncovered its prophetic essence more and more. It has led beyond the ritual and its ordinances into the "offering of praise", the "wordly offering" with which people open themselves to the Logos and thus become worship with him. In this way the Psalter has also become a bridge connecting the two Testaments. In the Old Testament its hymns had been considered to be the songs of David; this meant for Christians that these hymns had risen from the heart of the real David, Christ. In the early Church the psalms are prayed and sung as hymns to Christ. Christ himself thus becomes the choir director who teaches us the new song and gives the Church the tone and the way in which she can praise God appropriately and blend into the heavenly liturgy.

As a main connecting theme for my comments I would like to select one verse from the Psalter which appears again and again in the history of theological reflection on the foundations and path of church music, and this with justification since it mirrors something of the basic orientation of the book of Psalms as a whole. I am referring to the seventh verse of Psalm 47 [in some Bibles the eighth verse and/or Psalm 46; RSV-2CE 47:7]. The ecumenical Bible for German-speaking countries translates this verse in a rather vacuous way: Sing a psalm [Singt ein Psalmenlied]. It leaves it up to the one reading or praying to imagine what this—"a psalm"—could be. In contrast M. Buber and F. Rosenzweig had translated it: "Play as an inspiration" [Eine Eingebungsweise spielt auf]. They are emphasizing the artistic inspiration that should stand behind the requested song. A more distinctive interpretation of the word in question, "psalm", is offered by Alfons Deissler, who translates it as "artistic hymn".[1] In his outstanding commentary on the psalms, Hans-Joachim Kraus comes to a similar decision, for he writes: "Sing an art song."[2] The [French] translation of the Jerusalem Bible is along the same lines: "Play for God with all your art [with all your skill]."[3] The translation issued

---

[1] Alfons Deissler, Die Psalmen, pt. 2 (Düsseldorf, 1964), 192.

[2] Hans-Joachim Kraus, Psalmen, Biblischer Kommentar zum Alten Testament 15 (Neukirchen, 1960), 348.

[3] La Sainte Bible, traduite en français sous la direction de l'École biblique de Jérusalem (Paris, 1955), Ps 47 (46), verse 8: "sonnez pour Dieu de tout votre art!"

by the Italian Bishops' Conference also speaks of singing "con arte" (artistically). That more or less covers the spectrum of the attempts to approximate the Hebrew expression *maśkíl* in modern translations. But the old translations that reflect the efforts of the early Church are also important for us. The Septuagint, which became the Old Testament of Christianity, wrote *psalate synetōs*, which we might translate as: "Sing in an understandable way; sing with understanding"—in both senses of the word: that you yourselves understand it and that it is understandable. Of course there is more to this expression than our rationalistic idea of understanding and understandability: Sing from and toward the spirit; sing in a way worthy of and appropriate to the spirit, disciplined and pure. The translation that Jerome chose and that was taken up again in the Sixto-Clementine Vulgate is along the same lines: *psallite sapienter*. Singing psalms should have something of the essence of *sapientia* about it and in it. In order to plumb the enigmatic quality of this formulation we should ponder what is meant by *sapientia*: a behavior of man that certainly has the brilliance of understanding about it but also denotes an integration of the entire person who understands and is understandable not only from the perspective of pure thought, but with all the dimensions of his existence. In this respect there is an affinity between wisdom and music, since in it such an integration of humanness occurs and the entire person becomes a being in accordance with logos [with "reason"]. Finally we should also note that in the similar context of Psalm 33[32]:3 the Vulgate is acquainted with the expression "play the psalms well" or "sing well" (*bene cantare*), which Augustine, for example, quite naturally interprets as singing in the way the *ars musicae* teaches.[4] Thus, from the verse of a psalm, the Church became aware of the need for an artistic level of musical expression in the praise of God.

With these comments we have tried first of all to delineate the literal meaning of the biblical text and its reception in the Church. Now we have to ask: What follows for liturgical music from this biblical imperative and which conclusions were attached to it in the emerging Church? In such an analysis, which of course cannot go into scholarly details, two words in our psalm verse must be considered carefully; they are both momentous and have therefore been—and remain—laden with history. To begin with, there is the

---

[4] Augustine, *Enarrationes in Psalmos* 32, s. 1, 8, CChrSL (Turnhout, 1956), 38:253–54.

first word, which in German is translated somewhat innocuously as "sing". On the path from the Hebrew word *zāmîr* to the Greek phrasing *psalate*, however, a cultural and intellectual development had already occurred that had a determining influence on the entire history to come and that still has something very concrete to say to us as well. Just the choice of the Hebrew word already presupposes a cultural decision-making process that is based on a religious orientation and marks the peculiarity of Israel in the history of the religions of the Near East as well as of mankind in general. The word *zāmîr* is based on a stem found in all old Hamito-Semitic languages. The word means singing with or without instrumental accompaniment; the emphasis is on articulated singing, a singing with reference to a text, which is instrumentally supported as a rule but always ordered to a specific statement in regard to content.[5] Thus, *zāmîr* stands clearly apart from orgiastic cult music, which serves to intoxicate the senses and which, through the frenzy of sensual feelings, carries people away in the ecstatic "liberation" from mind and will. In contrast, *zāmîr* refers to logos-like music, if we can put it that way, which incorporates a word or wordlike event it has received and responds to it in praise or petition, in thanksgiving or lament. The Septuagint chose the word *psallein* in its translation, which for the Greeks meant "to touch, pluck, run with the fingers, particularly when playing strings", in general to play a stringed instrument, but never to sing.[6] The Greek Bible gave the Greek word a com-

---

[5] Cf. the extremely instructive article "zmr" by Christoph Barth, in *Theological Dictionary of the Old Testament* 4 (1980): 91–98. "The word *zamāru* (= the underlying Akkadian verb) never refers to instrumental 'music' without articulated singing" (92). "In Akkadian, the two meanings 'sing' and 'play' are so firmly linked that it would be more accurate to speak of two aspects of a single meaning: the single action is both 'vocal' and 'instrumental'" (93). "In the long series of words for hymnic praise, *zmr* occupies a middle position, being a term that covers both articulated praise that speaks in comprehensible words and unarticulated praise expressed in shouts and gestures; through it articulated praise takes on a breadth it does not otherwise exhibit, and unarticulated praise acquires a clarity it otherwise lacks" (98). In reference to our verse, Barth remarks: "Ps 47:8(7) (*zammerû maśkîl*) remains obscure" (96).

[6] Martin Hengel, "Das Christuslied im frühesten Gottesdienst", in *Weisheit Gottes— Weisheit der Welt: Festschrift für J. Ratzinger*, ed. Walter Baier et al., vol. 1 (St. Ottilien, 1987), 357–404 (quotation from 387). Barth, "zmr", has criticized this translation as a one-sided shift in emphasis to the instrumental, and in contrast he noted positively that in Jerome's second version of the Psalter he replaced *psallō* with *cano/canto*. In the process, however, the semantic change in meaning of *psallō* that occurs in the Septuagint is not taken into account.

pletely new meaning, and with that it also introduced a cultural change. Although the word *psalmos* had denoted a stringed instrument in Greek, it now meant the songs of Israel that arise from faith. The verb likewise acquired the meaning "to sing", but now in a sense that is quite clearly defined by the history of a civilization and religion: to sing as Israel sings to her God. In this sense the expression "to sing psalms" is a neologism of the Bible with which it also introduced a new phenomenon into the Greek world. It denotes a singing that found its clearly defined musical form in the prayer tradition of Israel; Martin Hengel describes this form as follows: "Since the number of syllables per line of verse was not fixed, it is not a matter of singing a thoroughly composed melody, but of a ... sprechgesang that probably only permitted melody-like movements of tone at the beginning and the end of the stichs." [7]

The analysis of the oft-repeated imperative *psallite* in the psalms thus allows us to draw a few concrete conclusions concerning our question about possible biblical directives for music in the Church:

1. This imperative runs through all of Scripture; it is the concrete version of the call to worship and glorify God that is revealed in the Bible as the most profound vocation of man. This means that musical expression is part of the proper human response to God's self-revelation, to his becoming open to a relationship with us. Mere speech, mere silence, mere action are not enough. That integral way of humanly expressing joy or sorrow, consent or complaint that occurs in singing is necessary for responding to God, who touches us precisely in the totality of our being. In the course of this discussion we have seen that the word *psallite* entails more than our word "to sing"; it does not necessarily require instrumental accompaniment, but because of its origin it does refer to instruments in which, as it were, creation is made to sound. Admittedly the biblical adaptation of this word has made singing—that is, making music vocally—primary. [8]

2. The musical imperative of the Bible is therefore not entirely unspecified but refers to a form that biblical faith gradually created for itself as the appropriate mode of its expression. There is no such thing as a faith completely undetermined by culture, so to speak, which

---

[7] Hengel, "Christuslied", 388.

[8] For interesting information on this point, see Hartmut Gese, "Zur Geschichte der Kultsänger am zweiten Tempel", in his *Vom Sinai zum Zion*, 2nd ed., BEvTh 64 (Munich, 1984), 147–58.

would then let itself be inculturated any way one likes. The faith decision as such entails a cultural decision; it forms the people, and by doing this it excludes a good many other cultural patterns as deformations. Faith itself creates culture and does not just carry it along like a piece of clothing added from the outside. This cultural given, which cannot be manipulated as one likes and which determines the extent of all subsequent inculturations, is neither rigid nor closed in on itself. The level of a culture is discernible by its ability to assimilate, to come into contact and exchange, and to do this synchronically and diachronically. It is capable of encountering other contemporary cultures as well as the development of human culture in the march of time. This ability to exchange and flourish also finds its expression in the ever-recurring imperative: "Sing the Lord a new song." Experiences of salvation are found not only in the past, but occur over and over again; hence they also require the ever-new proclamation of God's contemporaneity, whose eternity is falsely understood if one interprets it as being locked in decisions made "from time immemorial". On the contrary, to be eternal means to be synchronous with all times and to be ahead of all times.

The summons to sing a new song acquired a very special meaning for Christians. They saw it as the command to pass from the Old to the New Covenant, to transpose the psalms in a christological fashion. Particularly in the Toda-psalms one finds a type of prayer that grew out of the faith of Israel; this prayer, deep down inside, was on the path into the newness of the New Covenant.[9] The following characteristics belong to the schema of these psalms: asking for help in dire need, experiencing banishment into the abyss of death, vowing to proclaim God's great deed if one is saved, and keeping this vow by singing of God's favor before the congregation so as to give thanks and bring men the message of God's gracious power. This schema had been expanded into a new song time and again from the viewpoint of the various verifications of salvation. But the truly new, which had hitherto been merely awaited, happened only now, in the mystery of Jesus Christ. The "new song" praises his death and Resurrection and hence proclaims God's new deed to the whole world: that he himself

---

[9] Cf. Hartmut Gese, "Psalm 22 und das Neue Testament", ZThK 65 (1968): 1–22 (also in his *Vom Sinai zum Zion*, 180–201); Gese, "Die Herkunft des Herrenmahls", in his *Zur biblischen Theologie* (Munich, 1977), 107–27.

has descended into the anguish of the human state and into the pit of death; that he embraces all of us on the Cross with his stretched-out arms and, as the Risen One, takes us up to the Father across the abyss of the infinite divide separating Creator and creature, which only crucified love can cross. Thus, the old song has become new and must be sung as such over and over again. In this process of renewal, however, the song has not done away with the basic cultural decision of faith or with that which faith has culturally given as a directive but has opened them, on the one hand, even farther while simultaneously defining them more clearly. The first centuries of Christianity confront us with a dramatic struggle for the right determination of the relationship between this openness of the new, on the one hand, and the irrevocable and fundamental cultural form, on the other, which belongs to the essence of faith itself. This struggle must have been all the more provocative seeing that the transition worked by God from the old to the new song, from the prophetic to the christological version of the psalms, coincided with the historical transition from Semitic to Greek culture, so that in the cultural shift it was necessary to grapple very concretely with the questions of what was not relinquishable and of the possibility of a new form. Martin Hengel has shown how closely this cultural struggle was linked to the development of Christology itself, indeed, virtually coincided with it. We will have to come back to this, but for the moment we still have to complete our analysis of the psalm verse.[10]

3. We have already tried to probe the meaning of the second word in our psalm verse. We saw its range essentially delineated in the two translations *sapienter* and *cum arte*. It turned out that the meaning of *sapienter* leads in the same direction as the development in meaning given by the Greek Old Testament to the verb *psallein*. Speaking about singing in accordance with wisdom points to a word-oriented art, but the place of word must not be narrowed in the superficially rationalistic sense of an intelligibility of all words at all times. Instead, looking at it from the perspective of the early Church, we can call what is meant here music in accordance with logos [with "reason"]. There is an art form corresponding to God, who, from the beginning and in each life, is the creative Word that also gives meaning. This art form stands under the primacy of logos; that is, it integrates

---

[10] See Hengel, "Christuslied".

the diversity of man from the perspective of this being's highest moral
and spiritual powers, but in this way it also leads the spirit out of
rationalistic and voluntaristic confinement into the symphony of
creation.

The second translation, *cum arte*, told us that encountering God
challenges a person's highest abilities. Man can only correspond to
God's greatness if he also gives to his response, according to the
extent of his ability, the complete dignity of the beautiful, the height
of true "art". In this context we should recall the theory of art that
the book of Exodus develops in connection with the construction of
the sacred tabernacle.[11] Three elements are essential here. The artists
themselves do not plan what might be worthy of God and beautiful.
Man is not capable of inventing this on his own. It is rather God
himself who discloses to Moses the shape of the shrine, right down
to the details. Artistic creation reproduces what God has shown as
model. It presupposes the inner view of the exemplar; it is the conversion of a vision into form. Artistic creativeness as the Old Testament sees it is something completely different from what the modern
age understands by creativity. Today creativity is understood to be
the making of something that no one has made or thought of before,
the invention of something that is completely one's own and completely new. In comparison with this, artistic creativeness in the book
of Exodus is seeing together with God, participating in his creativity; it is exposing the beauty that is already waiting and concealed in
creation. This does not diminish the worth of the artist, but is in
fact its justification. For this reason it is also said that the Lord "has
called by name" Bezalel, the principal artist for the construction of
the sacred tabernacle (Ex 35:30): the same set phrase or formula is
valid for the artist as well as for the prophet. Furthermore, artists are
described as people to whom the Lord has given understanding and
skill so that they can carry out what God has instructed them to do
(36:1). Finally, the fact that every artist's "heart was stirred" (36:2)
belongs here as a third component. As far as I can see, what Exodus
says about the fine arts is in fact not explicitly applied to liturgical

---

[11] Cf. Ex 35–40. The parallels between the erection of the sacred tabernacle (Ex 40:16–
33) and the Priestly account of creation (Gen 1:1—2:4a) are interesting; the seven days of
creation correspond to the sevenfold saying "just as the Lord had commanded Moses";
Gen 2:1ff. is echoed in Ex 40:33: "So Moses finished the work", which is followed by the
theophany (in accord with the Sabbath after the six days of creation).

music anywhere in the Bible.[12] But the mere fact that the Psalter as a whole was ultimately dedicated to King David entails an analogous evaluation: David is the king who has given God his dwelling place in Israel, on the holy mountain; he is the new founder of the cult, and he has become this precisely by showing the Holy People the way in which they can praise God with dignity. For church music this means that everything the Old Testament has to say about art— its necessity, its essence, and its dignity—is concealed in the *bene cantare* of the psalms.

3. On the Adoption of the Biblical Directives in the Liturgical Life of the Church

We have thus returned to the question of the adoption of all this in the New Testament and consequently of the lasting significance of these biblical directives for the music of the Church. We had already seen that the Church regarded Christ, the true David, also as the true author of the psalms, and for this reason the Church embraced with a new hermeneutics the prayer and hymnbook of the Old Covenant as her primary book for worship. With the text she adopted the mode of singing, that is, that basic cultural decision which had occurred during the development of the psalmody. She saw in it the standard that served as orientation for any new singing of the new song. This is quite apparent in the organization of worship found in the First Letter to the Corinthians: "When you come together, each one has a song (*psalmon*), a lesson, a revelation, a tongue, or an interpretation. Let all things be done for building up" (14:26). At the beginning of the service there is the song that Paul describes with the word "psalm" and thus defines in its musical and theological form.[13] For the assessment of art in the apostolic Church it is important that the song appeared as a gift of the Spirit just like the lesson, tongue, prophecy, and interpretation. From Pliny we learn that the sung glorification of Christ in his divinity belonged to the core of the Christian religious service at the beginning of the sec-

---

[12] Hartmut Gese shows the high theological rank assigned to ritual music in the Old Testament ("Zur Geschichte der Kultsänger"). There are also helpful comments in Pellegrino M. Ernetti, *Principi filosofici e teologici della Musica*, vol. 1 (Rome, 1980).

[13] Cf. Hengel, "Christuslied", 387.

ond century, and we may consider the prologue of John and the hymn in Philippians as archetypes of such songs.[14] The early development of Christology, its ever-deeper recognition of Christ's divinity, probably occurred essentially and particularly in the hymns of the Church, in the blend of theology, poetry, and music.

At this point, though, a delaying factor set in that is of great significance for our reflections. To the extent that it distanced itself from the Semitic world, the development of christological art songs threatened more and more to turn into an acute Hellenization of Christianity, that is, to alienate itself from Christianity's own nature as culture and faith. The fascination of Greek music and Greek thinking led out of the faith by way of music so that the new music rapidly became the domain of Gnosticism—indeed, new music and gnosis virtually coalesced. For this reason the Church immediately and rigorously rejected the poetical and musical innovation and reduced church music to the Psalter in two senses: that the theology of the Psalter sufficed and set the standard in terms of content, but also in the sense that the way of making music specified by the Psalter became the musical model of emerging Christendom. This limitation of liturgical singing, which gradually began asserting itself from the second century, received its canonical expression in canon 59 of the Synod of Laodicea (364), which forbade the use of "private psalm compositions and non-canonical writings" in religious services. In addition, in canon 15 the singing of the Psalms is restricted to the choir, "whereas others should not sing in church". Somewhat later the so-called *Apostolic Constitutions* spoke in a similar way.[15] We can perhaps regret this phase of temporary restriction and lament the loss that occurred as a result of eradicating early Christian poetry. Nonetheless, this action was—historically speaking—essential for strengthening the Church's own cultural identity and, along with this, her identity in faith. Only in this way could she become a new source of cultural creativity, which began with renewed vigor in Alexandria already in the third century and then gave us the whole magnificent cultural inspiration that radiated from Christian faith in all the following centuries. Particularly in the area of music, the faith of the Church has become creative far beyond all other cultural spheres, not least of

---

[14] Cf. ibid., 382–83.
[15] Cf. ibid., 366–70.

all because, in terms of its creative expression, it has constantly judged itself on the biblical directives and with the passage of time has learned to plumb their inner wealth. Without diminishing its promising future, sung prayer has unfolded and concretized this standard above all in three basic forms: Gregorian chant, the great polyphonic music of the early modern age, and church hymns.

4. Consequences for Today

At the close there remains the question: What does all this mean for the present situation of faith and art? No one can answer this question in every detail at the moment. We only have approaches in which we must gradually try to learn to differentiate the right path from the wrong path in order to be of service to the daily practice of liturgical life, on the one hand, yet also show the sphere where lively development can productively flourish, on the other. At the outset we began with the modern art scene's schizophrenia between "pop" or popular music and elitist aestheticism. The two limits for church music have therefore already been indicated: if music crosses these boundaries, it sacrifices the culture of faith and hence stops being music from the word of God and for the word of God.

a. Against Aestheticism as an End in Itself

First of all, that hybrid aestheticism that excludes every function of art as service, that is, that can only regard art as having its own purpose and its own standard, is incompatible with the directives of the Bible. Wherever it is exhibited consistently this presumptuousness necessarily leads to a nihilistic lack of standards and therefore generates nihilistic parodies of art, but not a new creativity. The philosophy at work here belies the creaturely determination of man; it would like to elevate him to the level of a pure creator. But in this way it leads the him into untruth, into contradiction with his own nature; untruth, however, always drifts into the disintegration of what is creative. Earlier we had briefly touched on the problematic nature of the modern concept of creativity in which the anthropological problem of the modern age is present in a concentrated way. In idealistic philosophy the human spirit is no lon-

ger primarily receptive—it does not receive, but is only productive.[16]
In the existential radicalization of this approach, nothing meaningful at
all precedes human existence. Man comes from a meaningless factuality
and is thrown into a meaningless freedom. He thus becomes a pure
creator; at the same time his creativity becomes a mere whim and,
precisely for this reason, empty. According to Christian faith, however, it belongs to the essence of man that he come from God's "art",
that he himself is a part of God's art and as perceiver can think and
view God's creative ideas with him and translate them into the visible
and the audible. If this be the case, then to serve is not foreign to art;
only by serving the Most High does it exist at all. Music does not
become alienated from its own purpose when it praises God and praises
him in such a way that it becomes "proclamation in the great congregation" (Ps 22:25). On the contrary, only from this willingness does
it renew itself again and again. It is precisely the test of true creativity
that the artist steps out of the esoteric circle and knows how to form
his intuition in such a way that the others—the many—may perceive
what the artist has perceived. In the process, the three conditions for
true art specified in the book of Exodus are always valid: artists must
be moved by their hearts; they must have understanding, that is, be
skillful people; and they must have perceived what the Lord himself
has shown.

b. Against Pastoral Pragmatism as an End in Itself

Just like aesthetic elitism, pastoral pragmatism, which is only looking
for success, is also incompatible with the mission of church music.
When, in an earlier lecture entitled "Liturgy and Church Music", I
referred in this context to the incompatibility between rock and
pop music and the liturgy of the Church,[17] there quickly arose a
loud cry of protest from those who felt obliged to show once again
their progressive cast of mind. I heard very little of actual arguments

---

[16] Cf. the characterization of transcendental Idealism in contrast to the essence of Christian inwardness in Helmut Kuhn, *Romano Guardini—Philosoph der Sorge* (St. Ottilien, 1987),
47, also 80.

[17] See also Joseph Ratzinger, "Das Welt- und Menschenbild der Liturgie und sein Ausdruck in der Kirchenmusik" ["The Image of the World and of Man in the Liturgy and Its
Expression in Church Music"; JRCW 11:444–60; especially 455–58].

in these protests. My comments, though, were basically directed at rock music, whose radical anthropological opposition to both faith's image of man and its cultural intent has been amply and competently elucidated by others.[18] I touched on pop music only in passing, and so, as a matter of fact, one could argue that my comments were not justified. Pop music, as we have already said, wants to be popular music—"folk music" in contrast to elitist art music. For this reason we can understand the following questions: Is pop music not exactly what we need? Has the Church not always been the home of folk music? Has the high quality of the Church's musical expression not renewed itself again and again from the matrix of folk music?

Here we have to tread carefully. The audience to whom pop music refers is mass society. In contrast, folk music in its original sense is the musical expression of a clearly defined community held together by its language, history, and way of life, which assimilates and shapes its experiences in song—the experience with God, the experiences of love and sorrow, of birth and death, as well as the experience of communion with nature. Such a community's way of structuring music may be called naïve, but it does spring from original contact with the fundamental experiences of human existence and is therefore an expression of truth. Its naïveté belongs to that kind of simplicity from which great things can come. Mass society is something completely different from that community bound together for life which produced folk music in the old and original sense. The masses as such do not know experiences firsthand; they only know reproduced and standardized experiences. Mass culture is thus geared to quantity, production, and success. It is a culture of the measurable and marketable. Pop music joins up with this culture. As described by Calvin M. Johansson, it is the reflection of what this society is, the musical embodiment of kitsch.[19] It would be taking things too far to go into

---

[18] The essential arguments are carefully presented by M. Basilea Schlink, *Rockmusik—woher, wohin?* (Darmstadt and Eberstadt, 1989); literature is listed there as well. Cf. also Ulrich Bäumer, *Wir wollen nur deine Seele*, 4th ed. (Bielefeld, 1986).

[19] Cf. Calvin M. Johansson, *Music and Ministry: A Biblical Counterpoint* (Peabody, Mass., 1984), 50. I would emphatically like to endorse this work, which is thorough and balanced in its position but hitherto unfortunately hardly noticed in Germany.

Johansson's excellent analysis in detail here, but I would like to recommend it emphatically. Popular in the sense of pop music turns into something for which there is demand. Pop music is manufactured in industrial mass production like technical goods, in a totally inhuman and dictatorial system, as Paul Hindemith says.[20] For melody, harmony, orchestration, and the like, there are specialists at one's disposal who assemble the whole thing according to the laws of the market. Adorno commented: "The fundamental characteristic of popular music is standardization."[21] And Arthur Korb, whose book title *How to Write Songs That Sell* is already a telltale sign, quite candidly makes the point: popular music "is written and produced primarily to make money".[22] For this reason one has to offer something that does not anger or make profound demands on anyone according to the motto: Give me what I want now—no costs, no work, no effort. Paul Hindemith therefore used the term brainwashing for the constant presence of this kind of noise, which can hardly be called music any more. Johansson adds that it gradually makes us incapable of listening attentively, of hearing; "we become musically comatose."[23]

We still have to show in detail that this fundamental approach is incompatible with the culture of the Gospels, which seek to take us out of the dictatorship of money, of making, of mediocrity, and bring us to the discipline of truth, which is precisely what pop music eschews. Is it a pastoral success when we are capable of following the trend of mass culture and thus share the blame for its making people immature or irresponsible? The medium of communication and the communicated message must stand in a meaningful relationship to each other. As Johansson once again notes, this medium "kills the message".[24] Trivializing faith is not a new inculturation, but the denial of its culture and prostitution with the nonculture.

---

[20] Cf. Paul Hindemith, *A Composer's World* (Cambridge, 1952), 126; quoted in Johansson, *Music*, 51.

[21] Cited by Johansson, *Music*, 52.

[22] Arthur Korb, *How to Write Songs That Sell* (Boston, 1957), 8; Johansson, *Music*, 53. Cf. also H. Bryce, *How to Make Money Selling the Songs You Write* (New York, 1970).

[23] Cf. Hindemith, *Composer's World*, 211–12; Johansson, *Music*, 49: "We become musically comatose."

[24] Johansson, *Music*, 55, as a summary of an analysis of the basic spiritual direction of the Christian message, on the one hand, and of pop music, on the other.

c. Openness to Tomorrow in the Continuity of Faith

Let us admit it: faith and the culture of faith have a hard time of it in the interstice between aesthetic elitism and industrial mass culture. Their position is difficult simply because art and people themselves have a hard time of it in this situation and can hardly hold their ground. We certainly do not need to inflict upon ourselves the strict discipline the Church practiced in the second and third centuries when, in the face of the Gnostic temptation, she reduced church music to the Psalms. We do not need this if only because, in the meantime, an infinitely larger trove of music that is really appropriate to faith has become available. This trove makes creative attempts to recall and continue [the culture of faith] possible all the time. Undoubtedly we will also have to let considerable tolerance reign on the margins, at the points of transition to the two antitheses of liturgically appropriate music.

But even today it cannot be done without the courage of asceticism, without the courage to contradict. Only from such courage can new creativity arise. We are sure, however, that the creative potency of faith will suffice right up to the end of time: until all the dimensions of the human state have been traversed.

I would like to close my reflections with a quotation from the saintly pope Gregory the Great, which seems to me to formulate the spiritual center of liturgical music in a uniquely beautiful and convincing way.

If ... the singing of the psalmody rings out from the innermost reaches of the heart, the omnipotent Lord finds a way through this singing into the heart that he might pour the mysteries of prophecy or the grace of remorse into this attentively listening organ. For it is written: "A song of praise honors me, and this is the way on which I wish to show him the salvation of God" (Ps 49:23 [cf. RSV-2CE 50:23]). For the Latin *salutare*, salvation, means Jesus in Hebrew. Hence in the song of praise we gain access to where Jesus can reveal himself, for if remorse is poured out through the singing of psalms, then a way to the heart emerges in us at the end of which we reach Jesus.[25]

---

[25] Gregory the Great, *Homiliae in Ezechielem I*, hom. 1:15 (PL 76:793A–B). The German translation appears in *Homilien zu Ezechiel*, ed. Georg Bürke (Einsiedeln, 1983), 45 [translated into English from the German].

This is the loftiest service of music through which it does not deny its artistic grandeur but really discovers it to the full. Music uncovers the buried way to the heart, to the core of our being, where it touches the being of the Creator and the Redeemer. Wherever this is achieved, music becomes the road that leads to Jesus, the way on which God shows his salvation.[26]

---

[26] At about the same time this article appeared the book by Gianfranco Ravasi was published by Piemme (Casale Monferrato)—*Il canto della rana: Musica e teologia nella Bibbia* (1990). In the first part of the book there is poetry by Davide Maria Turoldo under the title "Cantate a Dio con arte" (7–50); in the second part (51–163) the well-known exegete Gianofranco Ravasi deals with music and theology in the Bible, with "the musical and the theological", with the silence of music, and finally, under the title "Sound in Pictures", with musical iconography. The author develops his presentation of the music of the Bible from the perspective of our psalm verse (47:7), whose translation "Sing artistically for God" (Cantate a Dio con arte) he justifies by referring to the commentary on the Psalms by Hans-Joachim Kraus, among others. This brilliantly written work is a treasure trove of insights that I would emphatically like to recommend to the reader.

VI. Professional Church Music as a Liturgical and Pastoral Ministry

I would like to present my topic in four theses.

Thesis 1: In accordance with Article 112 of the Constitution on the Liturgy of Vatican II, sacred music represents "a necessary or integral part of the solemn liturgy".

This means: sacred music is for the liturgy on the whole certainly not an essential but an integral component. Stated again in other words, it means: Sacred music is certainly not a requirement for the validity of each liturgical celebration, and therefore the Eucharist can also be celebrated licitly and appropriately as a *missa lecta* without any singing. So although sacred music is by no means necessary for every celebration of the Eucharist and for every liturgical action, the Church nevertheless would be neglecting an integral component of her mandate to glorify God if sacred music on the whole were to cease altogether. Sacred music, then, does not belong to every single liturgical celebration, but it must necessarily be present in the overall activity of the Church.

This intrinsic necessity of sacred music was predetermined for the Church by the continuity of her prayer with the prayer of Israel: the prayers of the Old Testament, the Psalms, are songs; they are the prayers of Jesus. Praying with him, and through him with the chosen people of the Old Covenant, the Church knows that she is called upon to use music in the service of prayer as the gesture of glorification that is accessible to man and in keeping with his nature and as a way of including creation in the glorification of God. Although one discovers here a reason for sacred music founded on creation theology and covenant theology, the whole notion is broadened in early Judaism and

Translated by Kenneth Baker, S.J., and Michael J. Miller.

early Christianity by the more Platonic-sounding idea of the heavenly liturgy with which the earthly liturgy joins in, singing along with the choirs of angels; yet the basic orientation of the statement remains the same.

Thesis 2: Sacred music is accordingly, by its very nature, a liturgical act, but it is just as much a musical act.

It is subordinate to the laws of the liturgy, but it is liturgical inasmuch as it fits the intrinsic nature of the musical act into the liturgical act. In this way two extreme positions are avoided: on the one hand, it rules out a merely aesthetic notion that is willing to understand music and liturgy each on its own terms alone and therefore necessarily rejects in principle the compound term "sacred music", regarding music as a task to be accomplished on the basis of purely artistic principles—a task that enters only into a casual relationship with the liturgy but not into an intrinsic connection with it. The church musician, then, would only have to be a musician whose workplace happens to be the church, without there being an intrinsic relation to the particular nature of the liturgical action. The reverse side of this approach starts out from the same premise: the impossibility of an intrinsic connection between the two realities, music and liturgy, but this time as a purely pastoral-liturgical solution that understands sacred music, not as music, but only in a strictly instrumental sense as a medium of liturgical action. From this perspective, music would not have to be musical, but only liturgically serviceable. The church musician would be just a liturgist for whom it would even be detrimental to know very much about music.

In contrast to that position, we will argue here that the liturgy is such that by its very nature it is not only open to music, but actually calls for it; hence piety and serviceability cannot take the place of intrinsic musical suitability and quality. That kind of substitution amounts instead to a misunderstanding of both piety and liturgy. At the same time, this advocates the viewpoint that music, too, is such that it does not require an exclusive attitude of "art for art's sake" in order to be able to maintain its own true nature; instead, it not only allows for an ancillary role in the act of community worship but, rather, by its very nature is open to it. The third and the fourth theses now follow automatically from this.

Thesis 3: Professional church music is therefore a truly liturgical and pastoral ministry.

If both words in the expression "church music" are understood in the full sense, as was just explained, then church music can be performed properly only by someone who understands it in terms of the nature of the liturgy and produces it with that nature in mind. Yet church music is not just aesthetic activity on the fringes of the Church but is itself liturgical ministry. This insight resolves two misunderstandings: on the one hand, the liturgical character of sacred music has led some sectors of Church tradition to conclude that the musician as a liturgist really cannot be a lay person—hence the inference that women were excluded and also that minor orders were required. Here we encounter either the previously rejected instrumentalization of music as something "merely liturgical" or a misunderstanding of liturgical action that denies that the whole Church is the subject of the liturgy and restricts that role to the clergy or else a combination of both errors. But then the complete separation of the functions should also be rejected: since music ministry is also liturgical ministry, it can be carried out very well as a form of pastoral and also priestly ministry. Church music that is truly performed in the name of the liturgy is a form of the apostolate and serves the building up of the worshipping community.

Thesis 4: Professional church music is also, however, a properly musical profession and demands real musical qualifications.

The church musician should be capable of making real music and, thus, of preserving a requisite dimension of the Church or of making it accessible to her once again. Of course, in this regard (as also in what has been said thus far), praxis no doubt sets limits, which the church musician will sense in proportion to his musicianship. Music that makes high artistic demands cannot be performed in every worshipping community; indeed, it will be possible only in a very few cases. But it would still be a mistake to conclude from this that music in the Church can be understood only in purely functional terms after all and that quality must be replaced completely by serviceability. Especially in communities with meager resources, the church musician needs genuine musicianship so as to recognize and accomplish, in the given circumstances, what is possible and worthy, including what is musically worthy.

This creates for him a duty of educating, which in turn ultimately serves the whole area of music as well, just as it serves the building up of the worshipping community: in such educational activity the pastoral and the musical are blended together. As difficult as it may be, it can be regarded as the particularly honorable service of the church musician to the Church and to humanity at the same time.

PART E

FURTHER PERSPECTIVES

I. Change and Permanence in Liturgy: Questions to Joseph Ratzinger

A Conversation with the Editor of the International Catholic Periodical Communio

Communio: There is no point looking for problems where there are none, so let us say at the outset that, insofar as liturgy has a form that is perceptible to the senses, it is changeable. Indeed, it must be changeable. For it is the existential presence of the celebrating, praying faithful that makes the liturgy into the worship of God; change is necessary so that their awareness of what is going on and of their part in it are not restricted by extraneous factors. Roman history reveals a most eloquent example of a form of worship that had become unintelligible. After three centuries no one any longer understood the ritual, the ceremonies, or the meaning it was all meant to express, with the result that religion dried up and became an empty shell, although it was no less practiced than before. The lesson is that, if liturgy is to retain its vitality and have an influence on individuals and society, there must be a continual process of adaptation to the understanding of believers. For believers, too, after all, are people of their time, people of their world.

Taking it as a fact that today, for the first time in history, the Church is really universal and encompasses the whole earth, not only in intention but *de facto*—apart from certain blank areas on the map of the Communist Far East—surely there has been far too little reform of the liturgy, of the Mass? What about the believers in mission lands? As far as they were concerned, the reform of the liturgy simply could not go far enough. Is it right that non-Western people, people with their own cultural setting, with their own and in some

From *The Feast of Faith: Approaches to a Theology of the Liturgy*, trans. Graham Harrison (San Francisco: Ignatius Press, 1986), 79–96.

ways totally different symbolic forms and gestures (the embrace, bow, genuflection, kiss) should be forced into the symbols and sign language that belong to the thought and feeling of the Mediterranean world and of Europe? For it is these European forms that have shaped our liturgy.

Cardinal Ratzinger: First of all it must be said that both the Constitution on the Liturgy and the Decree on the Church's Missionary Activity explicitly allow for the possibility of far-reaching adaptations to the customs and cultic traditions of peoples. In this respect, the new Missal is only providing a framework for mission lands. It is a feature of the new Missal that its very many *ad libitum* provisions give a great deal of scope for local variations. On the other hand, we must beware of seeing things too naïvely and simplistically. Only very slowly and with the greatest of caution did the growing Church take up certain of the external forms of pagan liturgies. At the beginning the Church operated within the form of the Jewish synagogue service—an extremely modest form from the point of view of ritual. She joined this to the celebration of the Eucharist, the basic structure of which was equally Jewish, namely, the great prayer of thanksgiving. At the core of this thanksgiving, she placed the account of the institution of the Eucharist. Hence this prayer also mediates the idea of sacrifice insofar as it is attuned to the prayer of Jesus Christ in his self-surrender to the Father and makes this self-offering present in time. These simple elements have constituted the basic structure of every Christian Eucharist right up to the present day. In the course of a gradual development, they have been furnished with various cultic forms, ultimately giving rise to the individual ritual genres. But this development presupposes the existence of a Christian identity that was able to create its own fundamental liturgical form. Only on the basis of a Christian consciousness of this kind could the existing elements be refashioned in a fruitful way and made to express Christian realities. In other words, the whole process presupposes the struggle to vindicate what was distinctively Christian, a struggle carried on by the martyrs over three centuries. Only once this had been done could the door be opened to the use of pagan customs, suitably purified. Moreover, much of what we are inclined to see as adaptation from the Roman sphere of influence was in fact the product of the Old Testament renaissance that began in the early Middle

Ages, that is, here, too, it was far more a case of Christianity returning to appropriate its own distinct origins.

Therefore it seems to me very dangerous to suggest that missionary liturgies could be created overnight, so to speak, by decisions of bishops' conferences, which would themselves be dependent on memoranda drawn up by academics. Liturgy does not come about through regulation. One of the weaknesses of the postconciliar liturgical reform can doubtless be traced to the armchair strategy of academics, drawing up things on paper that, in fact, would presuppose years of organic growth. The most blatant example of this is the reform of the Calendar: those responsible simply did not realize how much the various annual feasts had influenced Christian people's relation to time. In redistributing these established feasts throughout the year according to some historical arithmetic—inconsistently applied at that—they ignored a fundamental law of religious life. But to return to the missionary situation: conversion to Christianity means, initially, turning away from pagan forms of life. There was a very clear awareness of this in the first Christian centuries, even long after the so-called Constantinian settlement. Not until a strong Christian identity has grown up in the mission countries can one begin to move, with great caution and on the basis of this identity, toward christening the indigenous forms by adopting them into the liturgy and allowing Christian realities to merge with the forms of everyday life. It goes without saying that expressions that have no meaning in a particular country, or which have a contrary meaning, have been altered. I would not call this liturgical "reform", however, but the appropriate application of the existing form, something that is always necessary. What is more, I am convinced that a superficial or overhasty adaptation, far from attracting respect for Christianity, would only raise doubts as to its sincerity and the seriousness of its message. Then, too, we must remember that nowadays all indigenous cultures are overlaid by features of the technological world civilization, a fact that should caution us against haste and too much attention to externals.

Communio: I am sure you share my opinion that no reform can be meaningful unless it finds wide support. Otherwise it will fail to reach its goal. We see something similar in the field of law. A new law, unobjectionable in itself, will be useless if people do not understand it and do not accept it. In such a case jurists speak of a *lex non accepta*.

Having followed the debate about the reform of the liturgy, that is, of the Mass, that has been going on in recent years both here and abroad, I would like tentatively to suggest this: though small in numbers, there seems to be a definite stratum of the faithful, very committed in their Church membership, whose response to the reform ranges from surprise, puzzlement, discontent, right up to informal and even public protest. Perhaps Church leaders think "Let them be; the protests will die down eventually." I do not want to go into all the reasons adduced against the reform. But one thing is certain: the so-called "conservatives" who form this opposition, for whatever reason, feel that they have been betrayed and put in the wrong. Nor is this a wholly subjective matter. For instance, in 1947 we had *Mediator Dei*, the encyclical of Pius XII, and then, not twenty years later, came the reform. In other words, within twenty years a silent landslide took place, without the slightest assurance being given to those involved, the mass of traditional believers. I find it hard to understand how the Church could have so failed to carry out her pastoral responsibilities toward those under her care, leaving the believers of the old school almost defenseless against the tide of new thought and practice.

The people I am referring to had been taught certain things, had been brought up in a certain way. They had fought for these values. They had been committed to them. Now, overnight, all this was no longer supposed to be true. I am not so much interested in what is right and wrong here, the old belief or the new, but I do want to point out the situation as it appears in the minds of many of the faithful.

Cardinal Ratzinger: First of all I must take up the distinction you have just made between "the old belief" and "the new". I must emphatically deny such a distinction. The Council has not created any new matter for belief, let alone replaced an old belief with a new one. Fundamentally, the Council sees itself as continuing and deepening the work of earlier councils, in particular those of Trent and Vatican I. Its sole concern is to facilitate the same faith under changed circumstances, to revitalize it. That is why the reform of the liturgy aimed at making the faith's expression more transparent. But what we have is a renewed expression of the one faith, not a change in faith.

As to what led up to the reform: there seemed to be more going on in Germany, in terms of preparatory work, than anywhere else. Germany was the heartland of the Liturgical Movement, which had a great impact on the declarations of the Council. Many of the measures taken by the Council had long been anticipated here. Moreover, Pius XII had already carried out certain elements of liturgical reform—one thinks of the refashioning of the Easter Vigil. All the same I must admit that in the wake of the Council a lot of things happened far too quickly and abruptly, with the result that many of the faithful could not see the inner continuity with what had gone before. In part it is simply a fact that the Council was pushed aside. For instance, it had said that the language of the Latin Rite was to remain Latin, although suitable scope was to be given to the vernacular. Today we might ask: *Is* there a Latin Rite at all any more? Certainly there is no awareness of it. To most people the liturgy seems to be rather something for the individual congregation to arrange. Core groups make up their own "liturgies" from week to week, with an enthusiasm that is as amazing as it is misplaced. The really serious thing, in my view, is this fundamental breakdown of liturgical consciousness. Imperceptibly, the distinctions between liturgy and conviviality, liturgy and society, become blurred. Thus many priests, following the etiquette of polite society, feel that they must not receive Communion until all the others have been "served"; or they no longer feel able to say "I bless *you*" and so dissolve the basic liturgical relationship between priest and people. Here too is the origin of all those tasteless and banal forms of greeting—which many congregations endure with polite stoicism. In the period before the appearance of the new Missal, when the old Missal was already stigmatized as antiquated, there was a loss of the awareness of "rite", that is, that there is a prescribed liturgical form and that liturgy can only be liturgy to the extent that it is beyond the manipulation of those who celebrate it. Even the official new books, which are excellent in many ways, occasionally show far too many signs of being drawn up by academics and reinforce the notion that a liturgical book can be "made" like any other book.

In this connection I would like to make a brief reference to the so-called Tridentine liturgy. In fact, there is no such thing as a Tridentine liturgy, and until 1965 the phrase would have meant nothing to anyone. The Council of Trent did not "make" a liturgy. Strictly speaking, there is no such thing, either, as the Missal of Pius V. The Missal that appeared in 1570 by order of Pius V differed only in tiny details from the first printed edition of the Roman Missal of about a hundred years earlier. Basically the reform of Pius V was only concerned with eliminating certain late medieval accretions and the various mistakes and misprints that had crept in. Thus, again, it prescribed the Missal of the City of Rome, which had remained largely free of these blemishes, for the whole Church. At the same time it was felt that if the *Missale typicum* printed in Rome were used exclusively, it would help to get rid of the uncertainties that had arisen in the confusion of liturgical movements in the Reformation period, for in this liturgical confusion the distinction between Catholic and Reformed had been widely obscured. This is clear from the fact that the reform explicitly made an exception of those liturgical customs that were more than two hundred years old. In 1614, under Urban VIII, there was already a new edition of the Missal, again including various improvements. In this way each century before and after Pius V left its mark on the Missal. On the one hand, it was subject to a continuous process of purification, and, on the other, it continued to grow and develop, but it remained the same book throughout. Hence those who cling to the "Tridentine Missal" have a faulty view of the historical facts. Yet at the same time, the way in which the renewed Missal was presented is open to much criticism. We must say to the "Tridentines" that the Church's liturgy is alive, like the Church herself, and is thus always involved in a process of maturing that exhibits greater and lesser changes. Four hundred years is far too young an age for the Catholic liturgy—because in fact it reaches right back to Christ and the apostles and has come down to us from that time in a single, constant process. The Missal can no more be mummified than the Church herself. Yet, with all its advantages, the new Missal was published as if it were a book put together by professors, not a phase in a continual growth process. Such a thing has never happened before. It is absolutely contrary to the laws of liturgical growth, and it has resulted in the nonsensical notion that Trent and Pius V "produced" a Missal four hundred years ago. The Catholic liturgy was thus reduced to the level of a mere product of modern times. This loss of perspective is really disturbing. Although very few of those who express their uneasiness have a clear picture of these interrelated factors, there is an instinctive grasp of the fact that liturgy cannot be the result of Church regulations, let alone professional erudition, but, to be true to itself, must be the fruit of the Church's life and vitality.

Lest there be any misunderstanding, let me add that as far as its content is concerned (apart from a few criticisms), I am very grateful for the new Missal, for the way it has enriched the treasury of prayers and prefaces, for the new Eucharistic Prayers and the increased number of texts for use on weekdays, and so on, quite apart from the availability of the vernacular. But I do regard it as unfortunate that we have been presented with the idea of a new book rather than with that of continuity within a single liturgical history. In my view, a new edition will need to make it quite clear that the so-called Missal of Paul VI is nothing other than a renewed form of the same Missal to which Pius X, Urban VIII, Pius V, and their predecessors have contributed, right from the Church's earliest history. It is of the very essence of the Church that she should be aware of her unbroken continuity throughout the history of faith, expressed in an ever-present unity of prayer. This awareness of continuity is destroyed just as much by those who "opt" for a book supposed to have been produced four hundred years ago as by those who would like to be forever drawing up new liturgies. At bottom, these two attitudes are identical. It seems to me that this is the origin of the uneasiness to which you have referred. The fundamental issue is whether faith comes about through regulations and learned research or through the living history of a Church that retains her identity throughout the centuries.

Communio: Going on from the question of the method applied in the reform and the effects it had, perhaps we may ask about its *aims.* As early as *Mediator Dei* we find references to the active participation of the faithful in worship. What is meant by this active participation? Singing and praying together, responding to the priest? Sitting, standing, kneeling? In other words, it is not enough to be simply present in the church, as one could before the First World War, listening to the music of the choir or praying the Rosary at Mass. Now, surely, with the whole congregation, we need to be involved in what is going on at the altar.

But is it not true to say that there already was this kind of active participation, at least in Germany, before the Second World War, thanks to the Liturgical Movement of the twenties? And long experience has shown us, surely, that active participation, understood in this way, can itself become an empty form. I can sing "Holy God we praise thy name" or Credo III and at the same time be going over the details of my last income tax return. Active participation is no guarantee against the dangers of routine. The question is how to preserve and create a

V. Assessment and Future Prospects

I do not venture to suggest any conclusions; I have not had the time, the intellectual capability, or the physical strength to prepare anything. I can simply offer you a few remarks. But above all I would like to offer my deepest thanks to you, Father Abbot, for the spirit within this monastery, which has inspired us with the peace of the Church, the peace of our Lord, and which thus helps us to seek together that Catholic ecumenism within which there can be a reconciliation within the Church, in the midst of these differences that are both deep and hurtful.

What is it I want to say? I had been thinking of talking about four points: a first point, a further remark about the intellectual and spiritual makeup of the Liturgical Movement as I have known it; next, a word about the suggestions of Father Folsom and Professor Spaemann as to pluriformity within the Roman rite, about Roman rites within the Roman rite; a word about the "reform of the reform"; and also a word, in discussion with my friend Professor Spaemann, about the future of the 1962 Missal.

1. The Spiritual and Historical Components of the Liturgical Movement

Yesterday I talked about the origins of the academic discipline of liturgical studies (liturgiology), saying that, on the one hand, it had developed from historical studies and, on the other, from pastoral work; that was about academic liturgical studies, not about the Liturgical Movement. The Liturgical Movement originated in Germany from a

Translated by Henry Taylor. From Alcuin Reid, O.S.B., ed., *Looking Again at the Question of the Liturgy with Cardinal Ratzinger: Proceedings of the July 2001 Fontgombault Liturgical Conference* (Farnborough, Eng.: Saint Michael's Abbey Press, 2003), 145–53.

by Marx and the sacrament by a kind of "party" atmosphere. People wanted to "turn on" an immediate effect, as it were, from outside. Compared with the merely external busy-ness that became the rule in many places, the quiet "following" of Mass, as we knew it in former times, was far more realistic and dramatic: it was a sharing in the action at a deep level, and in it the community of faith was silently and powerfully mobilized. Of course, to say this is not to impugn "active participation" as I have defined it; the criticism only applies where this participation has degenerated into mere externals. There is simply no way of ensuring that everyone, always and on all occasions, is involved in the *actio*. Indeed, I think it is one of the crucial insights we have gained in the wake of the Council that the liturgy's effect cannot be achieved in a purely external manner. Faith requires a continual process of education, otherwise the words of faith begin to lose their meaning. In the Gospel, immediately after the first occurrence of a confession of faith in Christ, we read "he began to teach them" (Mk 8:29ff.). In other words, there is no such thing as a self-explanatory short formula of faith. The Creed is part of an organic context that includes teaching, education, and the life of a believing fellowship; both words and signs draw their life from this context.

Communio: I would like to ask you about the relationship between form and content in the celebration of Mass today. By content I have in mind the mysteries of faith represented by and through the Church. No experienced observer can fail to notice the change of emphasis in the Eucharist between the meal element, the sacrificial element, and the Liturgy of the Word. I am stating a fact, not making a judgment. No doubt the Liturgy of the Word has gained immeasurably as a result. But the question remains: Why this change of emphasis? Obviously it was not for some merely pragmatic reason, as if something had to be cut to make room for the extended Liturgy of the Word.

Let me give you my hypothesis: As long as there is no consensus with regard to the content of the celebration, there will be something wrong with the form and structure that manifest this content. What is the Mass? Is it a table fellowship? Or a sacrificial fellowship? You have given your answer on pages 33–60 of this book.* But I want to press

---

*JRCW 11:299–318.

The Mass was thus truly, as I wrote in the preface to my book, like a painted-over fresco. Thus, to rediscover that the liturgy in itself is living and is a reality experienced by the Church as such was a development that considerably enriched the Church. We have therefore left far behind those misunderstandings, those inadequate conceptions and deficient visions of the liturgy and of theology. I even think, too, that the explosive outbreak of the Reformation in the sixteenth century was possible because there was no longer any real understanding of the liturgy. For Luther, all that remained of the Mass was the Consecration and the distribution of Holy Communion.

Yet in this genuine progress that the Liturgical Movement brought—which led us toward Vatican II, toward *Sacrosanctum Concilium*—there lay also a danger: that of despising the Middle Ages as such and Scholastic theology as such. It was from that point onward that there was a parting of the ways: Dom Casel presented himself as an exclusive advocate of patristic theology, as he saw it, and of liturgical Platonism, as he conceived it. These one-sided ideas were then popularized with slogans that were most unfortunate and very dangerous; thus it already used to be said—I can recall quite well—"The consecrated bread is not there to be looked at but to be eaten." This was a slogan directed against eucharistic adoration; people thought that the whole business, the whole development in the course of the Middle Ages was mistaken. There was thus a liturgical rigorism and archaeologism, which in the end became very dangerous. People could no longer grasp that even the innovations of the Middle Ages—eucharistic adoration and popular piety and all that—were actually legitimate developments. Above all, a synthesis between the two currents of opinion was then no longer possible: Guardini split off from Maria Laach because he defended the Rosary, the Way of the Cross, eucharistic adoration, while the others had taken up a purist position that no longer allowed room for these later developments.

Therefore this question—which we discussed yesterday—remains open: What synthesis is possible between medieval theology and the Fathers, and what deeper vision do they share? I think that St. Thomas Aquinas is both a theologian who opens the door to a new vision of theology, with the integration of Aristotelian thought, and at the same time a perfectly patristic theologian: taking him as our starting point, it ought to be possible to discover this synthesis. At the beginning of the [nineteen] twenties, Guardini wrote a very interesting dialogue between an exegete

Rahner's intention was to remind us that Trent too had a very clear view of the words of institution and the inner finality of the realities of bread and wine, asserting that it is of the essence of this sacrament (and *mutatis mutandis* of all sacraments) that it is ordered to *reception*. But this awareness did not stop Trent from going on to say that this "reception" encompasses many factors: to "receive" Christ essentially involves "adoration". Receiving Christ must involve all the dimensions of Christ; so it cannot be limited to a physical process. It also implies belief in the Real Presence. It is so hard to define this adequately because nowadays we no longer have a philosophy that penetrates to the being of things. We are only interested in function. Modern science only asks "How does it work? What can I do with it?" It no longer asks "What *is* it?"; such a question would be regarded as unscientific, and indeed, in a strictly scientific sense, it is insoluble. The attempts to define the Eucharist by reference to the level of meaning and the goal (transsignification, transfinalization) were intended as a response to this new situation. Although these new concepts are not simply wrong, they are dangerously limited. Once sacraments and faith are reduced to the level of function, we are no longer speaking of God (for he is not a "function"), nor are we speaking of man, either (for he is not a function, although he *has* many functions). Here we can see how important it is, in a philosophically impoverished era, for sacramental faith to keep alive the question of being. This is the only way to break up the tyranny of functionalism, which would turn the world into one vast concentration camp. When nowadays we affirm that Christ is present at the level of being in the transformed gifts, we are doing something that, up to a point, is not backed up or "covered" by philosophy; therefore the affirmation becomes all the more significant as a human act.

On the relationship of the sacrifice and meal elements, I can only refer you back to the section on "Form and Content of the Eucharistic Celebration".* But I will say this: modern theology is rather against drawing parallels between the history of religions and Christianity. All the same I regard it as significant that, throughout the entire history of religions, sacrifice and meal are inseparably united. The sacrifice facilitates *communio* with the divinity, and men receive back the divinity's gift in and from the sacrifice. This is transformed

---

*JRCW 11:299–318.

the point at which we have to stand firm; we must rediscover the Church—the Body of Christ—as the true agent in the liturgy. Thus, we have to be aware that with a secularized exegesis, and with a hermeneutic system that is profoundly Protestant and secularized, we cannot find the basis of our faith in the New Testament; and that with the fragmentation of the liturgy, when it is considered as being the particular action of the local congregation, then we lose sight of the Church and, along with the Church, of faith and mystery. What we need, in contrast to this, is to return to an exegesis rooted in the living reality of the Church, the Church of all ages—especially the Church of the Fathers—but of the Church of truly *all* the ages: even the Church of the Middle Ages. We need also, therefore, to rediscover cultic reality and the sacral priesthood in the New Testament and to win back the essentials for the liturgy; in that sense, I wanted to say that, within the limitations that are certainly to be found in the documents of Trent, Trent remains the norm, as reread with our greater knowledge and deeper understanding of the Fathers and of the New Testament, as read with the Fathers and with the Church of all ages.

2. *The Problem of Roman Rites within the Roman Rite*

The fact of this coexistence of rites is obvious, as Father Folsom has shown us clearly and convincingly, and likewise Professor Spaemann. Father Folsom made explicit two consequences of this: there are no liturgical arguments against the plurality of rites, but there is a difficulty with canonical criteria and—as he remarked—with political criteria; I should say, rather, with pastoral criteria. And that is really the problem facing the authority of the Church: What are the criteria?

Personally, from the beginning I was in favor of the freedom to continue using the old Missal, for a very simple reason: people were already beginning to talk about making a break with the preconciliar Church and of developing various models of Church—a preconciliar and obsolete type of Church and a new and conciliar type of Church. This is at any rate nowadays the slogan of the Lefebvrists, insisting that there are two Churches, and for them the great rupture becomes visible in the existence of two Missals, which are said to be irreconcilable with each other. It seems to me essential, the basic step, to recognize that both Missals are Missals of the Church and belong to the Church,

II. Worship in the Parish Communities Fifteen Years After the Council

A Sermon Delivered to the Bishops' Conference in Fulda

"Worship in the parish communities fifteen years after the Council"— this was the main topic of our conference here in Fulda at the grave of St. Boniface. What then is our liturgical life like today? In asking this question we are bound to have mixed feelings. On the one hand, we are glad about the awakening of a new sense of common responsibility, a new experience of fellowship and of community participation in the eucharistic mystery; we rejoice in the new understanding that is abroad since the Church's liturgy has been brought from behind the veils of history to stand before us, fresh in its simplicity and greatness of stature. But, on the other hand, we are aware of the strife and dissension that have arisen concerning the liturgy and within it; we shiver a little in the face of too much talk, too little silence, and a lack of beauty; we are obliged to recall so much arbitrary action, which reduced the dignity of the Lord's institution to the level of something embarrassingly cobbled together. So we have cause for thanksgiving but also no less cause to examine our consciences, and to help us do so I would like to make a few suggestions in this evening hour.

My first consideration is this: Our topic refers to worship in the parish communities. "Community" is the new discovery of the post-conciliar period. We have called to mind once more that Eucharist, in the language of the ancient Church, was called, among other things, *synaxis*, the "meeting together", the assembly. It draws and binds men together, unites them, builds up community. Conversely, the community experiences Eucharist as fulfillment, as the center of its life, something in which it shares as a totality. All this is true, but we must remember that the scope of *synaxis* is much wider than the individual community. Behind it stand those words from the Gospel

---

From *The Feast of Faith: Approaches to a Theology of the Liturgy*, trans. Graham Harrison (San Francisco: Ignatius Press, 1986), 147–53.

an objective criterion. I am in *this* local Church, and I do not look for my friends there, I find my brothers and my sisters; and these brothers and sisters are not people we look for, we just find them there. This situation of the non-arbitrariness of the Church in which I find myself, which is not a church of my choice but rather the Church that presents itself to me, is a very important principle. It seems to me that the letters of St. Ignatius run very strongly along these lines: that this bishop is the Church; this is not my choice, as if I were to go with this or that group of friends; I am in the common Church, along with the poor, the wealthy, with people I like and people I do not like, with intellectuals and uneducated people; I am in the Church, which was there before me. Opening up the opportunity of choosing one's Church "*à la carte*" is something that could genuinely damage the structure of the Church.

One ought, therefore—it seems to me—to look for a non-subjective criterion with which to open up the opportunity of using the old Missal. That seems to me very simple, in the case of abbeys: this is a good thing; likewise it corresponds to the tradition by which there used to be orders with their own rite, for example, the Dominicans. Thus, abbeys that ensure the continuing presence of this rite and, likewise, religious communities, such as the Dominicans of St. Vincent Ferrer, or other religious communities or fraternities—they seem to me to offer an objective criterion. Naturally, the problem becomes more complicated with the fraternities, which are not religious orders but communities of non-diocesan priests who nevertheless are active in parishes. Perhaps the "personal parish" might be a solution, but that is not without difficulty, either. In any case, the Holy See should open up this opportunity and preserve this treasure for all the faithful; yet, on the other hand, it must also preserve and respect the episcopal structure of the Church.

3. The "Reform of the Reform"

Professor Spaemann is right: the "reform of the reform" refers, of course, to the reformed Missal, not to the Missal in previous use. What can we do, given that the goal we are all aiming for in the end—it seems to me—is liturgical reconciliation and not *rigid uniformity*? I am not in favor of *rigid uniformity*, but we should, of course, be opposed to *chaos*, to the fragmentation of the liturgy, and in that sense we should also be in favor of observing unity in the use of Paul VI's Missal. That seems to me a problem to be faced as a priority: How can we return to a *common* rite, reformed (if you like) but not fragmented or left to the arbitrary devices of local congregations, or that of a few commissions or groups of experts? Thus the "reform of the reform" is something that concerns the Missal of Paul VI, always with this aim of achieving reconciliation within the Church, since for the moment there exists instead a painful opposition, and we are still a long way from reconciliation, even though these days we have shared together here are an important step toward that reconciliation.

As for the Missal in current use, the first point, in my opinion, would be to reject false creativity, which is not a category of the liturgy. We have recalled more than once what the Council actually said on this subject: Only the ecclesiastical authority makes decisions; neither the priest nor any group of people has the right to change the liturgy. But in the new Missal we quite often find formulae such as: *sacerdos dicit sic vel simili modo* ... [the priest speaks thus or in a similar way ...] or *Hic sacerdos potest dicere* ... [Here the priest can say ...]. These formulae of the Missal in fact give official sanction to creativity; the priest feels almost obliged to change the wording, to show that he is creative, that he is giving this liturgy immediacy, making it present for his congregation; and with this false creativity, which transforms the liturgy into a catechetical exercise for *this* congregation, liturgical unity and the *ecclesiality* of the liturgy are being destroyed. Therefore, it seems to me, it would be an important step toward reconciliation if the Missal were simply freed from these areas of creativity, which do not correspond to the deepest level of reality, to the spirit, of the liturgy. If, by means of such a "reform of the reform", we could get back to a faithful, ecclesial celebration of the liturgy, then this would in my opinion be itself an important step, because the *ecclesial dimension* of the liturgy would once more be clearly apparent.

The second point about which we have spoken is the translations: Canon Rose said some important things to us; the crisis is almost more serious in the United States, in the English-speaking world, with permanent changes in the language, with the problem of what is *politically correct*, and the problem of "inclusive language". There are some congregations in the United States where, in the name of inclusive language, they no longer dare to say, "In the name of the Father, and of the Son, and of the Holy Spirit," because that is "male chauvinism"— the Father and the Son, two men. They then say, "In the name of the

the way of the Lord, in God himself. Its aim is to lead us to this breakthrough to God. This involves two further practical considerations: liturgy is not a matter of variety and change; it is concerned with an ever-deeper experience of something that is beyond change because it is the very answer that we are seeking. Secondly, liturgy is not only concerned with the conscious mind and with what can be immediately understood at the superficial level, like newspaper headlines. Liturgy addresses the human being in all his depth, which goes far beyond our everyday awareness; there are things we only understand with the heart; the mind can gradually grow in understanding the more we allow our heart to illuminate it.

I would like to mention a third aspect involved in the proper celebration of the Eucharist. It is one of the happy features of worship in the wake of the Council that more and more people participate fully in the Eucharist by receiving the Body of the Lord, communicating with him and, in him, with the whole Church of God. Yet do we not feel a slight uneasiness at times in the face of an entire congregation coming to Communion? Paul urgently insisted that the Corinthians should "discern" the Lord's Body (1 Cor 11:29): Is this still happening? Occasionally one has the feeling that "Communion" is regarded as part of the ritual—that it goes on automatically and is simply an expression of the community's identity. We need to regain a much stronger awareness that the Eucharist does not lose all its meaning where people do not communicate. By going to Communion without "discernment", we fail to reach the heights of what is taking place in Communion; we reduce the Lord's gift to the level of everyday ordinariness and manipulation. The Eucharist is not a ritual meal; it is the shared prayer of the Church, in which the Lord prays together with us and gives us himself. Therefore it remains something great and precious, it remains a true gift, even when we cannot communicate. If we understood this better and hence had a more correct view of the Eucharist itself, many pastoral problems—the position of the divorced and remarried in the Church, for instance—would cease to be such a burden.

One final remark: When we speak of worship in the parish community, we immediately think exclusively of the Eucharist. But this very fact expresses the regrettable narrowing and impoverishment that have overtaken us in these latter years. The Eucharist is the heart and understand quite well what Professor Spaemann was saying when he asserted that if you do not know the aim of a reform, however small it may be, if you are left to suppose that this is just an intermediate step toward a complete revolution, then people feel sensitive about it. And in that sense we have to be very careful about any possible changes. However, he did also say—and I emphasize this—that it would be fatal for the old liturgy to be, as it were, placed in a refrigerator, left like a national park, a park protected for the sake of a certain kind of people, for whom one leaves available these relics of the past. This would be—as Professor de Mattei said to us—a kind of inculturation: "There are also the conservationists, let that group have their own cultural version!" If it were to be reduced to the past in that way, we would not be preserving this treasure for the Church of today and tomorrow. In my view we should avoid, come what may, putting this liturgy into a deep freeze just for a certain type of people.

It must also be liturgy *of the Church* and under the authority of the Church; and only within this *ecclesial dimension*, in a *fundamental* relationship with the authority of the Church, can it give all that it has to offer. Naturally, one can say, "We no longer have any confidence in the authority of the Church, after all we have been through in the past thirty years." It is nevertheless a basic Catholic principle to trust in the authority of the Church. I have always been much impressed by something Harnack said in a discussion with Peterson, a Protestant theologian who at that time was moving toward converting to Catholicism; Harnack answered the questions of his younger colleague by saying: it is obvious that the Catholic principle of *Scripture and tradition* is better and that it is the correct principle and that it implies the existence of an authority in the Church; but even if the principle in itself, the Catholic principle, is correct, we are better off living without an authority and without the actions such an authority might take. He had confidence that the free use of reason in studying the Scriptures would bring men to the truth and that this was better than being subject to some authority, which could also make mistakes. That is true, authority can make mistakes, but being obedient to that authority is for us the guarantee of our being obedient to the Lord. That is certainly a very strong admonition to those people who are exercising authority not to exercise it in the way you exercise power. Having authority in the Church is always an exercise in obedience. When the Holy Father decided that the Church does not have the power to

III. In Memory of Klaus Gamber

Not long ago a young priest said to me, "Today we need a new liturgical movement." This expressed a concern that can be avoided nowadays only by deliberate superficiality. This priest was not interested in
winning even more audacious freedoms—really, what freedom has *not*
been taken already? He sensed that we again need a beginning from
within, as the Liturgical Movement at its best had intended, when it
was concerned not about making texts or inventing actions and forms
but rather about the rediscovery of the living heart, about entering
into the interior fabric of the liturgy to a new celebration that is shaped
from within. The liturgical reform, as it was carried out concretely,
distanced itself more and more from this origin. The result is not revival
but devastation. On the one side is a liturgy that has degenerated into
a show, in which people try to make religion interesting with trendy
antics and flippant moralizing, with momentary successes in the planning group and even more widespread alienation on the part of all
who look to the liturgy, not for clerical showmanship, but, rather, for
an encounter with the living God, in whose presence all our making
is insignificant, since the encounter with him can open up the true
wealth of being to all. The other side offers the extreme conservation
of ritual form, the greatness of which is still quite stirring, but, when
it becomes the expression of stubborn isolation, in the end it leaves
only sadness. Certainly, there is the middle way of the many good
priests and their congregations who celebrate the newly formed liturgy reverently and solemnly, but the contradiction on either side calls
it into question, and the lack of inner unity in the Church ultimately
makes even her fidelity seem to many people (unfairly) a merely private variety of neo-conservatism. That is how the matter stands, and
so a new spiritual impulse is necessary that will give the liturgy back

Translated by Michael J. Miller.

VI. Answer to the Open Letter of Olivier Bauer

Dear Professor Bauer:

I assume that you can understand German; allow me, therefore, to write to you in my mother tongue, because it would be very time-consuming for me to express my thoughts in acceptable French.

First of all, I would like to thank you cordially for reading my book on the liturgy so attentively and for having honored it with such a lengthy discussion. I appreciate it and personally find it very helpful that you have communicated to me your detailed, critical reflections. I am sure that you will understand if I reply in the same spirit of critical candor; it seems to me that there is much more mutual respect in this willingness to speak critically with one another than in a superficial friendliness.

Concerning your first point: frankly, I am somewhat surprised that you should say that the *point de départ* of my book is prayer facing east. Now in the second paragraph of your first point you did summarize very well the plan of my book—the tension between cosmos and history; the twofold view that looks both to the foundational past and also to the future, to the Lord who will come again; the importance of bodily posture and, generally, of the bodily and material dimensions in the liturgy; the connection with other religions and especially the connection between the Old and New Covenant. This broad outline does in fact define the perspective of my book. It is also correct to say that I do not begin with an analysis of the words at the Last Supper, because my book is not, strictly speaking, a theological interpretation of the Eucharist (the Last Supper) but intends, rather, to describe the essence of the liturgy as such within the context of Old and New Covenant, of world religions and biblical faith. But it is inaccurate to say that my starting point is prayer

---

Translated by Kenneth Baker, S.J., and Michael J. Miller.

making, the insipid product of the moment. Gamber opposed this falsification with the vigilance of a true seer and with the fearlessness of an honest witness and taught us the living fullness of real liturgy based on a tremendously thorough knowledge of the sources. As someone who knew and loved history, he showed us the manifold forms of its development and of its path; as someone who saw history from within, he saw precisely in this becoming and development the sacrosanct splendor of the eternal liturgy, which is not the object of our making but can continue to mature and unfold in a wonderful way if we are attuned to its mystery from within. The death of this great man and priest should cause us to listen attentively; his work could help us to make a fresh start.

exemplary objectivity.* I am pleased that these recent publications confirm in all essential points the positions that I have taken up in my book, even though they treat many of the historical aspects with more precision and additional distinctions. Having referred to these publications, I need not reply in detail to all your questions on this matter in point 2b of your letter.

Clearly you, as a Protestant Christian, cannot share my view in questions concerning "eucharistic reservation". Moreover, I do not question at all, in the pertinent paragraph, the fact that your "Protestant temple" is "bien vivant" [quite alive] when the faithful assemble to worship. The passage that you criticized is not about the congregation but, rather, about the significance of the church space when the community is not assembled in it. Here, even apart from belief in the abiding Real Presence, there is a considerable difference from a purely phenomenological viewpoint: the Protestant church space is living whenever the community is assembled there; outside of those times it is in itself an empty room. It is there for the congregation, bound up, as it were, with the functioning of the community and of its liturgical activity. On the other hand, where there is belief in the abiding Real Presence, "Eucharist" is always there, and the space is never empty. It is always "functioning" because the Lord who is present constantly goes to meet people and invites them to pray. I wanted to call attention to this difference in the significance of space apart from the liturgical assembly; it is evident—it seems to me—even independently of one's belief about the Eucharist.

Under point 2c you have reported very carefully and precisely my basic statements concerning sacred music, and then at the conclusion you have added your critical remarks. I confess that it is difficult for me to understand these questions, for I have not simply demanded a return to Gregorian chant, nor have I disputed the fact that the Spirit can inspire composers and musicians even today. Quite to the contrary: on page 156 I say, "Anyone who looks carefully will see that, even in our own time, important works of art, inspired by faith, have been produced and are being produced—in visual art as well as in music (and indeed literature). Today, too, joy in the Lord and contact with his presence in the liturgy has an inexhaustible

---

*Lang's book is available in English: *Turning towards the Lord* (San Francisco: Ignatius Press, 2004).—TRANS.

IV. The Theology of the Liturgy

1. The Definition of the Liturgy in Vatican II

The Second Vatican Council defined the liturgy as "an action of Christ the Priest and of his Body, which is the Church".[1] The work of Jesus Christ is referred to in the same text as the work of the redemption that Christ accomplished especially by the Paschal Mystery of his Passion, of his Resurrection from the dead, and his glorious Ascension. By this Paschal Mystery, by "dying He destroyed our death, and rising, restored our life."[2]

At first sight, in these two sentences, the phrase "the action/work of Christ" seems to have been used in two different senses. "The work of Christ" refers first of all to the historical, redemptive actions of Jesus, his death and his Resurrection; on the other hand, the celebration of the liturgy is called "the work of Christ".

In reality, the two meanings are inseparably linked: the death and Resurrection of Christ, the Paschal Mystery, are not just exterior, historic events. In the case of the Resurrection, this is quite obvious. It extends into history yet transcends it in two ways: it is not the action of a man but an action of God, and hence it carries the risen Jesus beyond history, to that place where he sits at the right hand of the Father. But the Cross is not a merely human action, either. The purely human aspect is present in the people who led Jesus to the Cross. For Jesus himself, the Cross is not primarily an action, but a passion, and a passion

---

"The Theology of the Liturgy", a lecture delivered during the Journées liturgiques de Fontgombault, July 22–24, 2001, trans. Margaret McHugh and Fr. John Parsons, published in *Oriens*, Journal of the Ecclesia Dei Society, vol. 7, no. 2; also in *Looking Again at the Question of the Liturgy with Cardinal Ratzinger: Proceedings of the July 2001 Fontgombault Liturgical Conference*, ed. Alcuin Reid, O.S.B. (Farnborough, Eng.: Saint Michael's Abbey Press, 2003), 18–31. Translation completed and revised by Michael J. Miller.

[1] SC 7, cf. CCC 107.
[2] SC 5; cf. CCC 1067.

VII. Fortieth Anniversary of the Constitution on the Sacred Liturgy

A Look Back and a Look Forward

1. It Happened Forty Years Ago

It was a great day for the Second Vatican Council and for the Church generally when, on December 4, 1963, the Constitution on the Sacred Liturgy was approved almost unanimously. The Council had made decisions of great importance, which have subsequently transformed the outward manifestation of the Church in ways that are not insignificant. The Fathers realized that they were thereby bringing in the harvest of a long prehistory and were amalgamating the various currents, findings, and experiences that had matured in the Liturgical Movement into a holistic vision, which was to usher in a new chapter in the history of the liturgy. The document itself expressed this connection with its prehistory in the words: "Zeal for the promotion and restoration of the sacred liturgy is rightly held to be a sign of the providential dispositions of God in our time, and as a movement (*transitus*) of the Holy Spirit in His Church" (SC 43). The Liturgical Movement of the nineteenth and twentieth centuries, to which these words allude, is thus interpreted as a divine disposition and as a pneumatic event, as a new wafting of the Holy Spirit through his Church. Actually, no council can create something entirely new: it can only give definitive form and binding force to what has previously reached maturity in the faith life of the Church. This can be observed in the trinitarian and christological councils of the early Church as well as in the councils of the Middle Ages and the modern period dealing with sacramental theology and ecclesiology. The task of the council, therefore, is not to bring forth something previously unknown; rather, it is supposed to filter out of the currents of a given era what is valid, what has truly developed from the faith of the Church, and in this way to

Translated by Kenneth Baker, S.J., and Michael J. Miller.

the same time the old Enlightenment positions still live on everywhere: accusations of magic and paganism, contrasts drawn between worship and the service of the Word, between rite and ethos, the idea of a Christianity that disengages itself from worship and enters into the profane world, Catholic theologians who have no desire to see themselves accused of anti-modernity.[5] Even if people want somehow or other to rediscover the concept of sacrifice, the end result is embarrassment and criticism. Thus Stefan Orth, in the vast panorama of a bibliography of recent works devoted to the theme of sacrifice, believed he could make the following statement as a summary of his research: "In fact, many Catholics themselves today ratify the verdict and the conclusions of Martin Luther, who says that to speak of sacrifice is 'the greatest and most appalling horror' and a 'damnable idolatry'; this is why we want to refrain from all that smacks of sacrifice, including the whole Canon, and retain only that which is pure and holy." Then Orth adds: "This maxim was also followed in the Catholic Church after Vatican II, or at least tended to be, and led people to think of divine worship chiefly in terms of the feast of the Passover related in the accounts of the Last Supper."[6] Citing a work on sacrifice, edited by two modern Catholic liturgists, he then said, in slightly more moderate terms,[7] that it clearly seemed that the notion of the sacrifice of the Mass—even more than the sacrifice of the Cross—was at best an idea very open to misunderstanding.

I certainly do not need to say that I am not one of the "numerous Catholics" who consider it the most appalling horror and damnable idolatry to speak of the sacrifice of the Mass. It goes without saying that the writer did not mention my book on the spirit of the liturgy,

---

[5] An anthology edited by Beate Ego, Armin Lange, and Peter Pilhofer in collaboration with Kathrin Ehlers reflects the current theological debate about these questions: *Gemeinde ohne Tempel—Community without Temple: Zur Substituierung und Transformation des Jerusalemer Tempels und seines Kultes im Alten Testament, antiken Judentum und frühen Christentum*, WUNT 118 (Tübingen, 1999). The review of this volume by Knut Backhaus in ThRv 97 (2001): 208–11 is instructive. Backhaus points out, among other things, the continued existence of the old anti-cultic prejudices in the essay by Folker Siegert, "Die Synagoge und das unblutige Opfer" (335–56). Worth reading is the article by Backhaus, "Kult und Kreuz", in ThGl 86 (1996): 517–33, in which the author convincingly sets right the persistent prejudice about the anti-cultic character of the New Testament.

[6] Stefan Orth, "Renaissance des Archaischen? Das neuerliche theologische Interesse am Opfer", *HerKorr* 55 (2001): 195–200, citation at 198.

[7] Albert Gerhards and Klemens Richter, eds., *Das Opfer: Biblischer Anspruch und liturgische Gestalt*, QD 186 (Freiburg, 2000).

Another characteristic of the Constitution on the Liturgy must be called to mind again before we get involved in analyzing some of its main points. In every chapter the document proceeds on two different levels. On the one hand, with respect to the individual sections of liturgical reality, it develops principles that quite fundamentally and generally concern the nature of liturgy and its celebration; based on these principles, it then gives normative instructions for the practical renewal of the Roman liturgy: it goes without saying that these directives are valid, not for the Church as a whole, but only for her Latin part and hence are also more products of their time than the statements of principle. Then in the new phase of liturgical history that began with the Council, another third level is added, namely, the reforms elaborated by the "Consilium for Implementation of the Constitution on the Sacred Liturgy", the most famous of which is the new edition of the Roman Missal published by order of Pope Paul VI. These forms of liturgical renewal established by church authority are obligatory for the Church of today, but they are not simply identical with the Council as such, whose directives (which for the most part are rather broad) allow for different realizations within a common framework. Someone who does not think that everything in this reform turned out well and considers many things subject to reform or even in need of revision is not therefore an opponent of the "Council". The aim of this lecture is to listen to the Council and to learn to understand better, if possible, some of the essential directives of the document. Naturally, at the same time the text should also be, as it were, newly "contextualized", that is, read in the light of its impact in recent history and of our present situation. Because completeness is quite impossible, I would like first of all to shed some light on the fundamental vision of cult and liturgy that is found in the Constitution and then consider a few focal points of its idea of reform—concepts like intelligibility, participation, simplicity.

2. The Definition of the Nature of the Liturgy in the Conciliar Document

Therefore let us try, first of all, to take a look at the basic understanding of liturgy that is developed in the Constitution. For through the liturgy, "the work of our redemption is accomplished", the document tells us, "most of all in the divine sacrifice of the Eucharist.... [The us that an up-to-date liturgy includes both a different expression of the faith and theological changes. Moreover, according to him, there are theologians, at least in the circles of the Roman Church and of her liturgy, who have not yet grasped the full import of the transformations in the field of dogmatic theology brought about by the liturgical reform.[11] The groundbreaking study by Reinhard Messner on Martin Luther's reform of the Mass and on the Eucharist in the early Church is much more serious. Messner, who says a great deal that is worth pondering, nonetheless arrives at the conclusion that Luther understood the early Church better than the Council of Trent did.[12]

The serious nature of these theories comes from the fact that frequently they pass immediately into practice. The thesis according to which each particular community as such is the subject of the liturgy is considered authorization to manipulate the liturgy according to each individual's understanding of it. So-called new discoveries and the forms that result from them are diffused with an astonishing rapidity and with a degree of conformity that has long ceased to exist where the norms of ecclesiastical authority are concerned. In the area of the liturgy, theories are transformed very rapidly today into practice, and practice, in turn, creates or destroys ways of behaving and thinking.

Meanwhile the problem has been aggravated by the fact that the most recent movement of "enlightened" thought goes much farther than Luther: whereas Luther still took literally the accounts of the institution and made them, as the *norma normans*, the basis of his efforts at reform, the hypotheses of historical criticism have long since caused a broad erosion of the texts. The accounts of the Last Supper are seen as the product of the liturgical construction of the community; behind the texts a historical Jesus is sought who could not have been thinking of the gift of his Body and Blood or understood his Cross as a sacrifice of expiation; we should, rather, imagine a farewell meal that included an eschatological perspective.[13] Not only the authority of the ecclesiastical Magisterium is downgraded

---

[11] Thaddäus Schnitker, review of the American *Book of Prayer*, in ThRv 78 (1982): 265–72, citation at 272.

[12] Reinhard Messner, *Die Messreform Martin Luthers und die Eucharistie der Alten Kirche*, IThS 25 (Innsbruck, 1989).

[13] The debate about these questions started by Hans Lietzmann is taken up again by Messner, *Messreform*, 31f., 38–45.

liturgy"—the Council tells us—"we take part in a foretaste of that heavenly liturgy which is celebrated in the Holy City of Jerusalem. . . . With all the warriors of the heavenly army we sing a hymn of glory to the Lord" (SC 8). And finally, a fundamental idea of the Council is the reference to the Paschal Mystery: In the Pasch all of salvation history is condensed, the whole "work of redemption" is present in concentrated form. One may indeed say that "Pasch" forms the central category of the liturgical theology of the Council. All other aspects are comprised in it: Pasch is the establishment and fulfillment of the covenant; Pasch is wedding; Pasch is *transitus*—is the dynamism of passage pure and simple, from life to death and from death to life, from world to God, from the visible to the invisible, from the stations of time into the new city, into the final Jerusalem. It is therefore also a breach through the walls, the places, and the periods that try to separate heaven and earth; it is the coinciding of heavenly and earthly liturgy: in the center of the heavenly liturgy, the book of Revelation tells us, stands the Lamb who was slain—the crucifixion of Jesus that was accomplished in the midst of history and on the soil of this earth and now has become the center of heaven. The Cross of Christ has torn heaven open—it is the bridge that joins together time and eternity.

Along with these must be included another passage that is not just important but quite essential: However much the Council emphasizes the centrality of the liturgy for Christian existence and for the nature of the Church, it tells us just as decisively also that it does not exhaust the entire activity of the Church (SC 9). It must always be preceded by preaching, which leads to faith and conversion. The works of love, of piety, and of the apostolate must always follow from it (SC 9). Precisely this passage is present in the nature of the Pasch itself. For the death of Jesus Christ, the Lamb who was slain, is by its very nature nothing other than the "love to the end" (see Jn 13:1) that is described by John as the great act of "departure" (see Jn 13:1).[3] It embraces the cosmos, the places, and times of all men. Love is the power that unifies what is separated, time and eternity. The Cross, center of the heavenly liturgy, stands not only on earth, as we just said—it also stands

---

[3] John 13:1 describes the "hour of Jesus" as the hour of Jesus' "departing" out of this world to the Father. Among commentators, Ulrich Wilckens in particular has emphasized this aspect of "transcending": *Das Evangelium nach Johannes*, NTD 4 (Göttingen, 1998), 206.

particularly his understanding of the relation between the Old and the New Testaments, of historical event and present moment in the Church, was such that the category of sacrifice, as he viewed it, could not help but seem idolatrous when applied to the Eucharist and the Church. The debate reported on by Stefan Orth shows how hazy and confused the concept of sacrifice is among almost all authors and, thus, makes clear how much work must be done here. For the believing theologian, it is clear that he must learn the essential definition of sacrifice from Scripture itself, indeed, from a "canonical" reading of the Bible, in which Scripture is interpreted as a unity and a dynamic movement, the individual stages of which receive their final meaning in terms of Christ, to whom this whole movement leads.[15] In this respect, the hermeneutic presupposed here is a hermeneutic of faith, founded on faith's internal logic. But that really ought to go without saying. For without faith, Scripture itself is not Scripture but, rather, an ill-assorted collection of literature that cannot have any normative significance for today.

Of course the task alluded to here far exceeds the limits of one lecture; so allow me to refer you to my book *The Spirit of the Liturgy*, in which I have tried to sketch the main lines of this question. It becomes evident, then, that the term sacrifice, over the course of the history of religion and of biblical history, has connotations that go well beyond the area of discussion that we usually associate with the concept of sacrifice. In fact, it opens the doorway to a comprehensive understanding of worship and liturgy: Here I would like to suggest briefly this wider perspective. Hence I must omit here specific exegetical questions, in particular the fundamental problem of interpreting the accounts of the institution; on this subject I have tried to provide some notes, not only in my book on the liturgy, but also in my essay "Eucharist and Mission".[16]

There is, however, one remark that I cannot refrain from making. In the aforementioned bibliographic review, Stefan Orth says that the neglect of the term sacrifice after Vatican II has "led people to think

---

[15] Cf. *L'interpretazione della Bibbia nella Chiesa: Atti del Simposio promosso dalla Congregazione per la Dottrina della Fede* (Vatican City, 2001); Ignace de la Potterie et al., *L'esegesi cristiana oggi* (Piemme, 1991).

[16] Joseph Ratzinger, "Eucharistie und Mission", FoKTh 14 (1998): 81–98 [trans. Henry Taylor as "Eucharist and Mission", in *Pilgrim Fellowship of Faith* (San Francisco: Ignatius Press, 2005), 90–122; JRCW 11:330–54].

and that we in turn can be healers only as reconciled and reconciling believers, not out of a spirit of protest, much less of hatred, but only by participating in the love that goes to the extreme. Now this, of course, is true Christian optimism: to believe and to know that love is victorious, even and precisely when it is defeated in martyrdom.

Taking the Paschal Mystery as our standard, however, reveals to us other aspects as well. When Jesus dies as Lamb, he enters into the tradition of Israel's Pasch, interprets it anew, and precisely thereby preserves it: not one iota is lost (see Mt 5:18). The currents of the Old Testament flow together in the Christian liturgy, and it is imperative to discover anew this profound unity of Old and New Testament, the unity of all salvation history. By no means can someone understand the New Testament without the Old; similarly, neither can the Christian liturgy be understood without the path along which it developed. We must take another step farther: Israel's Pasch, as it is normatively described in Exodus 12, for all its newness, did not simply fall from the sky but, rather, gathered into itself the ways of the previous history of religion. The novelty of Christianity, like the novelty of the old covenant revelation, is above all a path of distinguishing, of purifying, and of transcending, but in its discernment of the human quest it brings the elements of truth therein to their goal. This connection of Christian worship with the history of religion is of considerable importance. In the great period of the Liturgical Movement between the two world wars, theology was characterized to a large extent by oppositions: Christianity as opposed to world religions, the New Testament as opposed to the Old, or so it seemed. "Sacrifice" was viewed as something that stands in opposition to grace and belongs to the piety of good works that is abolished by grace. And "sacrifice", in turn, was viewed as the fundamental category of the world religions, but also of Old Testament worship. Today, on the contrary, we are tempted to regard everything as being of the same kind, just expressed in diverse cultural forms, and to consider the history of religion as a series of variations on the same theme, which per se never appears in the pure state. The one view is as false as the other. Yes, sacrifice is central to world religions and, in a different way, to the Old Testament. Through the Cross, it is also central to Christianity. The path from religions to the Old Testament and from there to Christ is, as we have said, a way of transcending and distinguishing, a path of transformations and of radical renewal, but the quest in the history of religion and above all Israel's pilgrimage is not simply rejected but, rather, purified and revived.

Anchoring the liturgy in the Paschal Mystery also includes its cosmic character, which was discussed previously. The whole Church is always present in the liturgy, even that of the smallest congregation, and that is why there are no strangers in the liturgical community and no self-contained "congregation". This essential openness and universality of every liturgy is one of the reasons why the liturgy cannot be devised and fashioned by a particular congregation or its liturgists but must instead have the form approved by the universal Church. Today, in speaking about the cosmic dimension of the liturgy, we would also emphasize its reference to creation, which is mentioned only indirectly in the conciliar document. The liturgy lives on the gifts of creation, which in it become gifts of redemption. As opposed to the Gnostics, who suspected creation to be the work of the demiurge, Irenaeus quite emphatically showed how the Eucharist inseparably joins creation and redemption to each other in the gifts of bread and wine that become the Body and Blood of Christ. There is only one God, who created the gifts and who gives himself in the transformation of the gifts.[5] By facing East, the early Church expressed the anchoring of the liturgy in creation and at the same time the orientation of creation toward the new heaven and the new earth. Creation groans under the footsteps of Adam; it awaits the appearance of the children of God, Paul tells us (Rom 8:18–24). Today we literally hear the groaning of creation, and that is why it is so important for the reference to creation in the liturgy to become physically audible also. Just as in the liturgy there should be only the open faith community, so too the worship space should have nothing in common with those cement constructions that close themselves off from creation and provide their own light and air, which nonetheless can come only from the supply in the world that God created. The church building—wherever possible—should be located in the expanse of creation, show contact with it, and thus at the same time set in motion a hopeful journey toward the Lord who is to come.[6]

---

[5] Cf. *Adversus haereses* IV, 17, 4ff. (SChr 100, ed. Adelin Rousseau, 2:590ff.).

[6] On the question of orientation, the most recent appraisal and evaluation of the discussion: U. M. Lang, *Turning towards the Lord: Orientation in Liturgical Prayer* (Ignatius Press: San Francisco, 2004).

our image of God has paled and come close to deism. One can no longer imagine that human guilt could offend God, much less that it could require expiation such as the Cross of Christ.

The same is true of vicarious substitution: we can hardly imagine such a thing anymore—our image of man has become too individualistic. In this respect, the crisis of the liturgy has its basis in central notions about man that cannot be overcome by trivializing the liturgy and making it into a simple gathering or merely a fraternal meal. But how can we find a way out of these disorientations? How can we grasp again the great truth conveyed by the message of the Cross and Resurrection? Ultimately not through theories and scholarly reflections, but only through conversion, by a radical change of life. Admittedly, clarifying one's thoughts can open the way to this change of heart, and I would like to attempt this with a few suggestions in three steps.[20]

The first step should be a preliminary clarification of the essential meaning of sacrifice. Commonly sacrifice is viewed as the destruction of some reality that is valuable to man, through which he intends to hand this reality over to God and to recognize his sovereignty. But destruction does not honor God. Great public sacrifices of animals or whatever else cannot honor God. "If I were hungry, I would not tell you, for the world is mine and all that is in it is mine. Do I eat the flesh of bulls, or drink the blood of goats? Offer to God a sacrifice of thanksgiving, and pay your vows to the Most High", says God to Israel in Psalm 50[49]:12–14. Of what, then, does sacrifice consist? Not in destruction, not in these or those things, but in the transformation of man; in the fact that he himself becomes conformed to God. He becomes conformed to God when he becomes love. "There is, then, a true sacrifice in every work which unites us in a holy communion with God", as Augustine puts it.[21] With this key from the New Testament, Augustine interprets the Old Testament sacrifices as symbols pointing to this real sacrifice, and that is why, he says, worship had to be changed, the sign had to give way to the reality. "All the manifold sacrificial precepts that were given by God concerning

---

[20] The following discussion is essentially a summary of the corresponding portions of my book on the liturgy. [JRCW 11:3–150, especially 20–30].

[21] *De civitate Dei* X, 6. Cited from *The City of God*, an abridged version from the translation of Gerald G. Walsh, S.J., et al., ed. Vernon J. Bourke (New York: Image Books, 1958), 192.

dose of ambiguity. The Council speaks five times about the desirable intelligibility (*intellegere*) of the liturgy.[7] The central passage pertaining to our question manages to do without this word; we just touched on it briefly: "The rites should be distinguished by a noble simplicity. They should be short, clear, and free from useless repetitions. They should be within the people's powers of comprehension, and normally should not require much explanation" (SC 34). This article should be understood against the background of a clerical liturgy that remained, for the most part, foreign to the people, and not just because of the Latin language: the long history of its development and the complications that resulted in the processes of growth and evolution had gradually produced the estrangement evident in the parallelism between the "Mass devotions" of the faithful and the liturgy celebrated by the priest, so that the faithful were connected only in a very indirect and very inadequate way to the liturgy that was taking place on the altar in front of them. It must have been an urgent concern to unite priest and faithful again in one single, common liturgy; to reopen the glass reliquary for common adoration in a "reasonable worship service", as one could translate the words *rationale obsequium* from the Roman Canon.

This little expression takes up again the Pauline concept of λογική λατρεία (Rom 12:1). It carries within it the baggage and fruit of a long path, in which the Bible seeks and finds ever greater clarity concerning the nature of right worship; but it also took up and assimilated a path of philosophical thinking that had moved ever closer to the biblical understanding of divine worship.[8] We must try to understand in terms of this expression what intelligibility and transparency of the liturgy means and what it does not mean. It conveys, first of all, the fact that biblical faith makes a claim to rationality and, thus, to communicability. It deals with the one Creator-God, whose invisible reality can be perceived by reason in the works of creation (Rom 1:20); it is faith in the Logos, the creative reason that assumed flesh in Jesus Christ. Christian liturgy is logos-liturgy, the worship of God "in spirit and truth" (Jn 4:23). A practical orientation results from this; Paul put it this way in writing to the Corinthians: "In church I would rather

---

[7] Cf. the list in the edition [of SC] by the Istituto per le scienze religiose di Bologna (1979), 83.

[8] Treated in greater detail in my *Geist der Liturgie*, 39 [*Spirit of the Liturgy*, 45–46; JRCW 11:27–28].

who therefore ought to be filled, not dissolved, and should fit into the free act of love. Difference is not abolished but becomes the means to a higher unity.

This philosophy of freedom, which is at the basis of the Christian faith and distinguishes it from the Asiatic religions, includes the possibility of denial. Evil is not merely the decline of being but the consequence of misused freedom. The way to unity, the way of love, is then a way of conversion, a way of purification: it takes the form of the Cross; it passes through the Paschal Mystery, through death and resurrection. It needs the Mediator, who in his death and in his Resurrection becomes for us the way, draws us all to himself, and thus exalts us (Jn 12:32).

Let us review. In presenting his definition "sacrifice = love", Augustine rightly relies on a saying found in several variations in the Old and New Testaments, which he cites from Hosea (6:6): "I desire steadfast love and not sacrifice, the knowledge of God, rather than burnt offerings." [25] But this saying does not merely pit ethos against worship—that would reduce Christianity to moral philosophy. It refers to a process that is more than morality—a process in which God takes the initiative. He alone can arouse man to start out toward love. Only in being loved by God does love for him grow. This fact of being loved is a process of purification and transformation, in which we are not only opened for God but also united with one another. God's initiative has a name: Jesus Christ, the God who himself becomes man and offers himself for us. That is why Augustine can summarize all this by saying: "Such is the sacrifice of Christians: 'We, the many, are one body in Christ.' This is the sacrifice, as the faithful understand, that the Church continues to celebrate in the Sacrament of the Altar, in which it is clear to the Church that she herself is offered in the very offering she makes to God." [26] Anyone who has understood this will no longer be of the opinion that talk about the sacrifice of the Mass is at the very least extremely ambiguous, or, rather, an appalling horror. On the contrary: if we do not rediscover this, we lose the grandeur that God discloses to us in the Eucharist.

I would like to suggest very briefly two other approaches. I regard the story of the cleansing of the Temple as an important guidepost,

---

[25] *De civitate Dei* X, 5.

[26] Ibid., X, 6; Bourke ed., 194.

comprehensibility of the banal. Nor can it be brought about simply through better translations and easier-to-understand gestures. The liturgy becomes accessible only in an interior way—it demands *eruditio*, openings of the soul in which the higher dimensions of reason are unsealed and a process of learning to see and hear takes place. I am afraid that the Council Fathers actually underestimated the complexity of this "intelligibility" and also presupposed a common Christian consciousness that no longer exists. The liturgy itself cannot be turned into a religion class, and it cannot be saved by trivializing it. There is a need for liturgical formation or, rather, for spiritual formation in general; searching for the ways and forms for this should be a major task of liturgical commissions and bishops' conferences. A majority of today's Christians are *de facto* in the catechumenate state, and it is high time for us to take this fact seriously in pastoral practice.

b. Participation

With that we have arrived at the concept of participation. The statements of the conciliar Constitution on this subject are complex. First of all, the document correctly emphasizes that the faithful should enter into the liturgy "with proper dispositions". For that reason, the pastors should see to it not only that the rules of a valid and licit celebration—and thus the external forms of participation—are observed, but also that the faithful take part in the liturgy "fully aware of what they are doing, actively engaged in the rite and enriched by it" (SC 11). Here the different dimensions of participation are by all means addressed; it should not be limited to external actions but must extend into the person's interior life. What is actually the main chapter on participation, too, explicitly emphasizes the necessity of liturgical formation, guidance in internal and external participation (SC 14; 19). All of this must be kept in view when one then reads the practical rules for participation, for example, in SC 30: "To promote active participation, the people should be encouraged to take part by means of acclamation, responses, psalms, antiphons, hymns, as well as by actions, gestures and bodily attitudes. And at the proper time a reverent silence should be observed." It is a question of what my professor of liturgics, Joseph Pascher, expressed in these words: It is not enough to observe the *rubrics*—the external ceremonial directions; much more important

Stephen, to the horror of the scribes and priests of the Temple, summarized in his great discourse with several citations, notably with this verse from Amos: "Did you offer to *me* slain beasts and sacrifices, forty years in the wilderness, O house of Israel? And you took up the tent of Moloch, and the star of the god Rephan, the figures which you made to worship" (Amos 5:25, Acts 7:42). This critique was the spiritual prerequisite for Israel to survive the destruction of the Temple and the time when there was no worship. Now believers had to explain anew and in greater depth what worship, atonement, and sacrifice are. From the time of the Hellenic dictatorship, when Israel was once again without temple or sacrifice, the book of Daniel has recorded for us this prayer:

> For we, O Lord, have become fewer than any nation. . . .
> And at this time there is no prince, or prophet, or leader,
>   no burnt offering, or sacrifice, or oblation, or incense,
>   no place to make an offering before you or to find mercy.
> Yet with a contrite heart and a humble spirit may we be accepted,
>   as though it were with burnt offerings of rams and bulls,
>   and with tens of thousands of fat lambs;
>   such may our sacrifice be in your sight this day,
>   and may we wholly follow you,
>   for there will be no shame for those who trust in you.
> And now with all our heart we follow you,
>   we fear you and seek your face. (Dan 3b:*14–18* RSV-2CE)

Thus the realization slowly matured that prayer, the word, the man who prays and himself becomes word, is the true sacrifice. Here the struggle of Israel could enter into fruitful contact with the search of the Hellenic world, which likewise was looking for a way out from the worship of substitution with its animal sacrifices, so as to arrive at authentic worship, true adoration, true sacrifice. Along this path the idea of λογικὴ θυσία (*logikē thysía*) developed—the idea of sacrifice in the word—which we encounter in the New Testament in Romans 12:1, where the Apostle exhorts the faithful "to present [their] bodies as a living sacrifice, holy and acceptable to God". This is described as *logikē latreia*, as logocentric, rational worship. We find the same thing expressed somewhat differently in Hebrews 13:15. "Through him [Christ] then let us continually offer up a sacrifice of praise to God, that is, the fruit of lips that acknowledge his name."

same set of ideas as intelligibility and openness to participation. The Christian liturgy has its origin in the Cenacle, the upper room of the Last Supper, in which the Paschal Mystery of death and resurrection was anticipated and opened up to cultic re-presentation. Thus it proceeds from the simple gesture of that great hour, in which is present, of course, the drama of the crucifixion of the Son of God and of his Resurrection that transformed the world. This drama was prepared for in the history of the Pasch, a perpetual part of which is the connection between dramatic reality (Exodus; Cross and Resurrection) and cultic transformation. The simplicity of the Cenacle is overwhelmingly deep and wide; it encompasses the whole history of mankind's worship and faith in this one gesture. In the theology of the second half of the twentieth century, there was a widespread tendency to interpret Christianity as a desacralization and anti-cultic.[11] The "simplicity" of the rites was then explained along lines suggesting that it should really not have a sacred, but only a pragmatic significance. This is not the place to wash out, so to speak, the nuggets of truth in this theory, as a miner pans for gold by swirling away the dirt and stones. The theory as a whole is false. The simple act of breaking bread and giving the chalice is a truly sacred act—the reconciliation of God and the world in the love of the Son. It is true that the liturgical structure, the individual signs, actions, and words should be transparent toward this center and in doing so must bear within themselves a "noble simplicity"—the ultimate simplicity that is in accordance with and points to the simplicity of the infinite God. But it is also true that this simplicity must be explained, that eye and heart must be opened in order to perceive it. Liturgy can be celebrated with great simplicity in a village church in the adversities of persecution; it can be celebrated with great solemnity in the beauty of a cathedral. The essential thing is that the great and solemn does not become autonomous but, rather, in humble service points to the real feast: God's Yes to the world, an affirmation won for each one of us by his suffering. For this is what makes life a feast: the fact that each one can say of himself: "I live by faith in the Son of God, who loved me and gave himself for me" (Gal 2:20). In the liturgy this profession becomes presence, for me, for everyone

---

[11] On this point, cf. the excellent study by Knut Backhaus, "Kult und Kreuz", ThGl 86 (1996): 517–33.

but is, rather, the presence of Christ's Paschal Mystery, which transcends and unites all times. When the Roman Canon cites Abel, Abraham, and Melchisedech and describes them as concelebrants of the Eucharist, it does so in the conviction that in them, too, those great men offering sacrifice, Christ was passing through time, or perhaps, more precisely, that in their search they were going forth to meet Christ. The theology of the Fathers that we find in the Canon did not deny the futility and insufficiency of the pre-Christian sacrifices; along with the figures of Abel and Melchisedech, moreover, the Canon includes also the "holy pagans" in the mystery of Christ. Here is what happens: the inadequacy and shadowlike character of what went before become visible, but also the fact that Christ draws everything to himself, that there is also a preparation for the gospel in the pagan world, that even detours lead to Christ, however many cleansings they may need.

This brings me to the conclusion. Theology of the liturgy means that God acts in the liturgy through Christ and that we can act only through him and with him. Of ourselves, we cannot construct the way to God. This way opens up only if God himself becomes the way. Moreover, the ways of man that do not lead to God are blind alleys. Theology of the liturgy means, furthermore, that in the liturgy the Logos himself speaks to us; not only does he speak, he comes with his Body and Soul, Flesh and Blood, Divinity and Humanity, in order to unite us with himself, to make of us one "body". In the Christian liturgy all of salvation history, indeed, the whole history of the human search for God is present, taken up, and brought to its goal. Christian liturgy is a cosmic liturgy—it embraces the whole of creation, which "waits with eager longing for the revealing of the sons of God" (Rom 8:19). Trent was not mistaken; it stood on the firm foundation of the Church's tradition. It remains a reliable standard. But we can and must understand it in a new, more profound way, drawing on the fullness of the biblical testimony and of the faith of the Church of all times. There are signs of hope that this renewed and deeper understanding of Trent can be made accessible to Protestant Christians through the mediation of the Eastern Churches as well.[28]

---

[28] Cf. the helpful remarks of Wolfhart Pannenberg in his work *Systematische Theologie*, vol. 3 (Göttingen, 1993), 337–52 [trans. as *Systematic Theology*, vol. 3 (Grand Rapids, Mich.: Eerdmans, 1998), 305–20].

One thing should be clear: the liturgy must not be an experimental field for studying theological hypotheses. Too rapidly, in recent decades, views of experts have been put into liturgical practice, to a great extent even bypassing ecclesiastical authority, by way of committees that knew how to spread their "consensus of the day" internationally and, practically speaking, to turn it into laws for liturgical activity. The liturgy derives its greatness from what it is, not from what we do with it. Of course, it is necessary for us to do something, but only by humbly complying with the spirit of the liturgy and serving him who is the true subject of the liturgy: Jesus Christ. Liturgy is not an expression of the community's consciousness, which in any case is diffuse and changing. It is revelation received in faith and prayer, and hence its standard is the Church's faith, which is the vessel of revelation. Liturgical forms can vary according to place and time, just as the rites are diverse. The essential thing is the connection with the Church, which for her part is bound by faith in the Lord. The obedience of faith guarantees the unity of the liturgy, beyond the frontiers of place and time, and thus allows us to experience the unity of the Church, the Church as the homeland of the heart.

Finally, the essence of the liturgy is summarized in the exclamatory prayer that St. Paul (1 Cor 16:22) and the *Didache* (10:6) have handed down to us: *Maran atha*—Our Lord is here—Our Lord, come! Even now the parousia is accomplished in the Eucharist, but in this way it causes us to reach out toward the Lord who is to come; thus it teaches us to cry, "Come, Lord Jesus." And it allows us again and again to hear the answer and to experience it as true: "Surely, I am coming soon" (Rev 22:17, 20).

sense of freshness and uniqueness on each occasion. What kind of active participation can help us to do this?

Cardinal Ratzinger: Perhaps I can begin by saying something about the idea of *participatio actuosa*—"active participation"—which is indeed a key phrase in the Constitution on the Liturgy of Vatican II. What lies behind it is the awareness that Christian liturgy, of its very nature, is something performed in the context of a community. It involves prayer dialogues, greetings, proclamation, praying together. People are referred to as "we" and "you"; the "I" occurs in only a few relatively late prayers. Here we are involved in an action, a "drama", in which we all play our part. This being so, the liturgical celebration, from its very structure, calls for the interplay of words and acts between the participants. Otherwise there would arise an inner conflict between the text and what actually takes place. This was the discovery made by the Liturgical Movement, and it gave a new immediacy to the old words and gestures. At this point the Council was simply lending its authority to something that was self-evident. Generally speaking, this insight proved most fruitful. If one were to remove the active involvement that exists in today's liturgy—and the Council facilitated this involvement—it would immediately be obvious how much growth there has been. No one would want to be without it. But it is always possible for any true insight to be diminished, interpreted one-sidedly, or distorted. Many protagonists of liturgical reform seemed to think that if we only did everything together and in a loud voice, the liturgy would automatically become attractive and effective. They forgot that the spoken words also have a *meaning*, and part *of participatio actuosa* is to carry out that meaning. They failed to notice that the *actio* consists not only or primarily in the alternation of standing, sitting, and kneeling, but in inner processes. It is these that give rise to the whole drama of the liturgy. "Let us pray"—this is an invitation to share in a movement that reaches down into our inner depths. "Lift up your hearts"—this phrase and the movement that accompanies it are, so to speak, only the "tip of the iceberg". The real action takes place in the deep places of men's hearts, which are lifted up to the heights. "Behold the Lamb of God"—here we have an invitation to a special kind of beholding, at a much deeper level than the external beholding of the Host. Where this inner dimension was neglected, the liturgy still seemed "boring" and "unintelligible", with the result that ultimately the Bible was replaced number of roots, about which Father Koster spoke to us very well; I should like to emphasize that it seems to me that the great Benedictine monasteries—Beuron most of all—were the true birthplace of the authentic Liturgical Movement. Beuron, a daughter-house of Solesmes, because the two Wolter brothers had been trained in the Benedictine life at Solesmes and had founded the Benedictine renewal first of all at Beuron and, then, at Maria Laach, a daughter-house of Beuron, and in the other abbeys. It is interesting to read, in the *Memoirs* of Guardini, that he himself had discovered the liturgy while taking part in the canonical hours at Beuron, sharing in the liturgical life experienced in the spirit of Solesmes, thus in the spirit of the Fathers, and how for him this was the discovery of a new world, of liturgy proper, which, it seems to me, offers a key to understanding what the fathers of this Movement were thinking in Germany—even if Father Anselm Schott did have a different idea, as likewise Father Odo Casel, and so on. It was in fact the discovery of the liturgy as a symbolical world filled with reality, full of meaning. In the context, on the one hand, of Neoscholastic theology, which was for the most part pretty dry, and, on the other, of rationalism and modernism—Guardini studied at Tübingen, at a time when modernism was rampant there—this movement offered a new vision of Christian reality on the basis of the liturgy.

For a certain kind of textbook theology, what mattered in the sacraments, and likewise in the Eucharist, was essentially their validity and, therefore, the moment of Consecration. Eucharistic theology had been reduced to an ontological and juridical problem, everything else being considered as beautiful ceremonies, interesting, and capable or incapable of interpretation in an allegorical sense, but not as the reality in which the Eucharist has its concrete existence. It was thus necessary to discover anew that the liturgy is not just a collection of ceremonies that aim to give length and solemnity to the Consecration, but that this is the world of the sacrament as such. This was a new vision, and in that sense they went beyond a narrow kind of theology and discovered a more profound vision, not only of theology, but of the whole Christian life. We can grasp the stature of the Liturgical Movement only in the historical context of an understanding of the liturgy that was severely lacking. For example, from the time of Leo XIII on, we used to recite the Rosary during Mass all through October—and that was still the custom when I was young.

you further: Is the Mass about the Real Presence of him who died on the Cross and was raised, or is it about symbols that speak of this mystery and are maybe surrogates for it? Moreover, do the ideas of transsignification and transfinalization do away with the doctrine of transubstantiation? The theologian cannot have it both ways. What are the realities involved? Is it the faith of the believers that causes the host to become the Body and Blood of Christ? Or does it become so only by being eaten—the *ut sumatur* of St. Thomas? And if we assume that such a view of the Eucharist has a place within the Church, do we need a priest with the power to consecrate? Cannot a faithful layman do it just as well? And what about the Consecration rite? Does it not detract from the mystery, does it not destroy the symbolism and open the door to ideas of magic and miracle? Such questions are not new to you. Where the sacrificial character of the Mass is concerned, it is all too easy to ask pointed questions. In 1966 Paul VI, in his encyclical *Mysterium Fidei*, still saw the sacrificial element as the core of the eucharistic mystery. The same applies to the eucharistic cult. All the questions I have touched on are in a state of flux. No doubt the theologians will say that the Real Presence and transubstantiation are quite safe; they are simply bearing a different emphasis. I am saying that they are being *differently interpreted*. Again, I am not so much concerned with the rights and wrongs of all these questions. The issue before us is "Change and Permanence in Liturgy" with reference to the celebration of the Eucharist. On the basis of the facts, we cannot exclude the possibility—without changing the premise that in and through the Mass the faithful serve and worship God, which is always true, of course—that there has been a greater change in the understanding of the Eucharist than its nature, the understanding of its origins, and the received faith of the Church permit.

Cardinal Ratzinger: The very many questions you have raised on this fourth point are so deeply involved with central dogmatic issues that it would be impossible to take them up within the space of this interview. One would need to undertake a substantial piece of catechesis. Here, a few remarks will have to suffice. I will begin with a single detail that has wider implications. The *ut sumatur* ("so that it may be consumed") that you quoted comes in fact from the Council of Trent (DS 1643); Karl Rahner pointed out that it is to be found there, in the chapter that concerns eucharistic adoration and Corpus Christi.

who was a university professor, rationalist but orthodox—of the kind that existed in the German universities at that time—a liturgical rigorist, and a director of *Caritas*, representing popular piety, especially keen on the Sacred Heart; in this *trialogue*, he was looking for a synthesis, and that still remains to be found.

It seems to me that as early as the 1950s, and certainly after the Council, the latent and, likewise, the patent risks in the Liturgical Movement constituted a great temptation, a serious danger for the Church. After the Council there was a new situation, because the liturgists had acquired a *de facto* authority: the authority of the Church was being recognized less and less, and now the expert became the authority. This transfer of authority to the experts transformed everything, and these experts in turn were the victims of an exegesis profoundly influenced by the opinions of Protestantism, that is to say, that the New Testament was against the category of sacredness, against cult and priesthood, and thus at the opposite pole to the great tradition, above all that of the Council of Trent. The view was maintained that the New Testament was against the cult because it separated itself from the Old Testament, from the Temple. The cult was now, they said, reality as it was lived, as it was suffered by Christ, who was crucified outside the walls of the city. That meant that now we should see the true cult in the realm of the *profane* and that the break with the levitical priesthood should be seen as a break with the sacral priesthood as such: the presbyterate, it was said, was not a sacral priesthood; sacral priesthood was something belonging to the Old Testament, or to paganism, not something belonging to Christianity. This interpretation of the New Testament by a point of view—a hermeneutic system—that was fundamentally Protestant and secularizing has become even stronger with the passage of time.

Finally, it seems to me that the transition from the universal Church to the local Church, and from the local Church to the local congregation—as Professor de Mattei told us—has been, and at present still is, one of our greatest difficulties. People say nowadays that the liturgy reflects the religious experience of the congregation and that the congregation is the only real agent in the liturgy; that leads in fact not only in the direction of a complete fragmentation of the liturgy but toward the destruction of the liturgy as such, for if the liturgy merely reflects the religious experience of the congregation, it no longer involves the presence of the mystery. This is therefore and deepened in many ways in the mystery of Jesus Christ: here the sacrifice itself comes from the incarnate love of God, so that it is God *who gives himself*, taking man up into his action and enabling him to be both gift and recipient. Perhaps I can illustrate what I mean here by taking up another small detail: you raised the question "Do we need a priest with the power to consecrate?" I would prefer not to speak of "power", although this term has been used since the early Middle Ages. I think it is better to approach it from another angle. In order that what happened *then* may become present *now*, the words "This is my body—this is my blood" must be said. But the speaker of these words is the "I" of Jesus Christ. Only he can say them; they are *his* words. No man can dare to take to himself the "I" and "my" of Jesus Christ—and yet the words must be said if the saving mystery is not to remain something in the distant past. So authority to pronounce them is needed, an authority that no one can assume and that no congregation, or even many congregations together, can confer. Only Jesus Christ himself, in the "sacramental" form he has committed to the whole Church, can give this authority. The word must be located, as it were, in sacrament; it must be part of the "sacrament" of the Church, partaking of an authority that she does not create, but only transmits. This is what is meant by "ordination" and "priesthood". Once this is understood, it becomes clear that, in the Church's Eucharist, something is happening that goes far beyond any human celebration, any human joint activity, and any liturgical efforts on the part of a particular community. What is taking place is the mystery of God, communicated to us by Jesus Christ through his death and Resurrection. This is what makes the Eucharist irreplaceable; this is the guarantee of its identity. The reform has not altered it: its aim was simply to shed new light upon it.

which remains the same as ever. The preface of Paul VI's Missal says explicitly that it is a Missal of the same Church and acknowledges its continuity. And in order to emphasize that there is no essential break, that there is continuity in the Church, which retains its identity, it seems to me indispensable to continue to offer the opportunity to celebrate according to the old Missal, as a sign of the enduring identity of the Church. This is for me the basic reason: what was until 1969 *the* liturgy of the Church, the most sacred thing for all of us, cannot become after 1969—with an incredible positivism—the most unacceptable thing. If we want to be credible, even with this slogan of modernity, we absolutely must recognize that what was fundamental before 1969 remains fundamental afterward: the realm of the sacral is the same, the liturgy is the same.

Observing the developments in how the new Missal was applied, I very quickly found a second reason, one which Professor Spaemann has also mentioned: the old Missal is a point of reference, a criterion—as he said, a semaphore signal. It seems to me most important for everyone that by its presence—which is a sign of the basic identity of the two Missals, even though they have differing modes of expression in ritual—this Missal of the Church should offer a point of reference and should become a refuge for those faithful who, in their own parish, no longer find a liturgy genuinely celebrated in accordance with the texts authorized by the Church. There is no doubt, on the one hand, that a venerable rite such as the Roman rite in use up to 1969 is a rite of the Church, a possession the Church, a treasure of the Church, and ought therefore to be preserved in the Church.

One problem, on the other hand, does remain: How are we to regulate the use of the two rites? To me it seems clear that, in law, the Missal of Paul VI is the Missal in current use and that using it is normal. We should therefore consider how to permit the use of the old Missal, and to preserve this treasure for the Church. I have often spoken along the same lines as our friend Professor Spaemann: If there used to be the Dominican rite, if there used to be—and, in fact, there still is—the Milanese rite, then why not likewise the rite, shall we say, "of St. Pius V"? Yet there is a very real problem here: if the *ecclesial community* becomes a matter of free choice, if there are, within the Church, ritual churches, chosen according to subjective criteria, that does create a problem. The Church is built on the bishops, in keeping with apostolic succession, in the form of local Churches, therefore with of John: Jesus wanted to die for the nation, and not only for the nation but "to gather into one the children of God who are scattered abroad" (Jn 11:52). The assembly to which Jesus Christ calls us is the assembly of all the children of God. The Lord does not assemble the parish community in order to enclose it but in order to open it up. The man who allows himself to be "assembled" by the Lord has plunged into a river that will always be taking him beyond the limits of his self at any one time. To be with the Lord means to be willing, with him, to seek all the children of God. It is a favorite theme of our time that the Church is "wherever two or three are gathered in my name", but the reverse is also true: the community is only "with the Lord" and "gathered in his name" provided it is entirely at one with the Church, wholly part of the whole. That is why, however much it lives in the here and now, in a particular place, seeking the consent of the local community, Christian liturgy is essentially Catholic, that is, it proceeds from the whole and leads back to it; it leads to unity with the pope, the bishops, and the faithful of all times and places. The Catholic element is not something added on externally, a legislative restriction of the community's freedom, but something from the Lord himself who seeks everyone and seeks to bring them all together. Liturgy is not "made" by the community; the community receives it from the whole, in the same way that it receives its own self, as community, from the whole. And it can only remain an ecclesial community by continually giving itself back in commitment to this whole. Two things are of immediate practical importance here: 1. The forms that are binding upon the whole Church, in which the whole Church shares, are not a kind of spoon-feeding of the local community; they are an expression of the authenticity and greatness of the liturgy. 2. Eucharist must never be allowed to be used to bolster up a community's self-affirmation or self-enclosure. Its genuineness and rightness are vindicated in those situations where not every erstwhile "parish community" can have its own priest and its own parish worship. Then we can see whether we are only looking for the Eucharist in our own community as a means of self-affirmation and togetherness or whether we are willing to be found by the Lord who opens us out and leads us beyond frontiers. Where parishes are opened up to one another, are received by one another, they are learning in a small way what catholicity means, namely, not priding oneself on one's own traditions but seeing, in the opening of the frontiers, a liberation into that great and wide realm for which the deepest yearnings of our souls are waiting.

There is something else: the Council reminded us most explicitly that the liturgy is, in the Church's language, *actio*, an action. Therefore it implies the *participatio actuosa*, the active participation of all the faithful. But here again the impression has been given, to a greater or lesser extent, that, if the liturgy is to be the work of the community, it must also be created by it; and, putting it crudely, this led to its being measured by its entertainment value. The idea was to make it as exciting as possible, shaking up the standoffish, the fringe members, and drawing them into community; but, strangely, what happened was that, as a result of all this, the liturgy actually lost its authentic inner vibrancy. For this does not arise from what *we* do but from the fact that something is being done here that all our concerted efforts cannot achieve. What has created the liturgy's special position, down the centuries, is the fact that in it a supreme authority is operative, an authority that no one can arrogate to himself. In the liturgy the absolutely Other takes place, the absolutely Other comes among us. In his commentary on the Song of Songs, that primally and profoundly human poem on the yearning and the tragic quality of love, Gregory of Nyssa describes man as the creature who wants to break out of the prison of finitude, out of the closed confines of his ego and of this entire world. And it is true: this world is too small for man, even if he can fly to the Moon or one day perhaps to Mars. He yearns for the Other, the totally Other, that which is beyond his own reach. Behind this is the longing to conquer death. In all their celebrations, men have always searched for that life which is greater than death. Man's appetite for joy, the ultimate quest for which he wanders restlessly from place to place, only makes sense if it can face the question of death. Eucharist means that the Lord's Resurrection gives us this joy which no one else can. So it is not enough to describe the Eucharist as the community meal. It cost the Lord his life, and only at this price can we enjoy the gift of the Resurrection. Therefore the Eucharist does not stand or fall by its effect on our feelings. Feelings come to an end, and ultimately all entertainment becomes tedious—as we know only too well nowadays. What we need is the presence in our lives of what is real and permanent so that we can approach it. No external participation and creativity is of any use unless it is a participation in this inner reality, in

Creator, of the Redeemer, and of the Holy Spirit". That is just one example to show the seriousness of the problem, and there is the insistence of some bishops (not of the bishops' conference as such) on using what they call "real language"—according to them, the other kind is no longer real language. The use of inclusive language involves the disappearance of essential things, such as, for example, in the Psalms, the whole christological dimension, because masculine words are forbidden. Thus the problem of translations is a serious one. There is a new document from the Holy See on this problem that constitutes, it seems to me, genuine progress. [Cf. Congregation for Divine Worship and the Discipline of the Sacraments, *Liturgicam Authenticam*, March 28, 2001.] I would just add this: we ought also to preserve some elements of Latin in the liturgy in ordinary use; the presence of a certain amount of Latin seems to me important, as constituting a bond of ecclesial fellowship and communion.

The third problem is the celebration *versus populum*. As I have written in my books, I think that celebration turned toward the east, toward the Christ who is coming, is an apostolic tradition. I am not however in favor of forever changing churches around completely; so many churches have now been restructured that starting all over again right now does not seem to me a good idea at all. But if there were always, on every altar, a cross, a quite visible cross, as a point of reference for *everyone*, for the priest and for the faithful, then we would have our east, because in the end the Crucified Christ is the Christian east; and we could, it seems to me, without any violence do as follows: we could offer the Crucified One, the Cross, as a point of reference and, thus, give the liturgy a new orientation. I think this is not a purely exterior thing: if the liturgy is celebrated within a closed circle, if there is only the dialogue between priest and people, then that is a false clericalization and an absence of a common path toward the Lord, toward whom we all turn. Thus, having the Lord as a point of reference for everyone, priest and people, seems to me something important that can perfectly well be put into practice.

4. The Future of the Missal of St. Pius V

I know very well the sensibilities of those faithful who love this liturgy— these are, to some extent, my own sensibilities. And in that sense, I center of our worshipping life, but in order to be this center, it must have a many-layered whole in which to live. Eucharist presupposes Baptism; it presupposes continual recourse to the Sacrament of Penance. The Holy Father has emphasized this most strongly in his encyclical *Redemptor Hominis.* The first element of the Good News, he stresses, was "Repent!" "The Christ who invites us to the eucharistic meal is always the same Christ who exhorts us to penance, continually saying 'Repent!'" (IV, 20). Where penance disappears, the Eucharist is no longer discerned and, as the Lord's Eucharist, is destroyed. But Eucharist also presupposes marriage and ordination, the social and the public structure of the Church. It presupposes personal prayer, family prayer, and the paraliturgical prayer of the parish community. I would just like to mention two of the richest and deepest prayers of Christendom, prayers that are able to draw us again and again into the vast river of eucharistic prayer: the Stations of the Cross and the Rosary. One of the reasons why, nowadays, we are so discountenanced by the appeal of Asiatic or apparently Asiatic religious practices is that we have forgotten these forms of prayer. The Rosary does not call for intense conscious efforts that would render it impossible but invites us to enter into the rhythm of quiet, peaceably bringing us peace and giving a name to this quietness: Jesus, the blessed fruit of the womb of Mary. Mary, who cherished the living Word in the recollected quiet of her heart and thus was privileged to become the Mother of the incarnate Word, is the abiding pattern for all genuine worship, the Star that illuminates even a dark heaven and shows us the way. May she, the Mother of the Church, intercede for us so that we may be enabled to fulfill more and more the Church's highest task: the glorification of the living God, from whom comes mankind's salvation. Amen.

ordain women, this was an exercise in obedience toward the great tradition of the Church and toward the Holy Spirit. For me, it is always most interesting to see the keenest progressives and the fiercest opponents of the Church's Magisterium saying to us, "Why, no, of course the Church can perfectly well do that! You ought to make use of the powers you have available!"—No, the Church cannot do everything, the pope cannot do everything. It seems to me that, toward an authority that in the present situation is becoming more than ever a conscious exercise in obedience, everyone can have, *must* have such confidence.

To speak in more concrete terms, I am not going to do anything in this sphere for the moment—that is clear. But, for the future, we ought to think—it seems to me—in terms of enriching the Missal of 1962 by introducing some new saints; there are now some important figures among the saints—I am thinking, for example, of Maximilian Kolbe, Edith Stein, the martyrs of Spain, the martyrs of Ukraine, and so many others—but I am also thinking of that little Bakhita in the Sudan, who came from slavery and came to freedom in her faith in the Lord; there are many really lovely figures whom we all *need*. Thus, opening up the calendar of the old Missal to new saints, making a well thought-out choice of these, that seems to me something that would be appropriate at present and would not have any destructive effect on the fabric of the liturgy. We might also think about the Prefaces, which also come from the storehouse of wealth in the Church Fathers, for Advent, for example, and then others; why not insert those Prefaces into the old Missal?

Thus, with great sensitivity and by showing a great deal of understanding for people's fears and preoccupations, maintaining contact with their leaders, we should be able to understand that this Missal is also a Missal *of the Church* and under the authority of the Church, that it is not an object preserved from the past, but a living reality within the Church, *very much* respected in its particular identity and for its historical stature, but also considered as something that is living and not as a dead thing, a relic of the past. The whole liturgy of the Church is always a living thing, a reality that is found above us and is not subject to our decisions and our arbitrary intentions. Those are the few remarks that I wanted to make.

to us as a communitarian action of the Church and snatch it away from the arbitrariness of the pastors or their liturgy committees.

We cannot "make" such a new liturgical movement, just as we generally cannot "make" a living thing, but we can foster its rise by striving personally to assimilate anew the spirit of the liturgy and also by publicly advocating what we receive in this way. A fresh start of this sort needs "Fathers" who are an example and show the way not only with their words. Anyone who looks today for such "Fathers" will inevitably come across the figure of Msgr. Klaus Gamber, who unfortunately has now been taken from us too soon; yet perhaps through his departure he is only now becoming fully present as a mighty pioneer. He has gone from our midst, but precisely thereby he is removed from partisan squabbles, and so in this hour of need he could become the "Father" of a new beginning. Gamber shared the enthusiasm and hope of the old Liturgical Movement wholeheartedly. Most likely because he came from a foreign school, on the German scene he remained an outsider who was not really taken seriously; even quite recently a dissertation met with considerable difficulty because the young scholar had dared to cite Gamber too extensively and favorably. But perhaps this outsider status, too, was providential, because it automatically forced Gamber to follow a path of his own and relieved him of the pressure to conform. It is hard to state in a few words what is really decisive and characteristic in the debate of the liturgists. The following reference may be helpful. Josef Andreas Jungmann, one of the really great liturgists of our [twentieth] century, had in his day characterized the Western understanding of liturgy, as it appeared above all through historical research, as "developed liturgy", probably also in contrast to an oriental concept that sees in the liturgy, not its historical becoming and growing, but simply the reflected splendor of the eternal liturgy, whose light shines through the sacred action into our changing time in unchanging beauty and greatness. Both concepts are right in their own way, and ultimately they are not irreconcilable. What happened to a great extent after the Council has quite a different significance: instead of the developed liturgy, some have set up their self-made liturgy. They have stepped out of the living process of growing and becoming and gone over to making. They no longer wanted to continue the organic *becoming* and *maturing* of something that had been alive down through the centuries, and instead they replaced it—according to the model of technical production—with facing east: this theme does not appear until the second chapter of part 2 and occupies only a small portion of the whole volume: pages 72–84 [in the English edition],* which is thirteen pages out of a 232-page book. Again and again I have been amazed that many reviewers have discussed those thirteen pages exclusively, as if the book consisted of them alone. Everything else seemed not to interest them, while you, thank God, have certainly paid attention to the other parts. Given the one-sided emphasis of many reviewers, I had even considered omitting that chapter from the book entirely in a new edition so as to provide an unobstructed view of its other contents. My starting point is not the *orient-ation* of prayer (prayer facing east) but, rather, the question about what "cult" or "liturgy" really is—what happens in it and what kind of reality it is. This question must be approached anthropologically and historically. We must ask: Why did "cult" come to be? What did people intend to accomplish by it? And what importance can this have today? For a Christian theology, however, this general anthropological question should be posed specifically, above all in terms of the Bible and its contents. Thus I have tried to find an answer to these fundamental questions and—without losing sight of the general anthropological interest—thereby, above all, to highlight the specific character of the concrete form that the liturgy assumed along the way from the Old to the New Testament. Allow me to refer to the summary of my findings in part 1 on pages 48–50.**

The question about the orientation of prayer is, in contrast, a question of detail, certainly an important one, because by it the interior direction of prayer and of a Logocentric understanding of the liturgy assumes a communitarian form. Praise God, the debate about this problem, which used to be conducted in a very ideological way, has become more objective in recent years. Allow me to refer you on this point to the article by Albert Gerhards, a liturgical scholar at the University of Bonn, in the *Theologische Revue* 98 (2002): 15–22; it is anticipated that a small book by Uwe Michael Lang, a young Oratorian living in England, will be published by Johannes Verlag (Freiburg-Einsiedeln) this autumn, probably with the title *Conversi ad Dominum*; the book summarizes the whole state of the question with

---

*JRCW 11:44–51.
**JRCW 11:29–30.

DISCUSSION OF *The Spirit of the Liturgy*

power of inspiration. The artists who take this task upon themselves need not regard themselves as the rearguard of culture."* I am not calling for a return to the past but, rather, for the great fundamental laws of the basic form of liturgical art to be taken as the standard. In the liturgy—as also in other areas of artistic life and even more so—the masterworks of the past still retain their place (who would ever wish, for example, to consider Bach as passé and no longer suited to our time?). Yet at the same time they are inspirations that do not stand in the way of what is new but, actually, call it forth.

As for point 3 in your letter, both the "question" and the "critique" essentially refer again to the question about the orientation of prayer to the east, and once again I refer you to the literature mentioned above.

Finally, as far as your "regret" is concerned, I think that I have presented the transition from the early Jewish-Christian communities to the developing Church in Rome in a manner that is much more differentiated than you insinuate with the reference to page 77 of my book. The statement in question is a summary that takes up and presupposes the previous individual points; the formula "cela va sans dire" [it goes without saying] finds its foundation in the previous exposition. I do not deny that the particulars of the process were complicated and that developments took place. But the scholarly literature, as far as I am acquainted with it, still confirmed my statement about the essential line of continuity, despite all the variations.

It is clear that 1 Corinthians 11 presupposes a community meal as the framework for the Eucharist, and I do not deny that. But the criticism of the conduct during the meal in verses 17–22 and the resulting advice in verse 34 show that Paul already saw this as an occasion for a separation of the two, which then did take place very quickly. I hoped that I had described that process in its totality, that is, as a gradual formation of the Eucharist in the apostolic and early post-apostolic Church, and that in doing so I had made clear to some extent

---

*"Wer aufmerksam zusieht, wird wahrnehmen, dass gerade auch in unserer Zeit aus den Inspirationen des Glaubens heraus bedeutende Kunstwerke sowohl im Bereich des Bildes wie im Bereich der Musik (und im Bereich der Literatur) entstanden sind und entstehen. Auch heute ist die Freude an Gott und die Berührung mit seiner Gegenwart in der Liturgie eine unerschöpfliche Macht der Inspiration. Die Künstler, die sich diesem Auftrag unterwerfen, brauchen sich wahrhaftig nicht als Nachhut der Kultur zu verstehen [...]." This quote appears on page 126 of the original German edition, *Einführung in den Geist der Liturgie.*—Trans. See JRCW 11:97.

that what determines the form of the Eucharist is not the paschal meal but, rather, the new feature added by the Lord—namely, the prayer of blessing and the gifts that were made "Word-like" by it and through it. . . . The form of the Eucharist, which has been the subject of long debates since the 1920s, cannot, after all, be deduced from a single point but, rather, belongs to the gradual process by which the Church herself took shape. It assumes the context of a living development and also presupposes the living Church as its responsible subject. I have attempted to say a few things about this in my book *Das Fest des Glaubens* (1981; English edition: *The Feast of Faith* [1986]).

The strong emotion experienced by the faithful at the coming of the Lord in the Eucharist is by no means a mechanical reaction—as is stated quite clearly in the sentence that you yourself quote in the last paragraph of your letter. I must vigorously deny that the words "ceux qui participant à l'Eucharistie dans la foi et dans la prière" are merely "une piteuse tentative de vous dédouaner" [a pitiful attempt to justify yourself]. The text in German [or English] is much clearer: "The moment [that is, the Consecration] cannot fail to stun, to the very core of their being, those who participate in the Eucharist by faith and prayer." It is inconceivable to me, frankly, how you could arrive at the opinion that I had maintained that there is a mechanical effect here. The indispensable involvement of the person and the necessity of interior participation is precisely the theme of this paragraph. I was afraid of having said too much about that for Protestant ears rather than too little.

In conclusion, I would like to thank you again for giving me the opportunity to engage in such an exchange of ideas regarding my book on the liturgy, and from my heart I wish you a blessed Easter and all the best in your theological work.

that signifies his oneness with the divine will—a union, the dramatic character of which is shown to us in the Garden of Gethsemane.[3] Thus the passive dimension of being put to death is transformed into the active dimension of love: death becomes the abandonment of himself to the Father for men. In this way, the horizon again extends, as it does in the Resurrection, far beyond the purely human aspect and far beyond the one-time fact of being nailed to a cross and dying. This surplus with respect to the mere historical event is what the language of faith calls a "mystery", and in the term "Paschal Mystery" it has summarized the real core of the redemptive event. If we can say accordingly that the "Paschal Mystery" constitutes the core of "the work of Jesus", then the connection with the liturgy is immediately evident: precisely this "work of Jesus" is the real content of the liturgy. In it, the "work of Jesus", through the faith and the prayer of the Church, continually penetrates history. Thus, in the liturgy, the present historical moment is transcended, leading into the permanent divine-human act of redemption. In it, Christ is really the responsible subject: it is the work of Christ; but in it he draws history to himself, into this permanent act which is the locus of our salvation.

If we go back to Vatican II, we find these connections described as follows: "In the liturgy, through which, especially in the divine Sacrifice of the Eucharist, 'the work of our Redemption is carried on,' the faithful are most fully led to express and show to others the mystery of Christ and the real nature of the true Church."[4]

2. The Current Debate about the Problem of Sacrifice

All this has become foreign to modern thinking and, only thirty years after the Council, has been questioned even among Catholic liturgists. Who still talks today about "the divine Sacrifice of the Eucharist"? Discussions about the concept of sacrifice have again become astonishingly lively, on the Catholic side as well as on the Protestant. People realize that an idea that under various forms has always preoccupied not only the history of the Church but the entire history of mankind must express something basic that concerns us as well. Yet at

---

[3] Cf. François-Marie Léthel, *Théologie de l'agonie du Christ* (Paris, 1979).
[4] SC 2; CCC 1068.

create common ground and to determine the direction of the path ahead. Naturally, this connection between the ways in which the sense of faith has matured and conciliar authority also causes the statements of a council to bear the stamp of a particular time, and that is once again very clearly evident in the councils of all periods of Church history: they do not formulate timeless words—not even Sacred Scripture does that, incidentally—but, rather, they condense and form what developed over time so that the words of a particular time open up a view that extends beyond time and thus express something permanently valid.[1]

The Constitution on the Sacred Liturgy gathered up the various brooks and streams of the Liturgical Movement and united them into one river that "makes glad the city of God" (Ps 46[45]:4). But of course backwaters, so to speak, remained, too, which could not enter into the river, and in the river itself the different streams that are united in it can still be recognized. One can still tell, so to speak, where the waters had their sources. Thus inner tensions remained also, which we will have to discuss: tensions between the desire to renew the liturgy of the early Church again in its originality and the need to settle the liturgy in the present; tensions between the conservative and the creative elements; tensions between the worship character of the liturgy and its catechetical and pastoral functions. These are of course tensions that ultimately are rooted in the nature of the liturgy itself and do not reflect merely different currents of the liturgy. The Council, in an impressive way, attempted to produce the right inner equilibrium among these different aspects, but in the implementation of the conciliar mandate it was easy for the balance of the conciliar document to be disrupted one-sidedly in a specific direction; that is why referring back to the actual words of the Council is always necessary. The casualness with which almost everyone simply claims "the Council" as the authority for his own wishes of the moment falsifies the great mandate that the assembly of the Council Fathers left behind.

---

[1] On the history of the Liturgical Movement, its relation to the Council, as well as its progress after the Council, there is an abundance of literature that does not have to be itemized here. An excellent summary of the perspectives beforehand and afterward is offered by Andreas Heinz, "Liturgiewissenschaftliche Forschung und liturgisches Leben der Pfarreien" in *Comment faire de la théologie aujourd'hui? Continuité et renouveau*, ed. Otto Hermann Pesch and Jean-Marie van Cangh, Académie Internationale des Sciences Religieuses, Session de Bose, 2002 (Paris, 2003), 279–89.

which analyzes the idea of sacrifice in detail. His diagnosis remains dismaying. Is it true? I do not know these numerous Catholics who consider it a damnable idolatry to understand the Eucharist as a sacrifice. The second, more circumspect diagnosis according to which the sacrifice of the Mass is open to misunderstandings is, on the other hand, easily shown to be correct. Even if one leaves to one side the first affirmation of the writer as a rhetorical exaggeration, there remains a troubling problem to which we should face up. A sizeable party of Catholic liturgists seems to have arrived in practice at the conclusion that Luther, rather than Trent, was substantially right in the sixteenth-century debate; one can detect much the same position in the post-conciliar discussions on the priesthood. The great historian of the Council of Trent, Hubert Jedin, pointed this out in 1975, in the preface to the last volume of his history of the Council of Trent: "The attentive reader . . . in reading this will not be less dismayed than the author when he realizes that many of the things—in fact, almost everything—that disturbed the men of the past is being put forward anew today." [8] Only against this background of the effective denial of the authority of Trent can one understand the bitterness of the struggle against allowing the celebration of Mass according to the 1962 Missal after the liturgical reform. The possibility of so celebrating constitutes the strongest and thus (for them) the most intolerable contradiction of the opinion of those who believe that the faith in the Eucharist formulated by Trent has lost its validity.

It would be easy to gather proofs to support this statement of the position. I leave aside the extreme liturgical theology of Harald Schützeichel, who departs completely from Catholic dogma and expounds, for example, the bold assertion that the idea of the Real Presence was not invented until the Middle Ages.[9] A modern liturgist such as David N. Power tells us that through the course of history, not only the manner in which a truth is expressed, but also the content of what is expressed can lose its meaning.[10] He links his theory in concrete terms with the statements of Trent. Thaddäus Schnitker tells

---

[8] Hubert Jedin, *Geschichte des Konzils von Trient*, vol. 4, pt. 1 (Freiburg: Herder, 1975), vi–vii.

[9] Harald Schützeichel, *Die Feier des Gottesdienstes: Eine Einführung* (Düsseldorf, 1996).

[10] David N. Power, *The Sacrifice We Offer: The Tridentine Dogma and Its Reinterpretation* (New York, 1987), 141ff.; on 120–28 the concept of atoning sacrifice is disputed, along with Christ's self-sacrifice in the Eucharist.

liturgy] is the outstanding means whereby the faithful may express in their lives, and manifest to others, the mystery of Christ and the real nature of the true Church." Because the liturgy is the accomplishment of redemption, it communicates to people this redemptive dynamic—from the visible to the invisible, from activity to contemplation, from the present to the future city we seek (see SC 2). In Origen's works there is a beautiful saying: "For everything must be passed through."[2] One should not stay definitively with any good thing until he has arrived at that good with which he may stay forever. Although in Goethe's *Faust* the desire "But stay, you are so beautiful" appears as temptation pure and simple, that wish contains and keeps alive a last remnant of knowledge of the dynamism of human existence about which the Fathers speak. The liturgy—so the Council shows us—leads us into this dynamism of transcendence that Augustine in his theology of the *sursum corda* [lift up your hearts] tried again and again in his sermons to bring home to the listeners. Liturgy tears us away from the visible, the present, the comfortable—and directs us toward the future city.

In order to describe the nature of liturgy positively, the Council cannot be content with one concept; it sets before us some of the great fundamental ideas of the biblical tradition, an overview of which should bring close to us that which transcends all our concepts. Here is the motif of the Church as bride—liturgy is the fulfillment of the bridal mystery between Christ and Church; it is a nuptial event, the coming of the Bridegroom and a movement toward the eternal celebration of God's love for his creature, man. It is a covenant event that, indeed, ultimately points in the same direction, yet makes other aspects clear, if we have before our eyes Sinai as the great model of covenant making and keep in mind the fact that Jesus' words at the Last Supper incorporate the Sinai tradition and continue it along the lines of the promise in Jeremiah 31 toward the definitive form of the covenant. Furthermore, knowledge about the cosmic, heaven-and-earth-embracing character of the liturgy is emphasized; in the liturgical tradition this is expressed in a way that is practically audible for the faithful at the conclusion of the Preface and in the *Sanctus* as participation in the Trisagion of the Seraphim: "In the earthly

---

[2] Origen, "Homily XXVII on Numbers", no. 12 (at Num 33:34), in *Origen*, trans. Rowan A. Greer (New York: Paulist Press, 1979), 265.

in the eyes of many, but Scripture, too; in its place are put changing pseudo-historical hypotheses, which then basically make room for any arbitrary practice and put the liturgy at the mercy of fashion. When, on the basis of such ideas, the liturgy is manipulated ever more freely, the faithful sense that, in reality, nothing is celebrated, and they understandably desert the liturgy and, with it, the Church.

Let us return to the fundamental question: Is it correct to describe the liturgy as a divine sacrifice, or is it damnable idolatry? In this discussion, one must first of all establish the basic presuppositions that, in any event, determine one's reading of Scripture and, thus, the conclusions drawn from it. For the Catholic Christian, two lines of essential hermeneutic orientation assert themselves here. The first: We trust Scripture, and we base ourselves on Scripture, not on hypothetical reconstructions that go behind it and, according to their own taste, reconstruct a history in which the presumptuous idea of our knowing what can or cannot be attributed to Jesus plays a key role; which, of course, means attributing to him only what a modern scholar may attribute to a man belonging to a time that the scholar himself has reconstructed.

The second is that we read Scripture in the living community of the Church and, therefore, on the basis of the fundamental decisions through which it has become historically efficacious, precisely those that laid the foundations of the Church. One must not separate the text from this living context. In this sense, Scripture and tradition form an inseparable whole, and this is what Luther, at the dawn of the awakening of historical awareness, could not see.[14] He believed that a text could have only one meaning, but such univocity does not exist, and modern historiography has long since abandoned the idea. The fact that in the nascent Church the Eucharist was understood from the beginning as a sacrifice, even in a document like the *Didache*, which is so difficult and marginal in relation to the great tradition, is an interpretative key of primary importance.

But there is another fundamental hermeneutical aspect in the reading and the interpretation of biblical testimony. Whether or not I can recognize a sacrifice in the Eucharist as our Lord instituted it depends quite essentially on what I understand sacrifice to be, hence, on the so-called preconception. Luther's preconception, for example, or more

---

[14] On this subject, cf. Marius Reiser, "Bibel und Kirche", TThZ 108 (1999): 62–81.

outside of the city and of the Temple (Heb 13:12) and embraces the world of everyday life, too, the world outside of the sanctuary. The Cross gives mankind a rereading of its sacrificial tradition in which sacrifice and love become identical; because of this, it is at the same time the supreme liturgy, that is, the assimilation of man to the God who is love and the most concrete reality of everyday life.[4] One meets the Redeemer in lowly circumstances: in prison, at a sick bed, in dwellings of the hungry and the poor (see Mt 25:31–46). The self-transcendence of the merely liturgical is inscribed in the core of Christian liturgy and proves its worth again and again in very practical ways in those who live most profoundly and purely on their participation in the earthly-heavenly liturgy.

It seems to me that most of the problems in the concrete implementation of the liturgical reform are connected with the fact that the Council's approach starting with the Pasch was not kept in mind sufficiently; people stuck too much to merely practical matters and thereby ran the risk of losing sight of the center. It seems to me, therefore, essential to take up this approach again as the guiding norm of renewal and to deepen further what was necessarily only suggested by the Council. Pasch means the inseparability of Cross and Resurrection, as it is portrayed especially in the Gospel of John. The Cross stands in the center of the Christian liturgy, with all of its seriousness: a banal optimism that banishes suffering and injustice from the world with mere talk and reduces being a Christian to niceness has nothing to do with the liturgy of the Cross. The redemption cost God the suffering and the death of his Son, and its *exercitium* [that is, the practice or exercise of redemption], which is what the liturgy is, according to the conciliar document, cannot take place without the purification and maturation involved in following the way of the Cross. There are no passages without the pain of departure, of renunciation: Christ drew the world's suffering into himself so as to be able to heal it in that way, and we can be healed and healers only if we are willing to take up our crosses and follow after him. Resurrection means that God has granted reconciliation

---

[4] I have attempted to portray in more detail this fundamentally new understanding of sacrifice that arose from the Cross of Christ in the reception and transformation of historical sacrifice traditions in *Der Geist der Liturgie* (Freiburg im Breslau, 2000), 30–43 [trans. John Saward as *The Spirit of the Liturgy* (San Francisco: Ignatius Press, 2000), 35–50; JRCW 11:20–30].

of divine worship primarily in terms of the Passover feast described in the accounts of the Last Supper".[17] At first sight this wording appears ambiguous: Is one to think about divine worship in terms of the Last Supper narratives or in terms of the Passover, which they mention as a chronological framework but do not describe in greater detail? It would be correct to say that the Jewish Passover, the institution of which is related in Exodus 12, acquires a new meaning in the New Testament, and, thus, a great historical movement becomes visible from that beginning to the Last Supper, Cross, and Resurrection of Jesus. The most astonishing thing about Orth's formulation, however, is the opposition set up between the idea of sacrifice and the Passover. That makes no sense in light of the Old Testament and Jewish practice, because ever since the legislation in Deuteronomy, the slaughter of the lambs was linked to the Temple; even in the early period, when the Passover was still a family celebration, the slaughter of the lambs already had a sacrificial character.[18] Thus, precisely via the Passover tradition, the idea of sacrifice extends right into the words and actions of the Last Supper, in which it is of course made present also in terms of a second Old Testament background, namely Exodus 24, the account of the sealing of the covenant on Sinai. This passage relates that the people were sprinkled with the blood of the victims that had been offered previously and that Moses said on this occasion: "Behold the blood of the covenant which the Lord has made with you in accordance with all these words" (Ex 24:8). The new Christian Passover is thus expressly interpreted in the accounts of the Last Supper as a sacrificial event, and, on the basis of the words of the Last Supper, the nascent Church knew that the Cross was a sacrifice, because the Last Supper would be an empty gesture without the reality of the Cross and Resurrection, which is anticipated therein and made accessible in its interior value for all time.

I mention this peculiar opposition between the Passover and sacrifice because it is the structural principle of a book recently published by the Society of St. Pius X, claiming that there was a dogmatic rupture between the new liturgy of Paul VI and the previous Catholic

---

[17] Orth, "Renaissance", 199.

[18] Cf., for example, Herbert Haag, article "Passah", in LThK, 2nd ed., 8:133–37, citation at 134f.

liturgical tradition. This rupture is seen precisely in the fact that every-thing is interpreted now on the basis of the "Paschal Mystery" instead of Christ's redeeming sacrifice of atonement; the category of the Pas-chal Mystery is said to be the soul of the liturgical reform, and this very fact appears to be proof of the rupture with the classic doctrine of the Church.[19] Plainly there are authors who provide occasions for this misunderstanding. Yet to anyone who looks more closely it is quite obvious that it is a misunderstanding. For the expression "Pas-chal Mystery" unambiguously refers to what happened in the days from Holy Thursday to Easter Sunday: the Last Supper as an antici-pation of the Cross, the event on Golgotha, and the Lord's Resurrec-tion. In the expression "Paschal Mystery" these happenings are seen synthetically as a single, coherent event, as "the action of Christ", as we heard the Council say in the introduction to this lecture—an action that takes place historically and at the same time transcends the moment. Because this event is interiorly an act of worship rendered to God, it could become divine worship and so be present to all times. The pas-chal theology of the New Testament at which we just looked briefly means precisely this: that the seemingly profane event of Christ's cru-cifixion is an atoning sacrifice, a healing act of reconciling love by the incarnate God. Paschal theology is theology of redemption, liturgy of the atoning sacrifice. The Shepherd has become Lamb. The vision of the lamb that appears in the story of Isaac—the lamb that gets entan-gled in the undergrowth and ransoms the son—has come true: the Lord becomes Lamb; he allows himself to be bound and sacrificed in order to set us free.

3. A Theology of Sacrifice and of Liturgy

All this has become very foreign to contemporary thought. Atone-ment or expiation can perhaps be imagined as something within the framework of human conflicts and the resolution of human interper-sonal liability, but its application to the relationship between God and man does not seem to work. This may be due largely to the fact that

---

[19] Fraternité Sacerdotale St-Pie X, *Le Problème de la réforme liturgique* (Condé-Noireau, 2001) [trans. as: Society of St. Pius X, *The Problem of the Liturgical Reform* (Kansas City: Angelus Press, 2001)].

3. The Basic Categories of the Reform:
Intelligibility—Participation—Simplicity

These remarks already show that considering the liturgy in terms of the Pasch does not lead us into theological eccentricities but, rather, has a very practical character. In this respect, the connection between theological vision and the orientation toward reform is assumed from the start. But now we still have to ask: How does the Council itself see the direction in which the reform must proceed in practice? Apart from the fact that all theological statements of the Council contain an inner orientation toward praxis, one must say that on this point it clearly reflects the different emphases of the Liturgical Movement, for example when the Constitution says, "Although the sacred liturgy is principally the worship of the divine majesty it likewise contains much instruction for the faithful" (SC 33). Unfortunately, it must be said that in postconciliar praxis the instructional character got quite out of hand almost everywhere and ended up turning the liturgy into a school. All of us have had to learn, often in a very drastic way, that word and talk are two different things. There is of course no reason to object to the above-cited sentence from the Council, for the very epiphany of the holy, which is expressed in symbols, gestures, and words, is in itself "instruction". For the Constitution had also added that the rites themselves should be "clear" (*perspicui*) and "should not require much explanation" (SC 34). It had also in fact explained that "directives" (*admonitiones*) could be inserted into the liturgy as aids to understanding (SC 35, 3; 36, 2). Although it had explicitly urged brevity in doing so and, at the very least, dependence on the prescribed text (SC 35, 3), it thereby opened a floodgate, out of which veritable torrents of talk have poured since the Council.

a. Intelligibility

That should lead us now, however, to examine somewhat more closely several of the practical basic categories of the Council, three of which I should like to single out. I think that the essential ones are: participation, intelligibility, simplicity. The central term is certainly "participation"; nevertheless I would like to begin with the "intelligibility" required for the liturgy, because that term contains perhaps the largest the services in the tabernacle or the Temple are therefore supposed to refer symbolically to the love of God and neighbor." [22] But Augustine knows also that love is true only when it leads man to God and thus directs him to his true goal; only there can the unity of men among themselves also come about. Thus the concept of sacrifice points to community, and the first definition that Augustine attempted is now broadened into the statement: "The whole of that redeemed city, that is, the congregation or communion of saints, is offered as a universal sacrifice to God through the High Priest who, 'taking the form of a servant,' offered himself...." [23] And even more simply: "It is we ourselves who constitute the whole sacrifice", or again: "Such is the sacrifice of Christians: 'We, the many, are one body in Christ.'" [24] Sacrifice consists, then, we shall say it once more, in a process of transformation, in the conforming of man to God, in his θείωσις (theōsis, in English "theosis"), as the Fathers would say. It consists, to express it in modern phraseology, in the abolition of difference—in the union between God and man, between God and creation: "that God may be all in all" (1 Cor 15:28, Douay-Rheims).

But how does this happen, this process by which we become love and one body with Christ, unification with God, the abolition of difference? First of all there is a clear boundary here between the religions founded on the faith of Abraham, on one hand, and the other forms of religion, such as we find especially in Asia, but also in the Plotinian style of Neoplatonism, which was probably based on Asiatic traditions. In them, unification means deliverance from finitude, which is ultimately unmasked as a façade, the abolition of self in the ocean of the completely Other, which compared to our world of façades is nothingness yet is the only true being. In the Christian faith, which fulfills the faith of Abraham, union is seen differently: it is the union of love, in which differences are not abolished but become a higher union of loving persons, as this is modeled in the trinitarian union of God. Whereas in Plotinus, for example, finitude—being a descent from unity and, so to speak, the kernel of sin—is at the same time the kernel of all evil, the Christian faith sees finitude, not as negation, but as creation, the product of a divine will that creates a free counterpart,

---

[22] Ibid., X, 5.
[23] Ibid., X, 6; Bourke ed., 193.
[24] Ibid., X, 6; Bourke ed., 193, 194.

speak five words with my mind, in order to instruct others, than ten thousand words in a tongue" (1 Cor 14:19).

Hence making the liturgy understandable is an entirely biblical plan. But what does it mean to understand? The complexity of this plan first became apparent after the liturgy had been translated into the vernacular languages. I offer an example: the reading from the Letter to the Galatians about the two sons of Abraham and its allegorical application to Judaism and the Church (Gal 4:21-31) is not understood just because it is proclaimed in the vernacular. Now it becomes quite clear that we do not understand it without a thorough explanation. The same is true for many Scripture passages, precisely for those that guide us to the heart of Christian life. It is true for the great fundamental statements of the Canon of the Mass: Who today really understands the significance of Christ's death as an act of atonement? What it means to say, "we are redeemed by his blood"; what it means when Paul says: "Because there is one bread, we who are many are one body" (1 Cor 10:17), and so forth. With all these statements, however, we are dealing with the heart of what takes place in the celebration of the Eucharist as the highest form of Christian liturgy. No one can deny that the unintelligibility of these great statements is actually increasing today, because along with our culture we are moving farther and farther away from the ways of seeing that are asserted in such words.

So what should we do? One can either interpolate more and more explanations and thus talk the liturgy to shreds, so that it becomes classroom instruction with dubious results. Or else—and unfortunately this happens quite often—one can trivialize the great statements, leave out the difficult Scripture passages, and dumb down the words of the liturgy to what one considers to be the level of general comprehension. But that ends up leaving nothing to happen in the liturgy; it disintegrates. Then we should not be surprised about declining attendance. In the end, one reaches then for ingredients from other religions in order to give the whole thing somehow the thrill of mystery again. Thus it becomes evident that intelligibility is a complex and challenging matter. Not without good reason did the early Church have the catechumenate, in which individuals who were seeking God were slowly trained in the thinking and life of the Church, thus gradually opening their inner feelings, their minds, and their hearts. The accessibility of the liturgy should not be confused with the immediate especially in the form handed down by John. This is because John records an interpretive statement by Jesus that appears in the Synoptics only during the trial of Jesus, on the lips of false witnesses and in a distorted form. The action taken by Jesus against the merchants and money changers in the Temple was, practically speaking, an attack on the animal sacrifices that were offered there, hence an attack on the existing form of worship and of sacrifice in general. To that extent the competent Jewish authorities rightly asked him by what sign he justified such a deed, which necessarily was considered an attack on the law of Moses and the sacred precepts of the covenant and could therefore be justified only by divine authority, a sign from on high. Thereupon Jesus replies: "Destroy this temple and in three days I will raise it up" (Jn 2:18–19). This subtle formula evokes a vision that, as John himself says, the disciples did not understand until after the Resurrection in retrospect and that then led them to "believe the scripture and the word which Jesus had spoken" (Jn 2:22). For they understand now that the Temple was abolished at the moment of Jesus' crucifixion: according to John, Jesus was crucified precisely at the moment when the paschal lambs were being slaughtered in the Temple. At the moment when the Son makes himself the lamb, that is, freely gives himself to the Father and hence to us, this puts an end to the old cultic ordinances, which could be only a sign of the reality. The Temple is "destroyed". Now his resurrected body—he himself— becomes the true Temple of mankind, in which worship in spirit and in truth takes place (Jn 4:23). But spirit and truth are not abstract philosophical concepts—HE is the truth, and the spirit is the Holy Spirit who proceeds from him. Here, too, it becomes clear, therefore, that worship is not replaced by moral philosophy, but, rather, the ancient worship, with its substitutes and its often tragic misunderstandings, comes to an end because the reality itself is manifested, the new Temple: the risen Christ who draws us to himself, transforms us, and unites us. And, on the other hand, it is clear that the Eucharist of the Church—to use Augustine's expression—is the *sacramentum* of the true *sacrificium*—the sacred sign in which what is signified comes to pass.

Finally, I would like to point out very briefly a third way in which the transition from the worship of substitution, from animal sacrifices, to the true sacrifice, to communion with Christ's self-offering, gradually became clearer. Among the prophets before the Exile there had been extraordinarily harsh criticism of Temple worship, which is the claim of the *nigrics*—the inner demand made by what is printed in black, that is, by the liturgical text itself, which as such includes interaction in hearing and responding, in prayer, acclamation, and song.

In all these areas, no doubt, advances have been made in recent decades over which we can rejoice. But one cannot overlook an externalizing trend as well: everyone has to have something to do. When pastors who are friends of mine tell me that not a few of their faithful think that they do not have to go to church on the Sundays when no functions have been assigned to them, this is evidence of an externalization that is appalling. There is no more talk then about the dynamism of transcendence from the visible to the invisible, from external to internal, from here to on high, from now to the One who is to come. Origen once described the essence of the world, from which we as Christians were supposed to have been set free, as "agitation".[9] Have we not succeeded a little too well here in being open to the world? Do we still feel that we are standing before the throne of the Most High, that the heaven above us is open? That we are surrounded by God's angels and saints? Origen said to his faithful in one of his homilies on the Gospel of Luke: "I do not doubt that angels are even present in our assembly—not just generally, to every church, but for each individual believer." And he imagines what would happen if someone like the prophet Elisha were to pray for us: "O Lord, open the eyes of this child."[10] Where bustling activity prevails, the eyes of the heart cannot open. And yet we would finally be participating properly in the liturgy if only we started to sense that open heaven. All the talking, singing, and doing should ultimately serve the purpose of guiding us into this movement of transcendence in which silence can convey its message.

c. Simplicity

In conclusion, I might make another short comment about the demand for the "noble simplicity" of the rites, which doubtless belongs to the

---

[9] Cf. Origen, "Homily XXVII", 257f.; ibid., 258: "Thus the first progress of the soul is to be taken away from earthly agitation."

[10] Origen, *Homilies on Luke, Fragments on Luke*, trans. Joseph T. Lienhard, S.J., *The Fathers of the Church*, vol. 94 (Washington, D.C.: Catholic Univ. of America Press, 1996); here homily 23, 8 and 9, p. 101.

Numerous examples from the patristic literature show how these ideas were further developed and became the connection between Christology, eucharistic faith, and the existential application of the Paschal Mystery. I would like to cite, by way of example, just a few lines from Peter Chrysologus; of course one would have to read his sermon on this subject in its entirety in order to be able to understand this synthesis:

> Truly it is an amazing sacrifice in which a body is offered without being slain and blood is offered without being shed. The Apostle says: *I appeal to you by the mercy of God to present your bodies as a living sacrifice.* Brethren, this sacrifice follows the pattern of Christ's sacrifice by which he gave his body as a living immolation for the life of the world.... Each of us is [therefore] called to be both a sacrifice to God and his priest.... God desires not death, but faith; God thirsts not for blood, but for self-surrender. God is appeased not by slaughter, but by the offering of your free will.[27]

Here, too, it is a question of something quite different from mere moral philosophy, since it demands so much of man in his totality: sacrifice in the word—the Greek thinkers had already referred this to the logos, the word itself, indicating that the sacrifice of prayer must be, not mere speech, but the transformation of our being into the logos, unification with it. Divine worship means that we ourselves become wordlike, that we conform ourselves to the creative Intellect. But again it is clear that we cannot do this on our own, and so everything seems to end again in futility—until the Logos, the True One, the Son comes, is made flesh, and draws us up to himself in the exodus of the Cross. This true sacrifice that turns us all into sacrifice, in other words, unites us with God and causes us to become godlike, is indeed fixed and founded on an historical event but does not lie behind us as a thing of the past but, rather, becomes contemporary with and accessible to us in the community of the believing, praying Church, in its sacrament: this is what "sacrifice of the Mass" means.

Luther's error lay, I am convinced, in a false concept of historicity, in a misunderstanding of what is unrepeatable. Christ's sacrifice is not behind us as a thing of the past. It touches all times and is present to us. Eucharist is not merely the distribution of something from the past

---

[27] Peter Chrysologus, *Sermo* 108 (PL 52:499f.). [English translation from the Office of Readings for Tuesday in the Fourth Week of Easter.]

who takes part in it with faith. Friedrich Nietzsche once said: "Feasts include: pride, exuberance, wantonness ... ; a divine affirmation of oneself out of animal plenitude and perfection—one and all states that the Christian cannot honestly welcome. The feast is paganism par excellence." [12] The opposite is true: Only if there is divine authorization to rejoice—only if God himself guarantees that my life and the world are reason for joy, can there be a real feast. And for this reason the Christian liturgy, in which the crucified love of God is present, is the feast par excellence. In this joyful certainty we celebrate it, and so we celebrate it correctly.

---

[12] *Der Wille zur Macht*, no. 916, quoted by Walter M. Neidl, *Christliche Philosophie—eine Absurdität?* Salzburger Universitätsreden, Heft 70 (Regensburg, 1981), 6.

VIII. The Organic Development of the Liturgy

In the last few decades, the matter of the right way to celebrate the liturgy has increasingly become one of the points around which much of the controversy has centered concerning the Second Vatican Council, about how it should be evaluated, and about its reception in the life of the Church. There are the relentless supporters of reform, for whom the fact that, under certain conditions, the celebration of the Eucharist in accordance with the most recent edition of the Missal before the Council—that of 1962—has once more been permitted represents an intolerable fall from grace. At the same time, of course, the liturgy is regarded as "semper reformanda", so that in the end it is whatever "congregation" is involved that makes "its" liturgy, in which it expresses itself. A Protestant "Liturgical Compendium" recently presented worship as a "project for reform"[1] and thereby also expressed the way many Catholic liturgists think about it. And then, on the other hand, there are the embittered critics of liturgical reform—critical not only of its application in practice, but also of its basis in the Council. They can see salvation only in total rejection of the reform. Between these two groups, the radical reformers and their radical opponents, the voices of those people who regard the liturgy as something living, and thus as growing and renewing itself both in its reception and in its finished form, are often lost. These latter, however, on the basis of the same argument, insist that growth is not possible unless the liturgy's identity is preserved, and they further emphasize that proper development is possible only if careful attention is paid to the inner

---

Translated by Henry Taylor. Published as the preface to Alcuin Reid, O.S.B., *The Organic Development of the Liturgy: The Principles of Liturgical Reform and Their Relation to the Twentieth-Century Liturgical Movement Prior to the Second Vatican Council*, 2nd ed. (San Francisco: Ignatius Press, 2005), 9–13.

[1] Christian Grethlein and Günter Ruddat, eds., *Liturgisches Kompendium* (Göttingen, 2003), 13–41.

structural logic of this "organism": Just as a gardener cares for a living plant as it develops, with due attention to the power of growth and life within the plant and the rules it obeys, so the Church ought to give reverent care to the liturgy through the ages, distinguishing actions that are helpful and healing from those that are violent and destructive.

If that is how things are, then we must try to ascertain the inner structure of a rite and the rules by which its life is governed in order thus to find the right way to preserve its vital force in changing times, to strengthen and renew it. Dom Alcuin Reid's book takes its place in this current of thought. Running through the history of the Roman rite (Mass and breviary), from its beginnings up to the eve of the Second Vatican Council, it seeks to establish the principles of liturgical development and thus to draw from history—from its ups and downs—the standards on which every reform must be based. The book is divided into three parts. The first, very brief part investigates the history of the reform of the Roman rite from its beginnings up to the end of the nineteenth century. The second part is devoted to the Liturgical Movement up to 1948. By far the longest part—the third—deals with liturgical reform under Pius XII up to the eve of the Second Vatican Council. This part is most useful, because to a great extent people no longer remember that particular phase of liturgical reform, yet in that period—as, of course, also in the history of the Liturgical Movement—we see reflected all the questions concerning the right way to go about reform, so that we can also draw out from all this criteria on which to base our judgments. The author has made a wise decision in stopping on the threshold of the Second Vatican Council. He thus avoids entering into the controversy associated with the interpretation and the reception of the Council. Yet he can nonetheless show its place in history and show us the interplay of various tendencies on which questions as to the standards for reform must be based.

At the end of his book, the author enumerates some principles for proper reform: it should keep openness to development and continuity with the tradition in a proper balance; it should include awareness of an objective liturgical tradition and therefore take care to ensure a substantial continuity. The author then agrees with the *Catechism of the Catholic Church* in emphasizing that "even the supreme authority in the Church may not change the liturgy arbitrarily, but only in the obedience of faith and with religious respect for the mystery of the liturgy".[2] As subsidiary criteria we then encounter the legitimacy of local traditions and the concern for pastoral effectiveness.

From my own personal point of view, I should like to give further particular emphasis to some of the criteria for liturgical renewal thus briefly indicated. I will begin with those last two main criteria. It seems to me most important that the *Catechism*, in mentioning the limitation of the powers of the supreme authority in the Church with regard to reform, recalls to mind what is the essence of the primacy as outlined by the First and Second Vatican Councils: The pope is not an absolute monarch whose will is law; rather, he is the guardian of the authentic tradition and, thereby, the premier guarantor of obedience. He cannot do as he likes, and he is thereby able to oppose those people who, for their part, want to do whatever comes into their head. His rule is not that of arbitrary power, but that of obedience in faith. That is why, with respect to the liturgy, he has the task of a gardener, not that of a technician who builds new machines and throws the old ones on the junk-pile. The "rite", that form of celebration and prayer which has ripened in the faith and the life of the Church, is a condensed form of living tradition in which the sphere using that rite expresses the whole of its faith and its prayer, and thus at the same time the fellowship of generations one with another becomes something we can experience, fellowship with the people who pray before us and after us. Thus the rite is something of benefit that is given to the Church, a living form of *paradosis*, the handing-on of tradition.

It is important, in this connection, to interpret the "substantial continuity" correctly. The author expressly warns us against the wrong path up which we might be led by a Neoscholastic sacramental theology that is disconnected from the living form of the liturgy. On that basis, people might reduce the "substance" to the matter and form of the sacrament and say: Bread and wine are the matter of the sacrament; the words of institution are its form. Only these two things are really necessary; everything else is changeable. At this point modernists and traditionalists are in agreement: As long as the material gifts are there, and the words of institution are spoken, then everything else is freely disposable. Many priests today, unfortunately, act in accordance with this motto; and the theories of many liturgists are unfortunately moving in the same direction. They want to overcome the

---

[2] CCC 1125; cf. Reid, *Organic Development* (2nd ed.), 307.

limits of the rite, as being something fixed and immovable, and construct the products of their fantasy, which are supposedly "pastoral", around this remnant, this core that has been spared and that is thus either relegated to the realm of magic or loses any meaning whatever. The Liturgical Movement was in fact attempting to overcome this reductionism, the product of an abstract sacramental theology, and to teach us to understand the liturgy as a living network of tradition that has taken concrete form, that cannot be torn apart into little pieces but that has to be seen and experienced as a living whole. Anyone who, like me, was moved by this perception at the time of the Liturgical Movement on the eve of the Second Vatican Council can only stand, deeply sorrowing, before the ruins of the very things for which they were concerned.

I should like just briefly to comment on two more perceptions that appear in Dom Alcuin Reid's book. Archaeological enthusiasm and pastoral pragmatism—which is in any case often a pastoral form of rationalism—are both equally wrong. These two might be described as unholy twins. The first generation of liturgists were for the most part historians. Thus they were inclined to archaeological enthusiasm: they were trying to unearth the oldest form in its original purity; they regarded the liturgical books in current use, with the rites they offered, as the expression of the rampant proliferation through history of secondary growths that were the product of misunderstandings and of ignorance of the past. People were trying to reconstruct the oldest Roman liturgy and to cleanse it of all later additions. A great deal of this was right, and yet liturgical reform is something different from archaeological excavation, and not all the developments of a living thing have to be logical in accordance with a rationalistic or historical standard. This is also the reason why—as the author quite rightly remarks—the experts ought not to be allowed to have the last word in liturgical reform. Experts and pastors each have their own part to play (just as, in politics, specialists and decision-makers represent two different planes). The knowledge of scholars is important, yet it cannot be directly transmuted into the decisions of pastors, for pastors still have their own responsibilities in listening to the faithful, in accompanying with understanding those who perform the things that help us to celebrate the sacrament with faith today and the things that do not. It was one of the weaknesses of the first phase of reform after the Council that to a great extent specialists were listened to almost exclusively. A greater independence on the part of pastors would have been desirable.

Because it is often all too obvious that historical knowledge cannot be elevated straight into the status of a new liturgical norm, this archaeological enthusiasm was very easily combined with pastoral pragmatism: people first of all decided to eliminate everything that was not recognized as original and was thus not part of the "substance", and then they supplemented the "archaeological remains", if these still seemed insufficient, in accordance with "pastoral insights". But what is "pastoral"? The judgments made about these questions by intellectual professors were often influenced by their rationalist presuppositions and not infrequently missed the point of what really supports the life of the faithful. Thus it is that nowadays, after the liturgy was extensively rationalized during the early phase of reform, people are eagerly seeking forms of solemnity, looking for "mystical" atmosphere and for something of the sacred. Yet because—necessarily and more and more clearly—people's judgments as to what is pastorally effective are widely divergent, the "pastoral" aspect has become the point at which "creativity" breaks in, destroying the unity of the liturgy and very often confronting us with something deplorably banal. That is not to deny that the eucharistic liturgy, and likewise the Liturgy of the Word, is often celebrated reverently and "beautifully", in the best sense, on the basis of people's faith. Yet since we are looking for the criteria of reform, we do also have to mention the dangers, which unfortunately in the last few decades have by no means remained just the imaginings of those traditionalists opposed to reform.

I should like to come back to the way that worship was presented, in a liturgical compendium, as a "project for reform" and, thus, as a workshop in which people are always busy at something. Different again, and yet related to this, is the suggestion by some Catholic liturgists that we should finally adapt the liturgical reform to the "anthropological turn" of modern times and construct it in an anthropocentric style. If the liturgy appears first of all as the workshop for our activity, then what is essential is being forgotten: God. For the liturgy is not about us, but about God. Forgetting about God is the most imminent danger of our age. As against this, the liturgy should be setting up a sign of God's presence. Yet what happens if the habit of forgetting about God makes itself at home in the liturgy itself and if in the liturgy we are thinking only of ourselves? In any and every liturgical reform, and every liturgical celebration, the primacy of God should be kept in view first and foremost.

With this I have gone beyond Dom Alcuin's book. But I think it has become clear that this book, which offers a wealth of material, teaches us some criteria and invites us to further reflection. That is why I can recommend this book.

Joseph Cardinal Ratzinger
July 26, 2004

IX. "Rouse Your Power and Come"

Advent Sermon in the Cathedral of Trier, Preached
on December 4, 2003, and Based on the Following
Scripture Readings: Is 26:1–6; Ps 118; Mt 7:11–27

Dear brothers in the episcopal, priestly, and diaconal ministry!

Dear sisters and brothers in the Lord!

"Stir up your might, O Lord, and come", the Church prays today
in her Collect with a cry that she has taken from Psalm 80: "Rouse
your power!"

This was the cry of Israel in exile, in an hour in which God seemed
to have withdrawn from history and his promises apparently no longer
mattered; an hour in which God seemed to be sleeping and Israel was
left alone: "Rouse your power and come; show us that you are here
even today."

This was the cry of the disciples on the Sea of Galilee, in a boat
that was being tossed back and forth as the waves washed over it,
while the Lord was sleeping in the same boat: "Wake up, O Lord, and
help us!"

This was the Advent prayer of the Church in times of persecution,
when the full force of the Roman Empire was arrayed against the little
flock of believers, who were delivered up and crushed by the power
of politics and military might: "Stir up your might and come!"

And throughout all of history the little bark of the Church travels
in stormy waters and is in danger of sinking, at least that is how it
seems. Again—in the times of the migration of peoples—she could
only cry out: "Stir up your might and come"; yet precisely in the era
when the Church was a political force, she was all the more in danger
of losing her way and had to cry out all the more insistently: "Stir up
your might and come!" And today, when to a great extent the faith
silently trickles away, when the Church seems to be a concern about
the past that has no future, when God seems to have abandoned her,
we must cry out with new urgency: "Stir up your might and come,

Translated by Kenneth Baker, S.J., and Michael J. Miller.

O Lord! It is high time. Come, and do not be a God of the past; rather, be a God who comes and opens up the future and leads us on into the coming centuries."

"Rouse your power and come!" But if we take a closer look at this prayer, it must be obvious that we are not simply saying to God: "Wake up", as if we were to assume that he was sleeping. We say: "Rouse your power." Therefore the question is: What is it, really, this might of God that seems to be asleep and must be awakened?

St. Paul gives us the answer in 1 Corinthians when he says: Christ, the crucified One, who is foolishness and weakness to men, is the wisdom and the power of God. Therefore, when we pray for this real power of God, we are not asking for more money for the Church, for more buildings, for more structures, for more political influence. We are praying for this special, entirely different power of God. We are praying with the awareness that he comes in a powerful way that seems to the world to be weakness and foolishness.

So it was—if we wander briefly through history once more— already in Israel: in defeated Israel, of all places, which had apparently been extinguished as a political entity, for the first time faith in the one God attained its pure form and for the first time the great visions of salvation were awakened; in fact, the song of praise to the living God came out of the fiery oven of affliction. And so it was again in the early Church that, in the midst of external helplessness, God's power was the witness of strong faith given by the martyrs, the witness of love for one another and for all the weak and oppressed, the witness that came out of the heart of the Church; God's power was the way in which he comes with his might, with crucified might— and so it is throughout history.

He does not come with military divisions; he comes instead with a wounded heart that apparently has nothing more to say yet then proves to be the true, wholly other power, the might of God. But if we now see how God has aroused his might in the suffering and believing men in Israel, in the martyrs and in the great witnesses of love and truth in the early Church, and again in Francis of Assisi and in Dominic and down through all the centuries, then this cry hits home, then it concerns us personally, for then it becomes evident that God has deposited his holy might with us abundantly through the holy sacraments of Baptism and Confirmation and through his word, and that this might sleeps in us. So this prayer applies to us:

Lord, wake us up from our drowsiness, in which we are incapable of perceiving you, in which we conceal and impede the coming of your holy power that is here in us.

Christianity is not a moral system by which we may merely roll up our sleeves and change the world. We see in the movements that have promised us a better world how badly that turns out. But just as God built up the world and man, so also in Christianity other efficient causes are at work besides God alone; we Christians are not merely spectators who have only to wait; rather, he involves us; he desires to be efficacious in us and through us—he wants to bring to bear in this world through us his holy and new power, the power of truth and love. And so in this cry we pray to him for ourselves and allow our own hearts to be touched: Your power is in us, rouse it, and help us not to be an obstacle to it but, rather, witnesses and vital strength.

Now let us take a quick look at the First Reading, the Responsorial Psalm, and the Gospel for today. The First Reading begins with a saying full of confidence: "We have a strong city; he sets up salvation as walls and bulwarks." It is impregnable. This is the same thing the Lord tells us when he gives us the gift of these words: "The powers of the Evil One, the powers of death will never overwhelm it—my Church, my living house, my holy city." And this is the same thing he tells us once more today in the Gospel: The house that is built on my word stands on rock, and the storms and floods of this world will not be able to sweep it away. The Advent liturgy intends to give us this holy confidence in the midst of all the turmoil, in the midst of all the affliction, in the midst of all the human wretchedness and sin that are found in the Church—she remains his house. She stands on rock, and with confidence we can be certain: This house will not be destroyed. The Church will pass through these storms, too, and prove once again that she is God's living city in the world.

But then comes a sentence that, according to our usual standards, seems to contradict the first one. For first it says: The Church, the house of God, the city of God has strong walls, ramparts, and towers and is unconquerable. And then the very next thing is the sentence: "Open the gates, that the righteous nation which keeps faith may enter in." The trustworthy Church, the house of God on its firm foundation, is nevertheless an open house and an open city—open so that the Lord can enter in and so that we can go forth to meet the Lord.

Closely related, then, to this verse from the book of Isaiah is today's Responsorial Psalm 118, which is an Entrance Psalm and speaks again about entering into the Holy City. It was the psalm for the Feast of Booths, for the solemn entrance into God's festival of light. But it was also the psalm that belonged to the Paschal liturgy and was prayed as a psalm after the fourth cup of wine—the psalm that Jesus sang with his disciples before he went to the Mount of Olives and to his Passion, his way of opening up the gates of the world.

"Open the gates of this city so he can enter in and so we can go forth to meet him." At the same time these verses indicate what liturgy is. Liturgy is the opening of the gates of this world so that God can enter in, so that people who believe can enter in and can meet God. The two movements go together: the spiritual awakening of men, the setting out of the people, the procession of history so as to be able to go meet the Lord in his city—and the coming of the Lord who approaches us; thus, the encounter in the mystery of the Eucharist, in which we set out to follow him and in which he comes to us and gives himself to us so that we can go farther with him and can open wide the gates of the world for his entrance and for our going forth to him.

In conclusion, let us return once again to the Church's prayer: "Rouse your power and come." In the second part of this prayer, we are told more exactly what kind of "coming" we are requesting. In German, the text says: "Send help so that your salvation, which we delay, may come more quickly."* The Latin text is even more reserved and does not specify what is to come; it leaves that up to God and says only "quod nostra peccata praepediunt".** We say to him: May it come, what you will to come, in whatever and however you will to come. We leave to God the manner of his coming, which is the right one for us.

The Church's prayer does not ask simply for the parousia, for the final coming of Christ. It seems to me that such a prayer would be too lofty for all of us, that we would not really dare to utter it seriously. No, we simply ask God to come in some way that is right for us, and we leave it up to him what sort of coming that may be. Thus it becomes clear in this prayer that there are many ways of

---

*Hilf, dass dein Heil schneller kommt, das wir aufhalten.
**That which our sins hinder.

God's coming in history, not only his first coming in Bethlehem, not only his Second Coming at the end of the world.

St. Bernard of Clairvaux explained very explicitly what had previously been thought out more or less clearly. Between the first advent of Christ and the last, definitive one, he says, there is a *medius adventus*, an "intermediate advent of God". He comes continually, he comes into souls, but he also comes into history in a new way. He entered into it in a new way in the twelfth century through Francis and the new movement of the Mendicant Orders, who wanted to bring the Church close to the Lord again and to make her a simple and humble people. He came in a new way through the great mystics of the sixteenth century. He came in a new way in the midst of the enlightened nineteenth-century world through the great movements of the religious orders that were now concentrating on social justice and education. We ask him: "Come today, Lord, come into each one of us, and, thus, come into this age as well: visibly, historically, in a new way, as this time requires and in a manner suited to it. Yes, Lord, come and help us, so that we may open the gates to you, that we may go with you when you enter. Amen."

APPENDICES

Editorial Notes

I. The Complete Edition

Joseph Ratzinger: Gesamelte Schrifter [*Collected Works of Joseph Ratzinger*] are meant to be the "polished, final edition" of the theologian Joseph Ratzinger in the German language. The goal is to present as completely as possible his published work, supplemented by texts that are previously unpublished or not yet published in German, in a systematic order that combines chronological and thematic perspectives.*

Joseph Ratzinger's monographs are included in the *Collected Works* and supplemented in each instance with additional thematically related texts. As has often been the author's practice in earlier anthologies, too, the expressly scholarly texts are accompanied by those that belong to other literary genres, for example, encyclopedia articles, book reviews, and finally even homilies and meditations.

The volumes of Joseph Ratzinger's articles that compile thematically related writings from particular stages of the career of the theologian, bishop, and Prefect of the Congregation for the Doctrine of the Faith are broken up, and the individual essays are incorporated into the new system.

The *Collected Works* start—with respect to the numbering of the volumes, though not necessarily to the actual date of publication— with the two scholarly works that Joseph Ratzinger wrote to qualify for university degrees: his dissertation on Augustine's understanding of the Church, and his *Habilitation* thesis on Bonaventure's theology of history and understanding of revelation. In each case, further studies and texts about Augustine or Bonaventure are added.

Volume 3 takes the inaugural lecture given by Professor Ratzinger at the University of Bonn in 1959, "The God of Faith and the God of the Philosophers", as its point of departure and coordinates it with all further texts on the subject of *fides et ratio* [faith and reason]. This collection also includes, for example, all his reflections on the foundations of Europe in intellectual history.

Volume 4 starts from the *Introduction to Christianity* (1968) and appends further texts on the topics of professing the faith, Baptism, conversion, the imitation of Christ, and Christian living.

Volumes 5 through 12 are arranged according to the canon of topics in systematic theology in the broadest sense.

Volume 5 assembles the texts that can be categorized as parts of the treatises on creation, anthropology, and grace, whereby Mariology is presented as the doctrine on grace made concrete in salvation history.

Volume 6, starting with *Jesus of Nazareth* (2007, 2011) brings together the studies on Christology.

Volume 7 and volume 8 on ecclesiology cover another topic emphasized in Joseph Ratzinger's work. Volume 7 first compiles all texts on the theology of the Council: those that came about as part of the preparation for the Second Vatican Council, but also the written reports based on firsthand experience of it as well as the commentaries composed afterward, and last but not least a series of reflections with regard to the reception of the conciliar documents. Volume 8 reprints the ecclesiological studies in the narrower sense and above all includes also Joseph Ratzinger's writings on ecumenism.

At the intersection of fundamental and dogmatic theology stands volume 9, a collection of Joseph Ratzinger's studies on theological epistemology and hermeneutics, which were written over the entire span of his career, and also especially his studies on the understanding of Scripture and on the specific coordination of revelation, tradition, Scripture, and Magisterium.

Volume 10 takes as its point of departure *Eschatology* (1977), the one textbook in dogmatic theology published by Joseph Ratzinger, and classifies with it all further studies and texts on the topics of hope, death, resurrection, and eternal life.

With volumes 11 and 12 the author explicitly underscores further chief concerns in his thought. With the *Theology of the Liturgy* in volume 11, with which the Holy Father intends to inaugurate the publication of his collected theological writings, he places his complete works under the general rubric of a logically consistent theocentrism. Volume 12 assembles in particular texts on clerical ministry that might otherwise be incorporated into ecclesiology or sacramental theology and presents them as volume 12 under the title *Preachers of the Word and Helpers of Your Joy.*

Volume 13 assembles Joseph Ratzinger's numerous interviews, both the earlier, shorter ones and the three that were published in book format, beginning with the discussion with Vittorio Messori in 1984–1985, followed by the three books by and with Peter Seewald (1996, and 2000, and 2010).

Volume 14 presents as large a selection as possible from the voluminous homiletic works of Joseph Ratzinger, whereby less well-known and previously unpublished addresses and meditations are taken into consideration as well.

Volume 15, starting with Joseph Ratzinger's autobiography, *Milestones*, which was published in 1997–1998, compiles further biographical texts and essays of a personal nature, for instance, his numerous reflections in relation to his predecessor Pope John Paul II, his brother, Georg Ratzinger, and many other speeches at jubilees, awards ceremonies, and so on.

Volume 16 will offer a complete bibliography of the works of Joseph Ratzinger in the German language as well as a detailed systematic index for all the volumes, which allows the complete works to be grasped as an interrelated network. The individual volumes will include detailed tables of contents as well as indices of names and scriptural passages.

Wherever possible in selecting titles for the volumes of JRCW, formulas were used that had already appeared in the original publications.

Cross-references to the author's own texts are noted with a reference in brackets to the appropriate volume and page number of JRCW, insofar as the status of the edition allows.

As a rule, the copy of the text reprinted is the most recent version reviewed by the author himself. Textual variants are noted only in extremely rare instances in which a substantial change is evident.

At the author's request, this edition dispenses with duplications and titles that are excessively dependent on a particular time or situation. These, however, are mentioned individually in the context of the editorial notes and are also listed in the overall bibliography that is planned as volume 16.

Endnotes are converted into footnotes. The abbreviation loc. cit. is omitted as a matter of principle. It is replaced with the author's name and an abbreviated form of the title. The full citation may be found at its first occurrence in the chapter. Series titles in works of secondary literature, insofar as they could be determined, are indicated at the first mention thereof.

A few misprints or obvious *errata* were corrected silently in the German edition. Similarly, occasional errors in a previously published English translation were corrected silently by the English editor.

Forewords by the author that are limited to formalities and contain nothing substantial are not included in the body of the text but are referenced within the context of the editorial notes.

After mature reflection it was decided not to note the pagination of the original edition in the margins because in most cases, besides the most recent version reprinted here, other editions having the same contents verbatim but different page numbers are also in circulation, so that marginal notes would offer guidance to only one part of the readership while causing confusion among the rest.

The JRCW use the following symbols and typography:

Superscript numerals	Author's footnotes
Asterisks	Additional notes by the editor or translator
Superscript lower-case letters	Footnotes by the editor to indicate textual variants of the author (earlier versions)
Italic type	Titles of books; words and phrases emphasized by the author.
Small capitals	headings and subheadings by the editor
[JRCW 11...]	Cross-references within this edition of the author's works are indicated: (JRCW volume: page).

II. The Present Volume 11 of the JRCW

Volume 11 of the *Collected Works of Joseph Ratzinger*, entitled *Theology of the Liturgy*, assembles texts that were composed over the course of forty years (1964–2004) and is divided into five parts.

Part A

Part A, THE SPIRIT OF THE LITURGY, is a complete and (apart from the formal standardization of the text and especially the bibliographic references) unchanged reprinting of the book *The Spirit of the Liturgy*, which was published in 2000 by Herder Verlag [and later that same year in John Saward's English translation by Ignatius Press]; in 2006 Herder released a special German edition adding the author's name Benedict XVI. The preface reprinted in the text is dated "Rome, The Feast of St. Augustine of Hippo, 1999". The division of the book into parts and chapters is likewise adopted in its entirety, naturally taking into consideration the overall structure of volume 11 and incorporating the work within it.

Part B

Part B, TYPOS—MYSTERIUM—SACRAMENTUM, combines two ground-breaking lectures on the theme of sacrament. "The Sacramental Foundation of Christian Existence" is an excerpt prepared by the author himself from a four-hour lecture that Joseph Ratzinger gave during the *Salzburger Hochschulwochen* [College Conference in Salzburg] in 1965. It first appeared in *"blätter": Zeitschrift für Studierende* (Vienna) and then was published as a separate brochure by Kyrios Verlag in Freising. The slim volume attracted much attention well into the 1970s and went through three more editions. Its title serves as the subtitle for volume 11 of JRCW.

"On the Concept of Sacrament" goes back to a guest lecture that Joseph Ratzinger gave as Archbishop of Munich and Freising at the invitation of the Catholic Theological Faculty of the *Gesamthochschule Eichstätt* on January 23, 1978, and was published as volume 15 of the *Eichstätter Hochschulreden*.

Part C

The centerpiece of Part C, THE CELEBRATION OF THE EUCHARIST—SOURCE AND SUMMIT OF CHRISTIAN LIFE, consists of the four Lenten sermons, *Eucharistie—Mitte der kirche* (Eucharist—Center of the Church), by the Archbishop of Munich, which he gave in 1978 during the-season in preparation for Easter in St. Michael's Church in Munich and which were published that same year as a monograph by Wewel Verlag in Munich. The introductory foreword, which is reprinted with the body of the text, is signed and dated "Rome, on the Feast of the Assumption of the Blessed Virgin Mary, 1978".

The publishing houses Wewel and Sankt Ulrich (Augsburg) published another unchanged edition of these sermons in 2005, after they had already served as the basis for the anthology edited by Vinzenz Pfnür and Stephan Otto Horn, *Gott ist uns nah: Eucharistie: Mutte des Lebens* (Augsburg: Sankt Ulrich Verlag, 2001), 25–95; English trans.: *God Is Near Us: The Eucharist, the Heart of Life* (San Francisco: Ignatius Press, 2003), 27–93.

These homilies on the Eucharist are preceded by three scholarly essays and two book reviews on the topics from eucharistic theology:

"On the Meaning of Sunday for Christian Prayer and Christian Life" was a lecture given as part of a priests' conference in Essen on January 7, 1985; it was published for the first time in the initial volume (1985) of the periodical *Forum Katholische Theologie* and appeared subsequently in various other periodicals and finally was included in the anthology *Ein neues Lied für den Herrn* (1995); English trans.: *A New Song for the Lord* (1996).

"Is the Eucharist a Sacrifice?" was published in 1967 in the journal *Concilium* and has not been reprinted since except in the *Theologisches Jahrbuch* (Leipzig).

Since its first appearance in the *Theologische Quartalschrift* (Tübingen), "The Problem of Transubstantiation and the Question about the Meaning of the Eucharist" was reprinted only in the *Theologisches Jahrbuch* (Leipzig) and otherwise was not published again. The text reproduces the guest lecture that Professor Joseph Ratzinger, who was teaching then in Münster, gave on July 8, 1964, at the Catholic theological faculty in Tübingen. The essay is dedicated "To Gottlieb Söhngen on his 75th birthday (May 21, 1967)".

The two book reviews printed after that (on studies by Schillebeeckx from the year 1967 and Averbeck also from 1967) discuss particular questions in the theology of the Eucharist.

The sermons on the Eucharist are followed by further texts that deal with questions that go beyond the classical repertoire of themes from dogmatic theology on the Eucharist and for the most part dwell on the intersection of Eucharist and liturgy.

"Form and Content of the Eucharistic Celebration" as well as "On the Structure of the Liturgical Celebration" first appeared in the German edition of *International Catholic Review "Communio"*. Both essays were included in the anthology *Das Fest des Glaubens* compiled in 1981 by Johannes Verlag in Einsiedeln (English trans.: *The Feast of Faith* [San Francisco: Ignatius Press, 1986]), where the first essay was expanded with two postscripts.

"Eucharist and Mission" began as a lecture by the Prefect of the Congregation for the Doctrine of the Faith given on September 10, 1997, at the Eucharistic Congress in Como on the general theme of "Eucharist as the Origin of Mission". With slight modifications, Joseph Ratzinger repeated the lecture on September 25, 1997, at the National Eucharistic Congress in Bologna. The German version appeared first in *Forum Katholische Theologie* and, finally, in the *Festschrift* compiled for the author's seventy-fifth birthday by his *Schülerkreis* [circle of former students], *Weggemeinschaft des Glaubens: Kirche als Communio* (Augsburg, 2002); English trans.: *Pilgrim Fellowship of Faith: The Church as Communion* (San Francisco: Ignatius Press, 2005).

The lecture "Eucharist—Communio—Solidarity" was given in Benevento on June 1, 2002, reprinted several times in Italian, and finally published in German by Sankt Ulrich Verlag (Augsburg, 2003) in the anthology *Unterwegs zu Jesus Christus*; English trans.: *On the Way to Jesus Christ* (San Francisco: Ignatius Press, 2004).

"Built from Living Stones" originated as a lecture within the context of the millennial jubilee of the Cathedral of Mainz in 1975; it appeared for the first time in the anthology *Kirche aus lebendigen Steinen*, published by Walter Seidel in 1975, and in 1995 was included in *Ein neues Lied für den Herrn* (English trans.: *A New Song for the Lord* [New York: Crossroad, 1997]).

Under the editorial heading ON THE QUESTION OF THE ORIENTATION OF THE CELEBRATION, two essays are grouped, which were written almost twenty-five years apart: "Note on the Question of the Orientation of the Celebration" is an expanded version of "Kleine Korrektur: Zur Frage der Eucharistie", which first appeared in *Internationale Katholische Zeitschrift "Communio"* and was then included in *Das Fest des Glaubens* (1981); English trans.: *The Feast of Faith* (1986).

It is followed by the "Foreword" dated "Laetare Sunday 2003" that the Prefect of the Congregation for the Doctrine of the Faith contributed to the study by Uwe Michael Lang, *Turning towards the Lord*.

Part C is rounded out with a series of homilies and meditations:

"On the Question of the Adoration of the Eucharist and Its Sacredness" was the theme of the homily by the Archbishop of Munich at the Chrism Mass on April 2, 1980, in the Liebfrauendom [Cathedral of Our Lady] in Munich.

While celebrating Mass with the Munich Cathedral Choir in his titular church of Santa Maria Consolatrice in Rome on September 2, 1979, Cardinal Ratzinger likewise addressed a eucharistic theme: "The Lord Is Near Us in Our Conscience, in His Word, in His Personal Presence in the Eucharist." Both homilies were included by Vinzenz Pfnür and Stephan Otto Horn in *Gott ist uns nah* (*God Is Near Us*).

The Corpus Christi homily entitled "Standing before the Lord—Walking with the Lord—Kneeling before the Lord", given by the Archbishop of Munich on May 25, 1978, on the Marienplatz [St. Mary's Square] in Munich, was also anthologized in *Gott ist uns nah* (*God Is Near Us*), after it had previously been an element in the collection of sermons and meditations *Suchen, was droben ist* (Freiburg: Herder, 1985); English trans.: *Seek That Which Is Above* (San Francisco: Ignatius Press, 2007).

Finally, "What Corpus Christi Means to Me" consists of three meditations that were broadcast on June 14, 1979, by Bavarian Radio for the Feast of Corpus Christi. In 1981 they were included in the anthology *Das Fest des Glaubens* (*The Feast of Faith*, 1986).

Part D

Part D, THEOLOGY OF CHURCH MUSIC, brings together five essays in all on the stated theme along with a discussion of the topic of "Professional Church Music".

"On the Theological Basis of Church Music" originated as an article in systematic theology for a *Festschrift* entitled *Gloria Deo—Pax hominibus* on the occasion of the one-hundredth anniversary of the Sacred Music School in Regensburg on November 22, 1974. This essay by the then professor of dogmatic theology in Regensburg was also reprinted in several periodicals and finally in 1981 was included in the anthology *Das Fest des Glaubens* (*The Feast of Faith*, 1986).

"'Sing Artistically for the Lord': Biblical Directives for Church Music" started as a lecture that the Prefect for the Congregation for the Doctrine of the Faith gave on September 28, 1990, in the reception hall of the major seminary in Brixen to open the symposium on "Gregorian Chant and Polyphony", organized by the association Brixener Initiative Musik und Kirche; in 1995 it was included in *Ein neues Lied für den Herrn* (*A New Song for the Lord*, 1997).

This was done also with "The Image of the World and of Man in the Liturgy and Its Expression in Church Music", whereby the latter essay—based on a lecture at the opening of the Eighth International Congress for Musica Sacra in Rome on November 17, 1985—was first published in its entirety in English under the title "Liturgy and Church Music" in 1985 in *Musica Sacra* and since 1987 has been available in German as a separate brochure published by Musikverlag Hans Sikorski.

On the occasion of the retirement of his brother, Professor Georg Ratzinger, from the position of cathedral choirmaster in Regensburg in 1994, Cardinal Ratzinger gave a lecture on the topic of "The Tension between the Regensburg Tradition and the Postconciliar Reform". Under the title "'In the Presence of the Angels I Will Sing Your Praise': The Regensburg Tradition and the Reform of the Liturgy", it was reprinted first in *Musica Sacra* and then also in *Ein neues Lied für den Herrn* (*A New Song for the Lord*).

"The Artistic Transposition of Faith: Theological Problems of Church Music" was given as a guest lecture in the Catholic Music department of the Staatliche Musikhochschule [National Conservatory] in Stuttgart; it was also first published there as a separate brochure, and in 1980 it was reprinted in *Internationale Katholische Zeitschrift "Communio"*.

Finally, "Professional Church Music as Liturgical and Pastoral Ministry" is the statement submitted by Professor Joseph Ratzinger on May 22, 1975, within the framework of a forum on the topic of "Professional Church Music Today" to commemorate the one-hundredth anniversary of the Church Music School in Regensburg; it appeared in print the following year, on the occasion of the jubilee in 1976, in a special volume in the series published by the Allgemeines Cäcilien-Verband, together with speeches, talks, greetings, and other contributions to the discussion.

Part E

The fifth and final Part E, FURTHER PERSPECTIVES, compiles mostly essays that originated in the course of the debate about the book *The*

Spirit of the Liturgy. These are prefaced by two older discussions and a commemorative preface.

The first is the 1977 interview with the German edition of *Communio* entitled "Change and Permanence in Liturgy", and the second is the sermon "Worship in the Parish Communities Fifteen Years after the Council", given on September 27, 1979, at the German Bishops' Conference in Fulda; both were incorporated into the book *Das Fest des Glaubens* (*The Feast of Faith*).

"In Memory of Klaus Gamber" was originally supposed to honor the Regensburg liturgist on his seventieth birthday, but then after Gamber's sudden death it became part of a commemorative volume.

"The Theology of the Liturgy" transcribes the lecture that the then Prefect of the Congregation for the Doctrine of the Faith gave at a liturgical conference at the abbey of Fontgombault (from July 22–24, 2001), the proceedings of which were published that same year in French as *Autour de la question liturgique*. [The English edition, edited by Alcuin Reid, O.S.B., *Looking Again at the Question of the Liturgy with Cardinal Ratzinger*, was published in 2003 by Saint Michael's Abbey Press.] In German the lecture was published in 2002 in the *Forum Katholische Theologie*. The title of the lecture has been assigned to volume 11 of the *Collected Works*.

At the conference in Fontgombault, Cardinal Ratzinger was also asked to make concluding remarks and to formulate some perspectives on the future. This concluding lecture, which was given in French, was reprinted with the title "Bilan et perspectives" in the French edition of the proceedings, *Autour de la question liturgique* [and as "Assessment and Future Prospects" in the English edition]. It was published in German for the first time, in a translation by Dr. Karl Pichler, in volume 11 of the *Gesammelte Schriften* [Collected Works].

On the occasion of the fortieth anniversary of the promulgation of the Second Vatican Council's Constitution on the Liturgy, *Sacrosanctum concilium*, Cardinal Ratzinger paid a visit on December 4, 2003, to the German Liturgical Institute in Trier. The Cardinal's commemorative lecture, entitled "Fortieth Anniversary of the Constitution on the Sacred Liturgy: A Look Back and a Look Forward", was published first in the *Liturgisches Jahrbuch* and was subsequently included also in the anthology edited by Walter Euler, *40 Jahre danach: Das Zweite Vatikanische Konzil und seine Folgen* (Trier, 2005).

Although it was originally composed in German, an "Answer" by Cardinal Ratzinger, in which he thoroughly responded to a discussion of *The Spirit of the Liturgy* cast in the form of an open letter by Olivier Bauer, a theologian then teaching in Geneva, was first published in French as "Réponse à la lettre ouverte d'Olivier Bauer" in the periodical *Revue de théologie et de philosophie*.

"Die organische Entwicklung der Liturgie" was the headline that the magazine *30 Tage* [the German edition of *30 Days*] gave to Cardinal Ratzinger's review of the book by Alcuin Reed, *The Organic Development of the Liturgy*; the review was then published without revisions in the first issue of the 2005 volume of *Forum Katholische Theologie*. It was the last book review by Cardinal Ratzinger before his election to the papacy.

The present volume concludes with the homily that Cardinal Ratzinger gave while celebrating Mass on December 4, 2003, in the Cathedral of St. Peter in Trier, the oldest episcopal see in Germany, on the scriptural and liturgical texts for the Thursday in the First Week of Advent; an audio version of the homily was broadcast over the electronic media, but until now it has not been in print.

With the exception of Part A, the structure and subdivisions of this volume were designed specifically for this volume.

Most of the texts [for the German edition of JRCW, vol. 11] were scanned, while a few of them were made available by the author on electronic recording media. [Sixteen elements in the English edition were previously published by Ignatius Press and most are reprinted here from the same electronic files; nine elements were translated into English for the first time by Kenneth Baker, S.J., and Michael J. Miller; five are reprinted from *A New Song for the Lord*, published by Crossroad, and the remaining four are reprinted from scholarly publications.]

For their great care and painstaking work in formatting the text uniformly and especially in copyediting it, the German editor cordially thanks the following theology students at the Theological Faculty in Trier: Isabel Nowak, Benjamin Heu, and Gabriel Weiten, who was also quite skilled in using various scanners, coordinated the revisions, and furthermore played an essential part in preparing the manuscript in a smooth and timely fashion.

Christian Schaller, Th.D., and Franz Xaver Heibel, M.Phil., M.Theol., of the Pope Benedict XVI Institute conscientiously reviewed the typeset text once more and were responsible for compiling the indices.

Bibliographical Notes

PART A: THE SPIRIT OF THE LITURGY

Der Geist der Liturgie: Eine Einführung. Freiburg: Herder, 2000; 2nd–
5th ed., 2000; 6th ed., 2002; special edition, 2006. JRGS 11:27–194.
English: *The Spirit of the Liturgy.* Translated by John Saward. San Francisco: Ignatius Press, 2000. JRCW 11:1–150.

PART B: TYPOS—MYSTERIUM—SACRAMENTUM

"Die sakramentale Begründung christlicher Existenz". Meitingen
and Freising: Kyrios, 1966; 2nd ed., 1967; 3rd ed., 1970; 4th
ed., 1973). Originally published in *blätter: Zeitschrift für Studierende*
(Vienna) 20 (1965/1966): 22–27; *Der grosse Entschluss: Monatsschrift
für lebendiges Christentum* (Vienna) 21 (1966): 392–97. JRGS
11:197–214.
English: "The Sacramental Foundation of Christian Existence". Translated by Kenneth Baker, S.J., and Michael J. Miller. JRCW
11:153–68.
"Zum Begriff des Sakramentes". *Eichstätter Hochschulreden* 15. Munich:
Minerva-Publikation, 1979. JRGS 11:215–32.
English: "On the Concept of Sacrament". Translated by Kenneth Baker,
S.J., and Michael J. Miller. JRCW 11:169–89.

PART C: THE CELEBRATION OF THE EUCHARIST—SOURCE AND
SUMMIT OF CHRISTIAN LIFE

I. "Vom Sinn des Sonntags". FoKTh 1 (3/1985): 161–75. Also in
Pastoralblatt 37 (1985): 258–69; KlBl 65 (1985): 209–14, and

also in various editions of *Communio*. Revised, expanded, and retitled "Auferstehung als Grundlegung christlicher Liturgie—Von der Bedeutung des Sonntags für Beten und Leben des Christen", in Joseph Ratzinger, *Ein neues Lied für den Herrn: Christusglaube und Liturgie in der Gegenwart*, 83–104 (Freiburg, 1995); new ed. (Freiburg, 2007), 84–108. JRGS 11:235–257.

English: "The Resurrection as the Foundation of Christian Liturgy—On the Meaning of Sunday for Christian Prayer and Christian Life". In Joseph Ratzinger. *A New Song for the Lord: Faith in Christ and Liturgy Today*. Translated by Martha M. Matesich, 59–77. New York: Crossroad, 1996; 2nd ed., 2005. JRCW 11:187–206.

II. "Ist die Eucharistie ein Opfer?" Conc (D) 3 (1967): 299–304. Also in ThJb (L) (1969): 315–23. JRGS 11:259–70.

English: "Is the Eucharist a Sacrifice?" Translated by J. Drury. *Concilium* [English-language edition] 4 (1967): 35–40. Also in *The Sacraments: An Ecumenical Dilemma*. New York: Paulist Press, 1967. JRCW 11:207–17.

III. "Das Problem der Transsubstantiation und die Frage nach dem Sinn der Eucharistie". ThQ 147 (1967): 129–58. Also in ThJb (L) (1969): 281–301. JRGS 11:271–98.

English: "The Problem of Transubstantiation and the Question about the Meaning of the Eucharist". Translated by Kenneth Baker, S.J., and Michael J. Miller. JRCW 11:218–42.

Two Book Reviews

Review of Edward Schillebeeckx, *Die eucharistische Gegenwart: Zur Diskussion über die Realpräsenz* (Düsseldorf: Patmos, 1967). ThQ 147 (1967): 493–96. JRGS 11:299–302.

English: Translated by Kenneth Baker, S.J., and Michael J. Miller. JRCW 11:243–46.

Review of Wilhelm Averbeck, *Der Opfercharakter des Abendmahls in der neueren evangelischen Theologie*, KKTS 19 (Paderborn: Bonifatius, 1967). ThPQ 118 (1970): 89f. JRGS 11:302–4.

English: Translated by Kenneth Baker, S.J., and Michael J. Miller. JRCW 11:246–48.

IV. *Eucharistie—Mitte der Kirche: Vier Predigten.* Munich: Wewel, 1978; 2nd ed., 2005. These four Lenten sermons are reprinted consecutively in Joseph Ratzinger, *Gott ist uns nah: Eucharistie—Mitte des Lebens*, ed. Stephan Otto Horn and Vinzenz Pfnür (Augsburg, 2001), 25–95. JRGS 11:305–58.

English: In Joseph Ratzinger. *God Is Near Us: The Eucharist, the Heart of Life.* Translated by Henry Taylor, 27–93. San Francisco: Ignatius Press, 2003. JRCW 11:249–98.

V. "Gestalt und Gehalt der eucharistischen Feier". IKaZ 6 (1977): 385–96. Reprinted with two postscripts in Joseph Ratzinger, *Das Fest des Glaubens: Versuche zur Theologie des Gottesdienstes*, 31–54 (Einsiedeln, 1981; 2nd ed., 1981; 3rd ed., 1993). JRGS 11:359–82.

English: "Form and Content of the Eucharistic Celebration". In Joseph Ratzinger. *The Feast of Faith: Approaches to a Theology of the Liturgy.* Translated by Graham Harrison, 33–60. San Francisco: Ignatius Press, 1986; 2nd ed., 2006. JRCW 11:299–318.

VI. "Zur Frage nach der Struktur der liturgischen Feier". IKaZ 7 (1978): 488–97. Reprinted in Ratzinger, *Fest des Glaubens*, 55–67. JRGS 11:383–95.

English: "On the Structure of the Liturgical Celebration". In Ratzinger, *Feast of Faith*, 61–78. JRCW 11:319–29.

VII. "Eucaristia come genesi della missione". *Il Regno* 42 (1997): 588–93. Also in: *Ecclesia orans* XV/2 (1998): 137–61.

German: "Eucharistie und Mission". FoKTh 14 (1998): 81–98. Also in: Joseph Ratzinger, *Weggemeinschaft des Glaubens: Kirche als Communio*, 79–106 (Augsburg, 2002). JRGS 11:397–423.

English: "Eucharist and Mission". *Irish Theological Quarterly* 65 (2000): 245–64. Also in Joseph Ratzinger. *Pilgrim Fellowship of Faith: The Church as Communion.* Translated by Henry Taylor, 90–122. San Francisco: Ignatius Press, 2005. JRCW 11:330–54.

VIII. "Eucaristia, comunione e solidarietà". OR, June 19, 2002: 6 and 8. *Communio* (It) 31 (2002): 131–46.

German: "Eucharistie—Communio—Solidarität: Christus gegenwärtig und wirksam im Sakrament". In Joseph Ratzinger, *Unterwegs zu Jesus Christus*, 109–30. (Augsburg, 2003.) JRGS 11:425–42.

English: "Eucharist—Communio—Solidarity: Christ Present and Active in the Blessed Sacrament". In Joseph Ratzinger. *On the Way to Jesus Christ.* Translated by Michael J. Miller, 107–30. San Francisco: Ignatius Press, 2004; 2nd ed., 2005. JRCW 11:355–70.

IX. "Auferbaut aus lebendigen Steinen". In *Kirche aus lebendigen Steinen*, edited by Walter Seider, 30–48. Mainz, 1975. Reprinted with expanded notes as "'Auferbaut aus lebendigen Steinen': Das Gotteshaus und die christliche Weise der Gottesverehrung", in Ratzinger, *Neues Lied für den Herrn*, 105–23. JRGS 11:443–461.

English: "'Built from Living Stones': The House of God and the Christian Way of Worshipping God". In Ratzinger, *New Song for the Lord*, 78–93. JRCW 11:371–87.

X. On the Question of the Orientation of the Celebration

  1. "Kleine Korrektur: Zur Frage der Eucharistie". IKaZ 8 (1979): 381f. Expanded as "Anmerkung zur Frage der Zelebrationsrichtung". In Ratzinger, *Fest des Glaubens*, 121–26. JRGS 11:463–68.

    English: "Eastward- or Westward-Facing Position?" In Ratzinger, *Feast of Faith*, 139–46. JRCW 11:388–92.

  2. "Geleitwort". In *Conversi ad Dominum: Zu Geschichte und Theologie der christlichen Gebetsrichtung*, by Uwe Michael Lang, 7–11. Neue Kriterien 5. Freiburg, 2003; 4th ed., 2006. JRGS 11:469–471.

    English: "Foreword", by U. M. Lang, 9–12. In Ratzinger, *Turning towards The Lord: Orientation In Liturgical Prayer.* San Francisco: Ignatius Press, 2004; 2nd ed., 2009. JRCW 11:393–95.

XI. Homilies

  1. "Zur Frage der Verehrung und Sakralität der Eucharistie". Retitled "Die Gegenwärtig-keit der Nähe des Herrn in den Alltag hinein" and published in Ratzinger, *Gott ist uns nah*, 97–105. JRGS 11:473–79.

    English: "The Immediacy of the Presence of the Lord Carried into Everyday Life: On the Question of the Adoration of the Eucharist and Its Sacredness". In Ratzinger, *God Is Near Us*, 94–101. JRCW 11:396–402.

2. "Predigt für den Münchener Domchor in der Titelkirche S.M.C. in Rom am 2.9.1979". *Münchener Ordinariats-Korrespondenz* 26 (September 6, 1979). Reprinted under the title "Der Herr ist uns nahe in unserem Gewissen, in seinem Wort, in seiner persönlichen Gegenwart, in der Eucharistie: Homilie über Dtn 4,7" in Ratzinger, *Gott ist uns nah*, 107–11. JRGS 11:479–83.

   English: "The Lord Is Near Us in Our Conscience, in His Word, in His Personal Presence in the Eucharist." In Ratzinger, *God Is Near Us*, 102–6. JRCW 11:402–5.

3. "Fronleichnamsansprache auf dem Münchener Marienplatz am 25.5.1978". MOK 19 (June 1, 1978). Retitled "Stehen vor dem Herrn—Gehen mit dem Herrn—Knien vor dem Herrn: Zur Feier des Fronleichnamsfestes" and reprinted in *Gott ist uns nah*, 113–19; previously printed also in Joseph Ratzinger, *Suchen, was droben ist*, 77–86 (Freiburg, 1985). JRGS 11:483–88.

   English: "Standing before the Lord—Walking with the Lord—Kneeling before the Lord". In *God Is Near Us*, 107–13. Previously printed also in Joseph Ratzinger. *Seek That Which Is Above.* Trans. Graham Harrison, 83–93. San Francisco: Ignatius Press, 1986. JRCW 11:405–10.

4. "Was bedeutet mir Fronleichnam?" BR, June 14, 1979 (28 min., 40 sec.). Under the title "Was bedeutet Fronleichnam für mich?—Drei Meditationen", in Ratzinger, *Fest des Glaubens*, 112–20. JRGS 11:488–97.

   English: "What Corpus Christi Means to Me". In Ratzinger, *Feast of Faith*, 127–38. JRCW 11:410–17.

PART D: THEOLOGY OF CHURCH MUSIC

1. "Zur theologischen Grundlegung der Kirchenmusik". In *Gloria Deo—Pax hominibus*, FS zum 100jährigen Bestehen der Kirchenmusik-schule Regensburg, edited by Franz Fleckenstein, 39–62. Regensburg, 1974. KlBl 55 (1975): 263–67, 305–7; partially reprinted in OR(D) 4:7f.; reprinted in Ratzinger, *Fest des Glaubens*, 86–110. JRGS 11:501–26.

English: "On the Theological Basis of Church Music". In Ratzinger, *Feast of Faith*, 97–126. JRCW 11:421–42.

II. "Liturgy and Church Music". *Sacred Music* 12 (1985): 13–22; German version: "Liturgie und Kirchenmusik", IKaZ 15 (1986): 243–56; published as a separate brochure (Hamburg: Sikorski, 1987); also reprinted as "Das Welt- und Menschenbild der Liturgie und sein Ausdruck in der Kirchenmusik", in Ratzinger, *Neues Lied für den Herrn*, 145–64 [2nd German ed., 152–73]. Partially reprinted in *Theologisches* (1985), 6879–83. JRGS 11:527–47.

English: "The Image of the World and of Human Beings in the Liturgy and Its Expression in Church Music". In Ratzinger, *New Song for the Lord*, 111–27. JRCW 11:443–60.

III. "In der Spannung zwischen Regensburger Tradition und nachkonziliarer Reform". *Musica sacra* 114 (1994): 379–89. Retitled "'Im Angesicht der Engel will ich dir singen': Regensburger Tradition und Liturgiereform", in Ratzinger, *Neues Lied für den Herrn*, 165–86. JRGS 11:549–70.

English: "'In the Presence of the Angels I Will Sing Your Praise': The Regensburg Tradition and the Reform of the Liturgy". In Ratzinger, *New Song for the Lord*, 128–46. JRCW 11:461–79.

IV. *Theologische Probleme der Kirchenmusik*. Kirchenmusik eine geistig-geistliche Diziplin: Gastvorträge an der kath. Musikabteilung der Staatl. Musikhochschule Stuttgart, vol. 1, edited by R. Walter in association with the consultants for church music in the diocese of Rottenburg-Stuttgart. Rottenburg, 1978. Reprinted under the title "Die künstlerische Transposition des Glaubens: Theologische Probleme der Kirchenmusik", MS(D) 99 (1979): 129–35; IKaZ 9 (1980): 148–57. JRGS 11:571–85.

English: "The Artistic Transposition of the Faith: Theological Problems of Church Music". In *Crux et cithara*, edited by R.A. Skeris, 214–22. Altötting, 1983. Also: *Sacred Music* 135 (2008)—http://musicasacra.com/theological-problems. Accessed September 3, 2012. JRCW 11:480–93.

V. "Biblische Vorgaben für die Kirchenmusik". In Brixener Initiative Musik und Kirche. *Drittes Symposion "Choral und Mehrstimmigkeit"*, 9–21. Brixen, 1990. Retitled "'Singt kunstvoll für Gott': Biblische Vorgaben für die Kirchenmusik".

In Ratzinger, *Neues Lied für den Herrn*, 125–44. JRGS 11:587–606.

English: "'Sing Artistically for God': Biblical Directives for Church Music". In Ratzinger, *New Song for the Lord*, 94–110. JRCW 11:494–511.

VI. "Kirchenmusikberuf als liturgischer und pastoraler Dienst". In *Kirchenmusik im Gespräch: Ansprachen, Reden, Grußworte, Diskussionsbeiträge zur 100-Jahrfeier der Kirchenmusikschule Regensburg vom 21.–27.5.1975*, edited by Franz Fleckenstein, 24–27. Schriftenreihe des Allgemeinen Cäcilien-Verbandes für die Länder der deutschen Sprache 12. Bonn, 1976. JRGS 11:607–10.

English: "Professional Church Music as a Liturgical and Pastoral Ministry". Translated by Kenneth Baker, S.J., and Michael J. Miller. JRCW 11:512–15.

PART E: FURTHER PERSPECTIVES

I. "Liturgie—wandelbar oder unwandelbar? Fragen an Joseph Ratzinger". IKaZ 6 (1977): 417–27. Also in MS(D) 98 (1978): 114–17; reprinted under the title "Liturgie—wandelbar oder unwandel? Ein Gespräch mit der Redaktion der Internationalen katholischen Zeitschrift 'Communio'". In Ratzinger, *Fest des Glaubens*, 71–85. JRGS 11:613–26.

English: "Change and Permanence in Liturgy". In Ratzinger, *Feast of Faith*, 79–96. JRCW 11:519–30.

II. "Das gottesdienstliche Leben in den Gemeinden fünfzehn Jahre nach dem Konzil: Predigt bei der Bischofkonferenz in Fulda". In Ratzinger, *Fest des Glaubens*, 127–32. JRGS 11:627–32.

English: "Worship in the Parish Communities Fifteen Years after the Council". In Ratzinger, *Feast of Faith*, 147–53. JRCW 11:531–35.

III. "Zum Gedenken an Klaus Gamber". In *Simandron—Der Wachklopfer*, Gedenkschrift für Klaus Gamber (1919–1989), edited by Wilhelm Nyssen, 13–15. Cologne, 1989. JRGS 11:633–35.

English: "In Memory of Klaus Gamber" (1919–1989). Translated by Michael J. Miller. JRCW 11:536–38.

IV. "Théologie de la liturgie". In *Autour de la question liturgique avec le Cardinal Ratzinger: Actes des journées liturgiques de Fontgombault, 22–24 juillet 2001*, 13–29. Fontgombault, 2001. German version: "Theologie der Liturgie", FoKTh 18 (2002): 1–13. JRGS 11:639–56.

English: "Theology of the Liturgy: A Lecture Delivered during the Journées Liturgiques de Fontgombault, 22–24 July 2001". *Oriens, Journal of the Ecclesia Dei Society*, vol. 7, no. 2. Also published in *Looking Again at the Question of the Liturgy with Cardinal Ratzinger: Proceedings of the July 2001 Fontgombault Liturgical Conference*, edited by Alcuin Reid, O.S.B., 18–31. Farnborough, Eng.: Saint Michael's Abbey Press, 2003. JRCW 11:541–57.

V. "Bilan et perspectives". In *Autour de la question*, 173–89. German translation in JRGS 11:657–82.

English: "Assessment and Future Prospects". In Reid, *Looking Again at the Question of the Liturgy*, 145–53. JRCW 11:558–68.

VI. "Réponse à la lettre ouverte d'Olivier Bauer". *Revue de théologie et de philosophie* 135/3 (2003): 253–56; [Cf. Olivier Bauer, "Lettre ouverte à propos de *L'esprit de la liturgie*, ouvrage du cardinal Joseph Ratzinger", *Revue de théologie et de philosophie* 135 (2003): 241–51]. German translation in JRGS 11:683–93.

English: "Answer to the Open Letter of Olivier Bauer". Translated by Kenneth Baker, S.J., and Michael J. Miller. JRCW 11:569–73.

VII. "40 Jahre Konstitution über die heilige Liturgie: Rückblick und Vorblick". *Liturgisches Jahrbuch* 53/4 (2003): 209–21. Reprinted in *40 Jahre danach: Das Zweite Vatikanische Konzil und seine Folgen*, edited by Walter Andreas Euler, 11–26 (Trier, 2005). JRGS 11:695–711.

English: "Fortieth Anniversary of the Constitution on the Sacred Liturgy: A Look Back and a Look Forward". Translated by Kenneth Baker, S.J., and Michael J. Miller. JRCW 11:574–88.

VIII. "Lo sviluppo organico della liturgia". Review of the book *The Organic Development of the Liturgy*, by Alcuin Reid, O.S.B. (Farnborough, 2004), in *30Giorni* (12/2004): 72–75.

Reprinted in German as "Die organische Entwicklung der Liturgie", FoKTh (2005): 36–39. JRGS 11:713–18.

English: Reprinted as preface to *The Organic Development of the Liturgy*, by Alcuin Reid, O.S.B., 9–14. San Francisco: Ignatius Press, 2005. JRCW 11:589–94.

IX. Homily during the Pontifical Mass in the Cathedral in Trier on December 4, 2003. JRGS 11:719–23 [previously unpublished].

English: "Rouse Your Power and Come". Translated by Kenneth Baker, S.J., and Michael J. Miller. JRCW 11:595–99.

Not included:

"Um die Erneuerung der Liturgie: Antwort auf Reiner Kaczynski". StdZ 126 (2001): 837–43.

" 'Der Geist der Liturgie' oder: Die Treue zum Konzil: Antwort an Pater Pierre-Marie Gy". *Gottesdienst* 36 (2002): 97–100.

Liturgie und Weltverantwortung. Kölner Beiträge, n.s. 20. Cologne, 1998 [largely incorporated into Ratzinger, *Geist der Liturgie*, 11ff.].

The following texts are incorporated into other volumes of JRGS:

"Grundgedanken der eucharistischen Erneuerung des 20. Jahrhunderts". KlBl 40 (1960): 208–11.

"Der Eucharistische Weltkongress im Spiegel der Kritik". In *Statio orbis*, vol. 1, ed. R. Egenter, O. Pirner, and H. Hofbauer, 227–42. Munich, 1961.

"Gemeinde aus der Eucharistie". In *800 Jahre St. Martini Münster*, ed. Werner Hülsbusch, 32–34. Münster, 1980. Reprinted in Joseph Ratzinger, *Vom Wiederauffinden der Mitte: Grundorientierung: Texte aus vier Jahrzehnten*, ed. Stephan Otto Horn et al., 35–37 (Freiburg im Breisgau: Herder, 1997).

Index of Scripture Passages

Index

Index

Index

Index of Names

Index

Index

Index